GRAMMAR

FOR THE WELL-TRAINED MIND

KEY TO RED WORKBOOK

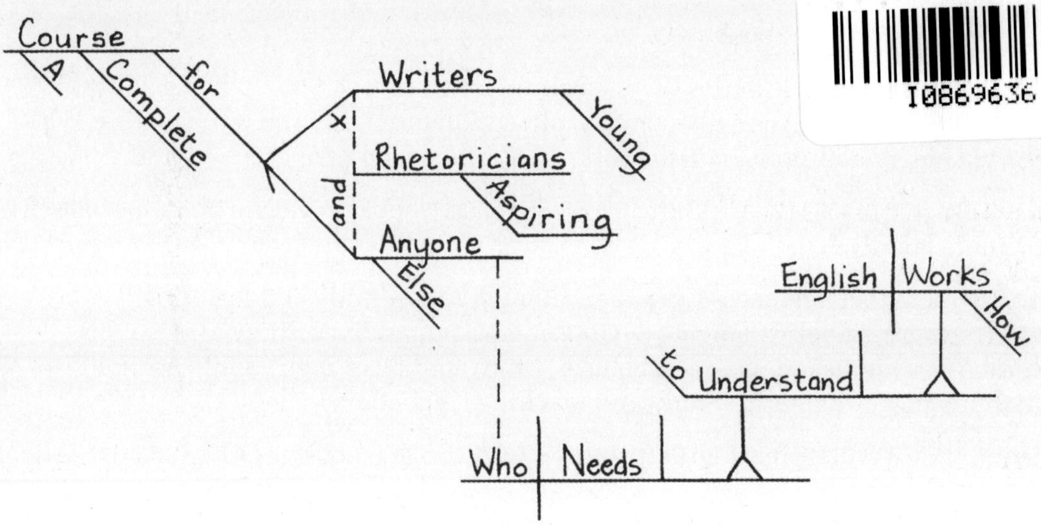

By Susan Wise Bauer

with Amanda Saxon Dean and Audrey Anderson,

Diagrams by Patty Rebne

WELL-TRAINED MIND PRESS

Publisher's Cataloging-In-Publication Data
(Prepared by The Donohue Group, Inc.)

Names: Bauer, Susan Wise. | Dean, Amanda Saxon. | Anderson, Audrey, 1986- | Rebne, Patty, illustrator. | Bauer, Susan Wise. Grammar for the well-trained mind. Red workbook.

Title: Grammar for the well-trained mind. Key to Red workbook / Susan Wise Bauer, with Amanda Saxon Dean & Audrey Anderson ; diagrams by Patty Rebne.

Other Titles: Key to Red workbook

Description: First edition. | [Charles City, Virginia] : Well-Trained Mind Press, [2018] | "A complete course for Young Writers, Aspiring Rhetoricians, and Anyone Else Who Needs to Understand How English Works." | For instructors of grades 5 and above.

Identifiers: ISBN 9781945841279 | ISBN 9781945841286 (ebook) | ISBN 9781945841606 (fixed format Kindle ebook)

Subjects: LCSH: English language--Grammar, Comparative--Study and teaching (Middle school) | English language--Grammar, Comparative--Study and teaching (Secondary) | English language--Rhetoric--Study and teaching (Middle school) | English language--Rhetoric--Study and teaching (Secondary)

Classification: LCC LB1631 .B394 2018 (print) | LCC LB1631 (ebook) | DDC 428.00712--dc23

For a list of corrections, please visit **www.welltrainedmind.com/corrections.**

TABLE OF CONTENTS

WEEK 1

Introduction to Nouns and Adjectives

— LESSON 1 —

Introduction to Nouns
Concrete and Abstract Nouns

Exercise 1A: Abstract and Concrete Nouns

Decide whether the underlined nouns are abstract or concrete. Above each noun, write *A* for abstract or *C* for concrete. If you have difficulty, ask yourself: Can this noun be touched or seen, or experienced with another one of the senses? If so, it is a concrete noun. If not, it is abstract.

> **Note to Instructor:** There may be some difference of opinion over these. If the student makes a strong argument for a different answer, you may accept it.

Our adventure (A) began with a tattered map (C).

Seeing the chocolates (C), the little girl's face (C) lit up with delight (A).

The orchestra (C) will be performing my favorite symphony (C).

My curiosity (A) led me to peek at the gift (C) before my birthday (C).

> **Note to Instructor:** We have labeled *birthday* as a concrete noun because it refers to one specific day that can be identified by the speaker. "Birthdays are fun" would refer to the idea of a birthday and could be defined as abstract. If the student disagrees and can articulate his reasoning, you may accept the answer abstract.

Charlotte's favorite book (C) is a mystery (A) about a lost princess (C).

Distracted by the loud noise (C), Bradley (C) forgot to finish combing his hair (C).

Mrs. Kim (C) was filled with pride (A) as her daughter (C) sang her solo (C).

A shadow (C) passed by the window (C) and gave us all a fright (A).

The baby (C) let out what was clearly a cry (C) of exhaustion (A).

Exercise 1B: Abstract Nouns

Each row contains two abstract nouns and one concrete noun. Find the concrete noun and cross it out.

amazement wonder ~~fireworks~~
~~notebook~~ neatness ideas
discovery interest ~~gold~~
danger ~~cliff~~ peril
conceit ~~mirror~~ arrogance
~~stomach~~ appetite satiety

— LESSON 2 —

Introduction to Adjectives
Descriptive Adjectives, Abstract Nouns
Formation of Abstract Nouns from Descriptive Adjectives

Exercise 2A: Descriptive Adjectives, Concrete Nouns, and Abstract Nouns

Decide whether the underlined words are concrete nouns, abstract nouns, or descriptive adjectives. Above each, write *DA* for descriptive adjective, *CN* for concrete noun, or *AN* for abstract noun.

The sentences below were taken from *Alice's Adventures in Wonderland*, by Lewis Carroll. Some have been slightly adapted.

By this time [AN] she had found her way [AN] into a tidy [DA] little [DA] room [CN] with a table [CN] in the window [CN].

Luckily for Alice [CN], the little [DA] magic [DA] bottle [CN] had now had its full [DA] effect [AN].

Alice [CN] noticed that the pebbles [CN] were all turning into little [DA] cakes [CN] as they lay on the floor [CN], and a bright [DA] idea [AN] came into her head [CN].

An enormous [DA] puppy [CN] was looking down at her with large [DA] round [DA] eyes [CN].

She had just succeeded in curving her neck [CN] down into a graceful [DA] zigzag [CN], when a sharp [DA] hiss [CN] made her draw back in a hurry [AN].

The Fish-Footman [CN] began by producing from under his arm [CN] a great [DA] letter [CN], nearly as large as himself.

Exercise 2B: Turning Descriptive Adjectives into Abstract Nouns

Change each descriptive adjective to an abstract noun by adding the suffix *-ness*. Write the abstract noun in the blank beside the descriptive adjective. Remember this rule: When you add the suffix *-ness* to a word ending in *-y*, the *-y* changes to *-i*. (For example, *grumpy* becomes *grumpiness*.)

smart	smartness
fretful	fretfulness
friendly	friendliness
marvelous	marvelousness
vicious	viciousness
merry	merriness
rich	richness
decisive	decisiveness

Exercise 2C: Color Names

Underline all the color words in the following paragraph. Then write *A* for adjective or *N* for noun above each underlined color word. If you are not sure, ask yourself, "*[Color name] what?*" If you can answer that question, you have found a noun that the color describes. That means the color is an adjective.

Keiko closed her eyes and considered different shades of green (N). She wanted the green (A) grass in her painting to look like the golden (A) sunlight was shining down on it through the trees. She chose two green (A) paints to mix together and began to paint. Green (N) was her favorite color, she thought—or was it red (N)? Then again, she loved the purple (A) flowers she'd painted below one of the trees. And the blue (A) sky had been fun to do as well. She even liked brown (N) or gray (N) when one of those was the right color for the job. "Actually," she said to herself, "there isn't a single color I don't like!"

— LESSON 3 —

Common and Proper Nouns
Capitalization and Punctuation of Proper Nouns

Exercise 3A: Capitalizing Proper Nouns

Write a proper noun for each of the following common nouns. Don't forget to capitalize all of the important words of the proper noun. Underline the name of the magazine you choose, to show that it should be in italics if it were typed. Use quotation marks around the title of the song you choose.

Note to Instructor: Answers will vary! Sample answers are given below.

Common Noun	**Proper Noun**
singer	Taylor Swift
restaurant	Cracker Barrel
country	The Republic of Ireland
park	Millennium Park
magazine	Highlights
song	"A Hazy Shade of Winter"

Exercise 3B: Proper Names and Titles

On your own paper, rewrite the following sentences properly. Capitalize and punctuate all names and titles correctly. If you are using a word processing program, italicize where needed; if you are writing by hand, underline in order to show italics.

The song **"**The **S**tar-**S**pangled **B**anner**"** is the national anthem for the **U**nited **S**tates.

"Himno **N**acional **M**exicano**"** is thought by many to be one of the most beautiful national anthems.

Germany sank the **L**usitania in **M**ay 1915.

Michael and **P**hyllis recited **W**illiam **M**akepeace **T**hackeray's poem **"A T**ragic **S**tory.**"**

In the book **C**harlotte's **W**eb, **W**ilbur is a pig who was born in the spring.

Keith's favorite show was **S**tar **T**rek; he especially loved the episode **"T**he **T**rouble with **T**ribbles.**"**

Exercise 3C: Proofreading for Proper Nouns

In the following sentences, indicate which proper nouns should be capitalized by underlining the first letter of the noun three times. This is the proper proofreading mark for *capitalize*. The first noun is done for you.

justinian was an emperor in byzantium, and his wife, theodora, was politically helpful to him.

The cathedral in constantinople known as the hagia sophia was built while justinian ruled.

justinian's general, belisarius, successfully conquered the barbarians living in the northern part of africa and proceeded into italy to retake rome from the ostrogoths.

The court historian, procopius, wrote a book called *the secret history*, which portrayed justinian in a very negative light.

— LESSON 4 —

Proper Adjectives
Compound Adjectives (Adjective-Noun Combinations)

Exercise 4A: Forming Proper Adjectives from Proper Nouns

Form adjectives from the following proper nouns. (Some will change form and others will not.) Write each adjective into the correct blank below. If you are not familiar with the proper nouns, you may look them up online at Encyclopaedia Britannica, Wikipedia, or some other source (this will help you complete the sentences as well). This exercise might challenge your general knowledge! (But you can always ask your instructor for help.)

Newton	Kentucky	Korea	China	Boston
June	America	Georgia	Germany	Monday
Gregory	Easter	Sherlock Holmes		

My favorite __German__ dish is sauerbraten, though nothing beats streuselkuchen when it comes to desserts!

The __Chinese__ New Year begins sometime in January or February of the __Gregorian__ calendar year.

Thoroughbred horses race each May in Louisville at the __Kentucky__ Derby.

The largest aquarium in the Western Hemisphere is the __Georgia__ Aquarium, located near the World of Coca-Cola in Atlanta.

Nina will go far as a detective, with her __Sherlock Holmesian__ deductive and observational skills.

Korean calligraphy had long used characters from China's writing system, but in the twentieth century calligraphers began using the *hangul* alphabet in response to nationalist feelings among the people.

Computer programmers will sometimes hide special features or messages in their work; these little Easter eggs can be fun to find.

They say that June brides are the most common, but my wedding was in December.

It's nice to have a long weekend, but a Monday holiday always throws me off for the rest of the week—I can't remember which day it is!

Non-Newtonian fluids have many interesting properties; for example, it's possible to run on top of oobleck!

The Boston Massacre, in which five colonists were killed by the British, was a key event leading to the American Revolution.

Exercise 4B: Capitalization of Proper Adjectives

In the following sentences:

- Correct each lowercase letter that should be capitalized by underlining it three times.
- Then, circle each proper adjective.
- Finally, put a check mark above each proper adjective that has not changed its form from the proper noun.

rube goldberg machines, which involve complicated ways of completing simple tasks, were named for an american cartoonist and inventor.

An associated press article by edward van winkle jones in 1950 marked the first mention of mysterious disappearances in the bermuda triangle.

> **Note to Instructor:** *Van* is sometimes left uncapitalized in names of Dutch origin, so you may accept *Edward van Winkle Jones* as an answer.

The pythagorean theorem is only true for euclidean geometry.

thomas jefferson, who was a philosopher, a musician, and an architect in addition to being a united states president, is an example of a renaissance man.

> **Note to Instructor:** *President* would be capitalized if it preceded a name as part of a title (President Jefferson), but in this sentence, a *president* (not one particular president) is a common noun.

The first olympic games in modern times were held in 1896 in the greek city of athens.

> **Note to Instructor:** The noun form of *Olympic* is *Olympics*.

In the southeastern asian kingdom of ayutthaya, the king trailokanat died; his two sons, ramathibodi II and boromarachathirat III, inherited his crown and divided the siamese territories between them.

Exercise 4C: Hyphenating Attributive Compound Adjectives

Hyphens prevent misunderstanding! Explain to your instructor the differences between each pair of phrases. The first is done for you. If you're confused, ask your instructor for help.

> **Note to Instructor:** These are intended to be fun, not frustrating. Use the suggestions below to help the student, and give the answers if the student is stumped.

the ten-gallon containers of soap *are multiple containers that each hold ten gallons*
the ten gallon containers of soap *are ten containers that each hold one gallon*
(both ten containers and gallon containers)

a private-eye company *is a company where private detectives work*
a private eye company *is an eye company that is nonpublic*
(both a private company and an eye company)

an assisted-living facility *is a facility where people are given help to live*
an assisted living facility *is a facility that is alive and receives help*
(both an assisted facility and a living facility)

the well-trained mind *is a mind that has been trained well*
the well trained mind *is a mind that is trained and not sick*
(both a well mind and a trained mind)

the second-place runner *is the runner who placed second*
the second place runner *is the second of two or more people who run places*
(both a second runner and a place runner)

(and if the student asks, we don't know what a place runner is either, but that's what the grammar tells us . . .)

WEEK 2

Introduction to Personal Pronouns and Verbs

— LESSON 5 —

Noun Gender
Introduction to Personal Pronouns

Exercise 5A: Introduction to Noun Gender

How well do you know your animals? Fill in the blanks with the correct name (and don't worry too much if you don't know the answers . . . this is mostly for fun).

Animal	Male	Female	Baby	Group of Animals
leopard	leopard	leopardess	cub	leap OR prowl of leopards
kangaroo	buck/boomer/jack	jill/doe/flyer/roo	joey	mob OR troop of kangaroos
donkey	jack	jenny	foal	herd OR drove of donkeys
alligator	bull	cow	hatchling	congregation of alligators
hamster	buck	doe	pup	horde of hamsters
hedgehog	boar	sow	hoglet	array of hedgehogs
turkey	tom	hen	poult	rafter of turkeys
jellyfish	boar	sow	planula	bloom OR fluther of jellyfish
squid	cock	hen	chick	audience of squid

Exercise 5B: Nouns and Pronouns

Write the correct pronoun above the underlined word(s). The first one is done for you.

James Watson and Francis Crick discovered the structure of DNA in 1953. James Watson and Francis Crick (They) built on the work of Rosalind Franklin.

Rosalind Franklin had done work on X-ray images of DNA. Rosalind Franklin (She) might have received Nobel Prizes for her work later on, but Rosalind Franklin (she) died at the age of 37.

Scientists all over the world worked on the Human Genome Project. The Human Genome Project [It] was an effort to determine what every single gene in the human body does.

When scientists mapped all the genes in the human body, scientists [they] declared the Human Genome Project complete in 2003.

Omar told his mother, "Mother [You] can get the ingredients ready, and Omar [I] can help mix them together!"

As soon as Ezra arrived home, Ezra called out with excitement, "Ezra and his family [We] won the competition!"

The teacher pulled Roxanne and Anita aside after class. "Roxanne and Anita [You] are going to represent our class at the assembly," the teacher [he/she] told them.

Exercise 5C: Replacing Nouns with Pronouns

Does the passage below sound awkward? It should, because it's not what the author Heather Vogel Frederick wrote in her novel *The Voyage of Patience Goodspeed.* Cross out the proper nouns (and any accompanying adjectives or modifying words such as *the*) that can be replaced by pronouns, and write the appropriate pronoun from the list at the beginning of this lesson over each crossed-out noun.

The narrator is Patience Goodspeed. The story is told from her viewpoint, in the first person—which means she refers to herself with the pronoun *I* when she's acting alone, and *we* when she's in a group with others.

Note to Instructor: The passage below has been corrected to match the original. Answers that replace other nouns by pronouns are acceptable as long as the pronouns are the correct gender and the passage reads well. It is not necessary for the student to replace every noun below, as long as the sentences no longer sound awkward.

Finally, the day came when ~~Patience Goodspeed and Papa and Tad~~ [we] were packed and ready. ~~Patience Goodspeed and Papa and Tad~~ [We] made the rounds of friends and neighbors to say our farewells, ~~Papa~~ [he] accepting their wishes of "greasy luck" — our Nantucket way of bidding whalemen a profitable voyage, with many barrels of oil — with all the dignity of a departing monarch. Which in a sense ~~Papa~~ [he] was, as were all whaling captains on the tiny kingdom that was our island...

On the evening prior to our departure, Papa took his leave in order to make the final arrangements aboard the *Morning Star.* After ~~Papa~~ [he] left, ~~Patience Goodspeed~~ [I] tossed and turned all night, my thoughts a jumble. Oh, why didn't ~~Patience Goodspeed~~ [I] have the courage to defy Papa!

But what was the use? Even if ~~Patience Goodspeed~~ I were to run away and hide, Papa would find me. And besides, my little brother needed me. It was me my little brother had looked to since Mama's death, not Papa, who was still a stranger to him. ~~Patience Goodspeed~~ I couldn't desert Tad now.

Martha awoke us at dawn, and ~~Tad and Patience Goodspeed~~ we tumbled groggily out of bed.

"Come along now, Tad," ~~Martha~~ she said, wrestling my sleepy and protesting brother into the small ell off the kitchen. "Won't do for the captain's son to step aboard looking like an orphan." ~~Tad~~ He emerged a few minutes later, unnaturally clean.

> **Note to Instructor:** Students who have already progressed once through this course may recognize that "It was me" is incorrect; "It was I" is correct, since *I* acts as a predicate nominative. However, in first person narratives, an author may choose to use the more colloquial "It is me" in order to preserve the feel of a conversation.

Exercise 5D: Pronouns and Antecedents

Circle the personal pronouns in the following sentences, and draw an arrow from each pronoun to its antecedent. If the noun and pronoun are masculine, write *m* in the margin. If they are feminine, write *f;* if neuter, write *n*. Look carefully: Some sentences may have more than one personal pronoun, and some personal pronouns may share an antecedent!

The sentences below were taken from C. S. Lewis's *The Voyage of the Dawn Treader*. Some have been adapted or condensed. The first one is done for you.

Eustace made the following diary entry: "*September 3*. The first day for ages when I have been able to write." m

If Caspian had been as experienced then as he became later on in this voyage he would not have made this suggestion; but at the moment it seemed an excellent one. m n

Eustace was surprised at the size of his own tears as they splashed on to the treasure in front of him. n

> **Note to Instructor:** "His" and "him" are also personal pronouns, but only subject pronouns are emphasized in this lesson. If the student circles either or both of those, the arrow(s) should point to Eustace as the antecedent.

"Please, Aslan," said Lucy, "what do you call *soon*?" "I call all times *soon*," said Aslan; and instantly he was vanished away and Lucy was alone with the Magician. m,m m

The Duffers are visible now. But they are probably all asleep still; they always take a rest n
in the middle of the day.

> **Note to Instructor:** *They* is neuter in this sentence because it is unclear whether the Duffers are masculine, feminine, or both.

Eustace now did the first brave thing he had ever done. m

"How beautifully clear the water is!" said Lucy, as she leaned over the port side early in f
the afternoon of the second day. And it was. n

— LESSON 6 —

Review Definitions
Introduction to Verbs
Action Verbs, State-of-Being Verbs
Parts of Speech

Exercise 6A: Identifying Verbs

Mark each underlined verb *A* for action verb or *B* for state-of-being verb.

The submarine, having accomplished her work, backs [A] off to a safe distance, explodes [A] these torpedoes by means of a galvanic battery, and up goes [A] the enemy, in more pieces than one can well count [A]. If a vessel under sail or steam is to be assaulted, the submarine dives [A] down and lies [A] hidden right under the track of her foe; then at the exact moment loosens [A] a torpedo furnished with a percussion apparatus; the enemy strikes [A] this, explodes [A] it, and up she goes [A] past all hope of redemption.

"We had [A] quite a sad accident yesterday," he wrote [A] in a letter home. "A 'machine' we had here and which carried [A] eight or ten men, by some mismanagement filled [A] with water and sank [A], drowning five men, one belonging to our vessel, and the others to the *Chicora*. They were [B] all volunteers for the expedition and fine men too, the best we had [A]."

"I am [B] part owner of the torpedo boat the *Hunley*," he began [A], and "have been interested in building this description of boat since the beginning of the war, and furnished [A] the means entirely of building the predecessor of this boat, which was lost in an attempt to blow [A] up a Federal vessel off Fort Morgan in Mobile Harbor. I feel [A] therefore a deep interest in its success."

The incoming rounds brought[A] with them a new sense of urgency. With the city now under the very guns of the Union Army, something had to be done to drive[A] the invaders away. The city's forts and batteries, while plentiful and powerful, were necessarily restricted to defensive action. Charleston's small flotilla of ironclads and warships was[B] not the answer either, for they were unable to effectively take[A] the offensive against the Federal warships steaming outside the bar. The situation facing Charleston was growing increasingly more desperate, and Battery Wagner on Morris Island was[B] under daily threat of collapse. Thus the hopes of many now rested[A] on the submarine *Hunley*.

Many in the Victorian Age considered[A] inventions such as submarine boats and underwater mines to be[B] "infernal machines," inhuman in their method of attack. If they were treated[A] as war criminals or on the order of spies, they could be hung[A] for their service. In an attempt to legitimize their endeavor—at least in the eyes of the Federals—Hunley placed[A] an order with Charleston's quartermaster on August 21 for "nine grey jackets, three to be trimmed in gold braid." Feeling the need to justify his request, he added[A] that "the men for whom they are ordered are[B] on special secret service and that it is necessary that they be clothed in the Confederate Army uniform."

—From Mark K. Ragan, *Submarine Warfare in the Civil War*

Exercise 6B: Choosing Verbs

Provide an appropriate action and state-of-being verb for each of the following nouns or pronouns. The first one is done for you.

Note to Instructor: The student's answers should be exactly the same as those listed in the State-of-Being column. The verbs in the Action column are samples; answers may vary and may be in any tense.

	State-of-Being	**Action**
Example: The camel	was (or is)	drank
A printer	was/is	prints
The professors	were/are	teach
Puppies	were/are	drool
We	were/are	enjoy
The flight	was/is	lands
The grass	was/is	sways
Friends	were/are	encourage
They	were/are	sing
Robert Louis Stevenson	was/is	wrote

Exercise 6C: Using Vivid Verbs

Good writers use descriptive and vivid verbs. First underline the action verbs in the following sentences. Then rewrite a different, vivid verb in the space provided. The first one is done for you. You may use a thesaurus if necessary.

Note to Instructor: Sample action verbs are provided, but answers may vary.

Example: The sudden noise scared the little girl.	startled
I looked at the man across the restaurant, trying to determine whether I knew him.	stared
When presented with the evidence, Lars finally said that he was the one who had stolen the money.	confessed
The thunder sounded from across the lake.	boomed
As she awaited the announcement of her scores, the figure skater shook with nervous energy.	trembled
Alexis saw a flaw in the plan.	perceived
The old woman walked down the street, carrying several heavy bags.	trudged
Marcus made a new system to increase the group's efficiency.	invented
After running the race, Oscar wanted some water.	craved
I ran to the finish line.	sprinted

— LESSON 7 —

Helping Verbs

Exercise 7A: Introduction to Helping Verbs

In each sentence below, underline the action verb once. Seven of the sentences also include helping verbs; underline each helping verb twice.

These sentences are from O. Henry's short story "After Twenty Years." Some have been slightly adapted or condensed.

The policeman on the beat moved up the avenue impressively.

Chilly gusts of wind with a taste of rain in them had well nigh depeopled the streets.

Now and then you might see the lights of a cigar store or of an all-night lunch counter.

The light showed a pale, square-jawed face with keen eyes, and a little white scar near his right eyebrow.

Twenty years ago to-night, I dined here at "Big Joe" Brady's with Jimmy Wells, my best chum, and the finest chap in the world.

He and I were raised here in New York, just like two brothers, together.

The policeman twirled his club and took a step or two.

Are you going to call time on him sharp?

I will give him half an hour at least.

The wind had risen from its uncertain puffs into a steady blow.

You may read it here at the window.

Exercise 7B: Providing Missing Helping Verbs

Fill in each blank with a helping verb. Sometimes, more than one helping verb might be appropriate.

This excerpt is adapted from Washington Irving's "Rip Van Winkle."

Note to Instructor: The original helping verbs are found below. You may accept any grammatical alternatives.

Whoever has made a voyage up the Hudson must remember the Kaatskill Mountains. They are a dismembered branch of the great Appalachian family, and are seen away to the west of the river, swelling up to a noble height and lording it over the surrounding country. Every change of season, every change of weather, indeed, every hour of the day produces some change in the magical hues and shapes of these mountains, and they are regarded by all the good wives, far and near, as perfect barometers. When the weather is fair and settled, they are clothed in blue and purple, and print their bold outlines on the clear evening sky; but, sometimes, when the rest of the landscape is cloudless, they will gather a hood of gray vapors about their summits, which, in the last rays of the setting sun, will glow and light up like a crown of glory.

At the foot of these fairy mountains, the voyager may have described the light smoke curling up from a village, whose shingle roofs gleam among the trees, just where the blue tints of the upland melt away into the fresh green of the nearer landscape. It is a little village of great antiquity, having been founded by some of the Dutch colonists in the early times of the province.

Certain it is that Rip Van Winkle was a great favorite among all the good wives of the village. The children of the village, too, would shout with joy whenever he approached. Not a dog would bark at him throughout the neighborhood.

The great error in Rip's composition was an insuperable aversion to all kinds of profitable labor. It could not be from the want of assiduity or perseverance, for he would sit on a wet rock, with a rod as long and heavy as a Tartar's lance, and fish all day without a murmur, even though he should not be encouraged by a single nibble. He would never refuse to assist a neighbor even in the roughest toil. But as to doing family duty and keeping his farm in order, he found it impossible.

In fact, he declared it was of no use to work on his farm; it was the most pestilent little piece of ground in the whole country; everything about it went wrong, and would go wrong, in spite of him. His fences were continually falling to pieces; his cow would either go astray or get among the cabbages; weeds were sure to grow quicker in his fields than anywhere else. Though his patrimonial estate had dwindled away under his management, acre by acre, until there was little more left than a mere patch of Indian corn and potatoes, yet it was the worst-conditioned farm in the neighborhood.

— LESSON 8 —

Personal Pronouns

First, Second, and Third Person

Capitalizing the Pronoun *I*

Exercise 8A: Capitalization and Punctuation Practice

Correct the following sentences. Mark through any incorrect small letters and write the correct capitals above them. Insert quotation marks if needed. Use underlining to indicate any italics.

Note: The name of a radio program should be treated like that of a television program.

Note to Instructor: The correct sentences are found below.

The first month of the year is January. January was named after the Roman god Janus, who is the god of transitions, because this month marks the transition to a new year. Numa Pompilius added this month to the Roman calendar around the year 700 BC.

When The Mercury Theatre on the Air broadcast an adaptation of H. G. Wells's novel The War of the Worlds on October 30, 1938, many people thought an alien invasion was actually happening. The radio program became a sudden huge hit, and Campbell Soup decided to sponsor it. The program was renamed The Campbell Playhouse.

In 1862, a Dutch ophthalmologist named Herman Snellen developed the Snellen Chart, which has a large E at the top and several more rows of letters, to measure visual acuity.

The first published crossword puzzle appeared in the Sunday edition of the New York World on December 21, 1913. The puzzle was written by Arthur Wynne, who was born in Liverpool, England, and its original title was "Word-Cross Puzzle."

The Summy Company, which was later acquired by Warner/Chappell Music, claimed for years that it owned the copyright to the song "Happy Birthday to You." On September 22, 2015, Judge George H. King ruled that this claim was invalid, and the song is now considered to be in the public domain.

After much debate over Prime Minister Lester B. Pearson's proposal for a new flag, Canada adopted its current flag with the image of a maple leaf on February 15, 1965. In 1996, February 15 became known in that country as National Flag of Canada Day.

In 1948, Eleanor Abbott made a game for children called Candy Land. The game was published by Milton Bradley beginning the next year, and it quickly became a bestseller. Children have enjoyed playing Candy Land for decades, and it was inducted into the National Toy Hall of Fame in 2005.

According to Guinness World Records (a reference book previously known as The Guinness Book of World Records), Robert Wadlow was the tallest man in medical history. Wadlow was born in Alton, Illinois, on February 22, 1918. When he was measured on June 27, 1940, he was found to be 8 feet, 11.1 inches tall.

Exercise 8B: Person, Number, and Gender

Label each personal pronoun in the following selection with its person (1, 2, or 3) and number (*s* or *pl*). For third person singular pronouns only, indicate gender (*m*, *f*, or *n*).

The first is done for you.

Note to Instructor: We have only addressed subject personal pronouns so far, but this passage contains personal pronouns that act as objects and possessives as well. The student may or may not mark these additional personal pronouns; the key below indicates these in parentheses. Answers NOT in parentheses are subject pronouns, which the student should be sure to mark.

Ermengarde began to laugh.

3sf 2s 2s
"Oh, Sara!" she said. "You *are* queer—but you are nice."

1s 1s 1s 3sf (3sf)
"I know I am queer," admitted Sara, cheerfully; "and I *try* to be nice." She rubbed her forehead
(3sf) (3sf)
with her little brown paw, and a puzzled, tender look came into her face. "Papa always laughed at
(1s) 3sf 1s (3sn) 3sm 1s 3sm (1s) 1s 1s
me," she said; "but I liked it. He thought I was queer, but he liked me to make up things. I—I can't
1s 1s 1s 3sf
help making up things. If I didn't, I don't believe I could live." She paused and glanced around the
1s 1s 3sf
attic. "I'm sure I couldn't live here," she added in a low voice.

3sf 2s 3sf 3pl
Ermengarde was interested, as she always was. "When you talk about things," she said, "they
3pl 2s 3sm
seem as if they grew real. You talk about Melchisedec as if he was a person."

3sm 3sm 1pl 3sm
"He *is* a person," said Sara. "He gets hungry and frightened, just as we do; and he is married
1pl 3sm 1pl (3sm) 3sm
and has children. How do we know he doesn't think things, just as we do? His eyes look as if he
1s (3sm)
was a person. That was why I gave him a name."

— From *A Little Princess*, by Frances Hodgson Burnett

WEEK 3

Introduction to the Sentence

— LESSON 9 —

The Sentence
Parts of Speech and Parts of Sentences
Subjects and Predicates

Exercise 9A: Parts of Speech vs. Parts of the Sentence
Label each underlined word with the correct part of speech AND the correct part of the sentence.

part of speech — pronoun, verb

We saw the huge tree.

part of the sentence — subject, predicate

part of speech — noun, verb

The leaves were red.

part of the sentence — subject, predicate

part of speech — noun, verb

A squirrel scampered up the trunk.

part of the sentence — subject, predicate

part of speech — pronoun, verb

It jumped to the next tree.

part of the sentence — subject, predicate

Exercise 9B: Parts of Speech: Nouns, Adjectives, Pronouns, and Verbs

Label each underlined word with the correct part of speech. Use *N* for noun, *A* for adjective, *P* for pronoun, and *V* for verb.

The first night [N], then, I [P] went to sleep on the sand, a thousand [A] miles [N] from any human [A] habitation [N]. I was [V] more isolated than a shipwrecked [A] sailor on a raft [N] in the middle [N] of the ocean. Thus you [P] can imagine [V] my amazement [N], at sunrise, when I was awakened by an odd [A] little [A] voice. It [P] said:

"If you [P] please—draw [V] me a sheep!"

"What!"

"Draw me a sheep [N]!"

I jumped [V] to my feet [N], completely thunderstruck. I blinked [V] my eyes [N] hard. I [P] looked [V] carefully all around me. And I saw [V] a most extraordinary [A] small [A] person [N], who stood [V] there examining me with great [A] seriousness [N].

— From *The Little Prince*, by Antoine de Saint-Exupéry

Exercise 9C: Parts of the Sentence: Subjects and Predicates

In each of the following sentences, underline the subject once and the predicate twice. Find the subject by asking, "Who or what is this sentence about?" Find the predicate by saying, "Subject what?"

Example: Flamingos make nests out of mud.

Who or what is this sentence about? Flamingos.
Flamingos what? Flamingos make.

Flamingos eat brine shrimp or algae.

Their food contains carotenoids.

The carotenoids turn the flamingos' feathers pink.

Baby flamingos have white or gray feathers.

Lake Natron, in Tanzania, is the birthplace for over half the world's lesser flamingos.

Caribbean flamingos are the only flamingo species native to North America.

> **Note to Instructor:** Accept either "Caribbean flamingos" or simply "flamingos" as the subject of the preceding sentence.

South America is home to Chilean, Andean, James's, and Caribbean flamingos.

Greater flamingos live in Europe, Africa, and Asia.

> **Note to Instructor:** Accept either "Greater flamingos" or simply "flamingos" as the subject of the preceding sentence.

— LESSON 10 —

Subjects and Predicates
Diagramming Subjects and Predicates
Sentence Capitalization and Punctuation
Sentence Fragments

Exercise 10A: Sentences and Fragments

If a group of words expresses a complete thought, write *S* for sentence in the blank. If not, write *F* for fragment.

while jumping up and down	F
the girl saw a train approaching	S
made of popsicle sticks	F
the delectable meal set before us	F
the window was slightly ajar	S
three tall men in brown suits approached	S
because the elevator was broken	F

Exercise 10B: Proofreading for Capitalization and Punctuation

Add the correct capitalization and punctuation to the following sentences. In this exercise you will use proofreader's marks. Indicate letters which should be capitalized by underlining three times. Indicate ending punctuation by using the proofreader's mark for inserting a period: ⊙ Indicate words which should be italicized by underlining them and writing *ital* in the margin.

The first is done for you.

the name texas comes from a caddo word that means friends ⊙

the state of pennsylvania gets its name from its founder, william penn, and the latin word for woods ⊙

a spanish novel, las sergas de esplandián, described a fictional place called california; this is the likely source of the us state name ⊙ ital

the french king louis xiv was honored in the name louisiana ⊙

florida's name, chosen by juan ponce de león, came from the spanish phrase "pascua florida," meaning "feast of flowers" and referring to the easter season ⊙

michigan is the ojibwa word for "large lake" changed to a french form ⊙

Note: Look carefully at the next part! There are three separate sentences here, so you will need to insert three periods.

during the civil war, the confederates took an old union ship, the merrimack, covered it with iron plates, and renamed it the virginia ⊙ the virginia battled against another ironclad ship, the monitor ⊙ this first battle between two ironclad ships ended in a draw ⊙ ital ital ital

Exercise 10C: Diagramming

Find the subjects and predicates in the following sentences. Diagram each subject and predicate on your own paper. You should capitalize on the diagram any words that are capitalized in the sentence, but do not put punctuation marks on the diagram. If a proper name is the subject, all parts of the proper name go on the subject line of the diagram.

Example: Joseph jumped jubilantly.

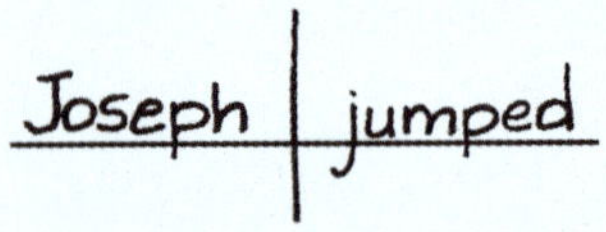

My big brother borrowed Ben's book.

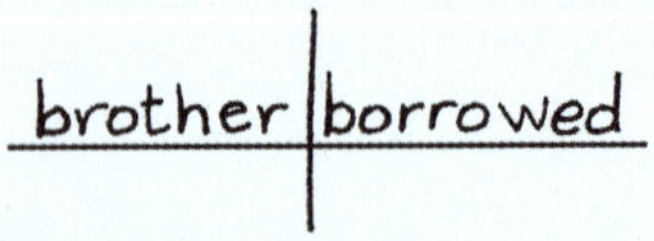

We watched Waldo's walrus on Wednesday.

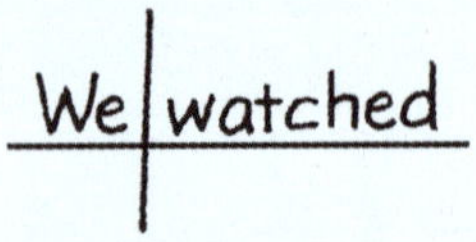

Isabella Ingalls itched in the igloo.

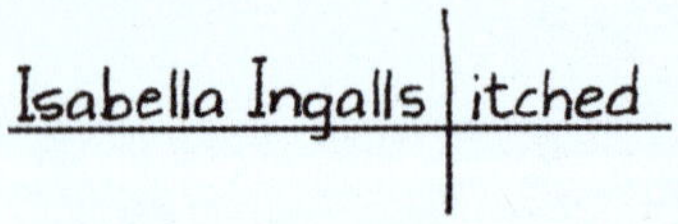

The enormous elephant entered the elevator.

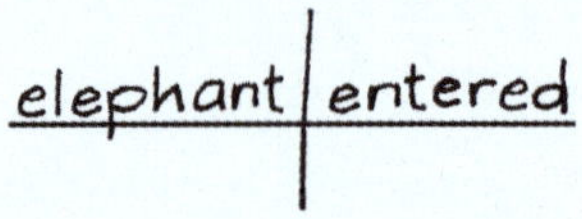

Six sleeping snails sat on the sill.

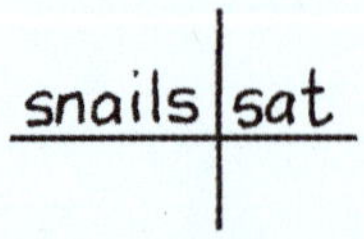

Clara clandestinely climbed the cliff.

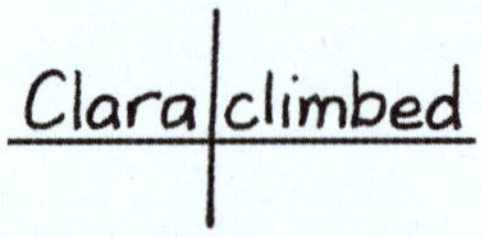

The floral fabric from Finland flatters Fiona's face.

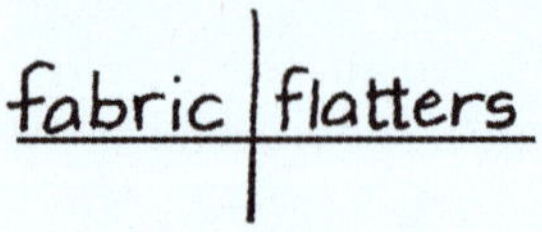

— LESSON 11 —

Types of Sentences

Exercise 11A: Types of Sentences: Statements, Exclamations, Commands, and Questions

Identify the following sentences as *S* for statement, *E* for exclamation, *C* for command, or *Q* for question. Add the appropriate punctuation to the end of each sentence.

Note to Instructor: For commands, periods and exclamation points are interchangeable.

	Sentence Type
Do you like to play basketball?	Q
Please dust the furniture.	C
I want to change clothes before going to the party.	S
Will you give me some advice?	Q
I love square dancing!	E
Don't get into any trouble!	C
What a huge volcano!	E
Daniel wanted a sandwich with strawberry jam.	S
Take off your hat.	C
How long would it take to hike to the top of that mountain?	Q

Exercise 11B: Proofreading for Capitalization and Punctuation

Proofread the following sentences. If a small letter should be capitalized, draw three lines underneath it. Add any missing punctuation.

what is your decision?

tell me the price of this game.

i want to start my own fashion design company.

the dog likes chasing his own tail.

pass me your plate.

that baby was cute as a button ! OR .

may we open the box now?

Exercise 11C: Diagramming Subjects and Predicates

On your own paper, diagram the subjects and predicates of the following sentences. Remember that the understood subject of a command is *you*, and that the predicate may come before the subject in a question.

We enjoyed lunch.

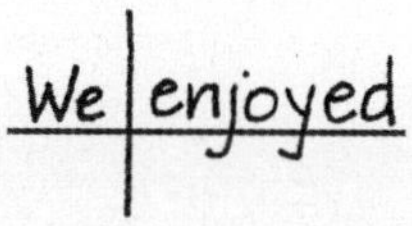

Were you happy?

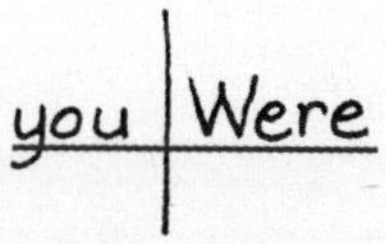

Eat your vegetables!

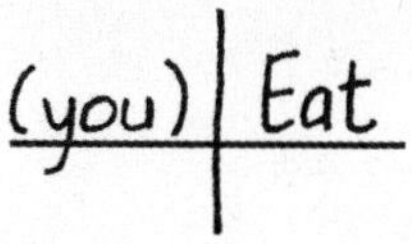

The tiger is beautiful.

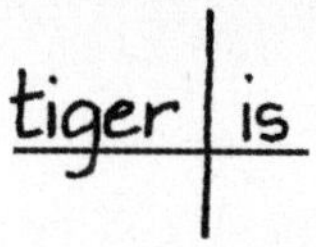

Please get your toys.

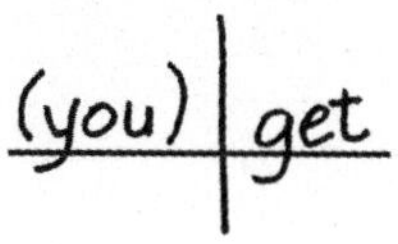

Harriet ambled into the store.

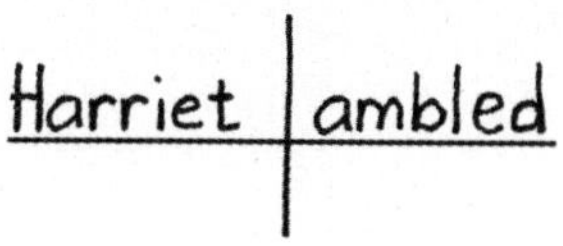

Are the geese by the lake?

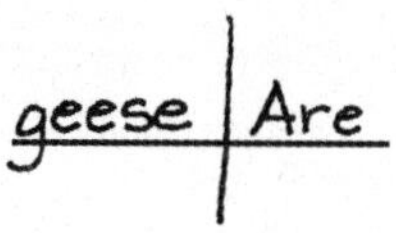

I see a mouse!

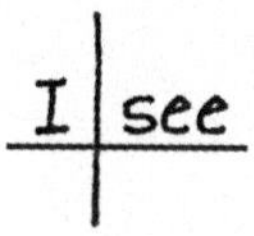

— LESSON 12 —

Subjects and Predicates
Helping Verbs
Simple and Complete Subjects and Predicates

Exercise 12A: Complete Subjects and Complete Predicates

Match the complete subjects and complete predicates by drawing lines between them.

The three children	pulled into the driveway.
Grandfather	was growing crystals on a string in a glass.
Last year, he	waited excitedly for their grandfather's arrival.
All that summer, they	smiled and hugged each of them.
Their favorite experiment	wondered what Grandfather would bring this time.
As they waited, the children	showed the children their new gift: a gardening kit!
Finally, Grandfather's car	always brought gifts when he came to visit.
With cries of delight, the children	had come with a chemistry kit that they could all use.
The elderly man	performed experiments and made discoveries with the kit.
Reaching into the car, Grandfather	opened the door and ran out to greet him.

Note to Instructor: The original sentences are listed below, but accept any reasonable answers.

The three children	waited excitedly for their grandfather's arrival.
Grandfather	always brought gifts when he came to visit.
Last year, he	had come with a chemistry kit that they could all use.
All that summer, they	performed experiments and made discoveries with the kit.
Their favorite experiment	was growing crystals on a string in a glass.
As they waited, the children	wondered what Grandfather would bring this time.
Finally, Grandfather's car	pulled into the driveway.
With cries of delight, the children	opened the door and ran out to greet him.
The elderly man	smiled and hugged each of them.
Reaching into the car, Grandfather	showed the children their new gift: a gardening kit!

Exercise 12B: Simple and Complete Subjects and Predicates

In the following sentences, underline the simple subject once and the simple predicate twice. Then, draw a vertical line between the complete subject and the complete predicate. The first is done for you.

These sentences are adapted from the Zulu story "The Day Baboon Outwitted Leopard," as told by Nick Greaves in *When Hippo Was Hairy: And Other Tales from Africa.*

Leopard | called her friend Baboon.

After a while, Baboon | dozed off.

Now an angry, hungry leopard | is not a very reassuring sight.

Despite their past friendship, she | opened her jaws for a bite.

Quick as a flash, Baboon | climbed up into the safety of the thickest thorns at the top.

Other animals | were gathering around.

Leopard's pride | could not stand it.

To this day, the leopard | hunts the baboon in preference to all other food.

Exercise 12C: Diagramming Simple Subjects and Simple Predicates

On your own paper, diagram the simple subjects and simple predicates from Exercise 12B.

Leopard called her friend Baboon.

Leopard | called

After a while, Baboon dozed off.

Baboon | dozed

Now an angry, hungry leopard is not a very reassuring sight.

leopard | is

Despite their past friendship, she opened her jaws for a bite.

she | opened

Quick as a flash, Baboon climbed up into the safety of the thickest thorns at the top.

Baboon | climbed

Other animals were gathering around.

animals | were gathering

Leopard's pride could not stand it.

pride | could stand

To this day, the leopard hunts the baboon in preference to all other food.

leopard | hunts

— REVIEW 1 —

Weeks 1-3

Topics
Concrete/Abstract Nouns
Descriptive Adjectives
Common/Proper Nouns
Capitalization of Proper Nouns and First Words in Sentences
Noun Gender
Pronouns and Antecedents
Action Verbs/State-of-Being Verbs
Helping Verbs
Subjects and Predicates
Complete Sentences
Types of Sentences

Review 1A: Types of Nouns

Fill in the blanks with the correct description of each noun. The first is done for you.

	Concrete / Abstract	Common / Proper	Gender (**M, F, N**)
cherry	C	C	N
Times Square	C	P	N
decision	A	C	N
Johnny Cash	C	P	M
hour	A	C	N
Cleopatra	C	P	F
sister	C	C	F
zipper	C	C	N
ram	C	C	M
Suwannee River	C	P	N

Review 1B: Types of Verbs

Underline the complete verbs in the following sentences. Identify any helping verbs as *HV*. Identify the main verb as *AV* for action verb or *BV* for state-of-being verb. The first is done for you.

Bones are (BV) both flexible and strong.

Collagen, a type of protein, gives (AV) bones their flexibility.

The strength of bones comes (AV) from minerals like calcium.

Have (HV) you ever broken (AV) a bone?

Bones may (HV) break (AV) with too much pressure.

A fracture can (HV) be (BV) open or closed.

HV AV
With an open fracture, bone has come through the skin.

HV AV
Closed fractures do not pierce the skin.

HV AV
Doctors must consider many factors for treatment of broken bones.

BV
The smallest bone in the human body is the stapes, a stirrup-shaped bone in the middle ear.

Review 1C: Subjects and Predicates

Draw one line under the simple subject and two lines under the simple predicate in the following sentences. Remember that the predicate may be a verb phrase with more than one verb in it.

Simon will visit the Rocky Mountains next month.

Natalie did not multiply the numbers correctly.

Throughout the show, the actors appreciated the audience's laughter.

The man with the untidy appearance was actually an undercover police officer.

Besides milk and stamps, I should add fruit to my shopping list.

The sad little girl wished for a friend.

An ominous knock sounded at the door.

Today may be the most exciting day of your life!

The storm had delayed our flight by three hours.

Review 1D: Parts of Speech

Identify the underlined words as *N* for noun, *P* for pronoun, *A* for adjective, *AV* for action verb, *HV* for helping verb, or *BV* for state-of-being verb.

The following excerpt is from Scott O'Dell's *Island of the Blue Dolphins.*

N P AV N N AV
After Kimki had been gone one moon, we began to watch for his return. Every day someone went
N AV A N P AV N AV
to the cliff to scan the sea. Even on stormy days we went, and on days when fog shrouded the
BV N A N AV
island. During the day there was always a watcher on the cliff and each night as we sat around
P AV N HV AV
our fires we wondered if the next sun would bring him home.

N AV AV BV N HV AV
But the spring came and left and the sea was empty. Kimki did not return!

A N A AV AV
There were few storms that winter and rain was light and ended early. This meant that
HV AV N A N AV
we would need to be careful of water. In the old days the springs sometimes ran low and no
AV N BV HV AV
one worried, but now everything seemed to cause alarm. Many were afraid that we would die
N
of thirst.

Review 1E: Capitalization and Punctuation

Use proofreader's marks to indicate correct capitalization and punctuation in the following sentences. The first has been done for you.

did enough students sign up for the september trip to new york city ?

in the twentieth century, the year 1935 had more solar eclipses than any other year; they occurred on january 5, february 3, june 30, july 30, and december 25 ⊙

the saturday evening post magazine featured artwork by norman rockwell for forty-seven years ⊙

what an amazing sunset !

have you ever seen george p. burdell at a georgia tech football game ?

a canadian newspaper editor, joseph coyle, invented egg cartons in 1911 ⊙

when inflation is taken into account, the highest-grossing film of all time is gone with the wind, starring clark gable and vivien leigh ⊙

"annabel lee" was the last poem edgar allan poe wrote ⊙

fred and i loved the performance of the phantom of the opera !

Review 1F: Types of Sentences

Identify the following sentences as *S* for statement, *C* for command, *E* for exclamation, or *Q* for question. If the sentence is incomplete, write *I*.

The following sentences are from *The Adventures of Tom Sawyer*, by Mark Twain. Some have been slightly adapted.

	Sentence Type
"I can."	S
"Can't!"	I
"What's your name?"	Q
"You're a liar!"	E
"Take a walk!"	C
"Why don't you do it?"	Q
"It's because you're afraid."	S
"Get away from here!"	C
"I'll tell my big brother on you."	S
"I've got a brother that's bigger than he is."	S
Both brothers were imaginary.	S
"Don't you crowd me now."	C
"You said you'd do it!"	E
At last the enemy's mother appeared and ordered Tom away.	S

WEEK 4

Verb Tenses

— LESSON 13 —

Nouns, Pronouns, and Verbs

Sentences

Simple Present, Simple Past, and Simple Future Tenses

Exercise 13A: Simple Tenses

	Simple Past	Simple Present	Simple Future
I	painted	paint	will paint
You	snored	snore	will snore
She	climbed	climbs	will climb
We	conquered	conquer	will conquer
They	bounced	bounce	will bounce

Exercise 13B: Using Consistent Tense

When you write, you should use consistent tense—if you begin a sentence in one tense, you should continue to use that same tense for any other verbs in the same sentence. The following sentences use two verb tenses. Cross out the second verb and rewrite it so that the tense of the second verb matches the tense of the first one.

The first sentence is done for you.

After the rain, we will go outside and the children ~~played~~ will play in the puddles.

I love the smell of the air after the rain, so I ~~closed~~ close my eyes to enjoy it.

Frances saw two little frogs hopping and ~~will take~~ took a picture of them.

The clouds will clear soon and the sky ~~is~~ will be bright blue.

Philip squealed when Kira ~~splashes~~ splashed him with water from a puddle.

An earthworm wriggles on the ground, and a robin ~~looked~~ looks at it hungrily.

Tomorrow it will be sunny and we ~~went~~ will go to the beach.

Exercise 13C: Forming the Simple Past Tense

Using the rules for forming the simple past, put each one of the verbs in parentheses into the simple past. Write the simple past form in the blank. Be sure to spell the past forms of regular verbs correctly, and to use the correct forms of irregular verbs.

These passages are condensed from *Five Children and It*, by E. Nesbit.

Then the postman was heard blowing his horn, and Robert rushed out in the rain to stop his cart and give him the letters. And that was how it happened that, though all the children meant to tell their mother about the Sand-fairy, somehow or other she never got to know.

The next day Uncle Richard came and took them all to Maidstone in a wagonette—all except the Lamb. Uncle Richard was the very best kind of uncle. He bought them toys at Maidstone. He took them into a shop and let them all choose exactly what they wanted, without any restrictions about price, and no nonsense about things being instructive. Robert chose, at the last moment, and in a great hurry, a box with pictures on it of winged bulls with men's heads and winged men with eagles' heads. He thought there would be animals inside, the same as on the box. When he got home it was a Sunday puzzle about ancient Nineveh! The others chose in haste, and were happy at leisure.

Then Uncle Richard took them on the beautiful Medway in a boat, and then they all had tea at a beautiful confectioner's and when they reached home it was far too late to have any wishes that day. . . .

Anthea woke at five. At the very moment when she opened her eyes she heard the black-and-gold clock down in the dining-room strike eleven. So she knew it was three minutes to five. The black-and-gold clock always struck wrong, but it was all right when you knew what it meant. She was very sleepy, but she jumped out of bed and put her face and hands into a basin of cold water. This is a fairy charm that prevents your wanting to get back into bed again. Then she dressed, and folded up her night dress.

Then she took her shoes in her hand and crept softly down the stairs. She opened the dining-room window and climbed out. It would have been just as easy to go out by the door, but the window was more romantic, and less likely to be noticed by Martha.

— LESSON 14 —

Simple Present, Simple Past, and Simple Future Tenses
Progressive Present, Progressive Past, and Progressive Future Tenses

Exercise 14A: Forming the Simple Past and Simple Future Tenses

Form the simple past and simple future of the following regular verbs

Past	Present	Future
wandered	wander	will wander
exercised	exercise	will exercise
searched	search	will search
delayed	delay	will delay
chopped	chop	will chop
confused	confuse	will confuse
stepped	step	will step
carried	carry	will carry
tamed	tame	will tame

Exercise 14B: Progressive Tenses

Circle the ending of each verb. Underline the helping verbs.

will be confessing

was preventing

were mourning

am tasting

will be drumming

are shivering

was decorating

is juggling

Exercise 14C: Forming the Progressive Past, Present, and Future Tenses

Complete the following chart. Be sure to use the spelling rules above.

Note to Instructor: This exercise drills progressive verbs and also prepares the student for the introduction of person in next week's lessons. If the student asks why the helping verbs change, you may either say, "You'll find out next week" or turn to Lesson 18 and do it out of order. (The first method is recommended for students who are doing this course for the first time; person has not yet been covered in order to allow the student to concentrate on the tenses being introduced.)

	Progressive Past	Progressive Present	Progressive Future
I chew	I was chewing	I am chewing	I will be chewing
I gather	I was gathering	I am gathering	I will be gathering
I encourage	I was encouraging	I am encouraging	I will be encouraging
I yawn	I was yawning	I am yawning	I will be yawning
You invent	You were inventing	You are inventing	You will be inventing
You breathe	You were breathing	You are breathing	You will be breathing
You shrug	You were shrugging	You are shrugging	You will be shrugging
You sail	You were sailing	You are sailing	You will be sailing
We remind	We were reminding	We are reminding	We will be reminding
We love	We were loving	We are loving	We will be loving
We spot	We were spotting	We are spotting	We will be spotting
We copy	We were copying	We are copying	We will be copying

Exercise 14D: Simple and Progressive Tenses

Fill in the blanks with the correct form of the verb in parentheses.

Leonhard Euler, a Swiss mathematician, became nearly blind in his right eye in 1738, and in 1766, he went blind in his left eye as well.

When he lost the use of his right eye, Euler said, "Now I will have less distraction."

Despite his almost total blindness, Euler was producing about one mathematical paper per week in 1775; his students helped him develop and record his ideas.

Students of mathematics today are learning many concepts Euler developed.

Euler introduced or standardized much mathematical notation that people are using today, such as the symbol π for the ratio of a circle's circumference to its diameter.

When you are studying algebra in high school, one thing you will be learning about is a special number named after Euler.

Euler said that "in the theory of numbers, observations will lead us continually to new properties which we will endeavor to prove afterwards."

— LESSON 15 —

Simple Present, Simple Past, and Simple Future Tenses
Progressive Present, Progressive Past, and Progressive Future Tenses
Perfect Present, Perfect Past, and Perfect Future Tenses

Exercise 15A: Perfect Tenses

Fill in the blanks with the missing forms.

Simple Past	Perfect Past	Perfect Present	Perfect Future
I planted	I had planted	I have planted	I will have planted
I ignored	I had ignored	I have ignored	I will have ignored
I glared	I had glared	I have glared	I will have glared
I flipped	I had flipped	I have flipped	I will have flipped
We pined	We had pined	We have pined	We will have pined
We objected	We had objected	We have objected	We will have objected
We refrained	We had refrained	We have refrained	We will have refrained
We napped	We had napped	We have napped	We will have napped
He pondered	He had pondered	He has pondered	He will have pondered
He escaped	He had escaped	He has escaped	He will have escaped
He contributed	He had contributed	He has contributed	He will have contributed
He jogged	He had jogged	He has jogged	He will have jogged

Exercise 15B: Identifying Perfect Tenses

Identify the underlined verbs as perfect past, perfect present, or perfect future. The first one is done for you.

perfect present
I have decided to make a quilt.

perfect present
I have purchased fabric and thread.

perfect past
I had practiced sewing straight lines before I decided to try a quilt.

perfect present
The quilt will be the same size as my brother's baby blanket; I have measured it carefully.

perfect past
Yesterday I was reading a book about quilting after I had watched some videos showing how to quilt.

perfect present
My grandmother has shown me several quilts she made.

perfect present
I have learned about the different steps in making a quilt.

perfect future
When I finish, I will have pieced nine blocks for my quilt.

Exercise 15C: Perfect, Progressive, and Simple Tenses

Each underlined verb phrase has been labeled as past, present, or future. Add the label *perfect*, *progressive*, or *simple* to each one. The first one has been done for you.

progressive FUTURE; progressive PRESENT
Maria will be turning thirteen soon. She is planning her birthday party.

perfect PAST; simple PAST
Maria had gone to the bakery with her father to look for a cake, but she decided to order cupcakes instead.

simple FUTURE; simple FUTURE
The baker will decorate the cupcakes so that each one will have a frosting soccer ball.

simple PRESENT; perfect PRESENT
Maria loves to play soccer. She has played since the age of four.

simple FUTURE; simple PRESENT; progressive FUTURE
Maria will invite all her teammates to her party. While music plays, everyone will be enjoying the soccer ball cupcakes!

progressive PAST; simple PAST
"I was hoping we could have the party on Saturday afternoon," said Maria, "but the coach scheduled practice for that time."

— LESSON 16 —

Simple Present, Simple Past, and Simple Future Tenses
Progressive Present, Progressive Past, and Progressive Future Tenses
Perfect Present, Perfect Past, and Perfect Future Tenses
Irregular Verbs

Exercise 16A: Irregular Verb Forms: Simple Present, Simple Past, and Simple Future
Fill in the chart with the missing verb forms.

Note to Instructor: We have not yet covered number and person of verbs, which affects some irregular forms. If the student uses an incorrect form, simply tell her the correct form. Have her cross out the incorrect answer and write the correct answer in its place.

	Simple Past	Simple Present	Simple Future
I	led	lead	will lead
You	built	build	will build
She	meant	means	will mean
We	grew	grow	will grow
They	understood	understand	will understand
I	spread	spread	will spread
You	fought	fight	will fight
He	drank	drinks	will drink
We	froze	freeze	will freeze
They	slept	sleep	will sleep
I	lost	lose	will lose
You	caught	catch	will catch
It	set	sets	will set
We	gave	give	will give
They	fell	fall	will fall
I	sought	seek	will seek
You	sent	send	will send
We	came	come	will come
They	hid	hide	will hide

Exercise 16B: Irregular Verbs, Progressive and Perfect Tenses

Fill in the remaining blanks. The first row is done for you.

Note to Instructor: This is only the first practice run with irregular verbs, designed to increase the student's familiarity—give all necessary help. Since we have not yet covered person and number in this workbook, the student should follow the pattern established in the first line of the chart.

Simple Present	Progressive Past	Progressive Present	Progressive Future	Perfect Past	Perfect Present	Perfect Future
send	was sending	is sending	will be sending	had sent	has sent	will have sent
grow	was growing	is growing	will be growing	had grown	has grown	will have grown
spread	was spreading	is spreading	will be spreading	had spread	has spread	will have spread
build	was building	is building	will be building	had built	has built	will have built
understand	was understanding	is understanding	will be understanding	had understood	has understood	will have understood
hide	was hiding	is hiding	will be hiding	had hidden	has hidden	will have hidden
mean	was meaning	is meaning	will be meaning	had meant	has meant	will have meant
drink	was drinking	is drinking	will be drinking	had drunk	has drunk	will have drunk
sleep	was sleeping	is sleeping	will be sleeping	had slept	has slept	will have slept
catch	was catching	is catching	will be catching	had caught	has caught	will have caught
lead	was leading	is leading	will be leading	had led	has led	will have led
fall	was falling	is falling	will be falling	had fallen	has fallen	will have fallen

Simple Present	Progressive Past	Progressive Present	Progressive Future	Perfect Past	Perfect Present	Perfect Future
set	was setting	is setting	will be setting	had set	has set	will have set
lose	was losing	is losing	will be losing	had lost	has lost	will have lost
freeze	was freezing	is freezing	will be freezing	had frozen	has frozen	will have frozen
give	was giving	is giving	will be giving	had given	has given	will have given
seek	was seeking	is seeking	will be seeking	had sought	has sought	will have sought
come	was coming	is coming	will be coming	had come	has come	will have come
fight	was fighting	is fighting	will be fighting	had fought	has fought	will have fought

WEEK 5

More About Verbs

— LESSON 17 —

Simple, Progressive, and Perfect Tenses
Subjects and Predicates
Parts of Speech and Parts of Sentences
Verb Phrases

Exercise 17A: Simple, Progressive, and Perfect Tenses

All of the bolded verbs are in the past tense. Label each bolded verb as *S* for simple, *PROG* for progressive, or *PERF* for perfect.

This passage has been adapted from *Oliver Twist*, by Charles Dickens.

It **chanced** [S] one morning, while Oliver's affairs **were** [S] in this auspicious and comfortable state, that Mr. Gamfield, chimney-sweeper, **was wending** [PROG] his way adown the High-street, and was deeply **cogitating** [PROG] in his mind, his ways and means of paying certain arrears of rent, for which his landlord **had become** [PERF] rather pressing. Mr. Gamfield's most sanguine calculation of funds could not raise them within full five pounds of the desired amount; and in a species of arithmetical desperation, he **was** alternately **cudgelling** [PROG] his brains and his donkey, when, passing the workhouse, his eyes **encountered** [S] the bill on the gate.

"Woo!" **said** [S] Mr. Gamfield to the donkey.

The donkey **was** [S] in a state of profound abstraction—wondering, probably, whether he was destined to be regaled with a cabbage-stalk or two, when he **had disposed** [PERF] of the two sacks of soot with which the little cart was laden; so, without noticing the word of command, he **jogged** [S] onwards.

Mr. Gamfield **growled** [S] a fierce imprecation on the donkey generally, but more particularly on his eyes. After he **had given** [PERF] the donkey a reminder that he **was** [S] not his own master, Mr. Gamfield **walked** [S] to the gate to read the bill. The gentleman with the white waistcoat **was standing** [PROG] at the gate with his hands behind him, and he **smiled** [S] joyously when Mr. Gamfield **came** [S] up to read the bill.

Exercise 17B: Identifying and Diagramming Subjects and Predicates, Identifying Verb Tenses

Underline the subject once and the predicate twice in each sentence. Be sure to include both the main verb and any helping verbs when you underline the predicate. Identify the tense of each verb or verb phrase (*simple past, present,* or *future*; *progressive past, present,* or *future*; *perfect past, present,* or *future*) in the blank. Then, diagram each subject and predicate on your own paper.

These sentences are adapted from *Oliver Twist*, by Charles Dickens.

The two boys had scoured with great rapidity through a most intricate maze of narrow streets and courts. perfect past

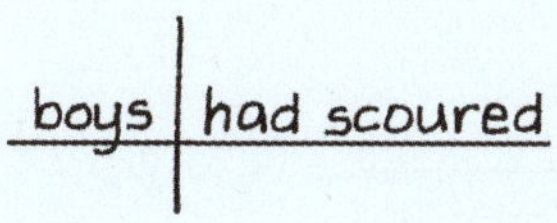

The Dodger made no reply. simple past

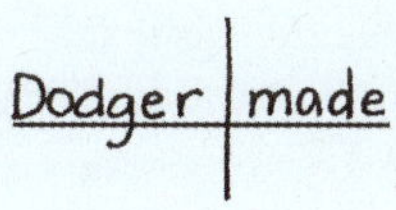

Will you speak? simple future

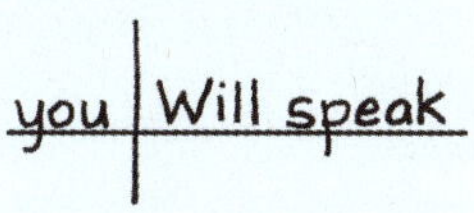

The dog coiled himself up in a corner very quietly without uttering a sound. simple past

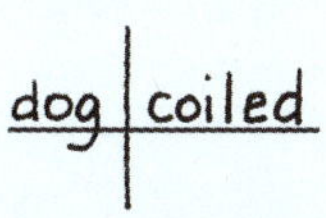

The old gentleman's eyes were vacantly staring on the opposite wall. progressive past

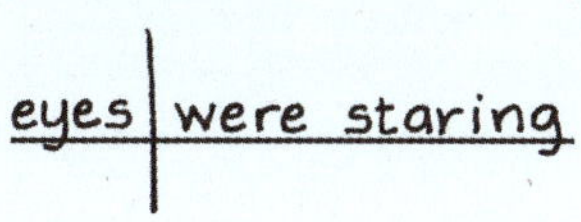

Miss Nancy arrived in perfect safety shortly afterwards. simple past

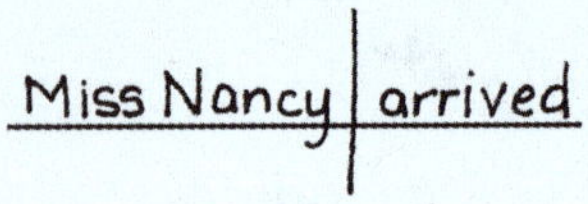

Mr. Brownlow's abrupt exclamation had thrown Oliver into a fainting-fit. perfect past

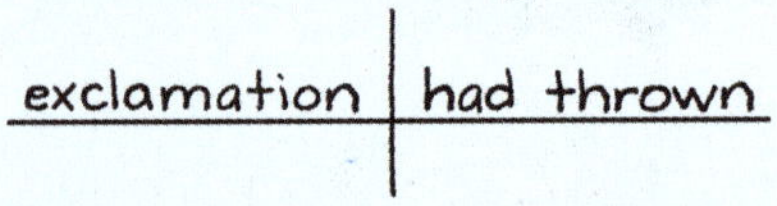

Oliver had never had a new suit before. perfect past

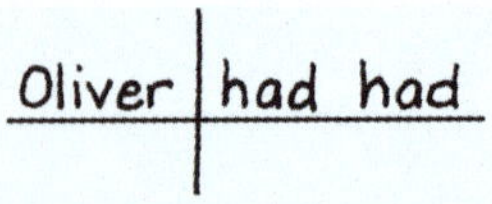

Oliver was talking to Mrs. Bedwin one evening. progressive past

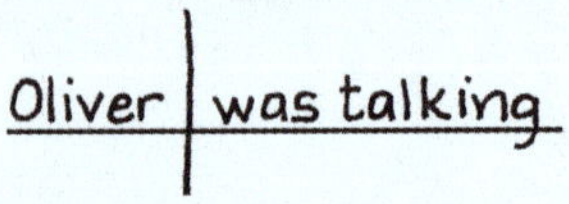

I will talk to you without any reserve. simple future

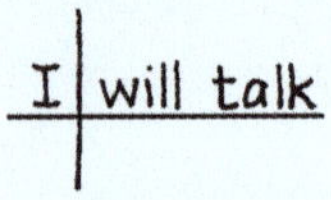

I feel strongly on this subject, sir. simple present

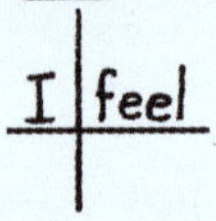

He is deceiving you, my dear friend. progressive present

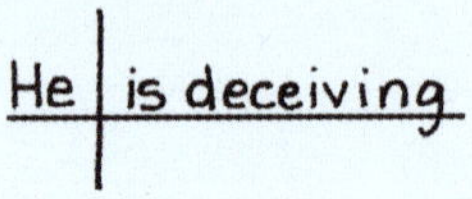

I know a great number of persons in both situations at this moment. simple present

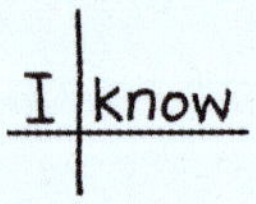

— LESSON 18 —

Verb Phrases
Person of the Verb
Conjugations

Exercise 18A: Third Person Singular Verbs

In the simple present conjugation, the third person singular verb changes by adding an *-s*. Read the following rules and examples for adding *-s* to verbs in order to form the third person singular. Then, fill in the blanks with the third person singular forms of each verb.

The first of each is done for you.

Usually, add *-s* to form the third person singular verb.

First Person Verb	Third Person Singular Verb	
I treat	he	treats
I fold	she	folds
I divide	it	divides

Add *-es* to verbs ending in *-s*, *-sh*, *-ch*, *-x*, or *-z*.

First Person Verb	Third Person Singular Verb	
we punish	she	punishes
we embarrass	it	embarrasses
we relax	he	relaxes

If a verb ends in *-y* after a consonant, change the *y* to *i* and add *-es*.

First Person Verb	Third Person Singular Verb	
I supply	it	supplies
I hurry	he	hurries
I identify	she	identifies

If a verb ends in *-y* after a vowel, just add *-s*.

First Person Verb	Third Person Singular Verb	
we stay	he	stays
we employ	she	employs
we obey	it	obeys

If a verb ends in *-o* after a consonant, form the plural by adding *-es*.

First Person Verb	Third Person Singular Verb	
I outdo	she	outdoes
I undergo	it	undergoes
I solo	he	soloes

Exercise 18B: Simple Present Tenses

Choose the correct form of the simple present verb in parentheses, based on the person. Cross out the incorrect form.

Zayan (~~love~~/loves) to play board games.

He (~~invite~~/invites) his friends over to play games whenever he can.

Sometimes, Zayan and his friends (play/~~plays~~) a game Zayan (~~own~~/owns). Other times, his friends (bring/~~brings~~) their games.

"I (want/~~wants~~) to play your newest game!" Zayan's friend Derek (~~announce~~/announces). "It really (~~sound~~/sounds) like a lot of fun!"

Zayan's brother Rehan (~~speak~~/speaks) up. "It is! I (enjoy/~~enjoys~~) playing it."

The other two friends (agree/~~agrees~~) to try out the new game.

Zayan (~~pick~~/picks) up the red player token, and Derek (~~choose~~/chooses) the yellow one. The others (select/~~selects~~) their player tokens as well, and they all (play/~~plays~~) for a while.

Then Zayan (~~bring~~/brings) out some snacks, and all the players (take/~~takes~~) a break from the game.

Exercise 18C: Perfect Present Tenses

Write the correct form of the perfect present verb in the blank.

These sentences are taken or adapted from *Redwall*, by Brian Jacques.

"Humph! After all the help and assistance that I __have given__, countless hours of study and valuable time. Really!"

"At least I hope I __have solved__ it."

The hare beckoned Sam. "C'm'ere, you dreadful little rogue! I __have got__ the very thing for you."

"Now that my son __has brought__ my new ingredients I can certainly give you medicine to make you sleep, sir."

"Look, Jess __has made__ it over the gutter! She's on the roof."

"It is all here, but as I __have said__ before, I will not concern myself with the fighting of a war."

— LESSON 19 —

Person of the Verb
Conjugations
State-of-Being Verbs

Exercise 19A: Forming Progressive Present Tenses

Fill in the blanks with the correct helping verbs.

Regular Verb, Progressive Present

	Singular	Plural
First person	I __am__ scribbling	we __are__ scribbling
Second person	you __are__ scribbling	you __are__ scribbling
Third person	he, she, it __is__ scribbling	they __are__ scribbling

Exercise 19B: Forming Progressive Present, Past, and Future Tenses

Regular Verb, Progressive Past

	Singular	Plural
First person	I __was__ learning	we __were__ learning
Second person	you __were__ learning	you __were__ learning
Third person	he, she, it __was__ learning	they __were__ learning

Regular Verb, Progressive Future

	Singular	Plural
First person	I __will be__ rejoicing	we __will be__ rejoicing
Second person	you __will be__ rejoicing	you __will be__ rejoicing
Third person	he, she, it __will be__ rejoicing	they __will be__ rejoicing

— LESSON 20 —

Irregular State-of-Being Verbs
Helping Verbs

Exercise 20A: Simple Tenses of the Verb *Have*

Try to fill in the missing blanks in the chart below, using your own sense of what sounds correct as well as the hints you may have picked up from the conjugations already covered. Be sure to use pencil so that any incorrect answers can be erased and corrected!

Simple Present

	Singular	Plural
First person	I __have__	we __have__
Second person	you __have__	you __have__
Third person	he, she, it __has__	they __have__

Simple Past

	Singular	Plural
First person	I had	we had
Second person	you had	you had
Third person	he, she, it had	they had

Simple Future

	Singular	Plural
First person	I will have	we will have
Second person	you will have	you will have
Third person	he, she, it will have	they will have

Exercise 20B: Simple Tenses of the Verb *Do*

Try to fill in the missing blanks in the chart below, using your own sense of what sounds correct as well as the hints you may have picked up from the conjugations already covered. Be sure to use pencil so that any incorrect answers can be erased and corrected!

Simple Present

	Singular	Plural
First person	I do	we do
Second person	you do	you do
Third person	he, she, it does	they do

Simple Past

	Singular	Plural
First person	I did	we did
Second person	you did	you did
Third person	he, she, it did	they did

Simple Future

	Singular	Plural
First person	I will do	we will do
Second person	you will do	you will do
Third person	he, she, it will do	they will do

WEEK 6

Nouns and Verbs in Sentences

— LESSON 21 —

Person of the Verb
Conjugations
Noun-Verb/Subject-Predicate Agreement

Exercise 21A: Person and Number of Pronouns

Identify the person and number of the underlined pronouns. Cross out the incorrect verb in parentheses. The first one is done for you.

These sentences are adapted from *The Story of Doctor Dolittle*, by Hugh Lofting.

	Person	Singular/Plural
He (~~talk~~/talks) every language—and Greek.	third	singular
I (am/~~is~~/~~are~~) never quite sure of my age.	first	singular
They (~~has~~/have) to stay at the Doctor's house for a week.	third	plural
John Dolittle was a strong man, though he (was/~~were~~) not very tall.	third	singular
It (~~am~~/is/~~are~~) a nasty thing to find under the bed.	third	singular
They (~~has~~/have) heard of you, and (beg/~~begs~~) you to come to Africa to stop the sickness.	third	plural
You (go/~~goes~~) and (ring/~~rings~~) it every half-hour.	second	singular
We (see/~~sees~~) the shores of Africa.	first	plural

Exercise 21B: Identifying Subjects and Predicates

Draw two lines underneath each simple predicate and one line underneath each simple subject in the following sentences. If a phrase comes between the subject and the predicate, put parentheses around it to show that it does not affect the subject-predicate agreement.

Okapis live in central Africa.

Giraffes are in the same family as okapis.

The two animals, (though very different in appearance,) have similar long, sticky tongues.

With their tongues, they can reach their eyes and ears.

They (also) walk with both legs on one side of the body, then both legs on the other side of the body.

Many other animals, (such as deer,) alternate sides of the body instead.

The okapi's striped legs camouflage it in the rainforest.

Exercise 21C: Subject-Verb Agreement

Cross out the incorrect verb in parentheses so that subject and predicate agree in number and person. Look out for any confusing phrases between the subject and predicate.

Yunseo (~~got~~/gets) a balloon, a funnel, and an empty bottle.
Ella (~~bring~~/brings) some vinegar and baking soda.
The girls carefully (work/~~works~~) together to add baking soda to the balloon with the funnel.
The other students in the lab (prepare/~~prepares~~) their balloons the same way.
Next, Yunseo (~~hold~~/holds) the bottle still while Ella (~~pour~~/pours) vinegar into it.
Ella then (~~wrap~~/wraps) the balloon's opening over the bottle.
Yunseo, a smile on her face, (~~shake~~/shakes) the baking soda from the balloon into the bottle.
All the students in the room eagerly (watch/~~watches~~) their balloons as the two materials in the bottles (react/~~reacts~~).

— LESSON 22 —

Formation of Plural Nouns
Collective Nouns

Exercise 22A: Collective Nouns

Write the collective noun for each description. Then fill in an appropriate singular verb for each sentence. (Use the simple present tense!) The first one is done for you.

Note to Instructor: Accept any verb that makes sense, as long as it is singular, simple present, third person.

Description		Collective Noun	Verb	
a large number of books	The	library	has	my favorite book.
people singing together	The	choir	performs	the piece.
flowers arranged together and held	The	bouquet	smells	lovely.
many grapes together	This	bunch	tastes	sour.
many airplanes	The	fleet	prepares	for battle.
a number of arrows all in the same place	The	quiver	appears	full.
many cookies made at the same time	This	batch	tastes	great.

Exercise 22B: Plural Noun Forms

Read each rule and the example out loud. Then rewrite the singular nouns as plural nouns in the spaces provided.

Usually, add *-s* to a noun to form the plural.

Singular Noun	Plural Noun
carpenter	carpenters
nut	nuts
queen	queens
basketball	basketballs

Add *-es* to nouns ending in *-s*, *-sh*, *-ch*, *-x*, or *-z*.

Singular Noun	Plural Noun
business	businesses
bush	bushes
peach	peaches
wax	waxes
waltz	waltzes

If a noun ends in *-y* after a consonant, change the *y* to *i* and add *-es*.

Singular Noun	Plural Noun
library	libraries
harmony	harmonies
industry	industries
party	parties

If a noun ends in *-y* after a vowel, just add *-s*.

Singular Noun	Plural Noun
way	ways
alley	alleys
turkey	turkeys
essay	essays

Some words that end in *-f* or *-fe* form their plurals differently. You must change the *f* or *fe* to *v* and add *-es*.

Singular Noun	Plural Noun
knife	knives
life	lives
self	selves
sheaf	sheaves

Words that end in *-ff* form their plurals by simply adding *-s*.

Singular Noun	Plural Noun
cuff	cuffs
mastiff	mastiffs
earmuff	earmuffs

Some words that end in a single *-f* can form their plurals either way.

Singular Noun	Plural Noun
dwarf	dwarfs/dwarves
handkerchief	handkerchiefs/handkerchieves

If a noun ends in *-o* after a vowel, just add *-s*.

Singular Noun	Plural Noun
studio	studios
kangaroo	kangaroos
scenario	scenarios
cameo	cameos

If a noun ends in *-o* after a consonant, form the plural by adding *-es*.

Singular Noun	Plural Noun
tomato	tomatoes
embargo	embargoes
torpedo	torpedoes
veto	vetoes

To form the plural of foreign words ending in *-o*, just add *-s*.

Singular Noun	Plural Noun
alto	altos
tango	tangos
casino	casinos
canto	cantos
libretto	librettos

Irregular plurals don't follow any of these rules!

Singular Noun	Irregular Plural Noun
ox	oxen
louse	lice
emphasis	emphases
crisis	crises
phenomenon	phenomena
nucleus	nuclei
moose	moose
sheep	sheep
elk	elk

Exercise 22C: Plural Nouns

Complete the following excerpt by filling in the plural form of each noun in parentheses.

The following is slightly condensed from L. M. Montgomery's *The Story Girl.*

Outside of the orchard the grass was only beginning to grow green; but here, sheltered by the spruce (hedge) hedges from uncertain (wind) winds and sloping to southern (sun) suns, it was already like a wonderful velvet carpet; the (leaf) leaves on the (tree) trees were beginning to come out in woolly, grayish (cluster) clusters; and there were purple-pencilled white (violet) violets at the base of the Pulpit Stone.

"It's all just as father described it," said Felix with a blissful sigh, "and there's the well with the Chinese roof."

We hurried over to it, treading on the (spear) spears of mint that were beginning to shoot up about it. It was a very deep well, and the curb was of rough, undressed (stone) stones. Over it, the queer, pagoda-like roof, built by Uncle Stephen on his return from a voyage to China, was covered with yet leafless (vine) vines.

"It's so pretty, when the (vine) vines leaf out and hang down in long (festoon) festoons," said the Story Girl. "The (bird) birds build their (nest) nests in it. A pair of wild (canary) canaries come here every summer. And (fern) ferns grow out between the (stone) stones of the well as far down as you can see. The water is lovely."

We then went to find our birthday (tree) trees. We were rather disappointed to find them quite large, sturdy ones. It seemed to us that they should still be in the sapling stage corresponding to our boyhood.

"Your (apple) apples are lovely to eat," the Story Girl said to me, "but Felix's are only good for (pie) pies. Those two big (tree) trees behind them are the twins' (tree) trees— my mother and Uncle Felix, you know. The (apple) apples are so dead sweet that nobody but us (child) children and the French (boy) boys can eat them. And that tall, slender tree over there, with the (branch) branches all growing straight up, is a seedling that came up of itself, and NOBODY can eat its (apple) apples, they are so sour and bitter. Even the (pig) pigs won't eat them. Aunt Janet tried to make (pie) pies of them once, because she said she hated to see them going to waste. But she never tried again. She said it was better to waste (apple) apples alone than (apple) apples and sugar too. And then she tried giving them away to the French hired (man) men, but they wouldn't even carry them home."

The Story Girl's (word) words fell on the morning air like (pearl) pearls and (diamond) diamonds. Even her (preposition) prepositions and (conjunction) conjunctions had untold charm, hinting at mystery and laughter and magic bound up in everything she mentioned. Apple (pie) pies and sour (seedling) seedling and (pig) pigs became straightway invested with a glamour of romance.

— LESSON 23 —

Plural Nouns
Descriptive Adjectives
Possessive Adjectives
Contractions

Exercise 23A: Introduction to Possessive Adjectives

Read the following nouns. Choose a person that you know to possess each of the items. Write the person's name in the first column. Then, in the second column, write the person's name, an apostrophe, and an *s* to form a possessive adjective.

Note to Instructor: Even if the person's name ends in *-s*, the student should still add 's to form the possessive: "Marcus's football."

Example: Clara	Clara's	stuffed animal
[Name]	[Name]'s	finger puppets
[Name]	[Name]'s	instrument
[Name]	[Name]'s	bedside table
[Name]	[Name]'s	bunny slippers
[Name]	[Name]'s	handwriting

Exercise 23B: Singular and Plural Possessive Adjective Forms

Fill in the chart with the correct forms. The first row is done for you. Both regular and irregular nouns are included.

Noun	Singular Possessive	Plural	Plural Possessive
sidewalk	sidewalk's	sidewalks	sidewalks'
lunch	lunch's	lunches	lunches'
bucket	bucket's	buckets	buckets'
deer	deer's	deer	deer's
woman	woman's	women	women's
kitten	kitten's	kittens	kittens'
hospital	hospital's	hospitals	hospitals'
army	army's	armies	armies'
creature	creature's	creatures	creatures'
foot	foot's	feet	feet's
stranger	stranger's	strangers	strangers'

Exercise 23C: Common Contractions

Drop the letters in grey print and write the contraction in the blank. The first one is done for you.

Full Form	Common Contraction	Full Form	Common Contraction
are not	aren't	she is	she's
we had	we'd	I have	I've
who is	who's	was not	wasn't
you will	you'll	I would	I'd
has not	hasn't	he would	he'd
she had	she'd	we will	we'll
did not	didn't	he has	he's
where is	where's	we have	we've

— LESSON 24 —

Possessive Adjectives
Contractions
Compound Nouns

Exercise 24A: Using Possessive Adjectives Correctly

Cross out the incorrect word in parentheses.

(~~Your~~/You're) standing too close to the experiment—(your/~~you're~~) hair could catch fire!

My lunch is over there. (~~Its~~/It's) the one in the superhero bag.

(His/~~He's~~) flight has arrived, but (~~his~~/he's) still waiting for his luggage.

The employees will call out (your/~~you're~~) number when (~~their~~/they're) ready for you.

(~~Hers~~/She's) going to be very surprised when she learns that the award is (hers/~~she's~~).

(~~Its~~/It's) time for the computer to download (its/~~it's~~) update.

Where are (your/~~you're~~) scissors? (~~Your~~/You're) going to need them for this project.

Did you hear about the lion that escaped from (its/~~it's~~) cage? (~~Its~~/It's) on the front page of today's newspaper.

(Your/~~You're~~) coach will not be pleased if (~~your~~/you're) late for practice.

(~~Its~~/It's) supposed to rain tomorrow. Will you bring (your/~~you're~~) umbrella, or should my sister bring (hers/~~she's~~)?

Exercise 24B: Compound Nouns

Underline each simple subject once and each simple predicate (verb) twice. Circle each compound noun.

The dishwasher will finish soon.

Li Na saw an inchworm on the windowsill.

My new keyboard has a green cover.

The babysitter played hide-and-seek with the five-year-old.

Jenna's high school prepared an excellent yearbook.

Rita's young granddaughter made a mess with her mother's makeup.

Fireflies lit the pathway.

In *A Charlie Brown Christmas*, Lucy van Pelt wishes for real estate.

Exercise 24C: Plurals of Compound Nouns

Write the plural of each singular compound noun in parentheses in the blanks to complete the sentences.

Did you bring extra (baseball) baseballs so we can play at the park?

It doesn't matter which of the (playground) playgrounds I take them to; the (six-year-old) six-year-olds I watch on Saturdays always want to play on (merry-go-round) merry-go-rounds.

Both of my (sister-in-law) sisters-in-law live on the other side of the country.

We ate lots of (hotdog) hotdogs when we went to see the (firework) fireworks.

The (police officer) police officers were chasing the (redhead) redheads.

My mother brought home (bucketful) bucketfuls of (blueberry) blueberries from the farm.

When we were serving as interns, my brother and I acted as (go-between) go-betweens for the two arguing (Congressman) Congressmen.

The celebrity made a fuss about the paparazzi, but in reality he loved having so many (hanger-on) hangers-on.

— REVIEW 2 —

Weeks 4-6

Topics
Simple, Progressive, and Perfect Tenses
Conjugations
Irregular Verbs
Subject/Verb Agreement
Possessives
Compound Nouns
Contractions

Review 2A: Verb Tenses

Write the tense of each underlined verb or verb phrase on the line to the right: simple past, present, or future; progressive past, present, or future; or perfect past, present, or future. The first one is done for you. Watch out for words that interrupt verb phrases but are not helping verbs (such as *not*).

These sentences are taken or adapted from Robert Louis Stevenson's *Treasure Island*.

	Verb Tense
Now, to tell you the truth, from the very first mention of Long John in Squire Trelawney's letter, I had taken a fear in my mind that he might	perfect past
prove to be the very one-legged sailor whom I had watched for so long at the old "Benbow."	perfect past
Another pause, and then, not a quarter of a mile in front of me, I beheld the Union Jack flutter in the air above a wood.	simple past
"Tom, my man," said I,	simple past
"you're going home."	progressive present
"They'll be glad to be packing in the schooner."	simple future
"These poor lads have chosen me cap'n, after your desertion, sir."	perfect present
He was whistling to himself, "Come, Lasses and Lads."	progressive past
I had already deserted my eastern loophole.	perfect past
But he stuck to it like a man, in silence.	simple past
Gray and I were sitting together at the far end of the blockhouse; and	progressive past
Gray took his pipe out of his mouth and fairly	simple past
forgot to put it back again, so thunderstruck he was at this occurrence.	simple past
"If I am right,	simple present
he's going now to see Ben Gunn."	progressive present
"I'll tell you one thing,"	simple future
says I:	simple present
"I'm not going back to Captain Kidd's anchorage."	progressive present

I began to fear that	simple past
something had gone wrong.	perfect past
"I dare you to thank me!"	simple present
cried the squire.	simple past
"And I'll be taking this to square the count."	progressive future

Review 2B: Verb Formations

Fill in the charts with the correct conjugations of the missing verbs. Identify the person of each group of verbs.

PERSON: Third

	Past	Present	Future
SIMPLE	she discovered	she discovers	she will discover
PROGRESSIVE	she was discovering	she is discovering	she will be discovering
PERFECT	she had discovered	she has discovered	she will have discovered

PERSON: First

	Past	Present	Future
SIMPLE	I followed	I follow	I will follow
PROGRESSIVE	I was following	I am following	I will be following
PERFECT	I had followed	I have followed	I will have followed

PERSON: Second

	Past	Present	Future
SIMPLE	you answered	you answer	you will answer
PROGRESSIVE	you were answering	you are answering	you will be answering
PERFECT	you had answered	you have answered	you will have answered

PERSON: Third

	Past	Present	Future
SIMPLE	they yelled	they yell	they will yell
PROGRESSIVE	they were yelling	they are yelling	they will be yelling
PERFECT	they had yelled	they have yelled	they will have yelled

Review 2C: Person and Subject/Verb Agreement

Cross out the incorrect verb in parentheses.

The following sentences are taken from the Malaya story "The Deceitful Pelican" in *Folk Tales and Fables of Asia and Australia*, by Robert Ingpen and Barbara Hayes.

Ruan (was/~~were~~) not clever. Few fish (~~is~~/are).

When he (was/~~were~~) not eating Ruan lay in the cool water at the bottom of the pool and tried to look like a mottled brown stone.

The great pouch under the pelican's large beak (was/~~were~~) empty.

The pelican tossed his head and said, "The creatures of this pool (~~lives~~/live) in times of dreadful danger. How I (~~admires~~/admire) their courage."

"I (~~has~~/have) a young family to consider."

"I (~~has~~/have) traveled the world," said the pelican. "I (~~knows~~/know) many things."

"You (~~has~~/have) found a new home of exquisite beauty for me and my wife and little ones."

His wife and young ones (~~was~~/were) confused at this startling news.

The baby fish pressed eagerly forward and showed that they (~~was~~/were) true children of their father.

Review 2D: Possessives and Compound Nouns

Complete the chart below, writing the singular possessive, plural, and plural possessive of each singular pronoun or compound noun. The first one has been done for you.

Noun	Possessive	Plural	Plural Possessive
notebook	notebook's	notebooks	notebooks'
I	my	we	our
hallway	hallway's	hallways	hallways'
it	its	they	their
butterfly	butterfly's	butterflies	butterflies'
chairwoman	chairwoman's	chairwomen	chairwomen's
he	his	they	their
president-elect	president-elect's	presidents-elect	presidents-elect's
you	your	you	your
ladybug	ladybug's	ladybugs	ladybugs'
spokesperson	spokesperson's	spokespeople	spokespeople's
she	her	they	their
jellyfish	jellyfish's	jellyfish	jellyfish's
toothpick	toothpick's	toothpicks	toothpicks'

Review 2E: Plurals and Possessives

In the following sentences, provide the possessive, the plural, or the plural possessive for each noun in parentheses as indicated.

These sentences are from *Pollyanna*, by Eleanor H. Porter.

To Mrs. Snow's unbounded amazement, Pollyanna sprang to her (foot, plural) feet and clapped her (hand, plural) hands.

"I like old (folk, plural) folks just as well, maybe better, sometimes—being used to the (Lady, plural possessive) Ladies' Aid, so."

(Nancy, possessive) Nancy's (lip, plural) lips parted abruptly, as if there were angry (word, plural) words all ready to come; but her (eye, plural) eyes, resting on (Pollyanna, possessive) Pollyanna's jubilantly trustful face, saw something that prevented the (word, plural) words being spoken.

She told me afterwards she reckoned she'd have gone raving crazy if it hadn't been for (Mr. White, possessive) Mr. White's (sister, possessive) sister's (ear, plural) ears.

Your aunt telephoned down to the (Harlow, plural possessive) Harlows' place across the way.

"I know it, poor little thing," crooned Pollyanna, tenderly, looking into the little (creature, possessive) creature's frightened (eye, plural) eyes.

"Yes; and I'd tell it better this time," hurried on Pollyanna, quick to see the (sign, plural) signs of relenting in the (boy, possessive) boy's face.

Review 2F: Contractions

Finish the following excerpt by forming contractions from the words in parentheses.

In the following transcript (which has been abridged), "LBJ" stands for Lyndon Baines Johnson, and "MLK" stands for Martin Luther King Jr. This conversation between them happened a few days after Johnson was inaugurated as President of the United States following the assassination of John F. Kennedy.

LBJ:. . . and a good many people told me that they heard about your statement. I've (I have) been locked up in this office, and I haven't (have not) seen it. But I want to tell you how grateful I am, and how worthy I'm (I am) going to try to be of all your hopes.

MLK: Well, thank you very much. I'm (I am) so happy to hear that, and I knew that you had just that great spirit, and you know you have our support and backing, because we know what a difficult period this is.

LBJ: It's (It is) just an impossible period. We've (We have) got a budget coming up that's (that is)—we've (we have) got nothing to do with it; it's (it is) practically already made. And we've (we have) got a civil rights bill that hadn't (had not) even passed the House, and it's (it is) November, and Hubert Humphrey told me yesterday everybody wanted to go home. We've (We have) got a tax bill that they haven't (have not) touched. We just got to let up—not let up on any of them and keep going and—

MLK: Yes.

LBJ: —I guess they'll (they will) say that I'm (I am) repudiated. But I'm (I am) going to ask the Congress Wednesday to just stay there until they pass them all. They won't (will not) do it. But we'll (we will) just keep them there next year until they do, and we just won't (will not) give up an inch.

MLK: Uh-uh. Well this is mighty fine. I think it's (it is) so imperative. I think one of the great tributes that we can pay in memory of President Kennedy is to try to enact some of the great, progressive policies that he sought to initiate.

LBJ: Well, I'm (I am) going to support them all, and you can count on that. And I'm (I am) going to do my best to get other men to do likewise, and I'll (I will) have to have y'all's help.

MLK: Well, you know you have it, and just feel free to call on us for anything.

WEEK 7

Compounds and Conjunctions

— LESSON 25 —

Contractions
Compound Nouns
Diagramming Compound Nouns
Compound Adjectives
Diagramming Adjectives
Articles

Exercise 25A: Contractions Review

Write the two words that form each contraction on the blanks to the right. Some contractions have more than one correct answer. The first is done for you.

Contraction	Helping Verb	Other Word
she's	is (or has)	she
who's	is	who
aren't	are	not
I'd	had (or would)	I
we've	have	we
shouldn't	should	not
can't	can	not
you'll	will	you
hasn't	has	not

Exercise 25B: Diagramming Adjectives and Compound Nouns

On your own paper, diagram every word of the following sentences.

Kristi's ice cream melted.

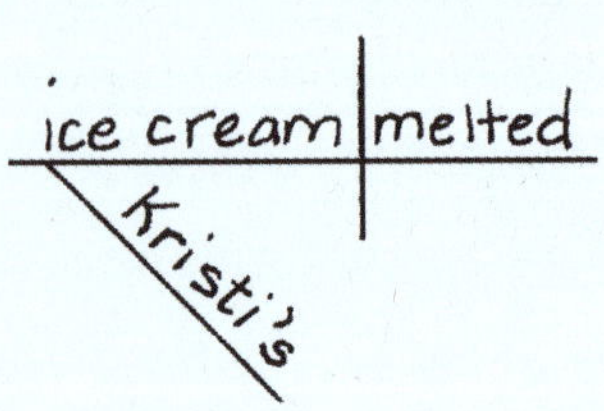

Our post office closed.

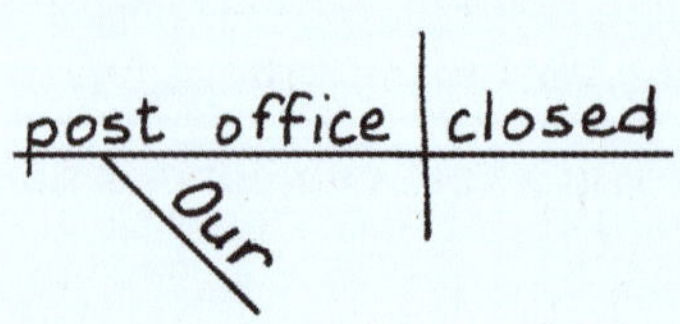

Humpty Dumpty has fallen.

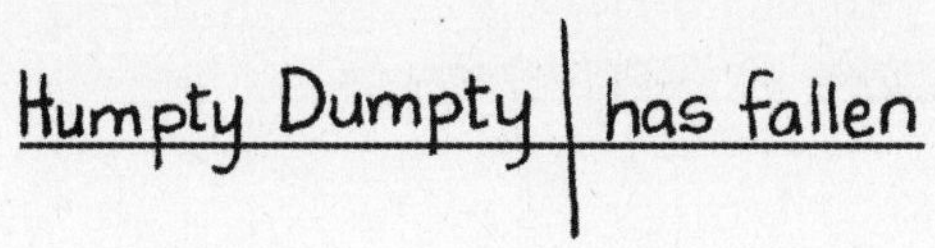

Marie Curie researched.

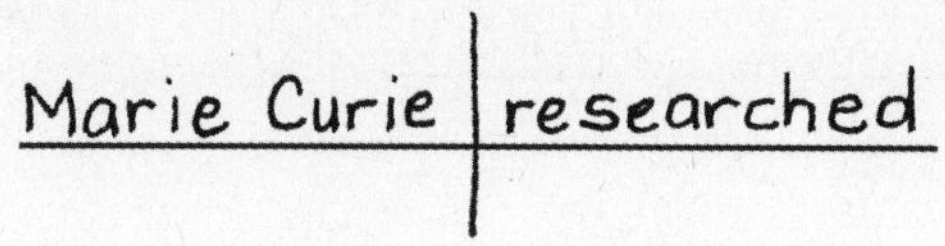

Exercise 25C: Compound Nouns

Draw a line to match each word in Column A with the correct word in Column B to form a single-word compound noun. Then rewrite the new compound noun on the space provided. The first is done for you.

Column A	Column B	New Compound Noun
base	book	baseball
key	crow	keyboard
note	ball	notebook
grape	worm	grapefruit
scare	fruit	scarecrow
earth	cake	earthworm
pan	board	pancake

Exercise 25D: Compound Adjectives

Correctly place hyphens in the following phrases.

forty-seven full-length novels
a part-time job
time-saving devices
the long-distance runner
three-fourths cup of sugar
a twelve-story building
twenty-four three-year-old children

Exercise 25E: Diagramming Adjectives, Compound Nouns, and Compound Adjectives

On your own paper, diagram every word in the following sentences. These are adapted from *The Secret Garden*, by Frances Hodgson Burnett.

The long-lasting rainstorm had ended.

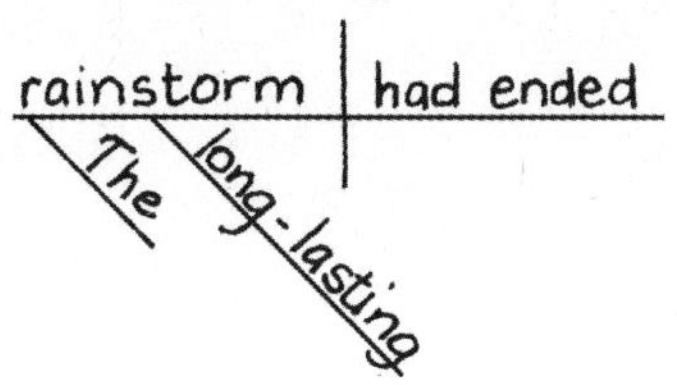

The rabbits' tremulous noses were sniffing.

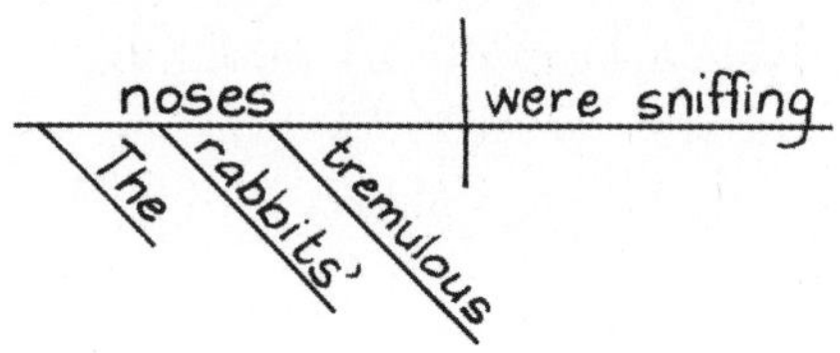

A laurel-hedged walk curved.

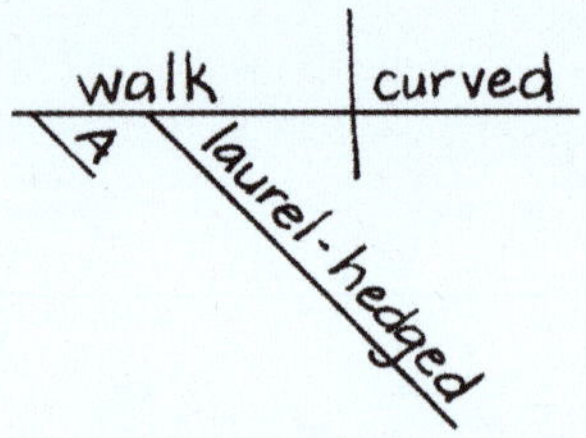

Pink-cheeked Mary Lennox was running.

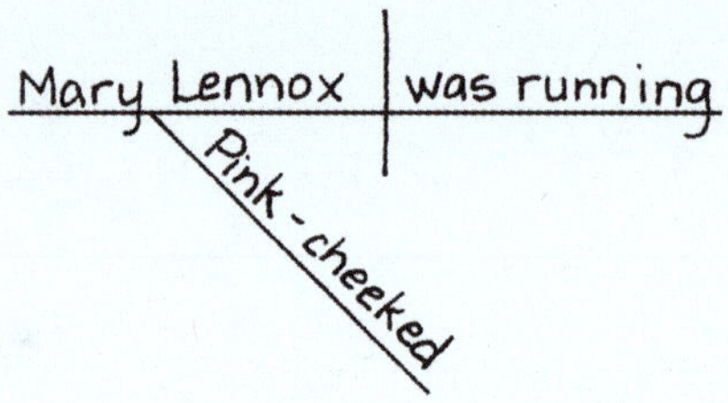

Fair fresh rosebuds uncurled.

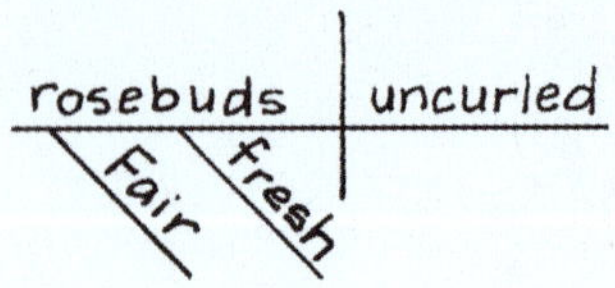

— LESSON 26 —

Compound Subjects
The Conjunction *And*
Compound Predicates
Compound Subject-Predicate Agreement

Exercise 26A: Identifying Subjects, Predicates, and Conjunctions

Underline the subject(s) once and the predicate(s) twice in each sentence. Circle the conjunctions that join them. The first one is done for you.

These sentences are adapted from E. L. Konigsburg's *From the Mixed-Up Files of Mrs. Basil E. Frankweiler.*

So she lay there in the great quiet of the museum next to the warm quiet of her brother and enjoyed the soft stillness around them: a comforter of quiet.

He felt its cool roundness and splashed his way over to Claudia.

Michelangelo, Angel, and the entire Italian Renaissance waited for them until morning.

We'll get our mailbox number, write it in, and take it to the museum office.

Jamie paid the rent, signed a form under the name Angelo Michaels and gave his address as Marblehead, Massachusetts.

They stood in line and got tickets for a tour.

Four Americans, two Englishmen, and one German have thus far examined the statue.

Exercise 26B: Diagramming Compound Subjects and Predicates

Underline the subject(s) once and the predicate(s) twice in the following sentences. Circle any conjunctions.

When you are finished, diagram the subjects (and any articles modifying the subjects), predicates, and conjunctions (ONLY) of each sentence on your own paper.

Alexandra and Raphael play tic-tac-toe together.

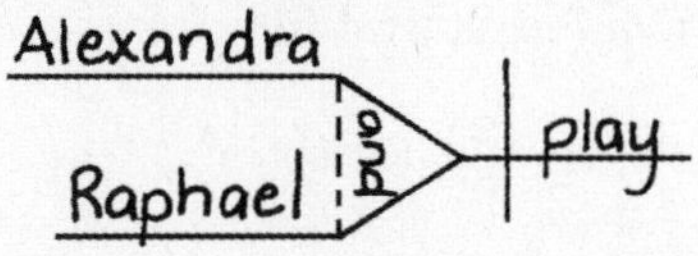

Bats and balls flew into the air and landed on the grass

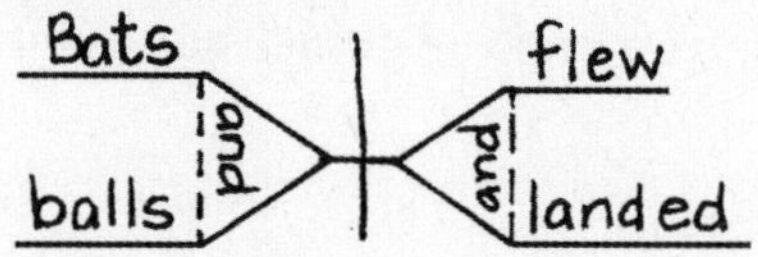

Megan calculated the answer and corrected her sister's work.

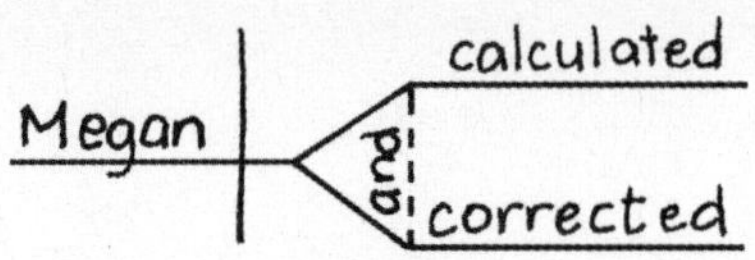

The puppy and the piglet study each other through the fence.

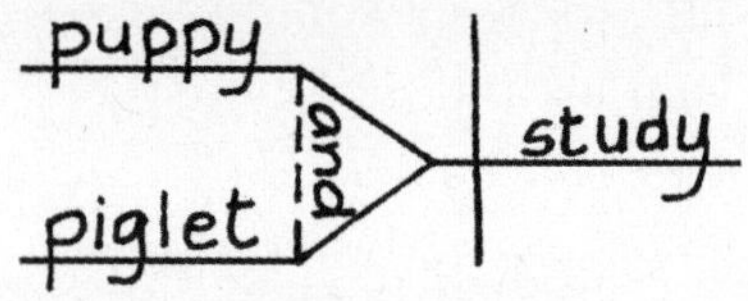

The vase on the nightstand teetered and fell.

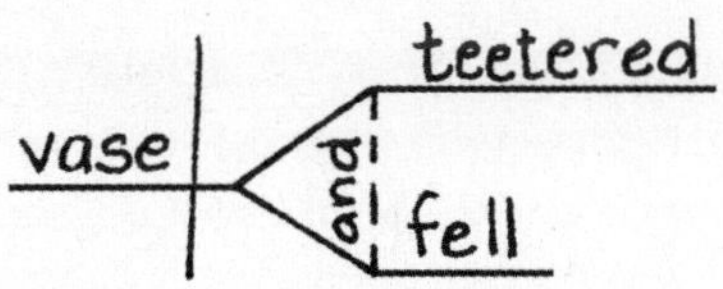

The newborn lambs and the curious rabbits delighted and amused the children during their visit to the petting zoo.

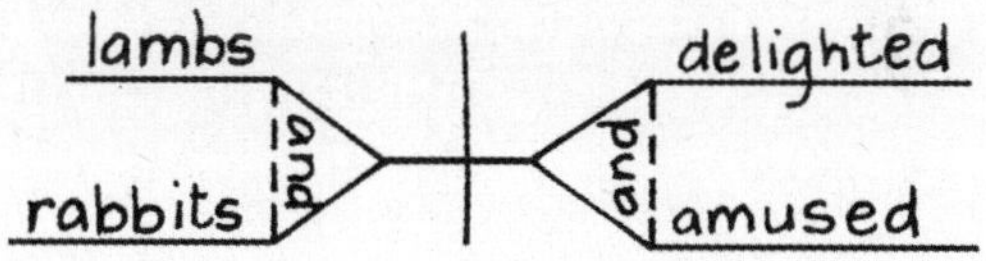

Exercise 26C: Forming Compound Subjects and Verbs

Combine each of these sets of simple sentences into one sentence with a compound subject and/or a compound predicate joined by *and*. Use your own paper.

Bimala parks the car.
Bimala locks the car.
Bimala parks and locks the car.

The fern needs watering.
The geranium needs watering.
The fern and the geranium need watering.

The hurricane has caused horrific damage to the town.
The tornado has caused horrific damage to the town.
The hurricane and the tornado have caused horrific damage to the town.

The red kangaroo clucks.
The red kangaroo hops.
The golden-mantled kangaroo hops.
The golden-mantled kangaroo clucks.
The wallaroo hops.
The wallaroo clucks.

The red kangaroo, the golden-mantled kangaroo, and the wallaroo hop and cluck.

OR

The red kangaroo and the golden-mantled kangaroo and the wallaroo cluck and hop.

Exercise 26D: Subject-Verb Agreement with Compound Subjects

Choose the correct verb in parentheses to agree with the subject. Cross out the incorrect verb.

The visitor (~~approach~~/approaches) the door and (~~knock~~/knocks) softly.
Louisa and Peter (run/~~runs~~) to open the door.
Louisa (~~ask~~/asks) if Mrs. Kim would like to see the new baby.
Mrs. Kim (~~smile~~/smiles) and (~~nod~~/nods).
Mother and Father (come/~~comes~~) into the room and (greet/~~greets~~) Mrs. Kim.
The tiny new baby (~~study~~/studies) the guest with wide eyes.

— LESSON 27 —

Coordinating Conjunctions
Complications in Subject-Predicate Agreement

Exercise 27A: Using Conjunctions

Fill the blanks in the sentences below with the appropriate conjunctions. You must use each conjunction at least once. (There is more than one possible answer for many of the blanks.)

These sentences are adapted from *A Wrinkle in Time*, by Madeleine L'Engle.

She has doctors' degrees in both biology and bacteriology.

Calvin held her hand strongly in his, but [yet/and] she felt neither strength nor reassurance in his touch.

Not only is there no need to fight me, but [yet] you will not have the slightest desire to do so. For [And] why should you wish to fight someone who is here only to save you pain and [or] trouble?

Charles Wallace slid down from his chair and trotted over to the refrigerator, his pajamaed feet padding softly as a kitten's.

On the dais lay—what? Meg could not tell, yet [but] she knew that it was from this that the rhythm came.

We could feel her heart, very faintly, the beats very far apart. And [But/Yet] then it got stronger. So [And/But/Yet] all we have to do is wait.

With a good deal of difficulty I can usually decipher Meg's handwriting, but [yet] I doubt very much if her teachers can, or [and] are willing to take the time.

You could learn it, Charles. But [Yet] there isn't time. We can only stay here long enough to rest up and [or] make a few preparations.

It had the slimness and lightness of a bicycle, yet [but/and] as the foot pedals turned they seemed to generate an unseen source of power, and [for/so] the boy could pedal very slowly yet [but/and] move along the street quite swiftly.

Charles Wallace continued his slow walk forward, and [but/yet/so/for] she knew that he had not heard her.

Exercise 27B: Subject-Predicate Agreement: Troublesome Subjects

Choose the correct verb in parentheses to agree with the subject noun or pronoun in number. Cross out the incorrect verb.

The invention of light bulbs (~~have~~/has) had a significant influence on society.
Now that pictures (have/~~has~~) been taken, the soccer team (have/~~has~~) returned to their classes.
Either this book or that poem (~~are~~/is) the most difficult thing I've studied this year.
The company of actors (take/~~takes~~) their places on the stage.
One hundred ten degrees (~~are~~/is) just too hot to play outside!
Seven days (have/~~has~~) passed since I made the decision to run for office.
The board (~~have~~/has) decided to enact the new rule.
The pie or the cupcakes (~~seem~~/seems) like a good choice for dessert.
The jury (~~wait~~/waits) for the judge to read the verdict.
The oranges on the tree (are/~~is~~) nearly ripe!
Sixteen dollars (~~are~~/is) a great deal for that coat!
The birds in the trees (are/~~is~~) chirping merrily.
About half of the attendees (were/~~was~~) planning to leave the conference after lunch.
Every Tuesday, Justine and Annika (sit/~~sits~~) on a bench in the park and (tell/~~tells~~) each other stories.
When I wake up in the morning, my mother or my father (~~have~~/has) made breakfast.
One-fourth of the money (~~were~~/was) intended for charity.
A band of outlaws (were/~~was~~) waiting for the stagecoach.
My brother, my sister, or I (take/~~takes~~) the trash out every week.

Exercise 27C: Fill in the Verb

Choose a verb in the present tense that makes sense to complete each sentence. Be sure the verb agrees in number with its subject!

Note to Instructor: Accept any reasonable answer as long as it is in the correct person and number.

The fog in the streets makes driving dangerous. **(3rd singular)**

The bevy of admirers ___surrounds___ the rock star. **(3rd singular)**

Your impudence ___forces___ me to eject you from this classroom! **(3rd plural)**

Nine dollars ___is___ not a large amount. **(3rd singular)**

Green, red, and purple ___are___ my favorite colors. **(3rd plural)**

The mice in the cage ___tremble___ with fright as the cat ___draws___ near. **(3rd plural first, 3rd singular second)**

I listen as either the old man or the clumsy child ___clambers___ up the stairs. **(3rd singular)**

Two-thirds of the children ___run___ as soon as they get to the playground. **(3rd plural)**

— LESSON 28 —

Further Complications in Subject-Predicate Agreement

Exercise 28A: Subject-Verb Agreement: More Troublesome Subjects

Choose the correct verb in parentheses and cross out the incorrect verb.

Mathematics (is/~~are~~) one of my favorite things to study.

Every ant in the colony (has/~~have~~) a job.

There (is/~~are~~) a little ice cream shop downtown near the park.

The criteria for the project (~~was~~/were) not made clear to the students.

The pianist and organist (is/~~are~~) also performing a trumpet solo.

Ham and cheese (is/~~are~~) my favorite kind of sandwich.

There (~~is~~/are) three children in the yard.

Each child (wants/~~want~~) a popsicle.

Each of the children (prefers/~~prefer~~) a particular flavor.

The Lion, the Witch, and the Wardrobe (was/~~were~~) the first book C. S. Lewis wrote in the Chronicles of Narnia.

My pants (~~is~~/are) too short!

Linguistics (is/~~are~~) a fascinating field of study.

The foci of an ellipse (~~determines~~/determine) what the ellipse will look like.

Romeo and Juliet (is/~~are~~) one of Shakespeare's tragedies.

Ginevra's left-handed scissors (~~has~~/have) green handles.

Spaghetti and meatballs (sounds/~~sound~~) like a great idea for dinner.

"Here (is/~~are~~) an interesting phenomenon in the skies," said the astronomy professor.

Each of the runners (was/~~were~~) determined to win the race.

The United Arab Emirates (is/~~are~~) a country on the Arabian Peninsula.

Every koala (loves/~~love~~) eucalyptus leaves.

Exercise 28B: Correct Verb Tense and Number

Complete each of these sentences by writing the correct number and tense of the verb indicated. When you are finished, read each sentence aloud to your instructor (don't read the bracketed instructions, though!).

These sentences are adapted from Lewis Carroll's *Through the Looking-Glass.*

> **Note to Instructor:** Make sure that the student reads the sentences out loud, not just to herself. Listening to how the correct tenses sound is an important part of developing grammar knowledge.

"There [simple present of am] is the effect of living backwards," the Queen [simple past of say] said kindly.

The Messenger, to Alice's great amusement, [progressive past of open] was opening a bag that hung round his neck.

The words of the old song [progressive past of play] were playing in Alice's mind.

There [simple past of am] were elephants that looked like bees.

The beautiful brown eyes of the Fawn [progressive present of fill] are filling with alarm.

The Knight with the odd inventions [simple past of am] was not a good rider.

Alice [simple past of think] thought to herself, "Thirty times three [simple present of make] makes ninety. I wonder if anyone [progressive present of count] is counting ?

The egg on the shelf [progressive past of become] was becoming larger and larger, and more and more human.

There [simple past of am] was a pause in the fight just then, and the Lion and the Unicorn [progressive past of pant] were panting while the King [simple past of call] called out "Ten minutes allowed for refreshments!"

Bread-and-butter [simple present of am] is what you get when you divide a loaf with a knife.

WEEK 8

Introduction to Objects

— LESSON 29 —

Action Verbs
Direct Objects

Exercise 29A: Direct Objects

In the following sentences, underline the subjects once and the predicates twice. Circle each direct object.

If the sentence is a command, write the understood subject in parentheses and underline it once.

Nate dragged the sled to the top of the hill.

The excited young girl shook the present too hard.

Would you pour the tea for us?

Place the candles on the cake. (you)

Victoria and Max will play the game.

The officers at the event direct traffic and answer questions.

After their performance in the ice skating competition, Yaroslav and Maria quenched their thirst and awaited their scores.

My new camera takes great pictures and videos.

Asami discarded the twos, threes, and fours, and dealt the rest of the cards.

The eccentric old man wore a fedora, a corsage, and a bright green apron.

In the bakery, I see and smell my favorite things.

Anya and Matthias popped their balloon and extracted the next clue for the game.

Camila, Tomás, and Maite crossed the bridge and waited.

Stamp and deliver this important letter! (you)

The angry boy slammed the door and hid.

Exercise 29B: Diagramming Direct Objects

On your own paper, diagram the subjects, verbs, and direct objects in the sentences from Exercise 29A.

Nate dragged the sled to the top of the hill.

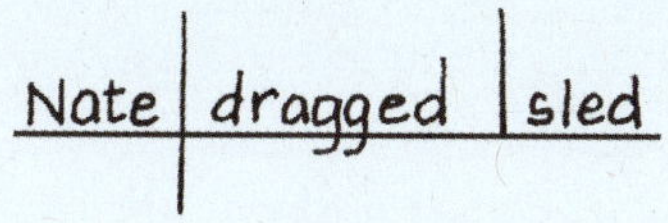

The excited young girl shook the present too hard.

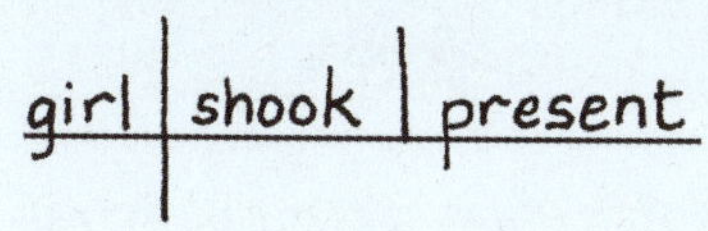

Would you pour the tea for us?

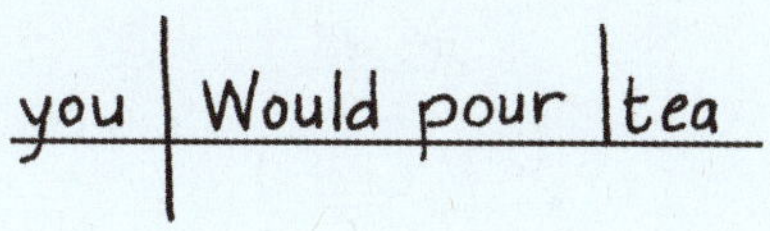

Place the candles on the cake. (you)

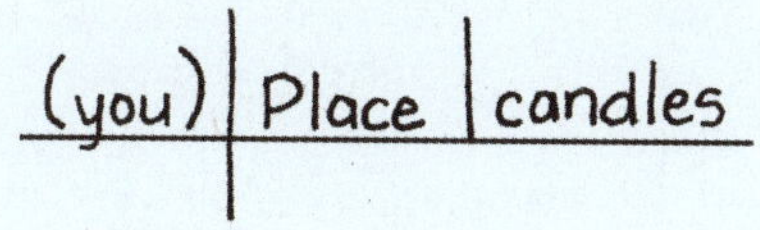

Victoria and Max will play the game.

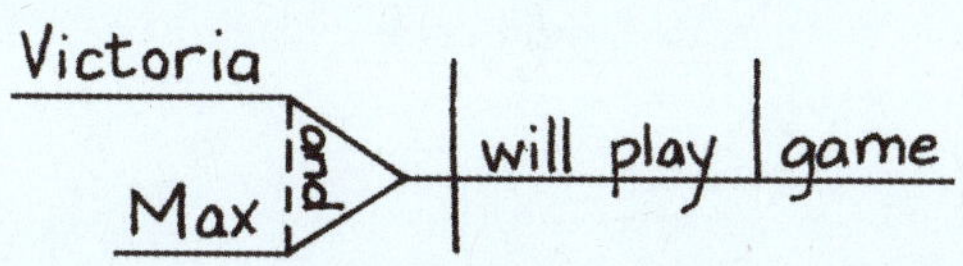

The officers at the event direct traffic and answer questions.

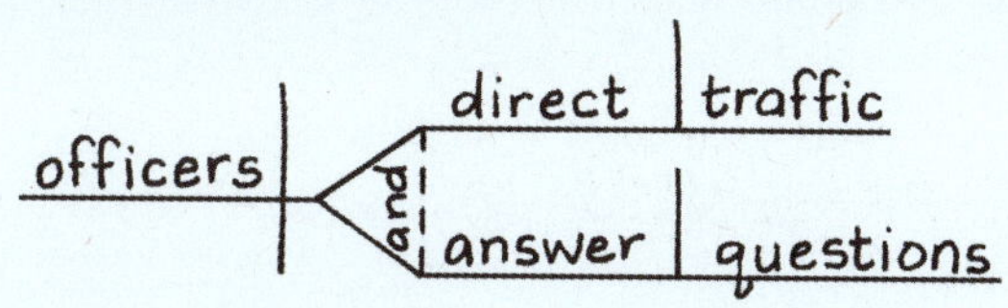

After their performance in the ice skating competition, Yaroslav and Maria quenched their thirst and awaited their scores.

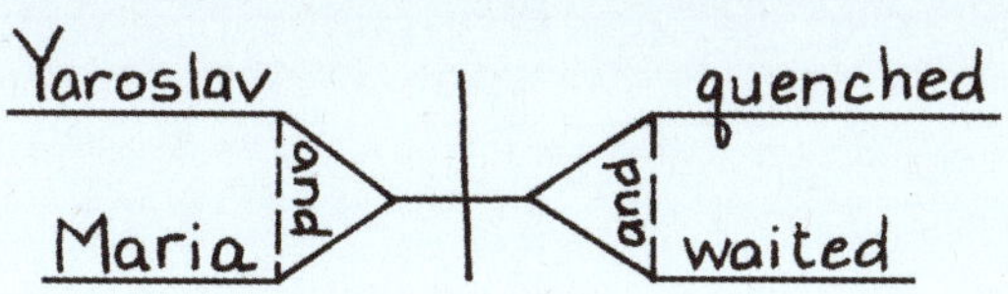

My new camera takes great pictures and videos.

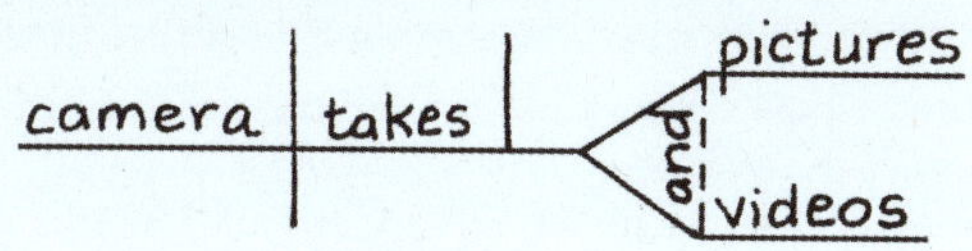

Asami discarded the twos, threes, and fours, and dealt the rest of the cards.

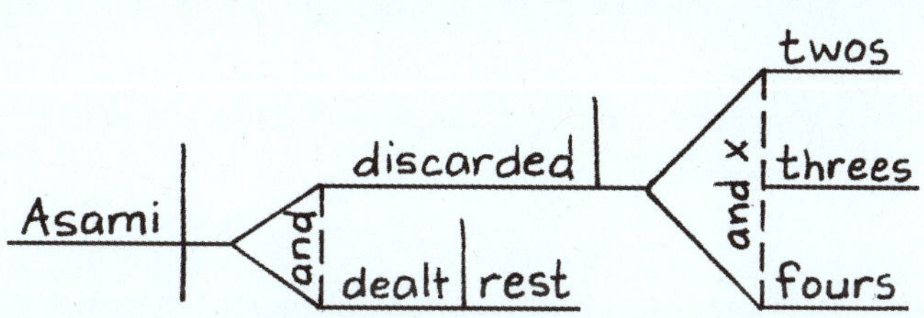

Note to Instructor: The *X* on the diagram stands for the comma, while the *and* is placed between the two direct objects it connects. Do not penalize the student if he simply writes *and* on the line, but show him the correct diagram and point out the placement of each element.

The eccentric old man wore a fedora, a corsage, and a bright green apron.

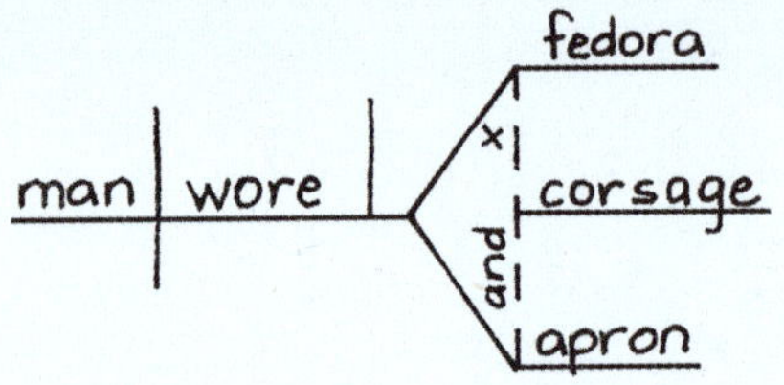

In the bakery, I see and smell my favorite things.

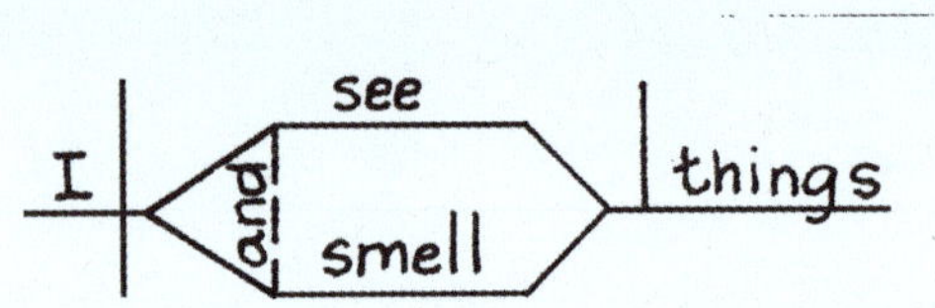

Anya and Matthias popped their balloon and extracted the next clue for the game.

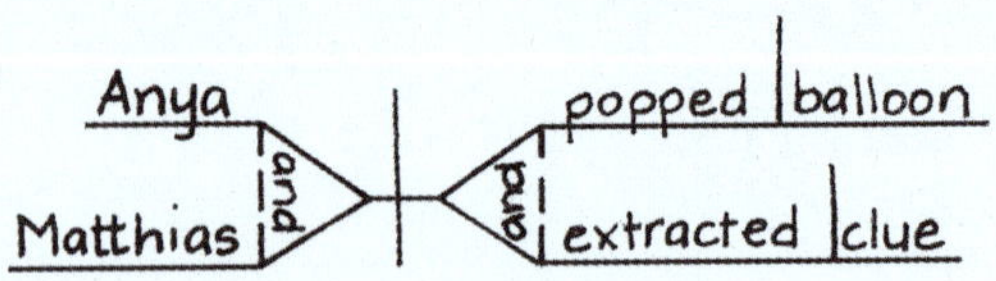

Camila, Tomás, and Maite crossed the bridge and waited.

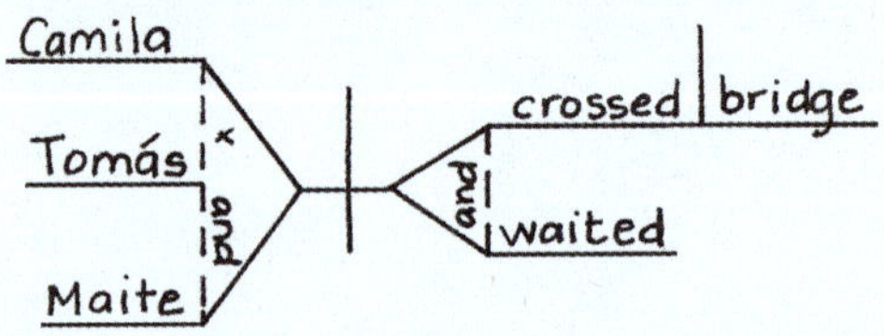

Stamp and deliver this important letter! (you)

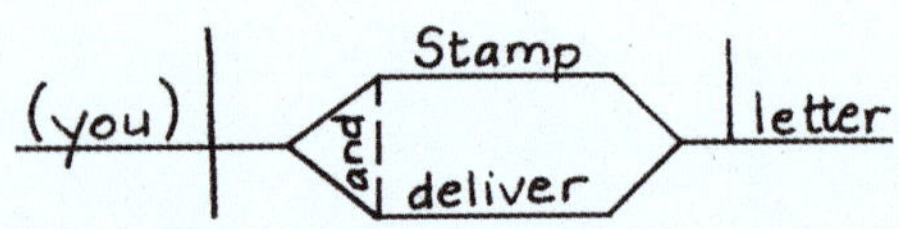

The angry boy slammed the door and hid.

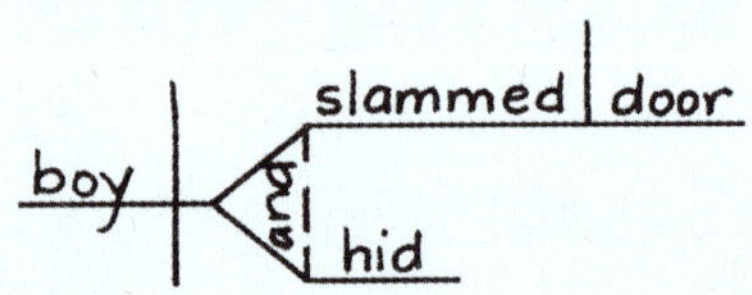

— LESSON 30 —

Direct Objects
Prepositions

Exercise 30A: Identifying Prepositions

In the following sentences (adapted from J. R. R. Tolkien's *The Hobbit*), find and circle each preposition. Be careful: One word on the preposition list is also on the list of conjunctions you learned in Lesson 27. Only circle it when it functions as a preposition!

Note to Instructor: In "for hats and coats," the word *for* is acting as a preposition, so it should be circled. In "for these were the only ones," *for* is acting as a conjunction and should NOT be circled.

It had a perfectly round door like a porthole, painted green, with a shiny yellow brass knob in the exact middle. The door opened to a tube-shaped hall like a tunnel: a very comfortable tunnel without smoke, with paneled walls, and floors tiled and carpeted, provided with polished chairs, and lots of pegs for hats and coats—the hobbit was fond of visitors. The best rooms were all on the left-hand side, for these were the only ones with windows, deep-set round windows looking over his garden, and meadows sloping to the river.

Exercise 30B: Word Relationships

The following sentences all contain action verbs. Underline each subject once and each action verb twice. If the sentence has an action verb followed by a direct object, write DO above the direct object. If the sentence contains a preposition, circle the preposition and draw a line to connect the two words that the preposition shows a relationship between. The first two are done for you.

The clothes hung on the line.

Genevieve remembered her grandmother's instructions.

The man charmed the snake.

Mrs. Wójcik teaches in the science lab.

The plumber with the green hat jumps very high.

The fidgety dog accidentally pressed the round purple button.

Jerome snapped his fingers.

The mighty ship with seven passenger decks rocked violently.

Enormous stones rolled down the hill.

A large black bear waited near the cave entrance.

My sister devoured her dinner.

The purple flowers by the curb were growing wildly.

Kiara reluctantly swallowed her pride.

I study at the library every Tuesday.

Exercise 30C: Diagramming Direct Objects

On your own paper, diagram the subjects, predicates, and direct objects only from the sentences above. If a sentence does not have a direct object, do not diagram it.

Genevieve remembered her grandmother's instructions.

The man charmed the snake.

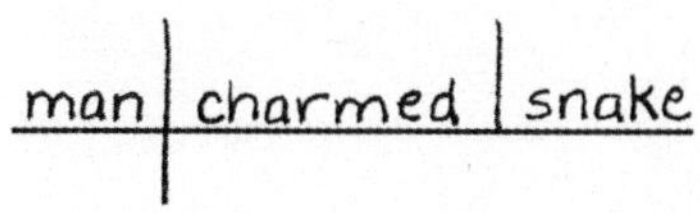

The fidgety dog accidentally pressed the round purple button.

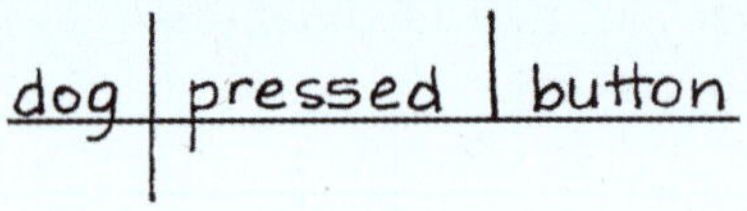

Jerome snapped his fingers.

My sister devoured her dinner.

Kiara reluctantly swallowed her pride.

— LESSON 31 —

Definitions Review
Prepositional Phrases
Object of the Preposition

Exercise 31A: Objects of Prepositional Phrases

Fill in the blanks with a noun as the object of the preposition to complete the prepositional phrases.

Note to Instructor: Answers will vary. Suggestions are provided in brackets.

Liliana placed her backpack near the ______________. [doorway, desk, bed]

The mouse scurried past the ______________. [trap, cat, mousehole]

Beyond the ______________ lies an ancient ruin. [hill, lake, fence]

The toddler's favorite toy was finally found beneath the ______________. [sofa, crib, dog]

With great ______________ , Mae climbed aboard the ______________.
[trepidation, anticipation, alacrity / elevator, roller coaster, horse]

Charles inched toward the ______________. [exit, tiger, fire]

Exercise 31B: Identifying Prepositional Phrases

Can you find all eleven of the prepositional phrases in the following excerpt from J. R. R. Tolkien's *The Hobbit*? (Beware words that can be prepositions but can also function as other parts of speech!) Underline the complete prepositional phrases. Circle each preposition. Label each object of the preposition with *OP*.

> Note to Instructor: In "for the autumn was come again," the word *for* is acting as a conjunction, introducing the complete sentence "The autumn was come again."

In a great hall with pillars hewn from the living stone sat the Elvenking on a chair of carven wood. On his head was a crown of berries and red leaves, for the autumn was come again. In the spring he wore a crown of woodland flowers. In his hand he held a carven staff of oak.

Exercise 31C: Remembering Prepositions

Can you remember all 46 prepositions without looking back at your list? On your own paper, write them down in alphabetical order. The first letter of each preposition and the number of prepositions that begin with that letter are found below, as a memory aid.

A	B	D	E	F	I	L
aboard	before	down	except	for	in	like
about	behind	during		from	inside	
above	below				into	
across	beneath					
after	beside					
against	between					
along	beyond					
among	by					
around						
at						

N	O	P	S	T	U	W
near	of	past	since	through	under	with
	off			throughout	underneath	within
	on			to	until	without
	over			toward	up	
					upon	

— LESSON 32 —

Subjects, Predicates, and Direct Objects
Prepositions
Object of the Preposition
Prepositional Phrases

Exercise 32A: Identifying Prepositional Phrases and Parts of Sentences

In the following sentences from L. M. Montgomery's *Anne of Green Gables*, circle each prepositional phrase. Once you have identified the prepositional phrases, underline subjects once, underline predicates twice, and label direct objects with *DO*.

By the end of the term Anne and Gilbert were promoted into the fifth class.

In geometry Anne met her Waterloo.

For Anne the real excitement began with the dismissal of school.

After the tea at the manse Diana Barry gave a party.

I bought the dye from him.

I shut the door and looked at his things on the step.

In the evening Miss Barry took them to a concert in the Academy of Music.

She went into her big house with a sigh.

The Avonlea hills beyond them appeared against the saffron sky.

A professional elocutionist in a wonderful gown of shimmering gray stuff like woven moonbeams was staying at the hotel.

The stout lady in pink silk turned her head and surveyed Anne through her eyeglasses.

Exercise 32B: Diagramming

On your own paper, diagram all of the uncircled parts of the sentences from 32A.

Anne and Gilbert were promoted.

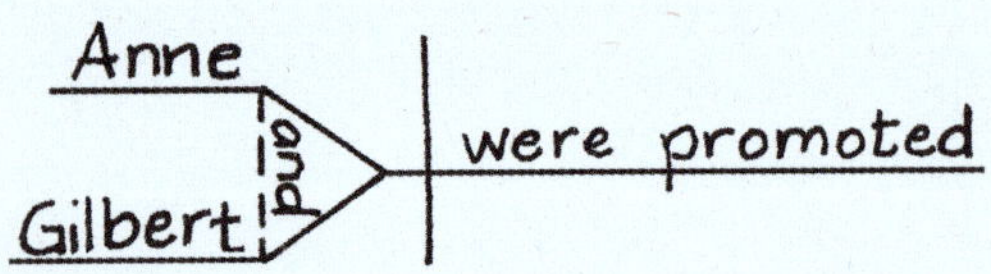

Anne met her Waterloo.

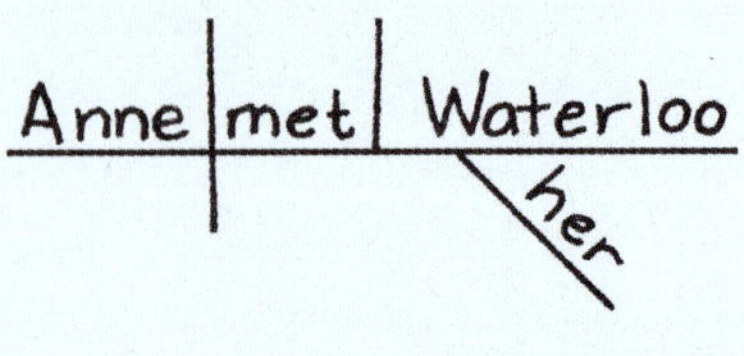

The real excitement began.

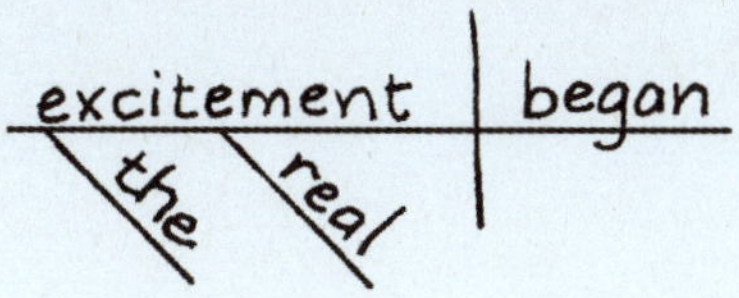

Diana Barry gave a party.

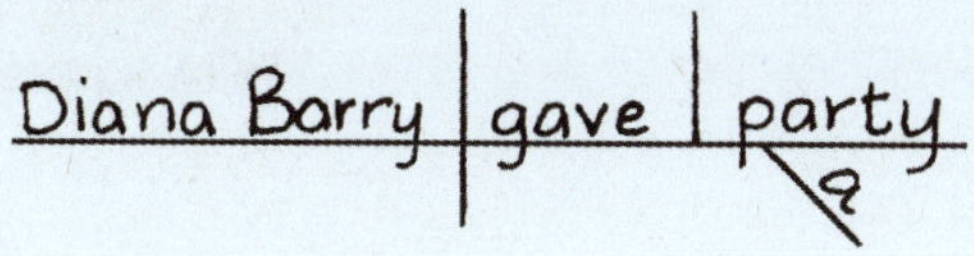

I bought the dye.

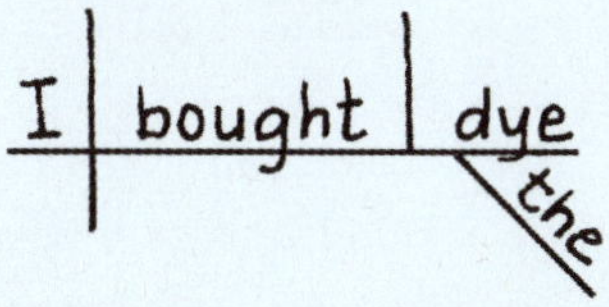

I shut the door and looked.

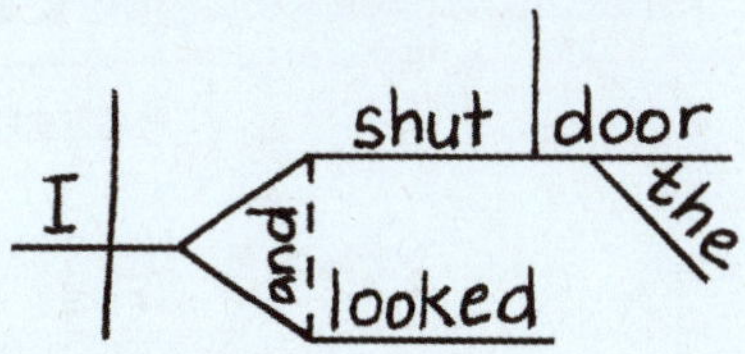

Miss Barry took them.

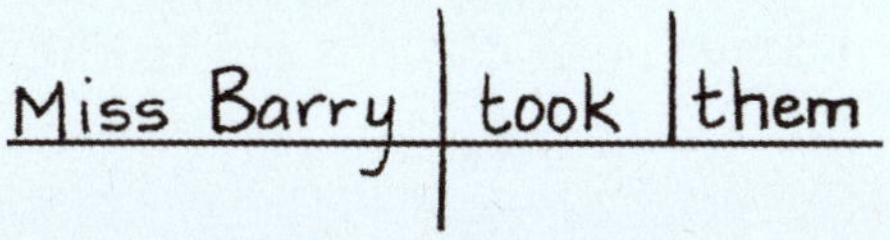

She went.

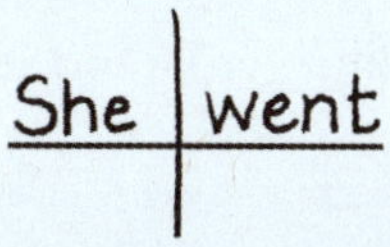

The Avonlea hills appeared.

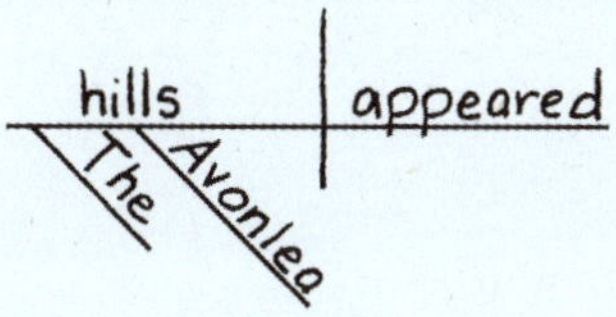

A professional elocutionist was staying.

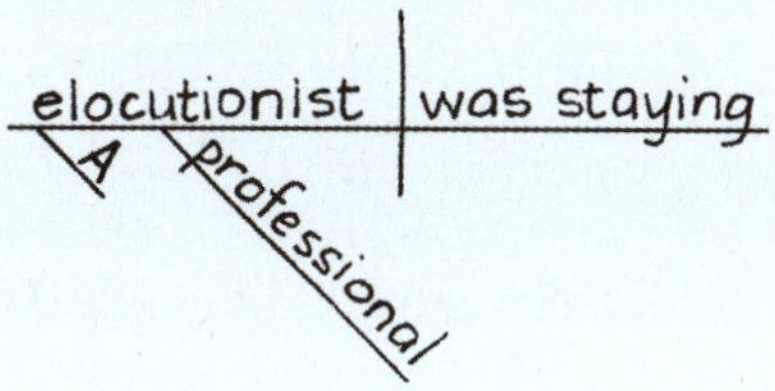

The stout lady turned her head and surveyed Anne.

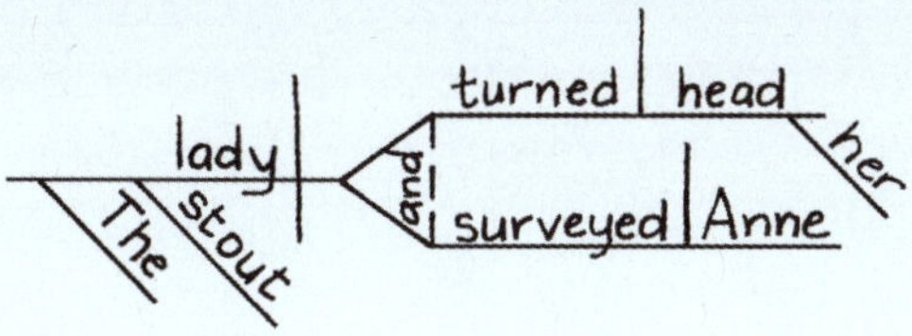

WEEK 9

Adverbs

— LESSON 33 —

Adverbs That Tell How

Exercise 33A: Identifying Adverbs That Tell How

Underline every adverb telling how in the following sentences, and draw arrows to the verbs that they modify.

These sentences are slightly adapted from *Imprudent King: A New Life of Philip II*, by Geoffrey Parker.

Ferdinand's obstinacy led Charles to exclaim angrily, "We need to establish who is emperor: you or me."

The ambassador dutifully informed his master.

Philip again complained selfishly.

He concluded briskly, "And so I am confident that you will gladly shoulder your part of the burden."

Philip scribbled grumpily, "If I were God and knew everyone's inner nature, this would be easy; but we are men, not gods."

Philip replied wearily that things were not nearly so bad.

He rode majestically through the streets of Genoa.

The prince spoke little and so softly that few could hear his words.

Some flatly refused to accept the posts that Philip offered them.

The condemned man unwisely appealed to the council again, and they recommended further clemency to the king.

The king sentenced him to be secretly strangled in his cell.

Exercise 33B: Forming Adverbs from Adjectives

Turn the following adjectives into adverbs.

Adjective	Adverb	Adjective	Adverb
useless	uselessly	unnecessary	unnecessarily
courageous	courageously	lazy	lazily
natural	naturally	owlish	owlishly
stern	sternly	dainty	daintily
limp	limply		

Exercise 33C: Diagramming Adverbs

On your own paper, diagram the following sentences.

The tired woman stared vacantly.

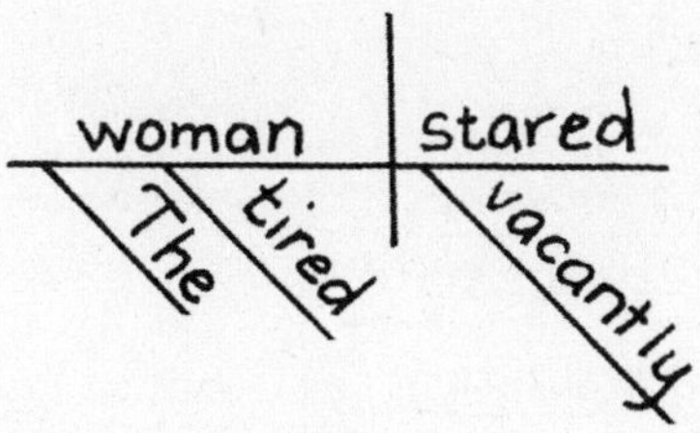

The new band enthusiastically plays songs.

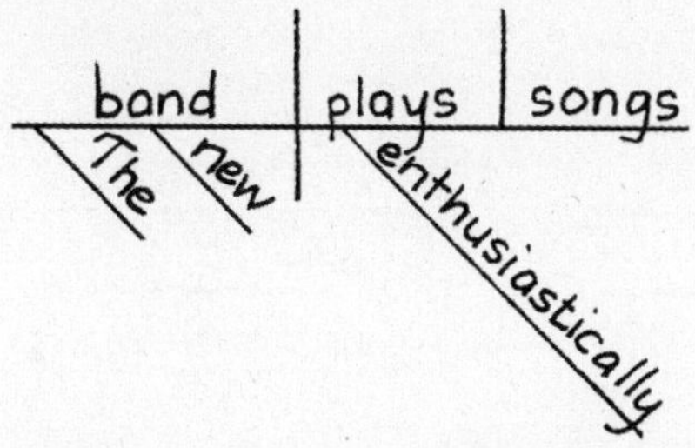

My old flashlight dimly lit the narrow passageway.

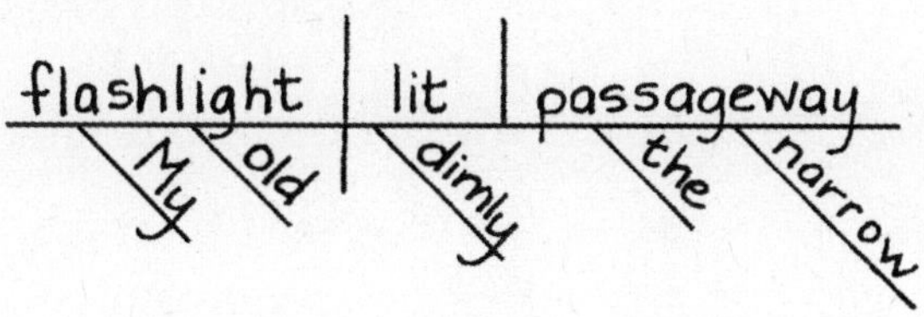

Adeline answered the question truthfully.

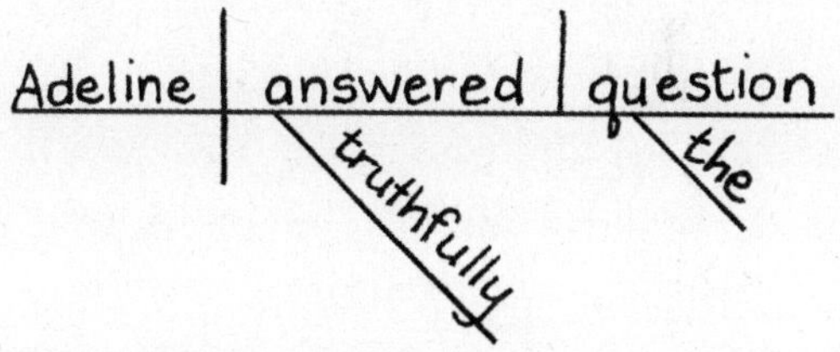

Sleepily, Travis answered the red phone.

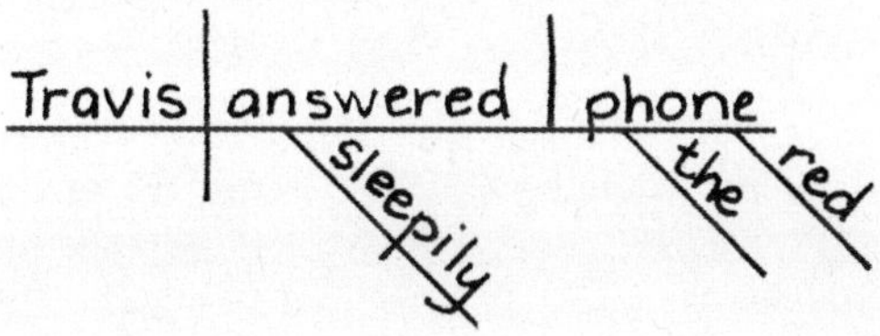

The furious bull snorted menacingly.

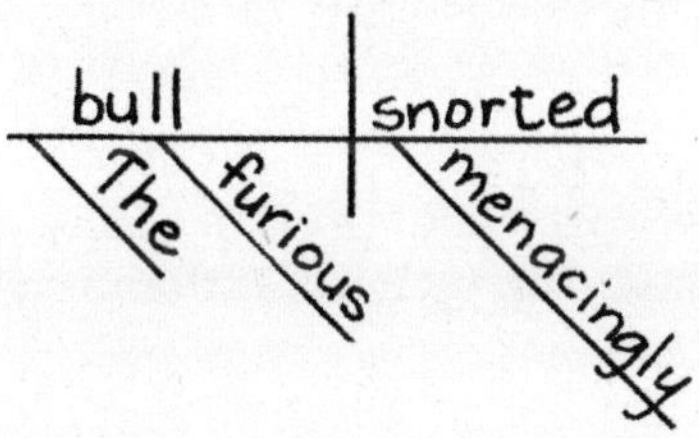

— LESSON 34 —

Adverbs That Tell When, Where, and How Often

Exercise 34A: Telling When

Calvin dropped his recipe cards for banana bread. Help him get organized by numbering the following sentences from 1 to 5 so he can make the bread.

4. ____ Later, combine the wet ingredients with the dry ingredients.

1. ____ First, mash the bananas in a bowl.

2. ____ Second, add the egg, sugar, and cooking oil to the bananas.

5. ____ Finally, cook for 50 to 55 minutes in a 350° oven.

3. ____ Next, mix flour, baking powder, baking soda, cinnamon, and salt in a separate bowl.

Exercise 34B: Distinguishing among Different Types of Adverbs

Put each of the following adverbs in the correct category according to the question it answers.

poorly	upstairs	sometimes	yesterday
fourth	regularly	sweetly	frequently
later	here	everywhere	happily

When	Where	How	How Often
yesterday	everywhere	sweetly	frequently
fourth	here	poorly	regularly
later	upstairs	happily	sometimes

Exercise 34C: Identifying Adverbs of Different Types

Underline the adverbs in the following sentences that tell when, where, or how often.

I will complete my homework later.

That stray cat often stays near the restaurant.

The coyote never catches the roadrunner.

Get your jacket now.

Quincy occasionally forgets a line, but he usually recovers from his mistakes.

Prairie dogs tunnel constantly.

The turtle was on that rock yesterday.

Tia is always changing her mind.

Antonio searched everywhere in the house for his keys.

I left my bag inside.

Exercise 34D: Diagramming Different Types of Adverbs

On your own paper, diagram the following sentences.

I was sneezing constantly yesterday!

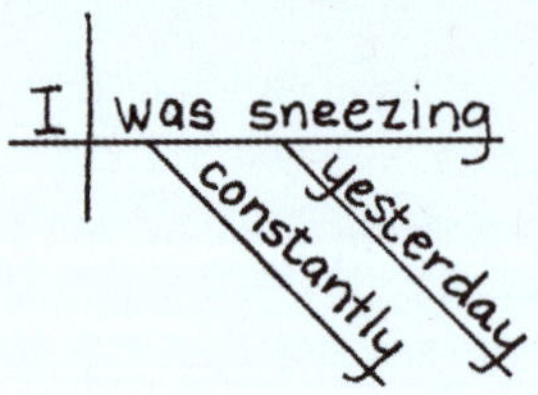

Tomorrow, greet the new student warmly.

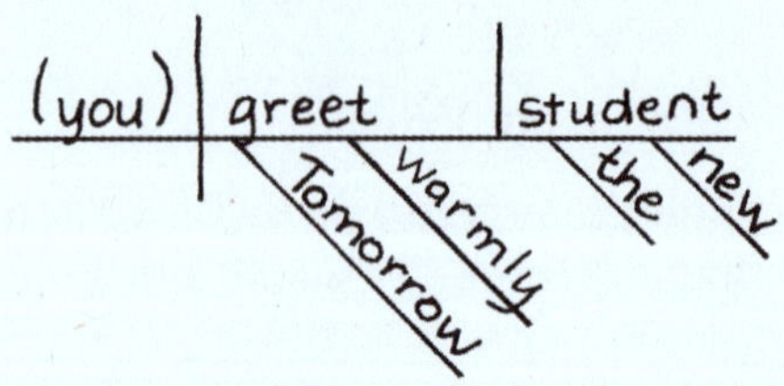

Cautiously, the timid girl stepped outside.

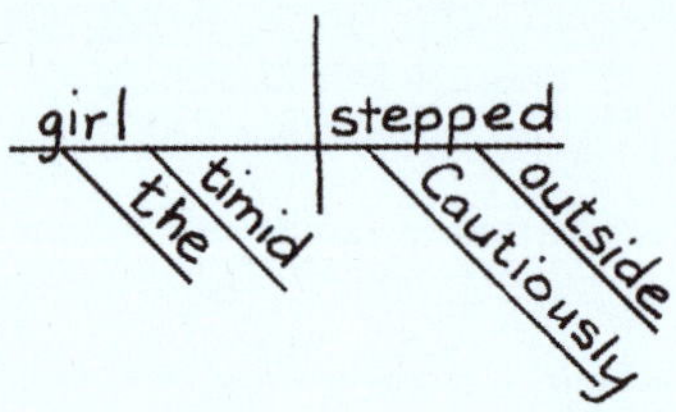

Bonnie and Reginald settled their differences yesterday.

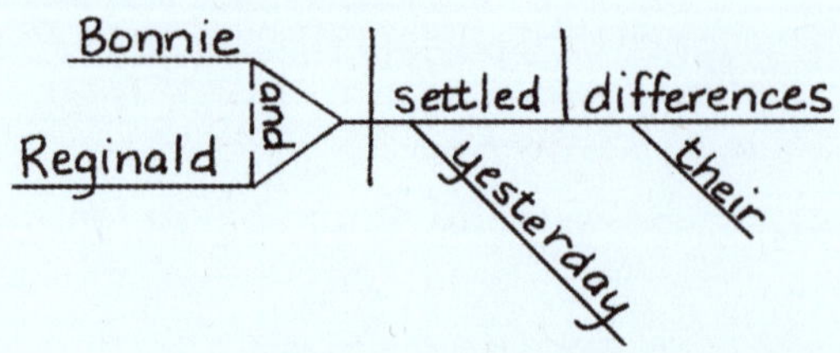

Our neighbors were playing baseball earlier and accidentally broke Mr. Larson's window.

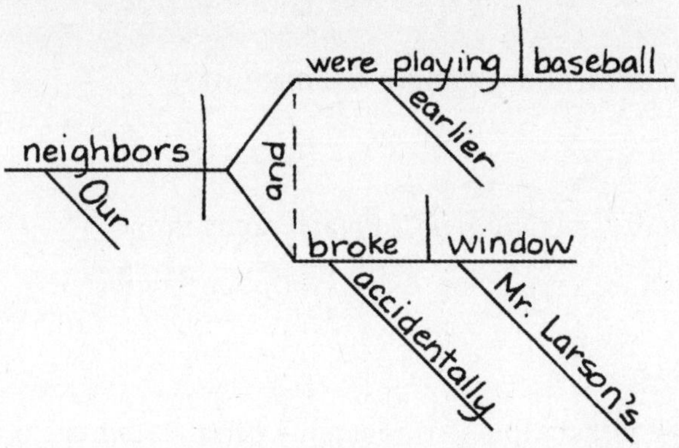

My dedicated instructor prepares lessons daily.

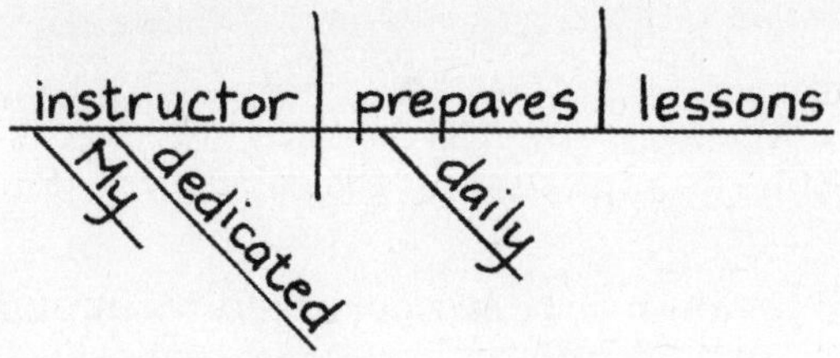

— LESSON 35 —

Adverbs That Tell To What Extent

Exercise 35A: Identifying the Words Modified by Adverbs

Draw an arrow from each underlined adverb to the word it modifies.

These sentences are slightly adapted from Stephen Jay Gould's *The Flamingo's Smile: Reflections in Natural History.*

He was barely able to reconstruct the story later from his sadly inadequate record.

No other theme so well displays the human side of science.

Mottled shells are equally inconspicuous (indeed remarkably camouflaged) when dappled sunlight filters through the vegetation.

I shall then summarize the three major arguments from modern biology for the surprisingly small extent of human racial differences.

What cause could yield a periodicity so regular, yet so widely spaced?

The chain of being had always vexed biologists because, in some objective sense, it doesn't seem to describe nature very well.

We know, in retrospect, that England and most of northern Europe were, quite recently, covered several times by massive continental ice sheets.

One question has always predominated in this case—individuality.

Many of these plants contain psychoactive agents, avoided by mammals today as a result of their bitter taste.

The alkaloids simply don't taste good (they are bitter); in any case, mammals have livers happily supplied with the capacity to detoxify them.

As an animal, or any object, grows (provided its shape doesn't change), surface areas must increase more slowly than volumes—since surfaces get larger as length squared, while volumes increase much more rapidly, as length cubed.

A master in the art of teaching, he exercised an almost irresistible influence over his students.

He never married, socialized little, and published less.

Exercise 35B: Diagramming Different Types of Adverbs

On your own paper, diagram every word of the following sentences.

The extremely old chair wobbled threateningly.

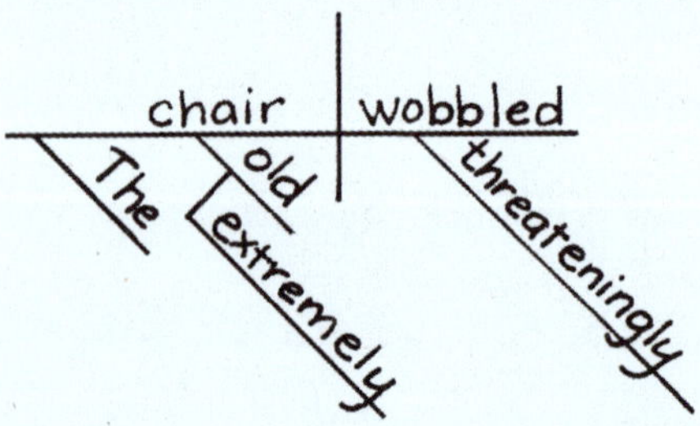

Angie and Brian presented a completely workable solution.

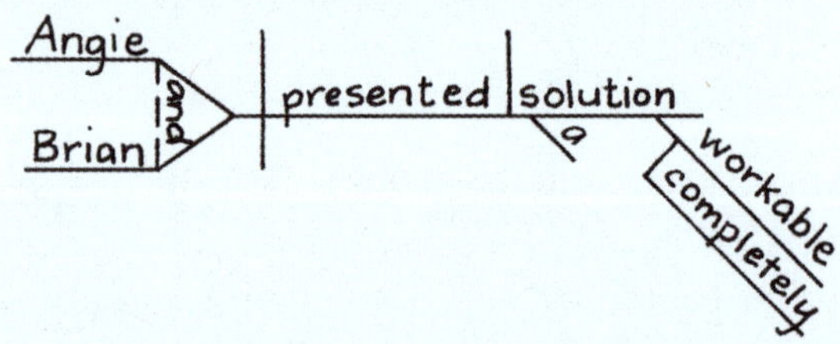

Somewhere, this very untidy room contains my completely finished project.

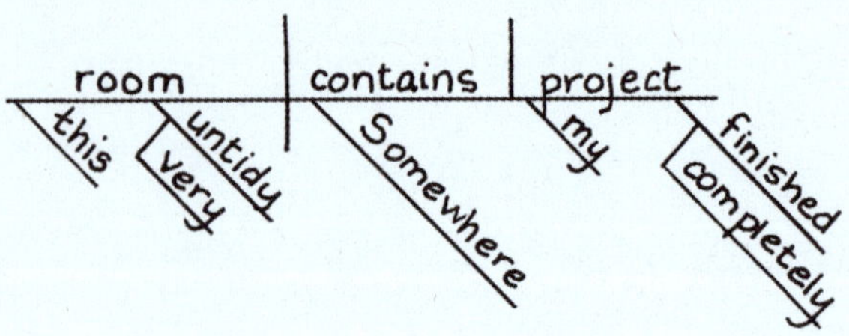

Kick the ball much more forcefully.

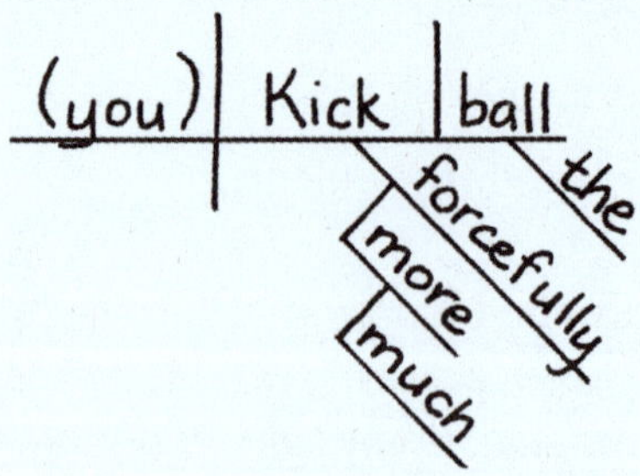

Sophia retrieved the next clue quite easily.

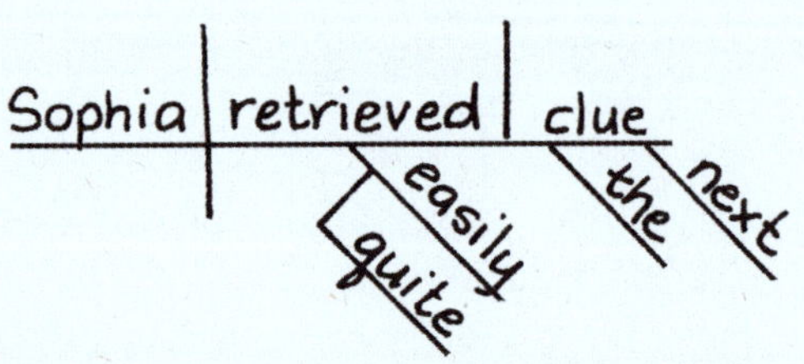

Where are you going so hurriedly?

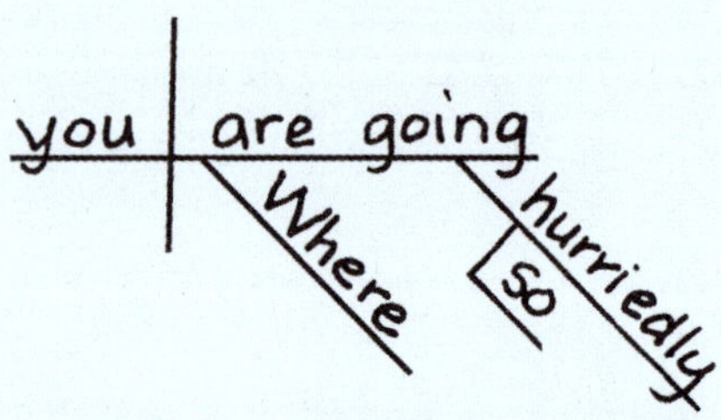

— LESSON 36 —

Adjectives and Adverbs
The Adverb *Not*
Diagramming Contractions
Diagramming Compound Adjectives and Compound Adverbs

Exercise 36A: Practice in Diagramming

On your own paper, diagram every word of the following sentences.

These sentences are adapted from *Rebecca of Sunnybrook Farm*, by Kate Douglas Wiggin.

I've almost broken my neck.

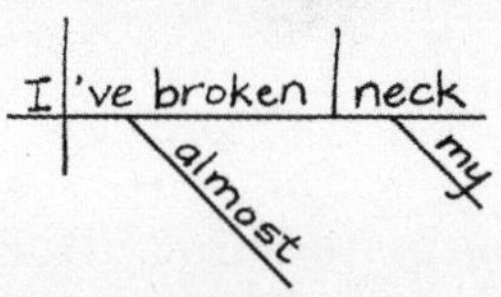

The thought gradually permeated Mr. Jeremiah Cobb's slow-moving mind.

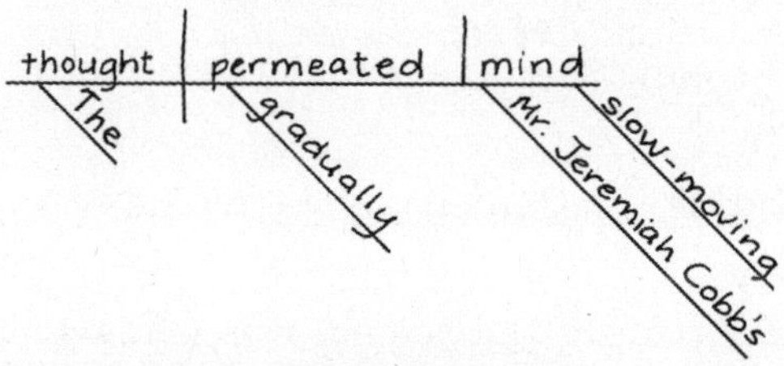

We don't use the front stairs.

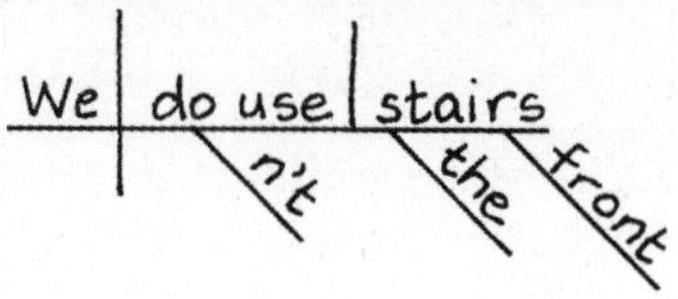

Miss Dearborn heard many admiring remarks.

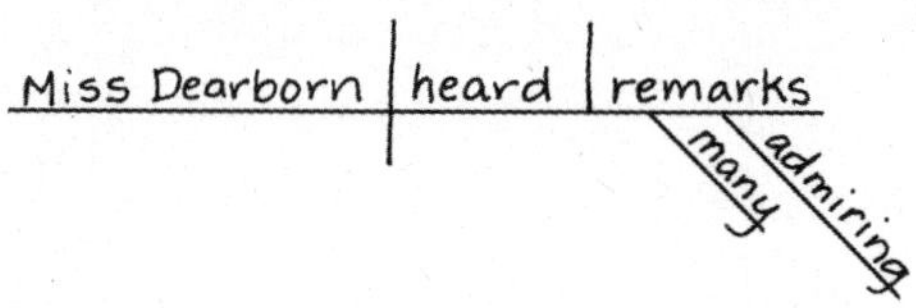

She smoothed it carefully and pinched up the white ruffle.

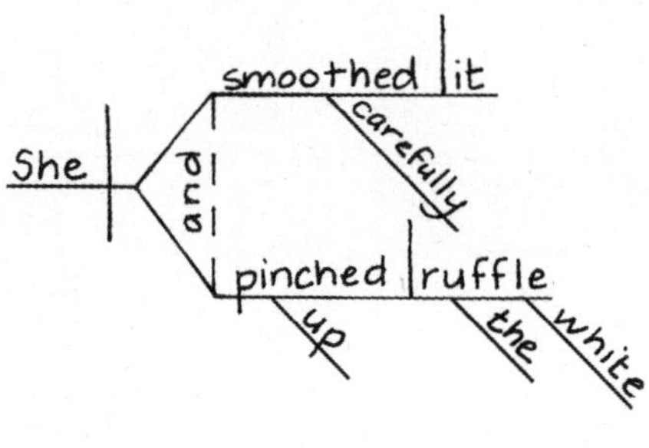

She extended her dress still farther.

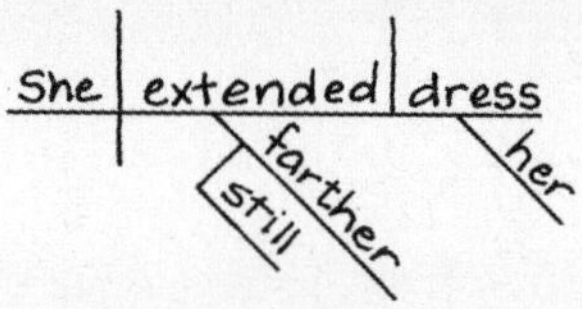

Mother always keeps her promises.

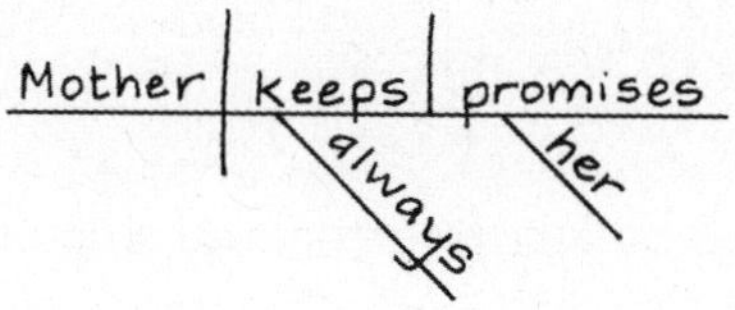

She fell down and wept very loudly.

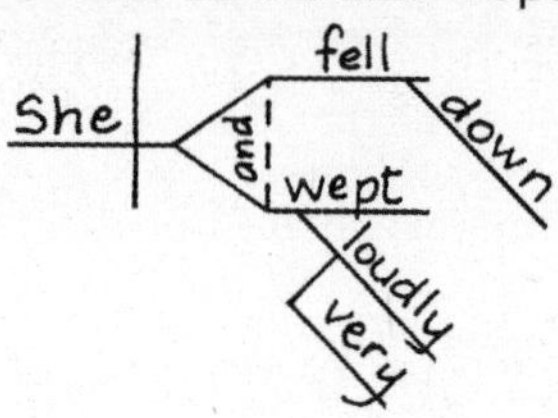

She did not tread the solid ground.

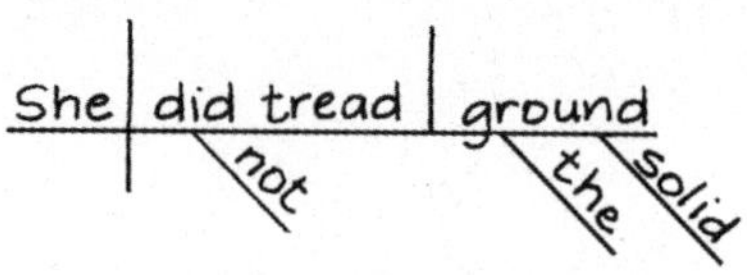

I didn't make a bad guess.

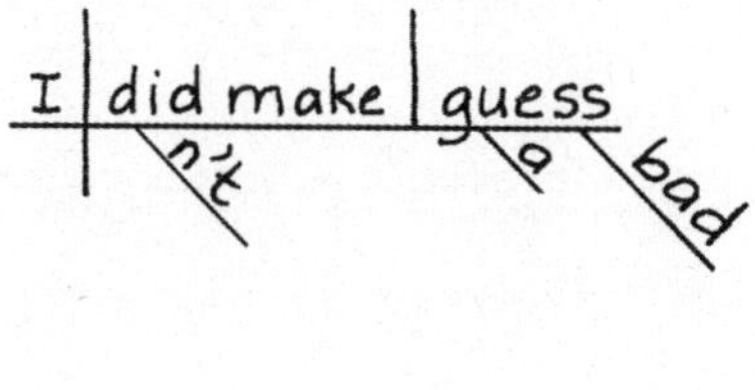

— REVIEW 3 —

Weeks 7-9

Topics
Parts of Speech
Compound Parts of Sentences
Prepositions
Prepositional Phrases
Objects of Prepositions
Subjects and Predicates
Subject-Verb Agreement
Verbs and Direct Objects

Review 3A: Parts of Speech

In the passage below, from Jules Verne's *Journey to the Center to the Earth*, identify the underlined words as *N* for noun, *ADJ* for adjective, *ADV* for adverb, *PREP* for preposition, or *CONJ* for conjunction. The first is done for you.

My uncle [N] said nothing. He was too [ADV] busy [ADJ] examining his papers, among [PREP] which of course was the famous [ADJ] parchment [N], and some letters [N] of introduction from [PREP] the Danish [ADJ] consul [N], which were to pave the way to [PREP] an introduction [N] to the Governor of [PREP] Iceland [N]. My only [ADJ] amusement [N] was looking out [ADV] of [PREP] the window. But as we passed through [PREP] a flat though fertile [ADJ] country, this occupation was slightly [ADV] monotonous [ADJ]. In three [ADJ] hours we reached Kiel [N], and [CONJ] our baggage was at once transferred to [PREP] the steamer [N].

We had now [ADV] a day before [PREP] us, a delay of about [ADV] ten [ADJ] hours [N], which fact [N] put my uncle in a towering [ADJ] passion. We had nothing to do but [CONJ] to walk about [PREP] the pretty [ADJ] town and [CONJ] bay. At length, however, we went on [PREP] board, and at half past ten were steaming down [PREP] the Great Belt [N]. It was a dark [ADJ] night, with [PREP] a strong breeze and a rough [ADJ] sea, nothing being visible but [CONJ] the occasional [ADJ] fires on [PREP] shore [N], with [PREP] here and there a lighthouse. At [PREP] seven in the morning we left Korsör, a little [ADJ] town [N] on the western [ADJ] side of [PREP] Seeland [N].

Review 3B: Recognizing Prepositions

Circle the 46 prepositions from your list in the following bank of words. Try to complete the exercise without looking back at your list of prepositions.

since against there during of before by small
after inside you past aboard went most
under in until now upon above ours pony
over behind near with he eat between
know beside like around and underneath grew about
from through beyond when sick oops their
toward among to off where without for but
up mine throughout they below been at
or within on hers beneath across down our
note along into star front except more

Review 3C: Subjects and Predicates

Draw one line under the simple subject and two lines under the simple predicate. These lines are from the poem "Wynken, Blynken, and Nod," by Eugene Field. Watch out for compound subjects and predicates!

Also, remember that in poetry, sometimes the order of words is different than in normal speech—once you have found the verb, ask "who or what?" before it to find the subject.

Wynken, Blynken, and Nod one night sailed off in a wooden shoe.
Where are you going?
And what do you wish?
The old moon asked the three.
The old moon laughed and sang a song.
The little stars were the herring fish.
Now cast your nets. (you)
All night long their nets they threw to the stars in the twinkling foam.
Then down from the skies came the wooden shoe.
Wynken and Blynken are two little eyes.
And Nod is a little head.
And you shall see the beautiful things.

Review 3D: Complicated Subject-Verb Agreement

Cross out the incorrect verb form in parentheses.

The economics quizzes (~~is~~/are) challenging.
Linguistics (is/~~are~~) my favorite class.
There (~~is~~/are) four beverage options; Sally (wants/~~want~~) lemonade.

There (is/~~are~~) a man with yellow glasses near the statues.
A one-eyed dragon or a seven-headed dog (lies/~~lie~~) behind that door!
The quarterback and captain of the team (is/~~are~~) inviting everyone to his house after the game.
My pants (~~is~~/are) on backwards!
The faculty (is/~~are~~) waiting in the auditorium for the principal's announcement.
The faculty (~~has~~/have) different theories about what the principal might say.
Every book in those three sections (has/~~have~~) been checked out.
Grandmothers and grandfathers (~~is~~/are) seated near the front for the performance.
Songs or poems (~~makes~~/make) memorization easier for many people.
Each criterion (has/~~have~~) been met.
Each of the buttons in the quilt (represents/~~represent~~) a different place the quilter visited.

Review 3E: Objects and Prepositions

Identify the underlined words as *DO* for direct object or *OP* for object of preposition. For each direct object, find and underline twice the action verb that affects it. For each object of the preposition, find and circle the preposition to which it belongs.

These sentences are adapted from Andrew Peterson's *On the Edge of the Dark Sea of Darkness.*

He lifted a ring [DO] (of) keys [OP] (from) the wall [OP], opened the barred door [DO], and shoved the children [DO] (into) a cell [OP].

People were walking, pushing carts [DO], driving carriages [DO], leading sheep [DO], and loading wagons [DO] (with) fish [OP].

Podo's weak voice echoed (from) the carriage [OP] again.

Immediately, Janner sensed a smell [DO] (in) the air [OP], or some subtle sound [DO] (on) the wind [OP].

He enjoyed the food [DO] and the fine filth [DO] (of) the place [OP].

Brimney Stupe strolled (through) the corridors [OP] (of) the mansion [OP] (at) night [OP] (with) a candle [OP] (above) his head [OP].

Peet fished a leather pouch [DO] (from) a small box [OP] (beside) him [OP] and sprinkled some [DO] (of) its contents [OP] (into) the pot [OP].

Tink wiped his brow [DO] and shook his head [DO].

Leeli hugged Mr. Reteep [DO] (around) his sizable waist [OP].

WEEK 10

Completing the Sentence

— LESSON 37 —

Direct Objects
Indirect Objects

Exercise 37A: Identifying Direct Objects

Underline the action verbs (and any accompanying helping verbs) and circle the direct objects in these sentences. Remember that you can always eliminate prepositional phrases first if that makes the task easier.

The sentences are adapted from the Aztec folktale "The Earth Giants," as told by Robert Ingpen and Barbara Hayes in *Folktales and Fables of the Americas and the Pacific.*

And can you not lift it?

Zipacna lifted the huge tree onto his shoulder.

I will take the tree there.

Zipacna pulled several hairs from his head and gave them to some ants.

They built a great house over the ditch.

The heavenly twins made a model of a large, delicious-looking crab and put it in the river at the foot of the mountain.

He rubbed his hand across his eyes.

Exercise 37B: Identifying Direct Objects, Indirect Objects, and Objects of Prepositions

Underline every object in the following sentences. Label each one: *DO* for direct object, *IO* for indirect object, or *OP* for object of the preposition.

Cornelius cut Ryan (IO) an enormous slice (DO) of cake (OP).

Jacques baked an enormous pie (DO) for his grandmother (OP).

I cannot guarantee you (IO) a role (DO) in the play (OP).

The first baseman lackadaisically tossed the pitcher (IO) the ball (DO).

Mr. Cruz assigned us (IO) forty math problems (DO) yesterday!

Has someone actually sent me (IO) a present (DO) in the mail (OP)?

IO DO DO
Rosa handed Corrie a pink backpack and a yellow pencil.

DO IO OP OP
Noora had a new idea and asked us for our opinions about it.

Exercise 37C: Diagramming Direct Objects and Indirect Objects

On your own paper, diagram the following sentences.

Lend me your ears!

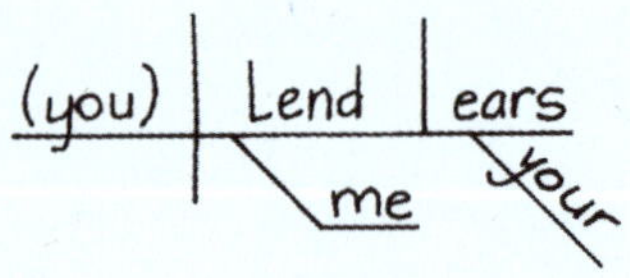

The teenager stood and offered the elderly lady his seat.

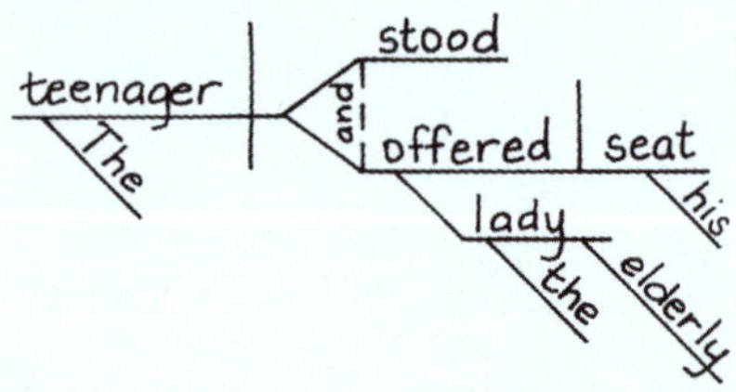

The mother gave her baby a toy and sang him a song.

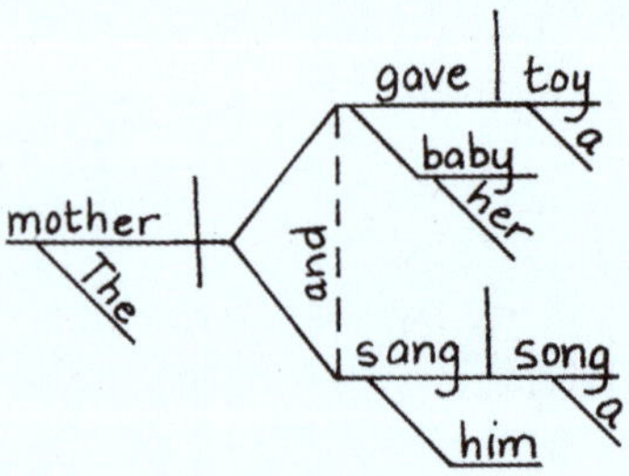

Will you read me a story?

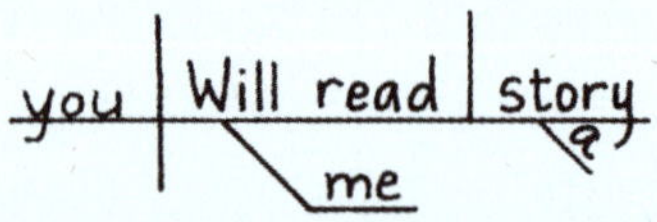

Gwendolen showed Rachna and Ethan the secret passage.

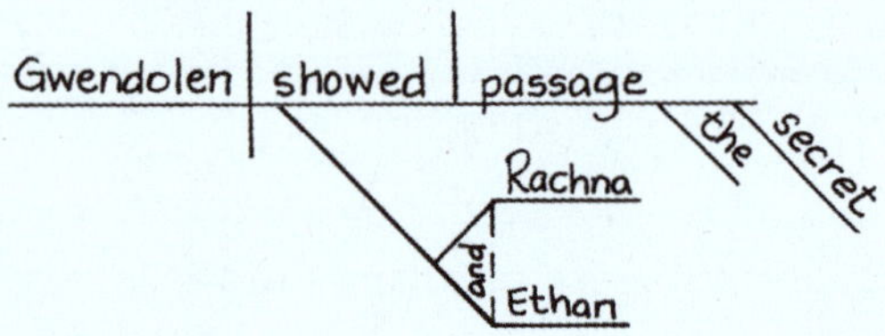

The artist sold him a unique painting.

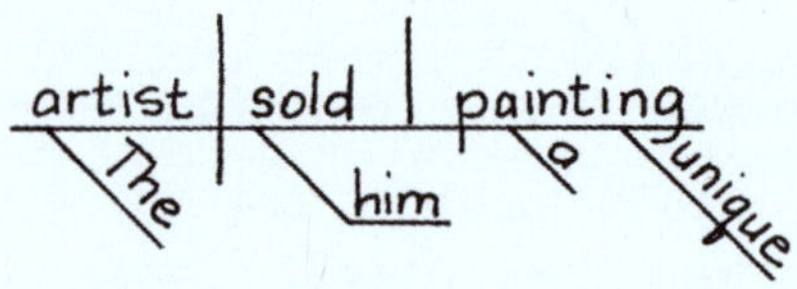

Ms. Fitzpatrick will bring us the leftover cake tomorrow.

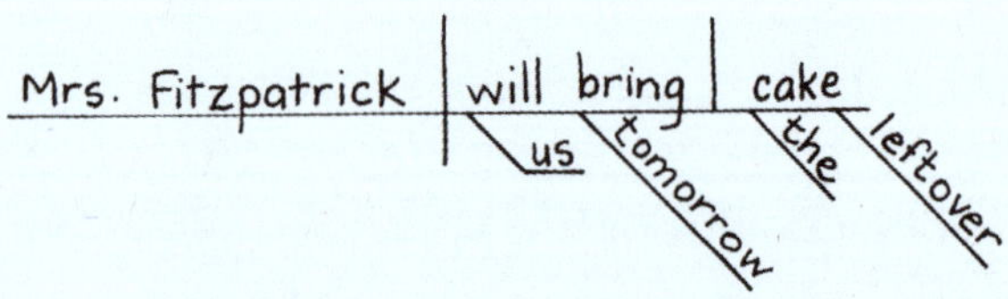

— LESSON 38 —

State-of-Being Verbs
Linking Verbs
Predicate Adjectives

Exercise 38A: Action Verbs and Linking Verbs

In the following sentences, adapted from a letter Christopher Columbus wrote describing his first voyage, underline the simple subjects once and the simple predicates twice. If the verb is a linking verb, write *LV* over it, circle the predicate adjective, and label it *PA*. If the verb is an action verb, write *AV* over it, circle the direct object, and label it *DO*. If the sentence also includes an indirect object, circle it and label it *IO*. The first is done for you.

The harbors are incredibly fine.

I found very many islands with large populations and took possession of them for their Highnesses.

The land is high and has many ranges of hills.

The trees, fruits, and plants are very different from those of Cuba.

They are amazingly timid.

All these islands are extremely fertile.

I gave them a thousand pretty things.

They gave me a good reception everywhere.

These men soon understood us.

Their hair is straight.

I will bring back a large cargo.

All was conjectural, without ocular evidence.

They should hold great celebrations.

Exercise 38B: Diagramming Direct Objects and Predicate Adjectives

On your own paper, diagram *only* the words you labeled (simple subjects, simple predicates, predicate adjectives, direct objects, and indirect objects), along with any conjunctions used to connect compounds, from the sentences in Exercise 38A.

The harbors are incredibly fine.

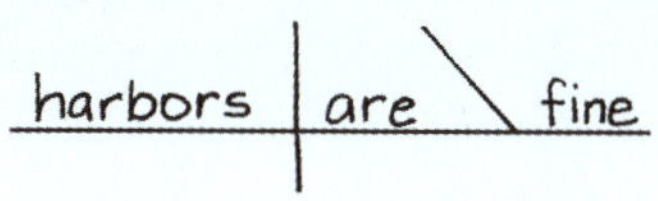

I found very many islands with large populations and took possession of them for their Highnesses.

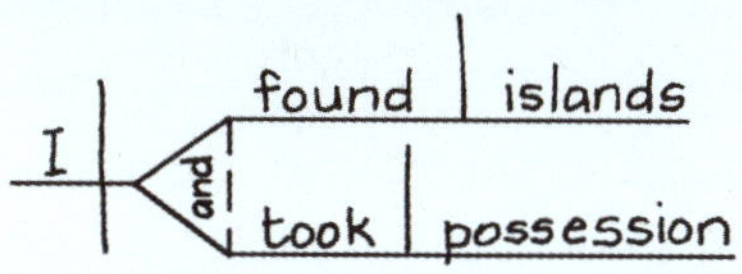

The land is high and has many ranges of hills.

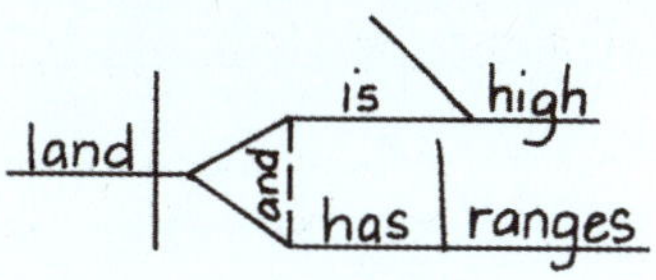

The trees, fruits, and plants are very different from those of Cuba.

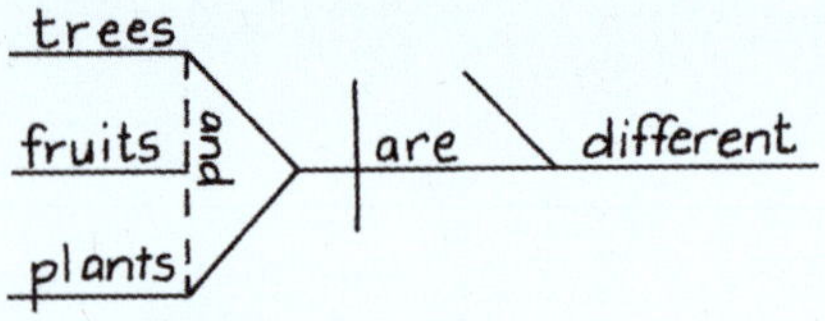

They are amazingly timid.

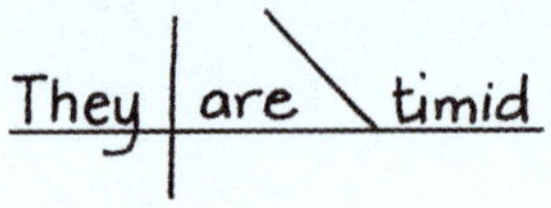

All these islands are extremely fertile.

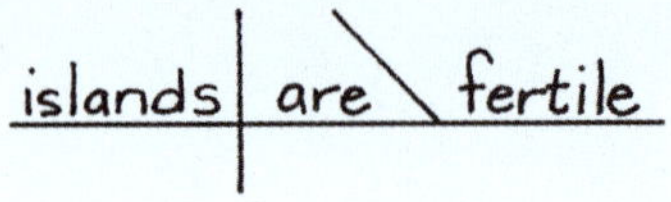

I gave them a thousand pretty things.

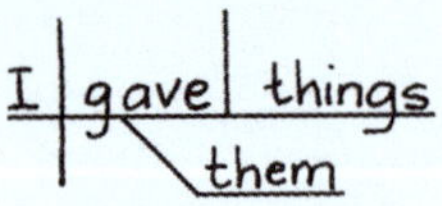

They gave me a good reception everywhere.

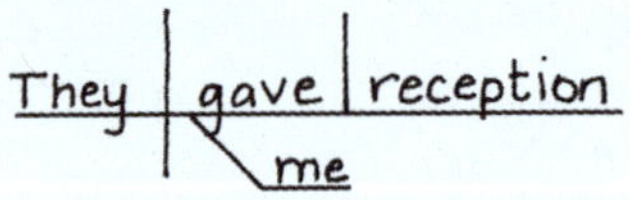

These men soon understood us.

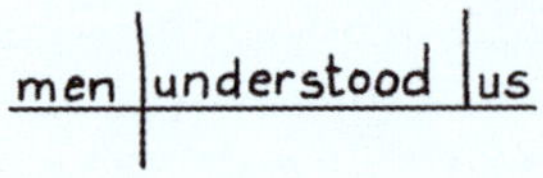

Their hair is straight.

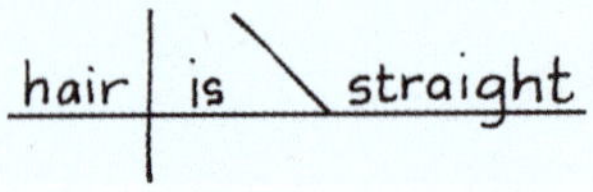

I will bring back a large cargo.

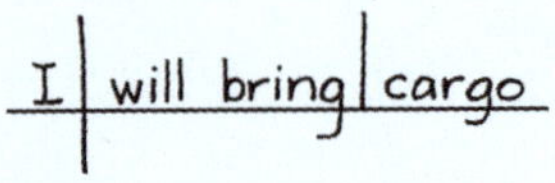

All was conjectural, without ocular evidence.

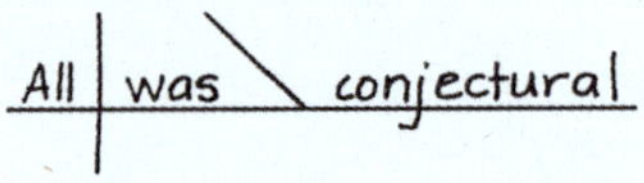

They should hold great celebrations.

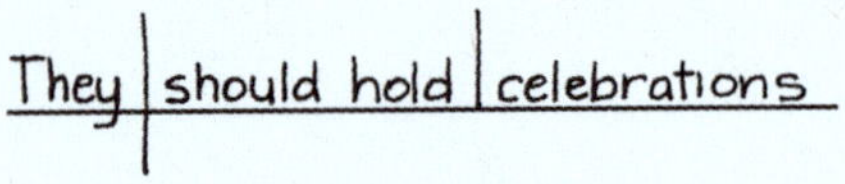

— LESSON 39 —

Linking Verbs
Predicate Adjectives
Predicate Nominatives

Exercise 39A: Identifying Predicate Nominatives and Adjectives

In the following sentences, underline the simple subjects once and the simple predicates twice. Circle the predicate nominatives or adjectives and label each one *PN* for predicate nominative or *PA* for predicate adjective. Draw a line from the predicate nominative or adjective to the subject that it describes. There may be more than one of each.

The octopus, the squid, and the cuttlefish are cephalopods. (PN: cephalopods)

Cephalopods are very intelligent. (PA: intelligent)

Salt water is home to cephalopods. (PN: home)

The blue-ringed octopus is poisonous and very dangerous. (PA: poisonous; PA: dangerous)

Note to Instructor: *Blue-ringed octopus* is a single compound noun, because "octopus" and "blue-ringed octopus" are two different things.

The colors on the blue-ringed octopus are a warning to predators. (PN)

The striped pyjama squid is actually a cuttlefish. (PN)

> **Note to Instructor:** *Striped pyjama squid* is a single compound noun, because "squid" and "striped pyjama squid" are two different things.

It is active at night. (PA)

A cephalopod's ink is a defense. (PN)

Exercise 39B: Writing Predicate Nominatives and Adjectives

Finish each sentence in two ways: with a predicate nominative and with a predicate adjective. If you need to use more than one word in a blank to complete your sentence, circle the word that is the predicate nominative or predicate adjective. The first is done for you.

> **Note to Instructor:** Answers will vary; possible answers are provided. Be sure the student has used a noun for each predicate nominative and an adjective for each predicate adjective. If the student mistakenly uses an adverb instead of an adjective (e.g., "here" for "My aunt's dog is"), remind the student that adjectives tell what kind, which one, how many, and whose.

Curling is ____my favorite sport____. (predicate nominative)
Curling is ____entertaining____. (predicate adjective)

The ice cream was ____a nice treat____. (predicate nominative)
The ice cream was ____delicious____. (predicate adjective)

My aunt's dog is ____a beagle____. (predicate nominative)
My aunt's dog is ____very friendly____. (predicate adjective)

The boy in the blue shirt is ____my neighbor____. (predicate nominative)
The boy in the blue shirt is ____thoughtful____. (predicate adjective)

The white fence is ____the boundary for our game____. (predicate nominative)
The white fence is ____old____. (predicate adjective)

The final clue was ____a jigsaw puzzle____. (predicate nominative)
The final clue was ____confusing____. (predicate adjective)

Exercise 39C: Diagramming

On your own paper, diagram every word of the following sentences.

Kittens are adorable.

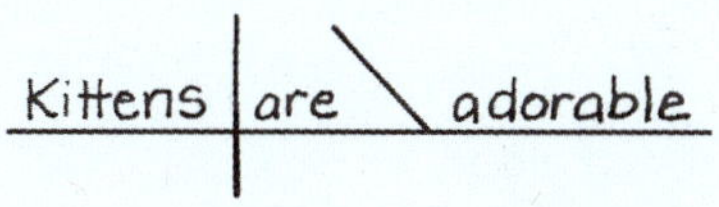

A crib is a baby's bed.

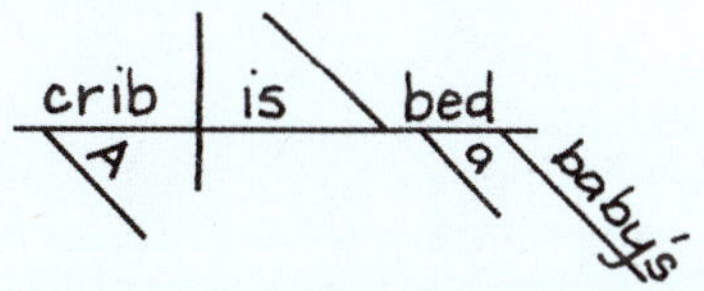

The bouquet was strikingly beautiful.

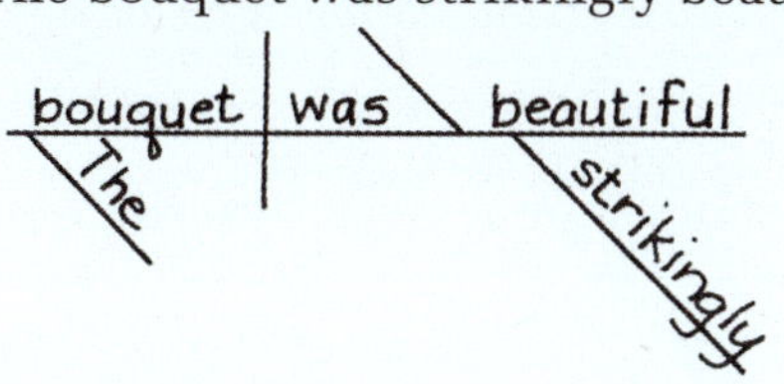

Diligent students check their work.

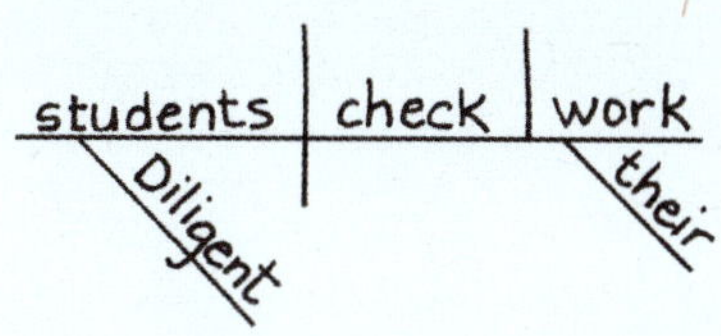

Tomatoes and pumpkins are fruits.

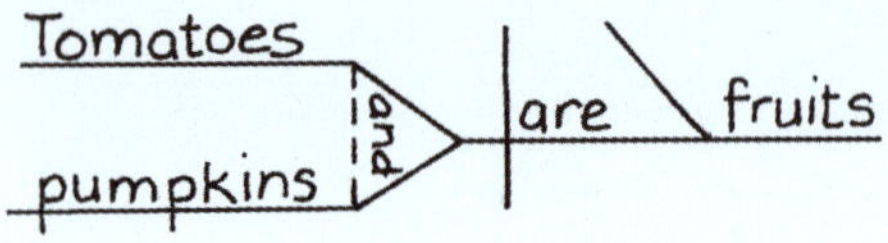

Be a good sport!

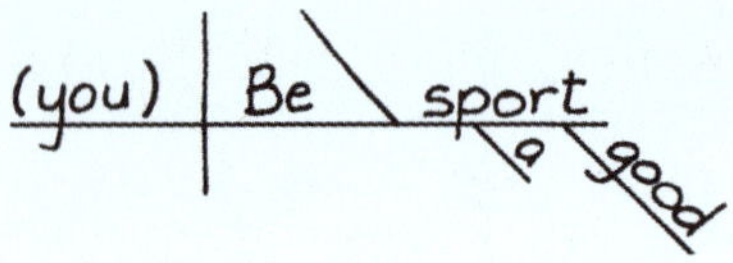

Thunder and lightning began.

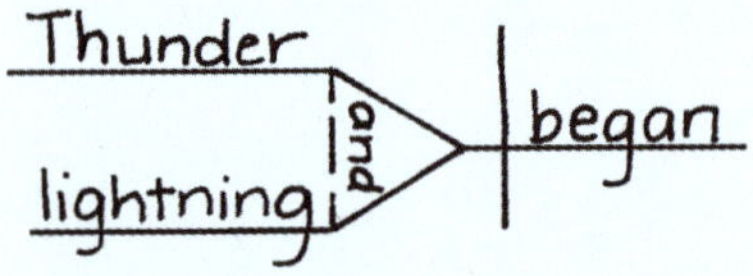

Will you be late?

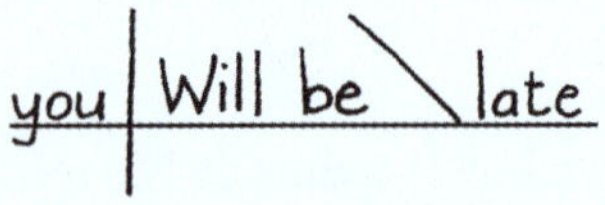

Forgetful Tim burned our breakfast.

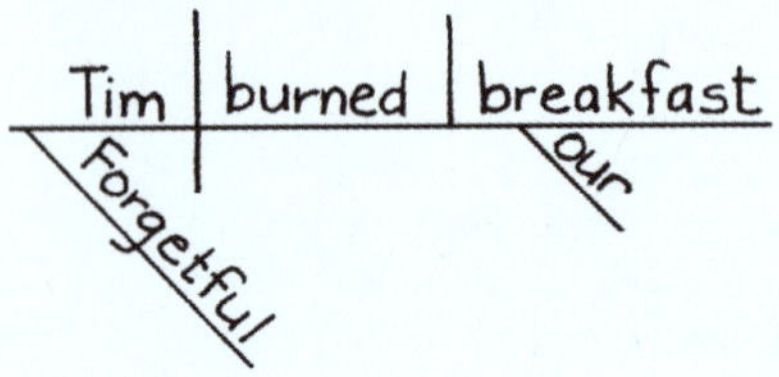

— LESSON 40 —

Predicate Adjectives and Predicate Nominatives

Pronouns as Predicate Nominatives

Object Complements

Exercise 40A: Reviewing Objects and Predicate Adjectives and Nominatives

Identify the underlined words as *DO* for direct object, *IO* for indirect object, *OP* for object of preposition, *PN* for predicate nominative, or *PA* for predicate adjective.

- For each direct object (or direct object/indirect object combination), find and underline twice the action verb that affects it. Include helping verbs!
- For each object of the preposition, find and circle the preposition to which it belongs.
- For each predicate nominative and predicate adjective, find and draw a box around the linking verb that it follows. Include helping verbs!
- When you are finished, answer the questions at the end of the selection.

The following passage is from L. M. Montgomery's *Anne of Green Gables.*

Note to Instructor: This is intended to be a challenging exercise. Give all necessary help.

"But they shouldn't call that lovely place [DO] the Avenue. There is no meaning in a name [OP] like that. They should call it [DO]—let me see—the White Way of Delight. Isn't that a nice imaginative name [PN]? When I don't like the name [DO] of a place or a person I always imagine a new one [DO] and always think of them [OP] so. There was a girl at the asylum [OP] whose name was Hepzibah Jenkins [PN], but I always imagined her as Rosalia DeVere. Other people may call that place The Avenue, but I shall always call it the White Way of Delight. Have we really only another mile to go before we get home? I'm glad and I'm sorry. I'm sorry because this drive has been so pleasant and I'm always sorry when pleasant things end. Something still pleasanter may come after, but you can never be sure. And it's so often the case that it isn't pleasanter. That has been my experience anyhow. But I'm glad to think of getting home. You see, I've never had a real home since I can remember. It gives me that pleasant ache again just to think of coming to a really truly home. Oh, isn't that pretty!"

They had driven over the crest of a hill. Below them was a pond, looking almost like a river so long and winding was it. A bridge spanned it midway and from there to its lower end, where an amber-hued belt of sand-hills shut it in from the dark blue gulf beyond, the water was a glory of many shifting hues—the most spiritual shadings of crocus and rose and ethereal green, with other elusive tintings for which no name has ever been found. Above the bridge the pond ran up into fringing groves of fir and maple and lay all darkly translucent in their wavering shadows. Here and there a wild plum leaned out from the bank like a white-clad girl tiptoeing to her own reflection. From the marsh at the head of the pond came the clear, mournfully-sweet chorus of the frogs. There was a little gray house peering around a white apple orchard on a slope beyond and, although it was not yet quite dark, a light was shining from one of its windows.

Find the compound adjective in this passage. Write it in the blank below and cross out the incorrect choice. amber-hued is in the (attributive/~~predicative~~) position.

Find the object complement in the first sentence. Write it in the blank below and cross out the incorrect choices. Avenue is (~~an adjective~~/a noun) that (~~describes~~/renames) the direct object.

Find the other object complement in the first paragraph! (It's a different name.) Write it in the blank below. White Way of Delight

Exercise 40B: Parts of the Sentence

Label the following in each sentence: *S* (subject), *LV* (linking verb), *AV* (action verb), *DO* (direct object), *OC-A* (object complement-adjective), *OC-N* (object complement-noun), *IO* (indirect object), or *PN* (predicate nominative).

S AV DO
The instructor found the students quickly.

S AV DO OC-A
The instructor found the students intelligent.

S AV DO OC-N
The instructor declared Marisa his apprentice.

S AV IO DO
The instructor gave Marisa an apprenticeship.

S AV DO OC-A
The circus made the children happy.

S AV DO OC-N
My sister named her puppy Aminga.

S AV DO OC-A
Can you keep the jewelry safe?

S AV DO
Can you keep the dog outside?

S LV PN
The president will be you.

S AV DO OC-N
The group elected you president.

S AV DO OC-A
The girl dyed her hair green yesterday.

Exercise 40C: Diagramming

Diagram the sentences from Exercise 40B on your own paper.

The instructor found the students quickly.

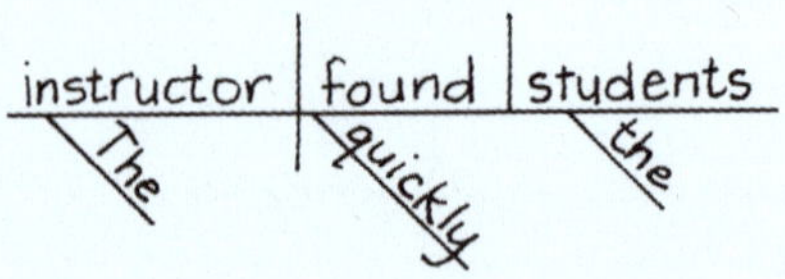

The instructor found the students intelligent.

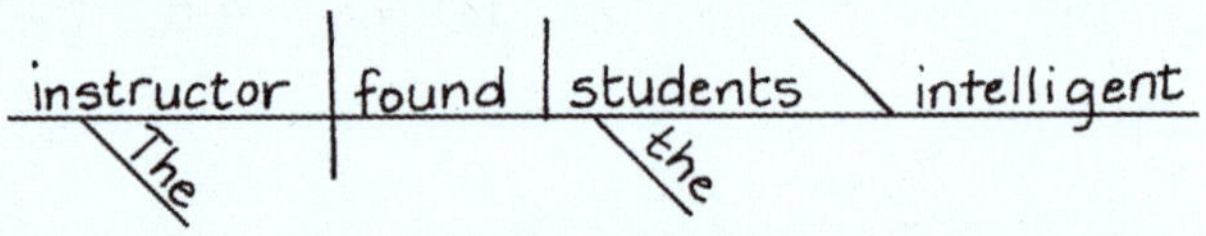

The instructor declared Marisa his apprentice.

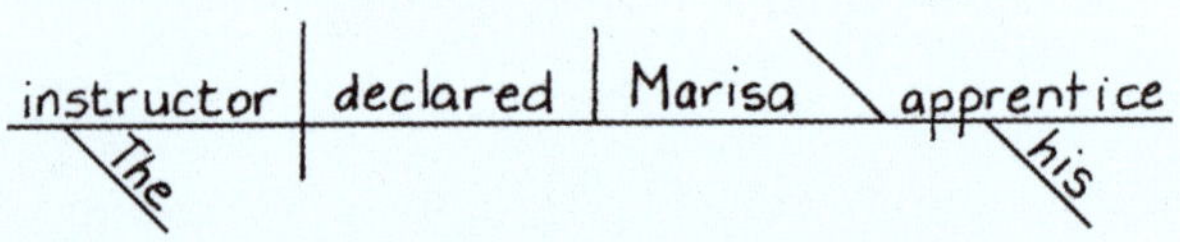

The instructor gave Marisa an apprenticeship.

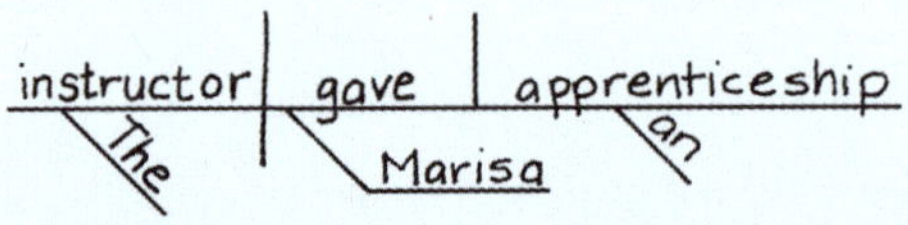

The circus made the children happy.

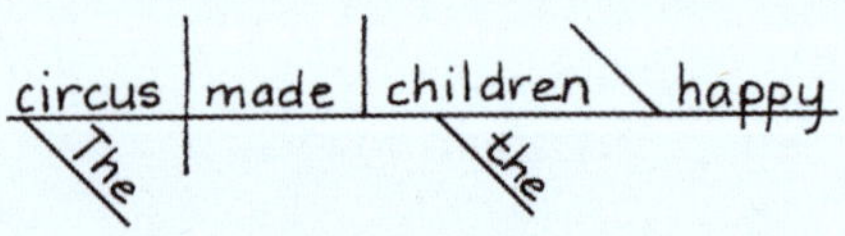

My sister named her puppy Aminga.

Can you keep the jewelry safe?

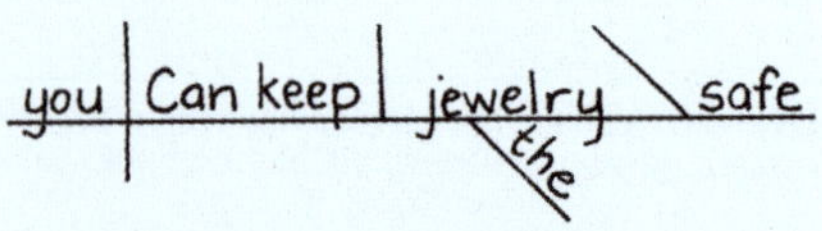

Can you keep the dog outside?

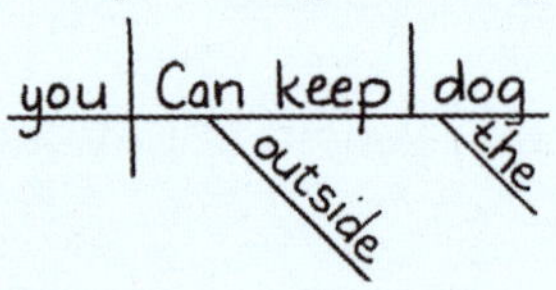

The president will be you.

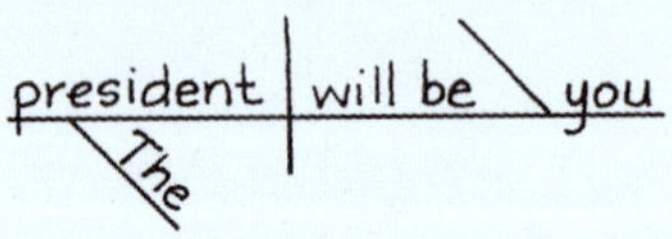

The group elected you president.

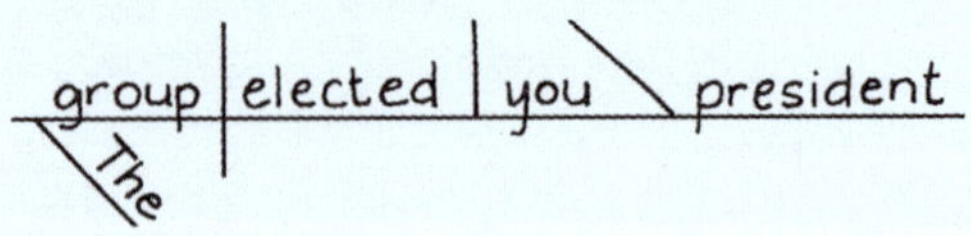

The girl dyed her hair green yesterday.

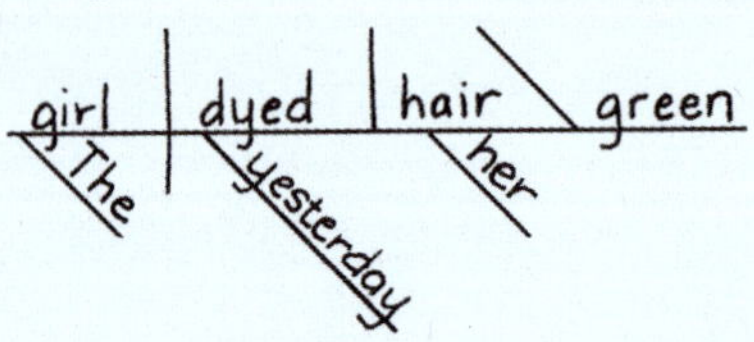

WEEK 11

More About Prepositions

— LESSON 41 —

Prepositions and Prepositional Phrases

Adjective Phrases

Exercise 41A: Identifying Adjective Phrases

Underline the adjective phrases in the following sentences. Draw an arrow from each phrase to the word it modifies. The first is done for you.

These sentences are adapted from *The Histories* by Herodotus, the fifth-century BC Greek historian (translation by Aubrey de Sélincourt).

The people of Samos did not want liberty.

Persians of the highest rank then placed chairs of state there.

I will keep the priesthood of Zeus.

The birds fly down and carry away the joints of meat.

Another tribe to the east is nomadic.

You have personal experience of the effect.

He destroys the structure of ancient tradition and law.

The anniversary of this day is now a red-letter day in the Persian calendar.

This was a further indication of the truth.

You are the son of Hystaspes.

Exercise 41B: Diagramming Adjective Phrases/Review

Diagram each sentence from Exercise 41A on your own paper. Follow this procedure, and ask yourself the suggested questions if necessary.

1. Find the subject and predicate and diagram them first.

    What is the verb?

    Who or what [verb]?

2. Ask yourself: Is the verb an action verb? If so, look for a direct object.

    Who or what receives the action of the verb?

    If there is a direct object, check for an indirect object.

    To whom or for whom is the action done?

    Remember that there may be no direct object or no indirect object—but you can't have an indirect object without a direct object. If there is an indirect object, it will always come between the verb and the direct object.

3. Ask yourself: Is the verb a state-of-being verb? If so, look for a predicate nominative or predicate adjective.

    Is there a word after the verb that renames or describes the subject?

4. Find all prepositional phrases. Ask yourself: Whom or what do they describe?

5. Place all other adjectives and adverbs on the diagram.

If you have trouble, ask for help.

The people of Samos did not want liberty.

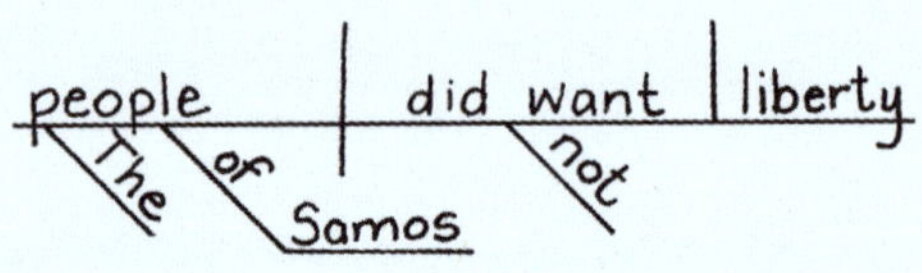

Persians of the highest rank then placed chairs of state there.

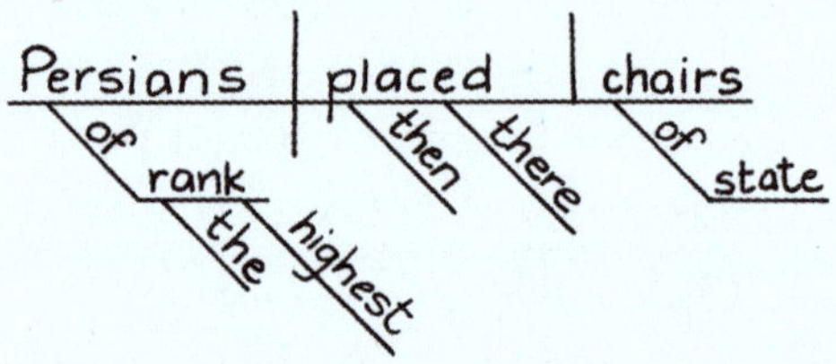

I will keep the priesthood of Zeus.

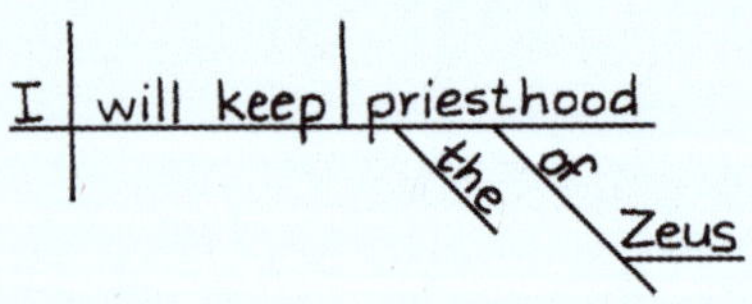

The birds fly down and carry away the joints of meat.

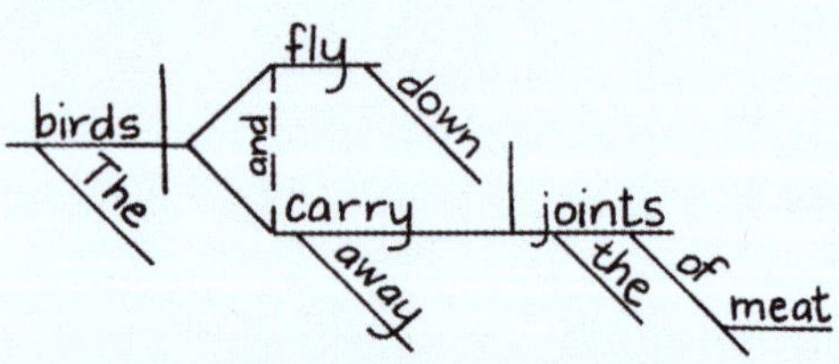

Another tribe to the east is nomadic.

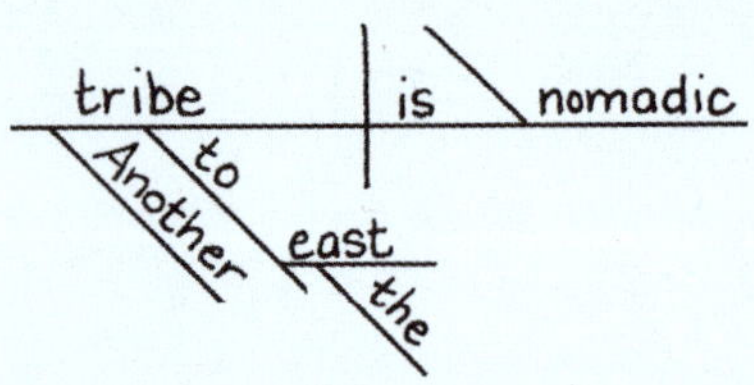

You have personal experience of the effect.

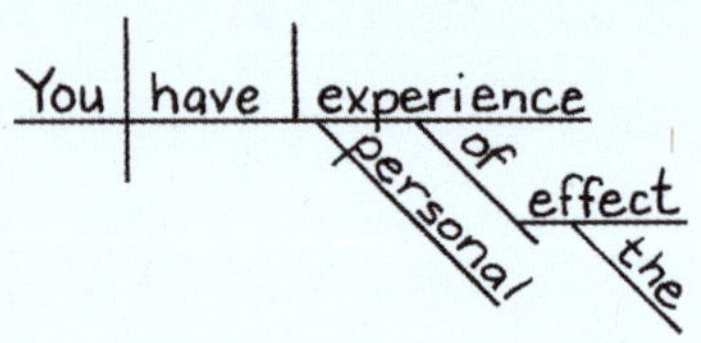

He destroys the structure of ancient tradition and law.

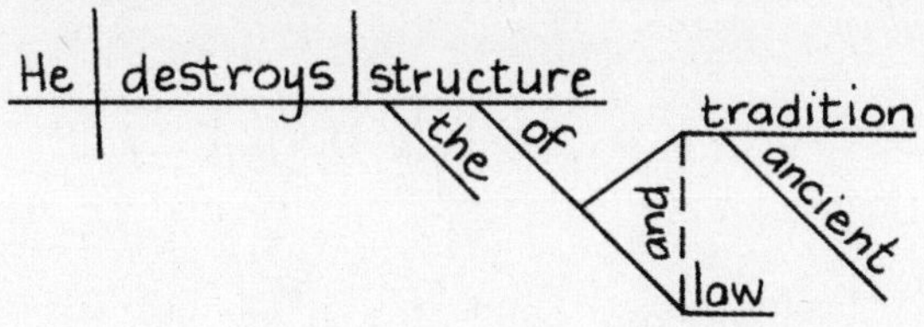

The anniversary of this day is now a red-letter day in the Persian calendar.

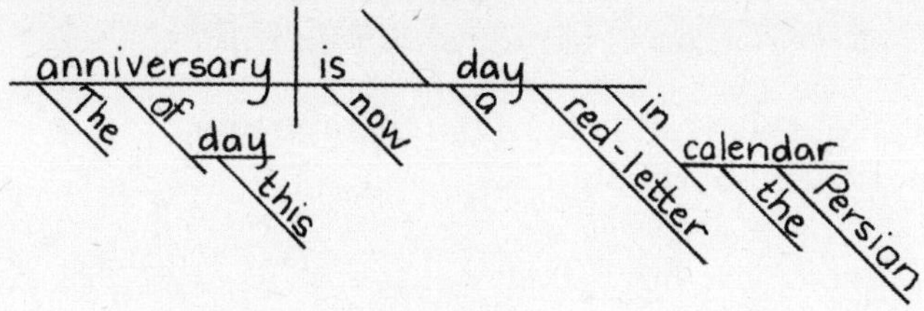

This was a further indication of the truth.

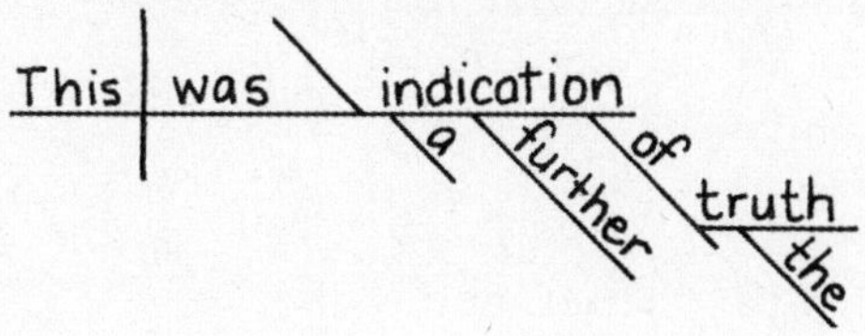

You are the son of Hystaspes.

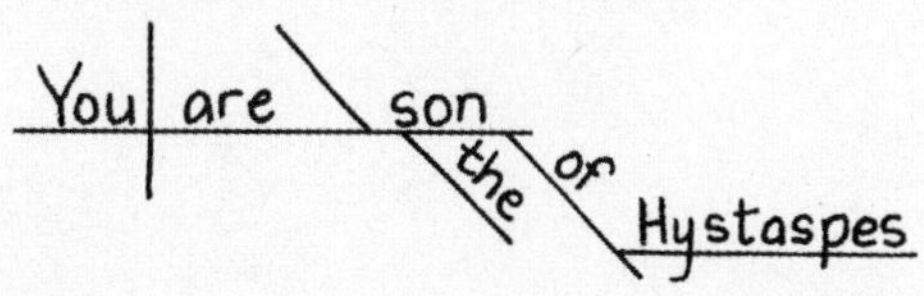

— LESSON 42 —

Adjective Phrases
Adverb Phrases

Exercise 42A: Identifying Adverb Phrases

Underline the adverb phrases in the following sentences and circle the preposition that begins each phrase. Draw an arrow from the phrase to the word it modifies. The first is done for you.

In the morning, we will walk over the hill.

Mrs. Puri encouraged the nervous performers with a smile.

The audience stared curiously at the first scene.

The race will begin in the Guru Nanak Stadium at noon.

Amanjit hid the gift with haste.

With reluctance, Jothi walked onto the stage and began her speech.

The tour guide described in great detail the building's history.

Please hang your umbrella on this hook.

The crowd quickly formed a line in an orderly fashion.

Sani yawned frequently during class.

You spilled lassi on my shirt!

In unison, the students nodded their heads.

Exercise 42B: Diagramming Adverb Phrases

On your own paper, diagram the following sentences, slightly adapted from the nineteenth-century botanical handbook *Punjab Plants.*

The purple fruit is found in the extreme northwest of the Punjab.

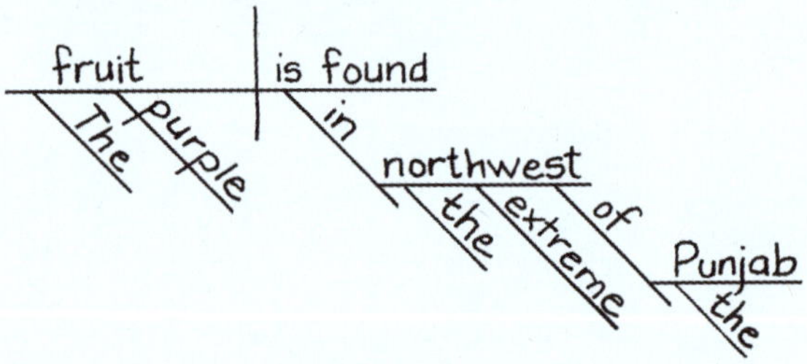

The seed is spread by birds on the tops of buildings.

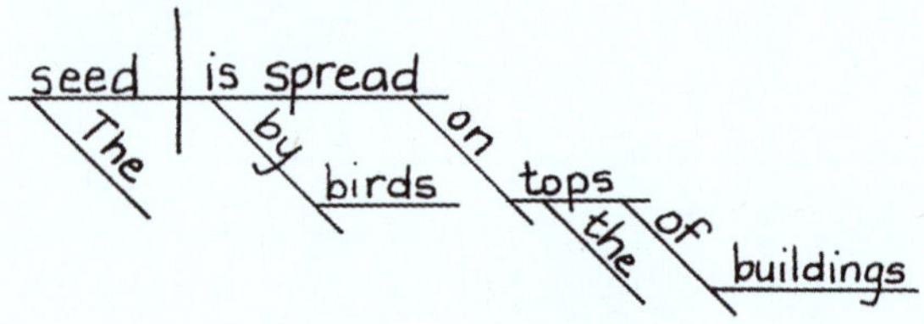

The European olive had been introduced into the Calcutta Botanical Gardens in 1800.

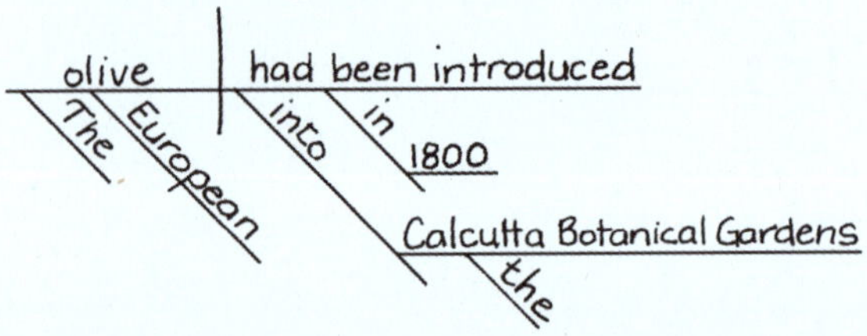

In Kashmir, a proportion of the fiber is mixed with the material for paper-making.

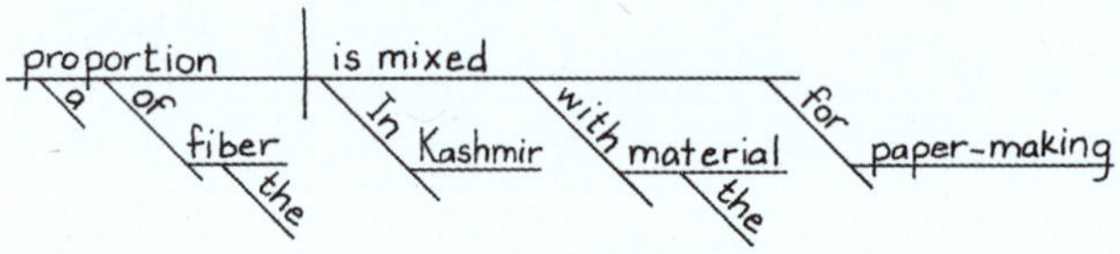

The fruit is commonly eaten without bad effects.

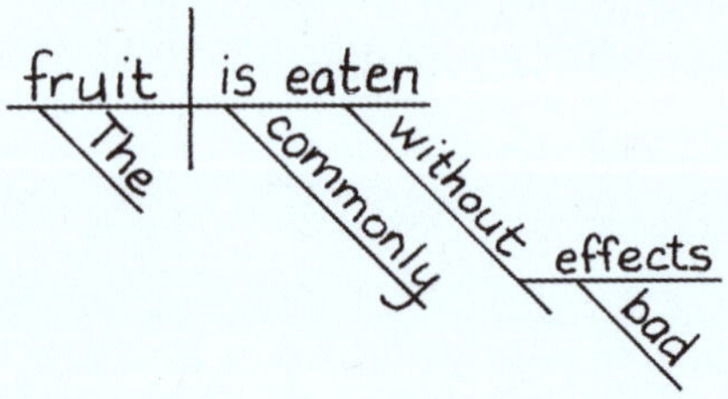

The tree is found below the Niti Pass.

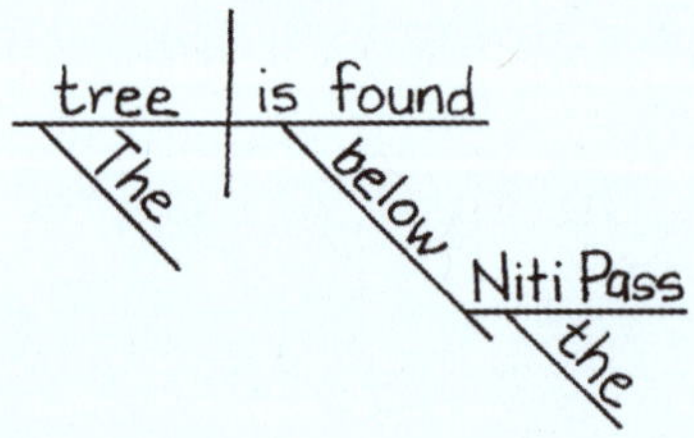

— LESSON 43 —

Definitions Review
Adjective and Adverb Phrases
Misplaced Modifiers

Exercise 43A: Distinguishing between Adjective and Adverb Phrases

Underline all the prepositional phrases in the following sentences. Write *ADJ* above the adjective phrases and *ADV* above the adverb phrases.

These sentences are adapted from *The Princess and the Goblin*, by George MacDonald.

ADV ADV ADJ
In the morning he had laid some bread in a damp hole in the rock.

ADV ADV
The growl continued in a low bass for a good while.

ADV
The goblins had a special evil design in their heads.

That place is swarming with wild beasts (ADV) of every description (ADJ).

At every moment (ADV) he was nibbling with his fingers (ADV) at the edges (ADV) of the hole (ADJ).

In a moment (ADV) the troop disappeared at a turn (ADV) of the way (ADJ).

At length (ADV), he had almost rushed into the middle (ADV) of the goblin family (ADJ).

The nurse left her with the housekeeper (ADV) for a while (ADV).

She emptied the contents of an old cabinet (ADJ) upon the table (ADV).

Through the passages (ADV) she softly sped.

A large oval bed stood in the middle (ADV).

Exercise 43B: Correcting Misplaced Modifiers

Circle the misplaced adjective and adverb phrases in the following sentences. Draw an arrow to the place where the phrase should be. The first is done for you.

The red book is on the shelf with the worn cover.

The dragons breathed fire with green tails.

The young boy on the baseball regarded the player's signature with awe.

Four squirrels are hiding nuts with bushy tails in the back yard.

Inside the nest, Gilbert saw three eggs.

Theodore showed a goldfish to his father in a tank.

The adorable kitty drank the milk with the long whiskers.

The clowns juggled the balls in the funny hats.

Mr. Dunlap under the sofa discovered the missing books.

My mother told me about how she learned at bedtime to ride a bicycle.

Note to Instructor: The arrow could also point to the beginning of the sentence.

Our teacher with chocolate loves to eat pretzels.

— LESSON 44 —

Adjective and Adverb Phrases

Prepositional Phrases Acting as Other Parts of Speech

Exercise 44A: Prepositional Phrases Acting as Other Parts of Speech

In each sentence below, circle any prepositional phrases. Underline the subject of the sentence once and the predicate twice. Then label the prepositional phrases as *ADJ* (adjective phrase), *ADV* (adverb phrase), *S* (subject), *PA* (predicate adjective), *PN* (predicate nominative), or *OP* (object of a preposition).

Our flight is on time.

The argument between the candidates was on the news.

Note to Instructor: The difference between the two sentences is that "on time" describes *what* the flight is, while "on the news" describes *where* the news is.

Beneath that tree is my favorite spot.

My favorite spot is beneath that tree.

We crawled through the tunnel and jumped across the stream.

Our father telephoned us from across the country.

The group's meetings are at the library.

In the sun is too hot today!

The house upon the hill was full of mystery.

Exercise 44B: Diagramming

On your own paper, diagram the sentences from 44A.

Our flight is on time.

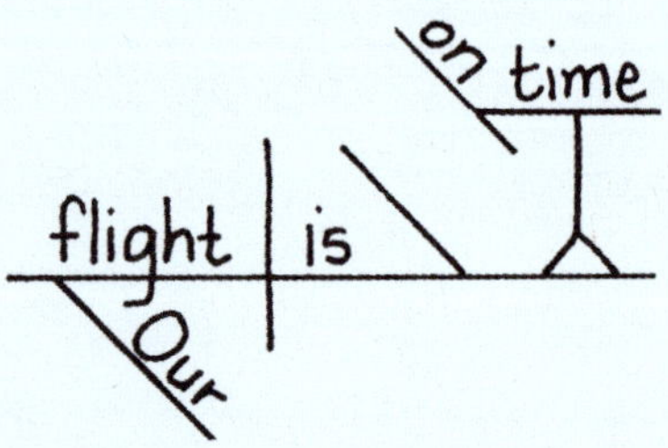

The argument between the candidates was on the news.

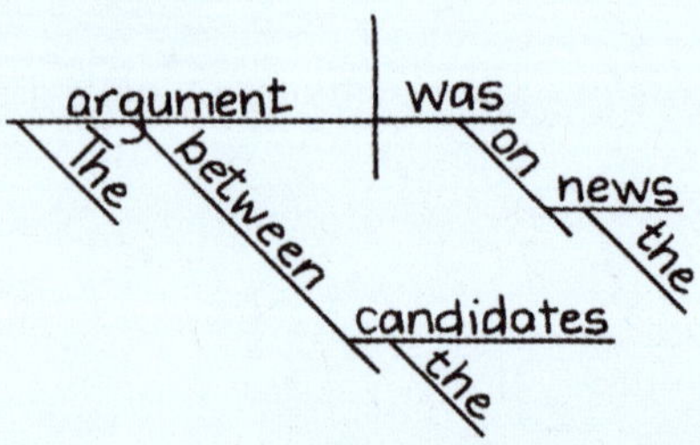

Beneath that tree is my favorite spot.

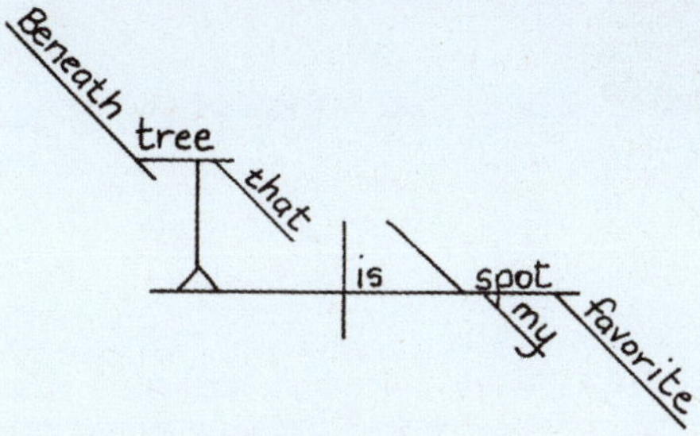

My favorite spot is beneath that tree.

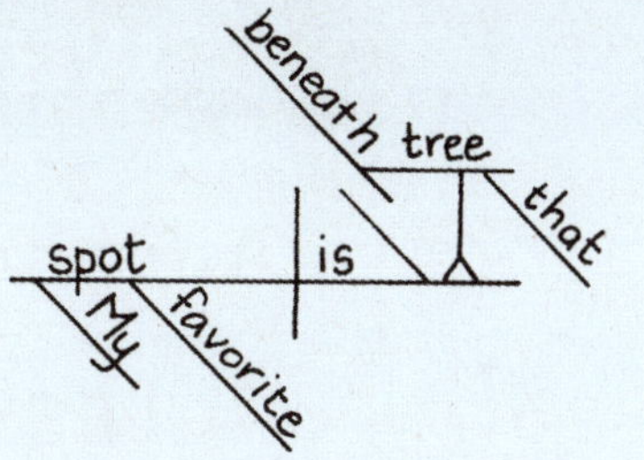

We crawled through the tunnel and jumped across the stream.

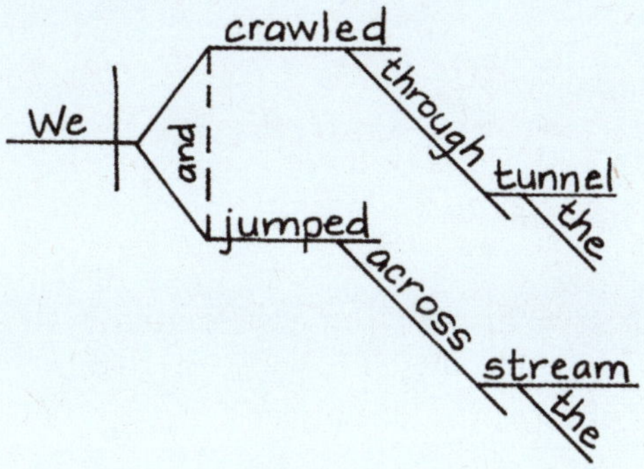

Our father telephoned us from across the country.

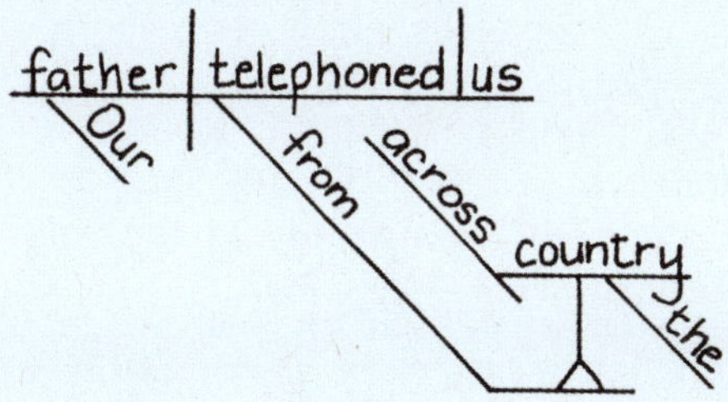

The group's meetings are at the library.

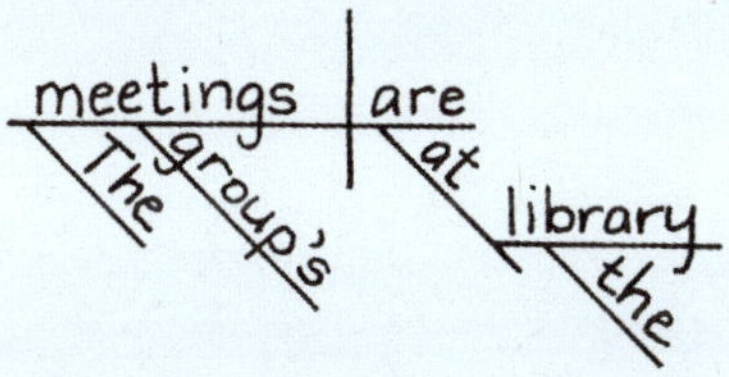

In the sun is too hot today!

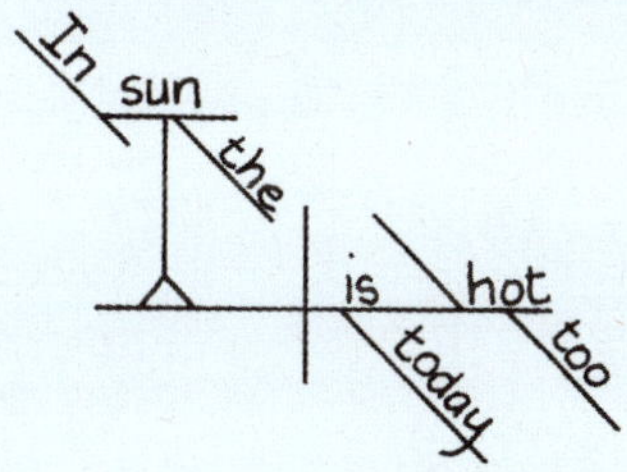

The house upon the hill was full of mystery.

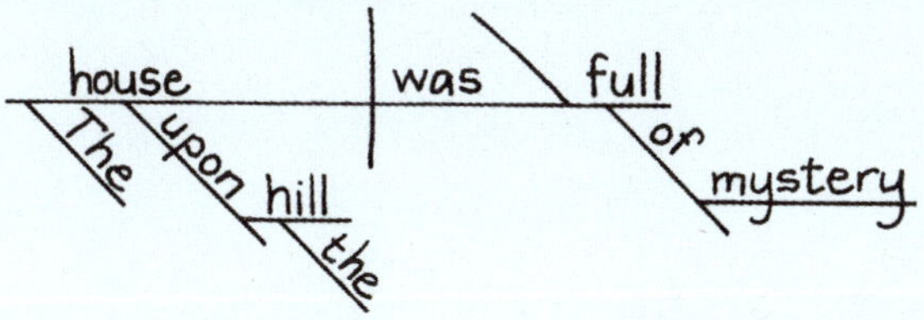

WEEK 12

Advanced Verbs

— LESSON 45 —

Linking Verbs
Linking/Action Verbs

Exercise 45A: Distinguishing between Action Verbs and Linking Verbs

Underline the verbs in the following sentences. Identify them as *AV* for action verb or *LV* for linking verb. If the verb is followed by a direct object (*DO*), predicate adjective (*PA*), or predicate nominative (*PN*), label it.

Remember that a verb with *no* direct object, predicate adjective, or predicate nominative will be an action verb, unless it is a state-of-being verb. Also remember that direct objects, predicate adjectives, and predicate nominatives are never found within prepositional phrases.

AV DO
Herman suspiciously tasted the new food.

LV PA
The food tasted wonderful!

AV DO
Herman ate everything on his plate.

LV PA
Please stay alert during the flight attendant's instructions.

AV
Stay in your seat during takeoff.

AV DO
Ana felt the edge of the platform with her foot.

LV PA
She felt somewhat nervous.

LV PA
She grew less nervous throughout the dance.

AV
Her mother and father looked at her.

LV PA
They looked proud.

LV PN
Ana proved a capable dancer.

AV DO
The mathematician proved her idea.

LV PA
It seemed reasonable.

LV PN
She became a renowned professor.

Exercise 45B: Distinguishing Different Kinds of Nouns

Underline all of the nouns in the following sentences. Identify them as *S* for subject, *OP* for object of a preposition, *IO* for indirect object, *DO* for direct object, or *PN* for predicate nominative.

Clara Lazen [S] discovered a new kind [DO] of molecule [OP].

She was a fifth-grade student [PN].

Her teacher [S] was using ball-and-stick models [DO] for molecules [OP].

She combined oxygen [DO], nitrogen [DO], and carbon [DO] into a new formation [OP].

Was her design [S] a real molecule [PN]?

Her teacher [S] sent a scientist [IO] a picture [DO] of it.

The scientist [S] told her teacher [IO] the good news [DO].

Clara's design [S] became tetranitratoxycarbon [PN].

Scientists [S] have not yet synthesized this new molecule [DO].

Exercise 45C: Diagramming Action Verbs and Linking Verbs

On your own paper, diagram the following sentences.

Pumpkins become ripe.

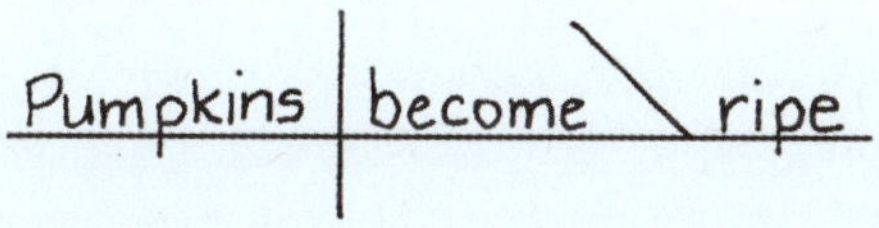

Jackson told me the truth.

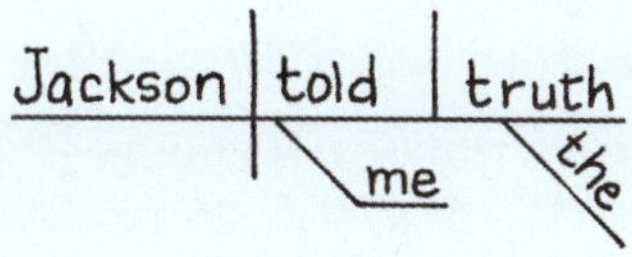

This smells funny.

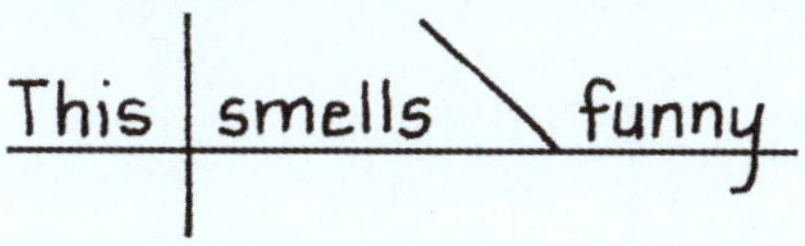

Bobcats are predators.

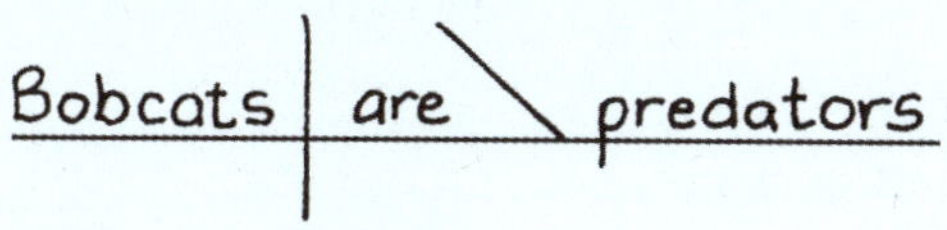

Bobcats hunt rabbits.

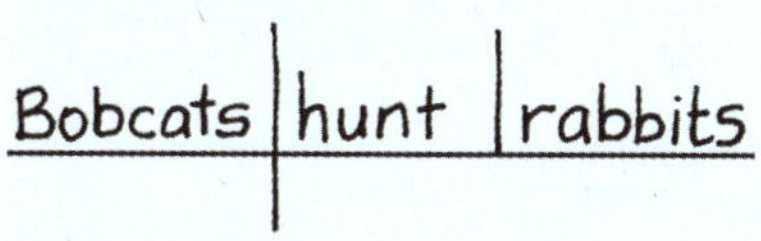

Bobcats are solitary.

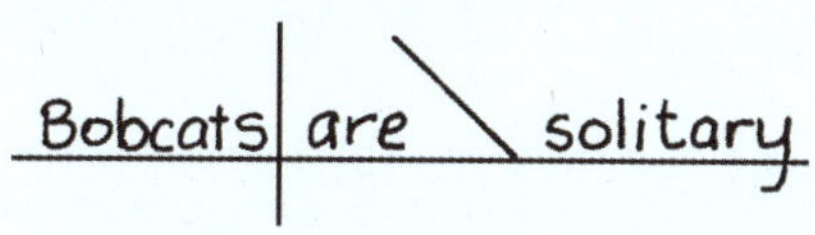

— LESSON 46 —

Conjugations
Irregular Verbs
Principal Parts of Verbs

Exercise 46A: Forming Simple, Perfect, and Progressive Tenses

Fill in the missing blanks in the chart below.

Simple Present

	Singular	Plural
First person	I zoom	We zoom
Second person	You zoom	You zoom
Third person	He, she, it zooms	They zoom

Simple Past

	Singular	Plural
First person	I zoomed	We zoomed
Second person	You zoomed	You zoomed
Third person	He, she, it zoomed	They zoomed

Simple Future

	Singular	Plural
First person	I will zoom	We will zoom
Second person	You will zoom	You will zoom
Third person	He, she, it will zoom	They will zoom

Perfect Present

	Singular	Plural
First person	I have zoomed	We have zoomed
Second person	You have zoomed	You have zoomed
Third person	He, she, it has zoomed	They have zoomed

Perfect Past

	Singular	Plural
First person	I had zoomed	We had zoomed
Second person	You had zoomed	You had zoomed
Third person	He, she, it had zoomed	They had zoomed

Perfect Future

	Singular	Plural
First person	I will have zoomed	We will have zoomed
Second person	You will have zoomed	You will have zoomed
Third person	He, she, it will have zoomed	They will have zoomed

Progressive Present

	Singular	Plural
First person	I am zooming	We are zooming
Second person	You are zooming	You are zooming
Third person	He, she, it is zooming	They are zooming

Progressive Past

	Singular	Plural
First person	I was zooming	We were zooming
Second person	You were zooming	You were zooming
Third person	He, she, it was zooming	They were zooming

Progressive Future

	Singular	Plural
First person	I will be zooming	We will be zooming
Second person	You will be zooming	You will be zooming
Third person	He, she, it will be zooming	They will be zooming

Exercise 46B: French and English Words

Draw lines to match the English word with its French equivalent. Because English and French have similar backgrounds, you should be able to complete this exercise easily, even if you've never learned any French!

Note to Instructor: The student's lines should connect the English words on the left to the French word placed directly across from them below.

English	French
insert	B. insérer
family	D. famille
negotiate	F. négocier
history	H. histoire
stomach	G. estomac
lemon	E. limon
flower	A. fleur
perfume	I. parfum
magnificent	J. magnifique
palace	C. palais

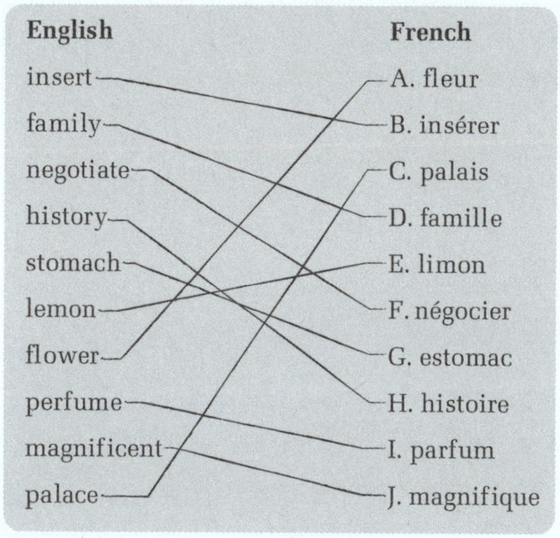

Exercise 46C: Principal Parts of Verbs

Fill in the chart with the missing forms.

	First Principal Part Present	Second Principal Part Past	Third Principal Part Past Participle
I	delay	delayed	delayed
I	embarrass	embarrassed	embarrassed
I	tumble	tumbled	tumbled
I	visit	visited	visited
I	remind	reminded	reminded
I	copy	copied	copied
I	borrow	borrowed	borrowed
I	skip	skipped	skipped
I	whistle	whistled	whistled
I	count	counted	counted

Exercise 46D: Distinguishing between First and Second Principal Parts

Identify each underlined verb as *1* for first principal part or *2* for second principal part.

These sentences are from Carol Berkin's *A Brilliant Solution: Inventing the American Constitution.*

The Virginia resolutions provided [2] a governmental skeleton, a structural blueprint for the new Constitution.

Sensibly, Madison turned [2] his days in Philadelphia to good use.

"I confess [1] there are several parts of this constitution which I do not at present approve."

John Mercer, the young, opinionated delegate from Maryland, arrived [2] in late July.

"I agree [1] to this Constitution with all its faults, if they are such."

— LESSON 47 —

Linking Verbs
Principal Parts
Irregular Verbs

No exercises this lesson.

— LESSON 48 —

Linking Verbs
Principal Parts
Irregular Verbs

Exercise 48A: Principal Parts

Fill in the blanks in the following chart of verbs.

Present	Past	Past Participle
fight	fought	fought
cut	cut	cut
drive	drove	driven
feed	fed	fed
grow	grew	grown
sell	sold	sold
quit	quit	quit
freeze	froze	frozen
teach	taught	taught
tear	tore	torn
pay	paid	paid
bleed	bled	bled
buy	bought	bought
jump	jumped	jumped
burst	burst	burst
bring	brought	brought
fly	flew	flown
draw	drew	drawn
sleep	slept	slept
make	made	made
send	sent	sent
cost	cost	cost
awake	awoke	awoken
stand	stood	stood
break	broke	broken
set	set	set
rise	rose	risen
think	thought	thought
tear	tore	torn
build	built	built
get	got	gotten

Present	Past	Past Participle
hit	hit	hit
hear	heard	heard
sniff	sniffed	sniffed
shake	shook	shaken
bring	brought	brought
say	said	said
find	found	found
shoot	shot	shot
fall	fell	fallen
forget	forgot	forgotten
keep	kept	kept

Exercise 48B: Forming Correct Past Participles

Write the correct third principal part (past participle) in each blank. The first principal part is provided for you in parentheses. The first is done for you.

Kristin had ___set___ (set) her bag near the stairs.

The dog has ___dug___ (dig) a new hole under the fence.

I had long ___sought___ (seek) the ancient treasure, and now I have ___found___ (find) it!

The announcer said Timothy had ___won___ (win) the award.

Timothy will get his award later; he was not feeling well and has already ___left___ (leave) the ceremony.

I have not ___ridden___ (ride) a horse since I was five years old.

Ouch! A mosquito has ___bitten___ (bite) me!

Asa has ___worn___ (wear) his favorite shirt three times this week.

Exercise 48C: Forming Correct Past Tenses

Write the correct second principal part (past) in each blank. The first principal part is provided for you in parentheses. The first is done for you.

Priscilla ___spoke___ (speak) to me about the event.

This shirt is on sale today; yesterday it ___cost___ (cost) thirty dollars!

Last year we ___grew___ (grow) zucchini in our garden.

Marcus ___read___ (read) the book before class.

Unhurriedly, my father ___drove___ (drive) through the mountain village and ___let___ (let) us see the lovely foliage.

On our vacation, I ___caught___ (catch) one fish, but my sister ___threw___ (throw) it back.

The alarm clock ___rang___ (ring) at least five times before I ___awoke___ (awake).

Exercise 48D: Proofreading for Irregular Verb Usage

In the passage below, adapted from Frances Hodgson Burnett's *A Little Princess*, you will find seven errors in irregular verb usage. Cross out the incorrect forms and write the correct ones above them.

He ~~thinked~~ thought that her eyes looked hungry because she had perhaps had nothing to eat for a long time. He did not know that they looked so because she ~~beed~~ was hungry for the warm, merry life his home ~~holded~~ held and his rosy face ~~speaked~~ spoke of, and that she had a hungry wish to snatch him in her arms and kiss him. He only ~~knowed~~ knew that she had big eyes and a thin face and a common basket and poor clothes. So he ~~putted~~ put his hand in his pocket and ~~finded~~ found his sixpence and walked up to her benignly.

Exercise 48E: Diagramming

On your own paper, diagram the following four sentences.

Who painted the sign on the lawn blue?

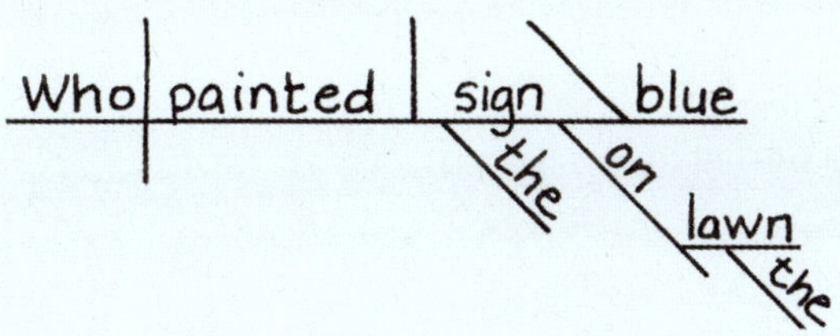

Ron tasted the ice cream and nodded his head approvingly.

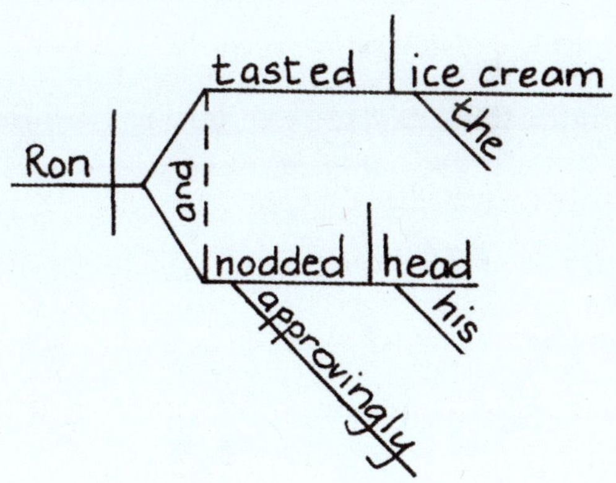

The time for questions is before the exam.

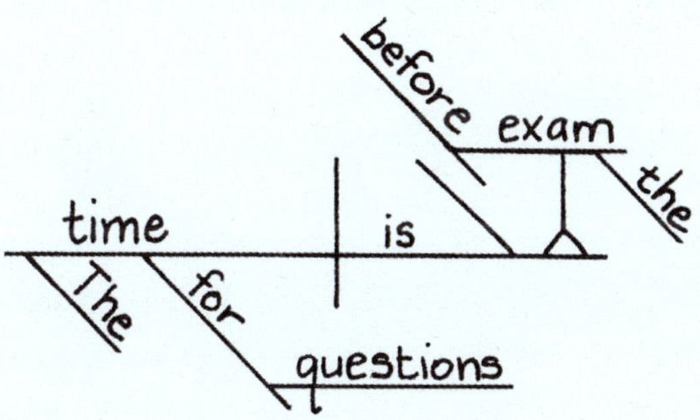

Outside the house, I felt very cold.

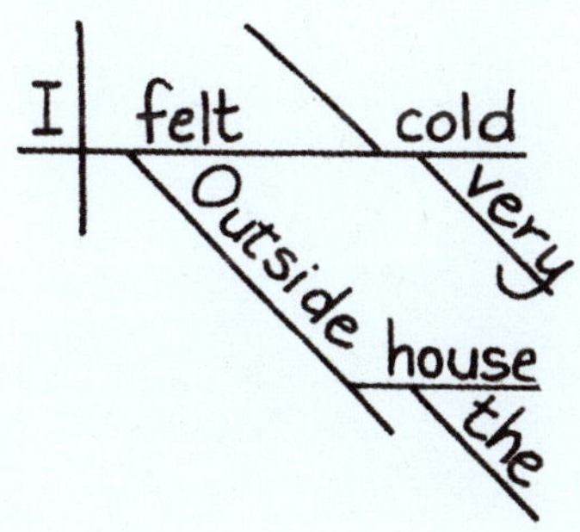

— REVIEW 4 —

Weeks 10-12

Topics:
Direct and Indirect Objects
Linking Verbs
Predicate Adjectives
Predicate Nominatives
Articles
Adjective Phrases
Adverb Phrases
Action vs. Linking Verbs
Irregular Verbs
Principal Parts (Present, Past, Past Participle)

Review 4A: Action vs. Linking Verbs

Identify the underlined verbs as *A* for action or *L* for linking.

Margaret smelled [A] the mystery container from the refrigerator.

The contents smelled [L] suspiciously strange, so Margaret emptied [A] the container into the trash.

Something else would probably taste [L] better.

Sound [A] the alarm! This sale sounds [L] like the biggest sale of the year!

These deals seem [L] fabulous.

With our new products, you look [L] great and feel [L] wonderful!

Come [A] to our store today and try [A] these amazing products for yourself!

You'll become [L] the envy of all your friends!

Review 4B: Predicate Adjectives and Predicate Nominatives

Underline the linking verb in each of the following sentences. If the sentence concludes with a predicate nominative or predicate adjective, circle each and write *PA* for predicate adjective or *PN* for predicate nominative above it.

The geese in the sky were ridiculously **loud** [PA].

Your cousin is a famous **actress** [PN] in our city.

Latin class seemed extremely **long** [PA] today.

The rabbits under the deck look **skittish** [PA].

The fresh bread at the bakery smelled delectable. (PA)

Jacques, Ricky, and Razak became a team. (PN)

For several hours, the human statue remained motionless. (PA)

Stephanie's locket was a keepsake from her grandmother. (PN)

Review 4C: Adjective and Adverb Phrases

In the following excerpt from Andrew Peterson's *North! Or Be Eaten*, identify each underlined prepositional phrase as *ADJ* for adjective phrase or *ADV* for adverb phrase.

Podo thought it would be funny to strike the tent with Oskar still sleeping in it (ADV), so after a quick breakfast (ADV) of dried fruit (ADJ), Janner and Tink helped Podo pull the stakes and lift the center stick that held the canvas aloft. They laughed and whispered to one another (ADV) as they raised it like a giant umbrella (ADV) and exposed Oskar to the sunlight (ADV), and still he snored. When the tent was rolled and lashed to Podo's pack (ADV), there was nothing left to do but rouse Mister Reteep. Leeli nudged his shoulder, and his only response was a slight shift in the tone (ADJ) of his snore (ADJ). Nia joined Leeli and prodded Oskar on the other side (ADV). Soon they were rocking him back and forth so hard that Podo, Tink, and Janner doubled over with laughter (ADV). Oskar snored and scratched at his belly (ADV).

Review 4D: Forming Principal Parts

Complete the following excerpt (from J. R. R. Tolkien's *The Two Towers*) by writing the correct principal part of the verb in parentheses (*1stPP*, *2ndPP*, or *3rdPP*).

> **Note to Instructor:** *Stride* is an irregular verb that was not included on the list in Lesson 47. Its principal parts are *stride, strode, stridden*. If the student answers "strided," explain that "stride" follows the same pattern in its principal parts as "ride."

"Good! Good!" said (*say*, 2nd PP) Treebeard. "But I spoke (*speak*, 2nd PP) hastily. We must not be (*be*, 1st PP) hasty. I have become (*become*, 3rd PP) too hot. I must cool (*cool*, 1st PP) myself and think (*think*, 1st PP); for it is easier to shout *stop!* than to do it."

He strode (*stride*, 2nd PP) to the archway and stood (*stand*, 2nd PP) for some time under the falling rain of the spring. Then he laughed (*laugh*, 2nd PP) and shook (*shake*, 2nd PP) himself, and wherever the drops of water fell (*fall*, 2nd PP) glittering from him to the ground they glinted (*glint*, 2nd PP) like red and green sparks. He came (*come*, 2nd PP) back and laid (*lay*, 2nd PP) himself on the bed again and was silent.

Review 4E: Irregular Verbs

Find and correct the FIVE errors in irregular verb usage in the following excerpt from *The Wonderful Wizard of Oz*, by L. Frank Baum. Cross out each incorrect form and write the correct form above it.

There ~~beed~~ were few birds in this part of the forest, for birds love the open country where there is plenty of sunshine; but now and then there ~~comed~~ came a deep growl from some wild animal hidden among the trees. These sounds ~~maked~~ made the little girl's heart beat fast, for she did not know what ~~maked~~ made them; but Toto ~~knowed~~ knew, and he walked close to Dorothy's side, and did not even bark in return.

Review 4F: Misplaced Modifiers

Circle the misplaced adjective and adverb phrases in the following sentences. Draw an arrow to the place where each phrase should be.

Our trip was a comedy of errors (to California).

(In the soda), Grandpa told me that there were 140 calories.

People are learning to swim (across the country).

The lady cuts my hair (with seven dogs).

The owner (in his pocket) of the restaurant has twenty dollars.

The quilt keeps the sick child (with green and purple squares) warm.

(In the trash can), the worried woman searched frantically for her wallet.

The monster frightened the boy (with two heads).

Review 4G: Diagramming

On your own paper, diagram the following sentences.

The moon appears largest near the horizon.

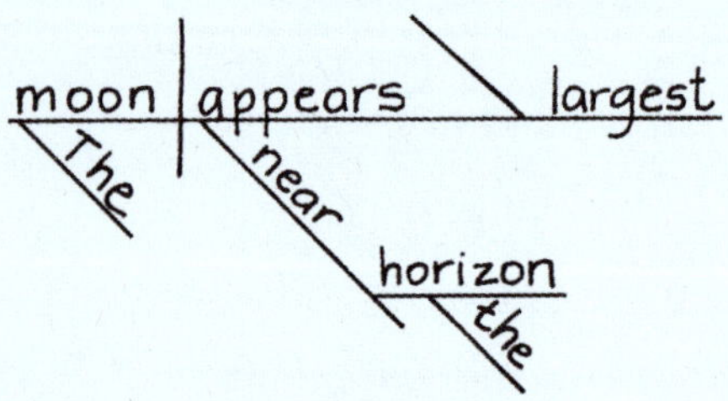

At that point, the moon's image is actually farther away.

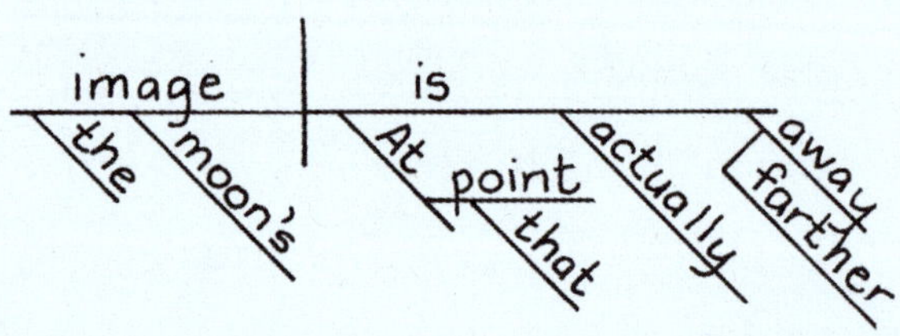

This optical illusion has given observers a puzzle for many centuries.

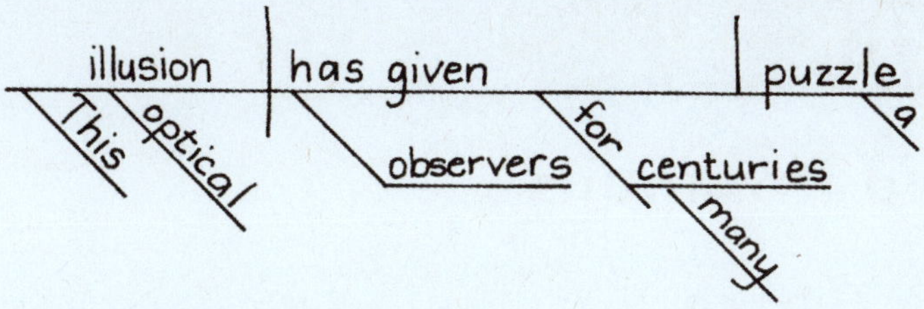

Aristotle and others declared the atmosphere responsible for the illusion.

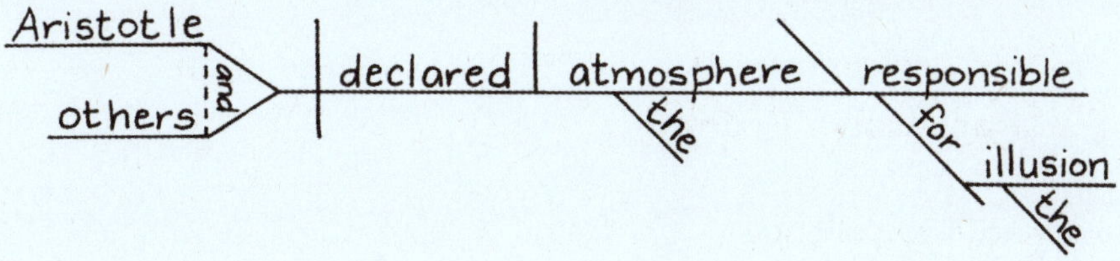

The atmosphere only changes our perception of the moon's colors.

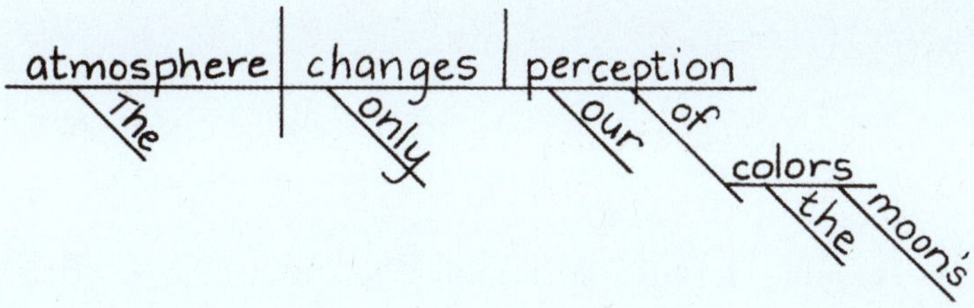

Smaller objects near the horizon might influence our ideas about the size of the moon.

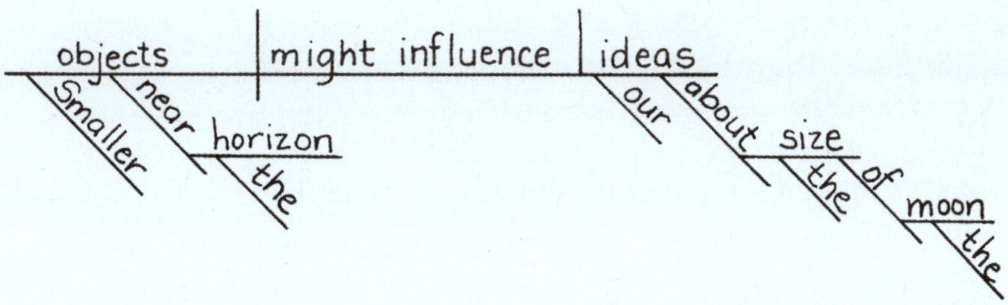

Have you looked at the moon lately?

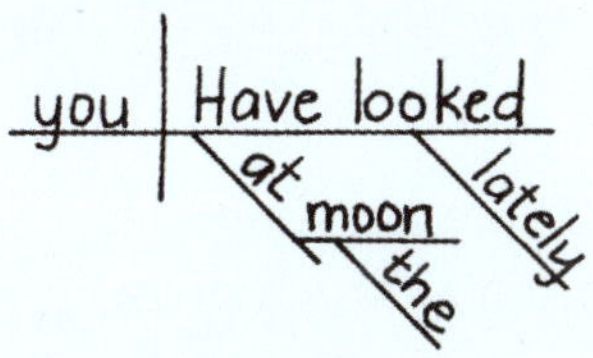

It may look different at different times of night!

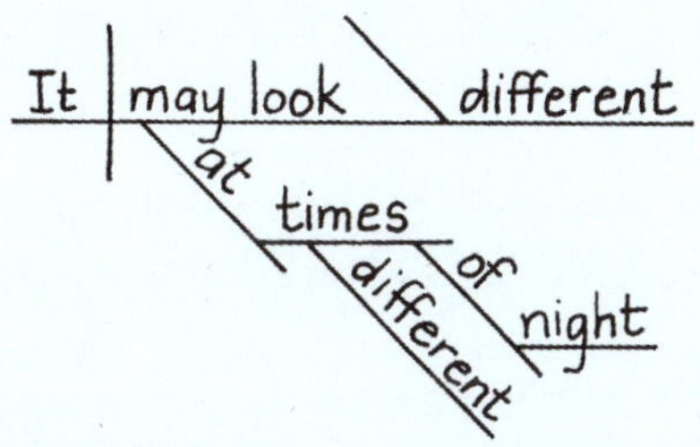

WEEK 13

Advanced Pronouns

— LESSON 49 —

Personal Pronouns
Antecedents
Possessive Pronouns

Exercise 49A: Personal Pronouns and Antecedents

Circle the personal pronouns in the following sentences, adapted from Margery Sharp's *The Rescuers*. Draw an arrow from each pronoun to the antecedent. In the margin, write the gender (*F*, *M*, or *N*) and number (*S* or *PL*) of each pronoun.

Miss Bianca recognized the model speedboat at once. It was the Boy's, a gift from the American Naval Attaché. N,S

Albert was Miss Bianca's favorite. He had a very noble, serene expression. Miss Bianca was convinced, she told Bernard, that Albert hadn't exactly come down in the world, but had renounced the world.) M,S F,S

Miss Bianca threw Bernard a grateful look. But she was very anxious there should be no bickering. F,S

For a moment Miss Bianca, Bernard, and Nils all thought about The Barrens. Then they all thought about the prisoner, and courage was renewed. N,PL

Exercise 49B: Identifying Possessive Pronouns

Underline the possessive pronouns in the following sentences from Thomas Streissguth's *The Transcontinental Railroad*. Each possessive pronoun is acting as an adjective. Draw an arrow from the pronoun to the noun it modifies. There may be other pronouns in these sentences as well; ONLY underline the possessive ones!

To cross California, however, his line would have to rise from Sacramento, at 50 feet above sea level, and cross the steep Sierra Nevada, where the lowest passes lay more than a mile higher.

The scheme gave the company a much-needed boost in its bank accounts in very lean times.

I remember very well, Mr. Lincoln looked at the map and said, "I have got a quarter-section of land right across there, and if I fix it there, they will say that I have done it to benefit my land."

The directors of the Union Pacific had to build their road as quickly as possible.

Exercise 49C: Using Possessive Pronouns

Write the correct possessive pronoun above the underlined word(s).

The little wren perched on the bird feeder and shook the wren's [its] tail.

Stacy and Nila worked diligently on Stacy's and Nila's [their] project.

I met Oscar because we had identical luggage; I had picked up Oscar's [his] suitcase, and he had grabbed my suitcase [mine].

Krista called out to Aziz, "Hey! You forgot Aziz's [your] jacket!"

On Luisa's [her] birthday, Luisa finally got the thing she'd been wanting for months.

Janet said, "My sister and I like to imagine what my sister's and my [our] future jobs will be."

Becoming an ornithologist is Janet's [my] plan; becoming a translator is my sister's [hers].

Saul's phone battery was drained of all the battery's [its] power.

Nate's father shook Nate's father's [his] head. "No," he answered, "we cannot add five puppies to Nate's and Nate's father's [our] household, no matter how cute they are."

Exercise 49D: Diagramming Pronouns

On your own paper, diagram every word in the following sentences. These sentences are adapted from Thomas Streissguth's *The Transcontinental Railroad*.

In 1865, twelve-year-old Robert Gifford walked the four miles from his home in Dutch Flat to Gold Run.

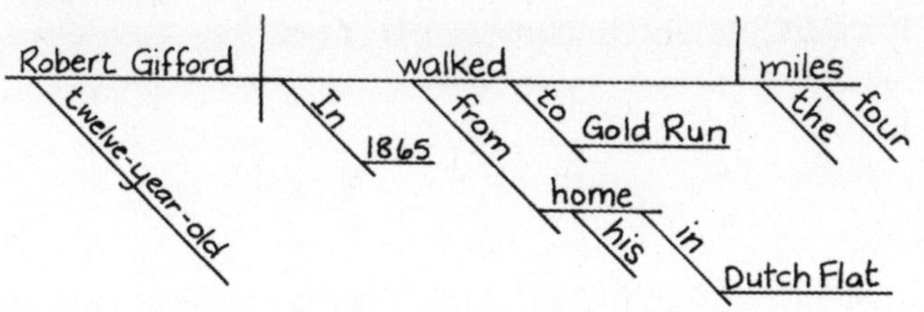

Theodore Judah had several bitter confrontations with his directors.

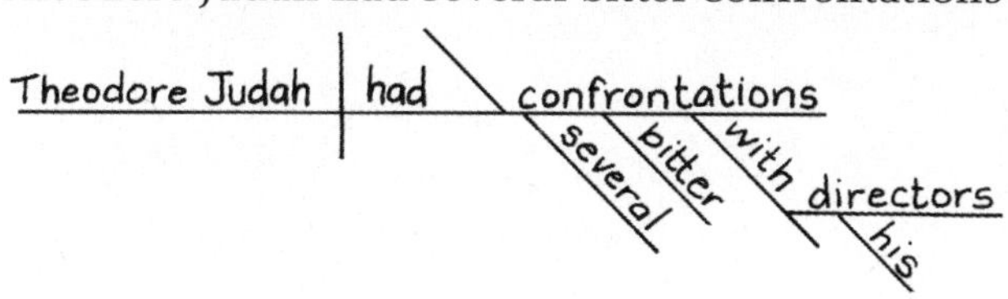

The workers of the Central Pacific were now compensating for their years of slow, heavy labor in the mountains.

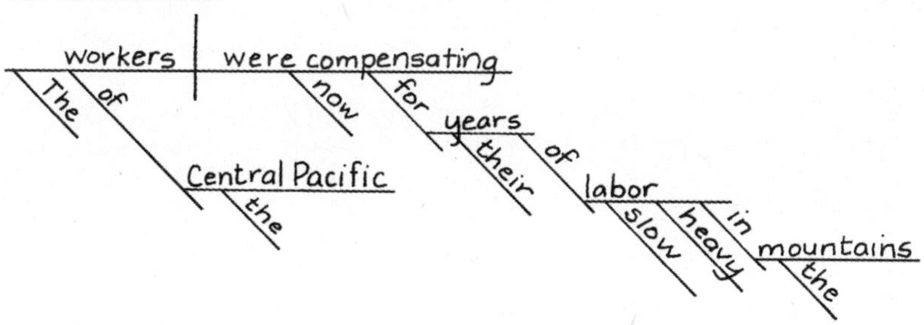

— LESSON 50 —

Pronoun Case

Exercise 50A: Subject and Object Pronouns

Underline all the personal pronouns in the following selections from *The Great Revolt of 1381*, by Charles Oman. Identify each personal pronoun as *S* for subject, *O* for object, or *P* for possessive.

Wraw's gang pillaged his[P] manor, and not finding his[P] plate and other precious goods in the house, went to seek them[O] in the church. They[S] broke open its[P] doors and distributed the silver, but did no further damage to the sacred edifice.

Then they[S] (the rebels) asked them[O] if they[S] had any traitors among them[O], and the townsfolk said that there were three, and named their[P] names. These three the commons dragged out of their[P] houses and cut off their[P] heads.

It[S] would have puzzled a much more capable set of men than those who now served as the ministers and councillors of his[P] grandson to draw England out of the slough into which she[S] had sunk. Her[P] present misfortunes were due to her[P] own fault.

When the king heard of their[P] doings he[S] sent his[P] messengers to them[O], on Tuesday after Trinity Sunday, asking why they[S] were behaving in this fashion, and for what cause they[S] were making insurrection in his[P] land. And they[S] sent back by his[P] messengers the answer that they[S] had risen to deliver him[O], and to destroy traitors to him[O] and his[P] kingdom.

Exercise 50B: Using Personal Pronouns Correctly

Choose the correct word(s) in parentheses and cross out the incorrect word. Be sure to select the grammatically correct choice for writing, which may not necessarily be the one that sounds best to your ear.

The person you are looking for is (I/~~me~~).

For Pearl and (~~I~~/me), the choice was clear.

Do you think Mr. Evans will help (~~we~~/us) with the painting?

Near the lake at the edge of the property, (we/~~us~~) found a large group of turtles.

Early this morning (he/~~him~~) went for a run.

We thought we saw (~~he~~/him), but the runner we saw was not (he/~~him~~).

(Martin and she/~~Martin and her~~) measured the room carefully.

Exercise 50C: Diagramming Personal Pronouns

On your own paper, diagram the following sentences. Personal pronouns are diagrammed exactly like the nouns or adjectives they replace.

The mayor is she.

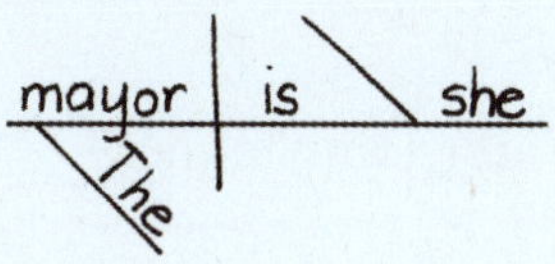

They read it.

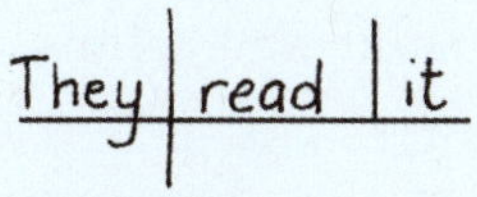

It was brief.

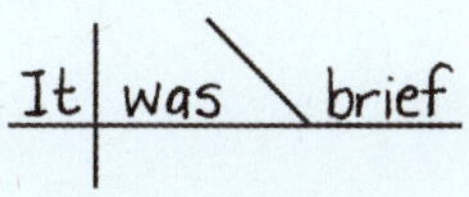

She understands us.

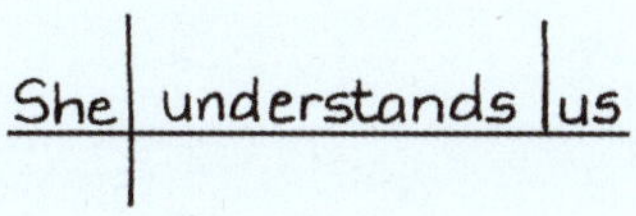

We sent her a letter.

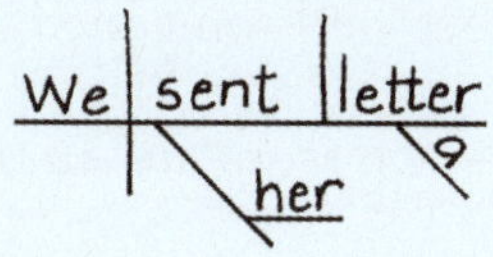

He wrote us a response.

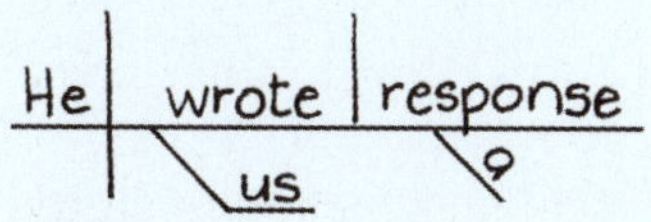

We appreciated it.

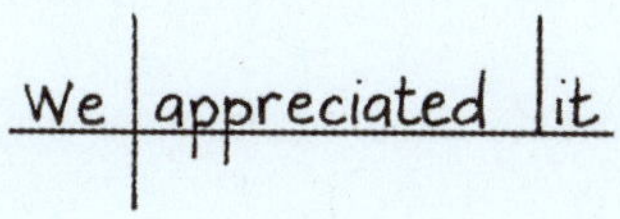

— LESSON 51 —

Indefinite Pronouns

Exercise 51A: Identifying Indefinite Pronouns

Underline all the indefinite pronouns in the following sentences. Each sentence may contain more than one pronoun. The sentences are adapted from Richard Peck's *The Ghost Belonged to Me.*

Inside, everything looked regular, and I was thinking seriously about checking around upstairs, though I could see from the cobwebs that nobody had been up there in quite some time.

I was not sure I followed Lucille's reasoning, since people have been known to attend a party out of nothing but curiosity. But I supposed she had all of it worked out in her own mind.

But if somebody will just tell me what all of the fuss is about, I'll be gone. You know I never rest till I know everything.

We neither of us had come all this way to be led around like children.

She'd have been a lot more pleased with the both of us if she could have gotten me to knuckle down and apply myself to scholarship.

Exercise 51B: Subject-Verb Agreement: Indefinite Pronouns

Choose the correct verb in parentheses. Cross out the incorrect verb.

Some of the choir members (~~is~~/are) preparing a surprise for the director.

Everyone (loves/~~love~~) her, and someone (has/~~have~~) learned that her birthday is today.

Both of the assistant directors (~~is~~/are) in on the surprise, and one of them (is/~~are~~) going to pick up the flowers.

Nobody (knows/~~know~~) the director's favorite kind of flower, but a few of us (~~remembers~~/remember) her saying white and yellow are her favorite colors, so all of the flowers (~~is~~/are) white and yellow.

Each of us (has/~~have~~) been asked to sign a birthday card for her.

Some of the rehearsal time (is/~~are~~) wasted because everyone (is/~~are~~) excited about the surprise.

One of the assistant directors (appears/~~appear~~) with the card and flowers, and all of us (~~shouts~~/shout), "Happy birthday!"

Exercise 51C: Diagramming Indefinite Pronouns

On your own paper, diagram the following sentences, adapted from Mary Norton's *The Borrowers*.

All of its feathers fell off.

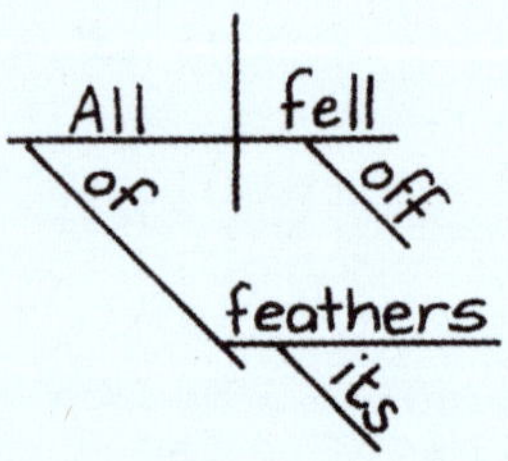

No one will ever believe me.

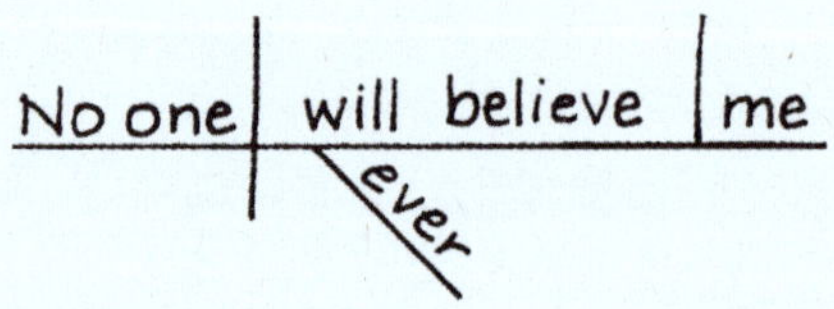

Something did happen.

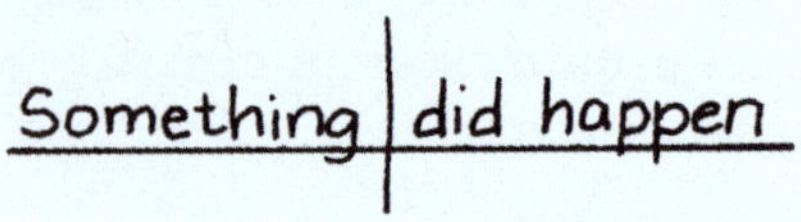

Someone saw one of them.

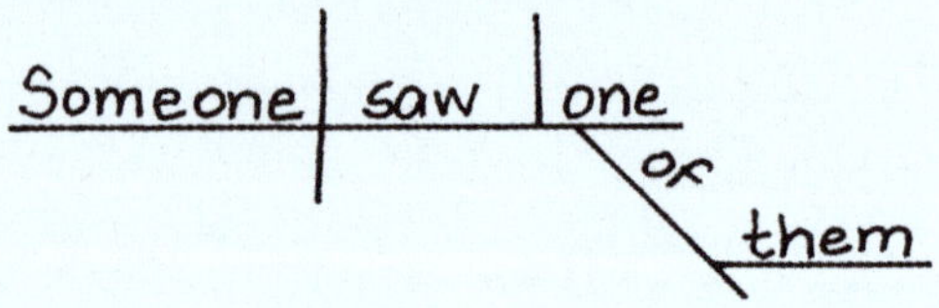

Your father's got nothing now.

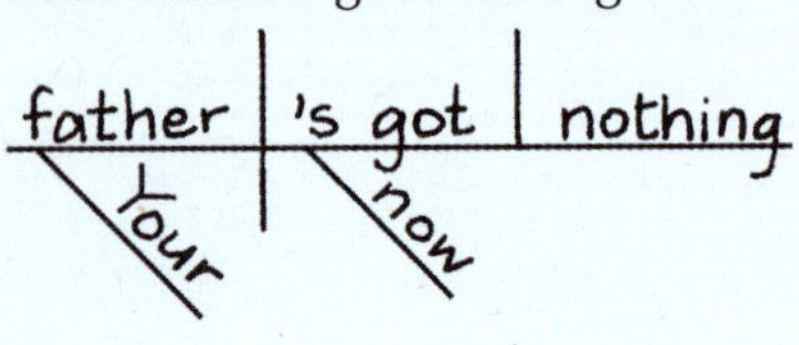

— LESSON 52 —

Personal Pronouns
Indefinite Pronouns

Exercise 52A: Subject and Object Pronouns

In the following sentences from Mary Norton's *The Borrowers*, cross out the incorrect pronouns.

(She/~~Her~~) had been lying under her knitted coverlet staring up at the ceiling.

"Oh," (he/~~him~~) said again and picked up two petals of cherry blossom which (he/~~him~~) folded together like a sandwich and ate slowly.

"(He/~~Him~~) means," said Pod, "that Lupy must have set off to come here and that (she/~~her~~) never arrived."

Pod held (~~she~~/her) tightly by the ankle. It was not easy to control (~~she~~/her) as (he/~~him~~) was lying on his back.

(She/~~Her~~) dragged (~~he~~/him) roughly across the hall.

(I/~~Me~~) showed (~~he~~/him) where it was.

(She/~~Her~~) lay back among the stalks of the primroses and (they/~~them~~) made a coolness between (~~she~~/her) and the sun.

(I/~~Me~~) led (~~he~~/him) into that one too!

(I/~~Me~~) will bring you some supper.

(They/~~Them~~) were making a bed-quilt.

It was Mrs. May who first told (~~I~~/me) about (~~they~~/them).

(They/~~Them~~) never asked anyone up there and (I/~~me~~), for one, never wanted to go.

Oh, (we/~~us~~) did have some lovely things!

(She/~~Her~~) shrieked and felt behind (~~she~~/her) for a chair. (She/~~Her~~) clambered on to it and it wobbled beneath (~~she~~/her) and (she/~~her~~) climbed, still shrieking, from the chair to the table.

(She/~~Her~~) brushed past (~~he~~/him).

Didn't (he/~~him~~) see (~~they~~/them) come out?

Exercise 52B: Possessive and Indefinite Pronouns

In these sentences adapted from Anna Sewell's *Black Beauty*, cross out the incorrect word in each set of parentheses.

It was all quite still except the clatter of my feet on the stones; everybody (was/~~were~~) asleep.

"We'll just go home by Farmer Bushby's, Beauty; and then if anybody (wants/~~want~~) to know, you and I can tell (him/~~them~~)."

Nobody (likes/~~like~~) to come too near his fist.

"O Harry! there never (was/~~were~~) anything so beautiful; Mrs. Fowler says we are all to go and live near her."

No one (was/~~were~~) ever kind to her, and why should she not bite?

Some of the sights (~~makes~~/make) me sad even now to think of.

Everybody (was/~~were~~) sorry; but the master began directly to make arrangements for breaking up his establishment and leaving England. We used to hear it talked about in our stable; indeed, nothing else (was/~~were~~) talked about.

Some of the men (~~was~~/were) standing together talking; some (~~was~~/were) sitting on their boxes reading the newspaper; and one (was/were) feeding (his/~~their~~) horse with bits of hay and a drink of water.

None of the other young colts (~~cares~~/care) for me, and I care for none of them.

Flies tease her more; anything wrong in the harness (frets/~~fret~~) her more.

"Of course I could not be warranted free from vice, so nothing (was/~~were~~) said about that."

"If anybody (has/~~have~~) been saying that about James, I don't believe it."

Several of the men (~~was~~/were) applauding this, till Jerry said, "That may sound well enough, but it won't do; everyone must look after (his/~~their~~) own soul."

As Smith's death had been so sudden, and no one (was/~~were~~) there to see it, there was an inquest held.

Exercise 52C: Writing Sentences from Diagrams

Use the diagrams below to reconstruct these sentences. Write the sentence on the blanks below each diagram. Pay careful attention to each part of speech! Punctuate each sentence properly.

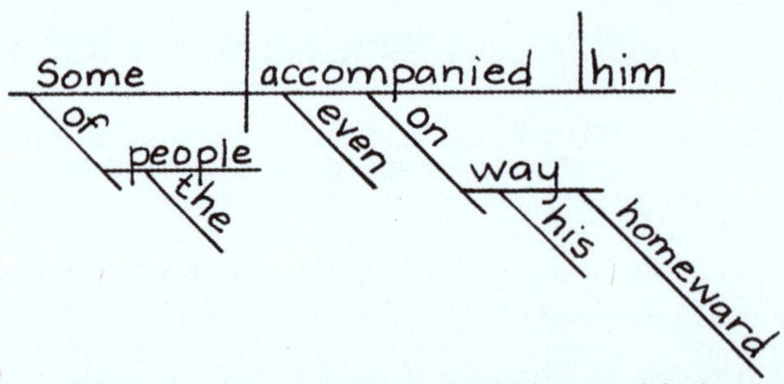

Some of the people even accompanied him on his homeward way.

OR Some of the people even accompanied him on his way homeward.

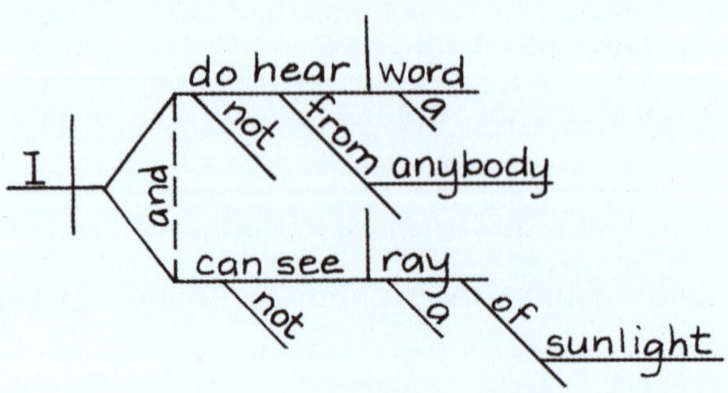

I do not hear a word from anybody and cannot see a ray of sunlight.

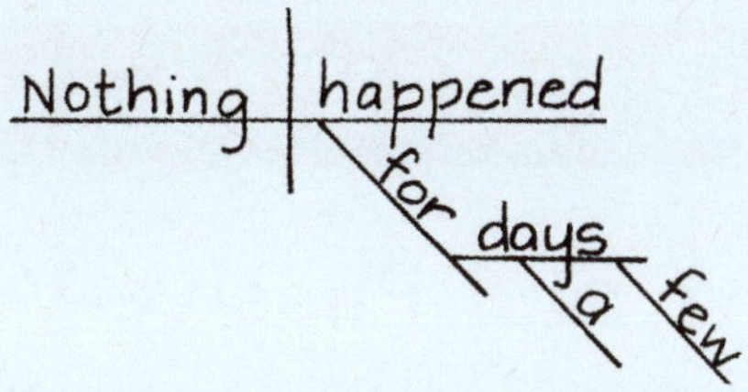

Nothing happened for a few days.

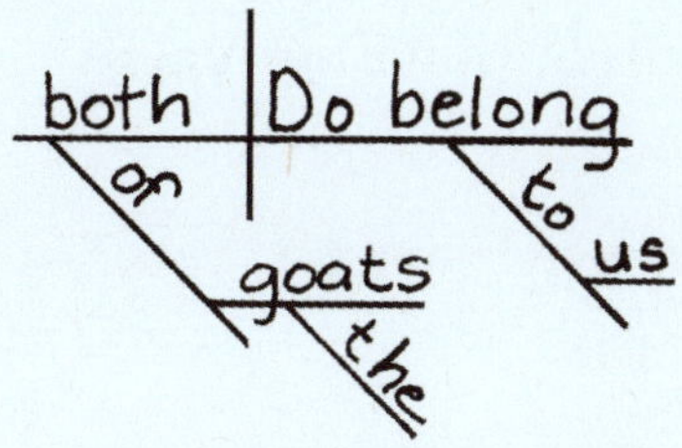

Do both of the goats belong to us?

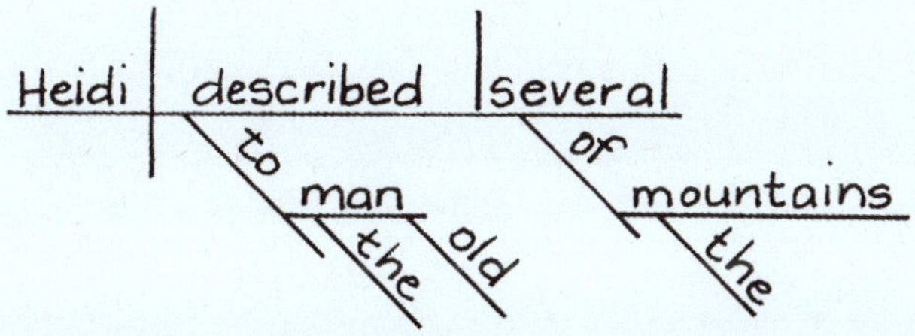

Heidi described several of the mountains to the old man.

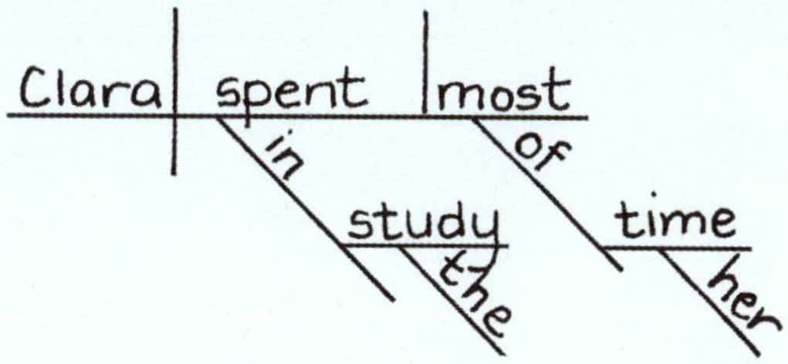

Clara spent most of her time in the study.

WEEK 14

Active and Passive Voice

— LESSON 53 —

Principal Parts
Troublesome Verbs

Exercise 53A: Principal Parts of Verbs

Fill in the chart with the missing forms.

	First Principal Part Present	Second Principal Part Past	Third Principal Part Past Participle
I	perform	performed	performed
I	eat	ate	eaten
I	win	won	won
I	cost	cost	cost
I	snore	snored	snored
I	bear	bore	born
I	bite	bit	bitten
I	feel	felt	felt

Exercise 53B: Using Correct Verbs

Choose the correct verb in parentheses. Cross out the incorrect verb.

The dancer (~~rose~~/raised) her arms gracefully above her head.

Don't (sit/~~set~~) down yet! I need you to (~~sit~~/set) these flowers on the table.

Before we (~~let~~/left) the stadium, the team members (let/~~left~~) us pose for pictures with them.

When Gabriella arrived home, she (~~lay~~/laid) her purse on the table and immediately fell asleep on the couch.

She has (~~laid~~/lain) there all afternoon.

I want to (~~rise~~/raise) money for my favorite charity. Will you (let/~~leave~~) me wash your car to earn some money?

Yesterday, Jasper (sat/~~set~~) near the back of the room, but today he has (~~sat~~/set) his things on a desk near the front.

Exercise 53C: Correct Forms of Troublesome Verbs

Fill in the blanks with the correct form of the indicated verb. The sentences below are from *The Wonderful Wizard of Oz*, by L. Frank Baum.

The house whirled around two or three times and ___ rose ___ slowly through the air. (rise)

They had taken the sparkle from her eyes and ___ left ___ them a sober gray. (leave)

Indeed, the old Witch never touched water, nor ever ___ let ___ water touch her in any way. (let)

The cyclone had ___ set ___ the house down, very gently—for a cyclone—in the midst of a country of marvelous beauty. (set)

The Scarecrow ___ sat ___ in the big throne and the others stood respectfully before him. (sit)

At last she crawled over the swaying floor to her bed, and ___ lay ___ down upon it; and Toto followed and ___ lay ___ down beside her. (lie)

It was some time before the Cowardly Lion awakened, for he had ___ lain ___ among the poppies a long while, breathing in their deadly fragrance; but when he did open his eyes and roll off the truck he was very glad to find himself still alive. (lie)

They carried the sleeping girl to a pretty spot beside the river, far enough from the poppy field to prevent her breathing any more of the poison of the flowers, and here they ___ laid ___ her gently on the soft grass and waited for the fresh breeze to waken her. (lay)

On the feet were some old boots with blue tops, such as every man wore in this country, and the figure was ___ raised ___ above the stalks of corn by means of the pole stuck up its back. (raise)

Exercise 53D: Proofreading for Correct Verb Usage

Find and correct SEVEN errors in verb usage by crossing out the incorrect verbs and writing the correct ones above them.

As the sun ~~raised~~ rose in the eastern sky, I ~~laid~~ lay in my bed and thought about my day. I knew it would be very busy. My father had ~~let~~ left me in charge of the family store while he went to a conference. I had done all the jobs before, but today I would be ~~raising~~ rising to a new level of responsibility, because my father would not be right there with me. I got dressed—I had ~~lain~~ laid out my clothes the night before—and had some breakfast, then walked over to the store. As soon as I ~~sat~~ set out the "OPEN" sign, one of our regular customers came in. "~~Leave~~ Let me help you with that," I said with confidence. I knew my father would be proud of me upon his return.

— LESSON 54 —

Verb Tense

Active and Passive Voice

Exercise 54A: Reviewing Tenses

Write the tense of each underlined verb above it. These sentences are from *The Lost World*, by Arthur Conan Doyle. The first is done for you.

If it will support [simple future] the weight of one and let him gently down, it will have done [perfect future] all that is required of it.

Oh, it was [simple past] rank nonsense about some queer animals he had discovered [perfect past]. I believe [simple present] he has retracted [perfect present] since.

I had been [perfect past] hopelessly in the wrong before, but this man's menaces were putting [progressive past] me in the right.

It was [simple past] a fearsome walk, and one which will be [simple future] with me so long as memory holds [simple present].

Flinging away my useless gun, I set [simple past] myself to do such a half-mile as I have never done [perfect present] before or since.

Exercise 54B: Distinguishing between the Active and Passive Voice

Identify the following sentences from William Makepeace Thackeray's *The Rose and the Ring* as *A* for active or *P* for passive. If you're not sure, ask yourself: Is the subject *doing* the verb, or is the verb *happening to* the subject?

She toddled down the great staircase into the hall.	A
He was pinned to the door.	P
He was turned into metal!	P
The painters dabbed him over the mouth and eyes.	A
She capered away on her one shoe.	A
Betsinda was not puffed up by these praises.	P
She thought her cousin very handsome, brave, and good-natured.	A
She was walking through the court of the Palace on her way to their Majesties.	A
Here a very pretty game may be played by all the children.	P
He was making fun of Prince Bulbo.	A
He made himself very comfortable in the straw.	A
The market-place was filled with soldiers.	P
She declined his invitation in her usual polite gentle manner.	A
His Majesty's agitation was not appeased by the news.	P
He sat down and began writing an adieu to Angelica.	A
He was treated with the greatest distinction by everybody.	P

Exercise 54C: Forming the Active and Passive Voice

Fill in the chart below, rewriting each sentence so that it appears in both the active and the passive voice. Be sure to keep the tense the same.

These sentences are adapted from Walter Farley's *The Black Stallion*. The first one is done for you.

ACTIVE	PASSIVE
Alec picked up the pail and cloths.	The pail and cloths were picked up by Alec.
They watched the falling snow.	The falling snow was watched by them.
His articles on the mystery horse aroused the people's curiosity.	The people's curiosity was aroused by his articles on the mystery horse.
This horse attacked me!	I was attacked by this horse!
Alec cut a long, slender staff from a tree.	A long, slender staff was cut from a tree by Alec.
A line of policemen kept the eager spectators away.	The eager spectators were kept away by a line of policemen.

— LESSON 55 —

Parts of the Sentence
Active and Passive Voice

Note to Instructor: You should adapt the following review to the student's level of knowledge. If the student is clear on the concepts learned so far and is able to diagram the sentences correctly, you do not need to follow every line of dialogue for every sentence. However, the student should be able not only to diagram the sentences, but to name the parts of the sentence and explain their use (for example, in the first sentence, if you ask the student, "What kind of phrase is *from his feet* and what does it do?" the student should be able to answer, "A prepositional phrase acting as an adverb).

(These sentences are adapted from Walter Farley's *The Black Stallion*.)

Sentence #1

Instructor: Read me the first sentence on your worksheet.

Student: Alec was lifted from his feet.

Instructor: What is the simple predicate?

Note to Instructor: In the dialogues that follow, prompt the student whenever necessary.

Student: Was lifted.

Instructor: Who or what was lifted?

Student: Alec.

Instructor: *Alec* is the subject. Diagram the subject and the simple predicate. Does the subject perform the action? Is Alec lifting something?

Student: No.

Instructor: *Alec* receives the action of the verb. Is *was lifted* an active or passive verb?

Student: Passive.

Instructor: Repeat after me: In a sentence with a passive verb, the subject receives the action.

Student: In a sentence with a passive verb, the subject receives the action.

Instructor: What part of speech is *from*?

Student: A preposition.

Instructor: What does a preposition do?

Student: A preposition shows the relationship of a noun or pronoun to another word in the sentence.

Instructor: This preposition shows the relationship between Alec and what?

Student: Feet.

Instructor: *Feet* is the object of the preposition *from*. What kind of pronoun is *his*?

Student: Possessive pronoun.

Instructor: What are possessive pronouns also known as?

Student: Possessive adjectives.

Instructor: *His* modifies *feet* in the prepositional phrase *from his feet*. This prepositional phrase answers the question *where*. What part of speech answers the questions *how, when,* ***where****, how often, to what extent?*

Student: An adverb.

Instructor: *From his feet* is a prepositional phrase acting as an adverb. Diagram it beneath the verb.

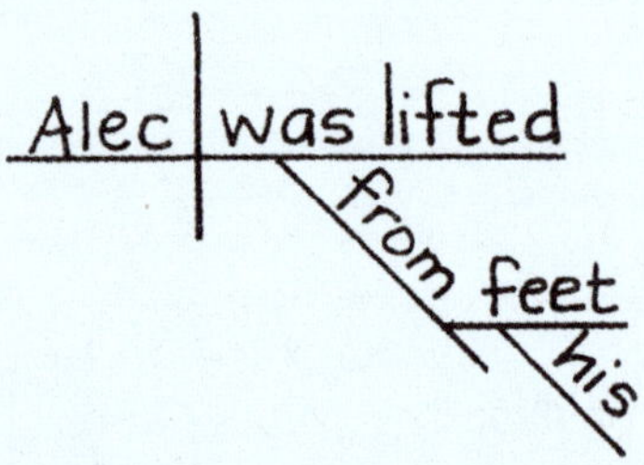

Sentence #2

Instructor: Read the second sentence out loud.

Student: Then the sound of a police siren reached Alec's ears.

Instructor: What is the simple predicate of the sentence?

Student: Reached.

Instructor: Who or what reached?

Student: Sound.

Instructor: *Sound* is the subject. Sound *reached what*?

Student: Ears.

Instructor: *Ears* receives the action of the verb *reached*. What part of the sentence is *ears*?

Student: Direct object.

Instructor: When a sentence has a direct object, you can be sure that the subject is performing the action! Repeat after me: In a sentence with an active verb, the subject performs the action.

Student: In a sentence with an active verb, the subject performs the action.

Instructor: Diagram the subject, predicate, and direct object on your paper. What article precedes *sound*?

Student: The.

Instructor: Articles are particular kinds of adjectives. What are the other two articles?

Student: A, an.

Instructor: Diagram *the* beneath the subject. What is the prepositional phrase in this sentence?

Student: Of a police siren.

Instructor: What is the object of the preposition *of*?

Student: Siren.

Instructor: It isn't always easy to know what word a prepositional phrase modifies. Ask yourself: Does this phrase answer one of the *adverb* questions (how, when, where, how often, to what extent)? Or does it answer one of the a*djective* questions? Repeat those after me: what kind, which one, how many, whose.

Student: What kind, which one, how many, whose.

Instructor: Which sound reached Alec's ears?

Student: The sound of a police siren.

Instructor: *Of a police siren* is a prepositional phrase acting as an adjective, because it answers the question *which one*. What part of speech do adjectives modify?

Student: Nouns.

Instructor: Diagram o*f a police siren* beneath the subject. Going back to the direct object, what word tells whose ears?

Student: Alec's.

Instructor: *Alec's* is an adjective modifying *ears*. Add it to your diagram. What is the one remaining word in this sentence that has not been placed on your diagram?

Student: Then.

Instructor: When did the sound reach Alec's ears?

Student: Then.

Instructor: What part of speech answers the question *when*?

Student: Adverbs.

Instructor: *Then* is an adverb that tells when. Diagram it beneath the verb.

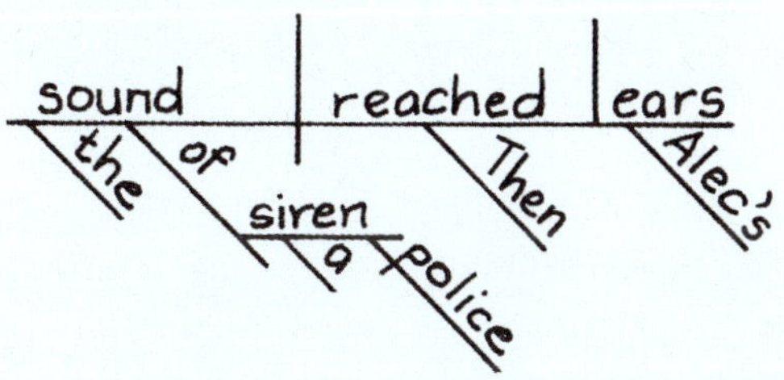

Sentence #3

Instructor: Read me the third sentence.

Student: Alec and Henry climbed into the front seat.

Instructor: What is the simple predicate in this sentence?

Student: Climbed.

Instructor: Who or what climbed?

Student: Alec and Henry.

Instructor: *Alec and Henry* is the compound subject. Diagram the compound subject and the predicate. Is *climbed* an active or passive verb?

Student: Active.

Instructor: The subjects *Alec and Henry* are *doing* the climbing, so the verb is active. What is the prepositional phrase in this sentence?

Student: Into the front seat.

Instructor: What question does that prepositional phrase answer?

Student: [Climbed] where?

Instructor: When a prepositional phrase answers *where*, what kind of prepositional phrase is it?

Student: Adverb phrase.

Instructor: Diagram *into the front seat* beneath the verb.

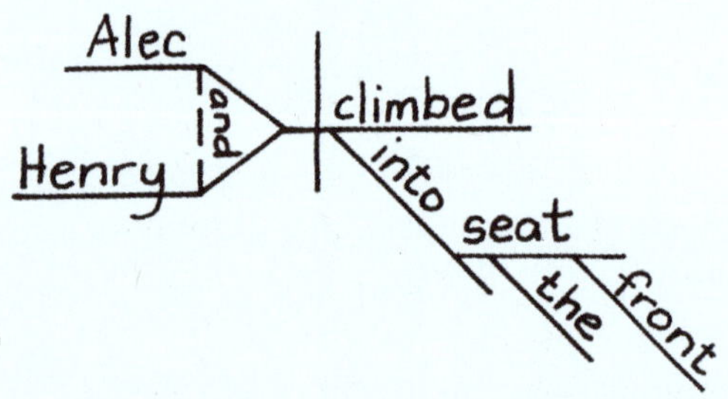

Sentence #4

Instructor: Read me the fourth sentence.

Student: Both of them were going to Chicago.

Instructor: What are the simple subject and predicate? Remember not to include any prepositional phrases when you answer.

Student: Both were going.

Instructor: Diagram those words on your paper. *Both* is the subject. What part of speech is *both*? What kind of word is it? (Hint: You learned about this word in Lesson 51.)

Student: Indefinite pronoun.

Instructor: What are indefinite pronouns?

Student: Indefinite pronouns are pronouns without antecedents.

Instructor: Is the indefinite pronoun *both* always singular, always plural, or sometimes singular and sometimes plural?

Student: Always plural.

Instructor: That's why it takes the plural helping verb *were* in this sentence. What prepositional phrase describes *both*?

Student: Of them.

Instructor: Add that prepositional phrase to your diagram beneath *both*. What prepositional phrase remains in the sentence?

Student: To Chicago.

Instructor: What question does this prepositional phrase answer?

Note to Instructor: If necessary, go through the adjective and adverb questions one at a time. Does *to Chicago* answer the questions what kind, which one, how many, whose? Or does it answer the questions how, when, where, how often, to what extent? The answer is where. Where were they going? To Chicago.

Student: Where.

Instructor: Is the phrase acting as an adjective or adverb?

Student: Adverb.

Instructor: Diagram it beneath the verb.

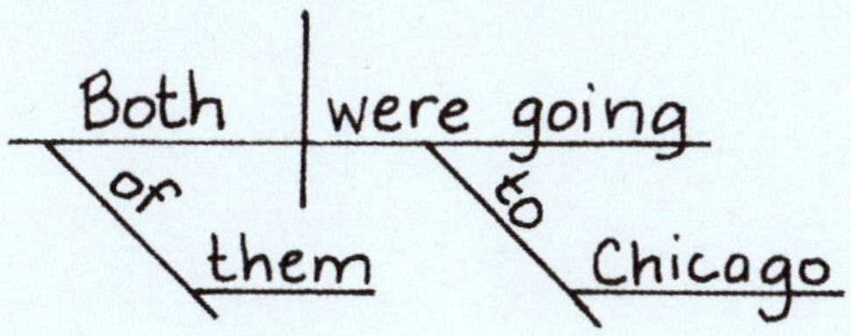

Sentence #5

Instructor: Read me the fifth sentence.

Student: The horse was awakened in the middle of the night.

Instructor: What are the subject and verb?

Student: Horse was awakened.

Instructor: Diagram the subject and verb on your paper. The action verbs *awake* and *awaken* are slightly different. *Awake* is an irregular verb. What are its principal parts?

Student: Awake, awoke, awoken.

Instructor: *Awaken* is a regular verb. What are its principal parts?

Student: Awaken, awakened, awakened.

Instructor: This sentence uses the past participle of *awaken*. In this sentence, is the verb active or passive? (Is the horse awakening on his own, or is something else awakening him?)

Student: Passive.

Instructor: The horse was *awakened*, which means someone or something else awakened him. The subject received the action of the verb, so the verb is passive. What article modifies *horse*?

Student: The.

Instructor: Diagram *the* beneath *horse*. What prepositional phrase follows the verb?

Student: In the middle.

Instructor: Now answer with another prepositional phrase: Which middle?

Student: [The middle] Of the night.

Instructor: *In the middle* answers what question?

Student: When.

Instructor: Is that phrase acting as an adjective or adverb?

Student: Adverb.

Instructor: Diagram it beneath the verb. *Of the night* answers the question *which one*. Is *of the night* acting as an adjective or adverb?

Student: Adjective.

Instructor: What noun is that adjective phrase modifying?

Student: Middle.

Instructor: It tells *which middle*, so it is modifying *middle*. Add *of the night* to your diagram beneath *middle*.

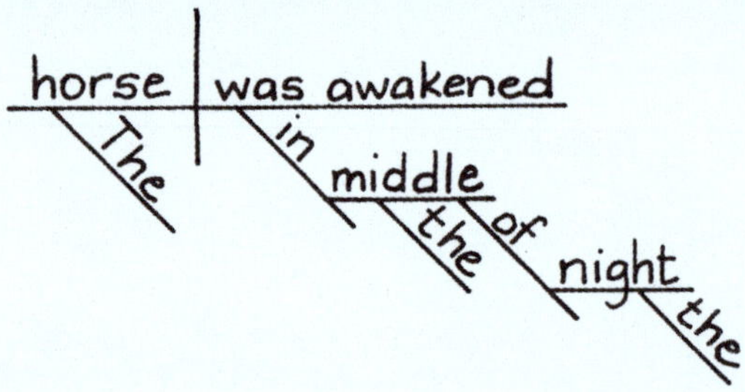

— LESSON 56 —

Active and Passive Voice

Transitive and Intransitive Verbs

Exercise 56A: Transitive and Intransitive Verbs

Underline each verb in the following sentences twice. Write *T* above each transitive verb and *IT* above each intransitive verb. Circle the direct object of each transitive verb.

These sentences are adapted from *Drought*, by Christopher Lampton.

The many farms in the Great Plains states provide food for people around the country.

In the 1930s, drought arrived in the Great Plains.

The Sahel region borders on the Saharan desert.

In the middle of a high-pressure system, you can expect fair weather with no rain.

Water also has a solid form.

In the 1980s, a mass famine in Africa lasted for much of the decade and took thousands of lives.

All living things need water for survival.

Plagues of grasshoppers and other insects descended on the Great Plains.

The dust storms blew across the plains and down the streets of cities.

They covered automobiles, homes, and people with thick layers of dust.

In Southeast Asia, monsoons provide rains after the dry winters.

Normally, the monsoon winds blow (IT) from south to north.

Every ring on the exposed surface of a tree stump represents (T) one (year) in the tree's growth.

After a few days a high-pressure system usually moves (IT) on.

With a stalled high-pressure system, the area underneath can go (IT) for long periods without rain.

Water in the ocean can take (T) the (form) of water vapor and enter the air.

Eventually, the droplets of water in the cloud will clump (IT) together into larger droplets.

Finally, water rationing began (T).

Exercise 56B: Active and Passive Verbs

In the blanks below, change each sentence from active to passive or from passive to active.

These sentences are adapted from *South Africa at the Crossroads*, by Jacqueline Drobis Meisel.

The Dutch were greatly disrupting the Khoikhoi way of life.

The Khoikhoi way of life was being greatly disrupted by the Dutch.

The German colony of South West Africa was defeated by South African forces.

South African forces defeated the German colony of South West Africa..

From the very beginning, some groups opposed the policy of apartheid.

From the very beginning, the policy of apartheid was opposed by some groups.

Note to Instructor: "From the very beginning" could instead be placed after "was opposed" or after "by some groups" in the sentence above. Similarly, in the sentence below, "in 1960" could be placed after "was organized" or after "by the Pan-African Congress."

In 1960, the Pan-African Congress organized a campaign of peaceful protest.

In 1960, a campaign of peaceful protest was organized by the Pan-African Congress.

Police and army vehicles patrolled the troubled township streets.

The troubled township streets were patrolled by police and army vehicles.

Significant political reforms were made by the government.

The government made significant political reforms.

More voices joined the call to economic action.

The call to economic action was joined by more voices.

Exercise 56C: Diagramming

On your own paper, diagram every word of the following sentences.

The sneeze from the elephant echoed across his enclosure at the zoo and startled many of the visitors.

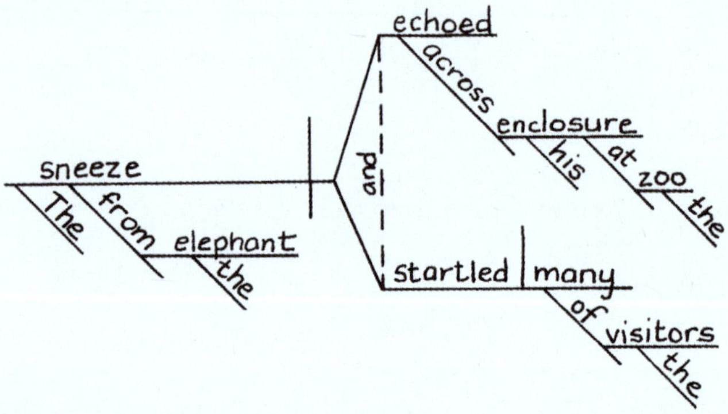

Mr. Williamson's amusement waned with the realization of Lucy's involvement in the prank.

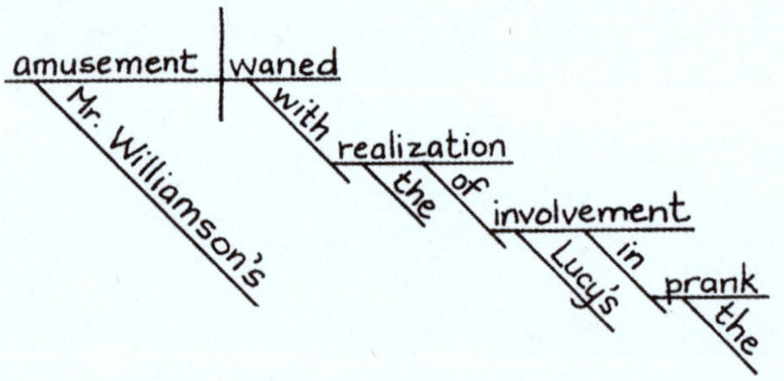

The little boy stumbled on the rickety bridge and became fearful.

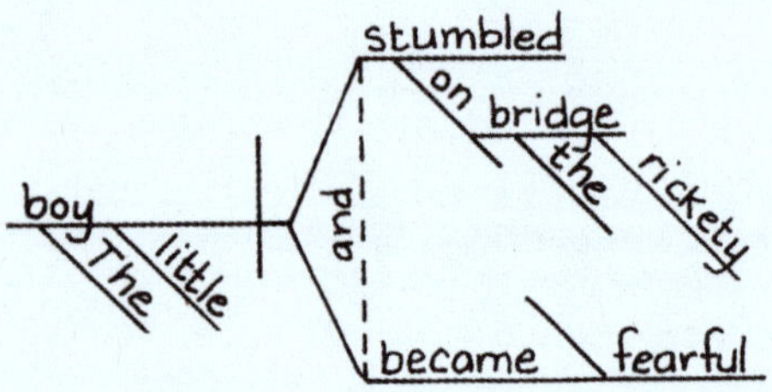

The unexpected knock at the door gave me a start and made me quite curious.

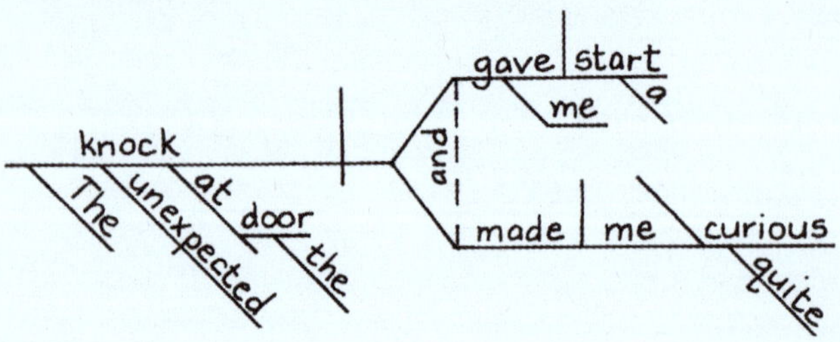

WEEK 15

Specialized Pronouns

— LESSON 57 —

Parts of Speech
Parts of the Sentence
Intensive and Reflexive Pronouns

Exercise 57A: Identifying Intensive and Reflexive Pronouns

Underline the intensive and reflexive pronouns in the following sentences. Above each pronoun, write *I* for intensive or *R* for reflexive. If the pronoun is reflexive, also mark it as *DO* (direct object), *IO* (indirect object), or *OP* (object of the preposition). The first is done for you.

These sentences are adapted from *Gulliver's Travels*, by Jonathan Swift.

I was struck with the utmost fear and astonishment, and hid myself (R DO) in the corn.

We brought the materials of diseases, folly, and vice, to spend among ourselves (R OP).

I myself (I) heard him give directions that one of his pages should be whipped.

They are dressed by men till four years of age, and then must dress themselves (R DO).

The author gives some account of himself (R OP) and family.

The farmer was glad enough to have his daughter preferred at court, and the poor girl herself (I) was not able to hide her joy.

Whenever he begins to praise you to others or to yourself (R OP), you are from that day forlorn.

She behaved herself (R DO) at our house as cheerfully as the rest.

But the danger is much greater when the ministers themselves (I) are commanded to show their dexterity.

We therefore trusted ourselves (R DO) to the mercy of the waves.

Exercise 57B: Using Intensive and Reflexive Pronouns Correctly

The following sentences may contain errors in the usage of intensive or reflexive pronouns. Cross out each incorrect word and write the correction in the blank. If a sentence has no errors, write "Correct" in the blank.

Silvia and myself will sing together in the talent show. I

The commencement address was given by the president hisself. himself

Susan B. Anthony herself died before all women in the United States were granted suffrage.	Correct
We all reminded ourself about the prize we would get if our team won.	ourselves
The basketball players got theirselves water after the game.	themselves
Take this to the office by yourself.	Correct
Please hand herself this note.	her

Exercise 57C: Diagramming Intensive and Reflexive Pronouns

Diagram every word in the following sentences.

The speaker carried himself to the podium with confidence.

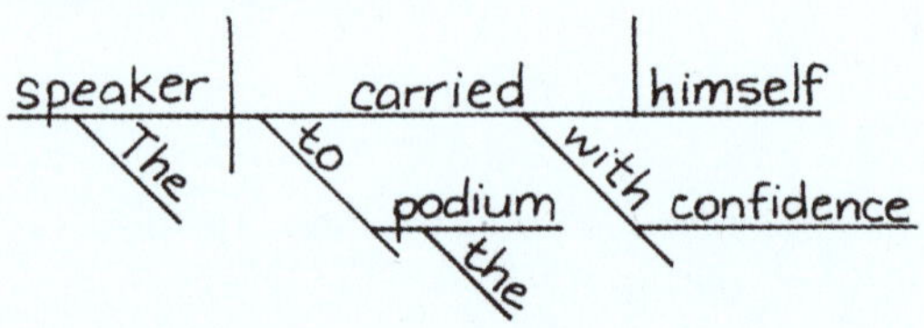

The key itself is scribbled in a corner of the map.

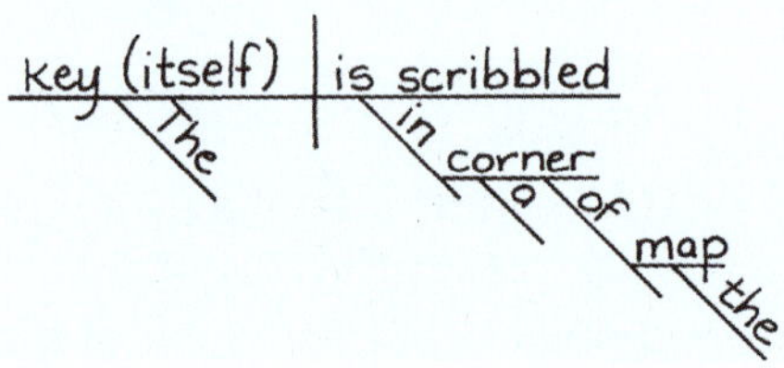

After their explanation, I approved the plan myself.

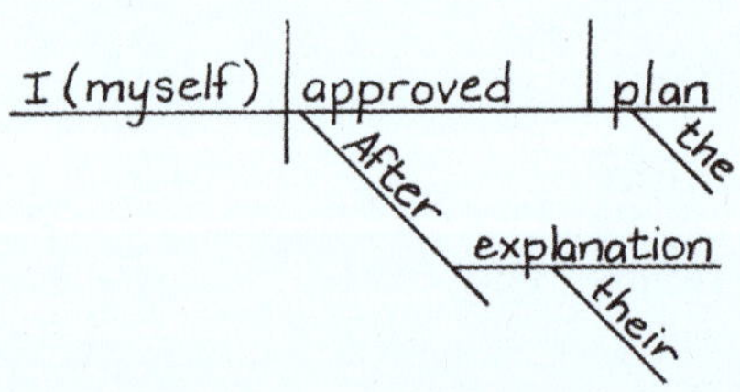

The two adventurers must discover the treasure by themselves.

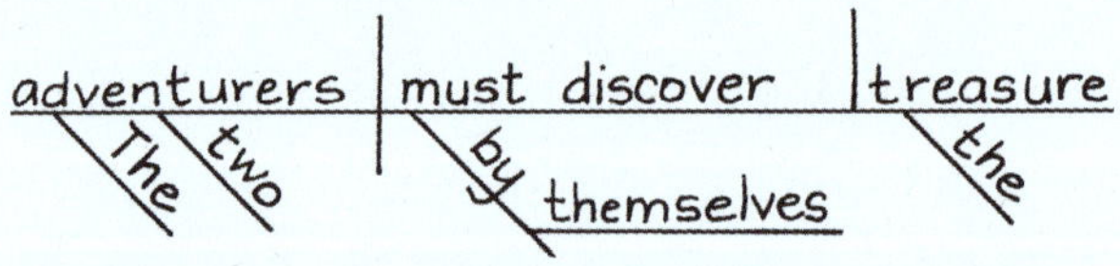

— LESSON 58 —

Demonstrative Pronouns
Demonstrative Adjectives

Exercise 58A: Demonstrative Pronouns and Demonstrative Adjectives

In the sentences below, label every occurrence of *this, that, these,* and *those* as either *DP* (for demonstrative pronoun) or *DA* (for demonstrative adjective). Draw an arrow from each demonstrative adjective to the noun it modifies. Label each demonstrative pronoun as *S* (subject), *DO* (direct object), *IO* (indirect object), or *OP* (object of the preposition).

The sentences below are from *The Merry Adventures of Robin Hood*, by Howard Pyle.

Now the Sheriff of Nottingham swore he himself would bring this (DA → knave) knave, Robin Hood, to justice.

"Now, Reynold Greenleaf," quoth the Sheriff, "thou art the fairest hand at the long bow mine eyes ever beheld, next to that (DA → knave) false knave, Robin Hood, from whose wiles Heaven forfend me!"

"I and these [DA] brethren were passing peacefully along the high-road with our packhorses, and a half score of men to guard them."

"Now yield thee," quoth the Tinker, "for thou art my captive." To this [DP OP] Robin Hood made no answer, but, clapping his horn to his lips, he blew three blasts, loud and clear.

But the Sheriff grew grave, for he did not like this [DP DO] so well.

So these [DP S] also came to the church, and there Sir Stephen leaped from his horse, and, coming to the litter, handed fair Ellen out therefrom.

"Come, busk thee, Little John! Stir those [DA] lazy bones of thine."

At this [DP OP] Will Scarlet laughed again. "Be not too sure of that, good uncle," quoth he.

"Now, thou art a man after mine own heart!" cried the Cook right heartily; "and, as thou speakest of it, that [DP S] is the very service for me."

Behind these [DP OP] were two of the higher brethren of Emmet.

Not far from the trysting tree was a great rock in which a chamber had been hewn. This [DP S] was the treasure-house of the band.

"It used to gall me to hear him speak up so boldly to my father, who, thou knowest, was ever a patient man to those [DP OP] about him."

Then next they met a stout burgher and his wife and their two fair daughters. These [DP DO] Little John saluted gravely.

> **Note to Instructor:** In the sentence above, the student may struggle to identify the function of the demonstrative pronoun *these* because it does not use the most familiar word order. It may be helpful to ask the student, "What is the verb in the sentence?" *Saluted.* "Who or what saluted?" *Little John.* "Saluted whom or what?" *These.* Since *Little John* is the subject and *these* receives the action of the verb, *these* is the direct object.

Some among them shouted, "Hey for Reynold Greenleaf!" for this [DP S] was the name Little John had called himself that [DA] day.

Exercise 58B: Demonstrative Pronouns

In the blank beneath each sentence, write a possible description of the thing or person that the underlined demonstrative pronoun stands for. Make sure to choose the correct number. (And use your imagination.)

> **Note to Instructor:** Any answers of the correct number are acceptable.

These are absolutely delicious!

Answer should be plural, e.g., *The cupcakes with pink frosting*

This is not very sturdy.

Answer should be singular, e.g., *The stool with one leg missing*

That may be the most adorable thing in the world.
Answer should be singular, e.g., *The kitten playing with the ball of yarn*

Those are quite ancient.
Answer should be plural, e.g., *The coins on display at the museum*

Exercise 58C: Diagramming

On your own paper, diagram every word in the following three sentences.

That object moves others, and is itself also moved by something from the outside.

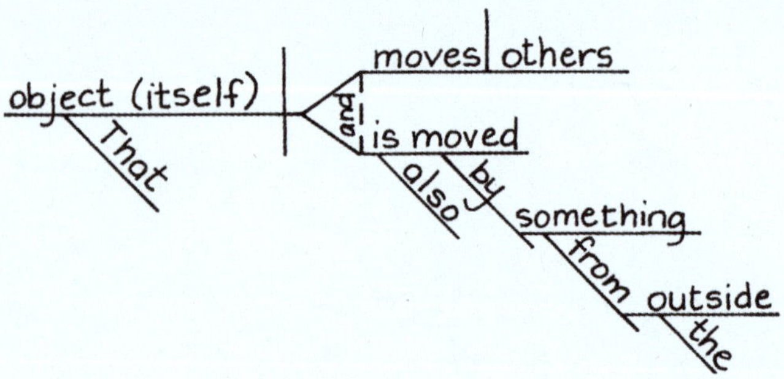

Of this, I myself am certain and am fully resolved.

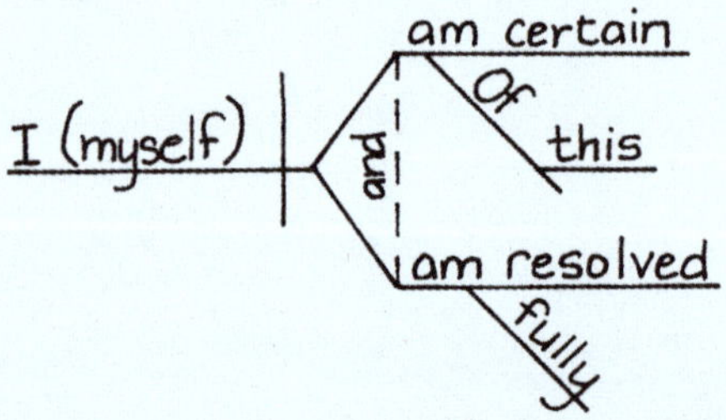

All of those, great and small, are problems, but can be resolved with fortitude and a certain determination.

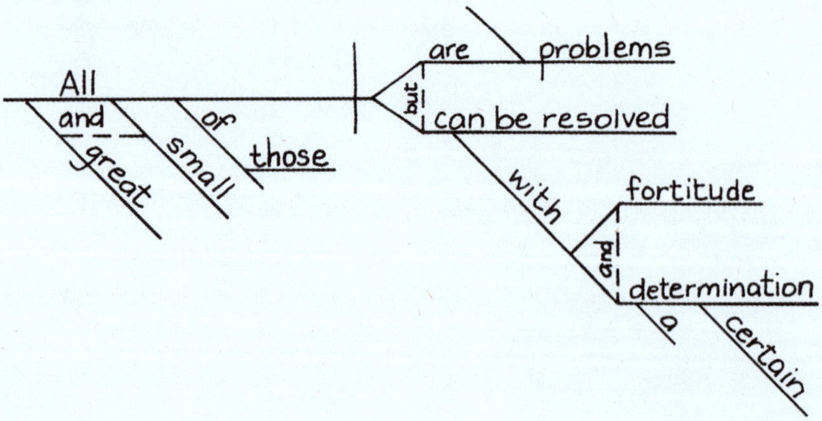

— LESSON 59 —

Demonstrative Pronouns
Demonstrative Adjectives
Interrogative Pronouns
Interrogative Adjectives

Exercise 59A: Identifying Demonstrative and Interrogative Pronouns

Underline all of the demonstrative and interrogative pronouns in these sentences, which are all from the plays of Gilbert & Sullivan. There may be more than one in each sentence.

Who has ventured to approach our all but inaccessible lair?

But who are you, sir? Speak!

Kind sir, you cannot have the heart
Our lives to part
From those to whom an hour ago
We were united!

Note to Instructor: In this sentence, *whom* is a pronoun but not an interrogative pronoun.

Who knows whose husband you are?

Note to Instructor: In this sentence, *whose* is an adjective, not a pronoun.

But which is it? There are two of them!

Dear, dear, dear! this is very tiresome.

She has twice as much money, which may account for it.

Note to Instructor: In this sentence, *which* is a pronoun but not an interrogative pronoun.

But heaven ha' mercy, whom wouldst thou marry?

I didn't anticipate that,
When I first put this uniform on!

You see before you
The men to whom you're plighted!

Note to Instructor: In this sentence, *whom* is a pronoun but not an interrogative pronoun.

Whom were you talking with just now?

Aye, she knows all about that.

Now what can that have been—
A shot so late at night,
Enough to cause a fright!

That's not true, but let it pass.

I say, which of us has married her?

Why, who is this whose evil eyes
        Rain blight on our festivities?

> **Note to Instructor:** In this sentence, *whose* is an adjective, not a pronoun.

Bless your heart, they've been staring at us through those windows for the last half-hour!

> **Note to Instructor:** In this sentence, *those* is an adjective, not a pronoun.

Those who would separate us woe betide!

> **Note to Instructor:** In this sentence, *who* is a pronoun, but not an interrogative pronoun.

But they're nothing at all, compared
        With those of his daughter-in-law elect!
And this is the certificate of his death.
What shall I do? Before these gentle maidens
        I dare not show in this alarming costume!

> **Note to Instructor:** In this sentence, *these* and *this* are both adjectives, not pronouns.

But which of you is married to which of us, and what's to become of the other?
These were my thoughts; I kept them to myself,
    For at that age I had not learnt to speak.

> **Note to Instructor:** In this sentence, *that* is an adjective, not a pronoun.

Exercise 59B: Using Interrogative and Demonstrative Pronouns Correctly

Choose the correct word in parentheses. Cross out the incorrect word.

(~~Who~~/Whom) are you going to choose to play the clown?

(Who/~~Whom~~) was shrieking so loudly last night?

(~~This~~/These) are the most comfortable pajamas I've ever worn.

For (~~who~~/whom) are the flowers in the graveyard?

(~~Who's~~/Whose) cousins are coming to visit?

(~~Who~~/Whom) did Aaron Burr challenge to a duel?

(This/~~That~~) is my calculator right here, so (~~this~~/that) one over there must be Nara's.

(~~Who's~~/Whose) is this clown makeup?

(This/~~These~~) is not very clean.

(Who/~~Whom~~) is the eccentric woman in the red and purple hat?

(Who/~~Whom~~) is the veterinarian in charge of delivering the new foal?

(Who's/~~Whose~~) delivering the cauliflower and caviar pizza?

Exercise 59C: Diagramming Interrogative and Demonstrative Pronouns

Diagram the following sentences.

Whose stomach is growling so loudly?

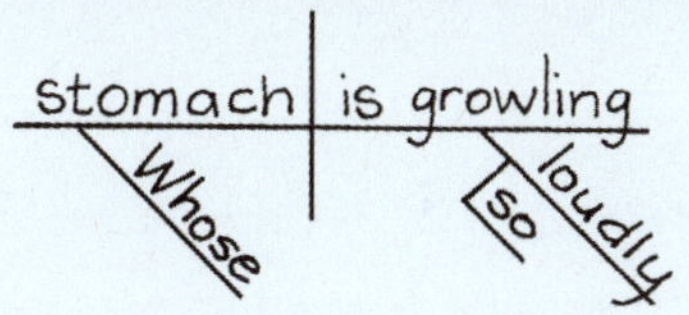

She ate what?

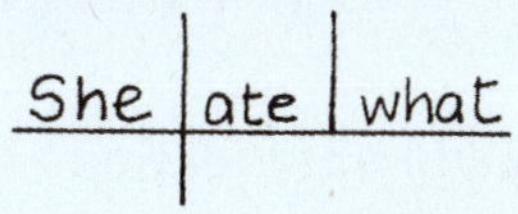

My sister ate all of that.

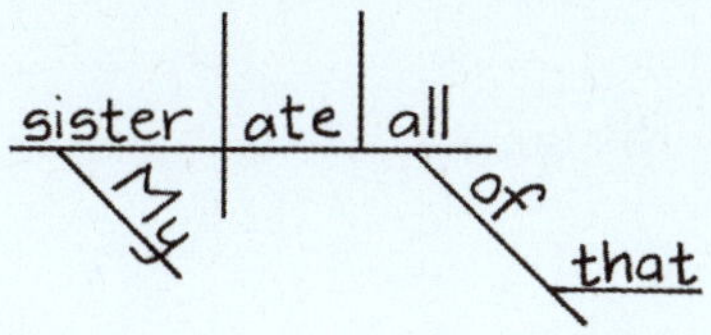

Who spilled this Smoking Bishop punch on the floor?

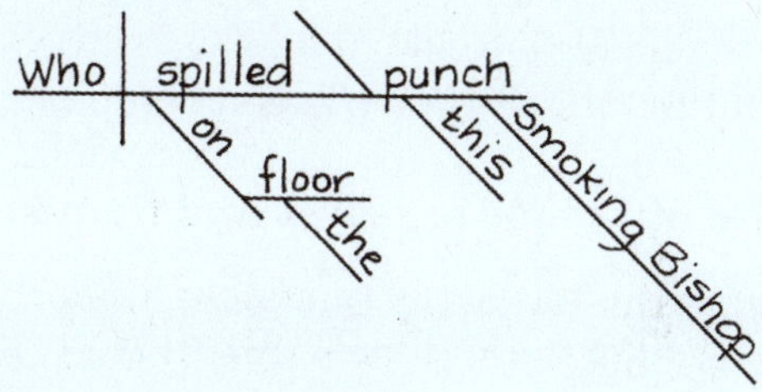

From whom did Charles Dickens get the recipe for Smoking Bishop punch?

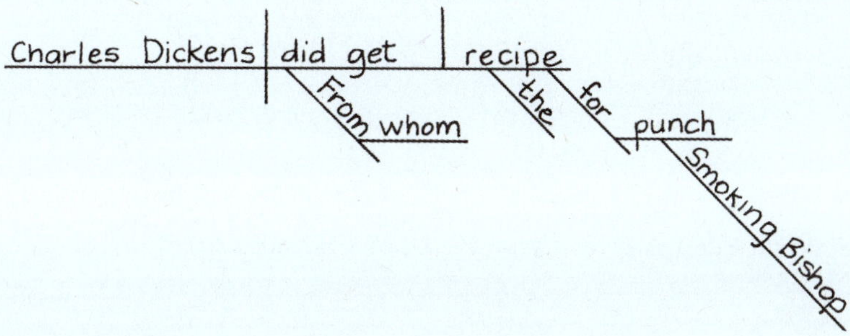

Petra gave you which box of salt caramel truffle chocolates?

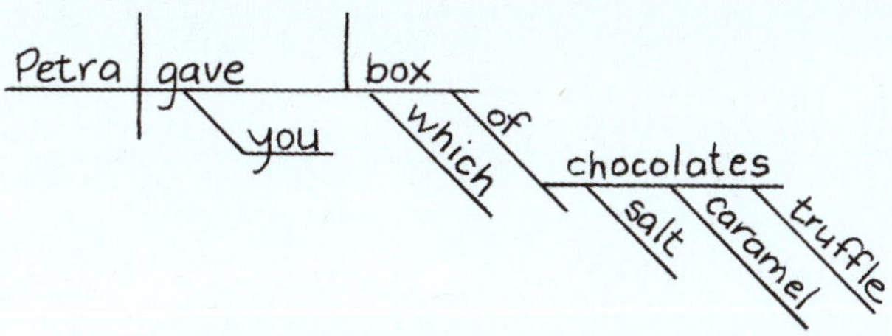

Note to Instructor: The student could also diagram *salt caramel truffle* as a single compound adjective modifying *chocolates*, or diagram *salt caramel* as one compound adjective and *truffle* as another adjective.

Do not forget this letter and that ring.

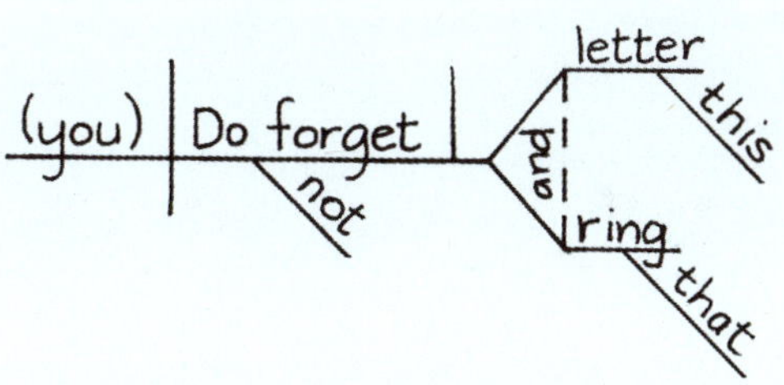

— LESSON 60 —

Pronoun Review

Sentences Beginning with Adverbs

Exercise 60A: Singular/Plural Indefinite Pronouns

Cross out the incorrect verb in each sentence.

Each of the villains (~~laugh~~/laughs) evilly.
"No one (is/~~are~~) able to stop us!" they cry.
Some of the heroes (narrow/~~narrows~~) their eyes.
"All of us (~~is~~/are) prepared for whatever you have planned," they promise.
Most of the villains (look/~~looks~~) nervous, but one (is/~~are~~) undaunted by the heroes.

Exercise 60B: Interrogatives and Demonstratives

In each of the following sentences, underline the interrogatives and demonstratives. If they are acting as adjectives, draw a line from each to the noun it modifies. If they are acting as other parts of the sentence, label them (*S* for subject, *DO* for direct object, *IO* for indirect object, or *OP* for object of the preposition).

These sentences are from Elizabeth George Speare's *The Witch of Blackbird Pond.*

S
So this is the orphan from Barbados?
S
What difference does that make?

Note to Instructor: *That* is the subject because *does make* is an action verb and *difference* is the direct object.

The next job is some new thatch for that roof.
DO
What am I offered for it?
There's scarce a house in this town but has a sick child in it.
S
Even that could not disturb her, poor child.
DO
What had poor Hannah ever done to them?
DO
Read that for us, child, beginning right there.
From that moment in the meadow Kit ceased to plan at all.

Exercise 60C: Diagramming Practice

Diagram every word of the following sentences.

These sentences are from Elizabeth George Speare's *The Witch of Blackbird Pond.*

This girl could have been the toast of a regiment!

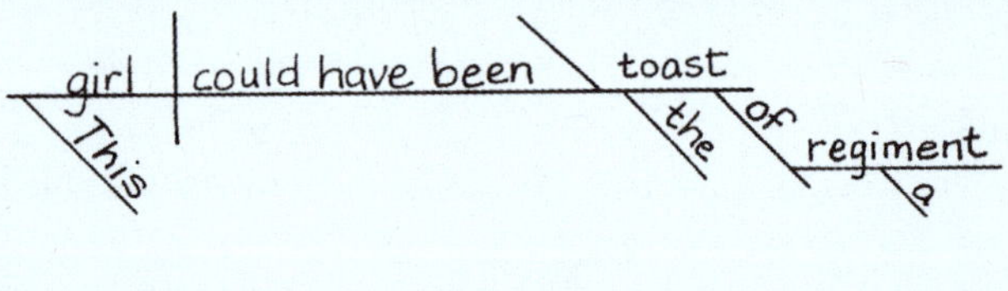

You're not making that fuss about one old wolf?

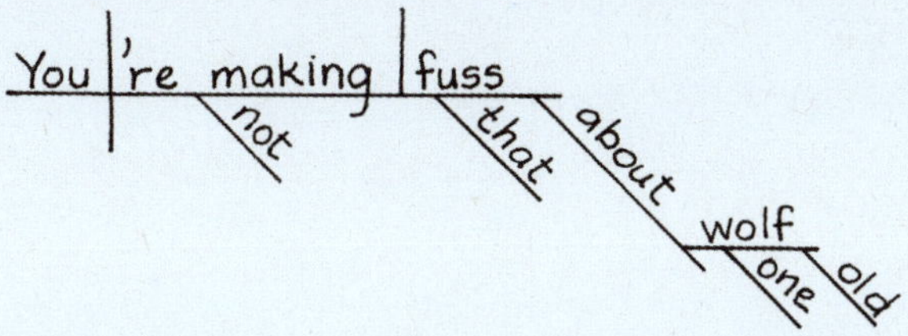

There, without a thought, she left the pathway, plunged into a field, and fell on the grass.

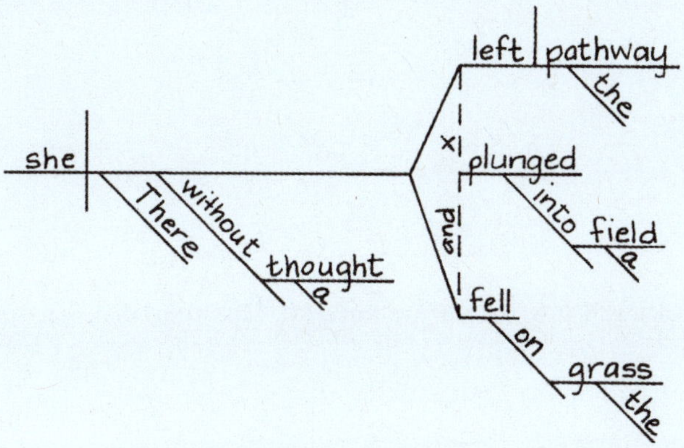

> **Note to Instructor:** In the diagram above, *without a thought* is diagrammed as though it modifies all three verbs. The student may also simply diagram the phrase under *left*. If the student asks how to diagram the phrase, show her the answer and explain that an adverb modifying more than one verb can be placed after the verb-dividing line on the diagram, but before the branches of the compound verbs.
>
> The student may also choose to place an X to represent the comma on the dotted line between left and *plunged*.

Hannah accepted the miracle and the prospect of a journey like a docile child.

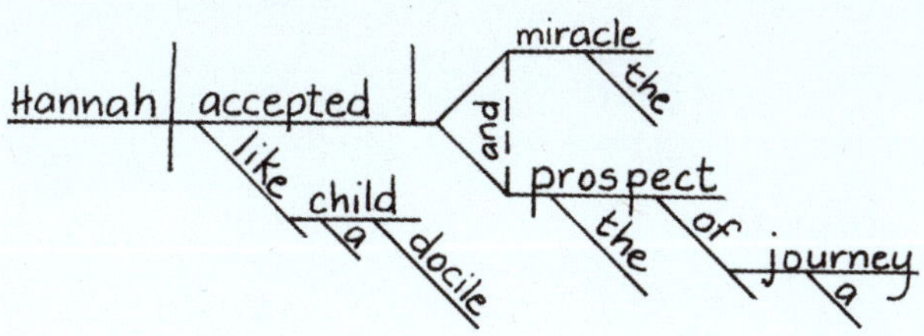

— REVIEW 5 —

Weeks 13-15

Topics

Pronouns and Antecedents
Possessive Pronouns
Subject and Object Pronouns
Indefinite Pronouns (and Subject-Verb Agreement)
Troublesome Verbs
Active and Passive Voice
Conjugating Passive Voice
Intensive and Reflexive Pronouns
Demonstrative and Interrogative Pronouns

Review 5A: Types of Pronouns

Put each pronoun from the word bank in the correct category. Some words may belong in more than one category.

her that he who
his myself them
we someone what ours
which it both
this yourself these many
herself

Personal Subject	he	we	it
Personal Object	her	them	it
Personal Possessive	her	his	ours
Indefinite	someone	both	many
Demonstrative	that	this	these
Interrogative	who	what	which
Intensive/Reflexive	myself	yourself	herself

Review 5B: Using Correct Pronouns

Circle the correct word in parentheses.

The actress with the blue hat was (her / she).

(There / Their / They're) were several obstacles in (there / their / they're) way, but (they / them) still got (there / their / they're) in time.

Marina and (herself / her / she) climbed over the fence and hurt (theirselves / themselves) on the way down.

All the purple properties in the game belong to (him / he).

(Who's / Whose) carrying Mrs. Prior's bags for (her / she)?

Jason, Titus, and (myself / me / I) are deciding (who's / whose) science project is the best.

(Who / Whom) was repeating (himself / hisself)?

(Who / Whom) is (your / you're) mother scolding?

Simeon and (he / him) are tossing the ball to (who / whom)?

(Who's / Whose) locket is over (there / their / they're) on the table?

Review 5C: Pronouns and Antecedents

Circle the THIRTEEN personal pronouns (subject, object, and possessive) in the following excerpt from *Betsy-Tacy* by Maud Hart Lovelace. Draw arrows to each pronoun's antecedent.

Then, find the single reflexive pronoun. Underline it. Draw an arrow to its antecedent.

Julia had already taken Betsy to the door, and had said to Miss Dalton, the teacher: "This is my little sister Betsy."

Now Katie said, "This is my little sister Tacy." And she added, "She's very bashful."

"Never mind," said Miss Dalton, smiling brightly. "I'll take care of that. I'll put her right by me." And she placed a little chair beside her desk and put Tacy into that.

Tacy didn't like that. Betsy could tell from the way she scrunched down and hid herself beneath her curls. She was less happy than ever when Betsy was put far away at a regular desk in one of the rows of desks filling the room.

Review 5D: Agreement with Indefinite Pronouns

Choose the correct word in parentheses to agree with the indefinite pronouns. Cross out the incorrect word.

No one (has/~~have~~) closed the door.

Most of the birds (~~has~~/have) flown away, but one (is/~~are~~) still sitting on the fence.

Everyone with a ticket (is/~~are~~) lined up by the door.

(Has/~~Have~~) anyone forgotten (his or her/~~their~~) lunch?

(~~Has~~/Have) all the dancers picked up (~~his or her~~/their) shoes?

In the sun, most of the snow (has/~~have~~) melted already, but some (remains/~~remain~~) in the shade.

Few of the tables at the restaurant (~~is~~/are) occupied.

Neither of the wounds (requires/~~require~~) stitches.

If anyone (wants/~~want~~) fabric, (he or she/~~they~~) should take a number at the cutting counter.

(Is/~~Are~~) either of the Collins twins coming on the trip?

Review 5E: Distinguishing between Active and Passive Voice

Identify each sentence as *A* for active or *P* for passive. These sentences are from *The Pony Express: Hoofbeats in the Wilderness*, by Joseph J. DiCerto.

The settlement of the West was made possible by people of great character and foresight.	P
Senator Gwin of California enthusiastically described the idea of a central-route mail service.	A
These locations were called relay stations.	P
Management increased the mail run service to twice each week.	A
Thousands of emigrants on their way west climbed the sloped walls of Independence Rock to engrave their names and dates for future historians.	A
The records of many of these stations were lost.	P
In 1860, Mark Twain was making a trip across the country by stagecoach.	A
The two men were paralyzed by fear.	P
Bill Cody had ridden an amazing 384 miles without a regular sleeping break.	A
By August 1861, most of the transcontinental telegraph line was completed.	P

Review 5F: Troublesome Verbs

Circle the correct verb form in parentheses. These sentences are from *The Golden Fleece and the Heroes Who Lived before Achilles*, by Padraic Colum.

The blue sky was above him, the great trees stood away from him, and the little child (laid/lay) at his feet.

In a quiet place he (sat/set) down, and for a while he lost sight of Pandora.

The Argonauts shouted, but the rude Bebrycians (raised/rose) their clubs to rush upon them.

The master of the ship (let/left) the sail take the breeze of the evening.

No sooner did they (sit/set) their feet upon the shore than the hero went off into the forest, to pull up a tree that he might shape into an oar.

Medea went to her couch and (laid/lay) down upon it.

And then, even as Telamon said these angry words, a strange figure (raised/rose) up out of the waves of the sea.

Straightaway he gave orders to his guard to (lay/lie) hands upon the youth.

The Graces put necklaces around her neck and (sat/set) a golden crown upon her head.

Once it came into the mind of Zeus that he would destroy the fourth race and (leave/let) the earth to the nymphs and the satyrs.

WEEK 16

Imposters

— LESSON 61 —

Progressive Tenses
Principal Parts
Past Participles as Adjectives
Present Participles as Adjectives

Exercise 61A: Identifying Past Participles Used as Adjectives

Underline the past participles used as adjectives in the following sentences, adapted from *Vitamins and Minerals* by Alvin Silverstein, Virginia Silverstein, and Robert Silverstein. Draw a line to each word modified.

Our bodies need balanced amounts of minerals.

In some areas, people eat mostly refined rice, and their diet lacks key vitamins.

The best way to get vitamins is through a diet with varied foods at each meal.

Fresh or frozen foods, rather than canned foods, can help you get more nutrients.

Milled grains and peeled vegetables lose some of their nutrients.

Exercise 61B: Identifying Present Participles Used as Adjectives

Underline the present participles used as adjectives in the following sentences, taken from *The Moffats* by Eleanor Estes. Draw a line to each word modified.

This consisted of a slight rocking motion from heel to toe.

And the red steed sent sparks from his nostrils that disappeared like shooting stars into the still night air.

A few heavy jerks and a harsh grating noise made Rufus realize what was happening.

Way off on the other side of the harbor they could just make out the slumbering form of the Sleeping Giant.

“At your service,” said he, and he gave Joe a meaning look.

Janey scuffled through the dry, crackling leaves in the gutter.

Her yellow eyes shone with a knowing gleam.

Exercise 61C: Diagramming Present & Past Participles Used as Adjectives

On your own paper, diagram the following sentences.

Flowering plants beautify gardens.

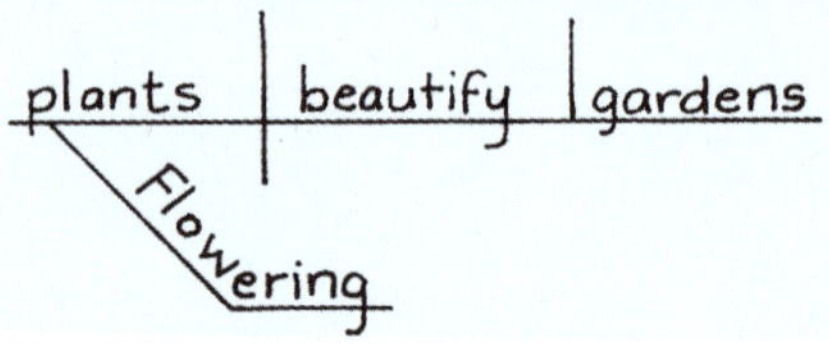

Menacing goblins brandished their curved swords.

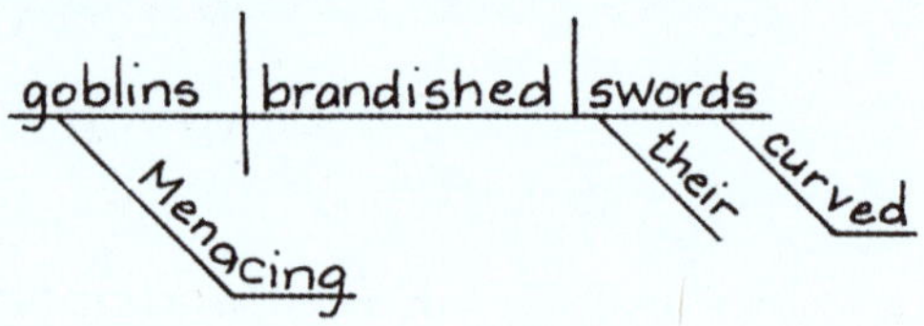

Her drumming fingers sounded rhythmic.

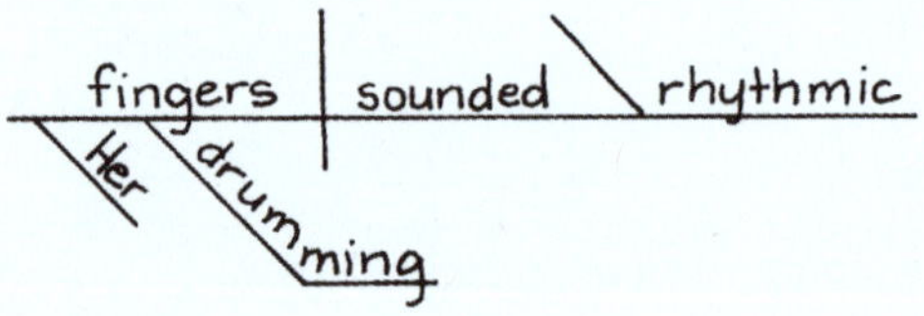

Jim replaced his torn jacket.

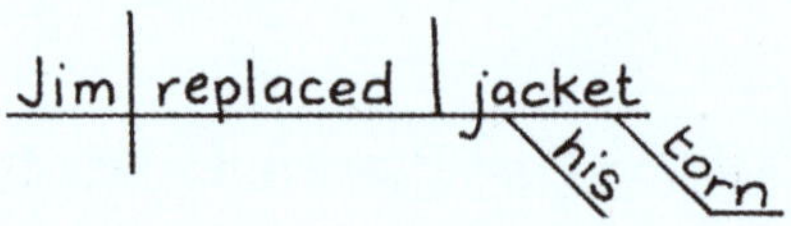

A watched pot never boils.

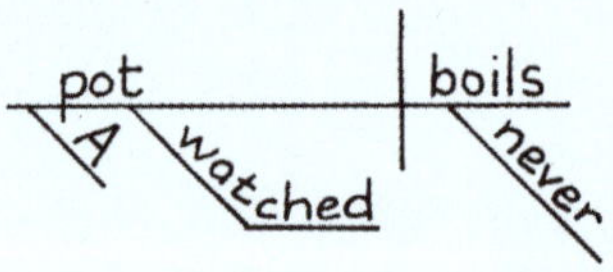

— LESSON 62 —

Parts of Speech and Parts of Sentences

Present Participles as Nouns (Gerunds)

Exercise 62A: Identifying Gerunds

In the following sentences, slightly condensed from George B. Schaller's *The Year of the Gorilla*, circle each gerund. Underline each subject once and each predicate twice. Write *DO* above any direct objects, *IO* above any indirect objects, and *OP* above any objects of prepositions.

Gorillas require two hours (DO) of feeding (OP) in the morning (OP), and each animal is intent on filling (OP) up.

Between nine (OP) and ten o'clock (OP), the foraging generally comes slowly to a stop (OP).

> **Note to Instructor:** The noun *ten o'clock* is a compound noun (remove either word and it no longer makes sense). *Nine* is shorthand for *nine o'clock* and so also serves as a noun. Both are objects of the preposition *between*.

The crackling of the undergrowth (OP) revealed the presence (DO) of the gorillas (OP) about forty yards (OP) ahead.

I heard rustling (DO) at my approach (OP).

Immediately after and sometimes during chest beating (OP), the animal runs sideways for a few steps (OP) before dropping (OP) to all fours (OP) and dashing (OP) along.

I give the charging animal (IO) all benefit (DO) of the doubt (OP).

Illegal hunting is a large industry.

Exercise 62B: Diagramming Gerunds

On your own paper, diagram every word in the following sentences.

Arguing will not solve your problems.

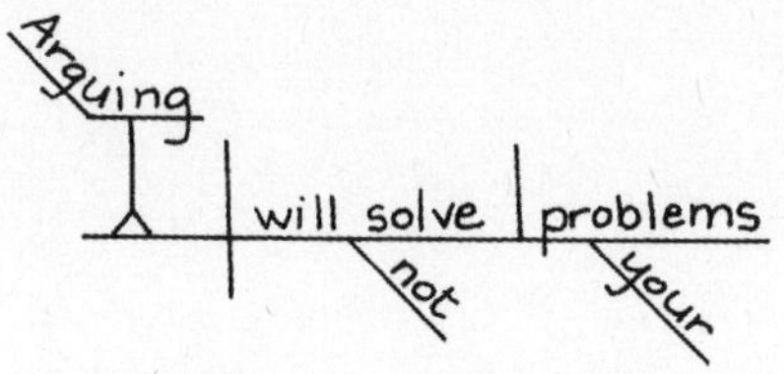

Tess earns extra money by coaching.

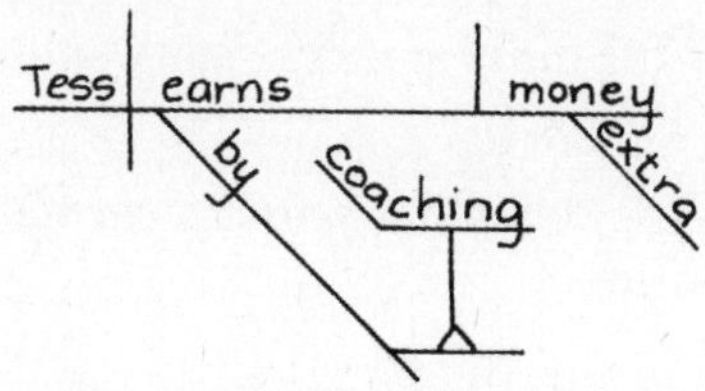

The suspect's confusing responses befuddled the detectives.

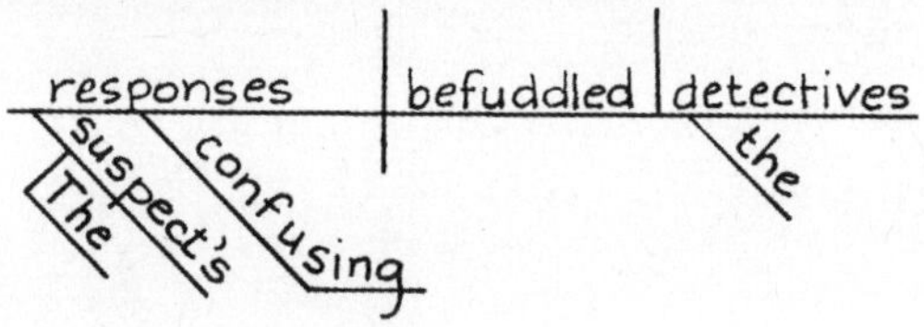

The owl is hunting mice.

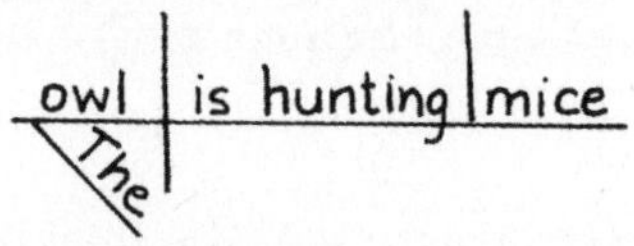

Joe enjoys hunting.

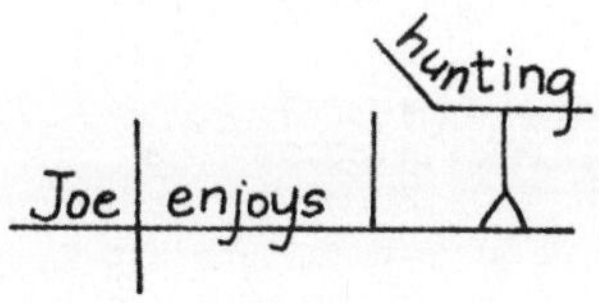

— LESSON 63 —

Gerunds
Present and Past Participles as Adjectives
Infinitives
Infinitives as Nouns

Exercise 63A: Identifying Gerunds and Infinitives

Underline the gerunds and infinitives in the following quotes. Identify the imposters as *G* for gerund or *I* for infinitive. Then, identify each gerund or infinitive as a subject (*S*), predicate nominative (*PN*), direct object (*DO*), or object of a preposition (*OP*).

The instinct of nearly all societies is to lock (I PN) up anybody who is truly free.
—Jean Cocteau

Learning (G S) is what most adults will do for a living (G OP) in the 21st century.
—Lewis Perelman

I S I PN
To exist is to change.
—Henri Bergson

G OP
I criticize by creation, not by finding fault.
—Cicero

G S
Avoiding danger is no safer in the long run than outright exposure.
—Helen Keller

G S G PN G PN
Living at risk is jumping off the cliff and building your wings on the way down.
—Ray Bradbury

I PN
One of the most important tasks of a manager is to eliminate his people's excuses for failure.
—Robert Townsend

G OP
He that is good for making excuses is seldom good for anything else.
—Benjamin Franklin

G DO
I don't mind lying, but I hate inaccuracy.
—Samuel Butler

G PN
Our whole life is solving puzzles.
—Ernő Rubik

> **Note to Instructor:** The phrase *is solving* isn't the progressive present of the action verb *solve*, because the subject *life* is not actively solving. Instead, the sentence tells us what life *is* (linking verb): [the] solving [of puzzles].

G S
Learning preserves the errors of the past, as well as its wisdom.
—Alfred North Whitehead

I DO I DO
We must learn to live together as brothers or perish together as fools.
—Martin Luther King Jr.

> **Note to Instructor:** Explain to the student that *perish* is the infinitive *to perish* with an understood *to* (borrowed from the previous infinitive, *to live*).

Exercise 63B: Diagramming Gerunds and Infinitives

On your own paper, diagram the following sentences.

Creating is my criticism.

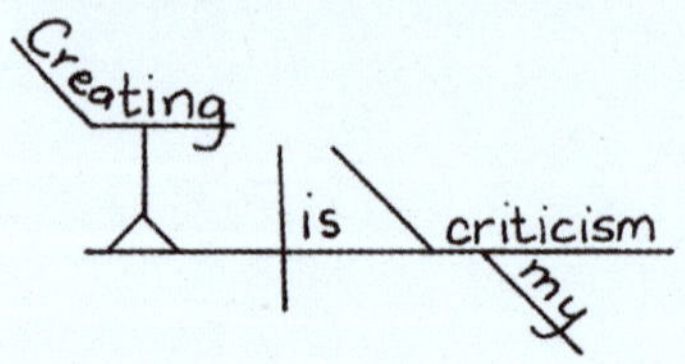

To exist is to change.

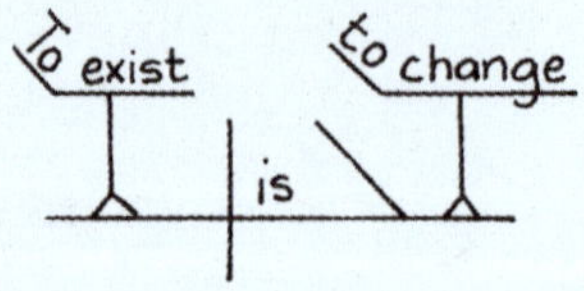

Learning preserves the errors of the past.

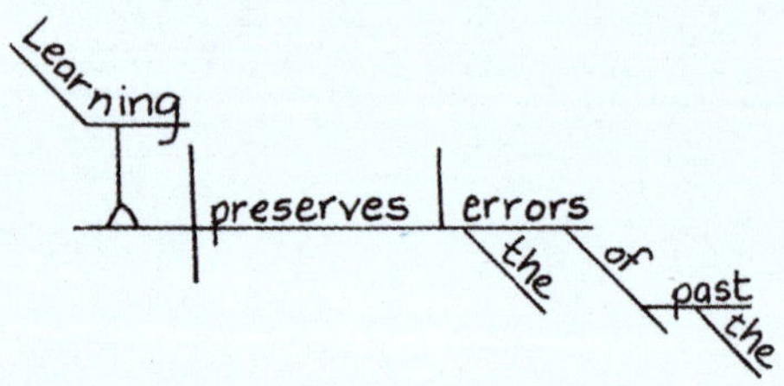

I don't mind lying, but I hate inaccuracy.

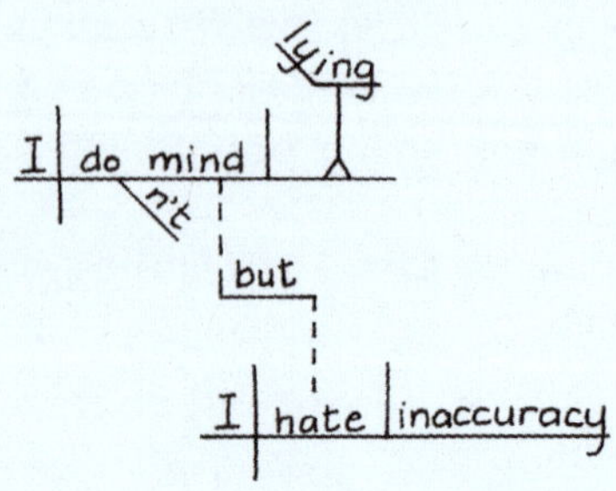

We must learn to live or to perish.

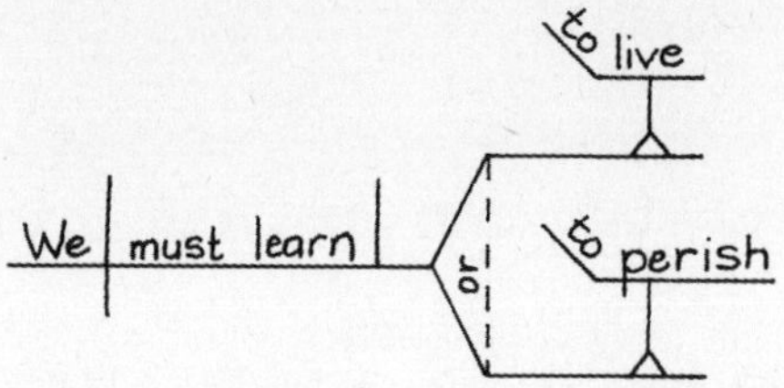

Living is jumping.

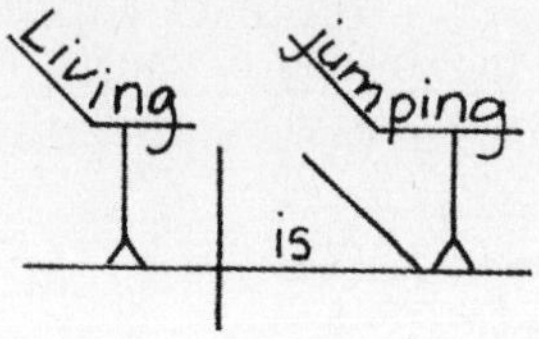

— LESSON 64 —

Gerunds
Present and Past Participles
Infinitives
Gerund, Participle, and Infinitive Phrases

Exercise 64A: Identifying Phrases that Serve as Parts of the Sentence

In the following sentences, begin by underlining each prepositional phrase.

- Then, circle each group of words that contains a gerund, infinitive, or past participle. Each one serves as a part of the sentence. (Those circled phrases might include some of your prepositional phrases!)
- Label each circled phrase. Your options are: *ADJ* (adjective), *ADV* (adverb), *S* (subject), *IO* (indirect object), *DO* (direct object), *OC* (object complement), *OP* (object of the preposition), *PN* (predicate nominative), or *PA* (predicate adjective).
- You might find that a circled phrase with a gerund, infinitive, or past participle in it contains other phrases with gerunds, infinitives, or past participles!

These sentences are taken from *The Matchlock Gun*, by Walter D. Edmonds.

OC [modifies *hair*]

She had black hair braided round her head.

PA

ADV

Now he seemed absorbed in examining his powder horn and filling it from the big horn beside the chimney.

Note to Instructor: The past participle phrase *absorbed in examining his powder horn and filling it from the big horn beside the chimney* describes *he* and serves as a predicate adjective. Within that past participle phrase, the gerunds *examining* and *filling* are both objects of the preposition *in*. But the entire prepositional phrase following *absorbed* is an adverb because it describes the past participle *absorbed*.

DO

They preferred to build their own house.

ADV [modifies *rode*] ADV [modifies *rode*]

John Mynderse rode down after lunch, carrying his musket in his hands, balancing it on the withers of his bright bay horse.

DO

Tell him not to worry about us.

Note to Instructor: The adverb *not* modifies *to worry*, so it is part of the infinitive phrase. If the student is uncertain whether to include it, ask him what *not* is modifying: not tell? not him? not worry?

ADJ

Gertrude had no trouble in leading them up the knoll beyond the garden.

Note to Instructor: The gerund *leading* is the object of the preposition *in*, so *in* should be included in the circle. The gerund phrase as a whole describes *trouble*, so it acts as an adjective.

S

To stay seemed the best way to her.

Exercise 64B: Diagramming

On your own paper, diagram all of the sentences from Exercise 64A.

She had black hair braided round her head.

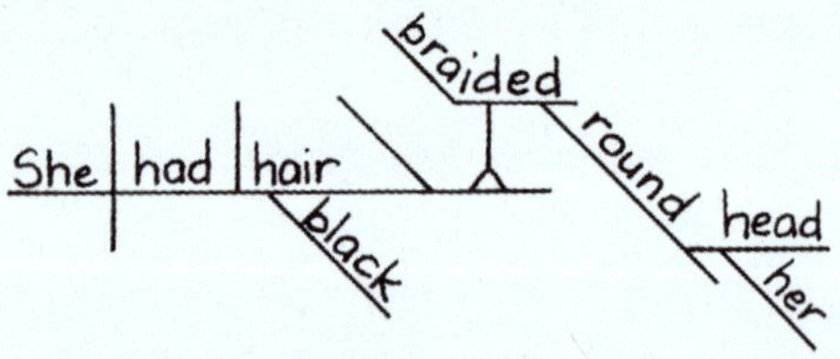

Now he seemed absorbed in examining his powder horn and filling it from the big horn beside the chimney.

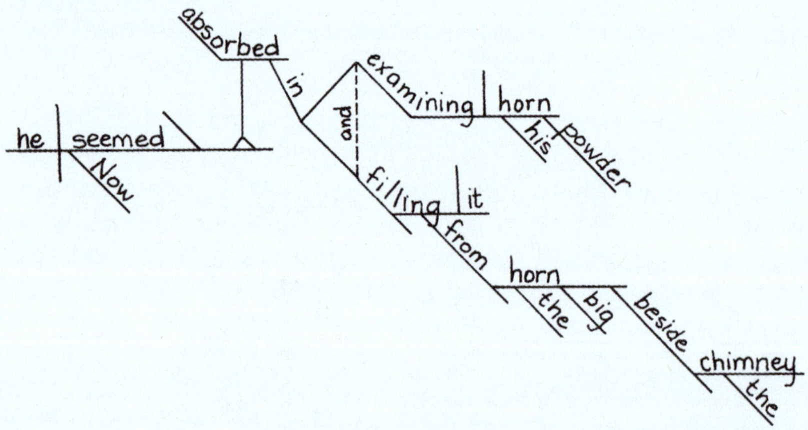

They preferred to build their own house.

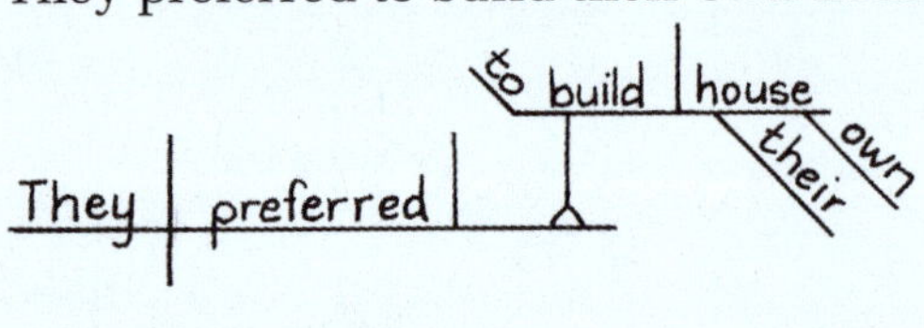

John Mynderse rode down after lunch, carrying his musket in his hands, balancing it on the withers of his bright bay horse.

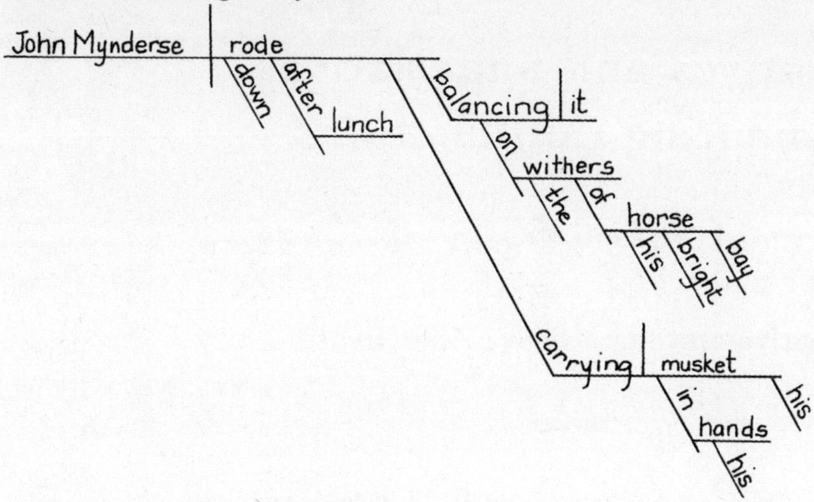

Tell him not to worry about us.

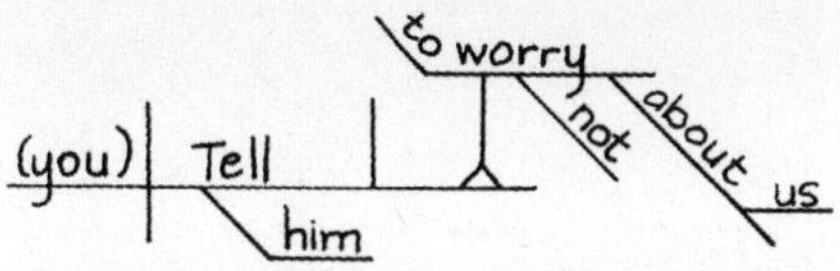

Gertrude had no trouble in leading them up the knoll beyond the garden.

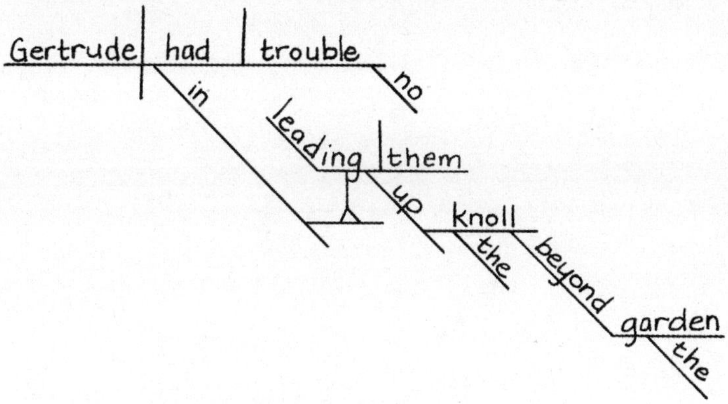

To stay seemed the best way to her.

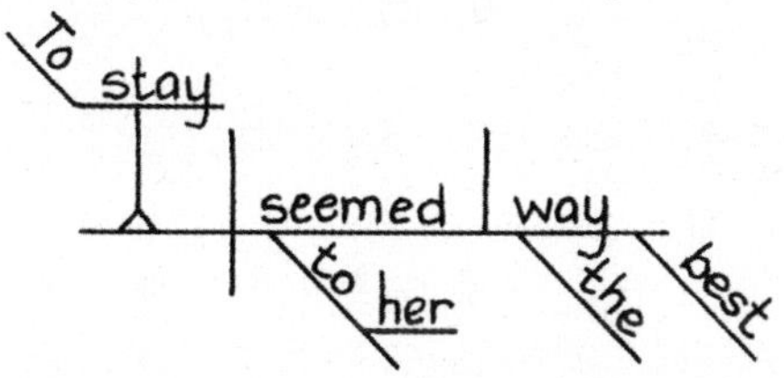

WEEK 17

Comparatives and Superlatives
Subordinating Conjunctions

— LESSON 65 —

Adjectives
Comparative and Superlative Adjectives

Exercise 65A: Identifying Positive, Comparative, and Superlative Adjectives

Identify the underlined adjective forms as *P* for positive, *C* for comparative, or *S* for superlative. These lines are from William Shakespeare's *A Midsummer Night's Dream.*

I am that merry wanderer of the night. ___P___

Or, rather, do I not in plainest truth ___S___
Tell you I do not, nor I cannot love you?

Effect it with some care, that he may prove
More fond on her than she upon her love. ___C___

The will of man is by his reason sway'd;
And reason says you are the worthier maid. ___C___
Things growing are not ripe until their season; ___P___
So I, being young, till now ripe not to reason. ___P___
[It] leads me to your eyes, where I o'erlook
Love's stories, written in love's richest book. ___S___

Injurious Hermia! most ungrateful maid! ___P,S___
Have you conspir'd, have you with these contriv'd
To bait me with this foul derision? ___P___

Exercise 65B: Forming Comparative and Superlative Adjectives

Fill in the blank with the correct form of the adjective in parentheses. Some of these adjectives use *more* or *most*, while others use *-er* or *-est* endings. You may consult a dictionary if you're not sure!

These sentences are taken from *The World's Great Explorers: Explorers of the Ancient World*, by Charnan Simon.

Egyptians found that they needed ___larger___, ___heavier___, ___more seaworthy___ boats than those they initially built. (large, heavy, seaworthy)

The Cretans of four thousand years ago were ___more modern___ than people living in the United States just two hundred years ago! (modern)

Timber from Phoenician cedar trees was always in great demand around the Mediterranean. But an even more desirable item was Phoenicia's exquisite purple dye. (desirable)

By 800 BC the Phoenician city of Carthage, located on the northern coast of Africa, was the largest and richest city in the western Mediterranean. (large, rich)

The most famous Greek historian and geographer of them all was Herodotus. (famous)

In 330 BC, Massilia was a thriving center of trade. Its greatest rival of all was the Phoenician port of Carthage. (great)

From the Yüeh-chih king, Chang Ch'ien learned of a rich country to the south and another to the southwest. And he learned of an even richer and more powerful country still farther to the west. (rich, powerful)

Exercise 65C: Diagramming Comparative and Superlative Adjectives

Diagram the following sentences.

A single tear revealed Commander Parrish's more tender side.

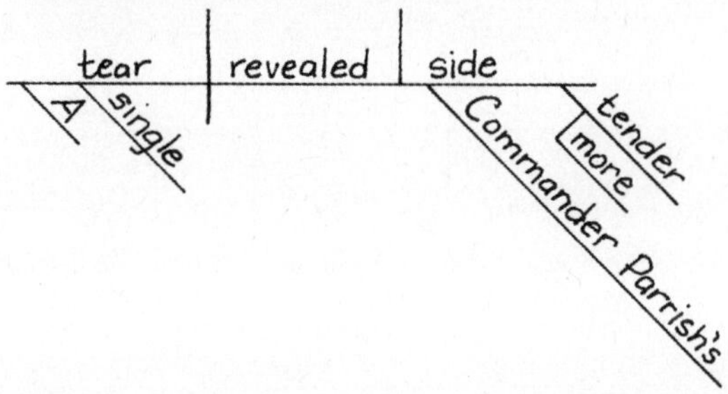

The shortest distance between two points is a straight line.

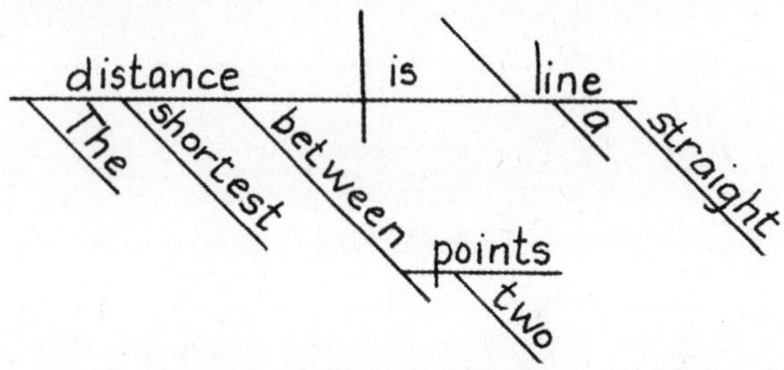

The leading actress appears more confident about tonight's performance.

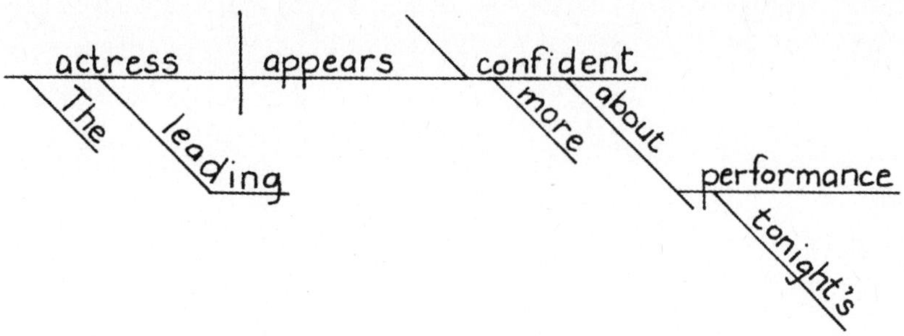

The tallest mountain in Africa is a volcano in Tanzania.

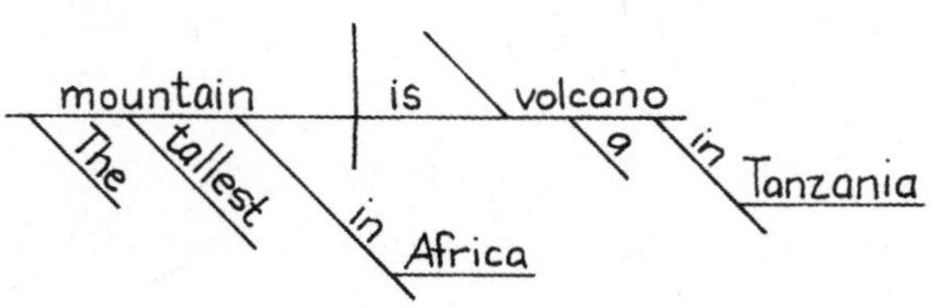

Will voters be more apathetic in the next election?

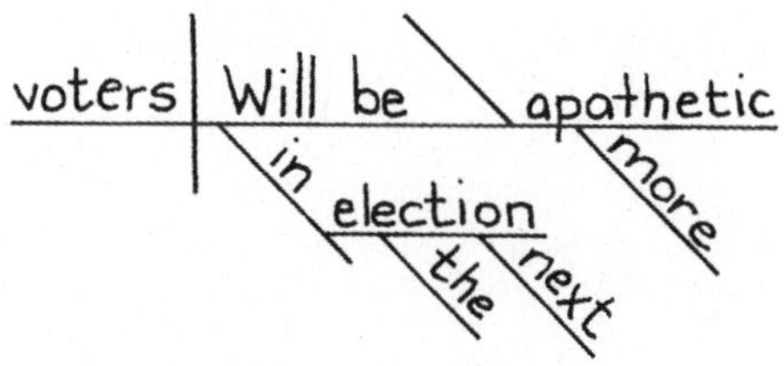

— LESSON 66 —

Adverbs
Comparative and Superlative Adverbs
Coordinating Conjunctions
Subordinating Conjunctions

Exercise 66A: Diagramming Comparatives

Diagram the first two sentences on the frames provided. Diagram the remaining sentences on your own paper.

The light in the hall shines more dimly than the one in the kitchen.

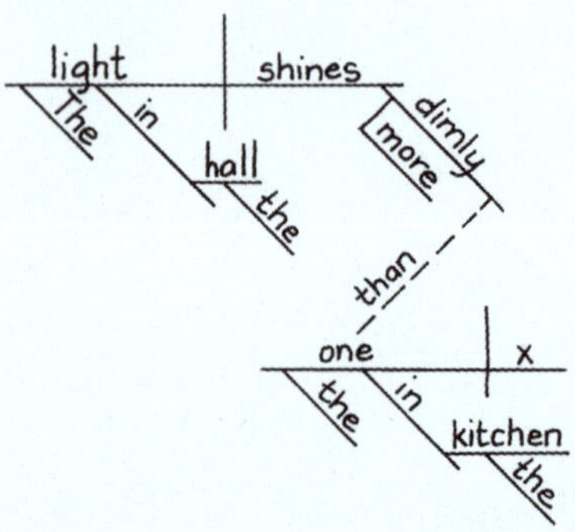

Greta reached the field more swiftly than her brother.

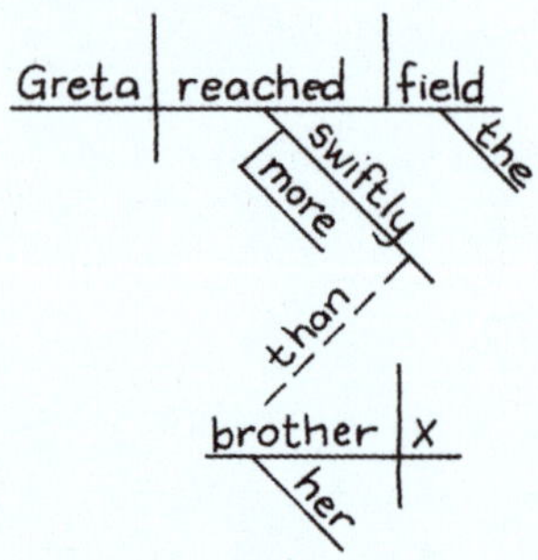

This story is even more bizarre than the last one was.

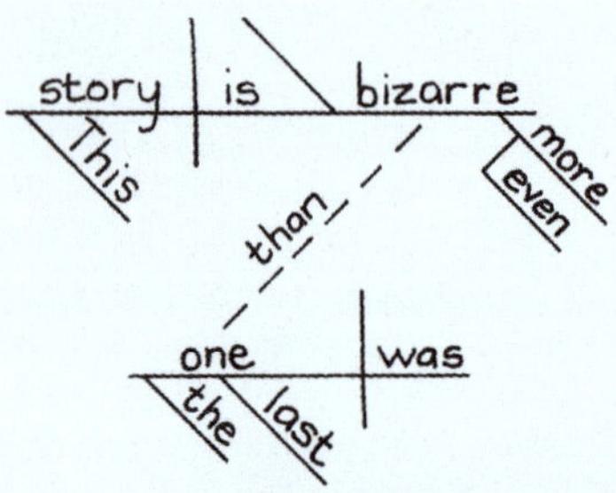

Note to Instructor: The student could choose to finish out the second diagram by adding the space for the repeated predicate adjective and placing an X in that space ("This story is even more bizarre than the last one was bizarre").

Jeffrey's comments during the debate were wittier than Sebastian's.

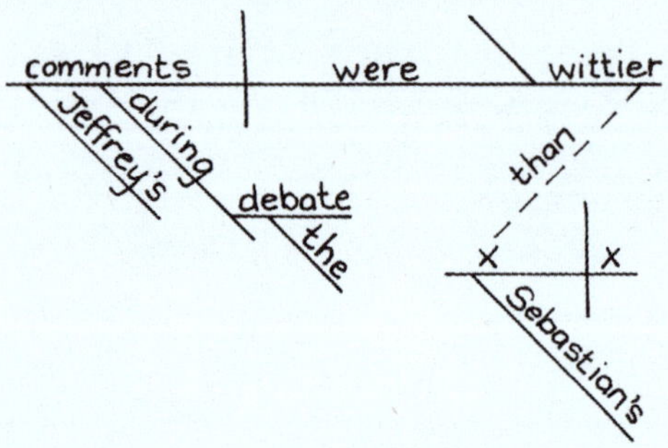

Sebastian has worked more diligently than Jeffrey.

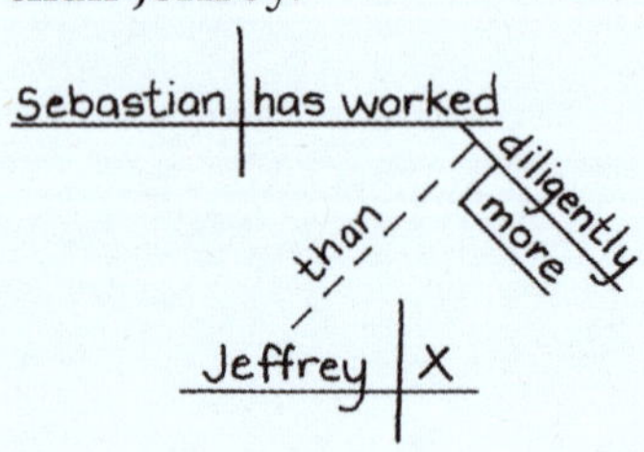

Exercise 66B: Identifying Positive, Comparative, and Superlative Adverbs

In the blanks, identify the degree of each underlined adverb form as *P* for positive, *C* for comparative, or *S* for superlative. These sentences are from Jane Austen's *Pride and Prejudice.*

After a polite request that Elizabeth would lead the way, which the other as politely and more earnestly negatived, she seated herself. C

Mrs. Bennet, who quarreled with no compliments, answered most readily. S

Oh! yes—it would be much better to wait till Jane was well, and by that time most likely Captain Carter would be at Meryton again. S

You will not find him more favorably spoken of by anyone. C

Steady to his purpose, he scarcely spoke ten words to her through the whole of Saturday, and though they were at one time left by themselves for half-an-hour, he adhered most conscientiously to his book, and would not even look at her. P S

They were of a respectable family in the north of England; a circumstance more deeply impressed on their memories than that their brother's fortune and their own had been acquired by trade. C

Mrs. Bennet and her daughters apologized most civilly for Lydia's interruption, and promised that it should not occur again, if he would resume his book. S

And when we got to the George, I do think we behaved very handsomely, for we treated the other three with the nicest cold luncheon in the world. P

Your conjecture is totally wrong, I assure you. My mind was more agreeably engaged. P,C

More than once did Elizabeth, in her ramble within the park, unexpectedly meet Mr. Darcy. P

Exercise 66C: Forming Comparative and Superlative Adverbs

Fill in the blank with the correct form of the adverb in parentheses.

Who will finish the race the fastest? (fast)

My sister usually wakes up earlier than I do. (early)

All three of my aunts have shipped me birthday gifts; I don't know which will arrive the soonest. (soon)

Morgan presented her project later than Kira. (late)

Excuse me, but I believe I have been waiting in this line longer than you have. (long)

The person who sits closest to me in class is James. (close)

Mr. Gilbert stands taller than anyone else I know! (tall)

— LESSON 67 —

Irregular Comparative and Superlative Adjectives and Adverbs

Exercise 67A: Best and Worst Jobs

Put the following jobs in the columns according to your opinion. (There are no correct answers—it all depends on you.)

Note to Instructor: The student may put these jobs on the list in any order.

ice cream taster
children's book illustrator
garbage collector
grass cutter
fashion designer
professional sky diver

good: ________________ **bad:** ________________
better: ________________ **worse:** ________________
best: ________________ **worst:** ________________

Exercise 67B: Using Comparative and Superlative Adverbs Correctly

Choose the correct form in parentheses. Cross out the incorrect form.

The disc golf tournament will raise money for a local charity; people are donating (~~more generous~~/more generously) this year than they did last year.

Monique can toss a flying disc (farther/~~more far~~) than Landon.

Landon's throws are (~~more accurately~~/more accurate) than Monique's, because he focuses (more deliberately/~~more deliberate~~) on his target.

Judith believes Landon will do (better/~~more well~~) than Monique overall; she watches the tournament (most enthusiastically/~~most enthusiastic~~).

Augustin looks (~~more naturally~~/more natural) tossing the disc than standing still.

When the players take a break for a snack, Augustin eats (more hungrily/~~hungrier~~) than anyone else.

Exercise 67C: Using Correct Comparative Forms of Modifiers

Choose the correct form in parentheses. Cross out the incorrect form.

The first seven sentences are from *A Christmas Carol* and the last four from *Oliver Twist*, both by Charles Dickens.

"You couldn't have met in a (better/~~best~~) place," said old Joe.

He was obliged to sit close to the fire, and brood over it, before he could extract the (~~less~~/least) sensation of warmth from such a handful of fuel.

But soon the steeples called good people all to church and chapel, and away they came flocking through the streets in their (best/~~most good~~) clothes.

I fear you (more/~~the most~~) than any specter I have seen.

No eye at all is (better/~~best~~) than an evil eye, dark master!

If he could have helped it, he and his child would have been (farther/~~more far~~) apart, perhaps, than they were.

That shirt is the (~~better~~/best) he had, and a fine one too.

The (~~worse~~/worst) of these women is, that a very little thing serves to call up some long-forgotten feeling; and the (~~better~~/best) of them is, that it never lasts.

Don't be (harder/~~more hard~~) upon the poor fellows than is indispensably necessary.

The dog advanced, retreated, paused an instant, turned, and scoured away at his (~~most hard~~/hardest) speed.

I have (~~more little~~/less) hesitation in dealing with two people, when I find that there's only one will between them.

Exercise 67D: Using Correct Adverbs and Adjectives

Choose the correct word in parentheses. Cross out the incorrect word.

Rachel mended this shirt very (~~good~~/well). I can't even tell where the hole was!

The new attorney argued his case (~~bad~~/badly); he isn't very (good/~~well~~) at cross-examination.

I can juggle pretty (~~good~~/well). I always feel (good/~~well~~) about making an audience smile.

Your statements prove my point (~~good~~/well); your words support my argument.

The character proved (good/~~well~~) in the end; he had supported the hero secretly all along.

The painting looks (bad/~~badly~~) above the sofa.

My nose healed (~~bad~~/badly) and is still a little crooked.

— LESSON 68 —

Coordinating and Subordinating Conjunctions
Correlative Conjunctions

Exercise 68A: Coordinating and Subordinating Correlative Conjunctions

In each of the following sentences, circle the correlative conjunctions. Underline the words or groups of words that the conjunctions connect. In the blank, write *C* for coordinating or *S* for subordinating.

These sentences are from T*he Call of the Wild*, *White Fang*, and *The Cruise of the Snark*, all by Jack London.

(Not only) did they not know how to work dogs, (but) they did not know how to work themselves.	C
For two days and nights he (neither) ate (nor) drank.	C
(Although) not wishing to offend, (yet) it would be madness to take to the bay in such a craft.	S
(Both) Dave (and) Sol-leks flew at him and administered a sound trouncing.	C
(Not only) did he not pick fights, (but) he avoided them whenever possible.	C
Here was (neither) peace, (nor) rest, (nor) a moment's safety.	C

Though following her, still he was dubious. S

If they could fast prodigiously, then they could feed prodigiously. C

Between him and all domestic animals there must be no hostilities. If not amity, then neutrality must obtain. C

He crawled to his feet, badly disheveled, hurt both in body and in spirit. C

Though bearing the marks of her teeth, yet they never replied in kind, never defended themselves against her. S

Exercise 68B: Subject-Verb Agreement

Cross out the incorrect word or words in each set of parentheses.

Neither the Big Dipper nor the Little Dipper (is a true constellation/~~are true constellations~~).

Not only the dippers but also Orion's Belt (is an asterism/~~are asterisms~~).

Not only Saturn but all the gas giants (~~has~~/have) rings.

Both Mercury and Venus (~~revolves~~/revolve) around the sun more quickly than Earth does.

Either mythology or Shakespeare's work (provides/~~provide~~) names for most moons in our solar system.

When NASA discovered bright spots on the minor planet Ceres early in 2015, a spokesperson said that either ice or salt (is/~~are~~) probably the cause.

Neither Pluto nor the other objects in the Kuiper belt (~~satisfies~~/satisfy) the International Astronomical Union's definition of a planet.

Both asteroids and comets (~~contains~~/contain) rocky materials, but their other components are different.

Exercise 68C: Diagramming

On your own paper, diagram every word of the following sentences. These sentences are adapted from *The Arabian Nights*, edited by Kate Douglas Wiggin and Nora A. Smith.

Aladdin not only commanded them to desist from their work, but ordered them to return all their jewels to the sultan.

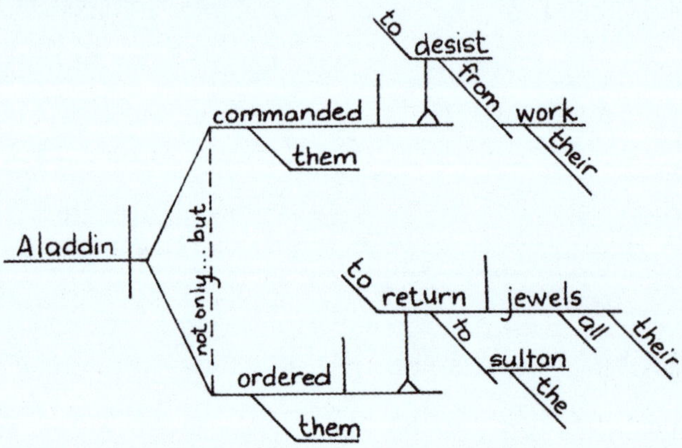

The sultan will either laugh at me or be in a great rage.

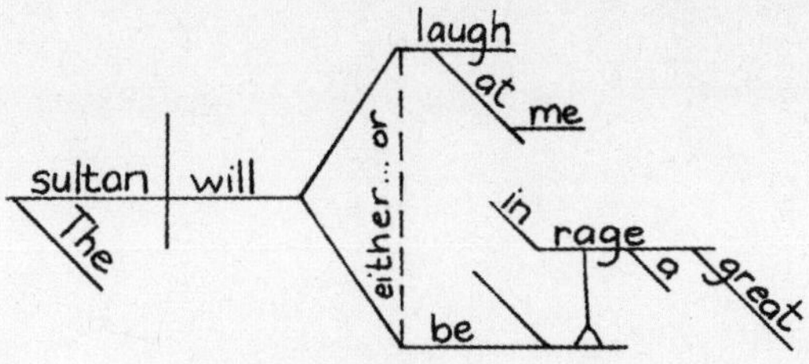

Note to Instructor: You may need to explain to the student that since the helping verb *will* goes with both *laugh* and *be* (The sultan *will* either laugh at me or *will* be in a great rage), it is placed after the subject/predicate dividing line and before the compound verb, as in the diagram above. Alternately, it can be placed on the same line as *laugh* and an *x* can be placed right before *be* to indicate that *will* is understood to precede the second verb as well.

Neither your discourse nor your remonstrances shall change my mind.

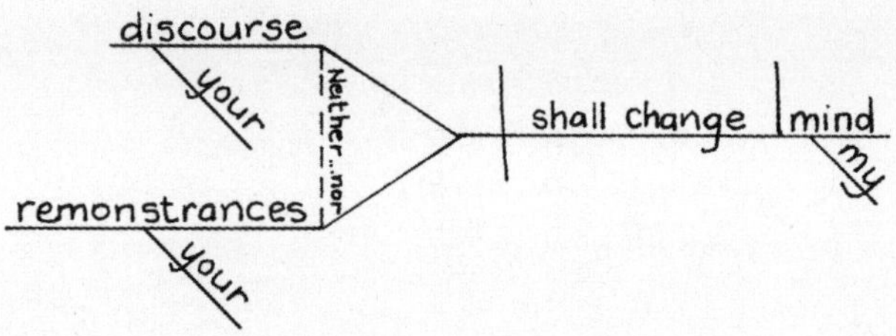

Both mother and son sat down and ate with relish.

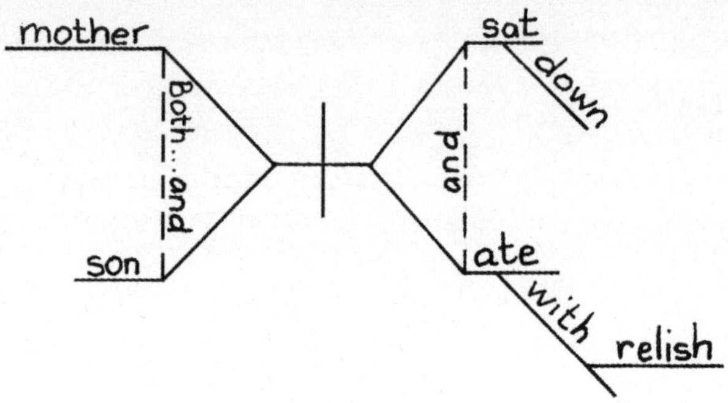

WEEK 18

Clauses

— LESSON 69 —

Phrases

Sentences

Introduction to Clauses

In the phrases and clauses below, the subjects are underlined once and the verbs twice for your reference.

Behind the dusty wardrobe.	***phrase***	*no subject or verb*
Lucy opened the door.	***clause***	*subject and verb*
Leaping and bounding.	***phrase***	*two verbs, no subject*
They did not believe her.	***clause***	*subject and verb*
He tasted the delicious candy.	***clause***	*subject and verb*
Because he wanted more.	***clause***	*subject and verb*

(Although) Jamie didn't mean to eat the entire cake.	D
(Whether) they won or lost.	D
He picked up the pieces.	I
That milk is from Uncle Louie's cow.	I
(Since) she was already covered in mud.	D

Exercise 69A: Distinguishing Between Phrases and Clauses

Identify the following groups of words as *phrases* or *clauses*. The clauses may be independent or dependent, but you only need to identify them as *clauses*. In each clause, underline the subject once and the verb twice.

Past the juggling clown	phrase
Orbiting the planet	phrase
When I was riding my bicycle	clause
Since the earliest days	phrase
Because of the late start	phrase
Although the assembly started late	clause
Eating her curds and whey	phrase
Since we began	clause
Wrestling with a dinosaur	phrase

I ate too many pickles	clause
Aboard the pirate ship	phrase
Danced and twirled	phrase

Exercise 69B: Distinguishing Between Independent and Dependent Clauses

Identify the following clauses as independent (*IND*) or dependent (*DEP*).

These clauses are taken from Edgar Allan Poe's "The Tell-Tale Heart." Some have been slightly adapted.

The disease had sharpened my senses	IND
Whenever the eye fell upon me	DEP
I looked in upon him	IND
While he slept	DEP
I kept quite still	IND
When I had waited a long time	DEP
It was the beating of the old man's heart	IND
The sound would be heard by a neighbor	IND
When I describe my precautions	DEP
As the bell sounded the hour	DEP
While I answered cheerily	DEP
The noise steadily increased	IND

Exercise 69C: Identifying Dependent Clauses in Complete Sentences

Circle the dependent clause in each sentence below. Within each dependent clause you circle, underline the subject once and the verb twice.

I will wait here (until you are ready).

(While the competitors dance), the judges will observe carefully.

(Before it changes direction), the train will go to the East Hill station.

The moon appears larger (when it is near the horizon).

My clock is wrong (because its battery died).

(As you watched the show), did you notice the leading actor's new haircut?

— LESSON 70 —

Adjective Clauses
Relative Pronouns

Intro 70: Introduction to Adjective Clauses

Match the dependent clause on the right with the correct independent clause on the left. The first one has been done for you.

1. George Orwell, B, worked as a teacher and as a bookstore assistant.
2. Elvis Presley, D, won three Grammy Awards.
3. Augusta, Georgia, is known for hosting the Masters golf tournament, E.
4. The honey badger is a carnivorous animal A.
5. Thomas Edison, C, was almost completely deaf.

A. that has the ability to use tools
B. who wrote *Animal Farm* and *1984*
C. whom people nicknamed "The Wizard of Menlo Park"
D. whose first single was "Heartbreak Hotel"
E. which takes place during the first full week of April each year

Exercise 70A: Identifying Adjective Clauses and Relative Pronouns

Underline the adjective clauses in the following sentences, and circle the relative pronouns. Draw an arrow from each relative pronoun to its antecedent.

John Dalton is the scientist whom we credit with the atomic theory of matter.

Dalton, who lived from 1766 to 1844, did not say anything about the internal structure of atoms.

"Atom" comes from a Greek word that means "uncuttable."

But atoms, which no one has ever seen, are actually made of even smaller particles.

Electrons, neutrons, and protons are the particles that comprise atoms.

Neutrons and protons, which are much heavier than electrons, are found in an atom's nucleus, or center.

Hydrogen, whose nucleus does not have any neutrons, is the element with the smallest atoms.

Exercise 70B: Choosing the Correct Relative Pronoun

In each sentence, cross out the incorrect relative pronoun. Above the correct pronoun, write *S* for subject, *OP* for object of the preposition, or *DO* for direct object to show how the relative pronoun is used within the dependent clause.

These sentences are adapted from the fairy tale "The Golden Goose," by the Brothers Grimm.

A man (who/~~whom~~) lived in the village had three sons. [S]

He had two sons (who/~~whom~~) thought themselves wise. [S]

His youngest son, (~~who~~/whom) they called Simpleton, was ridiculed by the others. [DO]

When the eldest and middle brothers, (who [S]/~~whom~~) went into the forest to cut wood, were asked to share their food and drink with an old man, they refused.

The youngest brother, to (~~who~~/whom [OP]) the other brothers had given more meager food and drink, was willing to share with the old man.

In exchange for this kindness, the old man, (who [S]/~~whom~~) knew of a goose with feathers of gold, told Simpleton where to find it.

Three sisters decided to take feathers from the goose, to (~~who~~/which [OP]) they became stuck.

The King of that kingdom had a daughter (who [S]/~~whom~~) never laughed.

The King declared that his daughter should marry the man (who [S]/~~whom~~) made her laugh.

When the princess saw Simpleton, the goose, and the people (who [S]/~~whom~~) were stuck behind them, she burst out laughing.

Simpleton was able to marry the princess because of the old man in the forest, to (~~who~~/whom [OP]) he had shown kindness.

Exercise 70C: Diagramming Adjective Clauses

On your own paper, diagram every word of the following sentences.

The birthday cake that Sarah made for Fritz was absolutely delicious!

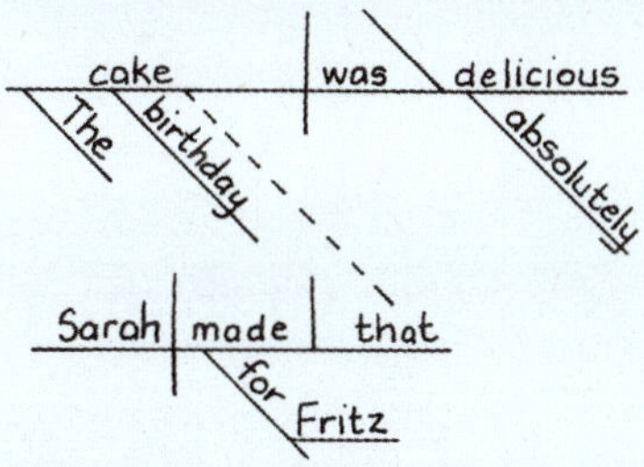

Alice, whose opinions we value, was sick and could not attend the meeting.

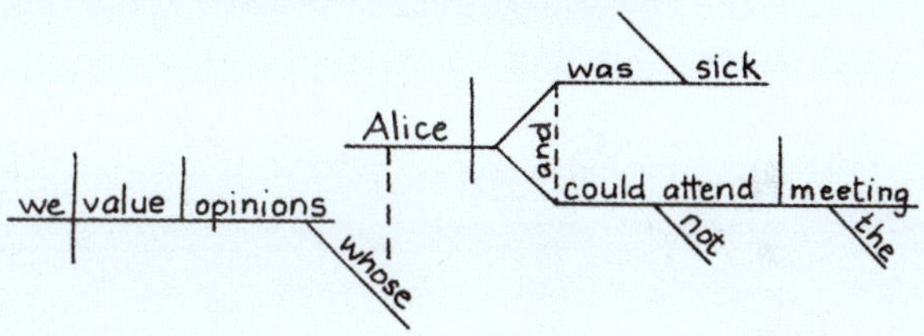

The ball bounced toward Jose, who was not paying attention.

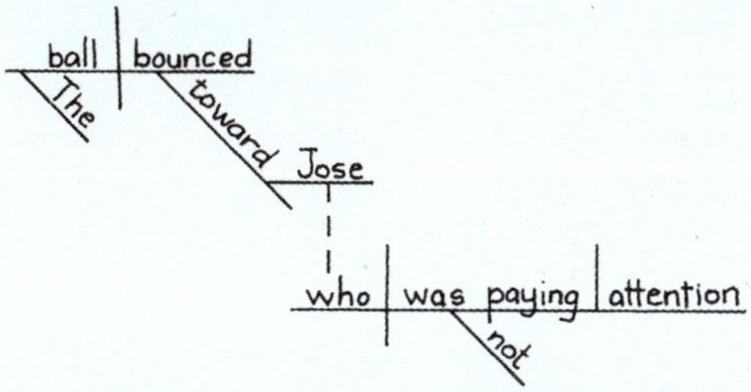

My new shirt, which I bought yesterday, already has a hole in the sleeve.

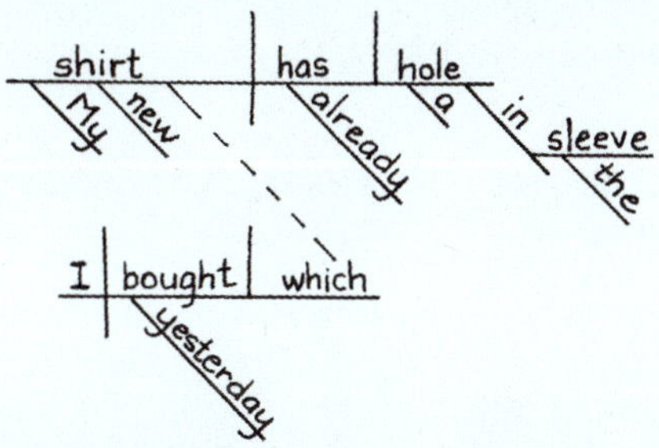

We will soon visit our cousin, who lives in Maryland.

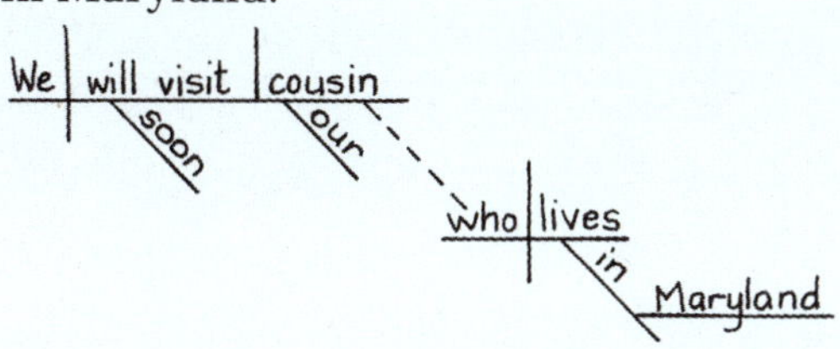

The young boy wanted the toy that made loud noises.

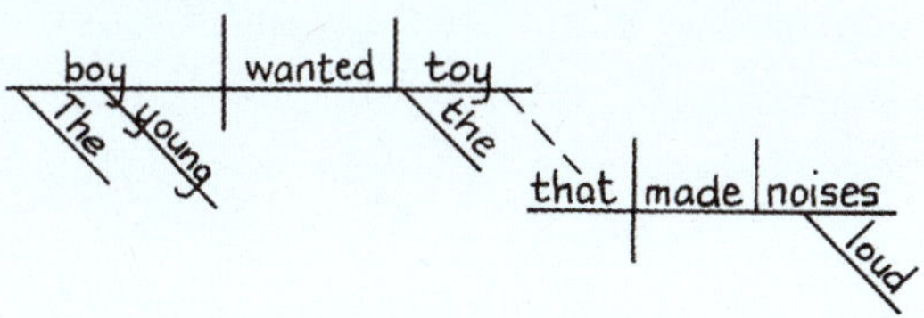

— LESSON 71 —

Adjective Clauses
Relative Adverbs
Adjective Clauses with Understood Relatives

Exercise 71A: Relative Adverbs and Pronouns

In the following sentences, underline each adjective clause. Circle each relative word and label it as *RP* for relative pronoun or *RA* for relative adverb. Draw an arrow from each relative word back to its antecedent in the independent clause.

Be alert—one sentence has *two* adjective clauses in it!

Christopher Columbus was influenced by a book (that)[RP] was called *The Travels of Sir John Mandeville*.

Mandeville, (who)[RP] told of his travels around the world, was probably not a real person.

The book was written at a time (when)[RA] faraway lands were mysterious to many Europeans.

Many of the places (where)[RA] Mandeville went were real places, but his descriptions were more fantasy than reality.

He mentioned one island (where)[RA] the people had human bodies but dog heads.

He also told of trees (whose)[RP] fruit contains little beasts (that)[RP] are like lambs.

The fantastic stories are interwoven with real facts from travelers (who)[RP] actually visited different places.

Scholars have different ideas about the actual author or authors (who)[RP] wrote Mandeville's *Travels*.

One possible reason (why)[RA] the name "Mandeville" was used is an earlier story about an imaginary heroic traveler named Mandevie.

Exercise 71B: Missing Relative Words

Draw a caret in front of each adjective clause and insert the missing relative pronoun. (For the purposes of this exercise, *which* and *that* may be used interchangeably.)

The drink of water ^[that/which] I had after the race was refreshing.

Jonathan introduced me to the librarian ^[whom] you had mentioned.

The sunrise ^[that/which] we saw this morning was breathtaking.

The screen on the computer ^[that/which] we just bought is smaller than the screen on our older computer.

Please put the bananas ^[that/which] you got at the market on the counter.

The little orange kitten loves the toy ^[that/which] Aiko selected.

The piano composition ^[that / which] Bria played was written by the composer ^[whom] you met at the party.

Beside the volcano ^[that / which] Annika made is my project.

Exercise 71C: Diagramming

On your own paper, diagram the following sentences from your first two exercises.

Christopher Columbus was influenced by a book that was called *The Travels of Sir John Mandeville.*

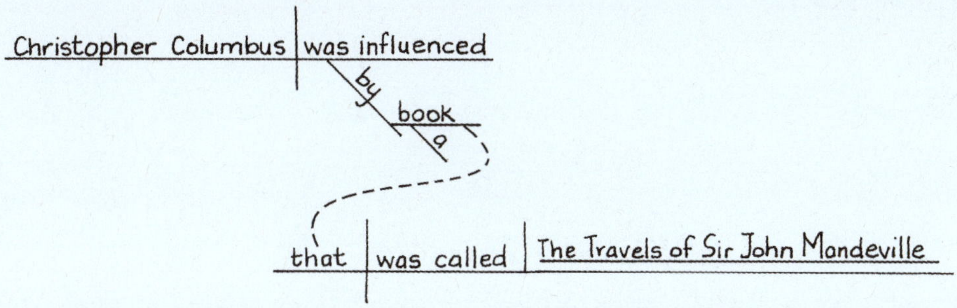

The book was written at a time when faraway lands were mysterious to many Europeans.

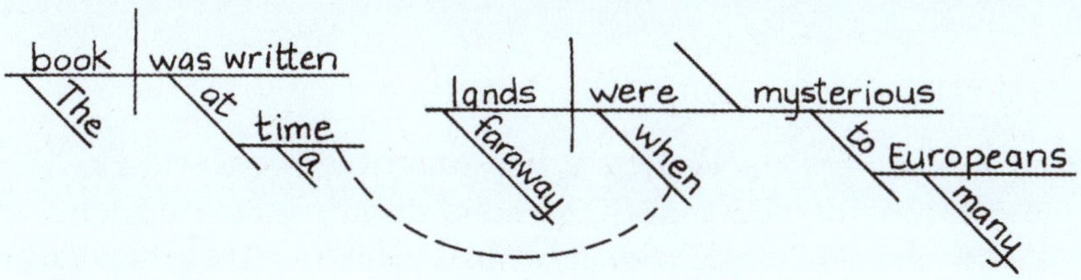

The fantastic stories are interwoven with real facts from travelers who actually visited different places.

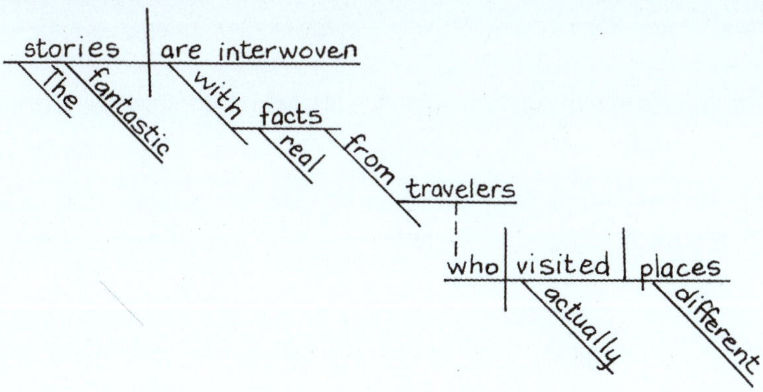

He mentioned one island where the people had human bodies but dog heads.

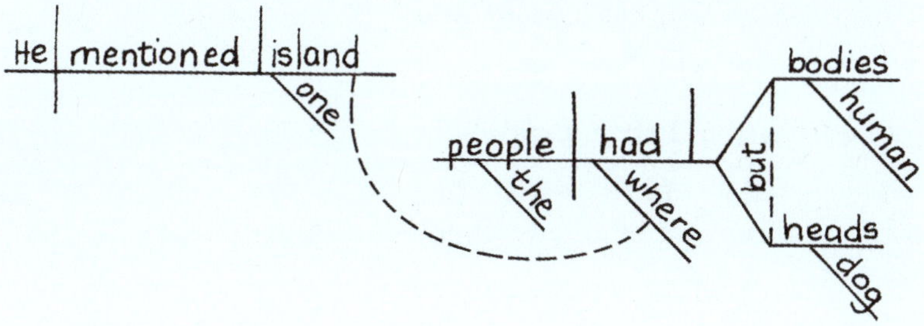

Please put the bananas you got at the market on the counter.

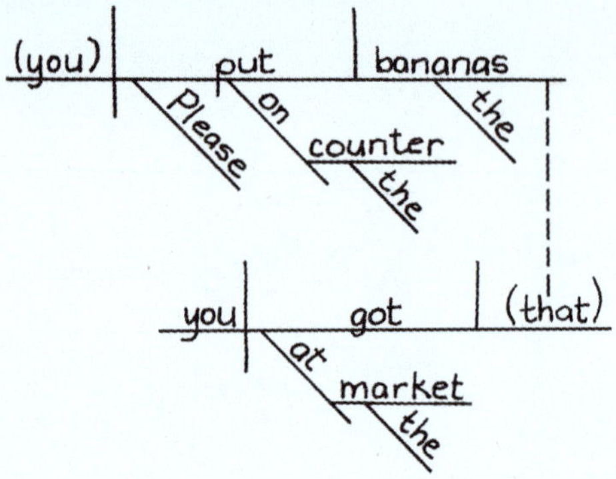

Beside the volcano Annika made is my project.

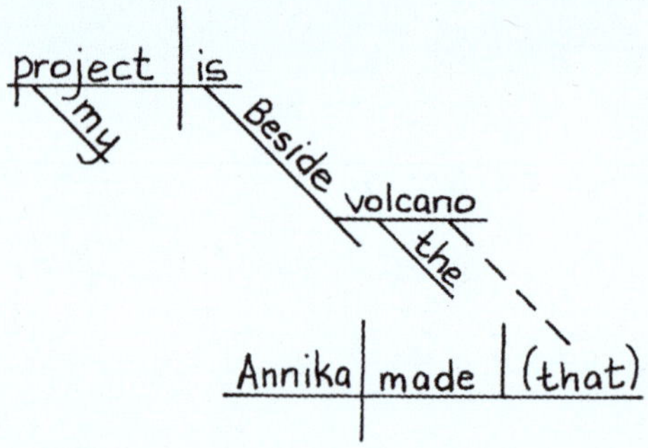

— LESSON 72 —

Adverb Clauses

Exercise 72A: Adverb Clauses

In the following sentences, underline each adverb clause. Circle the subordinating word(s) at the beginning of each clause and label it *ADV* for adverb or *SC* for subordinating conjunction. Draw an arrow from the subordinating word back to the verb, adverb, or adjective that the clause modifies.

These sentences are taken from Sir Arthur Conan Doyle's *The Hound of the Baskervilles*. Some have been adapted or condensed.

If we take this as a working hypothesis we have a fresh basis from which to start our construction of this unknown visitor.

He could not have been on the staff of the hospital, since only a man well-established in a London practice could hold such a position.

I laughed incredulously as Sherlock Holmes leaned back in his settee and blew little wavering rings of smoke up to the ceiling.

Note to Instructor: *As* can act as either an adverb or a subordinating conjunction. Here, it is adverbial because it is modifying *laughed* and answering the question *when*.

I said, if I remember right, amiable, unambitious, and absent-minded.

The appearance of our visitor was a surprise to me, since I had expected a typical country practitioner.

SC

A cast of your skull, sir, until the original is available, would be an ornament to any anthropological museum.

> **Note to Instructor:** *Until* is never an adverb, although the entire clause is adverbial and answers the question *when*.

SC

Because you are a practical man of affairs, you stand alone.

SC

But the young maiden, being discreet and of good repute, would ever avoid him, because she feared his evil name.

ADV SC

And while the revellers stood aghast at the fury of the man, one more wicked than the rest cried out for the hounds.

ADV

The man cried out, whence Hugo ran from the house.

Exercise 72B: Descriptive Clauses

Complete a dependent clause in each sentence using the subordinating word in bold print. After each sentence, circle *ADJC* or *ADVC* to show whether the clause is acting as an adjective or as an adverb.

> **Note to Instructor:** Sentence completions may vary; sample answers are provided below. Be sure that each of the student's answers includes a subject and a predicate to make a clause. Also, pay particular attention to the sentences using *who* and *whom*, making sure the student is using *who* as a subject and *whom* as either a direct object or the object of a preposition.

While I ran laps around the gym, Javier did thirty push-ups. ADJC or (ADVC)

Anna, **who** witnessed the cheating, encouraged her friends to tell the truth. (ADJC) or ADVC

For my birthday, I received a gift **that** I had wanted. (ADJC) or ADVC

You will be late **if** you do not hurry. ADJC or (ADVC)

The bookshelves, **which** had been built with cheap materials, looked somewhat unsteady. (ADJC) or ADVC

Ari began hesitantly **as though** he could not see the field clearly. ADJC or (ADVC)

We will eat dinner **whenever** your brother arrives at home. ADJC or (ADVC)

Ginevra, **whom** I saw outside, rushed into the room at the start of the meeting. (ADJC) or ADVC

Exercise 72C: Diagramming

On your own paper, diagram every word of the following sentences. These are adapted from Sir Arthur Conan Doyle's *The Hound of the Baskervilles.*

Down this walk is a gate which leads to the moor.

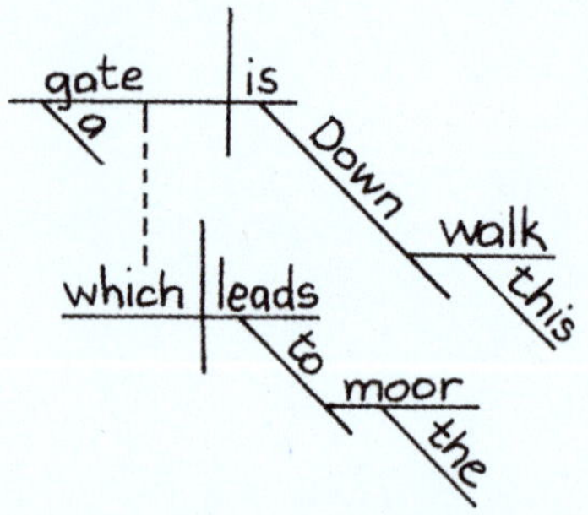

Since no practical good could result from it, I did not tell all that I knew.

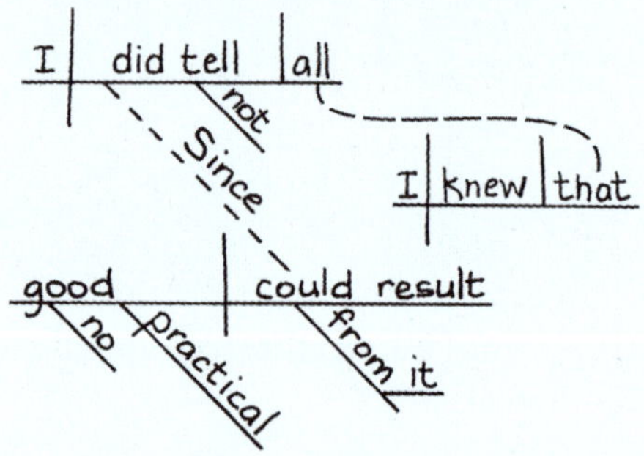

I went to the spot where the animal had been.

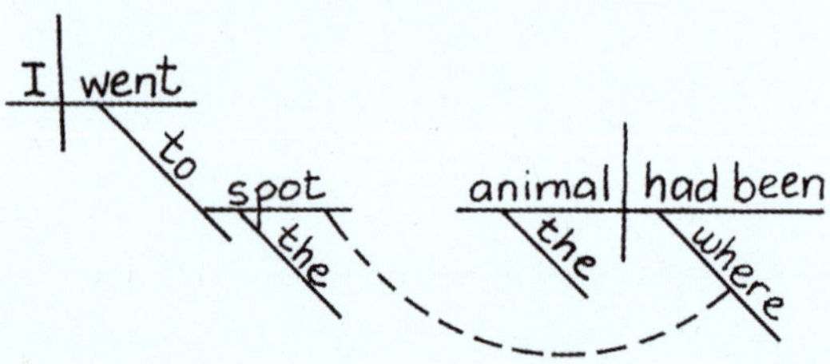

After the tragedy occurred, I heard about several incidents which seem unusual.

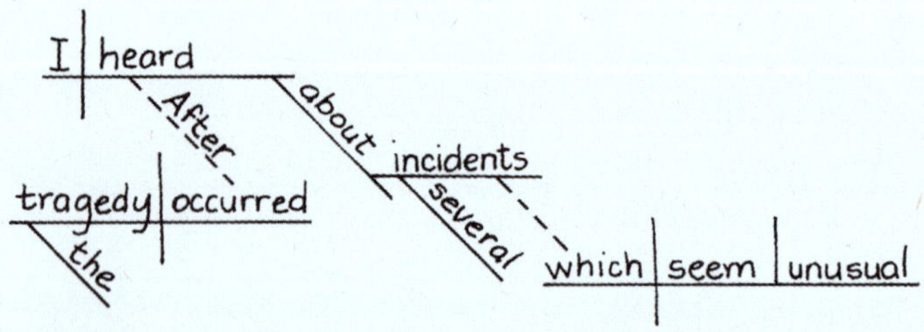

Although he would walk in his own grounds, nothing would induce him to go out upon the moor at night.

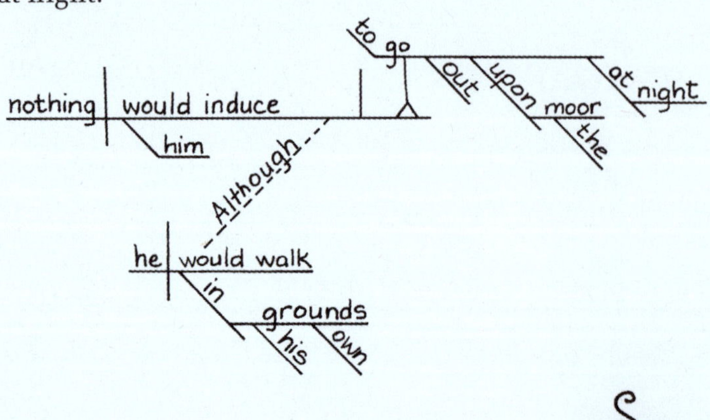

— REVIEW 6 —

Weeks 16-18

Topics
Personal Pronouns: Subject, Object, Possessive, Reflexive
Verb Voice (Active and Passive)
Verb Tense
Adjectives
Gerunds and Participles
Phrases
Clauses (Independent and Dependent)

Review 6A: Pronouns

In the following passage, circle each pronoun. Label each as *S* (subject form of pronoun), *O* (object form), *P* (possessive form), *R* (reflexive), *I* (indefinite), *D* (demonstrative), or *RP* (relative pronoun).

This passage is from Carol Ryrie Brink's *Caddie Woodlawn.*

Eyes round with wonder and anticipation, the young Woodlawns did as they [S] were told. To think of Father ever being small enough to wear those breeches and clogs, and dancing in them [O], too, in faraway England. How strange it [S] was! They [S] had heard so much [I] of Boston, but nobody [I] spoke of England where the strange little boy, who [RP] had grown to be Father, had danced in red breeches and clogs. Caddie thought of what Father had said about England on the night when the circuit rider had been with them [O]. How often she [S] had wondered about that [D] since then!

"You [S] have grown up in a free country, children," began Mr. Woodlawn. "I [S] want you [O] to think of yourselves [R] as young Americans, and I [S] want you [O] to be proud of that [D]. It [S] is difficult to tell you [O] about England, because there all men are not free to pursue their [P] own lives in their [P] own ways. Some men live like princes, while other men must beg for the very crusts that [RP] keep them [O] alive."

"And your [P] father's father was one [I] of those [D] who [RP] live like princes, children," cried Mrs. Woodlawn proudly.

Review 6B: Using Comparative and Superlative Modifiers Correctly

Choose the correct form in parentheses and cross out the incorrect form. These sentences are from *Call It Courage*, by Armstrong Sperry.

Into the (nearest/~~most near~~) canoe he flung half a dozen green drinking nuts, and his fish spear.

Mafatu found the cool liquid from the drinking nut (~~refreshinger~~/more refreshing) than spring water, cool on the (hottest/~~most hot~~) days, and as sustaining as food.

The island was high and peaked, its valleys blue-shadowed against the (paler/~~more pale~~) tone of the sky.

When he had bound on the leafy bandage with a twist of vine, it seemed that already his leg felt (better/~~more good~~).

He searched for a (smaller/~~more small~~) piece of the same wood, then propped the (larger/~~more large~~) piece against a rock.

It might be even (deeper/~~more deep~~) than he thought, for the clarity of the water confused all scale of distance.

There in submarine gloom a boy fought for his life with the (~~dreadedest~~/most dreaded) monster of the deep.

The measured booming grew (louder/~~more loud~~) with every inch that he advanced.

The warriors were a sight to quake the (stoutest/~~most stout~~) heart.

Review 6C: Verbs

Underline the main verb in each sentence. In the space above it, write the tense (*SIMP PAST, PRES, FUT*; *PROG PAST, PRES, FUT*; *PERF PAST, PRES, FUT*) and voice (*ACT* for active or *PASS* for passive) of the verb. If the verb is active, also note whether it is transitive (*TR*) or intransitive (*INTR*). The first is done for you.

These sentences are taken from *Save Our Forests*, by Ron Hirschi.

SIMP PRES, ACT, INTR
As winter approaches, grizzly bears <u>search</u> for a place to sleep through the coldest month.

PERF PRES, ACT, TR
Kids <u>have</u> already <u>made</u> a difference in helping wolves by adopting them as special animals for their school.

SIMP FUT, ACT, TR
Tangles of berry vines and a large variety of trees and shrubs <u>will make</u> a healthier and more meaningful forest.

SIMP PAST, PASS
A disease called chestnut blight <u>was introduced</u> into our country from Asia in about 1900.

PROG PRES, ACT, INTR
The disappearance of forests <u>is happening</u> right now in Oregon, California, Washington, Idaho, Montana, and Alaska.

PERF PRES, ACT, TR
No single animal in recent years has drawn our attention to the need for forest protection more than the northern spotted owl.

SIMP PAST, ACT, INTR
Trees grew on valley sides and on steep mountain slopes.

SIMP PRES, PASS
Under these regulations, erosion is allowed to continue, essentially unchecked.

SIMP FUT, ACT, TR
The survival of many animals will take lots of work and the help of many more people.

Review 6D: Identifying Dependent Clauses

Underline each dependent clause in the following sentences. Circle the subordinating word. Label each clause as either adjective (*ADJ*) or adverb clause (*ADV*), and draw a line from each subordinating word to the word it modifies.

These sentences are from Laura Baskes Litwin's *Benjamin Banneker: Astronomer and Mathematician.*

ADJ
The land that Benjamin Banneker was going to help map was still a marshy wilderness.

ADJ
For Banneker, who had never visited a large city before, the bustling activity on the wharves of the Alexandria seaport was strange and thrilling.

ADV
When a cow kicked over the pail, Molly Welsh was accused of stealing the milk.

ADV
As soon as the land was legally his, Robert Banneky went to work.

ADJ
Benjamin and his father also filled wheelbarrows with the rich, loamy marsh earth that ran along the river's edge.

ADV
Although the family was never prosperous, they were not hungry or wanting in any way.

ADJ
An ephemeris is an astronomical table that tells the positions of the sun, moon, and planets for every day of the year.

ADJ
There were many people at this time who doubted a black man's ability to figure an ephemeris.

ADV
While he contemplated his next steps, Banneker got word of his selection to accompany Major Ellicott on the survey of the Federal Territory.

ADV
Before he made any commitment he wanted to discuss it with his trusted friend George Ellicott.

ADJ
In one corner of the room was suspended a clock of his own construction, which was a true herald of departing hours.

ADJ
We must think well of that man, who uses his best endeavors to associate with none but virtuous friends.

Review 6E: Gerunds and Past Participles

Underline each gerund (present participle) and past participle in the following sentences. Indicate what part of the sentence each serves as with the labels *ADJ* for adjective, *ADV* for adverb, *S* for subject, *DO* and *IO* for direct and indirect object, and *OP* for object of the preposition. For adverbs and adjectives, draw an arrow back to the word modified.

These sentences are from *Microorganisms: The Unseen World*, by Edward R. Ricciuti.

Specialized structures within the single cell help with many of the vital functions accomplished by organs in multicellular organisms.

Protozoans eliminate their carbon dioxide waste by passing it through the cell membrane.

The volvox is a protozoan that lives in a colony composed of thousands of cells.

Despite their tiny size, microorganisms are much like all other living things on Earth.

The main functions of touch for protozoans seem to be to get food and to avoid becoming the food of something else.

This behavior may be related to feeding.

Getting food, storing it, and then converting it to energy involve chemical processes that keep organisms alive.

Trapped within the amoeba, this water droplet becomes an organelle called a food vacuole.

Lining the inside of a bacterium's cell wall is a flexible cell membrane.

In Holland, a self-taught scientist named Anton van Leeuwenhoek had become fascinated with making lenses for the simple microscopes in use at the time.

Review 6F: Diagramming

On your own paper, diagram every word of the following sentences from *A Treasury of Turkish Folktales for Children*, retold by Barbara K. Walker.

When he arrived, there was his uncle waiting by the path to greet him.

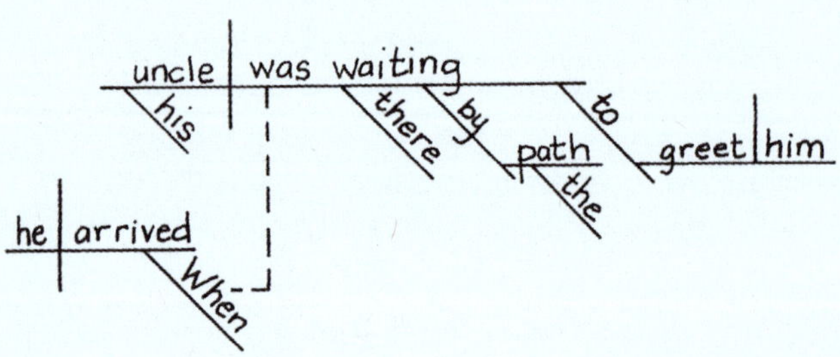

By poking his head way out, he could just see the doorstep.

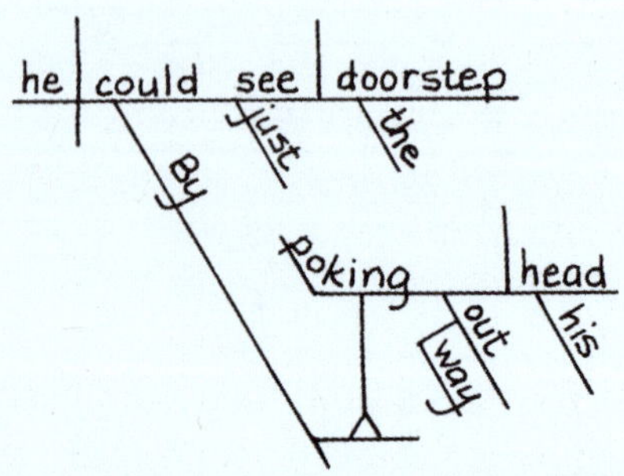

Boldly Hasan began to whistle the tune the village watchman whistled as he came down the street.

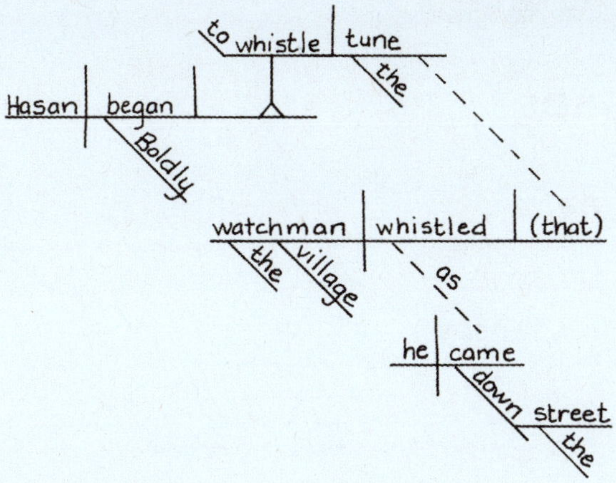

Leaving him in the sorry state in which the rabbit had come upon him, they went on their way.

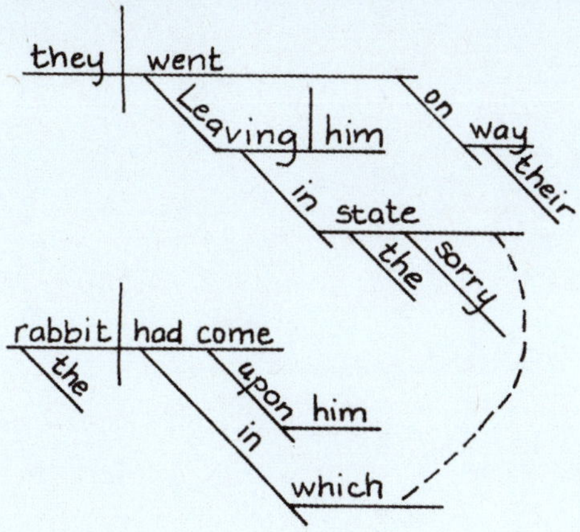

As Keloğlan finished speaking, the princess felt a strange prickling in her scalp.

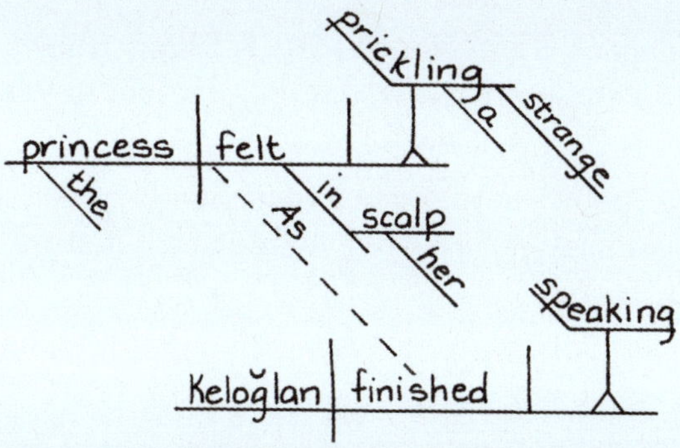

On the next day he encountered several of his students on the street that ran past the public fountain.

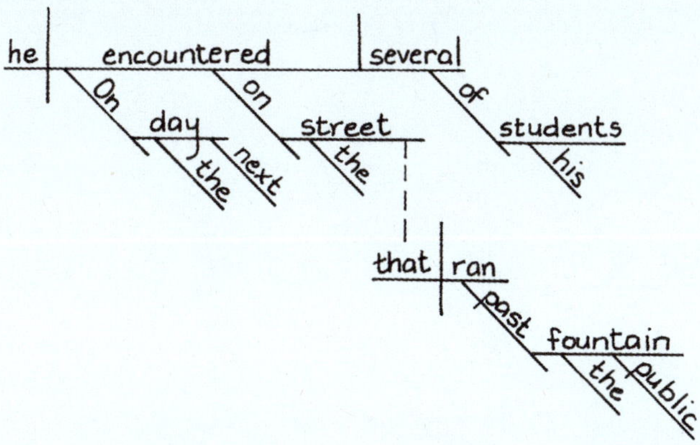

WEEK 19

More Clauses

— LESSON 73 —

Adjective and Adverb Clauses
Introduction to Noun Clauses

Exercise 73A: Identifying Clauses

In the following sentences, circle each dependent clause. Label each as *N* for noun, *ADJ* for adjective, or *ADV* for adverb.

- For noun clauses, indicate the part of the sentence that each noun clause fulfills (*S* for subject, *DO* for direct object, *IO* for indirect object, *PN* for predicate nominative, or *OP* for object of the preposition).
- For adjective and adverb clauses, draw a line from the subordinating word of each adjective and adverb clause back to the word it modifies. If the subordinating word is understood, draw a caret and insert the understood subordinating word in brackets.
- Dependent clauses may contain other dependent clauses! Do your best to find them all.

These sentences are from Laurence Yep's *Dragonwings*.

ADJ
This figure does not even reflect the large number of Tang men (who could not get into the country for the first time.)

N S
(What's here) belongs neither to us nor to the demons.

N OP
I remembered stories about (how the hills were made by burrowing dragons.)

ADV; N DO
I decided not to put my boots on, (because the echoes might tell Father [that] (I was behind him.))

ADV; N DO
(When I finally finished looking around her kitchen,) I realized [that] (I had gone through four more of the cookies.)

N DO
That very evening I found out (that there can be some bad demons too.)

ADV
He unbound his queue (until his hair hung down loose on his back.)

ADJ
That was a sign [that] (the Stove King had returned to his place above our stove.)

At that moment there was a loud explosion (that made us all duck) ADJ

I had my employer, (who knows your landlord) ADJ, call him and find out (what was the matter) N DO.

Exercise 73B: Creating Noun Clauses

For each of the following sentences, write a noun clause that fits into the blank.

If you have trouble coming up with a dependent clause, try starting out with one of the following subordinating words: *that, how, why, what/whatever, who/whoever* (these are always subjects within the dependent clause); *whom/whomever* (these are always objects within the dependent clause); or *where, whether.* (This is not an exhaustive list of the possibilities—just a jumping-off place for you.)

Note to Instructor: Answers will vary; the sentences below are examples of possible clauses.

I always love to see how Mr. Prather's plants are growing.

Whoever opened the secret passage was a huge help to us.

Please remember why you are here.

What you want us to do is exceedingly difficult.

Do you understand how I want the flowers arranged?

Exercise 73C: Diagramming

On your own paper, diagram every word of the following sentences, taken or adapted from Laurence Yep's *Dragonwings.*

I scooped up some of the sand and saw that it was really tiny sapphires that made noises like laughter when I rubbed some of them between my palms.

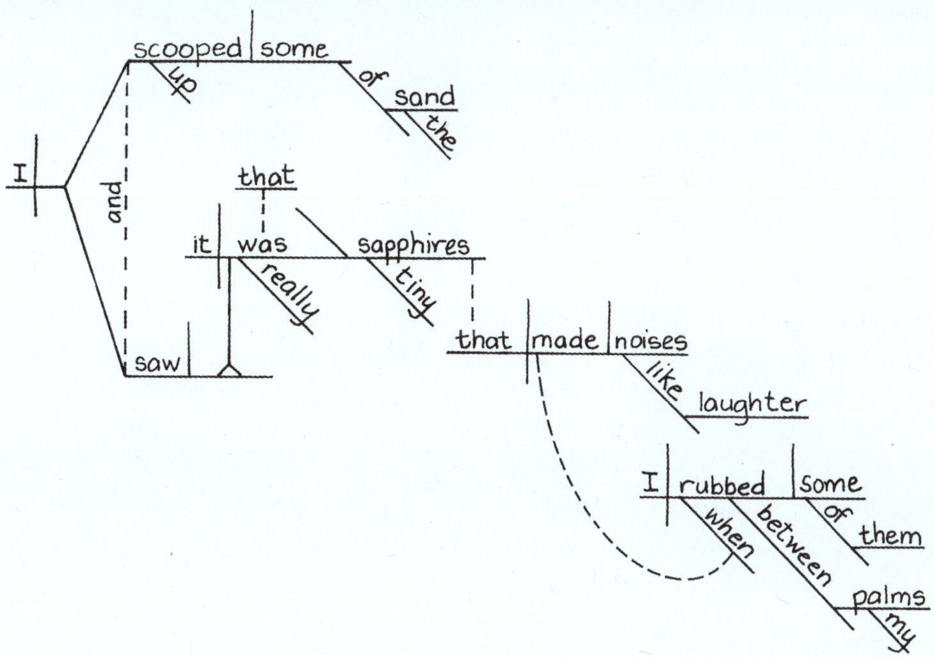

Anyone who could laugh and tell stories and jokes and sing while he was alone among the demons must know what he was doing.

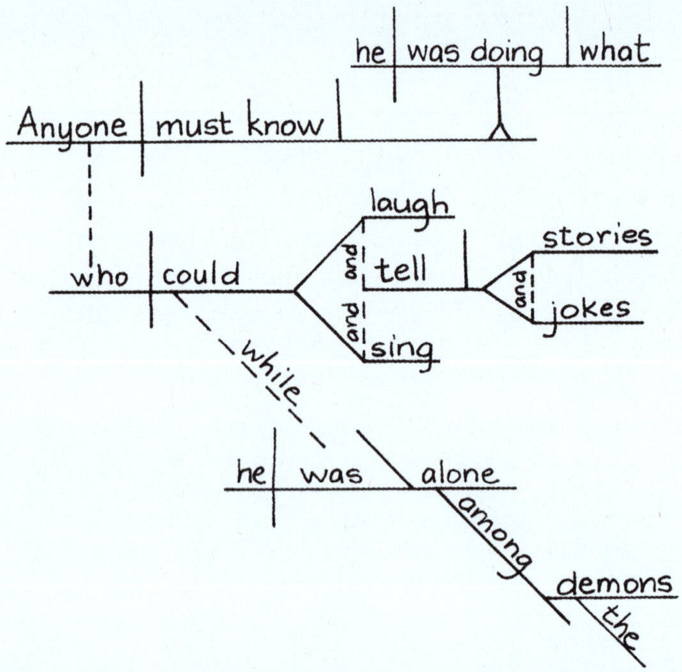

Finally they admitted that I was who I claimed to be.

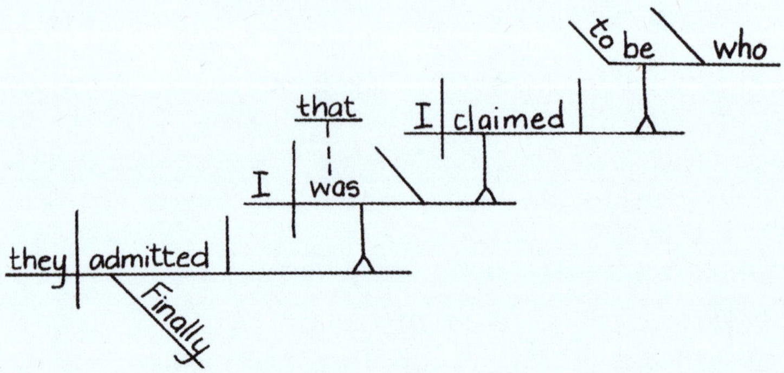

What was best about flying any of the kites was what it did for Mother.

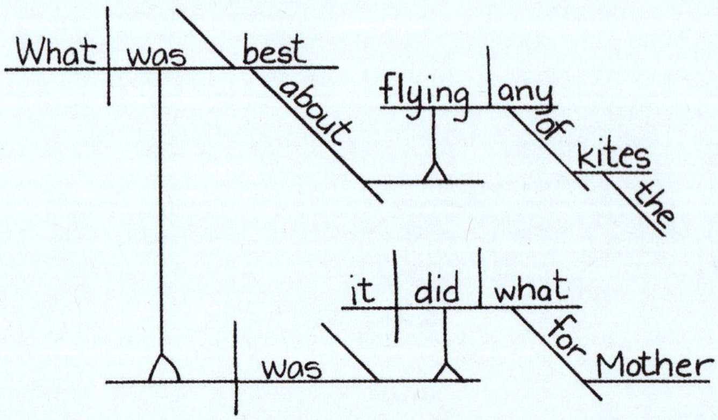

— LESSON 74 —

Clauses Beginning With Prepositions

Exercise 74A: Adjective Clauses Beginning with Prepositions

In the following sentences, circle each adjective clause. Draw a line from the subordinating word back to the word the clause modifies. If the clause begins with a preposition, underline that preposition and label its object with *OP*.

The sentences below are taken or adapted from H. D. F. Kitto's *The Greeks.*

The Dorian Greeks were preceded, by at least two centuries, by Achaean Greeks, about whom (OP) we know something, though not enough.

It is interesting to note one of the inaccuracies of the tradition on which (OP) Homer worked later.

Greek is well stocked with little words whose sole function is to make the structure clear.

Such was one side of Mediterranean trade, not only in this Dark Age, but in every other age too in which (OP) there has been no government strong enough to police the coasts and control the seas.

The imprecision into which (OP) English occasionally deviates and from which (OP) German occasionally emerges is quite foreign to Greek.

Homer does not forget those to whom (OP) another man's glory brings sorrow.

A very large number of these names go back to the period with which (OP) we are now concerned.

Just before the Peloponnesian War there were something like 125,000 slaves in Attica, of whom (OP) something like 65,000 were in domestic employment.

This is the way in which (OP) the earliest work of European literature opens.

Sparta was the only state which had a standing army.

But Philip's successor was not commonplace—he was Alexander the Great, one of the most astonishing men of whom (OP) we know.

From others he took hostages, and deposited them in one of the islands of which (OP) he had control.

It is hard to believe that the dramatists never, even by accident, portrayed the stunted creatures (among whom they actually lived)

OP (above *whom*)

Exercise 74B: Correct Use of Who and Whom

Choose the correct pronoun within the parentheses; cross out the incorrect pronoun.

(Who/~~Whom~~) will deliver the pizza?

(~~Who~~/Whom) will the pizza be delivered to?

It's nice to spend time with those (~~who~~/whom) you love.

Looking carefully at the picture, I zoomed in on the girl for (~~who~~/whom) we'd been searching.

I will give these cookies to the person (who/~~whom~~) wants them badly enough to clean the kitchen!

(Who/~~Whom~~) did you guess would be the winner?

> **Note to Instructor:** The main clause of the sentences is *you did guess*. *Who* is the subject of the noun clause *Who would be the winner*, which is the direct object of *did guess*. The entire clause is an object, but within that clause, *who* is the subject and must be a subject pronoun.

There's the man (~~who~~/whom) I bumped into earlier!

The client for (~~who~~/whom) we provided the samples would like to hire us for the whole project.

(~~Who~~/Whom) did you peel the apple for?

The referee (who/~~whom~~) blew the whistle is very upset.

Do you know (~~who~~/whom) they added to the list in the past week?

This letter is from my aunt, to (~~who~~/whom) we'll pay a visit next month.

There was only one child in the whole class (who/~~whom~~) remembered her pencil today.

Though their culture was different than mine, I became very fond of the people among (~~who~~/whom) I lived for three years.

Exercise 74C: Formal and Informal Diction

On your own paper, rewrite the following informal sentences in formal English, placing the preposition before its object. The first has been done for you.

Place a star by any sentence that sounds better in informal English.

> **Note to Instructor:** None of the informal sentences are "incorrect," and "sounds better" is a judgment call. Accept any answers from the student; the exercise is intended to begin to teach the student to read sentences out loud and listen to them.

Whom should I look for?
For whom should I look?

The rule everyone complained about has been changed.
The rule about which everyone complained has been changed.

Your sister is the one you should apologize to.
Your sister is the one to whom you should apologize.

The city he's returning to is much larger than this village.
The city to which he's returning is much larger than this village.

Whose account should I charge this to?
To whose account should I charge this?

The guests whom we contained the dogs for are leaving now.
The guests for whom we contained the dogs are leaving now.

Someone has taken the space I normally park in!
Someone has taken the space in which I normally park!

Josh, Delia, and Abram are some of the friends whom I like to play with at the park.
Josh, Delia, and Abram are some of the friends with whom I like to play at the park.

Exercise 74D: Diagramming

On your own paper, diagram every word of the following two sentences from Exercise 74A.

Homer does not forget those to whom another man's glory brings sorrow.

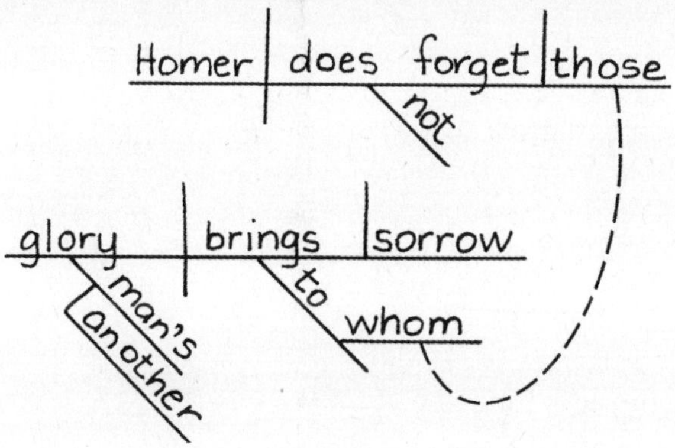

From others he took hostages, and deposited them in one of the islands of which he had control.

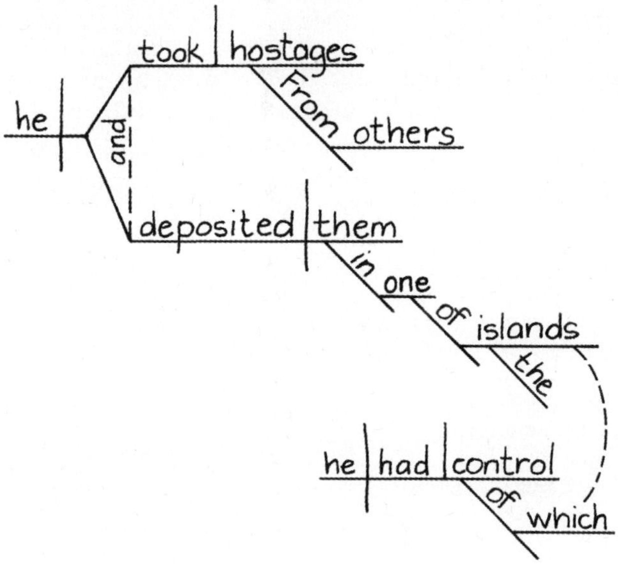

— LESSON 75 —

Clauses and Phrases
Misplaced Adjective Phrases
Misplaced Adjective Clauses

Exercise 75A: Correcting Misplaced Modifiers

Circle the misplaced adjective clauses and phrases in the following sentences. Draw an arrow to the place where each modifier should be. In the blank, indicate whether the modifier is a phrase or a clause by writing *P* or *C*.

The orange juice slaked my thirst that I found in the refrigerator. C

The clock is on the yellow wall made by the renowned clockmaker. P

The dog wearing the pink swimsuit belongs to the girl. P

Redwood trees provide homes for many animals, which can grow over 350 feet tall. C

The trucks that were grown by farmers in my hometown are carrying the tomatoes. C

My neighbor's son with a perfect shell searched high and low for a snail. P

A few buttons make a perfect addition to the little girl's dress shaped like flowers. P

The teacher's sneeze resulted in giggles from every student that echoed across the gymnasium. C

Neville drew a picture for his teacher that resembled a monster. C

Written with childish spellings, the mother smiled at her son's first story. P

This opal ring will be a wonderful addition to the museum, which belonged to my great-great-grandmother. C

Exercise 75B: Diagramming

Each of the following sentences has at least one misplaced clause or phrase. On your own paper, diagram each sentence correctly, and then read the corrected sentence out loud to your instructor.

The sentences below are adapted from L. M. Boston's *The Children of Green Knowe.*

He put his hand, which was real horsehair, on the rocking horse's mane.

He put his hand on the rocking horse's mane, which was real horsehair.

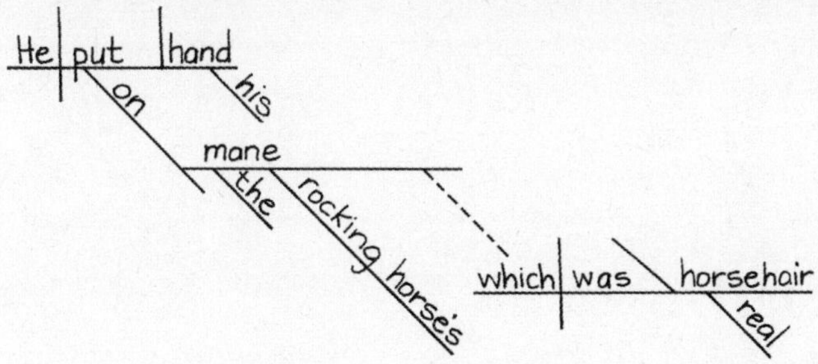

There was a high garden wall that must once have been windows with arched slits in it.

There was a high garden wall with arched slits in it that must once have been windows.

> **Note to Instructor:** The rewritten sentence provided is the original version. The student could also have chosen to place the misplaced clause between "slits" and "in."

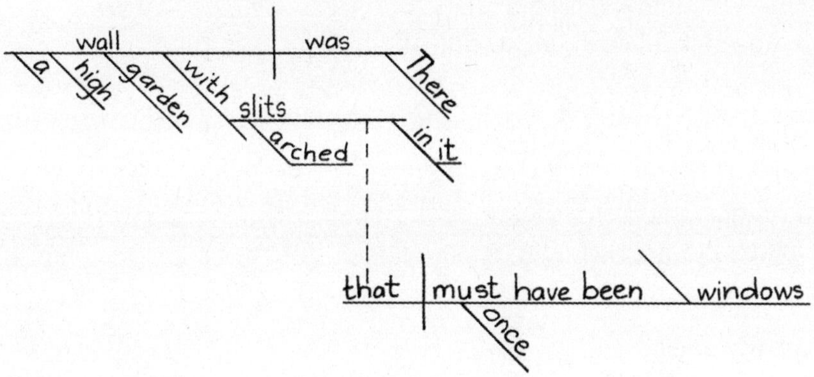

With a soft purr, each domino, which startled the inquisitive chaffinch up into the air, in turn fell forward.

With a soft purr, which startled the inquisitive chaffinch up into the air, each domino in turn fell forward.

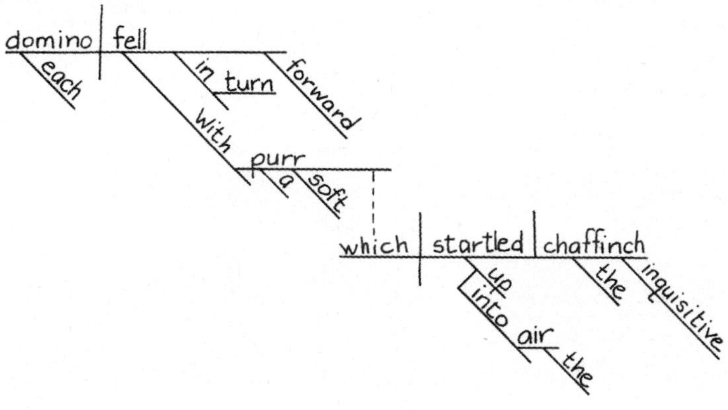

The horse nuzzled Toby's cheek, who had lowered his head to receive the bridle.

The horse, who had lowered his head to receive the bridle, nuzzled Toby's cheek.

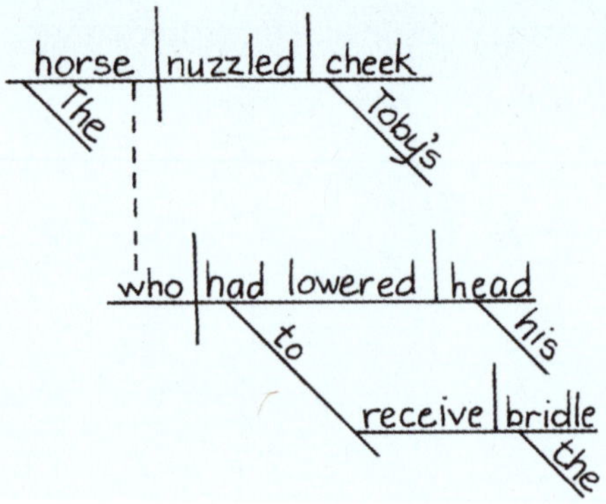

LESSON 76

Noun, Adjective, and Adverb Clauses

Restrictive and Non-Restrictive Modifying Clauses

Exercise 76A: Clause Review

For each of the three sentences below, complete these steps:

1. Find and circle the dependent clause. Label each one as adjective, adverb, or noun.
2. Identify and underline the subordinating word.
3. For the adverb and adjective clauses, draw a line from the subordinating word to the word modified. For the noun clauses, identify the part of the sentence that the clause is serving as.
4. Diagram each sentence on your own paper.

These sentences are from *The Book of Three* by Lloyd Alexander.

Noun Subject

Whatever had seized him made snorting noises.

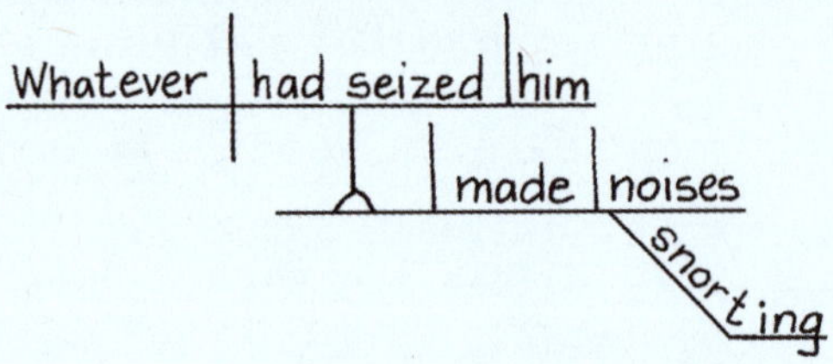

Adjective

At last he dropped the hammer and turned to Coll, who was watching him critically.

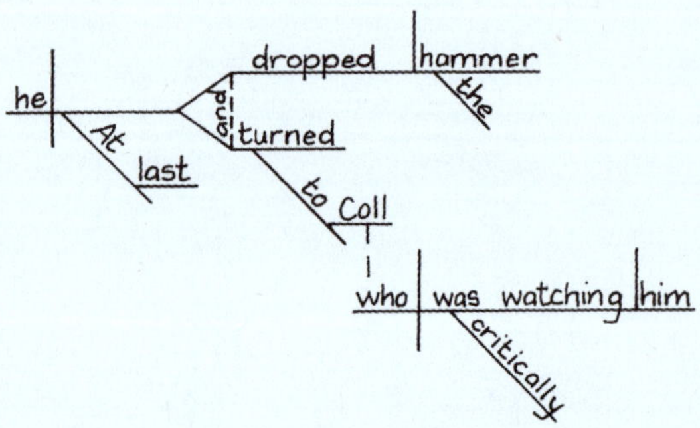

Adjective Adverb

Those who fell into his clutches would be counted fortunate if they perished quickly.

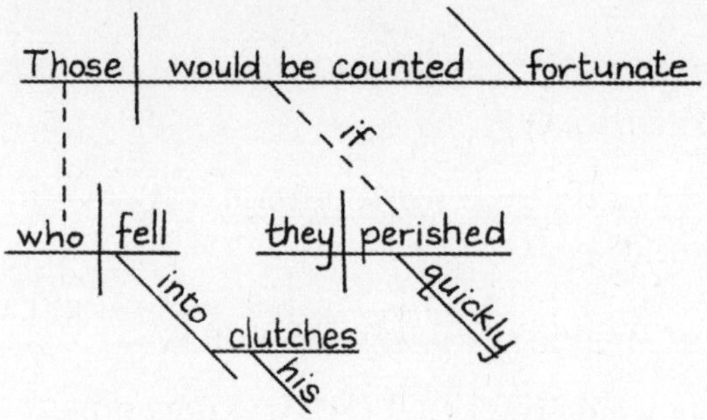

Exercise 76B: Non-Restrictive Clauses and Missing Commas

In the following sentences, taken from Sylvia Engdahl's *Enchantress from the Stars*, underline each dependent clause. If you find a dependent clause within another dependent clause, use a double underline for the inner one. Using proofreader's marks ^, place commas around each non-restrictive clause. Leave sentences with restrictive clauses as they are.

Although there was seldom more than dry bread or thin gruel on their table they were not miserable.

While our main objective is to study the Younglings there are occasions on which we do take action.

The place where we had come down was an idyllic one.

When I stopped to think about it I realized that she was of a race very much like the Andrecians.

It's chancy, but not impossible in a culture like this one which is very favorably disposed toward it.

It wasn't till then that I really took in what it meant!

I'm supposed to make them feel that I want them to succeed.

The cup remained poised in the air where she had placed it.

If there were no problems to solve no one would get very far.

Then all at once his eye fell upon the Stone which he now saw had been bound to his belt.

Exercise 76C: Restrictive Clauses and Unnecessary Commas

In the following sentences, taken from Rod and Ken Preston-Mafham's *Butterflies of the World*, underline each dependent clause. If you find a dependent clause within another dependent clause, use a double underline for the inner one. Delete the incorrect commas that have been placed around restrictive clauses. Use the proofreader's mark for delete: ℓ. Leave sentences with non-restrictive clauses as they are.

The way, in which holdings are established and defended, has been closely studied in the European speckled wood butterfly, Pararge aegeria.

That the crushed and withered stems of certain plants can prove irresistible to male danaines cannot be disputed.

In these instances, apparently, the surface of the soil or rock is first daubed with saliva, into which the salts dissolve, before it is re-imbibed.

Anyone who feels that such an event may occur too infrequently to be worth mimicking should take a walk in a tropical rain forest at night during a bout of heavy rain.

In this position it mimics the kind of leaf decay which is commonly found in the tropics.

Some tropical caterpillars positively bristle with an impenetrable thicket of interlocking spines, which probably serve to deter both vertebrate and invertebrate predators.

The mimetic concept was later expanded by the realization that unrelated unpalatable butterflies bore similar color patterns.

The fields and copses had been completely wiped out and replaced by the urban desert of a light industrial estate, which even today is creeping irrevocably outwards.

Butterfly species whose caterpillars are gregarious in their early stages seem to be particularly vulnerable.

A prime example of this may be found in the African swallowtail, which is widespread throughout sub-Saharan Africa.

WEEK 20

Constructing Sentences

— LESSON 77 —

Constructing Sentences

Exercise 77A: Making Sentences out of Clauses and Phrases

The independent clauses below are listed in order and make up a story—but they're missing all their supporting pieces.

- On your own paper, rewrite the story by attaching the dependent clauses and phrases in Lists 2 and 3 to the independent clauses in List 1 to make complete sentences. You may insert dependent clauses that act as adjectives or adverbs into the beginning, middle, or end of independent clauses (usually by putting them right before or after the word they modify), and you may change any capitalization or punctuation necessary. But do not add or delete words.
- The first sentence has been constructed for you.
- Crossing out each clause or phrase as you use it will help you not to repeat yourself! (The phrase "at night" appears twice in the story, so it appears twice in your list.)

List 1. Independent Clauses

~~There once was a King.~~
They all slept.
The King locked and bolted the door.
He saw.
The King said.
He should have forfeited his life.
A poor soldier met an old woman.
She told him.
She also gave him a cloak.
The Princesses descended.
The soldier put on his cloak and went down last.
He followed the Princesses.
He took a twig.
The soldier reported.
They confessed all.

List 2. Dependent Clauses

where the Princesses danced their shoes
where the trees had leaves
that the Princesses danced
when he unlocked the door
~~who had twelve daughters~~
that were silver, gold, and diamond
that he was going to find out
if a man tried and failed to discover the secret
when the Princesses saw
while he pretended to sleep
when they were
how that had come to pass
where he was going
that falsehood would be
when the King asked
who had watched everything

when he said
in which their beds stood side by side
that someone should find out
that would make him invisible
whoever could discover
that startled the youngest Princess
who asked him
where the Princesses danced
that their shoes were worn out
that he must pretend to be sound asleep

List 3. Phrases

with twelve Princes
for his wife
in the morning
should choose a princess
with the youngest
into holes
in one chamber
in an underground castle
from each type
through a secret opening
to a place
making sounds
in their beds
of tree
for an answer
at night
at night
after three nights
of no avail
with dancing

> **Note to Instructor:** The original sentences, adapted from The Brothers Grimm's "The Worn-Out Dancing Shoes," are provided below (in chronological order). However, any sentences that the student assembles are acceptable as long as they make sense.

There was once a King who had twelve daughters.

They all slept in one chamber, in which their beds stood side by side.

When they were in their beds at night, the King locked and bolted the door.

In the morning when he unlocked the door, he saw that their shoes were worn out with dancing.

The King said that someone should find out how that had come to pass.

Whoever could discover where the Princesses danced at night should choose a princess for his wife.

If a man tried and failed to discover the secret, he should have forfeited his life.

A poor soldier met an old woman who asked him where he was going.

When he said that he was going to find out where the Princesses danced their shoes into holes, she told him that he must pretend to be sound asleep.

She also gave him a cloak that would make him invisible.

While he pretended to sleep, the Princesses descended through a secret opening.

The soldier, who had watched everything, put on his cloak and went down last with the youngest.

He followed the Princesses to a place where the trees had leaves that were silver, gold, and diamond.

He took a twig from each type of tree, making sounds that startled the youngest Princess.

After three nights, when the King asked for an answer, the soldier reported that the Princesses danced in an underground castle with twelve Princes.

When the Princesses saw that falsehood would be of no avail, they confessed all.

— LESSON 78 —

Simple Sentences
Complex Sentences

Exercise 78A: Identifying Simple and Complex Sentences

In the sentences below, underline each subject once and each predicate twice. (Find the subjects and predicates in both independent and dependent clauses.) Write any understood subject in parentheses to the left of the sentence. In the blank at the end of each sentence, write *S* for simple or *C* for complex.

These sentences are adapted from *The King's Mirror*, translated from Old Norse by Laurence Marcellus Larson.

The man who is to be a trader will have to brave many perils. C

(you) Keep your table well provided and set with a white cloth, clean victuals, and good drinks. S

After the meal you may either take a nap or stroll about a little while for pastime. S

But although I have most to say about laws, I regard no man perfect in knowledge unless he has thoroughly learned and mastered the customs of the place where he is sojourning. C

Soon the east wind is crowned with a golden glory and robed in all his raiments of joy. S

Not long since, we mentioned a certain fact which must be thought exceedingly strange elsewhere. C

The farmers raise cattle and sheep in large numbers and make butter and cheese in great quantities. S

I gather from what you have said that the ocean is deep and also very salt and always in commotion. C

Since every question looks toward a reply, I shall explain this to you in a few words, as it seems most reasonable to me. C

His chief business, however, is to maintain an intelligent government and to seek good solutions for difficult problems and demands. S

You also heard in the earlier account how the king and the city of Themar perished because the king, being friendly to one side and very hostile to the other, had distorted a just decision. C

Exercise 78B: Forming Complex Sentences

On the blanks provided, rewrite each pair of simple sentences as a single complex sentence. The first is done for you. The sentences below are adapted from Washington Irving's *The Legend of Sleepy Hollow.*

There are peculiar quavers still to be heard in that church. They may even be heard half a mile off.

There are peculiar quavers still to be heard in that church, which may even be heard half a mile off.

> **Note to Instructor:** Variations on the sentences below are acceptable, as long as they are grammatical in construction and follow the instructions. For example, the third sentence might also be written as, *When Ichabod laid his eyes upon these regions of delight, the peace of his mind was at an end* (complex sentence), but not as *Ichabod laid his eyes upon these regions of delight, and the peace of his mind was at an end* (compound sentence with no dependent clauses).

She wore the ornaments of pure yellow gold. Her great-great-grandmother had brought the ornaments over from Saardam.

She wore the ornaments of pure yellow gold, which her great-great-grandmother had brought over from Saardam.

Ichabod laid his eyes upon these regions of delight. The peace of his mind was at an end.

After Ichabod laid his eyes upon these regions of delight, the peace of his mind was at an end.

Brom had a degree of rough chivalry in his nature. Brom would fain have carried matters to open warfare.

Brom, who had a degree of rough chivalry in his nature, would fain have carried matters to open warfare.

He approached the stream. His heart began to thump.

As he approached the stream, his heart began to thump.

A thief might get in with perfect ease. The thief would find some embarrassment in getting out.

Though a thief might get in with perfect ease, he would find some embarrassment in getting out.

Exercise 78C: Diagramming

On your own paper, diagram the following four sentences. Beside each diagram, write the number of vertical lines dividing subjects from predicates, along with the label *S* for simple or *C* for complex.

Along came a spider, who sat down beside her, and frightened Miss Muffet away.

2C

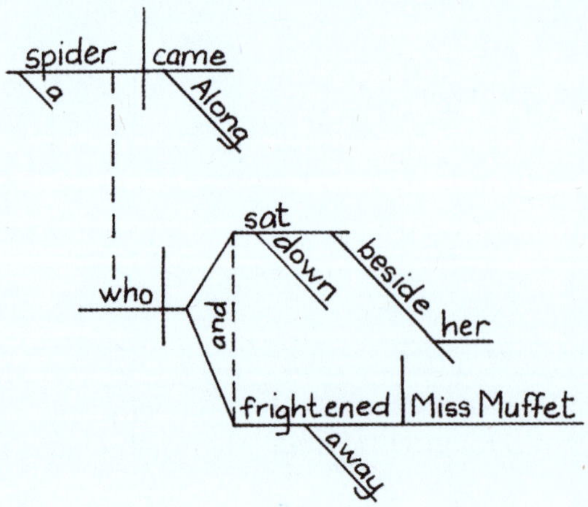

Little Bo-Peep has lost her sheep, and doesn't know where to find them.

1S

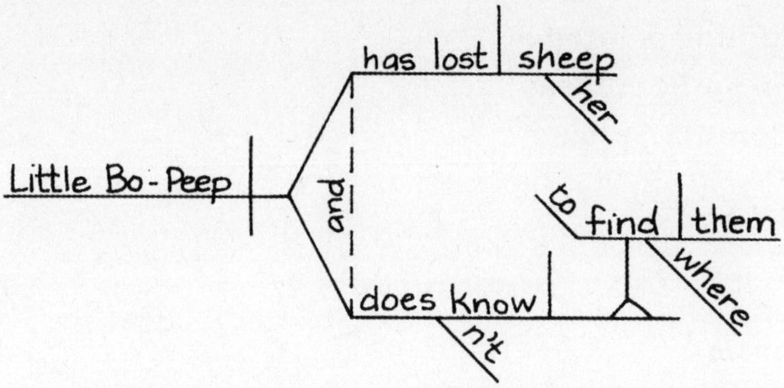

Pat it, and prick it, and mark it with T, and put it in the oven for Tommy and me.

1S

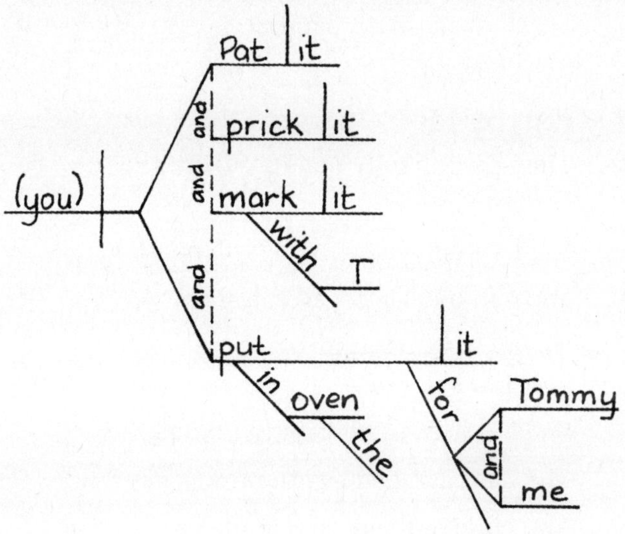

If Peter Piper picked a peck of pickled peppers, where's the peck of pickled peppers Peter Piper picked?

3C

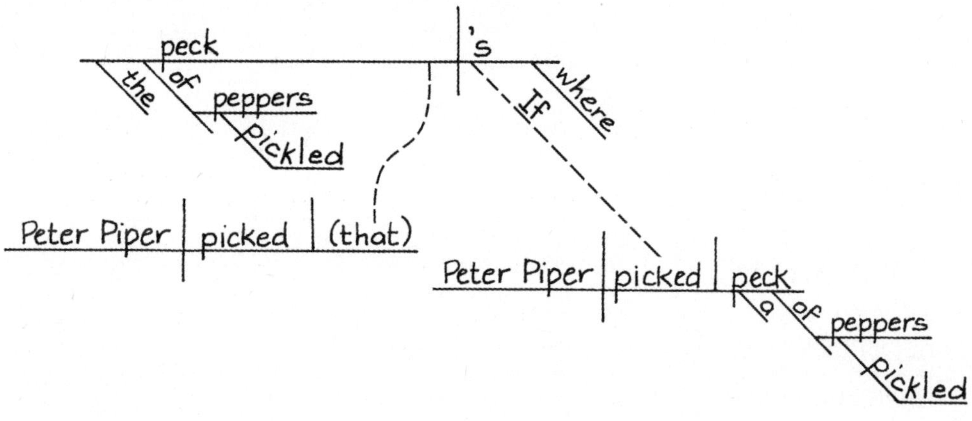

— LESSON 79 —

Compound Sentences
Run-on Sentences
Comma Splice

Exercise 79A: Forming Compound Sentences

Choose at least one independent clause from Column 1 and at least one independent clause from Column 2. Using correct punctuation and adding coordinating conjunctions as needed, combine the clauses into a compound sentence. (You may use more than two clauses, as long as your sentence makes sense!) Write your new compound sentences on your own paper. Use every clause at least once.

COLUMN 1	COLUMN 2
The dragon breathed fire.	They are the only marsupials in the United States.
The boy had never visited the town before.	Ducks were waddling by the pond.
The cat may pounce on the mouse.	You can buy six for five dollars.
Cows were grazing in the fields.	He felt his surroundings were familiar somehow.
Opossums carry their young in pouches.	She has a great interest in onomastics.
Eleanor knows the meanings of many names.	The hero avoided the flames.
She bought the item at this store.	The children may startle the cat.
Raffle tickets cost one dollar each.	She lost her receipt.

Note to Instructor: The student may form other sentences than those below, as long as they make sense. However, she should *only* use coordinating conjunctions. Watch out for subordinating conjunctions such as *before*, *while*, *because*, *after*, etc. Use of subordinating conjunctions transforms a clause from independent to dependent, and makes the sentence complex rather than compound.

No clauses should be joined with a comma splice (a comma without a coordinating conjunction), but all sentences can make use of either a semicolon (with or without coordinating conjunction) or a comma with a coordinating conjunction.

The dragon breathed fire, but the hero avoided the flames.

The boy had never visited the town before, yet he felt his surroundings were familiar somehow.

The cat may pounce on the mouse, or the children may startle the cat.

Cows were grazing in the fields, and ducks were waddling by the pond.

Opossums carry their young in pouches; they are the only marsupials in the United States.

Eleanor knows the meanings of many names, for she has a great interest in onomastics.

She bought the item at this store, but she lost her receipt.

Raffle tickets cost one dollar each, or you can buy six for five dollars.

Exercise 79B: Correcting Run-On Sentences (Comma Splices)

Using proofreader's marks (^ to insert a word, ^, to insert a comma, ^; to insert a semicolon), correct each of the run-on sentences below.

These sentences are from George Orwell's *Animal Farm.*

Note to Instructor: Answers may vary; each set of independent clauses should be connected by a semicolon (with or without a coordinating conjunction) or a comma and a coordinating conjunction.

and
The animals settled down in the straw,^the whole farm was asleep in a moment.

and
He was a brilliant talker^he had a persuasive way of skipping from side to side and whisking his tail. (^;)

for
Their efforts were rewarded,^the harvest was a big success.

but
The birds did not understand Snowball's long words^they accepted his explanation. (^;)

and
The earth was like iron^nothing could be done in the fields. (^,)

They were happy in their work^they grudged no effort or sacrifice. (^;)

for
The Commandment had not been violated^clearly there was good reason for killing the traitors. (^;)

Exercise 79C: Diagramming

On your own paper, diagram every word of the following sentences, adapted from Thomas Paine's *Common Sense.*

Society in every state is a blessing, but government even in its best state is a necessary evil; in its worst state it is an intolerable one.

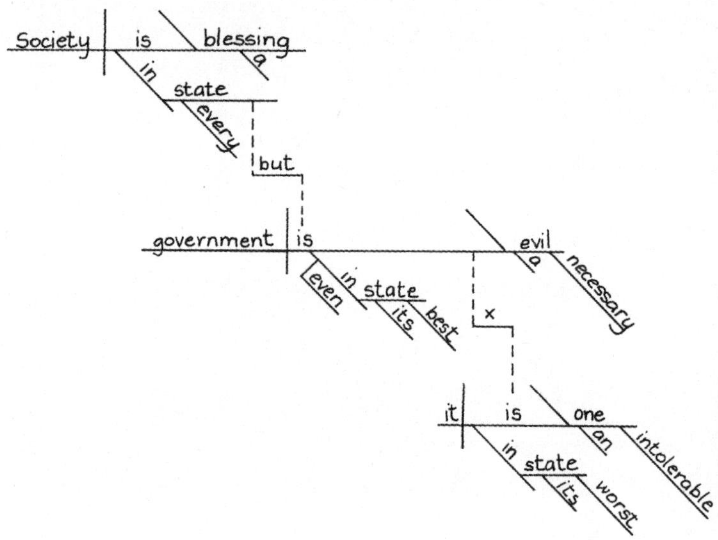

Note to Instructor: It is not incorrect to place *in every state* beneath *Society* as an adjectival prepositional phrase. Although the meaning is "Society is, in every state, a blessing" (adverbial, with in every state expressing how), it is also reasonable to interpret the phrase as an adjective describing *Society* ("Society, in every state, is a blessing.") This does not substantially change the meaning.

The student may not know where to put *even*. The prepositional phrase *in its best state* is acting as an adverb; *even* is another adverb that modifies the adverbial phrase; as long as the student connects it somewhere to the prepositional phrase, that is acceptable. (The best alternative would be beneath *best*.)

Government is the badge of lost innocence; the palaces of kings are built on the ruins of the bowers of paradise.

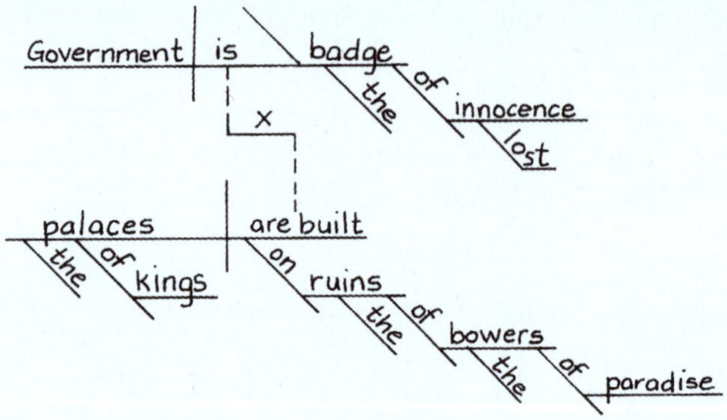

Five men united would be able to raise a tolerable dwelling in the midst of a wilderness, but one man might labor out the common period of life without accomplishing anything.

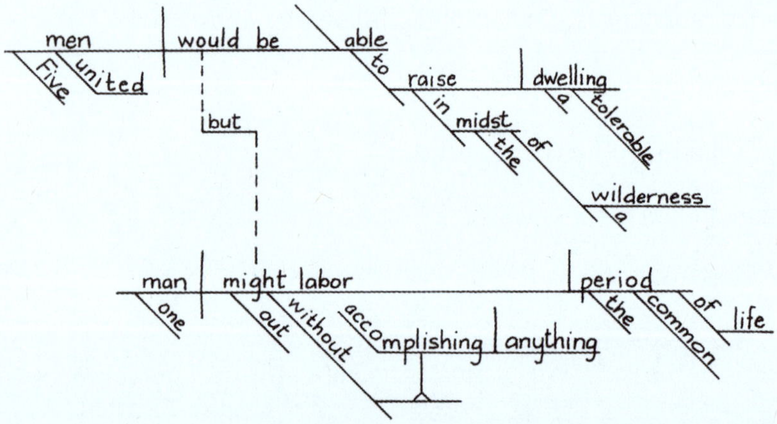

Men of all ranks have embarked in the controversy, from different motives, with various designs; but all have been ineffectual, and the period of debate is closed.

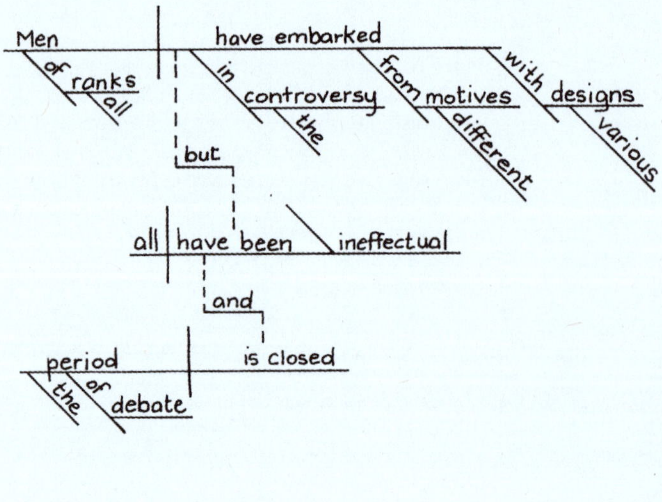

— LESSON 80 —

Compound Sentences
Compound-Complex Sentences
Clauses with Understood Elements

Exercise 80A: Analyzing Complex-Compound Sentences

The sentences below are all complex-compound sentences. For each sentence, carry out the following steps:

a. Cross out each prepositional phrase.

b. Circle any dependent clauses. Label them as *ADJ*, *ADV*, or *NOUN*. Draw a line from adjective and adverb clauses to the word modified. Label noun clauses with the part of the sentence that they function as.

c. Underline the subject of each independent clause once and the predicate twice.

d. Draw a vertical line between each simple and/or complex sentence.

e. Insert missing words (if any).

The first sentence has been done for you.

These sentences are adapted from *Cheaper by the Dozen*, by Frank B. Gilbreth Jr. and Ernestine Gilbreth Carey.

ADV

He hadn't remembered to count noses when he came down the gangplank, | and he didn't

ADV NOUN DO

notice, until the gangplank was pulled in, that Dan was missing.

NOUN SUBJECT NOUN SUBJECT

What would work in the home would work in the factory, | and what would work in the factory would work in the home.

that NOUN DO

Dad decided we were going to have to help them, | and he wanted us to offer the help of our own accord.

NOUN DO

He knows where the razor is, | but first he must locate it with his eye.

ADV

Most photographers prefer sunlight for their pictures, | but Dad liked it best when there was no sun.

ADJ

We had better success with another guest whom we set out deliberately to discourage; | she

ADJ

was a woman psychologist who came to Montclair from New York.

Exercise 80B: Constructing Complex-Compound Sentences

From each set of independent clauses, construct a single complex-compound sentence. You may turn any of the clauses into dependent clauses by adding subordinating words, insert any other words necessary, omit unnecessary words, and make any other needed changes, but try to keep the original meaning of each clause. You must use every clause in the set!

You may turn a clause into a prepositional phrase or another form, as long as your resulting sentence has at least two independent clauses and one dependent clause and contains all of the information in the listed clauses.

Write your sentences on your own paper. The first has been done for you. The other four sets of clauses are adapted from Patricia Lauber's *Fur, Feathers, and Flippers: How Animals Live Where They Do.*

Note to the Instructor: Sample answers are below. The student's may vary, as long as she has followed the rules in the instructions.

We usually go out for ice cream.
We go to the little ice cream shop.
The little ice cream shop is next to the grocery store.
We usually go after the club meetings.
The club meetings are on Tuesday evenings.

On Tuesday evenings, we have our club meetings, and then we usually go out for ice cream at the little shop that is next to the grocery store.

Leopards attack their prey from hiding.
Leopards hunt at night.
Leopards may drag their catch up into a tree.
Leopards hunt alone.
Leopards may finish eating their catch later.

Leopards, which hunt alone at night, attack their prey from hiding; they may drag their catch up into a tree and finish eating it later.

New England has cold winters.
The deeper soil does not freeze.
Tree roots can reach the deeper soil.
The New England region has forests and woods.
Forests are large areas.
Forests have thick growths of trees.
Woods are smaller areas of trees.

New England has cold winters, but tree roots are deep enough to reach where the soil does not freeze, so the region has forests, which are large areas with thick growths of trees, and woods, which are smaller areas of trees.

Many birds build their nests in the forest understory.
Birds in the understory are sheltered from storms.
Birds in the understory are out of reach of predators.
Young trees are in the forest understory.
Low-growing trees are in the forest understory.

Many birds build their nests in the forest understory, where they are sheltered from storms and out of reach of predators; this part of the forest is made up of young and low-growing trees.

Gila woodpeckers search for insects to eat in saguaros.
Saguaros are a type of giant cactus.
Gila woodpeckers make nest holes in saguaros.
Other birds use the same holes in subsequent years.
Some of these birds are sparrow hawks, screech owls, and flycatchers.

Gila woodpeckers search for insects to eat in saguaros, which are a type of giant cactus; they also make nest holes in saguaros, and other birds such as sparrow hawks, screech owls, and flycatchers use the same holes in subsequent years.

Exercise 80C: Diagramming

On your own paper, diagram the following sentences from Anne Frank's *The Diary of a Young Girl* (translated from the Dutch by B. M. Mooyaart).

I don't think I shall ever feel really at home in this house, but that does not mean that I loathe it here.

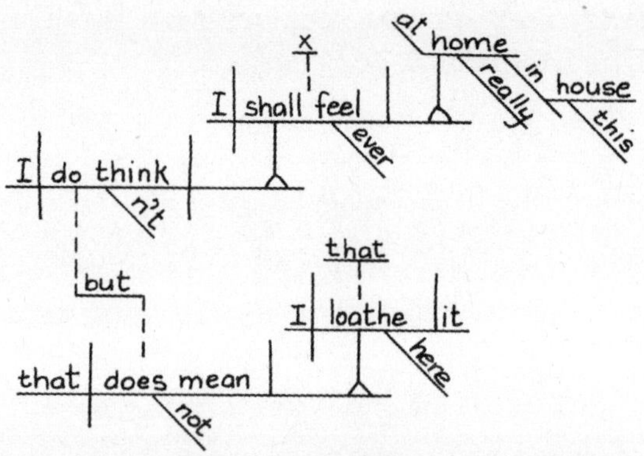

I have previously written about how much we are affected by atmospheres here, and I think that in my own case this trouble is getting much worse lately.

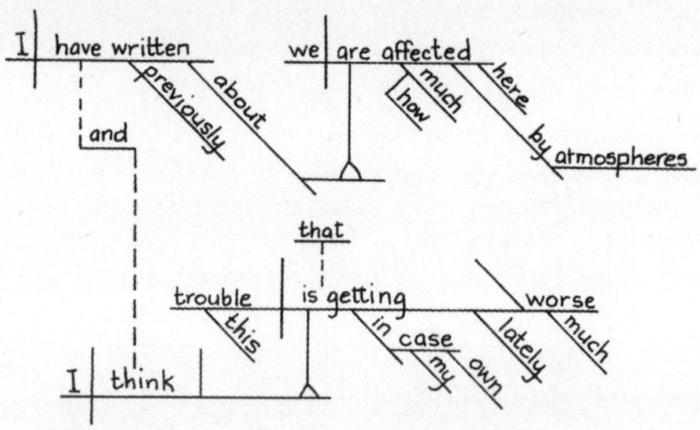

I know quite well that I'd be desperately jealous, but Margot only says that I needn't pity her.

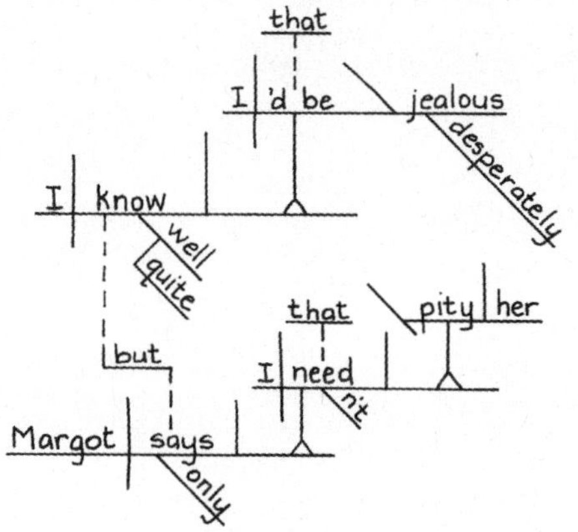

I have one outstanding trait in my character, which must strike anyone who knows me for any length of time, and that is my knowledge of myself.

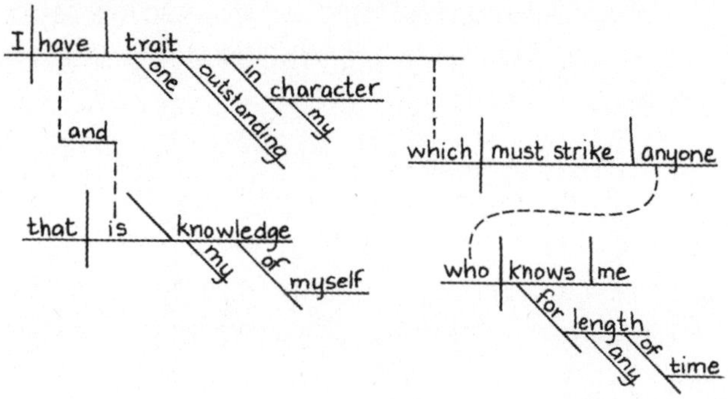

WEEK 21

Conditions

— LESSON 81 —

Helping Verbs
Tense and Voice
Modal Verbs

Exercise 81A: Using Do, Does, and Did

On your own paper, rewrite each sentence, putting it into the form described in brackets. Use the appropriate form of the helping verb along with any interrogatives or negatives necessary. Don't forget that you may have to change the form of the verb! The first is done for you.

These sentences are adapted from Irene Hunt's *Across Five Aprils.*

His body had need of green food. [Provide emphasis.]
His body did have need of green food.

Bill, talk about it more. [Turn into a negative command.]
Bill, don't talk about it [any] more.

This makes you want to throw up your hat and say that it's all about over. [Change into a question.]
Does this make you want to throw up your hat and say that it's all about over?

You have to be in such an all-fired hurry. [Turn into a negative statement.]
You don't have to be in such an all-fired hurry.

He knew how much he would tell about the ugly words of Guy Wortman and the others. [Turn into a negative statement.]
He did not know how much he would tell about the ugly words of Guy Wortman and the others.

The tragedy of that summer impressed Jethro deeply. [Provide emphasis.]
The tragedy of that summer did impress Jethro deeply.

Need I say that the men in the Army of the Potomac cheer General Burnside? [Turn the dependent clause into a negative statement.]
Need I say that the men in the Army of the Potomac do not cheer General Burnside?

The President removed General Grant. [Turn into a negative statement.]
The President did not remove General Grant.

You see Mr. Lincoln. [Change into a question.]
Do you see Mr. Lincoln?

You want to tell me more of the things on your mind. [Change into a question.]
Do you want to tell me more of the things on your mind?

Exercise 81B: Modal Verbs

Fill in the blanks below with an appropriate helping verb (*should, would, may, might, must, can, could*) to form a modal verb. There may be more than one correct answer for each sentence. Use each helping verb at least once.

These sentences are from Robert Newton Peck's *A Day No Pigs Would Die.* After you finish the exercises, be sure to read the original sentences in the key.

Note to Instructor: The underlined words below are Robert Newton Peck's originals. Other choices are acceptable as long as the resulting sentence makes sense.

He even said I __should__ feed her some new food, and to mix some meat scraps into her mash.

I __must__ have turned Rutland upside down just trying to find some soap.

And because I __could__ not read, I knew to listen with a full heart. It __might__ be the last and only time I __would__ learn its meaning.

I think I __may__ need a new winter coat.

The only other thing I'd wanted was a bicycle, but I knew we __could__ not afford it, so there was no sense in asking. Besides, both Mama and Papa __would__ have looked at a bicycle as a work of the Devil.

Well, nobody __could__ call Pinky a frill. Anybody who had half an eye __could__ see she was a pig.

With Pinky next to me that night, I guess I __must__ have been the luckiest boy in Learning.

Having a big hired man around like Ira __may__ be sinful.

Care taking of a pig __can__ keep a body as nervous as a longtail cat in a room full of rocking chairs.

And every man __must__ face his own mission.

"So," she said, writing as fast as she talked, "I am going to write out a sentence, and you __can__ diagram it."

Exercise 81C: Verb Tense and Voice

For each sentence below, underline each verb phrase (in both dependent and independent clauses) and identify the tense and voice of the verb. Do *not* mark gerunds, past participles, or infinitives. For state-of-being verbs, which are neither active nor passive in voice, identify the tense and write *state-of-being*. The first verb is done for you.

These sentences are from *The Journals of Lewis and Clark.*

As I, being surrounded, __was__ not __permitted__ (simple past, passive) by them to return, I __sent__ (simple past, active) all the men except two interpreters to the boat.

The fleas __are__ (simple present, state-of-being) so troublesome that I __have slept__ (perfect present, active) but little for two nights past.

If the boat __had struck__ (perfect past, active) the submerged tree, her bow __must have been knocked__ (perfect present, passive) off, and in course she __must have sunk__ (perfect present, active) in the deep water below.

perfect past state-of-being | simple past active | simple present state-of-being

Our men that had been sick for some time past recovered fast, and we are in hopes that they

perfect future passive | simple present state-of-being

will be fully recovered by the time that we are ready to proceed on down the river.

simple present active | simple present active

It appears to be navigable for canoes and perogues at this time, and I have no doubt but that it

simple present passive

might be navigated with boats of a considerable size in high water.

simple past active | simple past active

The chief drew me a kind of chart of the river, and informed me that a greater chief than himself

progressive past active | simple past passive

was fishing at the river half a day's march from his village; that he was called The Twisted Hair;

simple past active

and that the river forked a little below his camp.

simple present active | simple present active

We intend to delay a few days for the laying in of some meat, by which time we calculate that the

simple future active

snows will have melted off the mountains.

perfect present active | perfect past active

The beaver have cut great quantities of timber; we saw a tree nearly three feet in diameter that

perfect past passive

had been felled by them.

simple present active | perfect present passive

The French inform us that lead ore has been found in different parts of this river.

— LESSON 82 —

Conditional Sentences
The Condition Clause
The Consequence Clause

Exercise 82A: Identifying Conditional Sentences

Some of the sentences in this exercise are conditional sentences—and others are not! Identify each conditional sentence by writing a *C* in the margin. For each conditional sentence, label the clauses as *condition* or *consequence.*

Note to Instructor: If the student has trouble telling the difference, remind her that conditional sentences express situations that have not actually happened.

condition | consequence

After I finish my carrots, I will get some ice cream. C

consequence | condition

Mother will not be pleased if I do not clean my room. C

Though Shirin wondered about the noise, she did not investigate.

condition consequence
If he practices diligently, Michael will perform well in the violin competition. C

consequence condition
Don't answer the door unless you are expecting a visitor. C

As the minutes ticked by, the girl's family awaited the surgeon's report.

condition consequence
"If we don't hear something soon, I'll go and ask someone." C

consequence condition
"They will have news for us when the surgery is finished." C

While it took a long time, the procedure was successful.

Exercise 82B: Tense in Conditional Sentences

Fill in each blank below with the correct tense and form of the verb in brackets. Some sentences may have more than one possible correct answer.

First Conditional Sentences

> **Note to Instructor:** Accept any answers that make sense, as long as the first verb is in a present tense and the second verb is imperative, present, or future.

If you remember [remember] these guidelines, you will be [state-of-being verb] a good houseguest.

If your skin itches [itch], use [use] this cream to help.

If the audience applauds [applaud] for a long time, take [take] another bow.

If you pedal [pedal] too quickly, you will grow [grow] tired.

If Aaron trades [trade] his rare card for a chance to ride Benjamin's scooter, he will regret [regret] his decision tomorrow.

Second Conditional Sentences

> **Note to Instructor:** Accept any answers that make sense as long as the first verb is in a past tense and the second is simple present modal (the helping verbs *might*, *could*, *would*, and *should* can all be used).

If Maria tasted [taste] the bread, she might want [want] to eat the whole loaf.

If the ball bounced [bounce] onto the balcony, it could startle [startle] Grandpa.

If I knew [know] the correct tool for this job, I would use [use] it.

If I married [marry] royalty, I would be [state-of-being verb] rich and famous.

If the detective suspected [suspect] you, he could not tell [tell] you anything about the case.

Third Conditional Sentences

> **Note to Instructor:** Accept any answers that make sense as long as the first verb is in the perfect past tense and the second is either perfect present modal or simple present modal (the helping verbs *might*, *could*, *would*, and *should* can all be used).

If we had pressed [press] the red button, something horrible might have happened [happen].

If the nurse had injected [inject] you with this instead of with the correct medicine, you could have died [die].

If Melissa had multiplied [multiply] correctly in the first step, she would have [have] the right solution now.

If you had delayed [delay] us any longer, we would not have arrived [arrive] in time for the show.

I would have gotten [get] away with my crime, if those kids had not meddled [meddle]!

Exercise 82C: Diagramming

On your own paper, diagram these sentences from Sophocles's *Antigone* (translated by Dudley Fitts and Robert Fitzgerald). A conditional clause should be diagrammed like any other dependent clause.

All these men here would praise me were not their lips frozen shut with fear of you.

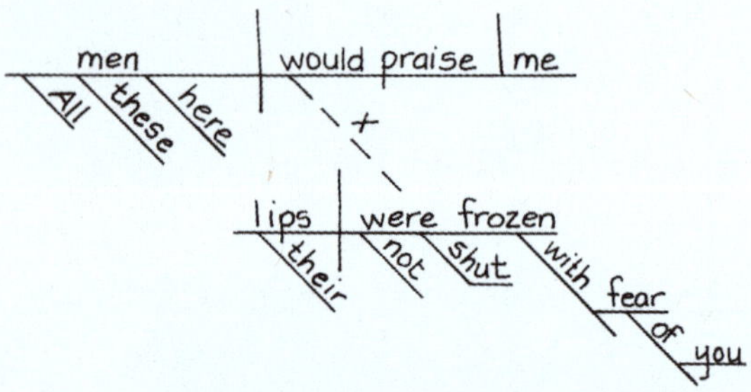

Note to Instructor: *Here* describes *men*, so in this sentence it is acting as an adjective. The prepositional phrases *with fear of you* could also be diagrammed beneath *shut*.

If I am young, and right, what does my age matter?

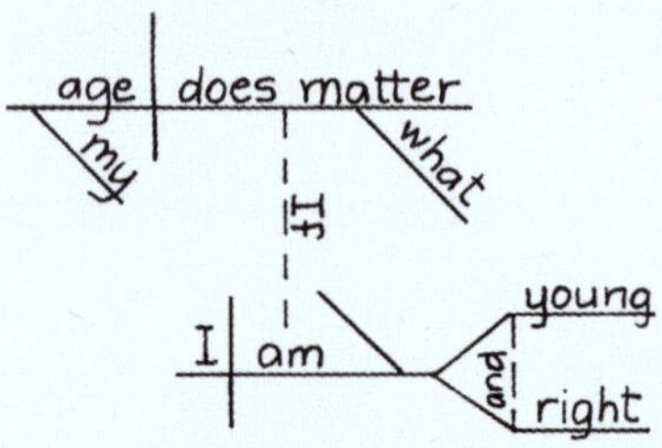

Note to Instructor: If the student diagrams *what* as a direct object, ask her to look up the verb *matter* in the dictionary. It is intransitive, so can't take a direct object. In this usage, *what* is expressing "to what extent or degree? how much?" and so is acting as an adverb.

It is no City if it takes orders from one voice.

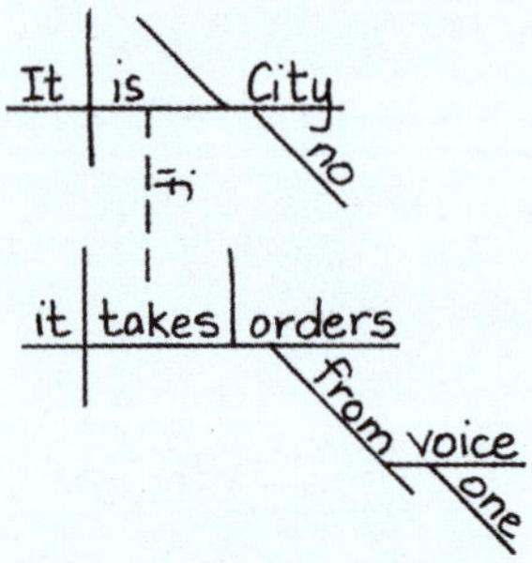

— LESSON 83 —

Conditional Sentences

The Subjunctive

Exercise 83A: Subjunctive Forms in Conditionals

Fill in the blanks with the correct verb forms to make the type of conditional indicated after each sentence. Circle each verb you write that is a different form because it is subjunctive.

The sentences below are from *What Katy Did Next,* by Susan Coolidge.

Note to Instructor: The answers below show Susan Coolidge's original sentences, with some slight adaptations. The student's answers may use different helping verbs to make modal verbs (*should, would, may, might, must, can, could*) and may use *will* in place of *shall.*

She would be [state-of-being verb] lonely if she (were) [state-of-being verb] left to herself. [second conditional]

If I have [have] her with me, I shall not be [state-of-being verb] afraid of anything. [first conditional]

If I (were) [state-of-being verb] going, I should simply stand [stand] on my head every moment of the time! [second conditional]

If it had been [state-of-being verb] for her to choose, she would have flown [fly] back to the shore then and there. [third conditional]

Oh, if ever the happy day comes [come] when Deniston consents to move into town, I never wish [wish] to set my eyes on the country again. [first conditional]

I shall consider [consider] your second cousin a lucky man if he persuades [persuade] her. [first conditional]

If this is [state-of-being verb] English history, I never mean [mean] to learn any more of it. [first conditional]

If he (were) [state-of-being verb] good, you would not mind [mind] his being big, would you? [second conditional]

I should be [state-of-being verb] very lonely sometimes if it (were) [state-of-being verb] not for my dear little fawn. [second conditional]

Polly's life would be [state-of-being verb] so lonely if Amy (were) [state-of-being verb] to die. [second conditional]

You are [state-of-being verb] perfectly right to go home if you feel [feel] so. [first conditional]

You have given me the loveliest six months' treat that ever was, and I should be [state-of-being verb] a greedy girl indeed if I found [find] fault because it is cut off a little sooner than we expected. [second conditional]

Exercise 83B: Subjunctive Forms in Complex Sentences

Cross out the incorrect verb forms in parentheses.

It is essential that the buyer (~~signs~~/sign) these papers before five o'clock.

Walking through the park, Min-jae sang as if she (~~was~~/were) on stage.
Mr. Nettles demanded that the receptionist (interrupt/~~interrupts~~) the board meeting.
The manager recommended that she (arrive/~~arrives~~) a few minutes early.
The mother suggested that the young child (~~carries~~/carry) his cup with both hands.
If the man (was/~~were~~) awake, he would hear our warnings.
The director (was/~~were~~) determined that Tobias (play/~~plays~~) the lead in the musical.
It (seems/~~seem~~) important that the student (~~corrects~~/correct) his work in order to learn.
Catherine's parents insist that she (~~removes~~/remove) her shoes before entering the house.
The guest has requested that the front desk (alert/~~alerts~~) him when the pizza arrives.

— LESSON 84 —

Conditional Sentences
The Subjunctive
Moods of Verbs
Subjunctive Forms Using *Be*

Exercise 84A: Parsing Verbs

Underline each predicate, in both main clauses and dependent clauses. Above each, write the tense, voice, and mood of the verb.

These sentences are from Kenneth Grahame's "The Reluctant Dragon."

Tense: Simple past, present, future; progressive past, present, future; perfect past, present, future
Voice: Active, passive
Mood: Indicative, subjunctive, imperative, modal, subjunctive/modal

(had been disturbed: perfect past, passive, indicative) (preoccupied: perfect past, passive, indicative) (came: simple past, active, indicative)

One evening the shepherd, who for some nights past had been disturbed and preoccupied, and off his usual mental balance, came home all of a tremble.

(was frightened: simple past, passive, indicative) (went: simple past, active, indicative) (could keep: simple present, active, modal)

"Of course I was terrible frightened," the shepherd went on; "yet somehow I couldn't keep away."

(had: simple past, active, indicative) (should say: simple present, active, modal) (was meditating: progressive past, active, indicative)

He had his chin on his paws, and I should say he was meditating about things.

(come: simple present, active, indicative) (wait: simple present, active, indicative) (leave: simple present, active, imperative) (will stroll: simple future, active, indicative) ('m: simple present, state-of-being, indicative) (will go: simple future, active, indicative) (have: simple future, active, indicative)

Rules always come right if you wait quietly. Now, please, just leave this all to me. And I'll stroll up tomorrow. Perhaps in the evening, if I'm quite free, I'll go up and have a talk to him.

('m going: progressive present, active, indicative) ('d guess: simple present, active, modal) (tried: simple past, active, subjunctive)

Now I'm going to tell you something! You'd never guess it if you tried ever so!

progressive present active indicative — simple future state-of-being indicative

I'm hoping the other neighbours will be equally agreeable.

perfect past active indicative — simple past active indicative

They had always left that branch to him, and they took his word without a murmur.

simple present passive modal/subjunctive

This sort of thing couldn't be allowed to go on.

> **Note to Instructor:** The form "thing be" has to be subjunctive; the modal verb turns it into a combined modal/subjunctive verb.

progressive present active indicative

I'm not seeing anybody at present.

perfect present active indicative — progressive present active indicative

I've never fought in my life, and I'm not going to begin now.

perfect past active subjunctive — simple present active modal — simple present active indicative — simple present active indicative — progressive present active indicative

And as soon as you'd really gone away, why, I'd come up again gaily, for I tell you frankly, I like this place, and I'm going to stay here!

simple past active indicative — simple present active imperative — simple future active indicative — simple present passive indicative

"St. George," said the dragon, "just tell him, please—what will happen after I'm vanquished in the deadly combat?"

Exercise 84B: Forming Subjunctives

Fill in the blanks in the following sentences with the correct verb form indicated in brackets.

Had I known [perfect past subjunctive of *know*] his position in the company, I would have chosen [perfect present modal of *choose*] my words more carefully.

The queen commands [simple present indicative of *command*] that the prisoner be set [simple present passive subjunctive of *set*] free immediately.

If the piano were [simple past subjunctive of *am*] in tune, it would sound [simple present modal of *sound*] much better!

It is recommended [simple present passive indicative of *recommend*] that the patient rest [simple present subjunctive of *rest*] while recovering from this illness.

I would not eat [simple present modal of *eat*] at that restaurant if I were [simple past subjunctive of *am*] you; the last time I was [simple past indicative of *am*] there, the chicken was not cooked [simple past passive indicative of *cook*] thoroughly.

Our teacher insists [simple present indicative of *insist*] that our papers be stapled [simple present passive subjunctive of *staple*] in this manner.

The event's director has requested [perfect present indicative of *request*] that traffic flow [simple present subjunctive of *flow*] in this direction; please move [simple present imperative of *move*] out of the way.

If Alejandro were [simple past subjunctive of *am*] here, we could be seated [simple present passive modal/subjunctive of *seat*] already.

Mother asked [simple past indicative of *ask*] that Dayana put [simple present subjunctive of *put*] her toys away before going outside.

Exercise 84C: Diagramming

On your own paper, diagram the following sentences from Andrew Peterson's *The Monster in the Hollows.*

A boy swaggered into the doorway and leaned against it as if he didn't have a care in the world.

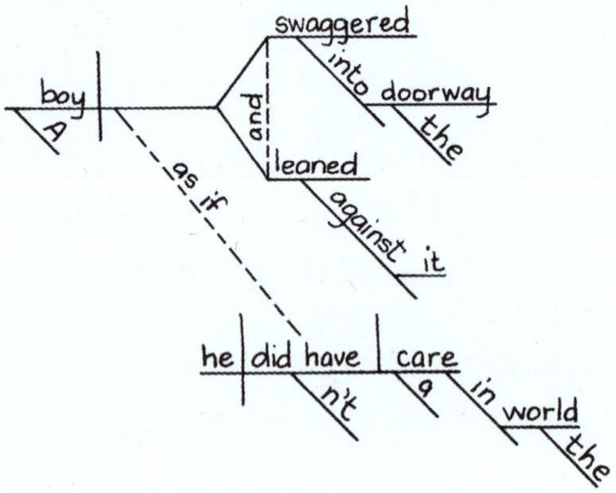

He wore a white shirt without sleeves, and his pants were held up with suspenders.

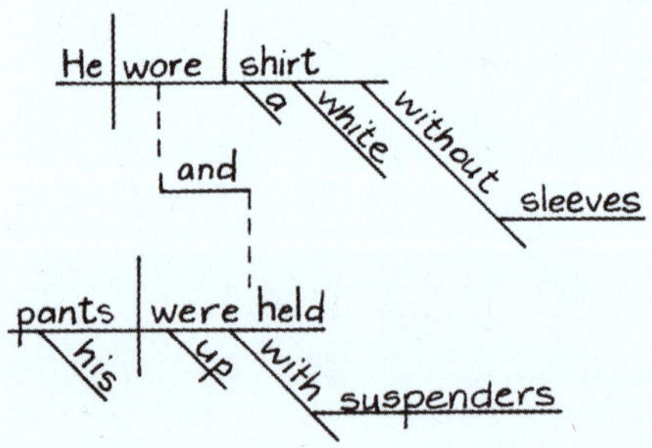

He tilted his head so the lock of his long black hair that wasn't slicked back didn't cover his eyes.

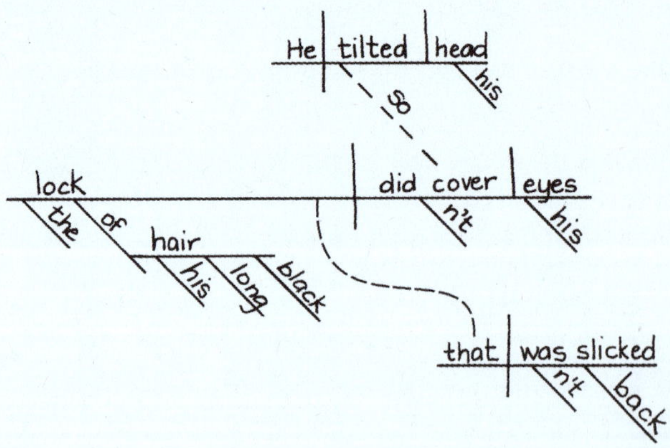

— REVIEW 7 —

Weeks 19-21

Topics
Phrases and Clauses
Adjective, Adverb, and Noun Clauses
Pronouns
Mood: Modal, Subjective, Imperative, Indicative
Conditional Sentences

Review 7A: Improving Sentences with Phrases

In the blanks below, supply phrases that meet the descriptions in brackets. You may supply more than one phrase in any blank, as long as at least one phrase fulfills the requirements (often, additional prepositional phrases may be needed). The first is done for you, with explanations provided.

The original sentences are taken from *A Tale of Two Cities*, by Charles Dickens. This is a challenging assignment—prepare to spend some time on it!

When you are finished, compare your sentences with the originals in the Answer Key.

[adverbial prepositional phrase answering the question *how* and describing *mashed*; preposition should have a compound object] [adverbial prepositional phrase answering the question *where*]

__________, the horses mashed their way __________.

[adverbial prepositional phrase answering the question *how* and describing *mashed*; preposition should have a compound object] [adverbial prepositional phrase answering the question *where*]

With drooping heads and tremulous tails, the horses mashed their way through the thick mud.

EXPLANATION: The phrase modifies the verb *mashed* and tells *how* the horses mashed.

EXPLANATION: The phrase modifies the verb *mashed* and tells where the horses *mashed*.

[adjectival prepositional phrase describing *linen*]
His linen, though not of a fineness in accordance with his stockings, was as white as
[adverbial prepositional phrase answering the question *where* and describing *broke*]
the tops of the waves that broke upon the neighbouring beach, or
[adverbial prepositional phrase answering the question *where* and describing *glinted*]
the specks of sail that glinted in the sunlight far at sea.

[adverbial prepositional phrase answering the question *where* and describing *laid*] [adverbial prepositional phrase answering the question *how* and describing *tended*]
She softly laid the patient on a sofa, and tended her with great skill and gentleness.

[adjectival present participle phrase describing *Mr. Jarvis Lorry* and *Miss Manette*]
Mr. Jarvis Lorry and Miss Manette, emerging from the wine-shop thus, joined Monsieur Defarge in the doorway to which he had directed his other company just before. It opened
[adverbial prepositional phrase answering the question *where* and describing *opened*]
from a stinking little black court-yard, and was the general public entrance to a great pile of
[adjectival past participle phrase describing *houses* and also including a prepositional phrase serving as the object of the past participle]
houses, inhabited by a great number of people.

[adverbial prepositional phrase answering the question *where* and describing *dropped*]
[adverbial prepositional phrase answering the question *how* and describing *lay*]

He had gradually dropped to the floor, and lay there in a lethargy,
[adverbial past participle phrase answering the question *how* and describing *lay*]
worn out.

[present participle phrase acting as a noun and serving as the object of the preposition *after*]
After bursting open a door of idiotic obstinacy with a weak rattle in its throat, you fell into
[adverbial prepositional phrase answering the question *where* and describing *came*]
Tellson's down two steps, and came to your senses in a miserable little shop.

[adverbial prepositional phrase with a compound object, answering the question *how* and describing *was dressed*]
He was plainly dressed in black, or very dark grey, and his hair, which was long and dark,
[adverbial prepositional phrase answering the question *where* and describing *was gathered*]
was gathered in a ribbon at the back of his neck..

[infinitive phrase acting as a noun and serving as the direct object of *told*]
"Ten o'clock at night?" "Yes, sir. Your honour told me to call you."

[adjectival prepositional phrase describing *way*]
This man stood still on his way across a silent terrace, and saw for a moment,
[adverbial present participle phrase answering the question *where* and describing *saw*]
lying in the wilderness before him, a mirage of honourable ambition, self-denial, and perseverance.

Review 7B: Improving Sentences with Clauses

Rewrite each sentence on your own paper, adding a dependent clause that meets the description in brackets.

The first is done for you, with explanations provided.

The original sentences are taken from *A Tale of Two Cities*, by Charles Dickens.

When you are finished, compare your sentences with the originals in the Answer Key.

[noun clause serving as the subject]
What the unknown prisoner had written will never be read, but he had written something.

EXPLANATION: The entire clause "What the unknown prisoner had written" is the subject, which will never be read (*never* is an adverb modifying *will be read*).

Those venerable and feeble persons were always seen by the public in the act of bowing, and were
[adverb clause telling *when*]
popularly believed, when they had bowed a customer out, still to keep on bowing in the
[adverb clause telling *when*]
empty office until they bowed another customer in.

[adjective clause describing *nobody*]
He was not missed; for, nobody who crossed the threshold looked for him.

[adverb clause telling *how*]
Defarge raised his head thoughtfully, as if there were something in that too.

[adverb clause telling *when*]
When it was yet light enough to work and read, she had neither engaged herself in her usual work, nor had she read to him.

My dear Manette, I am anxious to have your opinion, in confidence, on a very curious case
[adjective clause describing *case*]
in which I am deeply interested.

Presently, the château began to make itself strangely visible by some light of its own,
[adverb clause telling *how*]
as though it were growing luminous.

Review 7C: Conditional Clauses

Label the following sentences as first, second, or third conditional by writing *1*, *2*, or *3* in the blank next to each one. Underline each conditional clause. Circle each consequence clause.

These sentences are taken or adapted from *The Warden and the Wolf King*, by Andrew Peterson.

If I fight, I fight for the Hollows, not for a monster. 1

If they hadn't acted so weirdly, Janner would have suspected that there was some true danger at hand. 3

Unless he found more wood the little fire would weaken again. 2

I want him to have it if that's all right. 1

Of course, if you don't show up at Ban Rona for a week or so, we'll send out a search party to bring you home. 1

The thing stank, it was from a race of brutes, and it would happily squeeze them all to death if it were awake. 2

I can't rest until I finally learn what that means. 1

If he hadn't been so serious, and if there hadn't been real danger outside, it would have been humorous. 3

If he bore southward he would eventually run into a road that led to Ban Rugan. 2

Review 7D: Pronoun Review

The following paragraphs are taken from Katherine Paterson's *Bridge to Terabithia*. Circle every pronoun. Label each as personal (*PER*), possessive (*POSS*), reflexive (*REF*), demonstrative (*DEM*), relative (*REL*) or indefinite (*IND*). Beside this label, add the abbreviation for the part of the sentence (or clause) that the pronoun serves as: adjective (*ADJ*), subject (*SUBJ*), direct object (*DO*), indirect object (*IO*), or object of the preposition (*OP*).

The first has been done for you.

Jess pushed his [POSS/ADJ] damp hair out of his [POSS/ADJ] face and plunked down on the wooden bench. He [PER/SUBJ] dumped two spoonfuls of sugar into his [POSS/ADJ] cup and slurped to keep the hot coffee from scalding his [POSS/ADJ] mouth.

PER/SUBJ POSS/ADJ POSS/ADJ

"Oooo, Momma, (he) stinks." Brenda pinched (her) nose with (her) pinky crooked delicately.

PER/DO

"Make (him) wash."

REF/DO POSS/ADJ POSS/ADJ

"Get over here to the sink and wash (yourself)," (his) mother said without raising (her) eyes

PER/OP

from the stove. "And step on (it). These grits are scorching the bottom of the pot already."

"Momma! Not again," Brenda whined.

PER/SUBJ POSS/ADJ REL/SUBJ

Lord, (he) was tired. There wasn't a muscle in (his) body (that) didn't ache.

PER/SUBJ REL/DO POSS/ADJ

"(You) heard (what) Momma said," Ellie yelled at (his) back.

Review 7E: Parsing

In the sentences below, underline every verb or verb phrase that acts as the predicate of a clause (dependent *or* independent). Label each verb with the correct tense, voice, and mood.

Tense: Simple past, present, future; progressive past, present, future; perfect past, present, future

Voice: Active, passive (or state-of-being)

Mood: Indicative, subjunctive, imperative, modal, subjunctive/modal

The first is done for you.

The following paragraphs are taken from Milton Meltzer's *The Amazing Potato: A Story in Which the Incas, Conquistadors, Marie Antoinette, Thomas Jefferson, Wars, Famines, Immigrants, and French Fries All Play a Part.*

simple past active indicative — simple past state-of-being indicative

What finally did make the potato more acceptable to everyone? The commands of a king were

simple past active indicative — simple present active indicative

much less important than broad social changes. A French historian who studied the issue writes:

perfect present active indicative

"In all places and at all times the potato has always arrived in the baggage carts of distress. . . ."

simple present active indicative — simple past active indicative

He then cites the many wars and cereal-crop failures that ravaged Europe in the eighteenth

simple past active indicative — simple present active modal

century. When such disasters brought about hunger, the potato could save the day.

simple past passive indicative — simple past active indicative

The potato was planted in poor regions at first, and spread from there to meet food shortages.

simple past active indicative — simple past state-of-being indicative

Government officials soon realized how effective the new crop was. Given an equal surface of simple present / active / modal

land to grow on, the potato crop could feed five times as many people as wheat. So for the poor

simple past / active / indicative — simple past / active / indicative

farmer who held only a small bit of land, potatoes had great appeal. And when the wheat or rye

simple past / active / indicative — simple past / passive / indicative — simple past / active / subjunctive

crops failed, less harm was done to the community if potatoes were on hand.

The following sentences are taken from *The History and Social Influence of the Potato*, by Redcliffe N. Salaman and William Glynn Burton.

simple present / state-of-being / indicative — perfect future / passive / indicative

It is obvious that in thirty-five years many more advances will have been made.

perfect past / passive / indicative

In the interests of the army in the field, the countryside had been denuded of labour and horses;

perfect past / passive / indicative — simple past / passive / indicative

steam-tackle had been demobilized; the accessory trades, even that of the blacksmith, were closed

simple past / passive / indicative — simple present / passive / modal

down or brought to a standstill; to which must be added an acute shortage of potash and phosphate fertilizers.

Review 7F: Diagramming

On your own paper, diagram every word of the following sentence from J. R. R. Tolkien's *The Return of the King.*

Had I done so, I could have sent this thing hither to your keeping and spared myself and others much anguish.

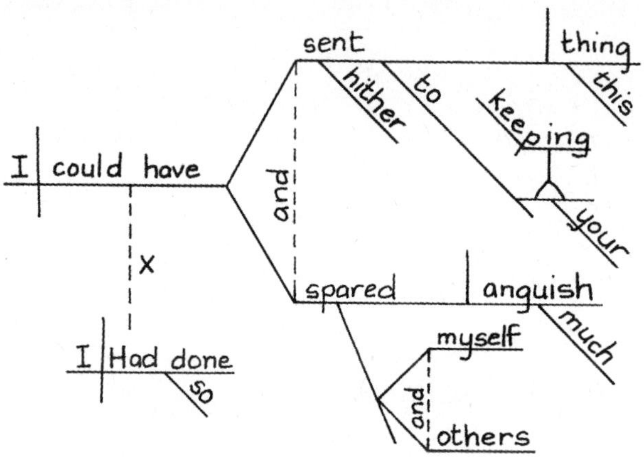

WEEK 22

Parenthetical Elements

— LESSON 85 —

Verb Review

Complete the following chart with the third-person-singular form of the verb indicated in the left-hand column. If you need help, ask your instructor.

Note to Instructor: Ask the student to make his best guess at any forms that confuse him. Then, show him the answers and have him erase (or scratch out) his incorrect answers and write in the correct ones.

INDICATIVE TENSES

		Active	Passive
SIMPLE			
hunt	Past	[he, she, it] hunted	[he, she, it] was hunted
film	Present	[he, she, it] films	[he, she, it] is filmed
bake	Future	[he, she, it] will bake	[he, she, it] will be baked
PROGRESSIVE			
notice	Past	[he, she, it] was noticing	[he, she, it] was being noticed
marry	Present	[he, she, it] is marrying	[he, she, it] is being married
release	Future	[he, she, it] will be releasing	[he, she, it] will be being released
PERFECT			
squash	Past	[he, she, it] had squashed	[he, she, it] had been squashed
pop	Present	[he, she, it] has popped	[he, she, it] has been popped
weigh	Future	[he, she, it] will have weighed	[he, she, it] will have been weighed

MODAL TENSES
(would OR should, may, might, must, can, could)

		Active	Passive
SIMPLE			
grip	Present	[he, she, it] would grip	
PERFECT			
claim	Past	[he, she, it] would have claimed	

SUBJUNCTIVE TENSES

		Active	Passive
SIMPLE			
balance	Past	[he, she, it] balanced	
chase	Present	[he, she, it] chase	

On your own paper, write sentences that use each of the forms above as the predicate of an independent or dependent clause. If you need help (or ideas), ask your instructor.

Note to Instructor: Model sentences using the forms in the chart are listed below. If the student needs assistance using a particular form, show him the sentence containing that form and then ask him to write a variation of it (different subject, different modifiers, etc.). Students should always be allowed to copy a model when they are confused.

Note that verbs are not used in exactly the same order as presented in the chart, since a number of them are in combination.

One child's balloon **has popped**, but the others **will be releasing** their balloons in a few minutes.

The new baby penguin **will have been weighed** many times to ascertain its growth rate before visitors see it at the zoo.

If you want to watch the royal wedding, turn on the television quickly; the princess **is being married** right now!

The prisoner **will be being released** on Thursday.

If Congress **balanced** the budget, everyone would be amazed.

Kira **is marrying** Luis this afternoon.

Martin, who **will bake** the wedding cake, **would have claimed** the wrong luggage at the airport, but Felicity corrected him.

The new TV show, which **is filmed** in Vancouver, **was being noticed** by critics all over the world.

In this game, it is imperative that each child **chase** the person with the balloon until the balloon **has been popped**.

Mr. Franks **hunted** all over for his contact lens, not realizing that he **had squashed** it as soon as he stood up.

Eliza **would grip** the handrail more carefully if she felt unsure of her footing.

The girl who **films** birthday parties **was noticing** that the child's largest present **had been squashed**.

If she keeps playing with the scales, Lorna **will have weighed** every toy she owns by tomorrow!

The pie that **will be baked** for the picnic should feed several people.

The Caribbean monk seal is an animal that **was hunted** to extinction.

— LESSON 86 —

Restrictive and Non-Restrictive Modifying Clauses

Parenthetical Expressions

Exercise 86A: Restrictive and Non-Restrictive Modifying Clauses

In the following sentences, mark each bolded clause as either *ADV* for adverb or *ADJ* for adjective, and draw an arrow from the clause back to the word modified. Some sentences contain more than one modifying clause.

Then, identify each bolded modifying clause as either restrictive (*R*) or non-restrictive (*N*).

Finally, set off all of the non-restrictive clauses with commas. Use the proofreader's mark ^ for comma insertion. When you are finished, compare your punctuation with the original.

These sentences are from Richard Peck's *The Ghost Belonged to Me.* The original commas around the non-restrictive clauses have been removed.

R ADJ

There are several opinions **that people hold** regarding ghosts, and not one of them would clinch an argument.

R ADJ
But she was a secret **I could not keep**, and so other people were drawn in.

R ADJ
There's hardly a topic **you can raise** without reminding Cousin Elvera of a point of interest down at the fair.

In seasonable weather, they run the open-sided cars, and you can hear the people talking
R ADV
as they glide behind the barn.

R ADV
She'll marry him **if she gets half a chance.**

N ADJ
Dad would have put him on the payroll at the business, **which is house construction.**

N ADV
When Gladys called me in to noon dinner, I found Mother and Lucille making a whole batch of paper roses.

N ADJ
The chauffeur, **who wore gaiters**, hopped out and darted up the steps to Mother.

N ADJ
Gladys took a supper tray upstairs to Mother, **who said she could not face anybody anymore that night or maybe ever.**

R ADJ
Here was a man **who would never believe anything told to him in a barnloft.**

R ADJ
But after a few steep yards we came to a path **that zigzagged down.**

R ADJ
The only voice **I could make out** was Dad's.

R ADV
We could all go down the cellar and hide out in the coal bin **until he's gone.**

N ADV
When I got down to the dining room, Dad was trying to finish his breakfast in peace.

R ADJ
She seemed to be passing the time of day with the men **who were unloading the train**..

Exercise 86B: Identifying Parenthetical Expressions

Identify each parenthetical expression as a phrase, dependent clause, or sentence.

CHALLENGE EXERCISE

- Provide a fuller description of each expression. What kind of phrase, clause, or sentence is it? What does it do or modify?
- When you are finished, ask your instructor for the fuller explanations. Compare your descriptions to these explanations.

The sentences below are adapted from Esther Hautzig's *The Endless Steppe.*

dependent clause,
acting as an adjective, modifying *millet*

At the state store, we lined up for bread, flour, millet (which tasted ghastly), and occasional treats.

phrase,
present participle phrase, acting as an adjective,modifying *movies*

The Russian movies (including some of the great ones) were all right, but nothing was as exciting as an American movie.

complete sentence,
providing more details about the setting and the noteworthiness of lights dimming

The light dimmed (there was electricity here, of course, the first I had seen since I left Vilna) and everyone quieted down and waited attentively.

complete sentence,
independent of the previous sentence

So Svetlana told me that her father had gotten a large quantity of hospital gauze. (How and why I did not know or care to ask.)

complete sentence,
providing a reason for Mother's "begging me to count the change carefully"

This she did, warning me to watch the thirty-ruble note for dear life—scarcely an exaggeration—and begging me to count the change carefully (for me, two and two did not always readily add up to four).

complete sentence,
providing more information about the socks the speaker wore

I ripped the red sweater with ice-cold fingers and a cold heart, and when it was too cold to stay out of bed, I knitted in bed, wearing socks (old socks of Father's had replaced my outgrown ones), my sweater, and often a shawl over my head.

phrase,
prepositional phrase, acting as an adjective, modifying *food*

One of the directors of the tractor factory, Yosif Isayevich, would give us food (in addition to our own rations) and lodging in exchange for caring for him and his house while his wife and children were away.

dependent clause,
acting as an adverb, modifying *help*

Shurik came to help us pack (as if our belongings couldn't have been packed in an hour) and his mother sent some flour and half a dozen eggs for us to bake some cookies for the road.

Exercise 86C: Punctuating Sentences with Parenthetical Expressions

Correct each of the following sentences, using the proofreader's marks listed below.

delete:
insert comma:
insert period:
insert exclamation point:
insert question mark:
move punctuation mark:

If the sentence is correct, write *C* in the margin next to it.

These sentences are adapted from *Cannibal Animals: Animals That Eat Their Own Kind*, by Anthony D. Fredericks.

Tiny black widow spiderlings often eat one another. (until they can build their own webs)

As larvae, midges develop inside their mother's body (and feed on her from the inside out.)

Skeletons indicate that the Tyrannosaurus rex may have been a cannibal (but scientists aren't sure!)

Note to Instructor: In the sentence above, the student could also choose to move the exclamation point to just after the closing parenthesis.

In some groups of tiger salamanders (particularly those living in crowded conditions,) the young eat one another.

The Chinese giant salamander grows up to 5 feet long and weighs about 220 pounds (is it bigger than you are)?

When they are hungry, horned frogs jump at anything that moves (including other horned frogs). C

The male damselfish guards the eggs laid by his mate (up to 300,000 of them)! but sometimes grows hungry and eats some of the eggs.

Did you know that a female gerbil may eat her own babies (when her diet is lacking in protein?)

Alaskan brown bear cubs (especially male cubs) are at risk of being eaten by adult male bears, C who want to ensure their control of a specific area.

— LESSON 87 —

Parenthetical Expressions

Dashes

Exercise 87A: Types of Parenthetical Expressions

Identify each parenthetical expression as a phrase, dependent clause, or sentence.

CHALLENGE EXERCISE

- Provide a fuller description of each expression. What kind of phrase, clause, or sentence is it? What does it do or modify?
- When you are finished, ask your instructor for the fuller explanations. Compare your descriptions to these explanations.

These sentences are from James Hilton's *Goodbye, Mr. Chips.*

phrase,
acting as an adjective, modifying *you*

When you are getting on in years (but not ill, of course), you get very sleepy at times, and the hours seem to pass like lazy cattle moving across a landscape.

And years later, when Colley was an alderman of the City of London and a baronet and various

phrase, prepositional phrase,
acting as an adjective, modifying *son*

other things, he sent his son (also red-haired) to Brookfield.

complete sentence,
letting the reader know that though the subject re-experienced things in his dreaming, he did not re-experience them in reality

But he resaw the glorious hump of the Gable (he had never visited the Lake District since), and the mouse-gray depths of Wastwater under the Screes; he could resmell the washed air after heavy rain, and refollow the ribbon of the pass across to Sty Head.

dependent clause,
acting as an adverb modifying *answering*

About a quarter to four a ring came, and Chips, answering the front door himself (which he oughtn't to have done), encountered a rather small boy wearing a Brookfield cap and an expression of anxious timidity.

complete sentence,
acting as an adjective, modifying *Head*

And then, in the shadows behind Merivale, he saw Cartwright, the new Head (he thought of him as "new," even though he had been at Brookfield since 1919), and old Buffles, commonly called "Roddy."

Exercise 87B: Punctuating Parenthetical Expressions

On either side of each bolded parenthetical expression, place parentheses, dashes, or commas. There are not necessarily "correct" answers for these, but compare them to the originals when you have finished.

These sentences are adapted from *A Dog on Barkham Street*, by M. S. Stolz.

Note to Instructor: The original punctuation of Stolz's sentences are below and reflect the author's intentions; any grammatical answers are acceptable, but where the student has chosen different punctuation, ask him to read first his version, and then Stolz's, out loud.

It was getting so he couldn't be interested in anything for very long — **not even dogs** — because the problem of Martin was always in the way.

In this**, as in so many matters concerning adults,** Edward failed to see the reason but accepted the fact.

As quietly as they could — **which was pretty noisily** — the fifth grade made itself ready.

And then Connie climbed the stepladder **(garlanded)** on the outside of the box and the lid flew back.

The man nodded and moved forward**, the young dog keeping at his side,** and put out his hand.

What bothers me is that we — **Edward and his father and I** — have discussed this matter for . . . oh, for years.

When she'd driven off, the two boys turned to the man**, their faces alight,** and waited for him to say something, anything.

It gave them a splendid, unchecked, adventurous feeling **(though they could not, <u>at the moment</u>, think of any forbidden thing they wished to do)**, but in another way they didn't altogether care for it.

Note to Student: The underlined phrase is a parenthetical expression within the longer parenthetical expression in bold print. Punctuate both expressions!

I was going to shout after him, but**, as I say,** he was kind of a big fellow with an ugly expression.

They asked Uncle Josh whether they could tie a rope around her neck so that Edward **(who certainly wouldn't leave Argess behind)** could accompany his friend.

They'd lasted till what they thought was three or four in the morning **(it turned out to be just short of midnight)**, and then had crept back in the house.

Exercise 87C: Using Dashes for Emphasis

On your own paper, rewrite the next four sentences, substituting dashes for the underlined punctuation marks and making any other capitalization or punctuation changes needed.

These sentences are taken from *Over Sea, Under Stone*, by Susan Cooper.

You stand in the doorway and look on both sides. The landing stops before it gets that far.

Would you like to go off swimming and come home for a late lunch (about one thirty)?

But they must have been behind it all, the ransacked books, the stolen maps, the attempt to look for a secret hiding-place under the floor.

It's like the way they searched the house, all at random, without any sort of plan.

You stand in the doorway and look on both sides--the landing stops before it gets that far.

Would you like to go off swimming and come home for a late lunch--about one thirty?

But they must have been behind it all--the ransacked books, the stolen maps, the attempt to look for a secret hiding-place under the floor.

It's like the way they searched the house--all at random, without any sort of plan.

— LESSON 88 —

Parenthetical Expressions
Dashes
Diagramming Parenthetical Expressions

Exercise 88A: Diagramming Parenthetical Expressions

On your own paper, diagram each of the following sentences (not including the citation in the grey box).

The next four sentences are drawn from Frederick Douglass's autobiography, *Narrative of the Life of Frederick Douglass.*

My mother and I were separated when I was an infant—before I knew her as my mother.

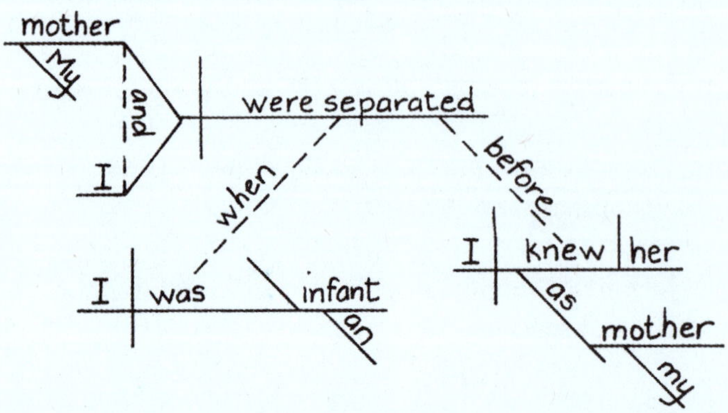

Aunt Hester went out once—where or for what I do not know—and happened to be absent when my master desired her presence.

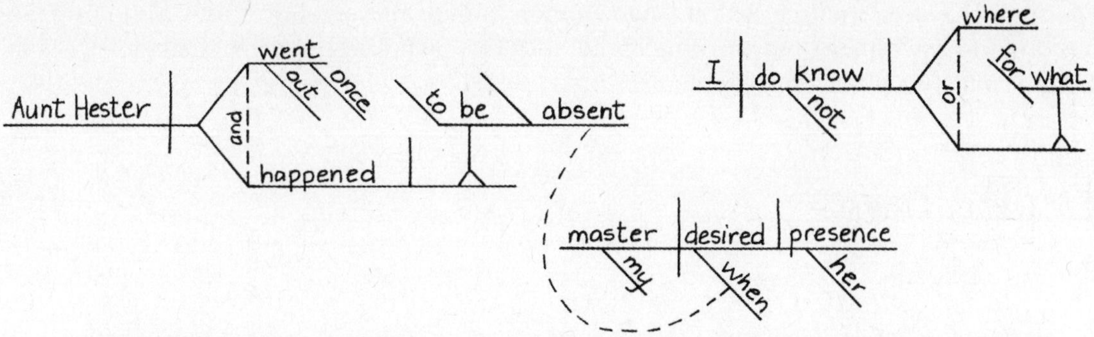

Note to Instructor: The student may have difficulty with *happened to be absent*. Although *to be absent* seems to describe *Aunt Hester, happened* is not a linking verb, so *to be absent* cannot be a predicate nominative. Instead, *happened* is acting as a transitive verb. In the parenthetical expression, *where* is acting as a pronoun.

During the summer months, people came from far and near—from Baltimore, Easton, and Annapolis—to see it.

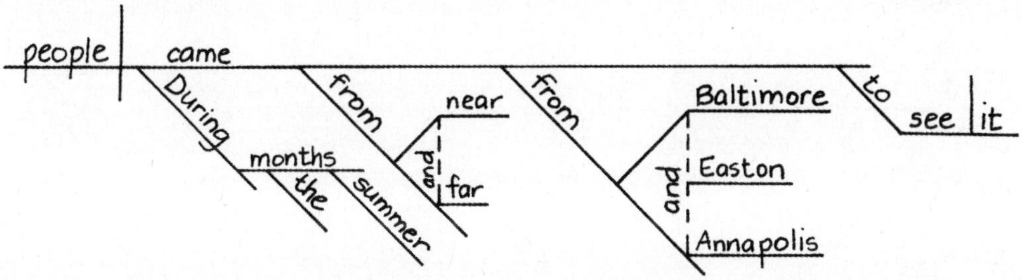

A single word from the white men was enough—against our wishes, prayers, and entreaties—to sunder forever the dearest friends, dearest kindred, and strongest ties known to human beings.

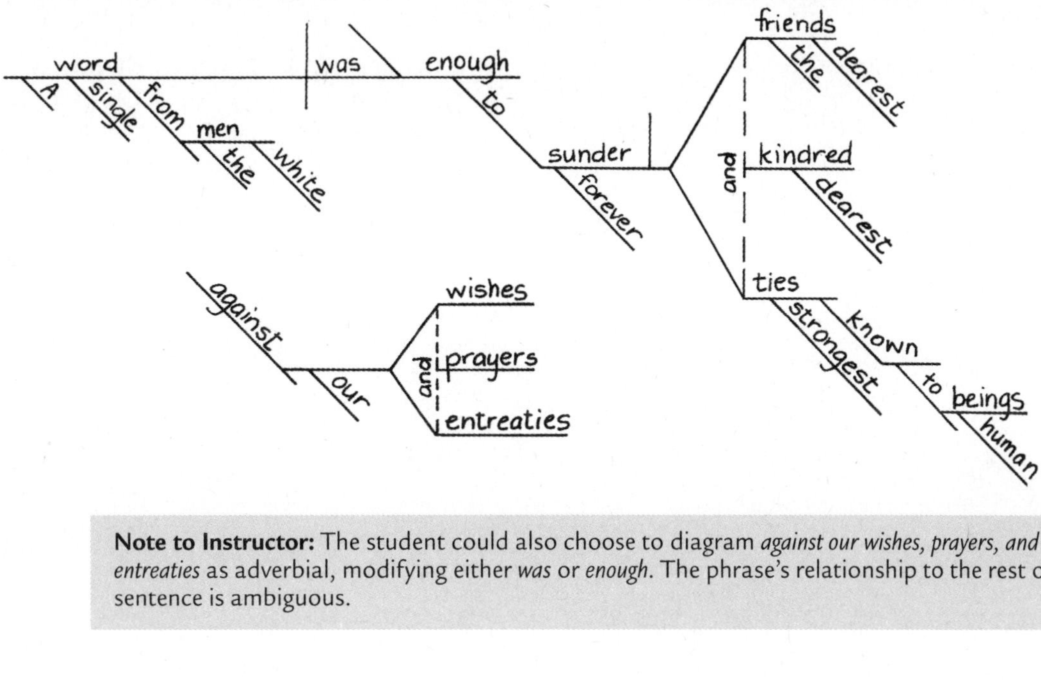

Note to Instructor: The student could also choose to diagram *against our wishes, prayers, and entreaties* as adverbial, modifying either *was* or *enough*. The phrase's relationship to the rest of the sentence is ambiguous.

The following sentences are slightly condensed from *David Copperfield*, by Charles Dickens.

When we got into the street (which was strange enough to me), and smelt the fish, and pitch, and oakum, and tar, and saw the sailors walking about, and the carts jingling over the stones, I felt that I had done so busy a place an injustice.

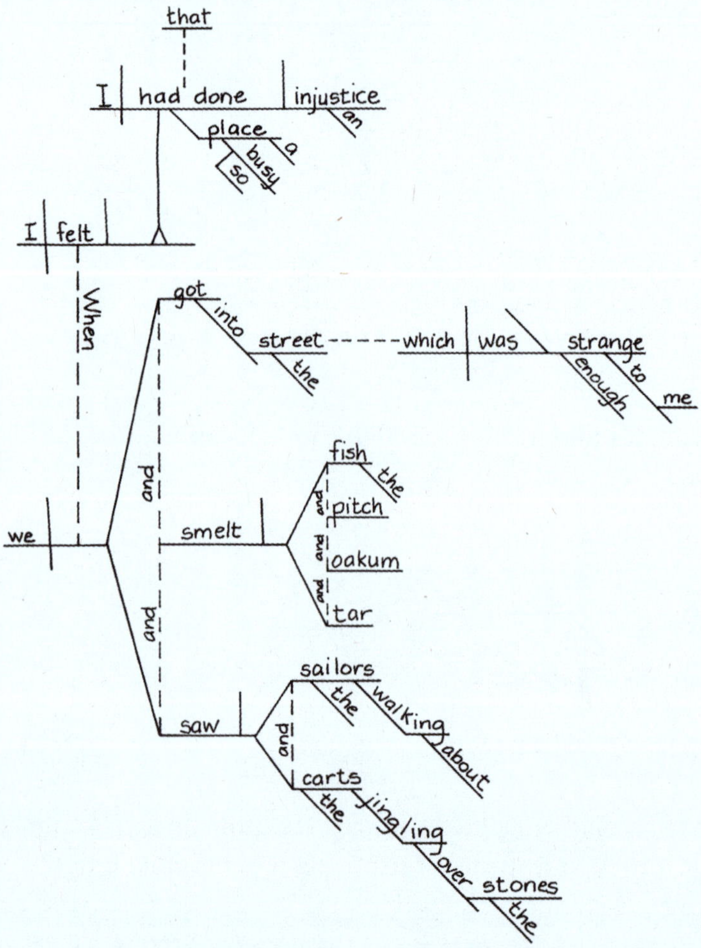

I listen to all they tell me with a vague feeling of solemnity and awe, which makes me glad that they are so near, and frightens me (though I feign to laugh) when Traddles pretends to see a ghost in the corner.

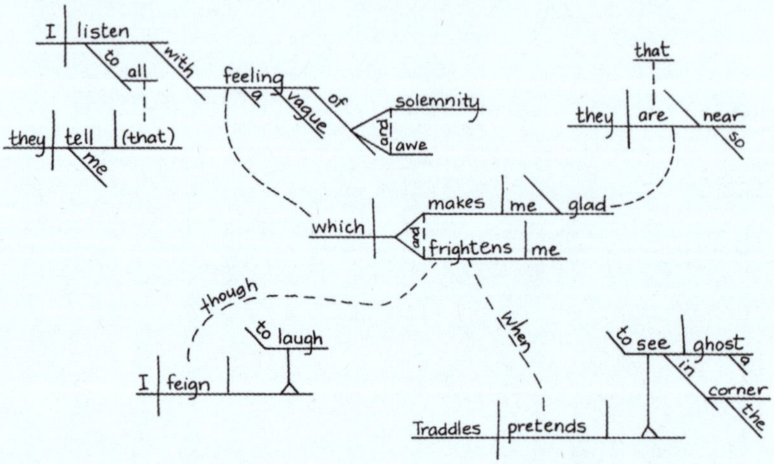

I passed the night at Peggotty's, in a little room in the roof (with the crocodile-book on a shelf by the bed's head) which was to be always mine, Peggotty said, and should always be kept for me in the same state.

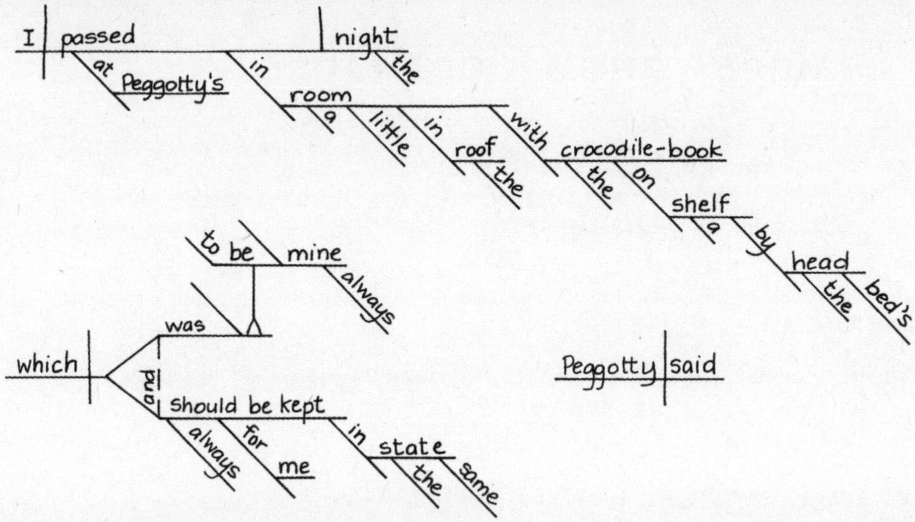

When I dress (the occupation of two hours), for a great ball given at the Larkins's (the anticipation of three weeks), I indulge my fancy with pleasing images.

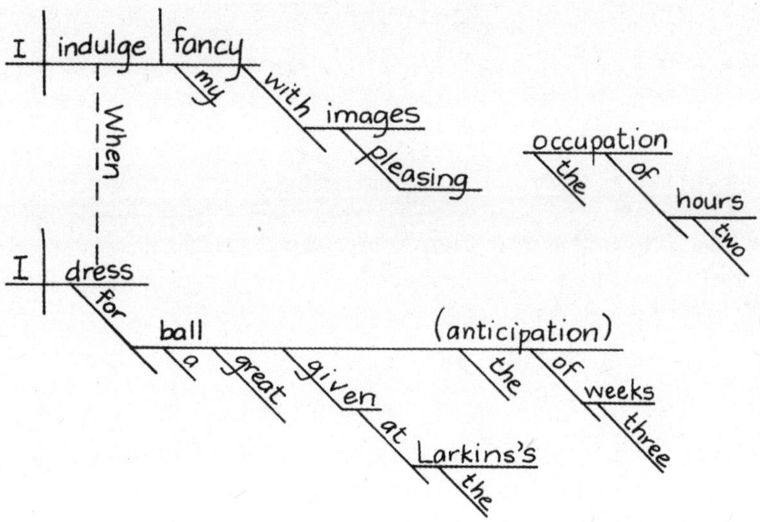

WEEK 23

Dialogue and Quotations

— LESSON 89 —

Dialogue

Exercise 89A: Punctuating Dialogue

The excerpt below is from Lois Lowry's *The Giver.* All of the dialogue is missing quotation marks, and some of it is missing ending punctuation as well. Do your best to supply the missing punctuation marks.

When you are finished, compare your versions with the originals.

"I felt very angry this afternoon," Lily announced. "My Childcare group was at the play area, and we had a visiting group of Sevens, and they didn't obey the rules at all. One of them—a male; I don't know his name—kept going right to the front of the line for the slide, even though the rest of us were all waiting. I felt so angry at him. I made my hand into a fist, like this." She held up a clenched fist and the rest of the family smiled at her small defiant gesture.

"Why do you think the visitors didn't obey the rules?" Mother asked.

Lily considered, and shook her head. "I don't know. They acted like . . . like . . ."

"Animals?" Jonas suggested. He laughed.

"That's right," Lily said, laughing too. "Like animals."

"Where were the visitors from?" Father asked.

Lily frowned, trying to remember. "Our leader told us, when he made the welcome speech, but I can't remember. I guess I wasn't paying attention. It was from another community. They had to leave very early, and they had their midday meal on the bus."

Mother nodded. "Do you think it's possible that their rules may be different? And so they simply didn't know what your play area rules were?"

Lily shrugged, and nodded. "I suppose."

"You've visited other communities, haven't you?" Jonas asked. "My group has, often."

Exercise 89B: Writing Dialogue Correctly

On your own paper, rewrite the following sentences as dialogue, using the past tense for the dialogue tags. Use the notations in parentheses to help you.

You may choose to place dialogue tags before, in the middle of, or after dialogue, or to leave the tags out completely. But you must use at least three of those four options.

When you are finished, compare your answers with the original, which is from George MacDonald's *The Shadows*. Note that Ralph Rinkelmann is the king's name.

(The Shadow repeats, solemnly) We are the Shadows.

(The king says) Well?

(The Shadow says) We do not often appear to men.

(The king says) Ha!

(The Shadow says) We do not belong to the sunshine at all. We go through it unseen, and only by a passing chill do men recognise an unknown presence.

(The king says again) Ha!

(The Shadow says) It is only the twilight of the fire, or when one man or woman is alone with a single candle, or when any number of people are all feeling the same thing at once, making them one, that we show ourselves, and the truth of things.

(The king says) Can that be true that loves the night?

(The Shadow answers) The darkness is the nurse of light.

(The king says) Can that be true which mocks at forms?

(The Shadow answers) Truth rides abroad in shapeless storms.

(Ralph Rinkelmann thinks) Ha! ha! it rhymes. The Shadow caps my questions with his answers. Very strange! And he grew thoughtful again.

(The Shadow says, resuming the conversation) Please, your majesty, may we present our petition?

(The king replies) By all means. I am not well enough to receive it in proper state.

Note to Instructor: Allow the student to compare her answers with the original text below, but accept any grammatical rewriting.

"We are the Shadows," repeated the Shadow, solemnly.

"Well?" said the king.

"We do not often appear to men."

"Ha!" said the king.

"We do not belong to the sunshine at all. We go through it unseen, and only by a passing chill do men recognise an unknown presence."

"Ha!" said the king again.

"It is only the twilight of the fire, or when one man or woman is alone with a single candle, or when any number of people are all feeling the same thing at once, making them one, that we show ourselves, and the truth of things."

"Can that be true that loves the night?" said the king.

"The darkness is the nurse of light," answered the Shadow.

"Can that be true which mocks at forms?" said the king.

"Truth rides abroad in shapeless storms," answered the Shadow.

"Ha! ha!" thought Ralph Rinkelmann, "it rhymes. The Shadow caps my questions with his answers. Very strange!" And he grew thoughtful again.

The Shadow was the first to resume.

"Please, your majesty, may we present our petition?"

"By all means," replied the king. "I am not well enough to receive it in proper state."

Exercise 89C: Proofreading

Using the following proofreading marks, correct these incorrect sentences. They are from the O. Henry short story "The Skylight Room."

Insert quotation marks:

insert exclamation point:

insert comma:

insert period:

delete:

move punctuation mark:

"It's that star" explained Miss Leeson, pointing with a tiny finger. "Not the big one that twinkles—the steady blue one near it. I can see it every night through my skylight. I named it Billy Jackson.

"Well, really"! said Miss Longnecker. "I didn't know you were an astronomer, Miss Leeson."

"Oh, yes, said the small star gazer, I know as much as any of them about the style of sleeves they're going to wear next fall in Mars."

"Well, really," said Miss Longnecker! "The star you refer to is Gamma, of the constellation Cassiopeia. It is nearly of the second magnitude, and its meridian passage is—"

"Oh," said the very young Mr. Evans. "I think Billy Jackson is a much better name for it."

"Same here, said Mr. Hoover, loudly breathing defiance to Miss Longnecker, "I think Miss Leeson has just as much right to name stars as any of those old astrologers had."

"Well, really!" said Miss Longnecker!

— LESSON 90 —

Dialogue

Direct Quotations

Exercise 90A: Punctuating Dialogue

The paragraphs below, from C. S. Lewis's *Prince Caspian*, are missing punctuation. Write in all of the missing punctuation marks (insert them directly rather than using proofreader's marks). When you are finished, compare your answers to the original sentences.

Note to Instructor: The original text is below.

"Look! Look! Look!" cried Lucy.

"Where? What?" asked everyone.

"The Lion," said Lucy. "Aslan himself. Didn't you see?" Her face had changed completely and her eyes shone.

"Do you really mean—?" began Peter.

"Where did you think you saw him?" asked Susan.

"Don't talk like a grown-up," said Lucy, stamping her foot. "I didn't think I saw him. I saw him."

"Where, Lu?" asked Peter.

"Right up there between those mountain ashes. No, this side of the gorge. And up, not down. Just the opposite of the way you want to go. And he wanted us to go where he was—up there."

"How do you know that was what he wanted?" asked Edmund.

"He—I—I just know," said Lucy, "by his face."

Exercise 90B: Punctuating Direct Quotations

Write in all of the missing punctuation marks (insert them directly rather than using proofreader's marks). When you are finished, compare your answers to the original sentences.

The following passages are from *The Fall of the Roman Empire*, by Don Nardo.

Note to Instructor: The original passages are below. Help the student to identify any differences between her answers and the source texts.

According to Rostovtzeff, the Roman Empire underwent a series of violent internal struggles between the lower classes and the upper classes, with the army increasingly taking the side of the peasants against the ruling aristocracy. "The army fought the privileged classes," he wrote, "and did not cease fighting until these classes had lost all their social prestige and lay powerless and prostrate under the feet of the half-barbarian soldiery."

Baynes finds little credence in the notion that the peasants and soldiers often found common cause in a struggle against the upper classes. Solomon Katz, formerly of the University of Washington, agrees. "There is little evidence," he contends, "that the army was made up of a class-conscious proletariat which hated the urban upper classes. On the contrary, in its greed the army plundered town and country alike."

According to Westermann, Egypt was a clear-cut example. "All the land of Egypt belonged to the sovereign," he wrote. "The mass of the native subject population . . . were increasingly bound to their villages, to their agricultural duties, and certain villein [feudal] services due to the state."

"Slavery grew," comments Walbank, "and as it invaded the various branches of production it led inevitably to the damping down of scientific interest."

Thus classical civilization inevitably decayed from within, in a sense rotted at the very roots from which it had once grown strong; as Walbank says, "an absolutely low technique and, to compensate for this, the institution of slavery."

The following passages are taken from *The Celtic Empire: The First Millennium of Celtic History 1000 BC–AD 51*, by Peter Berresford Ellis.

Appian of Alexandria, writing AD c.160, disapprovingly comments: "For this Didius was actually honoured with a triumph!"

Sotion, who wrote accounts of the philosophers of different schools, became a main source of Diogenes Laertius (writing in the third century AD), who says, "the study of this philosophy had its beginning among the barbarians."

Caesar was proud of his troops. "They did nothing unworthy of them," he reported.

Exercise 90C: Attribution Tags

In the following paragraphs, find and underline the direct quotes that are missing their attribution tags. In the blank below each paragraph, write an attribution tag for each quote; the source of each one is noted in parentheses. Place a caret (^) to show where you would insert the attribution tag. Do not worry about marking necessary punctuation changes for inserting the tag.

Note to Instructor: Answers provided below are samples. Direct quotes should be underlined, but attribution tags may be inserted before, after, or in the middle of quotes, and the wording of attribution tags may vary.

When an apple becomes ripe, it changes the starch inside of it into sugar.^"The presence of sugar, plus the bright light of the sun, produces chemical reactions in the apple. These reactions cause the cells in the apple's skin to produce a red pigment called anthocyanin." (quote from *Apple Trees*, by Sylvia A. Johnson)

As Sylvia A. Johnson writes in *Apple Trees,*

In Renaissance Europe, decisions to marry were not generally based on a couple's love for one another.^"Fathers chose husbands and wives for their children based on political and financial considerations." (quote from *Life During the Renaissance*, by Patricia D. Netzley)

According to Patricia D. Netzley,

Mexican leaders in 1844 were apprehensive about the US presidential election. "The unpleasant reality^was that if an annexationist won the 1844 election and Texas joined the Union, they would feel compelled to preserve Mexico's integrity by declaring war on the United States." Many of these leaders hoped this could be avoided. (quote from *The Mexican-American War*, by Don Nardo)

writes Don Nardo in *The Mexican-American War*

Apple growers must spend a long time caring for trees before they see the fruits of their labor. "A few varieties have been developed that bear apples when they are only 3 years old, but most other kinds of trees must be 7 to 10 years old before they reach their reproductive stage." ^ (quote from *Apple Trees*, by Sylvia A. Johnson)

writes Johnson

^ "Individual patrons were members of the middle class who wanted to gain prestige by offering economic support to artists." Renaissance artists could also receive support from a guild or from the Catholic Church. (quote from *Life During the Renaissance*, by Patricia D. Netzley)

In *Life During the Renaissance*, Netzley explains,

Following the battle of Cerro Gordo, Americans were able to learn about the nature of their enemy, by the actions of people like the Mexican army surgeons. ^ "What amazed the Americans was that these Mexican physicians, without being asked or coerced, also treated the American wounded, in one instance actually saving the life of an American officer who had sustained a serious head injury." (quote from *The Mexican-American War*, by Don Nardo)

Don Nardo describes those actions:

— LESSON 91 —

Direct Quotations
Ellipses
Partial Quotations

Exercise 91A: Using Ellipses

The following two paragraphs are taken from John Fiske's *The American Revolution*. This excerpt is 398 words long. On your own paper, rewrite it so that it has no more than 200 words. Use ellipses wherever you omit words. Do not cut the opening or closing words of any paragraph. Make sure that you don't end up with run-on sentences or fragments!

When you are finished, compare your version with the condensed version found in the key.

During the dreary winter at Valley Forge, Washington busied himself in improving the organization of his army. The fall of the Conway cabal removed many obstacles. Greene was persuaded, somewhat against his wishes, to serve as quartermaster-general, and forthwith the duties of that important office were discharged with zeal and promptness. Conway's resignation opened the way for a most auspicious change in the inspectorship of the army. Of all the foreign officers who served under Washington during the War for Independence, the Baron von Steuben was in many respects the most important. Member of a noble family which for five centuries had been distinguished in the local annals of Magdeburg, Steuben was one of the best educated and most experienced soldiers of Germany. His grandfather, an able theologian, was well known as the author of a critical treatise on the New Testament. His uncle, an eminent mathematician, had been the inventor of a new system of fortification. His father had seen half a century of honourable service in the corps of engineers. He had himself held the rank of first lieutenant at the beginning of the Seven Years' War, and after excellent service in the battles of Prague, Rossbach, and Kunersdorf he was raised to a position on the staff of Frederick the Great. At the end of the war, when the thrifty king reduced his army, and Blücher with other officers afterward famous left the service, Steuben retired to private life, with the honorary rank of General of the Circle of Swabia. For more than ten years he was grand marshal to the Prince of Hohenzollern-Hechingen. Then he went travelling about Europe, until in the spring of 1777 he arrived in Paris, and became acquainted with Franklin and Beaumarchais.

The American alliance was already secretly contemplated by the French ministry, and the astute Vergennes, knowing that the chief defect of our armies lay in their want of organization and discipline, saw in the scientific German soldier an efficient instrument for remedying the evil. After much hesitation Steuben was persuaded to undertake the task. That his arrival upon the scene might excite no heart-burning among the American officers, the honorary rank which he held in Germany was translated by Vergennes into the rank of lieutenant-general, which the Americans would at once recognize as more eminent than any position existing in their own army except that of the commander-in-chief.

Note to Instructor: A sample condensation is shown below. The student may choose to omit different parts of the passage. When she is finished, check her paragraphs for sense and readability. Ask her to read her paragraphs out loud, listening for meaning. Then, allow her to read the sample answer below.

Each omission must be marked by an ellipsis.

During the dreary winter . . .Washington busied himself in improving the organization of his army. The fall of the Conway cabal . . . opened the way for a most auspicious change in the inspectorship of the army . . . Baron von Steuben . . . was one of the best educated and most experienced soldiers of Germany. His grandfather . . . was well known as the author of a critical treatise on the New Testament. His uncle . . . had been the inventor of a new system of fortification . . . He . . . himself . . . was raised to a position on the staff of Frederick the Great. At the end of the war . . . Steuben retired to private life . . . Then he went travelling . . . until in the spring of 1777 he . . . became acquainted with Franklin and Beaumarchais.

The American alliance was already secretly contemplated by the French ministry, and . . . Steuben was persuaded to undertake the task. That his arrival upon the scene might excite no heart-burning among the American officers, the honorary rank . . . was translated by Vergennes into the rank of lieutenant-general, which the Americans would at once recognize as more eminent than any position . . . except that of the commander-in-chief.

Exercise 91B: Partial Quotations

On your own paper, rewrite the five statements below so that each one contains a partial quotation. Draw the partial quotation from the bolded sentences that follow each statement. The authors of the bolded sentences are provided for you—be sure to include an attribution tag for each direct quote!

You may change and adapt the statements freely.

One of your sentences should contain a very short one- to three-word quote; one should contain a preposition phrase, gerund phrase, participle phrase, or infinitive phrase; and one should quote a dependent clause.

If you need help, ask your instructor to show you sample answers.

Note to Instructor: If the student needs a jump-start, show her *one* of the three sample sentences that follow each statement.

Saint-Exupéry wrote the novella The Little Prince.

"As lost as Saint-Exupéry was, some of the best drawing rooms of Paris were open to him. His existence became a chaotic one of lavish dinners and low rents, skimpy meals and sumptuous lodgings, a habit to which he ultimately became accustomed. We have no record of how he dressed during these times, but he was neither the world's first nor last impoverished aristocrat, and was eccentric enough to have been allowed some latitude."
—Stacy Schiff, biographer

1–3 words

The biographer Stacy Schiff describes Saint-Exupéry, the author of *The Little Prince*, as an "impoverished aristocrat."

Infinitive phrase

Saint-Exupéry, the author of *The Little Prince*, is characterized by biographer Stacy Schiff as "eccentric enough to have been allowed some latitude" in his clothing choices.

Dependent clause

Saint-Exupéry, the author of *The Little Prince*, experienced an odd mixture of poverty and wealth, and biographer Stacy Schiff writes that this was "a habit to which he ultimately became accustomed."

During the Middle Ages, women were not encouraged to form friendships with others outside their families.

"In his book of instruction the wealthy merchant of Paris . . . advised his bride against such ties. In fact, he demanded that she walk through town, on those rare occasions when she went out at all, without stopping to speak to any man or woman on the road. This would presumably keep her from harm while protecting his reputation."
— Marty Williams and Anne Echols, historians

1–3 words

During the Middle Ages, women were not encouraged to form friendships with others outside their families, sometimes warned "against such ties" by their husbands, as historians Marty Williams and Anne Echols put it.

Prepositional, gerund, and infinitive phrases

During the Middle Ages, husbands sometimes wanted their wives to conduct business in town "without stopping to speak to any man or woman on the road," write historians Marty Williams and Anne Echols.

Dependent clause

A woman during the Middle Ages was instructed not to speak with others "on those rare occasions when she went out at all," write historians Marty Williams and Anne Echols.

Susan B. Anthony met with resistance from some women in her work for women's rights.

"Susan went from door to door during the cold blustery days of December and January 1854 to get signatures on her petitions for married women's property rights and woman suffrage. Some of the women signed, but more of them slammed the door in her face, declaring indignantly that they had all the rights they wanted."

—Alma Lutz, biographer

1–3 words

Not all women supported Susan B. Anthony's work for women's rights; some of them "slammed the door" when she came around seeking support, according to biographer Alma Lutz.

Prepositional phrase

When Susan B. Anthony attempted to garner support "for married women's property rights and woman's suffrage," writes biographer Alma Lutz, many of the women themselves refused to sign her petitions.

Dependent clauses

Many women told Susan B. Anthony "that they had all the rights they wanted" when she sought support for her women's rights efforts, as biographer Alma Lutz puts it.

All animals brought to a wildlife clinic are in danger of death.

"When animals arrive at the KSTR wildlife clinic, they are all essentially dying—some more quickly than others. That means our job is to reverse the path to death and heal them so they can make it back to where they belong—in the jungle. The only reason a person is ever able to physically pick up a wild animal is because it is injured, orphaned, or in shock and can't run away and save itself."

—Sam Trull, conservationist

1–3 words

All animals brought to a wildlife clinic are in danger of death, and according to conservationist Sam Trull, the workers at the clinic "reverse the path" if possible so the animals can return to the wild.

Infinitive phrase

All animals brought to a wildlife clinic are in danger of death, and as conservationist Sam Trull puts it, the goal of the clinic worker is "to reverse the path to death and heal them" in order to return the animals to the wild.

Dependent clause

An animal can only be picked up by a human and brought to a wildlife clinic if "it is injured, orphaned, or in shock and can't run away and save itself," writes conservationist Sam Trull.

Paper mills in the eighteenth century were not large enterprises.

"Hundreds of paper mills were established in North America in the eighteenth century. Most were small operations, using only one vat. Sometimes paper was made in mills that also ground grain or that were used as sawmills. Papermaking was done during only part of the year, in accordance with agricultural needs and the demands of boat traffic and competition with other mills for use of the river."

—Mark Kurlansky, author

1–3 words

According to author Mark Kurlansky, eighteenth-century paper mills were mostly "small operations."

Prepositional phrases

Author Mark Kurlansky writes that small paper mills were not run year-round, but had to be conducted "in accordance with agricultural needs and the demands of boat traffic and competition with other mills for use of the river."

Dependent clause

Most paper mills in the eighteenth century were not large enterprises, and many of them were "mills that also ground grain or that were used as sawmills," explains author Mark Kurlansky.

Exercise 91C: Diagramming

On your own paper, diagram every word of the following sentences. These are from *Glacier*, by Ronald H. Bailey.

These are difficult! Do your best, and then compare your answers with the key.

Meticulous ground surveys—ever more numerous and accurate with the passing of time—proved to be the key to understanding the complex processes of glacier movement.

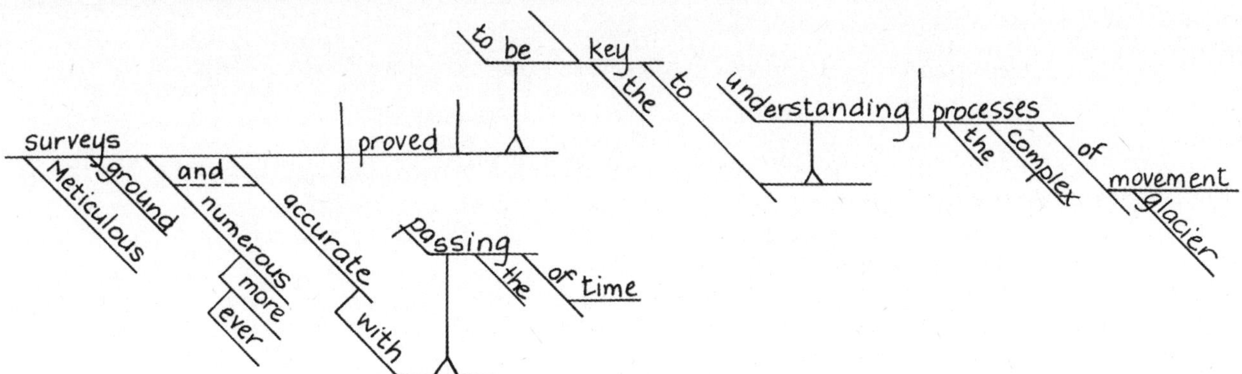

A transverse crevasse—across the direction of the ice's flow—occurs where there is a sudden change in the slope of the underlying bedrock and the glacier speeds up on the steeper slope.

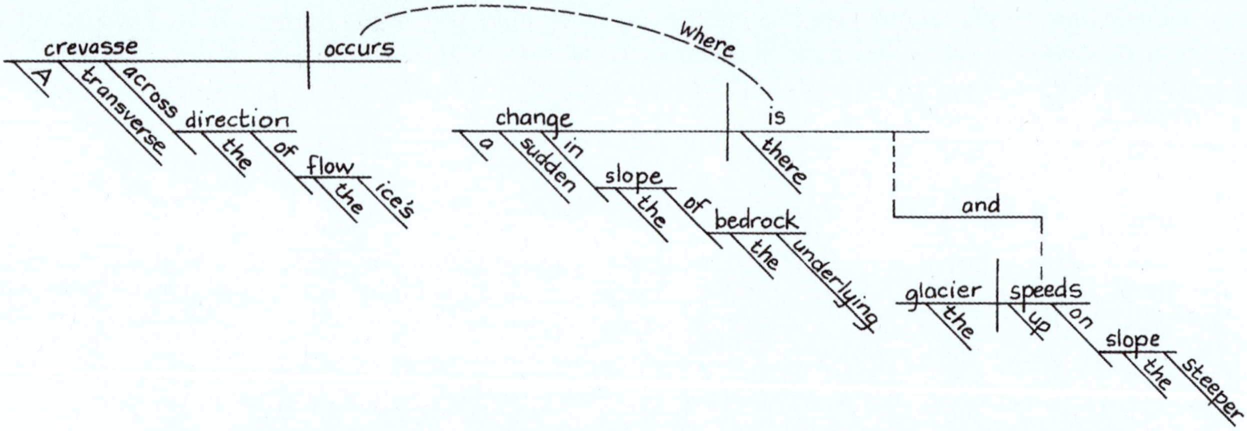

Note to Instructor: "Underlying" can also be diagrammed on a bent line as a present participle.

The problem is complicated by the fact that the bergs posing the gravest threat—the pinnacled, unstable ones—are also the most elusive.

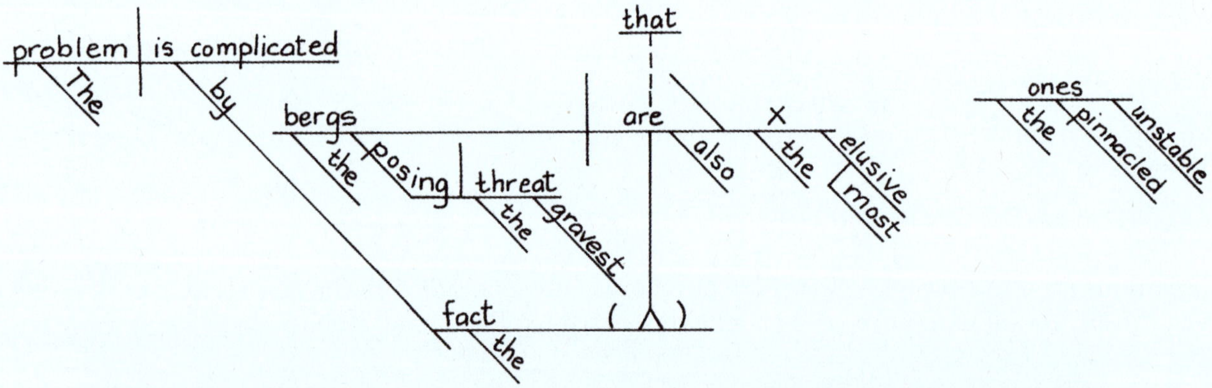

Note to Instructor: The phrase "the pinnacled, unstable ones" can also be diagrammed as an appositive following "bergs".

An expedition member called him "the strongest combination of a strong mind in a strong body that I have ever known."

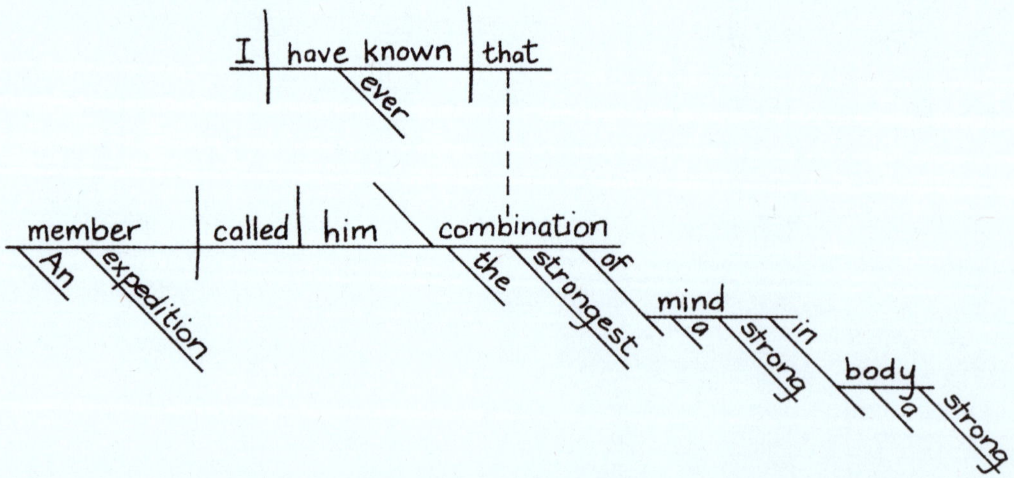

— LESSON 92 —

Partial Quotations
Ellipses
Block Quotes
Colons
Brackets

Exercise 92A:Writing Dialogue Correctly

The following speeches, from *Matilda* by Roald Dahl, are listed in the correct order, but are missing the dialogue tags. On your own paper, rewrite the speeches as dialogue, making use of the dialogue tags below. You must place at least one dialogue tag before a speech, one in the middle of a speech, and one following a speech.

A list of the rules governing dialogue follows, for your reference.

When you are finished, compare your dialogue to the original passage in the Key.

A. DIALOGUE (IN CORRECT ORDER)

Can you really turn the mileage back with an electric drill?

I'm telling you trade secrets. So don't you go talking about this to anyone else. You don't want me put in jug, do you?

I won't tell a soul. Do you do this to many cars, dad?

Every single car that comes through my hands gets the treatment. They all have their mileage cut to under ten thou before they're offered for sale.

And to think I invented that all by myself. It's made me a mint.

But daddy, that's even more dishonest than the sawdust. It's disgusting. You're cheating people who trust you.

If you don't like it then don't eat the food in this house. It's bought with the profits.

It's dirty money. I hate it.

B. DIALOGUE TAGS (NOT IN CORRECT ORDER)

Matilda said

Matilda, who had been listening closely, said

young Michael asked

the boy said

the father said

the father said

he added proudly

the father said

C. FOR REFERENCE: RULES FOR WRITING DIALOGUE

A dialogue tag identifies the person making the speech.

When a dialogue tag comes after a speech, place a comma, exclamation point, or question mark inside the closing quotation marks.

When a dialogue tag comes before a speech, place a comma after the tag. Put the dialogue's final punctuation mark inside the closing quotation marks.

Speeches do not need to be attached to a dialogue tag as long as the text clearly indicates the speaker.

Usually, a new paragraph begins with each new speaker.

When a dialogue tag comes in the middle of a speech, follow it with a comma if the following dialogue is an incomplete sentence. Follow it with a period if the following dialogue is a complete sentence.

> **Note to Instructor:** The original text is shown below. As long as the above rules are followed, the student's rewritten dialogue does not need to match the original exactly. Ask the student to point out the differences between her dialogue and the passage below.

"Can you really turn the mileage back with an electric drill?" young Michael asked.

"I'm telling you trade secrets," the father said. "So don't you go talking about this to anyone else. You don't want me put in jug, do you?"

"I won't tell a soul," the boy said. "Do you do this to many cars, dad?"

"Every single car that comes through my hands gets the treatment," the father said. "They all have their mileage cut to under ten thou before they're offered for sale. And to think I invented that all by myself," he added proudly. "It's made me a mint."

Matilda, who had been listening closely, said, "But daddy, that's even more dishonest than the sawdust. It's disgusting. You're cheating people who trust you."

"If you don't like it then don't eat the food in this house," the father said. "It's bought with the profits."

"It's dirty money," Matilda said. "I hate it."

Exercise 92B: Using Direct Quotations Correctly

On your own paper, rewrite the following three paragraphs, inserting at least one quote from each of the following three sources into the paragraph. Use the following guidelines:

- At least one quote must be a block quote.
- At least one quote must be a complete sentence.
- At least one quote must be a partial sentence incorporated into your own sentence.

In addition:

- Each quote must have an attribution tag.
- At least one quote must be condensed, using an ellipsis.
- You must make at least one change or addition that needs to be put in brackets.

A list of the rules governing direct quotations follows, for your reference.

When you are finished, compare your paragraphs to the sample answer in the Key.

A. PARAGRAPHS

The year 1860 saw national tensions grow even stronger, culminating with the secession of South Carolina in December. The pivotal point in the year was in early November, when the ballots were cast and Abraham Lincoln was selected as the country's next president. At the start of the year, however, Lincoln's selection as the Republican party's candidate was not at all certain.

Lincoln had been working for quite some time to lay the groundwork for his candidacy before the Republican nominating convention in May. He took every opportunity to make appearances and speeches around the nation in order to build his reputation. In line with the Republican party's position, he worked to stop slavery from expanding, but not to abolish it altogether.

At the start of the nominating convention, Republicans knew that their candidate was likely to win the election, particularly since the Democratic party had just split into different factions. The frontrunner for the Republican nomination was William H. Seward, but Seward proved to have some opinions that the Republicans worried might cause division among the electorate. Between Seward's perceived weaknesses and some deals made on Lincoln's behalf by those representing him at the convention, the delegates ultimately selected Lincoln as their candidate, leading to his election in November as President of the United States.

B. SOURCES

> **Note:** Two of the selections below include words that are themselves quoted from elsewhere. Because each full selection is in quotation marks, the smaller quotations are enclosed in single quotation marks. If you choose to use a block quote that includes a smaller quotation, you should change the single quotation marks back to double, since the block quote is not enclosed in quotation marks.

"On the first ballot, Lincoln had little more than half Seward's numbers but more than anyone else. On the second he was only a few short of Seward. After the third, the country discovered that the three-term state legislator and one-term moderate antislavery congressman, who had held no other office, who had no executive experience, who was resented for his opposition to the Mexican War, and whom many considered a clumsy Western primitive without formal education or drawing-room manners, was almost certain to be elected president."

—Fred Kaplan, biographer

"Certainly Lincoln occupied a surprisingly strong position as 1860 unfolded. His stature as a politician was noticeable, but not so noticeable as to appear threatening to Seward and the other front-runners. His 1858 Senate race and the Cooper Union speech had put him on the national stage—just. He had the support of those who knew him well—Illinois Republicans were solid for him—and competitors who did not yet know him well did not pay enough attention to him. He had devoted his energies to slavery expansion, the issue that defined his party—the 'question about which all true men do care,' he had called it at Cooper Union—without blotting his record with inconvenient positions on other issues."

—Richard Brookhiser, historian

"For many Republicans, Seward was entitled to the nomination by virtue of his clear, consistent, forceful argument against the extension of slavery. Almost every American knew that Seward believed that a 'higher law' dedicated the territories to freedom. But others opposed him for precisely this reason; they believed he was a radical who could not win moderate or conservative votes."

—Walter Stahr, author

C. FOR REFERENCE: RULES FOR USING DIRECT QUOTATIONS

When an attribution tag comes after a direct quote, place a comma, exclamation point, or question mark inside the closing quotation marks.

When an attribution tag comes before a direct quote, place a comma after the tag. Put the dialogue's final punctuation mark inside the closing quotation marks.

When an attribution tag comes in the middle of a direct quotation, follow it with a comma if the remaining quote is an incomplete sentence. Follow it with a period if the remaining quote is a complete sentence.

Direct quotes can be words, phrases, clauses, or sentences, as long as they are set off by quotation marks and form part of a grammatically correct original sentence.

An ellipsis shows where something has been cut out of a sentence.

Every direct quote must have an attribution tag.

If a direct quotation is longer than three lines, indent the entire quote one inch from the margin in a separate block of text and omit quotation marks.

If you change or make additions to a direct quotation, use brackets.

> **Note to Instructor:** You will need to check the student's paragraphs against the rules above. The sample answer below is just one way to insert the direct quotations.
>
> If the student needs prompting, allow her to read the sample answer below and then require her to use different parts of the sources in her own rewritten paragraphs.

The year 1860 saw national tensions grow even stronger, culminating with the secession of South Carolina in December. The pivotal point in the year was in early November, when the ballots were cast and Abraham Lincoln was selected as the country's next president. At the start of the year, however, Lincoln's selection as the Republican party's candidate was not at all certain.

Lincoln had been working for quite some time to lay the groundwork for his candidacy before the Republican nominating convention in May. He took every opportunity to make appearances and speeches around the nation in order to build his reputation. Writes historian Richard Brookhiser, "[S]lavery expansion . . . defined his party," and Lincoln followed the party's position, working to stop slavery from expanding, but not to abolish it altogether.

At the start of the nominating convention, Republicans knew that their candidate was likely to win the election, particularly since the Democratic party had just split into different factions. The frontrunner for the Republican nomination was William H. Seward, and indeed he had the support of many in the party because of his strong beliefs about slavery in the territories. "But others," notes author Walter Stahr, "opposed him for precisely this reason; they believed he was a radical who could not win moderate or conservative votes." Between Seward's perceived weaknesses and some deals made on Lincoln's behalf by those representing him at the convention, the delegates ultimately selected Lincoln as their candidate. As biographer Fred Kaplan describes the scene,

> After the third [ballot], the country discovered that the three-term state legislator and one-term moderate antislavery congressman, who had held no other office, who had no executive experience, who was resented for his opposition to the Mexican War, and whom many considered a clumsy Western primitive without formal education or drawing-room manners, was almost certain to be elected president.

Thus the stage was set for Lincoln's election in November as President of the United States.

WEEK 24

Floating Elements

— LESSON 93 —

Interjections
Nouns of Direct Address
Parenthetical Expressions

Exercise 93A: Using Floating Elements Correctly

On your own paper, rewrite the following sentences in List 1, inserting interjections, nouns of direct address, and parenthetical expressions from List 2. You must use every item in List 2 at least once. Every sentence in List 1 must have at least one insertion.

Interjections may either come before or after sentences on their own, or may be incorporated directly into the sentence.

List 1. Sentences

The pig got dirty.
This little girl was found walking along the street with a balloon in her hand.
The fundraiser will happen on Saturday.
Please eat these leftovers for lunch tomorrow.
We're going to the zoo today!
You are in favor of the proposed amendment.
We'll finish this project on time.

List 2. Interjections, Nouns of Direct Address, Parenthetical Expressions

no doubt
of course
Mr. Smith
in fact
come what may
everyone
hooray
Robert
rain or shine
Katherine
dear

Note to Instructor: The answers below are samples. Any grammatical, properly punctuated versions of these sentences are acceptable.

The pig got dirty, of course.

Mr. Smith, this little girl was, in fact, found walking along the street with a balloon in her hand.

Rain or shine, the fundraiser will happen on Saturday, everyone!

Please eat these leftovers for lunch tomorrow, dear.

Hooray! We're going to the zoo today, Robert!

You are, no doubt, in favor of the proposed amendment.

Katherine, we'll finish this project on time, come what may.

Exercise 93B: Parenthetical Expressions

In the following pairs of sentences, underline each subject once and each predicate twice. In each pair, cross out the parenthetical expression that is not essential to the sentences. If the expression is used as an essential part of the sentence, circle it and label it with the correct part of the sentence. If it acts as a modifier, draw an arrow back to the word it modifies.

The train, ~~in reality~~, is hardly ever on time.

prepositional phrase acting as an adverb

The train was present (in reality), not just in my imagination.

This isn't my first time speaking in front of an audience, ~~you know~~.

subject & verb

(You know) this isn't my first time speaking in front of an audience.

subordinating adverb / direct object

(After all) we've done, we deserve a break.

~~After all~~, tomorrow is another day!

Note to Instructor: *After all we've done* is a dependent clause, subordinated by *after*. The subject of the dependent clause is *we*, the predicate is *[ha]ve done*, and the object is *all*.

I believe, ~~in short~~, that our candidate will win this election.

prepositional phrase acting as an adverb (object is *order*; *short* modifies *order*)

The votes will be counted (in short) order.

infinitive phrase acting as direct object

We promise (to be brief) in our explanation.

~~To be brief~~, we need to borrow your car.

Exercise 93C: Diagramming

On your own paper, diagram every word of the following sentences. They come from Rudyard Kipling's *The Jungle Book*.

Rann had never seen Mowgli before, though of course he had heard of him.

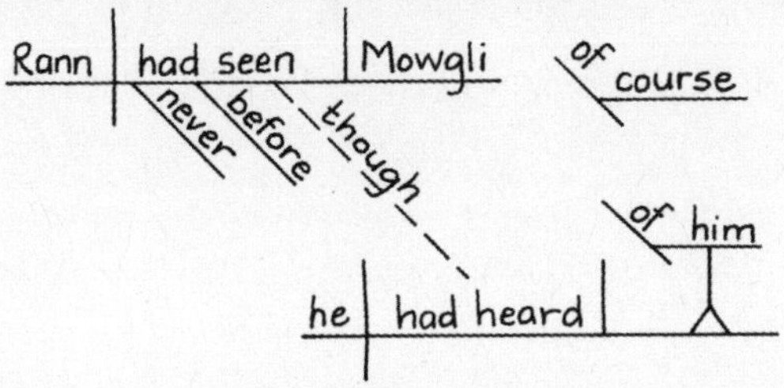

Because he had been appointed a servant of the village, as it were, he went off to a circle that met on a masonry platform under a great fig-tree.

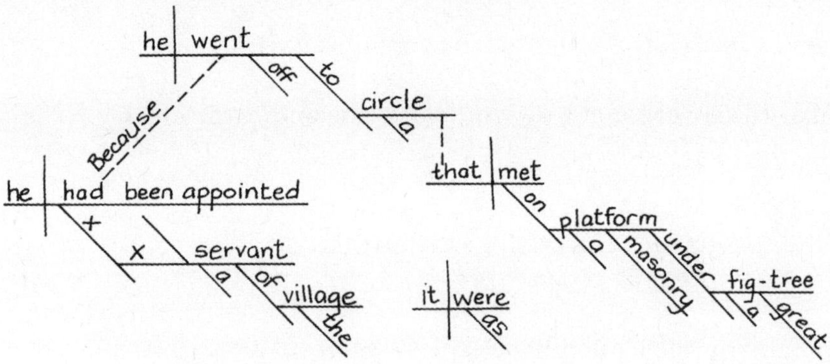

> **Note to Instructor:** The student will probably need help diagramming *a servant of the village*. It cannot be a direct object, because the verb is passive (so the subject is already receiving the acting of the verb), and it cannot be a predicate nominative because *appoint* is an action verb, not a state-of-being verb. So the phrase is best understood as including an understood infinitive: *he had been appointed [to be] a servant of the village*. The infinitive phrase answers the question how and modifies the verb (adverbial).
>
> This might be a good time to remind the student that language doesn't always fit neatly on a diagram!

Hm, tide's running strong tonight.

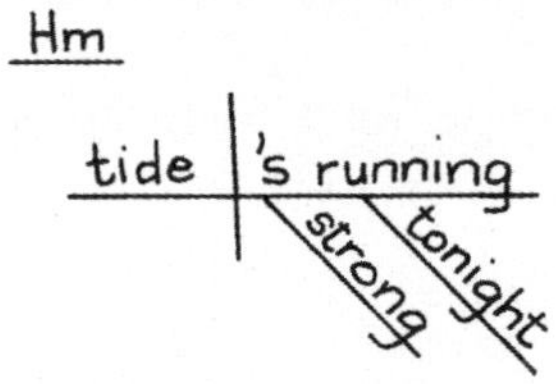

Well, if I am a man, a man I must become.

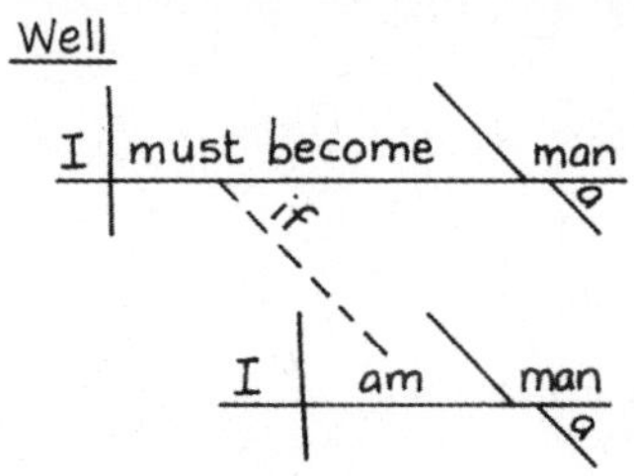

Mowgli, hast thou anything to say?

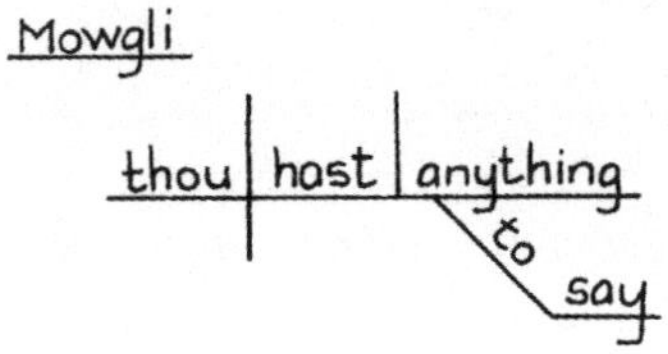

— LESSON 94 —

Appositives

Exercise 94A: Using Appositives

On your own paper, rewrite each group of sentences below as a single sentence using one or more appositives.

> **Note to Instructor:** The answers below are samples; other correct answers are possible. However, check to make sure the student has used appositives rather than other grammatical constructions.

The moon takes a little over 27 days to orbit the earth.
The moon is Earth's natural satellite.

The moon, Earth's natural satellite, takes a little over 27 days to orbit the earth.

Franklin Delano Roosevelt served as the governor of New York before becoming president.
Franklin Delano Roosevelt was the thirty-second president of the United States.
New York is nicknamed the Empire State.

Franklin Delano Roosevelt, the thirty-second president of the United States, served as the governor of New York, the Empire State, before becoming president.

Labor Day has been observed nationally in the United States since 1894.
Labor Day is the first Monday in September.

Labor Day, the first Monday in September, has been observed nationally in the United States since 1894.

The eardrum allows sound to pass through to the ossicles.
The eardrum is the tympanic membrane.
Ossicles are bones in the middle ear.

The eardrum, the tympanic membrane, allows sound to pass through to the ossicles, the bones in the middle ear.

Other than February 29, the days in the year when the smallest number of people have birthdays are December 25 and January 1.
December 25 is Christmas.
January 1 is New Year's Day.

Other than February 29, the days in the year when the smallest number of people have birthdays are December 25, Christmas, and January 1, New Year's Day.

Star Wars: Episode IV—A New Hope was released in US theaters in 1977.
Star Wars: Episode IV—A New Hope was the first movie in the original *Star Wars* trilogy.

The first movie in the original *Star Wars* trilogy, *Star Wars: Episode IV–A New Hope* was released in US theaters in 1977.

Exercise 94B: Identifying Appositives

In each of the following sentences, underline the subject once and the predicate twice. You do not need to mark subjects and predicates in dependent clauses, but watch for compound sentences! Circle each appositive or appositive phrase. Draw an arrow from each circled word or phrase back to the noun or pronoun it renames.

These sentences are slightly condensed from Rudyard Kipling's *The Jungle Book*.

It is I, Shere Khan, who speak!

And it is I, Raksha, who answer.

Akela, the great gray Lone Wolf, who led all the Pack by strength and cunning, lay out at full length on his rock.

It was Bagheera, the black Panther, inky black all over, but with the panther markings showing up in certain lights like the pattern of watered silk.

Perhaps Ikki, the Porcupine, had told him.

I am sleepy, Bagheera, and Shere Khan is all long tail and loud talk, like Mao, the Peacock.

He is a man—a man's child, and from the marrow of my bones I hate him!

But for the sake of the Honor of the Pack—a little matter that, by being without a leader, ye have forgotten—I promise that if ye let the man-cub go to his own place, I will not, when my time comes to die, bare one tooth against ye.

More I cannot do; but, if ye will, I can save ye the shame that comes of killing a brother against whom there is no fault—a brother bought into the Pack according to the Law of the Jungle.

I, the man, have brought here a little of the Red Flower.

Akela, the grim old wolf who had never asked for mercy in his life, gave one piteous look at Mowgli.

The boy could climb almost as well as he could swim, and swim almost as well as he could run; so Baloo, the Teacher of the Law, taught him the Wood and Water laws.

Exercise 94C: Diagramming

On your own paper, diagram every word of these sentences from Exercise 94B.

It is I, Shere Khan, who speak!

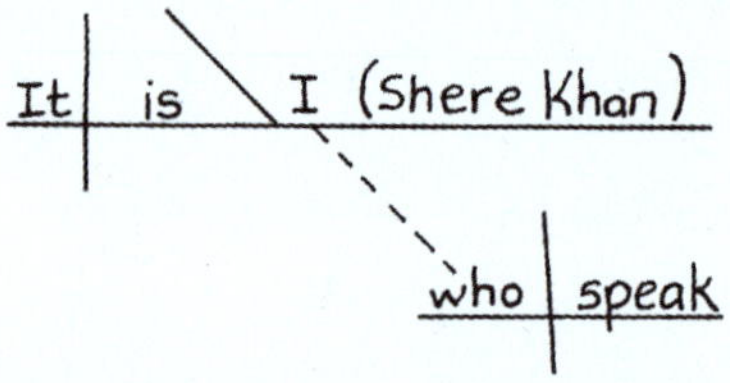

I, the man, have brought here a little of the Red Flower.

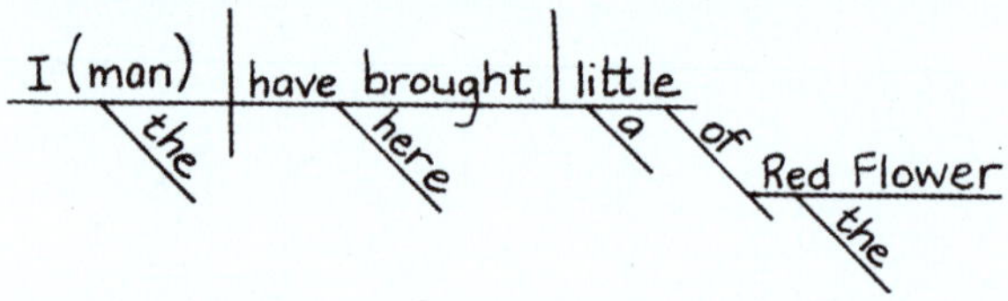

He is a man—a man's child, and from the marrow of my bones I hate him!

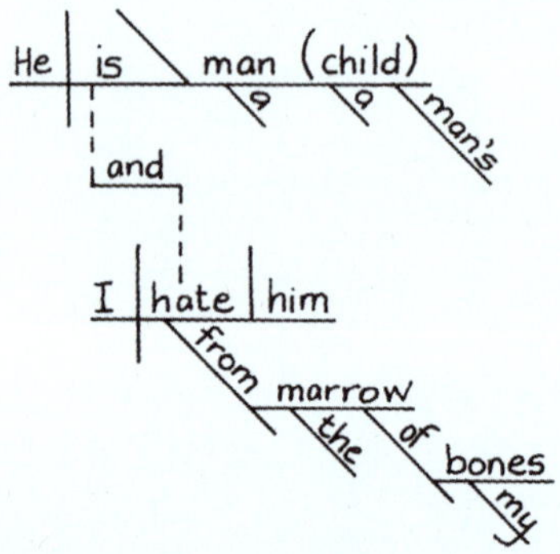

Akela, the grim old wolf who had never asked for mercy in his life, gave one piteous look at Mowgli.

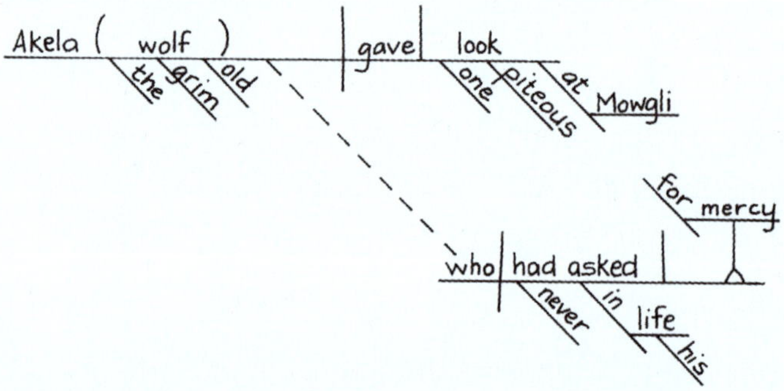

More I cannot do; but, if ye will, I can save ye the shame that comes of killing a brother against whom there is no fault—a brother bought into the Pack according to the Law of the Jungle.

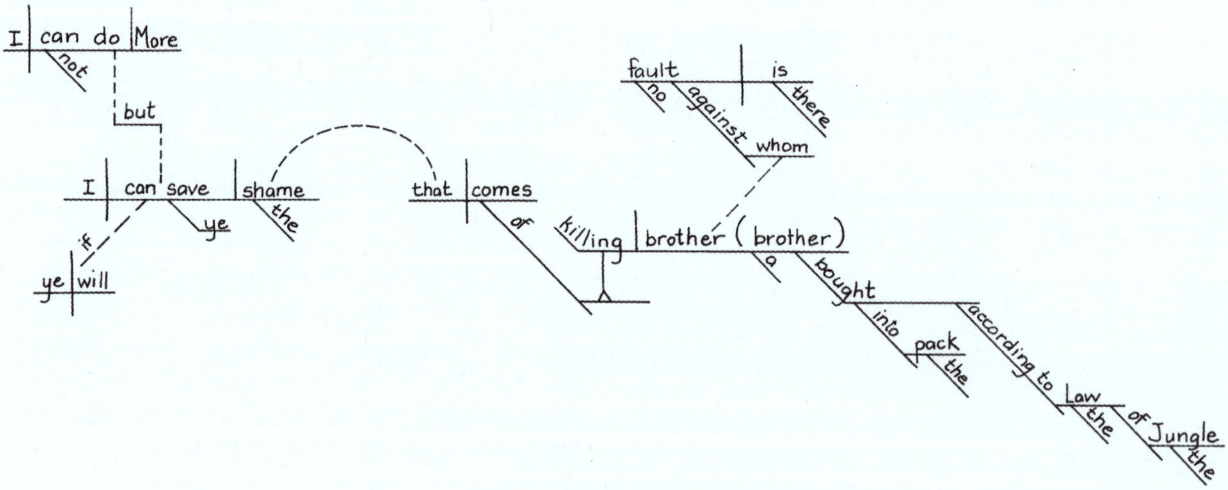

— LESSON 95 —

Appositives
Intensive and Reflexive Pronouns
Noun Clauses in Apposition
Object Complements

Exercise 95A: Reflexive and Intensive Pronoun Review

In the following sentences, slightly condensed from Oscar Wilde's *The Picture of Dorian Gray*, underline each reflexive or intensive pronoun. Put parentheses around each intensive pronoun. Label each reflexive pronoun with the correct part of the sentence (*DO*, *IO*, or *OP*).

Sin is a thing that writes itself (DO) across a man's face.

"Perhaps, after all, America never has been discovered," said Mr. Erskine; "I (myself) would say that it had merely been detected."

You know (yourself), Harry, how independent I am by nature.

In front of it, some little distance away, was sitting the artist (himself), Basil Hallward.

But the bravest man amongst us is afraid of himself (OP).

She consoled herself (DO) by telling Sibyl how desolate she felt her life would be, now that she had only one child to look after.

And, certainly, to him Life (itself) was the first, the greatest, of the arts, and for it all the other arts seemed to be but a preparation.

Don't flatter yourself (DO), Basil: you are not in the least like him.

You know we poor artists have to show ourselves (DO) in society from time to time, just to remind the public that we are not savages.

The praise of folly, as he went on, soared into a philosophy, and Philosophy (herself) became young.

I thought I would do myself (IO) the honour of coming round in person.

And what sort of lives do these people, who pose as being moral, lead (themselves)?

Exercise 95B: Distinguishing Noun Clauses in Apposition from Adjective Clauses

In the following sentences, identify each noun, noun phrase, or noun clause acting as an appositive by underlining it and writing the abbreviation *APP* above it. Draw an arrow from each appositive back to the noun it renames or explains. Circle each adjective clause and draw an arrow from each circle back to the noun that the adjective clause modifies.

The intricate doily, the only one of my grandmother's handmade projects (APP → doily) (that I owned → projects), was missing.

My alibi—what I needed the detective to accept as truth (APP → alibi)—was my presence at the concert.

The problem, how they were going to escape the locked cellar (APP → problem), was causing a bit of panic at that moment.

Oh, no! We've forgotten Morgan's stuffed bear (that he needs for bedtime → bear)!

Natalie's advice, that Soren skip the chicken at the roadside café (APP → advice), proved wise; three other people became ill from it.

I could never reveal the truth, that I was actually taking a pottery class.

Miss Kim gave me a suggestion, that we should ask local businesses to donate items for the auction.

Peregrine wished that he could find the book which Opal had loaned him.

Mother was much relieved by the result of the lab test, that Shelley did not have the flu.

Could you pick up the dress that is at the drycleaner?

The question, which competition I should enter, had been on my mind all week.

She stroked the cat, a purring ball of fur that had been her companion since childhood and considered the problem that her friend had mentioned.

Jensen's, the store at the end of Main Street, sells mailboxes that come in all sorts of animal shapes.

The prince knew his beloved had but one flaw, that she was not a princess.

Exercise 95C: Diagramming

On your own paper, diagram every word of these two sentences from G. K. Chesterton's *A Short History of England*. Do your best to place each word on the diagram, but ask your instructor if you need help.

This truth, that there was something which can only vaguely be called Tory about the Yorkists, has at least one interest, that it lends a justifiable romance to the last and most remarkable figure of the fighting House of York, with whose fall the Wars of the Roses ended.

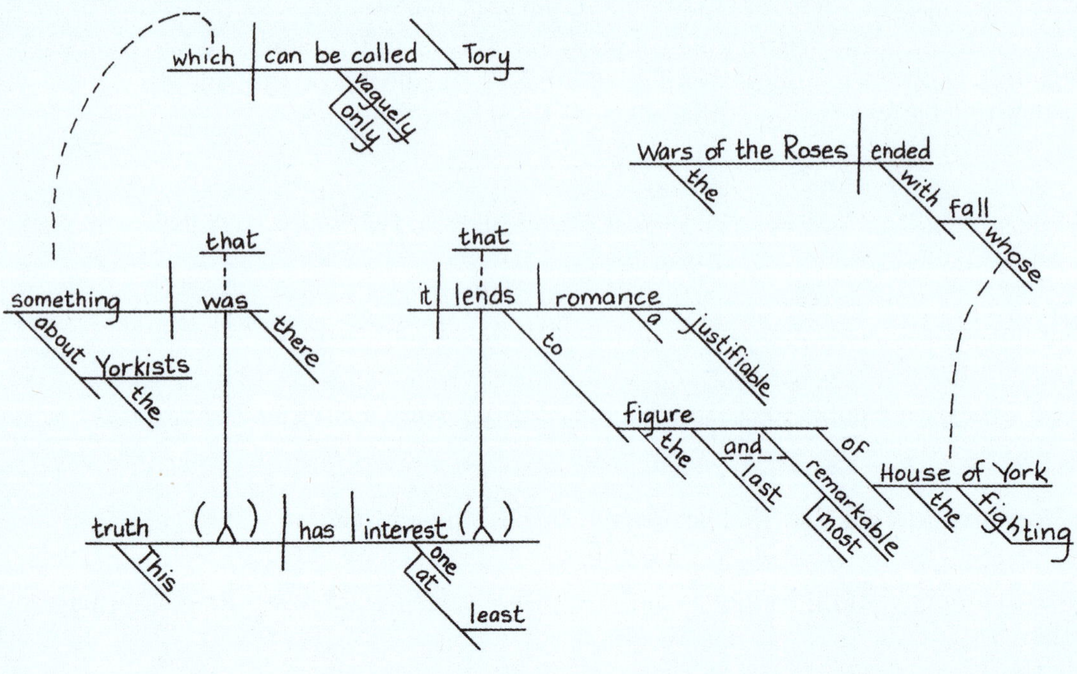

Henry of Anjou, who brought fresh French blood into the monarchy, brought also a refreshment of the idea for which the French have always stood: the idea in the Roman Law of something impersonal and omnipresent.

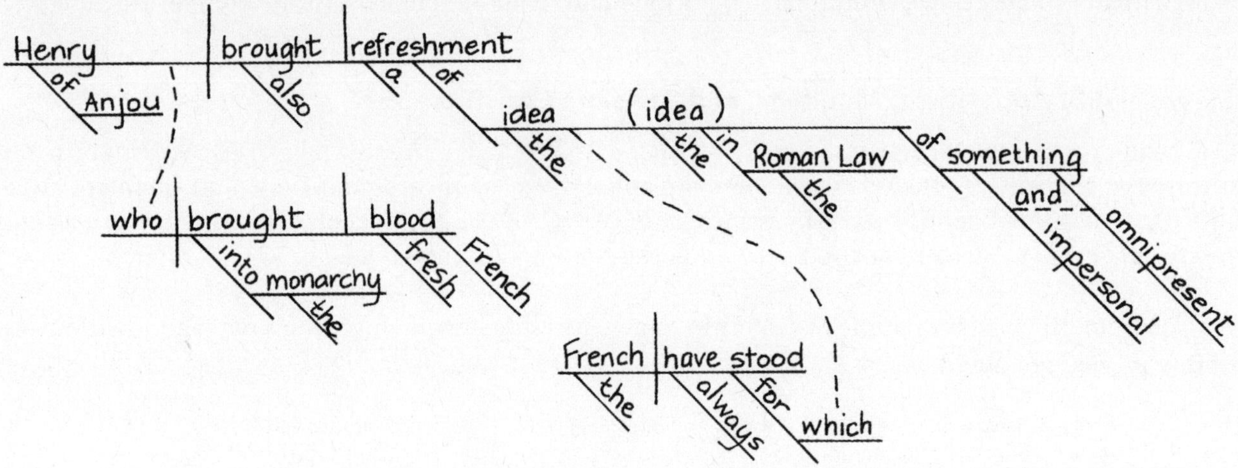

— LESSON 96 —

Appositives
Noun Clauses in Apposition
Absolute Constructions

Exercise 96A: Identifying Absolute Constructions

Circle the absolute construction in each sentence. Label each absolute construction as *CL* for clause or *PHR* for phrase. For clauses, underline the subject of each clause once and the predicate twice.

PHR
The geese having safely crossed the road, we continued our drive to the hospital.

PHR
Her brow furrowed in concentration, Zoe knelt to examine the antique chair.

PHR
He left the room hurriedly, his hat and glasses askew, and ran to his car.

PHR
Tours of the facility must be rescheduled, the educational director being sick today.

PHR
Travis answered with clipped sentences, his eyes on the sidewalk.

PHR PHR
They proceeded with the unpleasant task, Nora whistling absentmindedly and John mumbling about his plans for the weekend.

CL
Marilyn, her heart racing as she gasped for breath, thought that perhaps she wasn't quite ready to run a marathon after all.

PHR

Its midafternoon nap complete, the cat stretched and searched for a place to begin its late-afternoon nap.

CL

The British athletes, (as we should have mentioned,) arrived too late to join the competition.

Exercise 96B: Appositives, Modifiers, and Absolute Constructions

The sentences below, taken from *And Then There Were None* by Agatha Christie, each contain phrases or clauses set off by dashes. Some are appositives, some are modifiers, and some are absolute constructions. Identify them by writing *APP, MOD,* or *AC* above each one. For appositives and modifiers, draw an arrow back to the word being renamed or modified.

AC AC APP

An accurate diagnosis, a couple of grateful women patients—women with money and position—and word had got about.

> **Note to Instructor:** *An accurate diagnosis* and *a couple of grateful women patients* are also set off by the dashes from the main sentence, *word had got about*. They are not compound subjects with *word*--only the word *had got about.*

MOD

This island place ought to be rather good fun—if the weather lasted.

AC

One of them must wait till the slow train from Exeter gets in—a matter of five minutes.

APP

That bluff cheery gent—he wasn't a real gentleman.

APP

Over it, in a gleaming chromium frame, was a big square of parchment—a poem.

APP

On the table was a gramophone—an old-fashioned type with a large trumpet attached.

MOD

We got orders—by letter again—to prepare the rooms for a houseparty and then yesterday by the afternoon post I got another letter from Mr. Owen.

APP

I've no doubt in my own mind that we have been invited here by a madman—probably a dangerous homicidal lunatic.

AC

Lombard laughed—a sudden ringing laugh.

AC

If there's a lunatic hiding on this island, he's probably got a young arsenal on him—to say nothing of a knife or dagger or two.

AC

Murder—and I've always been such a law-abiding man!

APP

It came again—someone moving softly, furtively, overhead.

MOD

There is plenty of food, sir—of a tinned variety.

APP

Our main preoccupation is this—to save our lives.

We all went into the next room with the exception of Miss Brent who remained in this room—

MOD

alone with the unconscious woman.

Exercise 96C: Diagramming

On your own paper, diagram every word of the following sentences, taken from G. K. Chesterton's *The Man Who Knew Too Much*.

I believe Hoggs—I mean my cousin Howard—was coming down specially to meet him.

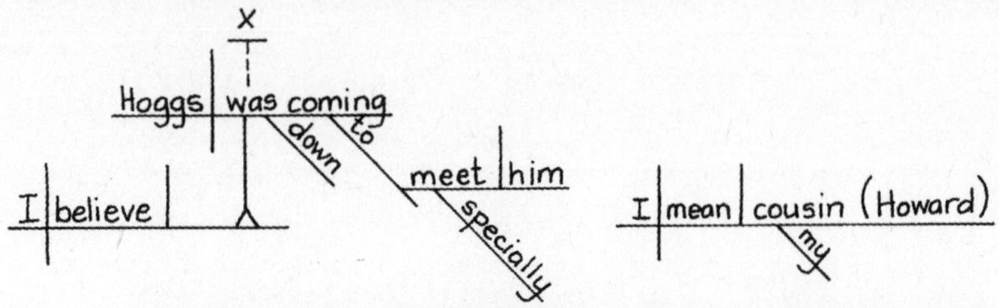

Note to Instructor: *Specially* could also be diagrammed beneath *was coming*, since it is ambiguous whether he was *coming down specially*, or whether he was coming down *specially to meet him*.

March followed him to the bar parlor with some wonder, and his dim sense of repugnance was not dismissed by the first sight of the innkeeper, who was widely different from the genial innkeepers of romance, a bony man, very silent behind a black mustache, but with black, restless eyes.

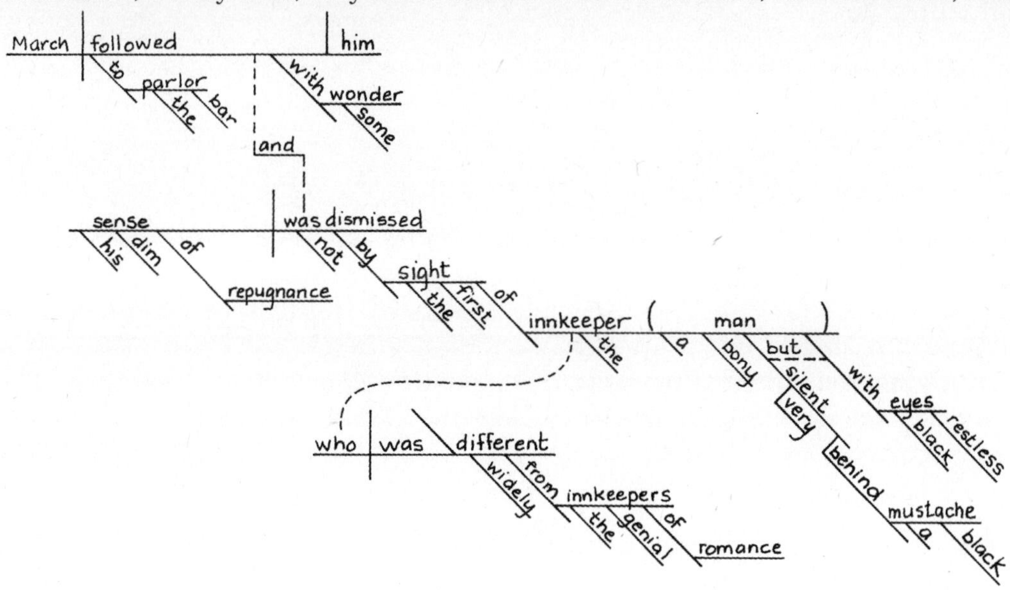

Morton had just placed himself in front of the nearest window, his broad shoulders blocking the aperture.

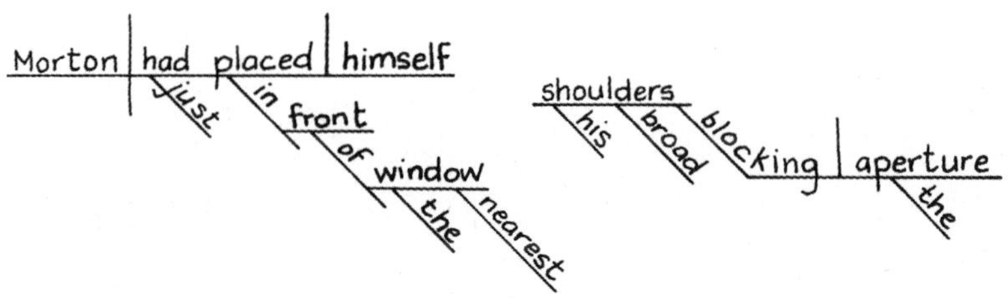

— REVIEW 8 —

Weeks 22-24

Topics
Parenthetical Expressions
Dashes, Colons, and Brackets
Dialogue and Dialogue Tags
Direct Quotations and Attribution Tags
Ellipses and Partial Quotations
Block Quotes
Interjections
Nouns of Direct Address
Appositives
Noun Clauses in Apposition
Absolute Constructions

Review 8A: Definition Review

You've learned many definitions in the past three weeks! Look at each statement below and write *TRUE* or *FALSE* in the box to the right. If a statement is false, cross out and add words as necessary to make it true.

Note to Instructor: Allow the student to look back through the workbook and find definitions as necessary; the value of the exercise comes in the student's reviewing each definition, whether from memory or not.

A ~~nonrestrictive~~ restrictive modifying clause defines the word that it modifies. Removing the clause changes the essential meaning of the sentence.	FALSE
A nonrestrictive modifying clause describes the word that it modifies. Removing the clause ~~changes~~ doesn't change the essential meaning of the sentence.	FALSE
Only a nonrestrictive modifying clause should be set off by commas.	TRUE
Parentheses can enclose words that are not essential to the sentence.	TRUE
A parenthetical expression is ~~always very important~~ often irrelevant to the rest of the sentence.	FALSE
Punctuation goes inside the parentheses if it applies to the parenthetical expression; all other punctuation goes outside the parentheses.	TRUE
A parenthetical expression only begins with a capital letter if it is a complete sentence with ending punctuation.	TRUE
A parenthetical expression can also be set off by commas.	TRUE

Short parenthetical expressions such as the following are ~~never~~ usually set off by commas: in short, in fact, in reality, as it were, as it happens, no doubt, in a word, to be sure, to be brief, after all, you know, of course.	FALSE
Dashes can enclose words that are not essential to the sentence.	TRUE
Dashes can also be used singly to separate parts of a sentence.	TRUE
Commas ~~cannot~~ make a parenthetical element a part of the sentence.	FALSE
Dashes ~~minimize~~ emphasize a parenthetical element.	FALSE
Parentheses ~~emphasize~~ minimize a parenthetical element.	FALSE
The independent clauses of a compound sentence must be joined by a comma and a coordinating conjunction, a semicolon, or a semicolon and a coordinating conjunction. They ~~can also~~ cannot be joined by a comma alone.	FALSE
When a dialogue tag comes before a speech, place a comma after the tag. Put the dialogue's final punctuation mark inside the closing quotation marks.	TRUE
Speeches do not need to be attached to a dialogue tag as long as the text clearly indicates the speaker.	TRUE
Usually, a new paragraph begins with each new speaker.	TRUE
When a dialogue tag comes in the middle of a speech, follow it with a ~~period~~ comma if the following dialogue is an incomplete sentence. Follow it with a ~~comma~~ period if the following dialogue is a complete sentence.	FALSE
When an attribution tag comes after a direct quote, place a comma, exclamation point, or question mark ~~outside~~ inside the closing quotation marks.	FALSE
When an attribution tag comes before a direct quote, place a comma after the tag. Put the dialogue's final punctuation mark inside the closing quotation marks.	TRUE
When an attribution tag comes in the middle of a direct quotation, follow it with a comma if the remaining quote is an incomplete sentence. Follow it with a period if the remaining quote is a complete sentence.	TRUE
Every direct quote must have an attribution tag.	TRUE
An ellipsis shows where something has been ~~added to~~ cut out of a sentence.	FALSE
A second or third quote from the same source does not need another attribution tag, as long as context makes the source of the quote clear.	TRUE

Direct quotes can be words, phrases, clauses, or sentences, as long as they are set off by ~~commas~~ quotation marks and form part of a grammatically correct original sentence.	FALSE
If a direct quotation is longer than ~~two~~ three lines, indent the entire quote one inch from the margin in a separate block of text and omit quotation marks.	FALSE
If you change or make additions to a direct quotation, use brackets.	TRUE
When using a word processing program, leave ~~no~~ an additional line space~~s~~ before and after a block quote.	FALSE
Block quotes should be introduced by a ~~semicolon~~ colon (if preceded by a complete sentence) or a comma (if preceded by a partial sentence).	FALSE
~~Conjunctions~~ Interjections express sudden feeling or emotion. They are set off with commas or stand alone with a closing punctuation mark.	FALSE
Nouns of direct address name a person or thing who is being spoken to. They are set off with commas. They are capitalized only if they are proper names or titles.	TRUE
An appositive is a noun or noun phrase that usually follows another noun and renames or explains it.	TRUE
A dependent clause can act as an appositive if it ~~modifies~~ renames the noun that it follows.	FALSE
An absolute construction has a strong semantic relationship but no grammatical connection to the rest of the sentence.	TRUE

Review 8B: Punctuating Restrictive and Non-Restrictive Clauses, Compound Sentences, Interjections, and Nouns of Direct Address

The sentences below contain restrictive clauses, non-restrictive clauses, interjections, and nouns of direct address. Some are compound sentences. But all of them have lost their punctuation! Insert all necessary punctuation directly into the sentences (use the actual punctuation marks rather than proofreader's marks).

These sentences are from *The Mystery of Drear House*, by Virginia Hamilton.

Note to Instructor: The original sentences are below; explanations have been inserted where necessary.

On weekends they often helped his father and old Pluto in the great cavern, where they polished the priceless glass.

Note to Instructor: In the original, the comma after *cavern* makes *where they polished the priceless glass* a nonrestrictive clause. The student may have opted to leave out the comma, making the clause restrictive. In the absence of the book's context, either choice is acceptable.

Macky was a huge bear that came straight at him, lumbering right over him like a grizzly over a log.

They crossed the old covered bridge and the stream that was so like a moat protecting the house.

Well, Thomas, you came back.

"Thomas, it's a grand old house," she said, finally, as they took her by the arms and gently helped her from the car.

> **Note to Instructor:** The comma before *finally* is optional.

From within, the sound of the night's blizzard that had awakened Thomas was faint.

After that he would have time for lunch at home; his mama would pick him up in the car.

> **Note to Instructor:** A comma may be inserted following *After that*. A semicolon is the only way to form the compound sentence correctly with only the insertion of punctuation; however, if the student has placed a comma there *and* inserted a coordinating conjunction, her answer is grammatically correct.

"When can I meet her?" Pesty asked.

"Move on out, Mr. Thomas," she told him.

Grandmother Rhetty, I'm sorry, but we have to be going.

> **Note to Instructor:** The comma and coordinating conjunction *but* connect the two independent sentences.

"Well! Martha, this is so sweet of you!" she said.

> **Note to Instructor:** Either or both exclamation points may be replaced with commas.

Billy covered his mouth to keep in the giggle that was bubbling up inside him.

He was going down the hall to the parlor room, which had become his study.

"Well, I know Grandmother Rhetty when she makes up her mind about something," his papa said.

Review 8C: Dialogue

In the following passage of dialogue, taken from Louisa May Alcott's *Little Women*, all of the punctuation around, before, and after the lines of dialogue is missing. Insert all necessary punctuation directly into the sentences (use the actual punctuation marks rather than proofreader's marks).

> **Note to Instructor:** The original punctuation is below. Student answers may vary (for example, the exclamation point between *A letter! a letter!* could be a comma). Accept any answers that follow the punctuation rules. Where there is a difference, ask the student to compare her work with the original.

As they gathered about the table, Mrs. March said, with a particularly happy face, "I've got a treat for you after supper."

A quick, bright smile went round like a streak of sunshine. Beth clapped her hands, regardless of the biscuit she held, and Jo tossed up her napkin, crying, "A letter! a letter! Three cheers for father!"

"Yes, a nice long letter. He is well, and thinks he shall get through the cold season better than we feared. He sends all sorts of loving wishes for Christmas, and an especial message to you girls," said Mrs. March, patting her pocket as if she had got a treasure there.

"Hurry and get done! Don't stop to quirk your little finger, and simper over your plate, Amy," cried Jo, choking in her tea, and dropping her bread, butter side down, on the carpet, in her haste to get at the treat.

Beth ate no more, but crept away, to sit in her shadowy corner and brood over the delight to come, till the others were ready.

"I think it was so splendid in father to go as a chaplain when he was too old to be drafted, and not strong enough for a soldier," said Meg warmly.

"Don't I wish I could go as a drummer, a vivan—what's its name? or a nurse, so I could be near him and help him," exclaimed Jo, with a groan.

"It must be very disagreeable to sleep in a tent, and eat all sorts of bad-tasting things, and drink out of a tin mug," sighed Amy.

"When will he come home, Marmee?" asked Beth, with a little quiver in her voice.

"Not for many months, dear, unless he is sick. He will stay and do his work faithfully as long as he can, and we won't ask for him back a minute sooner than he can be spared. Now come and hear the letter."

They all drew to the fire, mother in the big chair with Beth at her feet, Meg and Amy perched on either arm of the chair, and Jo leaning on the back, where no one would see any sign of emotion if the letter should happen to be touching.

Review 8D: Parenthetical Expressions, Appositives, Absolute Constructions

Each one of the sentences below (taken or adapted from David Lindley's *Uncertainty: Einstein, Heisenberg, Bohr, and the Struggle for the Soul of Science*) contains an element not closely connected to the rest of the sentence: parenthetical, appositive, or absolute.

- In each sentence, find and circle the unconnected element (word, phrase, or clause).
- Above it, write *PAR* for parenthetical, *APP* for appositive, or *AB* for absolute.
- In the blank at the end of the sentence, note whether the element is set apart with commas (*C*), parentheses (*P*), or dashes (*D*).

Rising early, he taught himself German (nouns and their declensions before breakfast [APP], his diary records [PAR], conjugation of auxiliary verbs afterward [APP]) so that he could master the considerable German literature on botany, his chosen subject. P, C

An admirer of Boltzmann's dense and, frankly [PAR], long-winded monographs [APP], Einstein had become fascinated by statistical questions in physics and by the attendant controversy over the existence of atoms. C

PAR
Physicists, it turned out, had been making X-rays for years without knowing it. C

PAR
Some years before, working with his young colleague Hans Geiger (of Geiger counter fame), he had finally pinned down the identity of radioactive alpha emanations. P

APP
These two processes, in other words—the radioactive decay of a nucleus and the hopping of an electron from one orbit to another—were not only both spontaneous, but spontaneous in the same way. D

APP
It was now August 1914, a fateful month. C

AB
The mechanics of the orbits followed entirely from old physics—the electrons obeying
PAR
Newtonian rules (with occasional modifications from Einstein), controlled by an inverse square law of attraction between electrons and nucleus. D, C

Finishing *Gymnasium* just as the war was ending, Werner had to serve in the local militia,
APP
a ragtag collection of teenagers charged with keeping order in the strife-torn city. C

AB
Sommerfeld having come back from Madison in the spring of 1923, Heisenberg returned to Munich from Göttingen to finish his doctorate. C

Review 8E: Direct Quotations

The following excerpt from *The Narnian*, a biography of C. S. Lewis by Alan Jacobs, contains two different direct quotations. Those quotations are bolded, but they are not properly punctuated. Rewrite the paragraph on your own paper, spacing and punctuating both quotations correctly.

- When you are finished, circle any places where words have been left out of the direct quotations.
- Underline any places where words have been added to the direct quotations.

Compare your paragraph with the original in the Key.

A knowledge of Lewis's miseries in school reveals that some scenes in the Narnia books are more important than they might appear. In *The Lion, the Witch, and the Wardrobe*, when Edmund is being nasty to his younger sister, Lucy, their older brother, Peter, tells him **You've always liked being beastly to anyone smaller than yourself; we've seen that at school before now.** But after Edmund has met Aslan and fought on Aslan's behalf, we have this scene **When at last [Lucy] was free to come back to Edmund she found him . . . looking better than she had seen him look—oh, for ages; in fact ever since his first term at that horrid school which was where he began to go wrong. He had become his real old self again and could look you in the face**. Edmund, then . . . is a "product of the system" as much as George Orwell was.

Note to Instructor: The original passage is shown below. Note that the student MUST set the second quotation as a block quote, because of its length.

A knowledge of Lewis's miseries in school reveals that some scenes in the Narnia books are more important than they might appear. In *The Lion, the Witch, and the Wardrobe*, when Edmund is being nasty to his younger sister, Lucy, their older brother, Peter, tells him, "You've always liked being beastly to anyone smaller than yourself; we've seen that at school before now." But after Edmund has met Aslan and fought on Aslan's behalf, we have this scene:

> When at last [Lucy] was free to come back to Edmund she found him . . . looking better than she had seen him look—oh, for ages; in fact ever since his first term at that horrid school which was where he began to go wrong. He had become his real old self again and could look you in the face.

Edmund, then . . . is a "product of the system" as much as George Orwell was.

Review 8F: Diagramming

On your own paper, diagram every word of the following sentences from historical letters (as they appear in *Letters of a Nation*, edited by Andrew Carroll).

I have sat and watched the cornfields of Iowa darken, seen the homesteads pass by—a white house, a red barn and a brave cluster of green trees in the midst of oceans of flat fields—like an oasis in a desert.

—From a letter from Anne Morrow Lindbergh to Charles Lindbergh (1944)

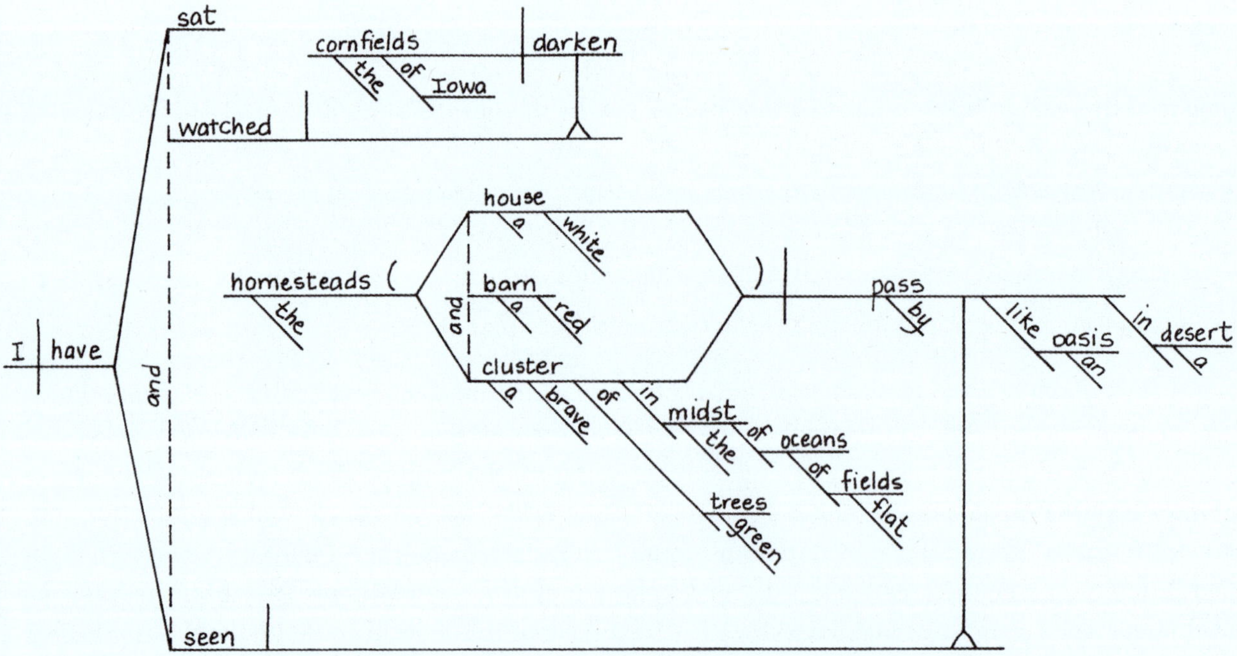

The prisoners lived in rows of one-story, green wooden barracks—the men being segregated from the women.

—Joseph Fogg, describing a Nazi concentration camp in a letter to his parents (1945)

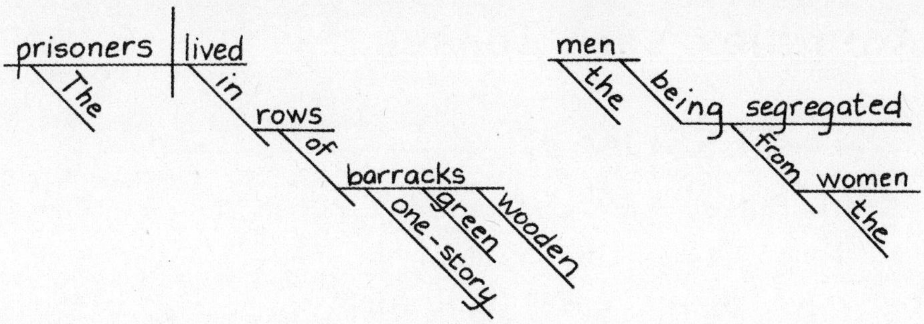

Tell Mildred I got a beautiful Dutch doll for little Emma Jones—one of those crying babies that can open and shut their eyes and turn their head.

—From a letter from Robert E. Lee to his wife, Mary (1856)

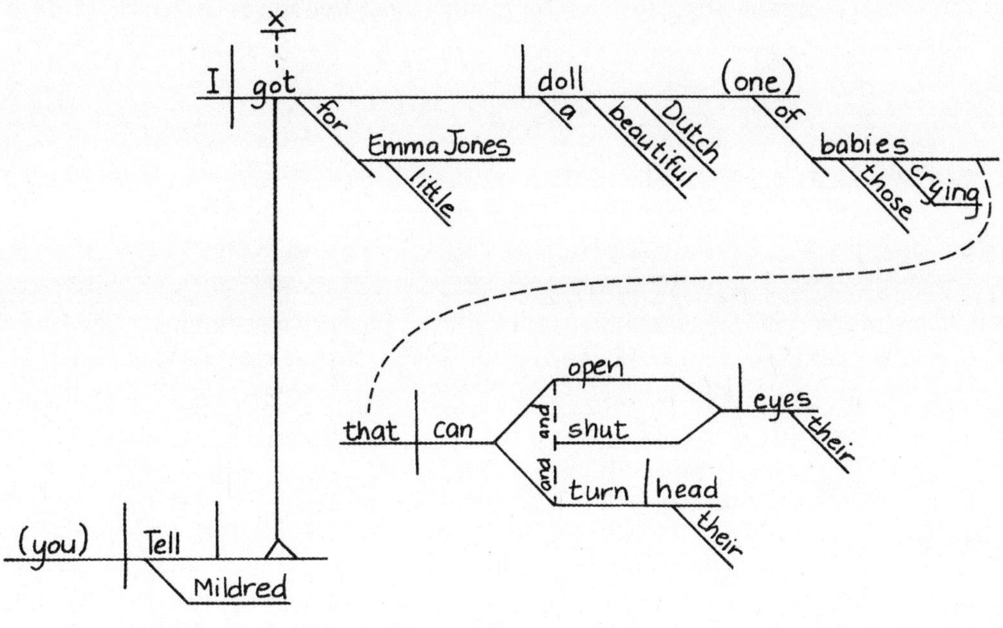

WEEK 25

Complex Verb Tenses

— LESSON 97 —

Verb Tense, Voice, and Mood
Tense Review (Indicative)
Progressive Perfect Tenses (Indicative)

Exercise 97A: Review of Indicative Tenses

The following partially completed chart shows the active and passive tenses of the regular verb *scold* (in the third-person singular), the irregular verb *choose* (in the third-person plural), and the irregular verb *lead* (in the first-person singular). Review your indicative tenses by completing the chart now.

		Active	Passive
SIMPLE TENSES			
	Past	he scolded they chose I led	he was scolded they were chosen I was led
	Present	he scolds they choose I lead	he is scolded they are chosen I am led
	Future	he will scold they will choose I will lead	he will be scolded they will be chosen I will be led
PROGRESSIVE TENSES			
	Past	he was scolding they were choosing I was leading	he was being scolded they were being chosen I was being led
	Present	he is scolding they are choosing I am leading	he is being scolded they are being chosen I am being led
	Future	he will be scolding they will be choosing I will be leading	he will be being scolded they will be being chosen I will be being led

		Active	Passive
PERFECT TENSES			
	Past	he had scolded they had chosen I had led	he had been scolded they had been chosen I had been led
	Present	he has scolded they have chosen I have led	he has been scolded they have been chosen I have been led
	Future	he will have scolded they will have chosen I will have led	he will have been scolded they will have been chosen I will have been led

Exercise 97B: Parsing Verbs

In the following sentences, underline the main verb of every clause (both independent and dependent). Above each verb, write the tense and voice. (All verbs are in the indicative mood.)

You may abbreviate: *PROG, PERF, SIMP, PAST, PRES, FUT, ACT, PASS, ST-OF-BE.*

PROG PAST, ACT — SIMP PAST, ACT — PERF PAST, PASS
As she was cleaning the empty theater, she reflected on how well the cast had been prepared for the performance.

PERF PRES, ACT — SIMP FUT, ACT
After seven to ten days have elapsed, the seeds will sprout.

PROG PERF FUT, ACT
Mr. Quinn will have been working at the library for ten years this October.

PROG PERF PRES, ACT — ST-OF-BE
The baby has been sleeping wonderfully, but only when her parents are awake!

PROG PERF PRES, PASS — SIMP PAST, ACT — SIMP PRES, ST-OF-BE
I have been being asked for a contribution to your organization six times a year since I moved to this city, and I am unhappy about it!

SIMP PRES, ACT — PROG PAST, ACT — PERF PRES, ACT
I see that the girl who was wearing your hat has returned it.

SIMP PRES, ACT — PROG PERF FUT, PASS
We expect that by the end of Tuesday, this amusement park will have been being enjoyed by over a million people.

PERF PAST, ACT — SIMP PAST, ACT
The old man had whistled on his way to work every day since the factory opened.

SIMP PAST, ACT — SIMP PAST, ST-OF-BE — PROG PERF PAST ACT — SIMP PAST, ST-OF-BE
Sam pretended that he was unfamiliar with the game, but he'd been playing it since he was four.

SIMP PAST, ACT — PROG PAST, ACT — SIMP FUT, ACT — PERF PRES, ACT
The scarf that I found while I was shopping with my best friend will go perfectly with the dress I've chosen for Saturday.

Exercise 97C: Completing Sentences

Complete the following sentences by providing an appropriate verb in the tense and voice indicated beneath each blank. (All verbs are in the indicative mood.)

Note to Instructor: Accept any verbs that make sense, as long as they are in the correct tense and voice.

Paula has been eating (progressive perfect present, active) waffles for breakfast every day for a month.

Since last Tuesday, I have been wanting (progressive perfect present, active) a puppy.

Several of the young children had been being frightened (progressive perfect past, passive) by Tristan's costume.

Some of the flowers had been blooming (progressive perfect past, active) before the family departed (simple past, active).

Certain facts had been omitted (progressive perfect past, passive) from the county's reports before they were released (simple past, passive) to the press.

Ana will have been sharpening (progressive perfect future, active) that pencil for two full minutes soon!

In August, the game show will have been being hosted (progressive perfect future, passive) by the same celebrity for forty years.

Your phone has been ringing (progressive perfect present, active) nonstop since you stepped (simple past, active) away from your desk.

Millions of people will have been celebrating (progressive perfect future, active) the election results all night, while just as many will have been lamenting (progressive perfect future, active) them.

The singer had been practicing (progressive perfect past, active) for his recital for three months.

— LESSON 98 —

Simple Present and Perfect Present Modal Verbs
Progressive Present and Progressive Perfect Present Modal Verbs

Exercise 98A: Parsing Verbs

Write the tense, mood, and voice of each underlined verb above it. The first is done for you.

These sentences are from *Pippi Longstocking*, by Astrid Lindgren.

simple present, modal, active

Why, she could lift a whole horse if she wanted to!

simple present, indicative, active — perfect present, modal, active

I wonder what you would have said if I had come along walking on my hands the way they do in Farthest India.

progressive present, modal, active

"Now you must be lying," said Tommy.

perfect present, modal, passive — perfect present, modal, active

He should have been left at home to pick fleas off the horse. That would have served him right.

perfect present, modal, active

No doubt they would have liked a little pie too.

simple present, modal, active

His ears were so big that he could use them for a cape.

simple present, modal, active

Annika sighed with relief and hoped that the meeting would last a long time.

simple present, modal, passive

Tommy let out a terrified shriek that could be heard all through the woods.

perfect present, modal, active — simple past, indicative, active

"Oh, Pippi, I could have died of fright," said Annika.

simple present, modal, passive — perfect past. indicative, active

He said that no new food should be prepared for Peter until he had eaten a swallow's nest for Daddy.

simple past, indicative, active — progressive present, modal, active

Tommy and Annika looked around cautiously, just in case the king of the Cannibal Isles might be sitting in a corner somewhere.

simple present, modal, active

"Oh, I can answer all right," said Pippi.

Exercise 98B: Forming Modal Verbs

Fill in the blanks with the missing modal verbs. Using the helping verbs indicated, put each action verb provided into the correct modal tense.

The customer may have been complaining about the small number of employees in the store today, but her ranting was so incoherent that we're not completely sure.

helping verb: may
progressive perfect present active of *complain*

I did not think his ravenous appetite would have been satisfied by such a meager meal, but I was wrong.

helping verb: would
perfect present passive of *satisfy*

Our grandparents should be arriving on tomorrow's earliest flight from Atlanta.

helping verb: should
progressive present active of *arrive*

Last year, Mrs. Hannachi would have allowed me to get away with shoddy work, but her expectations have increased.

helping verb: would
perfect present active of *allow*

The remaining cookies might have been eaten by your brother and his friends.

helping verb: might
perfect present passive of *eat*

The birds should migrate to a warmer place within the next few weeks.

helping verb: should
simple present active of *migrate*

My flower must have opened last night while I was asleep.

helping verb: must
perfect present active of *open*

Kwame's favorite book can be found on the bottom shelf.

helping verb: can
simple present passive of *find*

— LESSON 99 —

Modal Verb Tenses
The Imperative Mood
The Subjunctive Mood
More Subjunctive Tenses

Exercise 99A: Complete the Chart

Fill in the missing forms on the following chart. Use the verbs indicated above each chart, in order. The first form on each chart is done for you.

INDICATIVE

(establish, delight, ignore, spot, compare, borrow, report, roll, attack, need, question, obey)

Indicative Tense	Active Formation	Examples	Passive Formation	Examples
Simple present	Add *-s* in third-person singular	I establish he, she, it establishes	am/is/are + past participle	I am established you are established he, she, it is established
Simple past	Add *-d* or *-ed*, or change form	I delighted	was/were + past participle	I was delighted you were delighted

Indicative Tense	Active Formation	Examples	Passive Formation	Examples
Simple future	+ will OR shall	they will ignore	will be + past participle	it will be ignored
Progressive present	am/is/are + present participle	I am spotting you are spotting he, she, it is spotting	am/is/are being + past participle	I was being spotted you are being spotted he, she, it is being spotted
Progressive past	was/were + present participle	I was comparing you were comparing he, she, it was comparing	was/were being + past participle	I was being compared you were being compared he, she, it was being compared
Progressive future	will be + present participle	I will be borrowing	will be being + past participle	it will be being borrowed
Perfect present	has/have + past participle	I have reported you have reported he, she, it has reported	has/have been + past participle	I have been reported you have been reported he, she, it has been reported
Perfect past	had + past participle	they had rolled	had been + past participle	you had been rolled
Perfect future	will have + past participle	we will have attacked	will have been + past participle	they will have been attacked
Progressive perfect present	have/has been + present participle	I have been needing he, she, it has been needing	have/has been being + past participle	I have been being needed he, she, it has been being needed

Indicative Tense	Active Formation	Examples	Passive Formation	Examples
Progressive perfect past	had been + present participle	you had been questioning	had been being + past participle	you had been being questioned
Progressive perfect future	will have been + present participle	you will have been obeying	will have been being + past participle	they will have been being obeyed

MODAL

(request, carry, complete, store)

Modal Tense	Active Formation	Examples	Passive Formation	Examples
Simple present	modal helping verb + simple present main verb	I could request you could request he, she, it could request	modal helping verb + be + past participle	I could be request-ed they could be requested
Progressive present	modal helping verb + be + present participle	I could be carrying	modal helping verb + be + being + past participle	it could be being carried
Perfect present	modal helping verb + have + past participle	you could have completed	modal helping verb + have + been + past participle	it could have been completed
Progressive perfect present	modal helping verb + have been + present participle	I could have been storing	modal helping verb + have been being + past participle	we could have been being stored

IMPERATIVE
(worry, change)

Imperative Tense	Active Formation	Examples	Passive Formation	Examples
Present	Simple present form without subject	Worry ! Change !	be + past participle	Be worried ! Be changed !

SUBJUNCTIVE
(support, supply, include, notice, provide, rule, stretch, spare)

Subjunctive Tense	Active Formation	Examples	Passive Formation	Examples
Simple present	No change in any person	I support you support he, she, it support we support you support they support	be + past participle	I be supported they be supported
Simple past	**Same as indicative:** Add *-d* or *-ed*, or change form	I supplied you supplied he, she, it supplied	were + past participle	he were supplied you were supplied
Progressive present	**Same as indicative:** am/is/are + present participle	I am including you are including he, she, it is including	**Same as indicative:** am/is/are being + past participle	I am being included you are being included he, she, it is being included
Progressive past	were + present participle	I were noticing you were noticing he, she, it were noticing	were being + past participle	I were being noticed you were being noticed he, she, it were being noticed

Subjunctive Tense	Active Formation	Examples	Passive Formation	Examples
Perfect present	**Same as indicative:** has/have + past participle	I have provided he, she, it has provided they have provided	**Same as indicative:** has/have been + past participle	I have been provided he, she, it has been provided they have been provided
Perfect past	**Same as indicative:** had + past participle	we had ruled	**Same as indicative:** had been + past participle	we had been ruled
Progressive perfect present	**Same as indicative:** have/has been + present participle	I have been stretching you have been stretching he, she, it has been stretching	**Same as indicative:** have/has been being + past participle	I have been being stretched you have been being stretched he, she, it has been being stretched
Progressive perfect past	**Same as indicative:** had been + present participle	you had been sparing	**Same as indicative:** had been being + past participle	you had been being spared

Exercise 99B: Parsing

Write the mood, tense, and voice of each underlined verb above it. These sentences are taken from Laura Ingalls Wilder's *Little House on the Prairie.*

The first one is done for you.

indicative, simple past active — imperative present active — indicative simple future active — indicative simple present active

He said to Ma: "Take your time, Caroline. We won't move the wagon till we want to."

indicative simple past active — indicative progressive past active

When the sun rose, they were driving on across the prairie.

subjunctive perfect past active — modal perfect present passive

If we hadn't come by, there's no telling when they would have been found.

indicative simple present state-of-being — indicative simple present active — modal perfect present active — subjunctive perfect past active

Pet and Patty are good swimmers, but I guess they wouldn't have made it if I hadn't helped them.

subjunctive progressive present active — modal simple present active — modal simple present active — indicative simple present active

If we are going this year, we must go now. We can't get across the Mississippi after the ice breaks.

A shadow came [indicative simple past active] over the prairie just then because the sun had gone [indicative perfect past active] down, and Pa said, "I'll tell [indicative simple future active] you about it later."

He wore [indicative simple past active] fringed leather leggings, and his moccasins were covered [indicative simple past passive] with beads.

That big fellow trotted [indicative simple past active] by my stirrup as if he were [subjunctive simple past state-of-being] there to stay.

I guess [indicative simple present active] they had just eaten [indicative perfect past active] all they could hold [modal simple present active].

At milking-time Ma was putting [indicative progressive present active] on her bonnet, when suddenly all Jack's hair stood [indicative simple past active] up stiff on his neck and back, and he rushed [indicative simple past active] out of the house. They heard [indicative simple past active] a yell and a scramble and a shout: "Call [imperative present active] off your dog! Call off your dog!"

— LESSON 100 —

Review of Moods and Tenses
Conditional Sentences

Exercise 100A: Conditional Sentences

Identify the following sentences from George Selden's *The Cricket in Times Square* as first, second, or third conditional by writing *1*, *2*, or *3* in the blank to the right.

If a leaf in a green forest far from New York had fallen at midnight through the darkness into a thicket, it might have sounded like that.	3
If we come down with peculiar diseases—out he goes!	1
He saw the cardboard shells that open up into beautiful paper flowers if you put them in a glass of water.	1
He was afraid that if he moved, he would be buried under an avalanche of Chinese novelties.	2
She would certainly have known if he had two dollars to leave anybody.	2
They might have gone on bowing all night if Sai Fong hadn't said something in Chinese to his friend.	3
If the Bellinis find me gone, they'll think I set the fire and ran.	1
What good is it to be famous if it only makes you unhappy?	1
If Mario couldn't find him in a few minutes, Chester would give a quick chirp as a hint.	1
If a thief had taken it, he would have taken the money from the cash register too.	2

Exercise 100B: Parsing

Write the correct mood, tense, and voice above each underlined verb. These sentences are taken or adapted from *South American Jungle Tales*, by Horacio Quiroga.

The first one is done for you.

indicative simple past active — indicative simple past passive — indicative simple past active

The panther understood that the rays were packed close in along the shore; and he figured that if

modal simple present active — modal simple present active

he could jump away out into the stream he would get beyond them and their stingers.

subjunctive simple present active — indicative simple future active

"If you don't get out of the way, we will eat every ray, and every son of a ray, and every grandson of a ray, not counting the women and children!" said the panthers.

indicative progressive past passive — indicative simple past active

Though many more of the rays were being trampled on, and scratched and bitten, they held their ground.

indicative perfect past passive — modal simple past active

Sometimes when a ray had been tossed into the air by a panther's paw, he would return to the

indicative perfect past active

fight after he had fallen back into the water.

indicative perfect past active — indicative simple past active

One day when the cubs had grown to be quite large sized raccoons, their mother took them up all

modal simple present active

together to the top of an orange tree—you must know that in South America orange trees, which

indicative simple past active — indicative simple present active — indicative simple past active

came originally from Spain, now grow wild in the forest—and spoke to them.

modal simple present state-of-being — imperative present active

Cublets, there is one thing more you must all be afraid of: dogs! dogs! Never go near a dog! Once I

indicative simple past active — indicative simple present active — indicative simple past active

had a fight with a dog. Do you see this broken tooth? Well, I broke it in a fight with a dog! And so

indicative simple present active — indicative progressive present active — subjunctive simple present active — imperative present active

I know what I am talking about! . . . Whenever you hear a dog, or a man, or a gun, jump for your

imperative present active

lives no matter how high the tree is, and run, run, run!

Exercise 100C: Diagramming

On your own paper, diagram every word of the following sentences adapted from *South American Jungle Tales*, by Horacio Quiroga.

I should not have gotten into that trouble if I had worked, like the other bees.

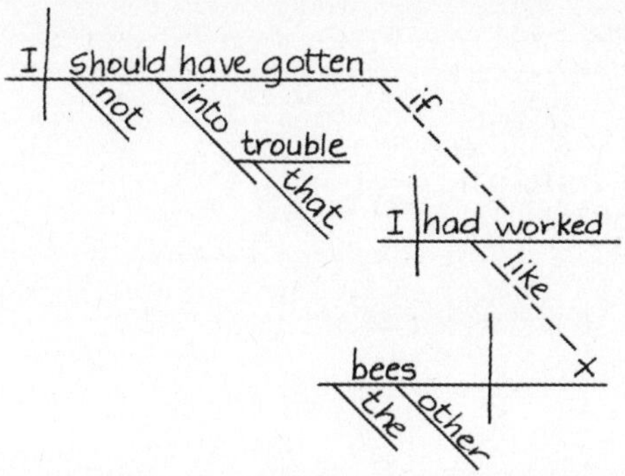

The snake understood that if his trick of spinning the top with his tail was extraordinary, this trick of the bee was almost miraculous.

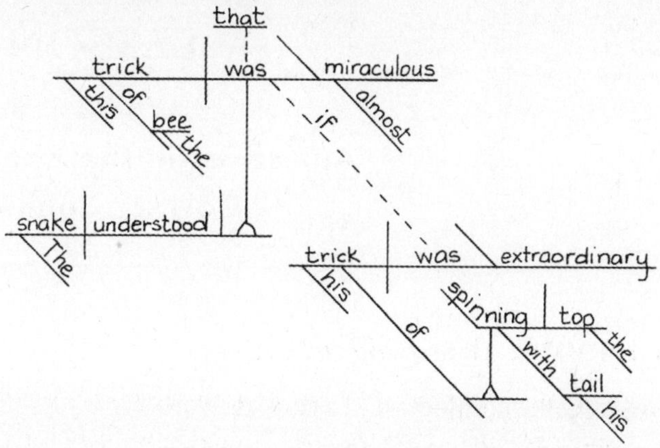

He fell ill, and the doctors told him he would never get well unless he left town and went to live in the country where there was good air and a warm climate.

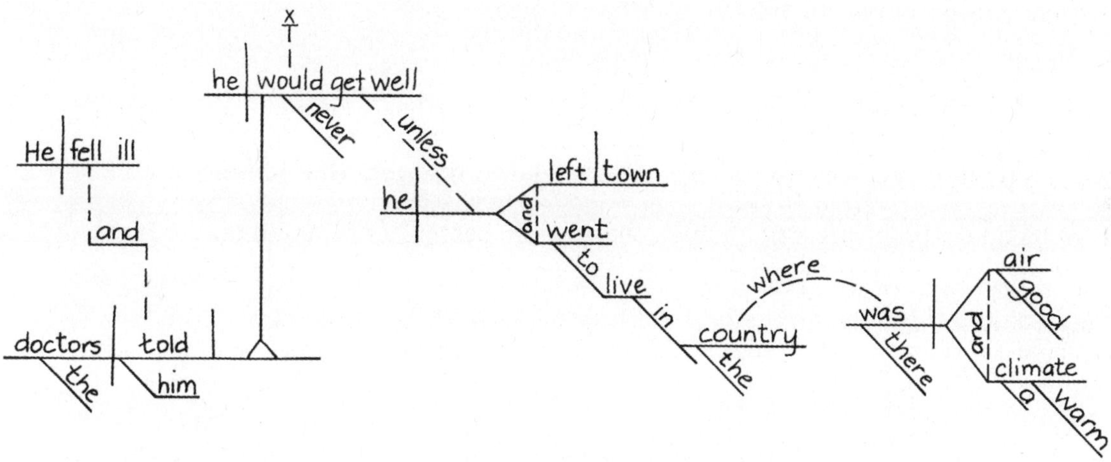

Note to Instructor: The phrase *fell ill* works here as a single verb. *Felt ill* would combine a linking verb with a predicate adjective, but since *fall* is not a linking verb, *ill* cannot be a predicate adjective. Rather, *fell ill* is an idiom (see Week 31 for more on idioms) that functions as a verb meaning to *sicken*.

The phrase *get well* functions in the same way. It is not unreasonable for the student to diagram *well* as an adverb modifying *get*, but you may want to point out that the subject is not "getting" anything; rather, he is "achieving health" or "healing," a single action.

WEEK 26

More Modifiers

— LESSON 101 —

Adjective Review

Adjectives in the Appositive Position

Correct Comma Usage

Exercise 101A: Identifying Adjectives

Underline every adjective (including verb forms used as adjectives) in the following sentences. Above each adjective, write *DESC* for descriptive or *POSS* for possessive. Then, label each as in the attributive (*ATT*), appositive (*APP*), or predicative (*PRED*) position. Finally, draw an arrow from each adjective to the word it modifies. Do not underline articles.

These sentences are from Edith Wharton's *Ethan Frome*.

I had been sent up by my (POSS ATT) employers on a job connected (DESC APP) with the big (DESC ATT) power-house at Corbury Junction, and a long-drawn (DESC ATT) carpenters' (POSS ATT) strike had so delayed the work that I found myself anchored (DESC PRED) at Starkfield—the nearest (DESC ATT) habitable (DESC ATT) spot—for the best (DESC ATT) part of the winter.

Note to Instructor: "Anchored" comes immediately after "myself," but it is an object complement (refer to Lesson 40) and therefore in the predicate position rather than the appositive.

I simply felt that he lived in a depth of moral (DESC ATT) isolation too remote (DESC APP) for casual (DESC ATT) access, and I had the sense that his (POSS ATT) loneliness was not merely the result of his (POSS ATT) personal (DESC ATT) plight, tragic as I guessed that to be, but had in it, as Harmon Gow had hinted, the profound (DESC ATT) accumulated (DESC ATT) cold of Starkfield (DESC ATT) winters.

His (POSS ATT) unfinished (DESC ATT) studies had given form to his (POSS ATT) sensibility and even in his (POSS ATT) unhappiest (DESC ATT) moments field and sky spoke to him with a deep (DESC ATT) and powerful (DESC ATT) persuasion.

DESC APP DESC APP
And there were sensations, less definable but more exquisite, which drew them together with a
DESC ATT DESC ATT DESC ATT
shock of silent joy; the cold red of sunset behind winter hills, the flight of cloud-flocks over slopes
DESC ATT DESC ATT DESC ATT
of golden stubble, or the intensely blue shadows of hemlocks on sunlit snow.

DESC ATT
The sunrise burned red in a pure sky, the shadows on the rim of the wood-lot were darkly
DESC PRED DESC ATT DESC ATT DESC ATT
blue, and beyond the white and scintillating fields patches of far-off forest hung like smoke.

Note to Instructor: In this sentence, *red* is acting as an adverb describing *burned.*

DESC APP DESC ATT POSS ATT
The cat, unnoticed, had crept up on muffled paws from Zeena's seat to the table, and was
POSS ATT
stealthily elongating its body in the direction of the milk-jug, which stood between Ethan and Mattie.

Exercise 101B: Punctuation Practice

The sentences below are missing all of their punctuation marks! Using everything you have learned about punctuation, insert correct punctuation. You may simply write the punctuation marks in, rather than using proofreader's marks.

These sentences are taken or adapted from Frances Hodgson Burnett's *A Little Princess.*

Note to Instructor: The original sentences are below. You may accept alternate answers if they are grammatically correct.

Her short, black locks tumbled about her ears, and she sat still.

Note to Instructor: Both commas could also be omitted.

She was a pretty, little, curly-headed creature, and her round eyes were like wet forget-me-nots.

Note to Instructor: The first two commas could be omitted, but the hyphen in *curly-headed* is necessary.

When she spoke it was in a quiet, steady voice; she held her head up, and everybody listened to her.

Her show pupil had melted into nothingness, leaving only a friendless, beggared little girl.

The fact was that Miss Minchin's pupils were a set of dull, matter-of-fact young people.

And at last, evidently in response to it, a gray-whiskered, bright-eyed head peeped out of the hole.

I am sure the Large Family have fat, comfortable armchairs and sofas, and I can see that their red-flowery wallpaper is exactly like them.

It was the picturesque white-swathed form and dark-faced, gleaming-eyed, white-turbaned head of a native Indian man-servant—"a Lascar," Sara said to herself quickly.

I only spare you because I am a princess, and you are a poor, stupid, unkind, vulgar old thing, and don't know any better.

And it was a baker's shop, and a cheerful, stout, motherly woman with rosy cheeks was putting into the window a tray of delicious newly baked hot buns, fresh from the oven—large, plump, and shiny, with currants in them.

"Yesterday, when she was out," he said, "I entered, bringing with me small, sharp nails which can be pressed into the wall without blows from a hammer."

"You insolent, unmanageable child!" she cried.

Exercise 101C: Diagramming

On your own paper, diagram the following sentences from *Ethan Frome*, by Edith Wharton.

His unfinished studies had given form to his sensibility and even in his unhappiest moments field and sky spoke to him with a deep and powerful persuasion.

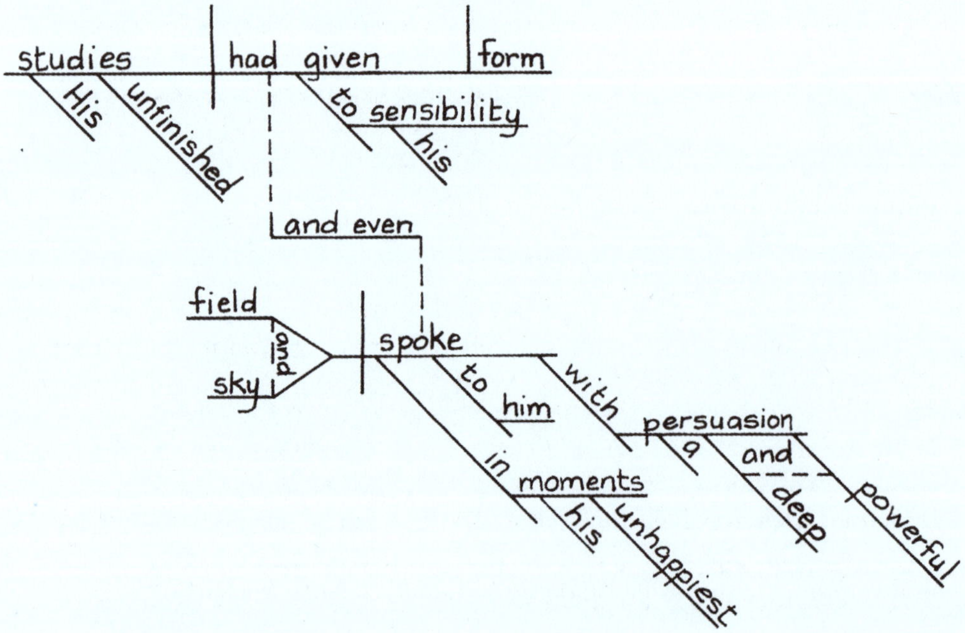

Note to Instructor: In this sentences, *and even* is acting as a compound conjunction between the two sentences. However, an argument could also be made for diagramming *even* as a modifier to *unhappiest*. Accept either answer.

Unfinished is not diagrammed as a past participle because *unfinish* is not an English verb. (*Finished* would be diagrammed as a past participle because *finish* is a verb.)

The sunrise burned red in a pure sky, the shadows on the rim of the wood-lot were darkly blue, and beyond the white and scintillating fields patches of far-off forest hung like smoke.

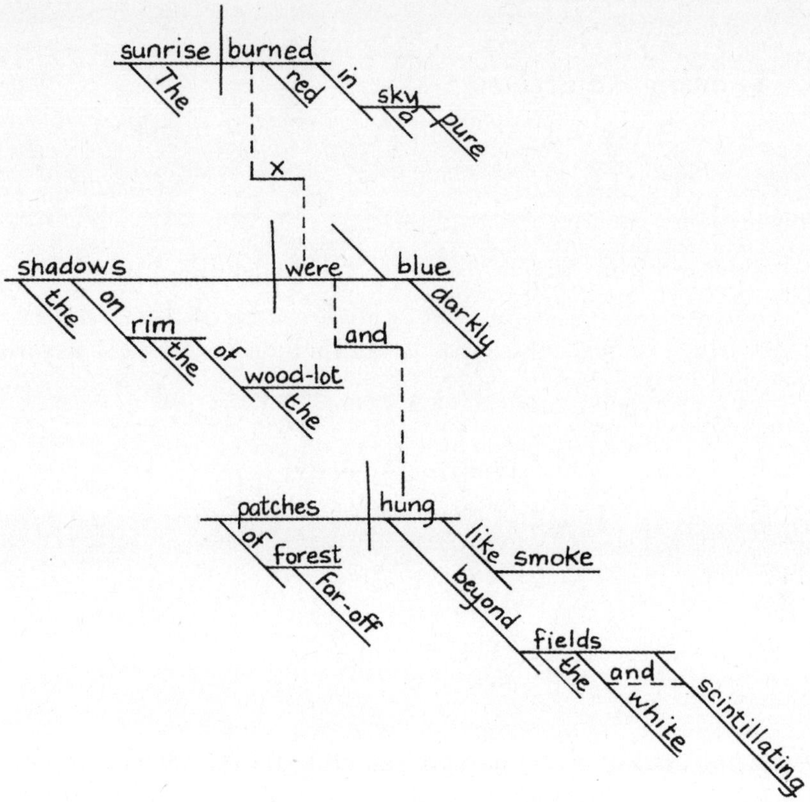

The cat, unnoticed, had crept up on muffled paws from Zeena's seat to the table, and was stealthily elongating its body in the direction of the milk-jug, which stood between Ethan and Mattie.

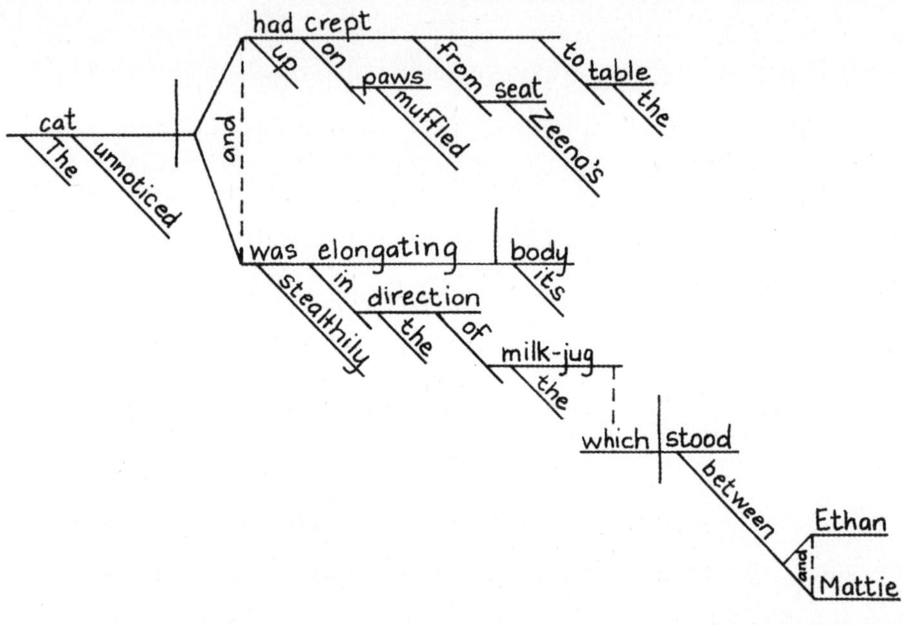

Note to Instructor: Like *unfinished*, *unnoticed* isn't a past participle because *unnotice* isn't a verb.

— LESSON 102 —

Adjective Review
Pronoun Review
Limiting Adjectives

Exercise 102A: Identifying Adjectives

The following paragraph is slightly condensed from *Moby Dick*, by Herman Melville. Underline every word that acts as an adjective.

Do not include phrases or clauses acting as adjectives. Also, do not include articles. (There are just too many!)

Label each one using the following abbreviations:

Descriptive Adjectives		**Limiting Adjectives**	
Regular	*DA-R*	Possessives	*LA-P*
Present participles	*DA-PresP*	~~Articles~~	~~*LA-A*~~
Past participles	*DA-PastP*	Demonstratives	*LA-D*
		Indefinites	*LA-IND*
		Interrogatives	*LA-INT*
		Numbers	*LA-N*

LA-IND DA-R DA-PastP DA-PastP
For some time past, though at intervals only, the unaccompanied, secluded White Whale had
LA-D DA-PastP DA-R
haunted those uncivilised seas mostly frequented by the Sperm Whale fishermen. But not all
LA-P
of them knew of his existence; only a few of them had knowingly seen him; while the number
DA-R
who as yet had actually and knowingly given battle to him, was small indeed. For, owing to the
DA-R DA-R DA-R DA-R
large number of whale-cruisers; the disorderly way they were sprinkled over the entire watery
LA-P DA-R
circumference, many of them adventurously pushing their quest along solitary latitudes, so as
DA-R DA-R DA-PresP
seldom or never for a whole twelvemonth or more on a stretch, to encounter a single news-telling
LA-IND DA-R LA-IND DA-R
sail of any sort; the inordinate length of each separate voyage; the irregularity of the times of
LA-IND DA-R DA-R
sailing from home; all these, with other circumstances, direct and indirect, long obstructed
DA-R DA-R DA-R DA-PresP
the spread through the whole world-wide whaling-fleet of the special individualizing tidings
LA-IND
concerning Moby Dick. It was hardly to be doubted, that several vessels reported to have
DA-R
encountered, at such or such a time, or on such or such a meridian, a sperm whale of uncommon
LA-INT DA-R LA-P
magnitude and malignity, which whale, after doing great mischief to his assailants, had
LA-IND DA-R
completely escaped them; to some minds it was not an unfair presumption, I say, that the whale
DA-R
in question must have been no other than Moby Dick. Yet as of late the Sperm Whale fishery had
DA-R DA-R DA-R
been marked by various and not unfrequent instances of great ferocity, cunning, and malice in

the monster attacked [DA-PastP]; therefore it was, that those who by accident ignorantly gave battle to Moby Dick; such [LA-D] hunters, perhaps, for the most [DA-R] part, were content [DA-R] to ascribe the peculiar [DA-R] terror he bred, more, as it were, to the perils of the Sperm Whale [DA-R] fishery at large, than to the individual [DA-R] cause. In that [LA-D] way, mostly, the disastrous [DA-R] encounter between Ahab and the whale had hitherto been popularly regarded.

> **Note to Instructor:** *Sperm whale* is a compound noun that also functions as a compound descriptive adjective.

Exercise 102B: Analysis

> **Note to Instructor:** This exercise is intended to engage statistically inclined thinkers in a way that grammar usually doesn't. You may certainly skip it if the student finds this sort of calculation frustrating or unhelpful.

The passage above shows you how a good writer uses adjectives: a mix of colorful descriptive adjectives and sparer, simpler limiting adjectives.

The total word count of the excerpt is 317 words. Now count each type of adjective and fill out the chart below. For the purpose of our calculations, hyphenated words (e.g., news-telling) should be counted as single words, while compound adjectives that are not hyphenated (e.g., Sperm Whale) should be counted as separate words.

Descriptive Adjectives		**Limiting Adjectives**	
Regular	30	Possessives	3
Present participles	2	~~Articles~~	
Past participles	4	Demonstratives	3
		Indefinites	6
		Interrogatives	1
		Numbers	0

Total Descriptive Adjectives 36 — Total Limiting Adjectives 13

Total Adjectives Used 49

Good prose can't be reduced to *just* formulas—but formulas can give you some extra help in writing well. The total word count of the excerpt is 317 words. You can figure out what fraction of the total word count is taken up by adjectives by dividing the total word count by the total number of adjectives used. Determine that quotient now, and ask your instructor for help if necessary.

$$317 \div 49 = 6 \text{ r.}23 \quad (317 - 294 = 23)$$

The sum above tells you that 1 out of every 6 r. 23 [insert answer to division problem!] words in this passage is an adjective. In other words, adjectives do not make up more than about 1/6 [or between 1/7 and 1/6] of this descriptive writing.

Now let's look at the relationship between limiting and descriptive adjectives. Complete the following division problem:

[number of limiting adjectives] 13 ⟌ 36 [number of descriptive adjectives] = 2 r. 10

The quotient above tells you that 1 out of every 2 r. 10 [insert answer to second division problem!] adjectives used is a limiting adjective. In other words, limiting adjectives do not make up more than about 1/3 [or between 1/3 and1/2] of this descriptive writing.

Ask your instructor to share the last part of this exercise with you.

Note to Instructor: Share the following conclusion with the student.

1/7 to 1/6 of Melville's words are adjectives (one out of every 6 or 7 words).

Of those adjectives, 1/3 to 1/2 are limiting (one out of every 2 or 3 adjectives). The rest are descriptive.

Exercise 102C: Using Adjectives

On your own paper, rewrite the passage below. It is taken from Herman Melville's short story "The Apple Tree Table"—but all of the adjectives (except for articles) have been removed.

Where adjectives could be removed without making the sentence ungrammatical, they have simply been deleted without a trace. Where removing an adjective made the sentence unreasonable, a blank has been inserted instead. So you know that adjectives go in the blanks—but you'll have to find a lot of other places to put them as well!

You can also insert adverbs, additional articles, and conjunctions as necessary to make your insertions work.

Use the same proportions as the passage in Exercise 102B. This excerpt originally had 326 words, so use:

- 47–54 total adjectives, not including articles.
  - Use between 15 and 27 limiting adjectives:
    - Use at least three different kinds of limiting adjectives (your choice!).
  - The remainder should be descriptive adjectives:
    - Use at least three participles (present or past) as adjectives.

When you are finished, compare your work with the original passage in the Key.

Notes to Instructor: The original passage, found below, actually had 59 adjectives, of which 15 were limiting adjectives. When the student has finished, show her the original and point out that proportions can change depending on the purpose of the passage. This exercise is intended to make students more aware of, and sensitive to, the presence and proportion of adjectives in good descriptive writing—not to establish some sort of firm rule.

You may need to remind her that she can add more than one descriptive adjective to any given noun or pronoun.

If she gets frustrated, show her one or more lines of the original and encourage her to use a thesaurus.

Under the apex of the roof was a rude, narrow, decrepit step-ladder, something like a Gothic pulpit-stairway, leading to a pulpit-like platform, from which a still narrower ladder—a sort of Jacob's ladder—led somewhat higher to the lofty scuttle. The slide of this scuttle was about two feet square, all in one piece, furnishing a massive frame for a single small pane of glass, inserted into it like a bull's-eye. The light of the garret came from this sole source, filtrated through a dense curtain of cobwebs. Indeed, the whole stairs, and platform, and ladder, were festooned, and carpeted, and canopied with cobwebs; which, in funereal accumulations, hung, too, from the groined, murky ceiling, like the Carolina moss in the cypress forest. In these cobwebs, swung, as in aerial catacombs, myriads of all tribes of mummied insects. . . .

Wishing to shed a clearer light through the place, I sought to withdraw the scuttle-slide. But no sign of latch or hasp was visible. Only after long peering, did I discover a little padlock, imbedded, like an oyster at the bottom of the sea, amid matted masses of weedy webs, chrysalides, and insectivorous eggs. Brushing these away, I found it locked. With a crooked nail, I tried to pick the lock, when scores of small ants and flies, half-torpid, crawled forth from the keyhole. . . . As if incensed at this invasion of their retreat, countless bands darted up from below, beating about my head, like hornets. At last, with a sudden jerk, I burst open the scuttle. And ah! what a change. As from the gloom of the grave and the companionship of worms, men shall at last rapturously rise into the living greenness and glory immortal, so, from my cobwebbed old garret, I thrust forth my head into the balmy air, and found myself hailed by the verdant tops of great trees, growing in the little garden below—trees, whose leaves soared high above my topmost slate.

— LESSON 103 —

Misplaced Modifiers
Squinting Modifiers
Dangling Modifiers

Exercise 103A: Correcting Misplaced Modifiers

Circle each misplaced modifier and draw an arrow to the place in the sentence that it should occupy.

Note to Instructor: After the student completes the exercise (or if the student asks for help because all of the options seem awkward), point out that some of these modifiers, once moved, would need commas placed around them. And some of the sentences would be better rewritten entirely. When the student is finished, show him the rewritten sentences that follow the answers.

The gold belonged to the queen in the treasure chest.

The giraffe ate lettuce from my hand that I saw at the zoo.

After wrapping the present, the table was beautifully decorated by my mother.

The couple strolled in the center of the park past the ornate fountain.

Note to Instructor: The student could also have circled "in the center of the park" and drawn an arrow pointing to the space after "fountain."

Sitting in the top row of the bleachers, the football game was hard for us to see.

The arcade game required three quarters, on which I had the high score.

Molly ate the dinner her father had prepared with a voracious appetite.

> **Note to Instructor:** The student could also have drawn the arrow pointing back to the space before "Molly."

Shane had promised to perform in the New Year's Day concert in October.

Packed with souvenirs, we couldn't fit our suitcases into the car.

I learned how to knit with great difficulty.

> **Note to Instructor:** The student could also have drawn the arrow pointing back to the space before "I."

The gold in the treasure chest belonged to the queen.

The giraffe that I saw at the zoo ate lettuce from my hand.

The table was beautifully decorated by my mother after wrapping the present.
BETTER: The table was beautifully decorated by my mother after she wrapped the present.
ALSO BETTER: After wrapping the present, my mother decorated the table beautifully.

The couple strolled past the ornate fountain in the center of the park.

The football game was hard for us, sitting in the top row of the bleachers, to see.
BETTER: The football game was hard for us to see while we were sitting in the top row of the bleachers.

The arcade game, on which I had the high score, required three quarters.

Molly ate with a ravenous appetite the dinner her father had prepared.
OR: With a ravenous appetite, Molly ate the dinner her father had prepared.

Shane had promised in October to perform in the New Year's Day concert.

We couldn't fit our suitcases, packed with souvenirs, into the car.

I learned with great difficulty how to knit.
OR: With great difficulty, I learned how to knit.

Exercise 103B: Clarifying Squinting Modifiers

Circle each squinting modifier. On your own paper, rewrite each sentence twice, eliminating the ambiguity by moving the squinting modifier to produce sentences with two different meanings. Insert commas and change capitalization/punctuation as needed.

The first is done for you.

Note to Instructor: If the student has difficulty, use the italicized questions to help her identify the ambiguity.

Zoe sang the second song at least as loudly as the soloist.

Zoe sang at least the second song as loudly as the soloist.
Zoe sang the second song as loudly, at least, as the soloist.

Did Zoe sing several songs loudly, with at least the second one having her as loud as the soloist? Or did Zoe sing the second song at least as loudly as the soloist but perhaps even more so?

Jasper wished immediately to disappear.

Jasper immediately wished to disappear.
Jasper wished to disappear immediately.

What was immediate—the wishing, or the wished-for disappearance?

The governor vowed earnestly to defend the proposal against criticism.

The governor earnestly vowed to defend the proposal against criticism.
The governor vowed to defend the proposal earnestly against criticism.

Did the governor make an earnest vow, or did she vow to make an earnest defense?

Tell Micah if he has the book I will read to him.

If he has the book, tell Micah I will read to him.
Tell Micah I will read to him if he has the book.

What is the consequence of "if he has the book"—the instruction to deliver a message to Micah, or the reading?

The director instructed us poorly to redo the scene.

The director poorly instructed us to redo the scene.
The director instructed us to redo the scene poorly.

Did the director give poor instructions? Or did the director want the actors to try a poor rendition of the scene?

The red sweater I bought yesterday got a snag.

The red sweater I bought got a snag yesterday.
Yesterday, the red sweater I bought got a snag.

What happened yesterday—the purchase, or the snag?

The smell of the bread she baked slowly filled the air.

The smell of the bread she baked filled the air slowly.
The smell of the bread she slowly baked filled the air.

Did she bake slowly, or did the smell fill the air slowly?

The athlete who had been training (intensely) stared at his opponent.

The athlete who had been intensely training stared at his opponent.
The athlete who had been training stared intensely at his opponent.

Which was intense—the training, or the stare?

My cousin realized (eventually) the toy would be worth a lot of money.

My cousin eventually realized the toy would be worth a lot of money.
My cousin realized the toy would eventually be worth a lot of money.

Was the realization eventual, or would the increased worth happen eventually?

Morgan decided (during the class) to work more diligently.

During the class, Morgan decided to work more diligently.
Morgan decided to work during the class more diligently.

Did Morgan, during the class, make a decision about his work (a decision that may or may not have applied to the work in that class)? Or did Morgan decide that he would use the class time to work more diligently?

Exercise 103C: Rewriting Dangling Modifiers

On your own paper, rewrite each of these sentences twice, using each of the strategies described in the lesson.

Note to Instructor: Answers may vary; as long as they follow the rules in "how to fix a dangling modifier," you may accept different versions.

Reading the instructions, the bookshelf appeared simple enough to put together.

Reading the instructions, we thought the bookshelf appeared simple enough to put together.
After we had read the instructions, the bookshelf appeared simple enough to put together.

Flying above the clouds, the town grew smaller and smaller.

Flying above the clouds, Jack watched the town grow smaller and smaller.
As Jack flew above the clouds, the town grew smaller and smaller.

Left without supervision, a baseball went through the window.

Left without supervision, the brothers hit a baseball through the window.
While the brothers were left without supervision, a baseball went through the window.

Terrified out of their wits, the knocks at the door continued.

Terrified out of their wits, the children heard the continued knocks at the door.
As the children sat terrified out of their wits, the knocks at the door continued.

The bus pulled away from the curb, having hugged our parents.

Having hugged our parents, we waved from the bus as it pulled away from the curb.
The bus pulled away from the curb, after we had hugged our parents.

— LESSON 104 —

Degrees of Adjectives

Comparisons Using More, Fewer, and Less

Exercise 104A: Positive, Comparative, and Superlative Adjectives

Using the following chart to review spelling rules for forming degrees of adjectives. Then, fill in the blank in each sentence with each adjective indicated in brackets (properly spelled!).

These sentences are all drawn from Charlotte Bronte's classic novel *Jane Eyre*.

Spelling Rules:

If the adjective ends in *e* already, add only *–r* or *–st*.

noble	nobler	noblest
pure	purer	purest
cute	cuter	cutest

If the adjective ends in a short vowel sound and a consonant, double the consonant and add *–er* or *–est*.

red	redder	reddest
thin	thinner	thinnest
flat	flatter	flattest

If the adjective ends in *–y*, change the *y* to *i* and add *–er* or *–est*.

hazy	hazier	haziest
lovely	lovelier	loveliest

When thus gentle, Bessie seemed to me the best, prettiest, kindest being in the world. [in order, the superlatives of good, pretty, and kind]

But I believed in the existence of other and more vivid kinds of goodness, and what I believed in I wished to behold. [comparative of vivid]

Could not even self-interest make you wiser? [comparative of wise]

Then she ought to look more cheerful. [comparative of cheerful]

Take your palette, mix your freshest, finest, clearest tints; choose your most delicate camel-hair pencils; delineate carefully the loveliest face you can imagine; paint it in your softest shades and sweetest hues, according to the description given by Mrs. Fairfax of Blanche Ingram. [in order, the superlatives of fresh, fine, clear, delicate, lovely, soft, and sweet]

The one who went with me appeared some years younger. [comparative of young]

I would fain exercise some better faculty than that of fierce speaking. [comparative of good]

It was Mr. Brocklehurst, buttoned up in a surtout, and looking longer, narrower, and more rigid than ever. [comparatives of long, narrow, and rigid]

Until she heard from Bessie and could discover by her own observation that I was endeavoring in good earnest to acquire a more sociable and child-like disposition, a more attractive and sprightly manner—something lighter, franker, more natural, as it were—she really must exclude me from privileges intended only for contented, happy little children. [in order, the comparatives of sociable, attractive, light, frank, and natural]

Miss Miller was more ordinary. [comparative of ordinary]

I felt physically weak and broken down: but my worst ailment was an unutterable wretchedness of mind. [superlative of bad]

But the three most distinguished —partly, perhaps, because the tallest figures of the band—were the Dowager Lady Ingram and her daughters, Blanche and Mary. They were all three of the loftiest stature of women. [in order, the superlatives of distinguished, tall, and lofty]

I believed he was naturally a man of better tendencies, higher principles, and purer tastes than such as circumstances had developed, education instilled, or destiny encouraged. [in order, the comparatives of good, high, and pure]

Exercise 104B: Forming Comparisons

Rewrite each set of independent clauses so that they form a comparative sentence making use of *more, less, fewer,* and/or comparative forms of the adjectives indicated. The first is done for you.

When you are finished, ask your instructor to show you the original sentences, which are taken from Carl von Clausewitz's nineteenth-century classic *On War,* a guide to military strategy.

Our political object is small.
We shall set less value upon it.

The smaller our political object, the less value shall we set upon it.

We ascend higher.
The difficulties increase.

The higher we ascend, the more the difficulties increase.

We demand a small sacrifice from our opponent.
Our opponent employs a smaller means of resistance.

The smaller the sacrifice we demand from our opponent, the smaller will be the means of resistance which he will employ.

The motives of a War are great and powerful.
A war affects the whole existence of a people.

The greater and the more powerful the motives of a War, the more it affects the whole existence of a people.

We go back farther.
Military history becomes less useful.
It gets much more meagre and barren of detail.

The farther we go back, the less useful becomes military history, as it gets so much more meagre and barren of detail.

This victory is sought for near our own frontiers.
It is easier.

The nearer our own frontiers that this victory is sought for, the easier it is.

Exercise 104C: Using "Fewer" and "Less"

Complete the sentences by filling in each blank with either "fewer" or "less."

The original sentences are taken from Carl von Clausewitz's nineteenth-century classic *On War*, a guide to military strategy.

While the number of cavalry and guns is the same, there are fewer horses, and therefore, there is less forage required.

It is certainly always of advantage to strengthen the flanks in this manner, as fewer troops are then required at those points.

He who uses force unsparingly, without reference to the bloodshed involved, must obtain a superiority if his adversary uses less vigour in its application.

The fewer favourable circumstances exist, the more will all depend on superior skill in combination, and promptitude and precision in the execution.

Napoleon always showed great foresight in the provision he made in this manner in the rear of his Army; and in that way, even in his boldest operations, he incurred less risk than might be imagined at first sight.

Exercise 104D: Diagramming

On your own paper, diagram every word of the following sentences from various stories in Andrew Lang's *The Blue Fairy Book*.

The more she hunted for it the more frightened she got, and at last she began to cry.
—from "The Yellow Dwarf"

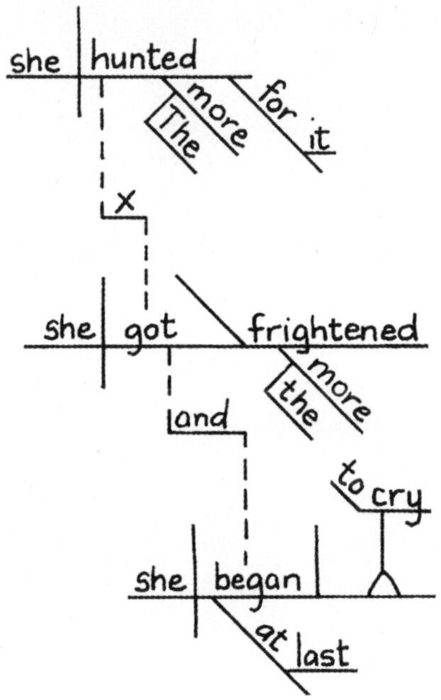

The slower he went, the more time had everyone to stare and look at him; and they used it too, and no one can imagine how tired out and ragged he looked after his dance with the calf.

—from "The Master-Maid"

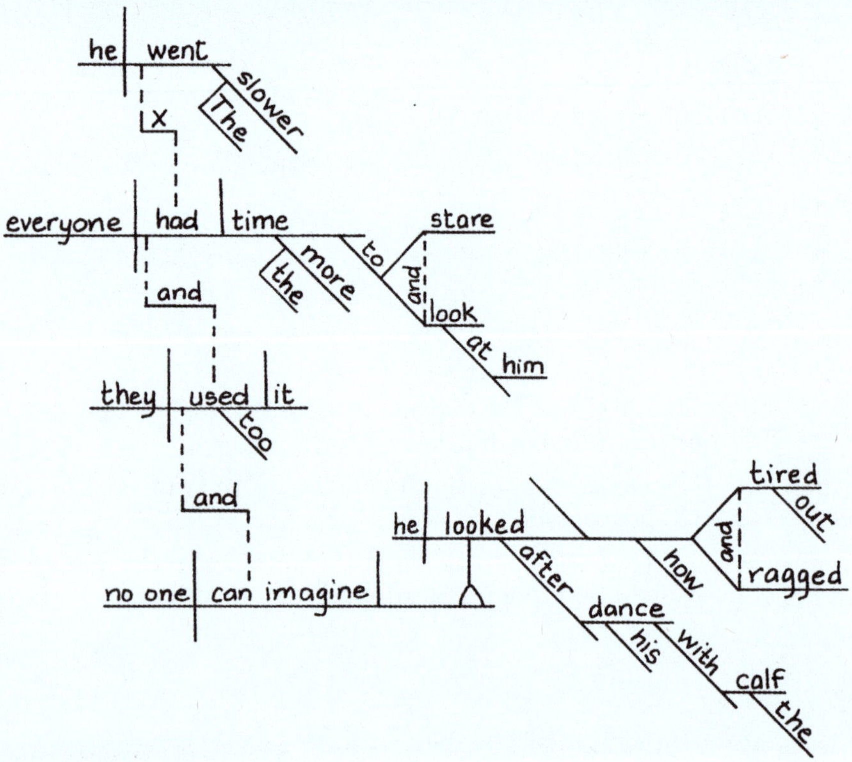

The more difficult it became to obtain the fruit, the more the Queen was determined that have it she would.

—from "The White Cat"

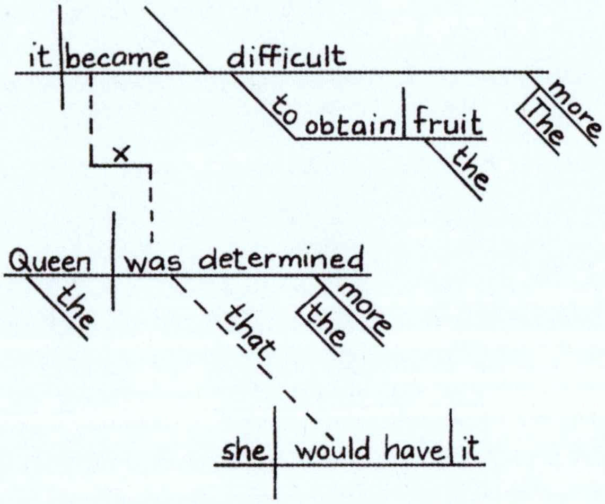

WEEK 27

Double Identities

— LESSON 105 —

Clauses with Understood Elements
Than as Conjunction, Preposition, and Adverb
Quasi-Coordinators

Exercise 105A: Comparisons Using *Than*

Each of the following sentences, taken from Robert B. Kebric's *Greek People*, contains a comparison clause introduced by *than* and missing some of its words. Using carets, do your best to insert the missing words.

> **Note to Instructor:** The student's phrasing may differ. Words in brackets can be inserted by the student, but do not mark the answer as wrong if they are left out. When the student is finished, ask him to compare his work to the answers below.

Since [the hoplite soldier] fought in a formation called the "phalanx," which was several ranks
was [vulnerable]
deep, he was less vulnerable than an individual warrior fighting by himself^.

Soldiers, not the state, provided their own equipment, and although hoplite armor was far more
was [expensive]
expensive than what they had previously worn as support troops^, their improved status as first-line heavy infantry made most members of the newly wealthy families willing to absorb the cost.

This one passage probably did more to disturb aristocrats of [Archilochus's] own generation—and
did [to disturb them]
later—than any other he wrote^.

enjoyed [celebrity]
No athlete in antiquity enjoyed greater celebrity than Milo of Croton^, whose wrestling prowess endeared him to fans of his own generation and those that followed.

No painter blended war, art, and politics better than the most famous Greek muralist, Polygnotus
blended [them]
of Thasos^.

was [bad]
Even worse than the death of a loved one^was the knowledge that he had died a dishonorable death, an embarrassment with which his family had to live.

> **Note to Instructor:** This one is tricky because of the word order in the sentence. If the student struggles, have him try rewriting the sentence with "than" and the comparison clause at the end: *The knowledge that he had died a dishonorable death, an embarrassment with which his family had to live, was even worse* ***than the death of a loved one***. This may help the student determine the missing word(s) more easily.

Exercise 105B: Identifying Parts of the Sentence

In the following sentences, drawn from Andrew Lang's *The Blue Fairy Book*, identify each bolded word or phrase as *SC* for subordinating conjunction, *QC* for quasi-coordinator, *PREP* for preposition, or *ADV* for adverb.

PREP
They said that the yellow water-lily could be none **other than** their sister, who was not dead, but transformed by the magic ball.

QC
Not to mention the richness of the furniture, which was inestimable, there was such profuseness throughout that the Prince, instead of ever having seen anything like it, owned that he could not have imagined that there was anything in the world that could come up to it.

QC
It is calculated that eleven hundred persons have at different times suffered death **rather than** break their eggs at the smaller end.

ADV
You will find the effect of it in **less than** an hour's time.

SC
Now this man was no other **than** the father of the boy's mother.

ADV
She has carried off **more than** one Prince like this, and she will certainly have anything she takes a fancy to.

SC
"O admirable potion!" she said: "it has wrought its cure much sooner **than** you told me it would."

QC
A lovely princess like you must surely prefer to die **rather than** be the wife of a poor little dwarf like myself.

ADV
In **less than** three hours I was raised and slung into the engine, and there tied fast.

SC
"I ask for no more **than** I am able to carry with me," said the prince.

Exercise 105C: Diagramming

On your own paper, diagram every word of the following sentences from Exercise 105B.

They said that the yellow water-lily could be none other than their sister, who was not dead, but transformed by the magic ball.

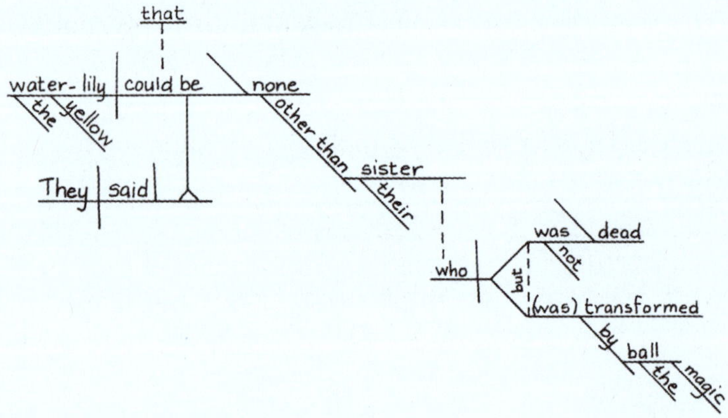

It is calculated that eleven hundred persons have at different times suffered death rather than break their eggs at the smaller end.

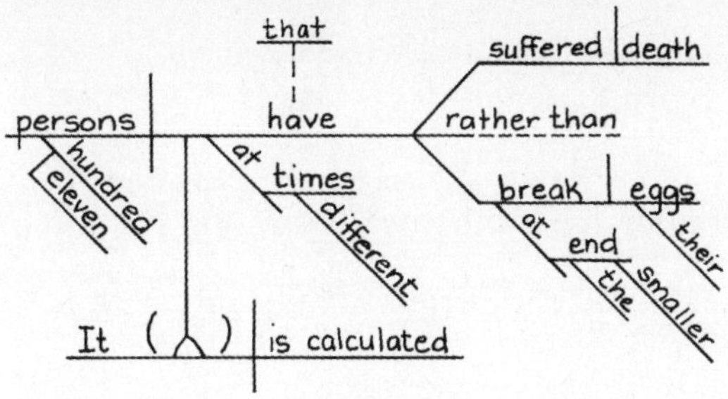

Note to Instructor: *Eleven hundred* can also be diagrammed on a single adjective line beneath *persons*; I have broken it into the adjective *hundred* modified by *eleven* because it is not hyphenated, but diagramming it as a single adjective is also acceptable.

A lovely princess like you must surely prefer to die rather than be the wife of a poor little dwarf like myself.

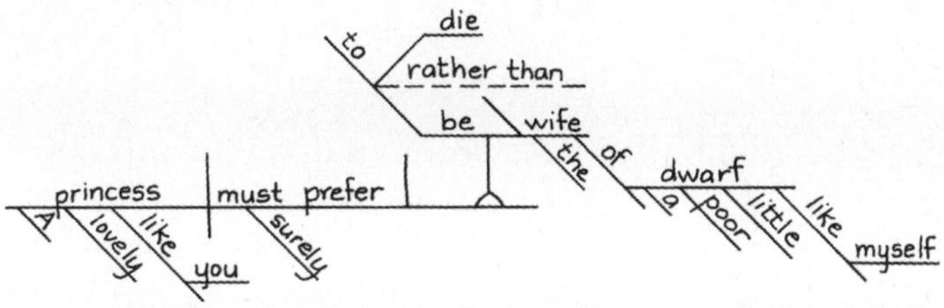

In less than three hours I was raised and slung into the engine, and there tied fast.

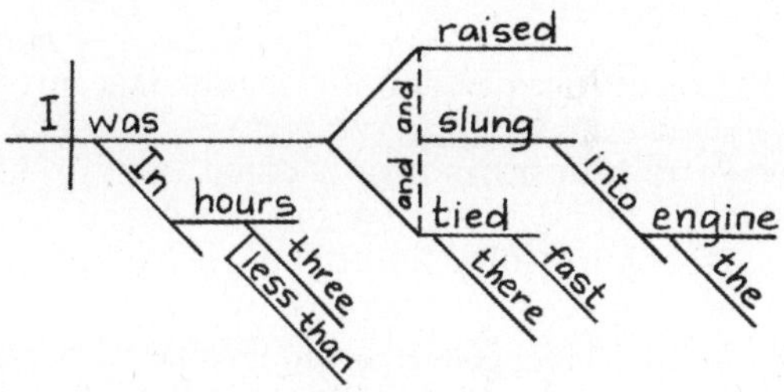

— LESSON 106 —

The Word *As*

Quasi-Coordinators

Exercise 106A: Identifying Parts of the Sentence

In the following sentences, find and underline every adverb, preposition, conjunction, and quasi-coordinator. Then label each as *ADV* for adverb, *PREP* for preposition, *CC* for coordinating conjunction, *SC* for subordinating conjunction, and *QC* for quasi-coordinator. Remember that a quasi-coordinator can be a short phrase as well as a single word.

These sentences are adapted from Robert Louis Stevenson's *The Strange Case of Dr. Jekyll and Mr. Hyde.*

Note to Instructor: The inserted parts of the understood clause are included for your reference only.

ADV ADV PREP SC [I was disappointed in]
I was never more disappointed in any man than^Lanyon.

CC ADV PREP CC
And then he condemned the fear as a disloyalty, and broke the seal.

PREP ADV CC PREP
He was the usual cut and dry apothecary, <u>of</u> <u>no</u> particular age <u>and</u> colour, <u>with</u> a strong
ADV ADV SC
Edinburgh accent, and <u>about</u> <u>as</u> emotional <u>as</u> a bagpipe.

> **Note to Instructor:** *Particular* is an adjective modifying *age* and *colour*; *no* is an adverb modifying the adjective *particular*.

ADV PREP ADV ADV PREP PREP
<u>But</u> he had an approved tolerance <u>for</u> others, <u>sometimes</u> wondering, <u>almost</u> <u>with</u> envy, <u>at</u> the high
PREP PREP CC PREP QC
pressure <u>of</u> spirits involved <u>in</u> their misdeeds; <u>and</u> <u>in</u> any extremity inclined to help <u>rather than</u>
to reprove.

ADV ADV PREP SC
The lawyer liked this letter <u>well</u> <u>enough</u>; it put a better colour <u>on</u> the intimacy <u>than</u> he had
PREP
looked <u>for</u>.

ADV PREP PREP SC
He could have wished it otherwise; <u>never</u> <u>in</u> his life had he been conscious <u>of</u> <u>so</u> sharp a wish to
CC SC ADV ADV PREP
see and touch his fellow-creatures; <u>for</u> struggle <u>as</u> he might, <u>there</u> was borne <u>in</u> <u>upon</u> his mind a
PREP
crushing anticipation <u>of</u> calamity.

> **Note to Instructor:** I have classified *otherwise* as an object complement (see the second diagram in Exercise 106B), but if the student makes an argument that otherwise is an adverb modifying *could have wished*, you may accept it. In that case, it would be diagrammed beneath the verb in the exercise below (as noted).

SC
"I see you feel <u>as</u> I do," said Mr. Enfield.

CC SC ADV
He must know his own state <u>and</u> that his days <u>are</u> counted; and the knowledge is more <u>than</u> he
can bear.

ADV PREP ADV PREP PREP
<u>There</u> he opened his safe, took <u>from</u> the <u>most</u> private part <u>of</u> it a document endorsed <u>on</u> the
PREP PREP ADV
envelope <u>as</u> Dr. Jekyll's Will, and sat <u>down</u> <u>with</u> a clouded brow to study its contents.

PREP PREP SC ADV PREP CC ADV
This was brought <u>to</u> the lawyer <u>on</u> the next morning, <u>before</u> he was <u>out</u> <u>of</u> bed; <u>and</u> he had <u>no</u>
ADV SC ADV
<u>sooner</u> seen it, and been told the circumstances, <u>than</u> he shot <u>out</u> a solemn lip.

CC ADV ADV
<u>But</u> I have been <u>pedantically</u> exact, <u>as</u> you call it.

CC ADV SC ADV PREP
<u>But</u> it is <u>more than</u> ten years <u>since</u> Henry Jekyll became <u>too</u> fanciful <u>for</u> me.

SC ADV CC PREP PREP
The tradesmen came <u>while</u> we were <u>yet</u> speaking, <u>and</u> we moved <u>in</u> a body <u>to</u> old Dr. Denman's
PREP ADV ADV
surgical theatre, <u>from</u> which (as you are <u>doubtless</u> aware) Jekyll's private cabinet is <u>most</u>
ADV
<u>conveniently</u> entered.

Exercise 106B: Diagramming

On your own paper, diagram every word of the following sentences from Exercise 106A.

He was the usual cut and dry apothecary, of no particular age and colour, with a strong Edinburgh accent, and about as emotional as a bagpipe.

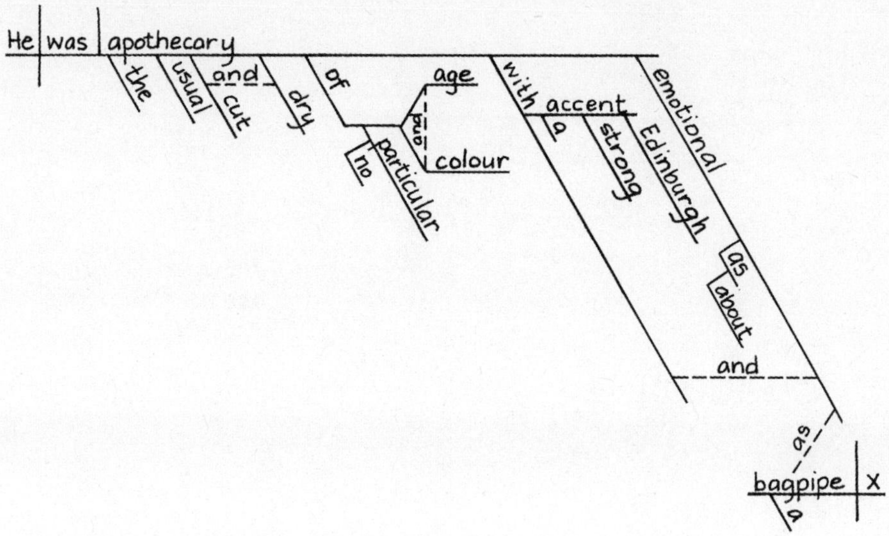

He could have wished it otherwise; never in his life had he been conscious of so sharp a wish to see and touch his fellow-creatures; for struggle as he might, there was borne in upon his mind a crushing anticipation of calamity.

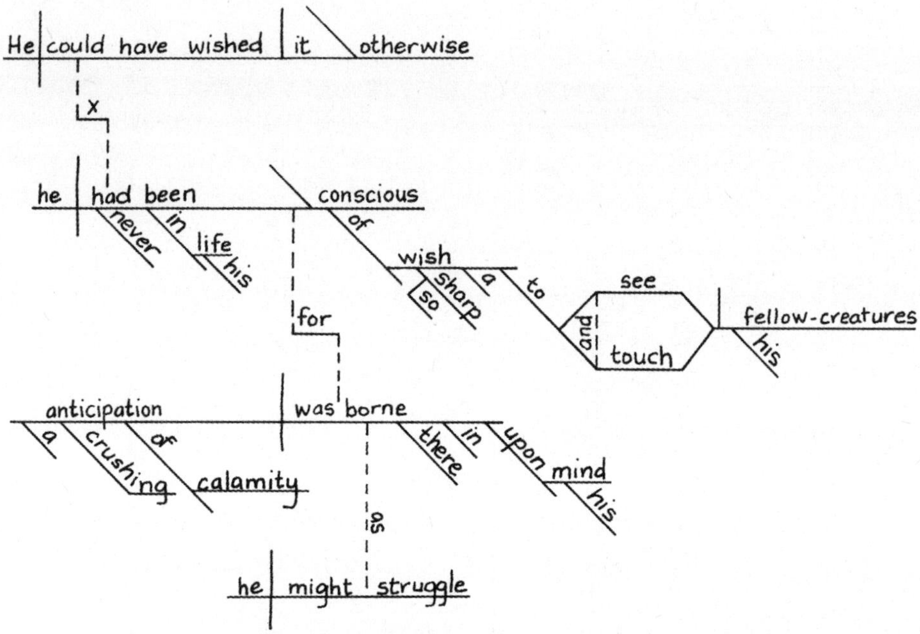

Note to Instructor: If the student has classified *otherwise* as an adverb in the exercise above, it should be diagrammed beneath the verb.

There he opened his safe, took from the most private part of it a document endorsed on the envelope as Dr. Jekyll's Will, and sat down with a clouded brow to study its contents.

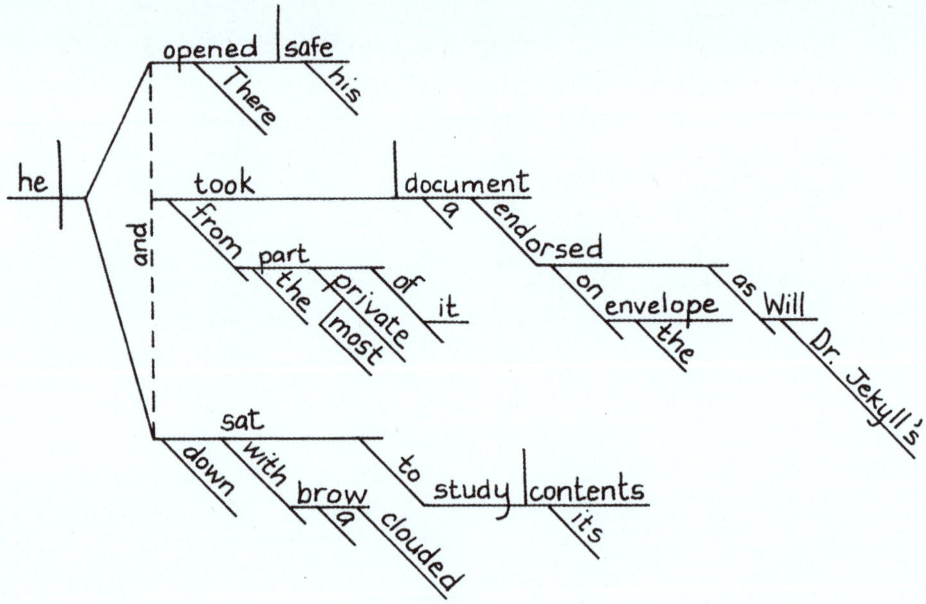

The tradesmen came while we were yet speaking, and we moved in a body to old Dr. Denman's surgical theatre, from which (as you are doubtless aware) Jekyll's private cabinet is most conveniently entered.

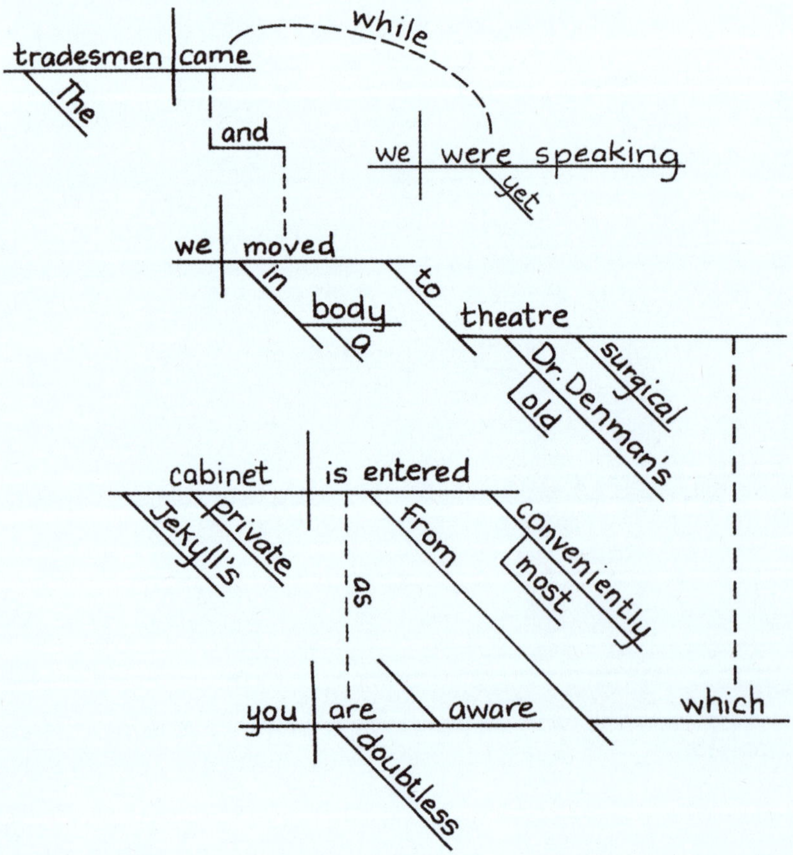

— LESSON 107 —

Words That Can Be Multiple Parts of Speech

Exercise 107A: Identifying Parts of Speech

Identify the part of speech of each underlined word by writing the correct abbreviation above it: *N* (noun), *PRO* (pronoun), *V* (verb), *ADJ* (adjective), *ADV* (adverb), *PREP* (preposition), *CC* (coordinating conjunction), or *SC* (subordinating conjunction).

The following sentences are from Charles Dickens's *A Tale of Two Cities.*

The nose, beautifully formed otherwise [ADV], was very slightly pinched at the top of each [ADJ] nostril.

He added the last [ADJ] words after [ADV] there had been a vivid flash which had shown him lounging in the window.

It is fifteen years since [SC] we—since I—came last [ADV] from France.

After [PREP] this odd description of his daily routine of employment, Mr. Lorry flattened his waxen wig upon his head with both hands (which was most unnecessary, for [CC] nothing could be flatter than its shining surface was before [ADV]), and resumed his former attitude.

This [ADJ] time a pair of haggard eyes had looked at the questioner before [ADV] the face had dropped again.

Take that [ADJ] message back, and they will know that I received this [PRO].

The banker would not have gone so far [ADV] in his expression of opinion on any [ADV] less solid ground than moral certainty.

He had a wild, lost manner of occasionally clasping his head in his hands, that had not been seen in him before [ADV]; yet [CC] he had some [ADJ] pleasure in the mere sound of his daughter's voice, and invariably turned to it when she spoke.

At last the top of the staircase was gained, and they stopped for [PREP] the third [ADJ] time.

His linen, though not of a fineness [N] in accordance with his stockings, was as white as the tops of the waves that broke upon the neighboring beach, or the specks of sail that glinted in the sunlight far [PREP] at sea.

A gentleman of sixty, formally dressed in a brown suit of clothes, pretty [ADV] well worn, but [CC] very well kept, with large square cuffs and large flaps to the pockets, passed along on his way to breakfast.

"You do me too much honour," said the Marquis; "still [CC], I prefer that supposition."

I think a messenger was sent after [PREP] him to beg the favour of his waiting for [PREP] me here.

The Lord above [ADJ] knows what the compromising consequences would be to numbers of people if some of our documents were seized or destroyed.

With the same intention he drew the key across it, three or four times before [SC] he put it clumsily into the lock, and turned it as [ADV] heavily as [SC] he could.

"True," said he, "and fearful to reflect upon [ADV]."

You are a pretty [ADJ] fellow to object and advise!

He had no good-humour left in his face, nor any [ADJ] openness of aspect left, but [CC] had become a secret, angry, dangerous man.

But [CC] the time was not come yet [ADV].

I should be so much more at my ease about [PREP] your state of mind.

The coachman was sure of nothing but [PREP] the horses.

Many leaves of burning red and golden yellow still [ADV] remained upon the trees.

A few passers turned their heads, and a few shook their fingers at him as [PREP] an aristocrat; otherwise [ADV], that a man in good clothes should be going to prison was no more remarkable than that a labourer in working clothes should be going to work.

The plane tree whispered to them in its own way above [PREP] their heads.

Her knitting was before [PREP] her, but [CC] she had laid it down to pick her teeth with a toothpick.

There was a character about [PREP] Madame Defarge, from which one [PRO] might have predicted that she did not often make mistakes against herself in any [PRO] of the reckonings over which she presided.

Darnay, unable to restrain himself any [ADJ] longer, touched Mr. Stryver on the shoulder, and said: "I know the fellow."

No one heard them as [SC] they went about [ADV] with muffled tread.

Mr. Lorry got his arm securely round [PREP] the daughter's waist and held her; for [CC] he felt that she was sinking.

He found them safe, and strong, and sound, and still [ADJ], just as [SC] he had last seen them.

The majesty of the law fired blunderbusses in among [PREP] them, loaded with rounds [N] of shot and ball.

He stopped there, and faced round [ADV].

A supper-table was laid for two [N], in the third [N] of the rooms; a round [ADJ] room, in one [N] of the chateau's four extinguisher-topped towers.

Exercise 107B: Diagramming

On your own paper, diagram every word of the following sentences from *A Tale of Two Cities.*

His judges sat upon the bench in feathered hats; but the rough red cap and tricoloured cockade was the headdress otherwise prevailing.

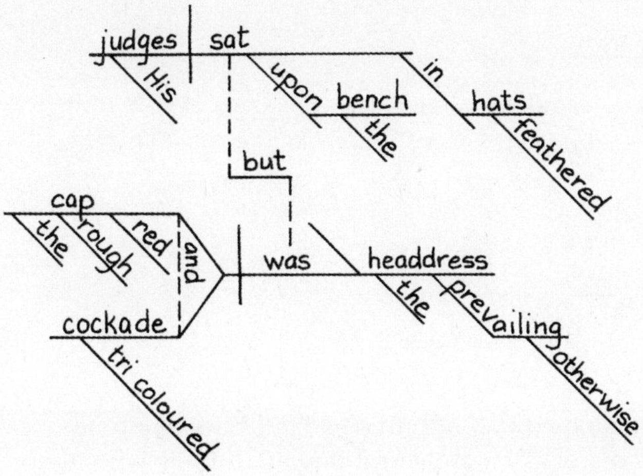

I don't suppose anything about it but what Ladybird tells me.

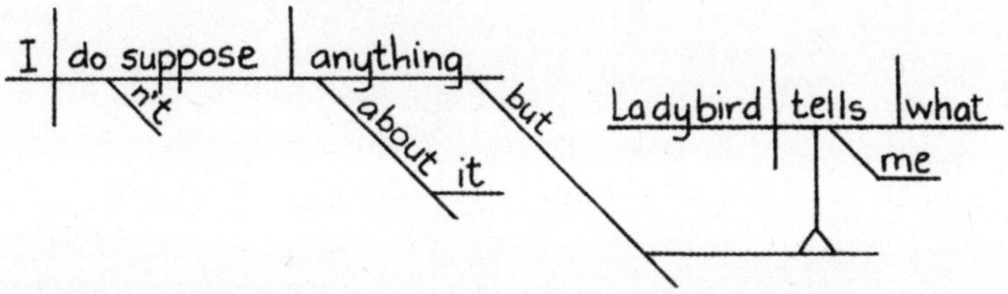

His hurried right hand parcelled out the herbs before him into imaginary beds of flowers in a garden; and his efforts to control and steady his breathing shook the lips from which the colour rushed to his heart.

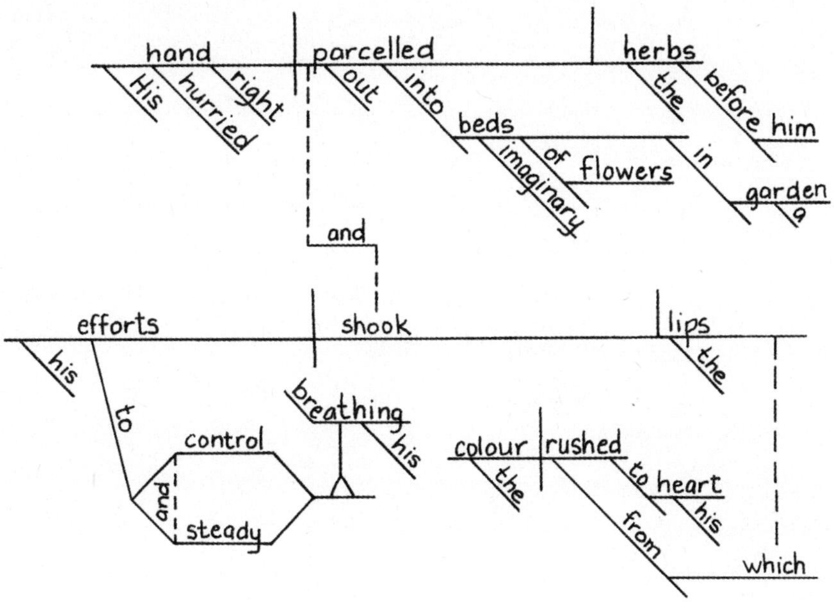

For some minutes after he had emerged into the outer presence of Saint Antoine, the husband and wife remained as he had left them, lest he should come back.

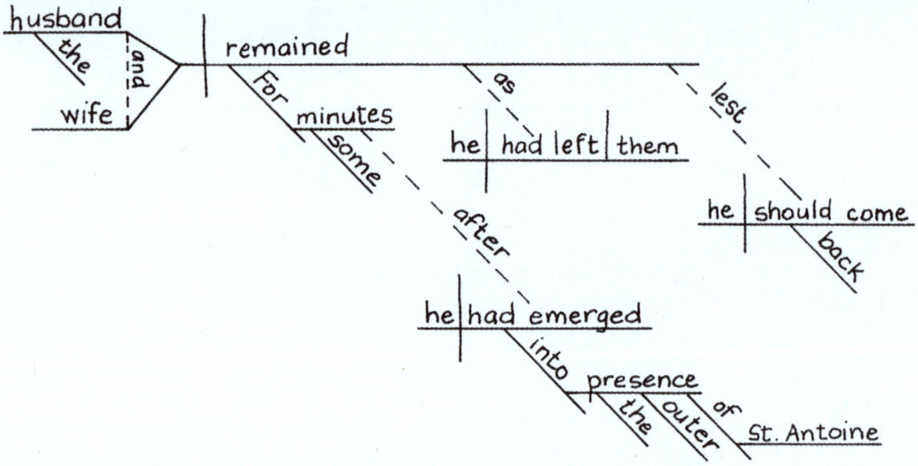

Little Lucie sat by her grandfather with her hands clasped through his arm; and he, in a tone not rising much above a whisper, began to tell her a story of a great and powerful fairy who had opened a prison-wall and let out a captive who had once done the fairy a service.

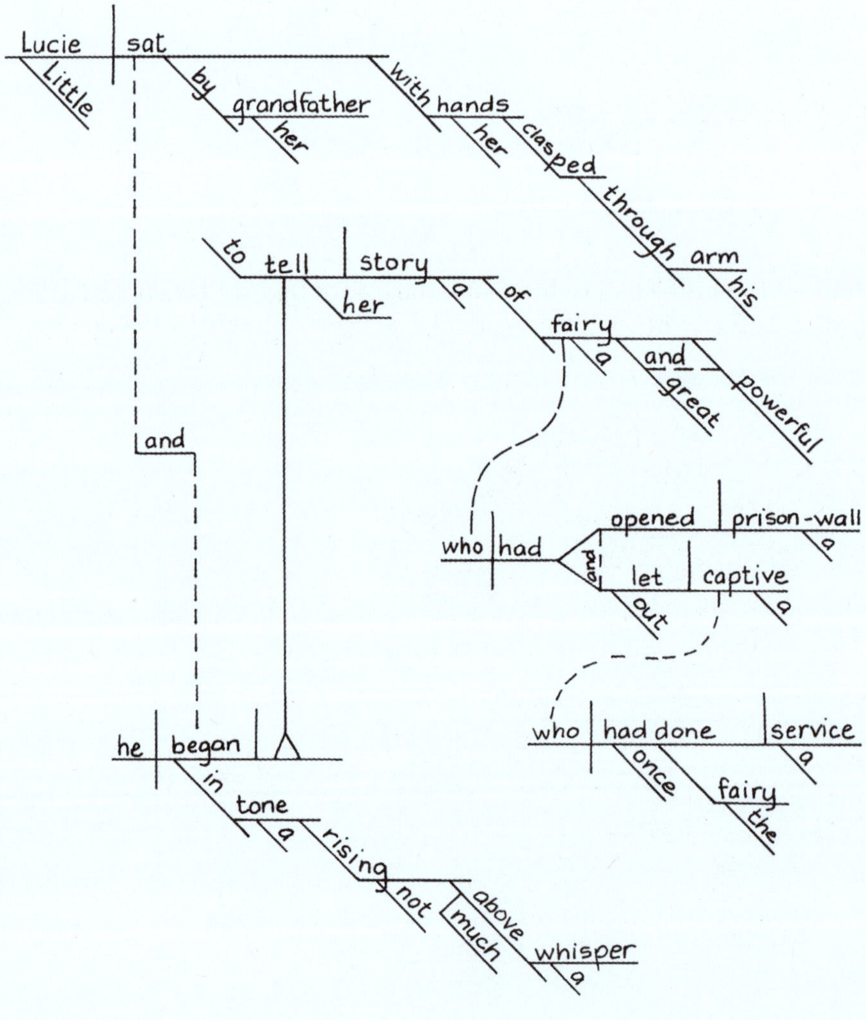

— LESSON 108 —

Nouns Acting as Other Parts of Speech
Adverbial Noun Phrases

Exercise 108A: Nouns

In the five sentences below, identify the part of the sentence or clause that each underlined noun plays by labeling it as *S* for subject, *DO* for direct object, or *OP* for object of the preposition.

Please select chicken, beef, fish, or none of the above. (OP: above)

I watched through the window as a glorious morning dawned. (S: morning)

Charlotte opted to rest for a little while before the evening's festivities. (OP: while)

Once you have finished your work, you may choose how to spend the rest of the afternoon. (DO: work)

The pillow filled with down belongs in the other bedroom. (OP: down)

Exercise 108B: Nouns as Other Parts of Speech

Each of the following sets of sentences is missing one of the nouns from the exercise above. Your task: figure out which noun can fill every blank in one set of sentences. Each set must use the *same* noun in each blank!

In the __morning__ I will begin my journey. (noun)
The sound of the __morning__ bells awakened me. (adj)

We will continue to __work__ on this problem until we reach a solution agreeable to everyone. (verb)
I need to do laundry this evening; all of my __work__ clothes are dirty. (adj)
Dr. Klein has done important __work__ in the field of linguistics. (noun)

I watered each plant carefully; Mr. Minton stared at me all the __while__. (noun)
Sigourney liked to __while__ away the rainy afternoons with her cousin, playing charades, hide-and-seek, and dress-up. (verb)
__While__ you clean the kitchen, I will wrap Joel's birthday presents. (subordinating conjunction)

As we walked into the room, something flew at us from __above__. (noun)
Miguel watched the birds soaring __above__. (adv)
The clouds __above__ formed curious shapes; one of them, I was certain, was a monkey holding a fish. (adj)
The hat you're looking for is on the shelf __above__ you. (prep)

The baby bird, covered in soft, fluffy __down__, captured the children's attention immediately. (noun)
Gary can __down__ the rest of his soda in one long gulp. (verb)
Hearing their grandmother's voice, the children ran excitedly __down__ the stairs. (prep)
"__Down__, Rover!" said the man to the overly enthusiastic dog. (interjection)
Our usual teacher is __down__ with the flu, so we have a substitute today. (adj)
A solitary leaf floated __down__ as I sat beneath the chestnut tree. (adv)

Exercise 108C: Identifying Parts of Speech

Identify the part of speech of each underlined word by writing the correct abbreviation above it: *N* (noun), *ADV-N* (adverbial noun), *PRO* (pronoun), *V* (verb), *ADJ* (adjective), *ADV* (adverb), *PREP* (preposition), *CC* (coordinating conjunction), *SC* (subordinating conjunction), or *QC* (quasi-coordinator).

These sentences are taken from Oscar Wilde's *The Importance of Being Earnest.*

Note to Instructor: Explanations are provided in brackets; give all necessary help to the student.

ADV
The happiness of more than one life depends on your answer. [*more than* is an adverb modifying the adjective *one*]

ADV SC
As far as the piano is concerned, sentiment is my forte. [the first *as* is an adverb modifying *far*; the second *as* introduces the subordinate clause *the piano is concerned*]

SC
Nothing annoys people so much as not receiving invitations. [*as* introduces a subordinate clause with an understood verb: *not receiving invitations [does]*]

PREP
Oh! it is absurd to have a hard-and-fast rule about what one should read and what one shouldn't. [*about* is a preposition; the noun clauses *what one should read* and *what one shouldn't* are the two objects of the preposition; the complete prepositional phrase acts as an adjective modifying *rule*]

ADV ADV
I haven't quite finished my tea yet! and there is still one muffin left. [*yet* modifies the verb *have finished*; *still* modifies the verb *is*]

ADV
Tell it to come round next week, at the same hour. [*round* modifies *to come*]

CC
I don't really know what a Gorgon is like, but I am quite sure that Lady Bracknell is one. [*but* joins the two independent clauses]

ADV CC QC QC
Surely such a utilitarian occupation as the watering of flowers is rather Moulton's duty than yours? [*such* is an adverb modifying the adjective *utilitarian*; *as* introduces a subordinate clause with understood elements: *the watering of flowers [is utilitarian]; rather than,* while split in this sentence, is a quasi-coordinator joining the adjectives *Moulton's* and *yours*]

SC
I forgave you before the week was out. [*before* introduces the adverbial clause *the week was out*]

ADV
Memory, my dear Cecily, is the diary that we all carry about with us. [*about* modifies the verb *carry*]

PREP
The gentleman whose arm is at present round your waist is my dear guardian, Mr. John Worthing. [*round* is a preposition; *round your waist* is an adverbial prepositional phrase modifying the *is* that precedes it]

PREP
I have never loved anyone in the world but you. [*but* is a preposition; *but you* is an adjectival prepositional phrase modifying the pronoun *anyone*]

ADV SC
Miss Fairfax, ever since I met you I have admired you more than any girl . . . I have ever met since . . . I met you. [*more* is an adverb modifying *admired*; *than* introduces the subordinate clause *[I have admired] any girl*]

PREP
I have introduced you to everyone as Ernest. [*as* is a preposition; the prepositional phrase *as Ernest* modifies *introduced*]

ADV SC
I'll reveal to you the meaning of that incomparable expression as soon as you are kind enough to inform me why you are Ernest in town and Jack in the country. [the first *as* modifies the adverb *soon*; the second *as* introduces the subordinate clause that begins *you are kind enough*]

ADV
I have never met any really wicked person before. [*before* modifies the verb *met*]

ADV
I have a country house with some land, of course, attached to it, about fifteen hundred acres, I
CC
believe; but I don't depend on that for my real income. [*about* modifies *fifteen hundred*; *but* links the two independent clauses]

SC ADV
While I am making these inquiries, you, Gwendolen, will wait for me below in the carriage. [*While* introduces the subordinate clause *I am making these inquiries*; *below* modifies the verb *wait*]

Exercise 108D: Adverbial Noun Phrases

Circle each adverbial noun or noun phrase, and draw an arrow from the circle to the word modified. Be careful—in one sentence, an understood element is being modified! You should insert it with a caret and then draw the arrow.

These sentences are adapted from *The Autobiography of Benjamin Franklin*.

In this manner we lay (all night), with very little rest; but the wind abating (the next day), we made a shift to reach Amboy before night, having been (thirty hours) on the water, without victuals, or any drink but a bottle of filthy rum, the water we sailed on being salt.

In walking through the Strand and Fleet Street (one morning) at seven o'clock, I observed there was not one shop open, though it had been daylight and the sun ^had been up above (three hours).

I had been absent (seven months), and my friends had heard nothing of me; for my brother Holmes was not yet returned, and had not written about me.

He told me that, when he had been detained (a month), he acquainted his lordship that his ship was grown foul to a degree that must necessarily hinder her fast sailing.

Each pine made three palisades (eighteen feet) long, pointed at one end.

In this journey I spent the summer, traveled about sixteen hundred miles, and did not get home till the beginning of November.

Philadelphia was a hundred miles farther; I set out, however, in a boat for Amboy, leaving my chest and other things to follow me round by sea.

Exercise 108E: Diagramming

On your own paper, diagram every word of these sentences from Exercise 108D.

In this manner we lay all night, with very little rest; but the wind abating the next day, we made a shift to reach Amboy before night, having been thirty hours on the water, without victuals, or any drink but a bottle of filthy rum, the water we sailed on being salt.

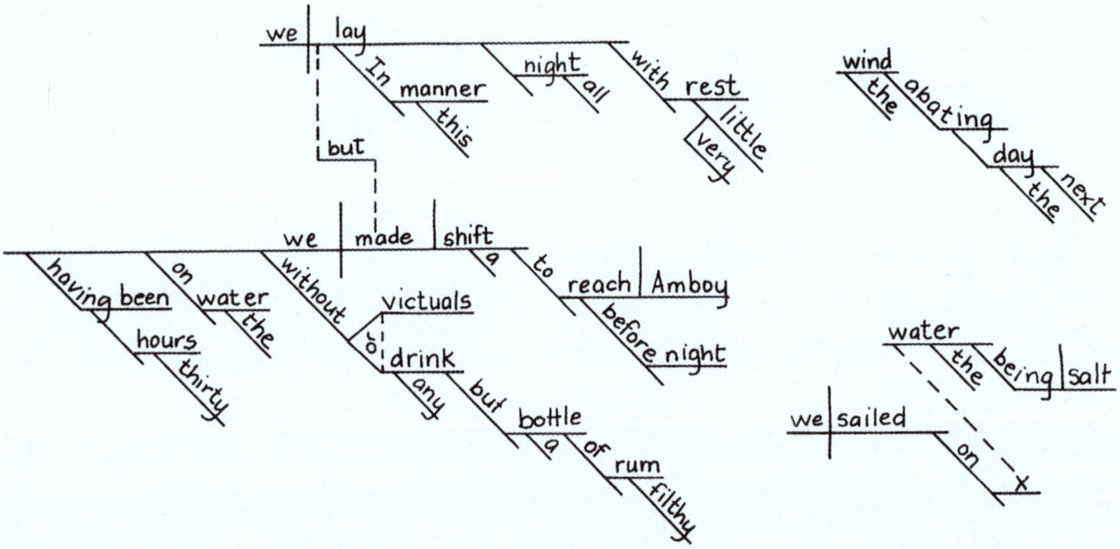

In walking through the Strand and Fleet Street one morning at seven o'clock, I observed there was not one shop open, though it had been daylight and the sun up above three hours.

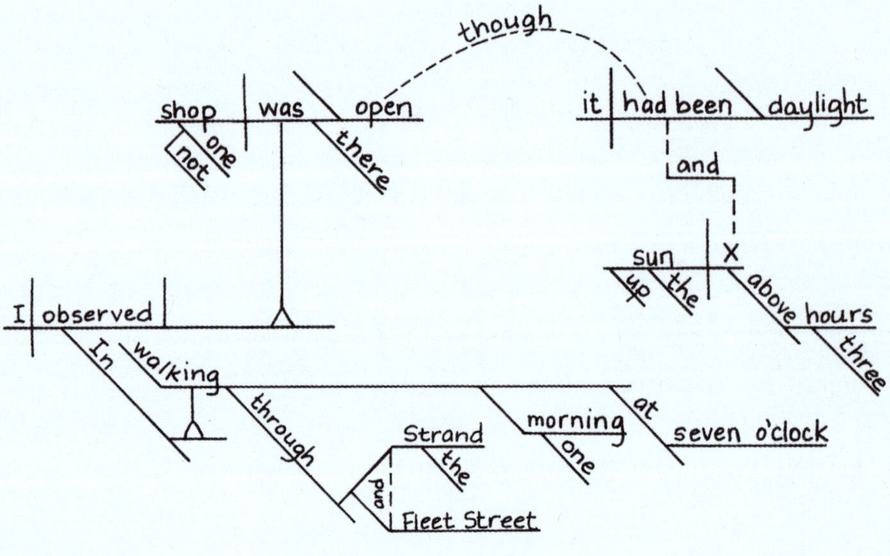

I had been absent seven months, and my friends had heard nothing of me; for my brother Holmes was not yet returned, and had not written about me.

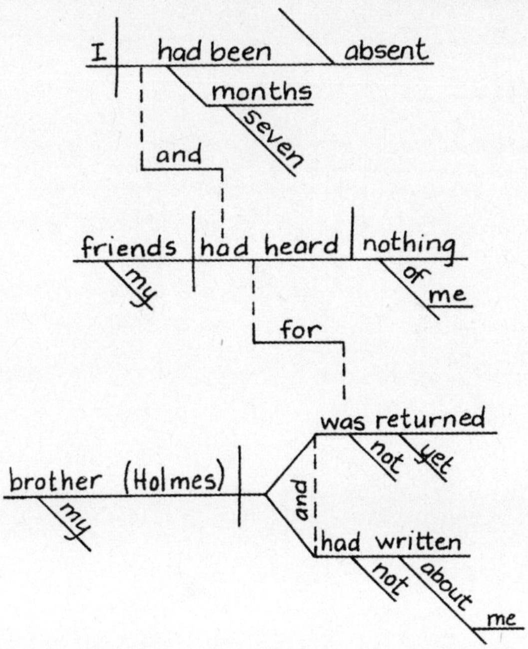

In this journey I spent the summer, traveled about sixteen hundred miles, and did not get home till the beginning of November.

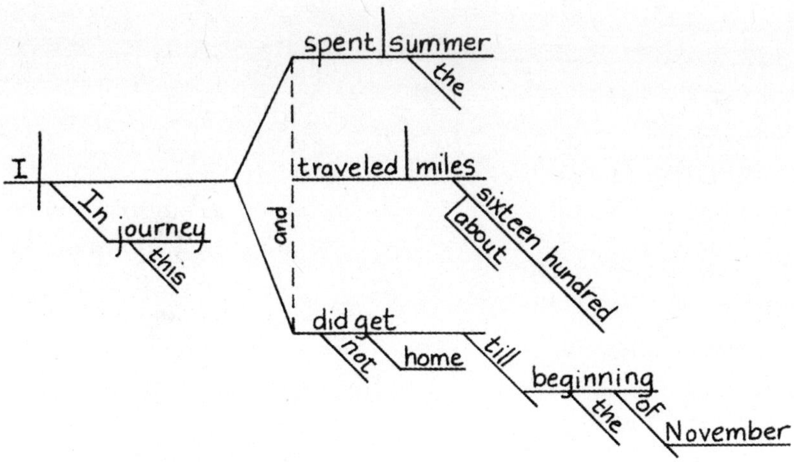

WEEK 28

— REVIEW 9 —

Weeks 25-27

Topics
Progressive Perfect Indicative Tenses
Progressive Present and Progressive Perfect Present Modal Verbs
Conditional Sentences
Adjectives in the Appositive Position
Correct Comma Usage
Limiting Adjectives
Misplaced, Squinting, and Dangling Modifier Comparisons
Using "More," "Fewer," and "Less" Quasi-Coordinators
Words That Can Be Multiple Parts of Speech
Nouns Acting as Other Parts of Speech
Adverbial Nouns

Review 9A: Definition Fill-in-the-Blank

In the last three weeks, you learned (and reviewed) even more definitions than in Weeks 22, 23, and 24! Fill in the blanks in the definitions below with one of the terms from the list. Many of the terms will be used more than once.

abstract noun
adjectives
adverbs
attributive
comma
compound preposition
dangling modifier
descriptive adjective
imperative
indicative
less
modal
passive
perfect
plural
predicative
progressive present
simple
squinting modifier
subordinating conjunction
active
adverb
apostrophe
cardinal numbers
commas
comparative
demonstrative adjectives
fewer
indefinite adjectives
interrogative adjectives
misplaced modifier
noun
past
perfect past
positive
progressive
quasi-coordinators
simple present
state of being
superlative
adjective
adverbial noun
appositive
clause
compound modifiers
coordinating conjunction
demonstrative pronouns
First Conditional
indefinite pronouns
interrogative pronouns
present
ordinal numbers
past participle
perfect present
possessive adjective
progressive perfect
Second Conditional
singular
subjunctive
Third Conditional
future

__Indicative__ verbs express real actions.

__Subjective__ verbs express situations that are unreal, wished for, or uncertain.

__Imperative__ verbs express intended actions.

__Modal__ verbs express possible actions and situations that have not actually happened.

In a sentence with an __active__ verb, the subject performs the action.

In a sentence with a __passive__ verb, the subject receives the action.

A __simple__ verb simply tells whether an action takes place in the past, present, or future.

A __progressive__ verb describes an ongoing or continuous action.

A __perfect__ verb describes an action which has been completed before another action takes place.

A __progressive perfect__ verb describes an ongoing or continuous action that has a definite end.

The present passive imperative is formed by adding the helping verb *be* to the __past participle__ of the verb.

The present passive subjunctive is formed by pairing *be* with the __past participle__ of a verb.

Use the simple past subjunctive __state of being__ verb, plus an infinitive, to express a future unreal action.

__First Conditional__ sentences express circumstances that might actually happen. The predicate of the condition clause is in a __present__ tense. The predicate of the consequence clause is an __imperative__ or is in a __present__ or __future__ tense.

__Second Conditional__ sentences express circumstances that are contrary to reality. The predicate of the condition clause is in a __past__ tense. The predicate of the consequence clause is in the __simple__ or __progressive present__ modal tense.

__Third Conditional__ sentences express past circumstances that never happened. The predicate of the condition clause is in the __perfect past__ tense. The predicate of the consequence clause is in the __perfect present__ modal or __simple present__ modal tense.

A __descriptive adjective__ tells what kind.

A __descriptive adjective__ becomes an __abstract noun__ when you add *-ness* to it.

A __possessive adjective__ tells whose.

A __noun__ becomes an __adjective__ when it is made possessive.

Form the possessive of a __singular__ noun by adding an __apostrophe__ and the letter *s*.

Form the possessive of a __plural__ noun ending in *-s* by adding an __apostrophe__ only.

Form the possessive of a plural noun that does not end in *-s* as if it were a singular noun.

An adjective that comes right before the noun it modifies is in the attributive position.

An adjective that follows the noun it modifies is in the predicative position.

Appositive adjectives directly follow the word they modify.

When three or more nouns, adjectives, verbs, or adverbs appear in a series, they should be separated by commas.

When three or more items are in a list, a coordinating conjunction before the last term is usual but not necessary.

When three or more items are in a list and a coordinating conjunction is used, a comma should still follow the next-to-last item in the list.

When two or more adjectives are in the attributive position, they are only separated by commas if they are equally important in meaning.

Demonstrative pronouns demonstrate or point out something. They take the place of a single word or a group of words.

Demonstrative adjectives modify nouns and answer the question "which one."

Indefinite prounouns are pronouns without antecedents.

Indefinite adjectives modify nouns and answer the questions "which one" and "how many."

Interrogative prounouns take the place of nouns in questions.

Interrogative adjectives modify nouns.

Cardinal numbers represent quantities (one, two, three, four . . .).

Ordinal numbers represent order (first, second, third, fourth . . .).

A misplaced modifier is an adjective, adjective phrase, adverb, or adverb phrase in the wrong place.

A squinting modifier can belong either to the sentence element preceding or the element following.

A dangling modifier has no noun or verb to modify.

The positive degree of an adjective describes only one thing.

The comparative degree of an adjective compares two things.

The superlative degree of an adjective compares three or more things.

Most regular adjectives form the comparative by adding *-r* or *-er*.

Most regular adjectives form the superlative by adding *-st* or *-est*.

Many adjectives form their comparative and superlative forms by adding the word *more* or *most* before the adjective instead of using *–er* or *–est*. In comparative and superlative adjective forms, the words *more* and *most* are used as adverbs.

Use "fewer" for concrete items and "less" for abstractions.

In comparisons using *more . . . fewer* and *more . . . less*, *more* and *less* can act as either adverbs or adjectives and *the* can act as an adverb.

In comparisons using two comparative forms, the forms may act as either adverbs or adjectives, and *the* can act as an adverb.

A coordinating conjunction joins equal words or groups of words together.

A subordinating conjunction joins unequal words or groups of words together.

When *than* is used in a comparison and introduces a clause with understood elements, it is acting as a subordinating conjunction.

Other than is a compound preposition that means "besides" or "except."

More than and *less than* are compound modifiers.

Quasi-coordinators link compound parts of a sentence that are unequal.

Quasi-coordinators include *rather than, sooner than, let alone, as well as,* and *not to mention.*

An adverbial noun tells the time or place of an action, or explains how long, how far, how deep, how thick, or how much. It can modify a verb, adjective, or adverb.

An adverbial noun plus its modifiers is an adverbial noun phrase.

Review 9B: Parsing

Above each underlined verb, write the complete tense, the voice, and the mood. These sentences are adapted from *Jane Goodall: 40 Years at Gombe*, by Jennifer Lindsey.

The first is done for you.

(bows: simple present, active indicative) (is wrinkled: simple present, passive indicative)

Yahaya Almasi bows his head; his weathered, brown face is wrinkled up in deep concentration.

(pointed: simple past, active indicative) (would find: simple present, active modal)

I pointed out that the little creatures would find it altogether too hot and stuffy beneath the feathers.

This insatiable curiosity about life, its origins and complexities, its mysteries and failures,

(has left: perfect present, active indicative)

has never left her.

By observing Flo, Fifi and her offspring, the other community members, and the relationships

simple past active indicative — simple present active indicative — simple present active indicative (state of being)

among them, Jane learned that young chimpanzees stay with their mothers until they are at

simple present active indicative

least seven years old, that adult chimpanzees form strong bonds, and, to her dismay, that rival

simple present active modal

communities can engage in brutal and bloody warfare.

simple present active indicative — simple future active indicative

Each chimpanzee builds a new nest for itself each night, although infants will sleep with their

simple present active indicative

mothers until the age of five, or until the next infant is born.

simple present passive indicative — simple present active indicative

Leaves are used to make sponges, which the chimpanzees use to sop up moisture in the hollow of a tree trunk.

progressive past active indicative — simple past active indicative — simple past active indicative

He was resting peacefully when Fifi hurled herself onto him. He indulgently pushed her to and fro with one hand.

simple future active indicative — simple present active indicative (state-of-being) — simple present active modal

A mother will touch her child when she is about to move away, and may tap on a tree trunk when

simple present active modal

she wants the youngster to come down.

perfect past active indicative

The researchers at Gombe had observed a phenomenon rarely recorded in field studies.

perfect past passive subjunctive — perfect present active modal

If he had not been rescued, young Kipara would have met with a cruel fate.

simple present active imperative — simple present active indicative

Refuse to buy products from companies, corporations, that do not conform to new environmental standards.

Review 9C: Provide the Verb

Complete each line below by providing an appropriate verb in the tense indicated. You may want to use the chart in Lesson 99 for reference. The original lines are from William Shakespeare's *Julius Caesar*; when you are finished, compare your answers to the original.

If you can't think of a verb, ask your instructor for help.

Note to Instructor: The original verbs are inserted below. You may accept any answers that make sense. Show the student the original sentences after she completes the exercise.

Caesar:	
The valiant never __taste__ of death but once.	*simple present, active, indicative*
Of all the wonders that I yet __have heard__,	*perfect present, active, indicative*

It seems to me most strange that men should fear,	*1: simple present, active, indicative;* *2: simple present, active, modal*
Seeing that death, a necessary end,	
Will come when it will come.	*1: simple future, active, indicative;* *2: simple future, active, indicative*

Brutus:	
Those that will hear me speak, let 'em stay here;	*1: simple future, active, indicative;* *2: simple present, active, imperative*
Those that will follow Cassius, go with him;	*1: simple future, active, indicative;* *2: simple present, active, imperative*
And public reasons shall be rendered	*simple future, passive, indicative*
Of Caesar's death.	

Antony	
Friends, Romans, countrymen, lend me your ears;	*simple present, active, imperative*
I come to bury Caesar, not to praise him.	*simple present, active, indicative*
The evil that men do lives after them;	*1: simple present, active, indicative;* *2: simple present, active, indicative*
The good is oft interred with their bones;	*simple present, passive, indicative (oft is an adverb)*
So let it be with Caesar. The noble Brutus	
Hath told you Caesar was ambitious:	*1: perfect present, active, indicative;* *2: simple present, active, indicative (state of being)*
If it were so, it was a grievous fault;	*1: simple present, active, subjunctive (state of being);* *2: simple past, active, indicative (state of being)*
And grievously hath Caesar answer'd it.	*perfect present, active, indicative (Caesar is the subject)*
Here, under leave of Brutus and the rest,—	
For Brutus is an honourable man;	*simple present, active, indicative (state of being)*

So __are__ they all, all honourable men,—	*simple present, active, indicative (state of being)*
__Come__ I to speak in Caesar's funeral.	*simple present, active, indicative*
Lucilius:	
When you __do find__ him, or alive or dead,	*simple present, active, indicative, with do for emphasis*
He __will be found__ like Brutus, like himself.	*simple future, passive, indicative*

Review 9D: Identifying Adjectives and Punctuating Items in a Series

In the following lines (from the poem "Rain in Summer," by Henry Wadsworth Longfellow), do the following:

a) Underline once and label all adjectives (except for articles), using the following abbreviations:

Descriptive Adjectives		Limiting Adjectives	
Regular	DA-R	Possessives	LA-P
Present participles	DA-PresP	~~Articles~~	~~LA-A~~
Past participles	DA-PastP	Demonstratives	LA-D
		Indefinites	LA-IND
		Interrogatives	LA-INT
		Numbers	LA-N

b) Circle all adjectives that are in the predicate or in the predicative position and draw an arrow from each to the noun it modifies.

How beautiful (DA-R) is the rain!

Note to Instructor: In this first sentence (and its reoccurences), the complete predicate *How beautiful is* and the complete subject *the rain* are reversed. Even though *beautiful* comes before the verb, it is located in the predicate of the sentence, and so is in the predicative position.

After the dust and heat,

In the broad (DA-R) and fiery (DA-R) street,

In the narrow (DA-R) lane,

How beautiful (DA-R) is the rain!

How it clatters along the roofs,

Like the tramp of hoofs

How it gushes and struggles out

From the throat of the overflowing (DA-PresP) spout!

Across the window-pane

It pours and pours;

And swift and wide,

DA-R
With a muddy tide,

Like a river down the gutter roars

DA-R
The rain, the welcome rain!

DA-R LA-P
The sick man from his chamber looks

DA-PastP
At the twisted brooks;

DA-R
He can feel the cool

LA-IND DA-R
Breath of each little pool;

LA-P DA-PastP
His fevered brain

DA-R
Grows calm again,

And he breathes a blessing on the rain.

DA-PastP
From the neighboring school

Come the boys,

LA-P DA-R
With more than their wonted noise

And commotion;

DA-R
And down the wet streets

LA-P DA-R
Sail their mimic fleets,

DA-R
Till the treacherous pool

LA-P DA-PresP
Ingulfs them in its whirling

DA-R
And turbulent ocean.

LA-IND
In the country, on every side,

Where far and wide,

LA-P DA-R DA-PastP
Like a leopard's tawny and spotted hide,

Stretches the plain,

DA-R DA-R
To the dry grass and the drier grain

DA-R
How welcome is the rain!

DA-PastP
In the furrowed land

DA-R DA-R
The toilsome and patient oxen stand;

Lifting the yoke encumbered (DA-PastP) head,

> **Note to Instructor:** Although Longfellow did not hyphenate *yoke encumbered*, it functions as a compound adjective.

With their (LA-P) dilated (DA-PastP) nostrils spread (DA-PastP),

They silently inhale

The clover-scented (DA-PastP) gale,

And the vapors that arise

From the well-watered (DA-PastP) and smoking (DA-PresP) soil.

For this (LA-D) rest in the furrow after toil

Their (LA-P) large (DA-R) and lustrous (DA-R) eyes

Seem to thank the Lord,

More than man's (LA-P) spoken (DA-PastP) word.

Review 9E: Correcting Modifiers

The following sentences all have modifier problems! Correct each sentence, using proofreader's marks, and be ready to explain the problems to your instructor. The first is done for you.

> **Note to Instructor:** Use the explanations below to prompt the student if necessary. These sentences may also be rewritten/corrected in other ways as long as the central error is corrected.

The man chased the monkey in the yellow hat.

Explanation: The adjective phrase "in the yellow hat" is misplaced; it should describe the man, not the monkey.

Joy believed spring was the ^most wonderful~~lest~~ time of the year.

Explanation: The superlative form of the adjective "wonderful" is formed with the adverb "most."

^While we were ~~S~~leeping soundly, the tent protected us from the rain outside.

Explanation: The adjectival participle phrase at the beginning is a misplaced modifier missing the words being modified—the tent was not sleeping; we were!

Wednesday's soccer game will be played on the ^larger ~~more large~~ field.

Explanation: "Large" is a regular adjective and forms a regular comparative.

^As the baby sucked ~~Sucking~~ contentedly on her thumb, the mother placed ^her ~~the baby~~ gently into the crib.

Explanation: The adjectival participle phrase at the beginning is a misplaced modifier—the baby was the one sucking on her thumb.

The worm startled the little boy wriggling on the ground.

Explanation: The participle phrase describes the worm, not the little boy.

The whistle sounded loudly in my ears that signaled the end of the game.

Explanation: The adjectival clause is misplaced. My ears did not signal the end of the game; the whistle did.

Our annual fundraising walk attracted over three hundred walkers organized by Marcia Trostle.

Explanation: The participle phrase is misplaced—the walk was organized by Marcia Trostle, not the walkers.

My uncle, who had just broken the school record for home runs, clapped enthusiastically for the player.

Explanation: The adjective clause is misplaced; the player was the one who had broken the record.

He's sleeping peacefully now, but that panther can be one of the fiercest ~~most fierce~~ animals in the zoo.

Explanation: "Fierce" is a regular adjective and forms a regular superlative.

My sister is a more diligent~~er~~ student than I am.

Explanation: The comparative form of the adjective "diligent" is formed with the adverb "more."

Gloria instructed us quickly to tidy the room.

OR

Gloria instructed us quickly to tidy the room.

Explanation: The word "quickly" is a squinting modifier; it could apply to "instructed" or to "tidy." The intended meaning determines where the word should be placed. If the student comes up with one answer but not the other, ask if there is another possibility with a different meaning.

The money is for spending at the circus in my wallet.

Explanation: Most of us don't keep circuses in our wallets; the adjective phrase is misplaced.

Our area gets fewer ~~less~~ earthquakes than the area where my cousins live.

Explanation: "Earthquakes" can be quantified, so "fewer" is more appropriate than "less."

The city hosts a famous golf tournament in which I grew up.

Explanation: The adjective clause is misplaced; the speaker did not grow up in a golf tournament, but in a city.

Review 9F: Identifying Adverbs

In the following sentences, taken from Frances Hodgson Burnett's *The Secret Garden*, carry out the following three steps:

a) Underline each word, phrase, or clause that is acting as an adverb.

b) Draw a line from the word/phrase/clause to the verb, adjective, or adverb modified.

c) Above the word or phrase, note whether it is a regular adverb (*ADV*), an adverbial noun (*AN*), a prepositional phrase (*PrepP*), an infinitive phrase (*INF*), a present participle phrase (*PresP*), a past participle phrase (*PastP*), or an adverbial clause (*C*).

Remember: within a phrase or clause acting as an adverb, there might also be an adverb modifying an adjective or verb form within the phrase or clause. Underline these adverbs a second time.

The guard lighted the lamps in the carriage, and Mrs. Medlock cheered up very much over her tea and chicken and beef.

She had never thought much about her looks, but she wondered if she was as unattractive as Ben Weatherstaff and she also wondered if she looked as sour as he had looked before the robin came.

She looked at the key quite a long time.

She liked the name, and she liked still more the feeling that when its beautiful old walls shut her in no one knew where she was.

Her hair was ruffled on her forehead and her cheeks were bright pink.

No one believes I shall live to grow up.

After another week of rain the high arch of blue sky appeared again and the sun which poured down was quite hot.

The fox was lying on the grass close by him, looking up to ask for a pat now and then, and Dickon bent down and rubbed his neck softly and thought a few minutes in silence.

He had lifted his head and whinnied softly the moment he saw Dickon and he had trotted up to him and put his head across his shoulder and then Dickon had talked into his ear and Jump had talked back in odd little whinnies and puffs and snorts.

Ben Weatherstaff had not quite got over his emotion, but he had recovered a little and answered almost in his usual way.

ADV ADV PrepP AN ADV PrepP

Review 9G: Comma Use

The following sentences have lost all of their commas. Insert commas directly into the text (no need to use proofreader's marks) wherever needed.

The first ten sentences are adapted from *Owls Aren't Wise and Bats Aren't Blind*, by Warner Shedd; the remaining sentences are adapted from *Fifty Animals that Changed the Course of History*, by Eric Chaline.

Note to Instructor: The original sentences are below; you may accept variations as long as they follow the rules of comma use.

Given the near ubiquity of beavers today, most people shouldn't find it difficult to locate a beaver dam that they can scrutinize at leisure.

These "dispossessed" beavers must now seek new territory, find mates, and begin new colonies.

While the beaver's tail is rounded and relatively short, very wide, and flattened top to bottom, the muskrat's is long, quite slender, and flattened from side to side.

Such behavior, though it might seem unjust, probably results in something like a fair exchange in most cases.

However, it most certainly was given great credence by that famous Roman, Pliny the Elder, who died in the cataclysmic eruption of Vesuvius that buried Pompeii and Herculaneum in AD 79.

The bat's fifth finger, or "thumb," incidentally, far from being elongated in the manner of its other digits, is a small hook used for climbing or walking.

Possums aren't, to use a current expression, the brightest bears in the woods, and they don't think in terms of playing dead to deceive an enemy.

On dark, rainy days, however, efts emerge in daylight hours to forage and wander about.

Based on two personal experiences, I would say that owls regard mice and voles in about the same light as we might view lobster, steak, or a rich chocolate dessert.

Suburban sprawl, timber cutting, wetland drainage, development, and other human disturbances are slowly but surely nibbling away at this critical nesting habitat, which rarely has any legal protection.

The English word "mosquito" is derived from a diminutive of the Spanish word for "fly," mosca, and translates as "little fly."

At first this consisted of the hunting of smaller species that came into inshore coastal waters.

The crusaders, whose ostensible aim was the liberation of the Holy Land, conquered the Christian Byzantine Empire.

After the war, silk was not able to regain its earlier preeminence.

Although the camel has now been supplanted by the truck and motorcar, it remains an important source of milk, wool, and meat in the Arab world.

In Europe, where the horse and oxen did the heavy lifting, the traditional roles of the dog have been in hunting and in animal husbandry.

Horse-drawn chariots were important weapons in Bronze Age ancient Egypt, Minoan Crete, and Mycenaean Greece.

Even after it became a protected species, the eagle, like the falcon and other birds of prey, fell victim to pesticides that almost caused its extinction from across much of the continental US.

Squanto was a member of the Patuxet tribe, a tributary of the Wampanoag, who had been kidnapped and forcefully taken to Europe by British sailors in 1614.

As we have seen in earlier entries, fiber can be obtained from a variety of animals, including goats, rabbits, and camels, but with selective breeding, the sheep has become the animal that produces the largest quantities of white wool.

Review 9H: Conjunctions

In the following sentences from L. Frank Baum's *The Marvelous Land of Oz*, find and circle every conjunction. Label each as coordinating (*C*), subordinating (*SUB*), coordinating correlative (*CC*), subordinating correlative (*SC*), or quasi-coordinator (*QC*).

He ran up beside her (and) [C] tried to keep pace with her swift footsteps—a very difficult feat, (for) [C] she was much taller (than) [SUB] he, (and) [C] evidently in a hurry.

Note to Instructor: The clause *than he* has understood elements: *than he [was tall].*

He is a proud man, (as) [SUB] he has every reason to be, (and) [C] it pleases him to be termed Emperor (rather than) [QC] King.

Mombi had (no sooner) [SC] arrived at the royal palace (than) [SC] she discovered, by means of her secret magic, that the adventurers were starting upon their journey to the Emerald City.

Note to Instructor: The student may not have encountered the subordinating correlative conjunction set *no sooner. . . than* before. If she cannot find the conjunctions, point them out to her and let her decide whether they are coordinating or subordinating correlatives. If she chooses coordinating, point out that *arrived at the royal palace* doesn't have a subject, while *she discovered* does; therefore, the conjunctions join unequal groups of words.

It is nearly dark, (and) [C] (unless) [SUB] we wait until morning to make our flight we may get into more trouble.

The throne of the Emerald City belongs (neither) [CC] to you (nor) [CC] to Jinjur, (but) [CC] to this Pastoria from whom the Wizard usurped it.

C C
I ought to know by heart every step of this journey, and yet I fear we have already lost our way.

SUB C
Although I am of tin, I own a heart altogether the warmest and most admirable in the whole world.

SUB C
Tip also noticed that Jack's pumpkin head had twisted around until it faced his back; but this was easily remedied.

Review 91: Identifying Independent Elements

The following sentences, taken from *The Secret Garden*, all contain independent elements: absolutes (*ABS*), parenthetical expressions (*PE*), interjections (*INT*), nouns of direct address (*NDA*), appositives (*APP*), and/or noun clauses in apposition (*NCA*). Locate, underline, and label each one.

Some elements may legitimately be labeled in more than one way. The difference between an absolute and a parenthetical expression is particularly tricky; generally, a parenthetical element can be removed without changing the meaning of the sentence, while an absolute construction cannot.

Be ready to explain your answers.

PE
She did not miss her at all, in fact, and as she was a self-absorbed child she gave her entire
PE
thought to herself, as she had always done.

PE
And there's nothing likely to improve children at Misselthwaite—if you ask me!

ABS NDA
I don't know anythin' about anythin'—just like you said. I beg your pardon, Miss.

ABS
He turned about to the orchard side of his garden and began to whistle—a low soft whistle.

INT
Eh! there does seem a lot of us then.

NCA
The sun was shining and a little wind was blowing—not a rough wind, but one which came in delightful little gusts and brought a fresh scent of newly turned earth with it.

APP
I never did many things in India, but there were more people to look at—natives and soldiers marching by—and sometimes bands playing, and my Ayah told me stories.

NCA
You could not do any harm, a child like you!

PE
For one thing, he's afraid he'll look at him some day and find he's growed hunchback.

The nurse, Mrs. Medlock and Martha had been standing huddled together staring at her,
ABS
their mouths half open.

INT NDA
Well, sir, you'll scarcely believe your eyes when you see him.

PE
And this, if you please, this is what Ben Weatherstaff beheld and which made his jaw drop.

ABS
The robin used to secrete himself in a bush and watch this anxiously, his head tilted first on one side and then on the other.

Review 9J: Words with Multiple Identities

In the following sentences, taken from *Ozma of Oz* by L. Frank Baum, identify each underlined word as an adverb (*ADV*), adjective (*ADJ*), noun (*N*), pronoun (*PRO*), preposition (*PREP*), subordinating conjunction (*SC*), coordinating conjunction (*CC*), or quasi-coordinator (*QC*).

He accomplished the feat without breaking any [ADJ] bones.

Their battle-axes were poised as if [SC] to strike down [ADV] their foes; yet [CC] they remained motionless as [SC] statues, awaiting the word of command.

I make but [PREP] one condition.

So she sat down [ADV] in a corner of the coop, leaned her back [N] against the slats, nodded at the friendly stars before [SC] she closed her eyes, and was asleep in half [ADJ] a minute [N].

It would not be enough [ADJ] to fill one of my back [ADJ] teeth.

Then the bell above [PREP] the throne, which sounded whenever an enchantment was broken, began to ring.

This the private managed to do, waiting until [PREP] a time when he was nearest the ground and then letting himself drop upon the Scarecrow.

If none of the eleven objects you touch proves to be the transformation of any [PRO] of the royal family of Ev, then you will yourself become enchanted.

They walked slowly down [PREP] the path between the rocks, Tiktok going first [ADV], Dorothy following him, and the yellow hen trotting along [ADV] last of all.

You'll be sorry for [PREP] treating me in this way.

He gave a sort of gurgle and stopped short [ADV], waving his hands frantically until [SC] suddenly he became motionless, with one arm in the air and the other held stiffly before [PREP] him with all the copper fingers of the hand spread out like [PREP] a fan.

They turned and fled madly into the cavern, and refused to go back [ADV] again.

Ozma of Oz and her people, as well as [QC] Dorothy, Tiktok and Billina, were splendidly entertained by the Queen mother.

So she retraced her steps until [SC] she found the entrance to the palace.

But [CC] the little Prince was shy, and shrank away from the painted Scarecrow because he did not yet [ADV] know his many excellent qualities.

Oh, no; you are mistaken about [PREP] that.

He won't need to be wound up [ADV] any more, for [CC] he has now become a very neat ornament.

"There is no rea-son to be a-fraid of the Wheel-ers," said Tiktok, the words coming more slowly

SC ADV
than before.

CC SC PREP
But as the yellow hen tried to enter after them, the little maid cried "Shoo!" and flapped her apron in Billina's face.

Review 9K: Verb Forms Functioning in Other Ways

The following sentences are from *Sophie's Diary*, by Dora Musielak. The book gives a fictionalized account of the life of mathematician Sophie Germain, who was a young teen living in Paris during the French Revolution.

In these sentences, present participles, past participles, and infinitives are used as nouns and modifiers. Circle each of these verb forms and label each one as noun (*N*), adjective (*ADJ*), or adverb (*ADV*).

For adjectives and adverbs, draw a line lto the word modified. For nouns, add a label describing the part of the sentence it fulfills: subject (*S*), direct object (*DO*), indirect object (*IO*), predicate nominative (*PN*), or object of the preposition (*OP*).

The first one is done for you.

ADJ
Father says the privileged aristocrats are fiercely opposed, and they will do anything

ADV N DO
to avoid losing their wealth and property.

ADJ
Armed with pitchforks, the women walked for six hours to Versailles.

ADJ
Thus, I also must know the amount of water displaced by a certain amount of gold and a certain amount of silver.

N DO
Even after moving to the Tuileries Palace in Paris, the king cannot resolve the social conflicts and the financial crisis of the nation.

ADJ
Now I just imagine the huge numbers on the squares of the fourth row and the remaining squares on the chessboard.

N OP N DO
My sister was enchanted and was more interested in learning to play.

N PN N OP
My dream is to devote my life to seeking out answers to difficult questions.

N DO
At home we try to preserve a sense of normality.

ADJ
Actors waved banners inscribed with the names of Voltaire's plays.

Review 9L: Diagramming

On your own paper, diagram every word of the following sentences, adapted from Charlotte Bronte's *Jane Eyre.*

Had I attended to the suggestions of pride and ire, I should immediately have left him: but something worked within me more strongly than those feelings could.

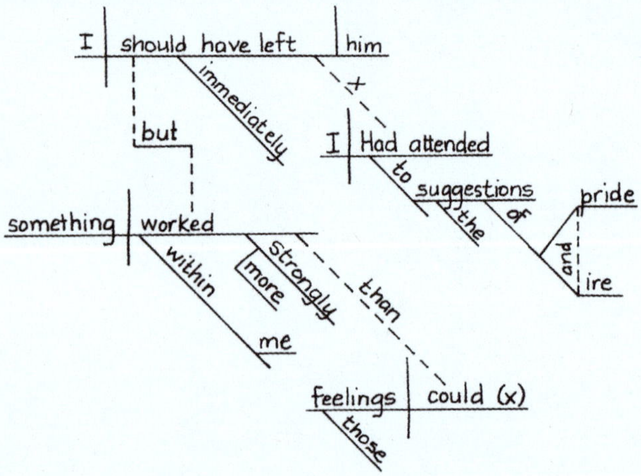

He was never married, and had no near kindred but ourselves, and one other person, not more closely related than we.

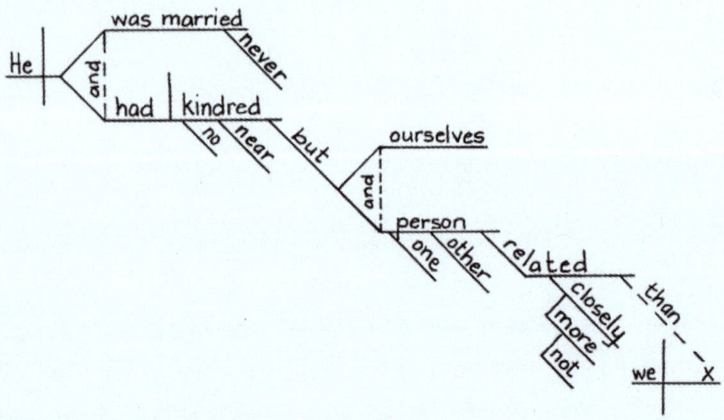

Tell me now, fairy as you are—can't you give me a charm, or a philter, or something of that sort, to make me a handsome man?

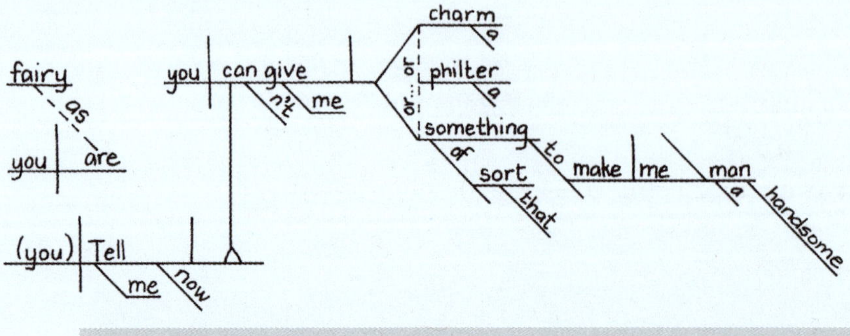

Note to Instructor: Any arrangement of *fairy as you are* is acceptable, as long as it is diagrammed as an absolute component of the sentence (it is a conversational and idiomatic phrase, so does not fit neatly into the diagramming system).

I burned for the more active life of the world—for the more exciting toils of a literary career—for the destiny of an artist, author, anything rather than that of a priest.

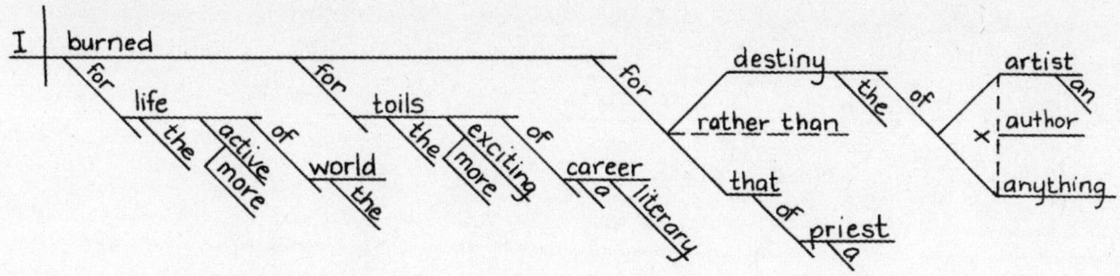

Of course (as St. John once said) I must seek another interest in life to replace the one lost: is not the occupation he now offers me truly the most glorious man can adopt or God assign?

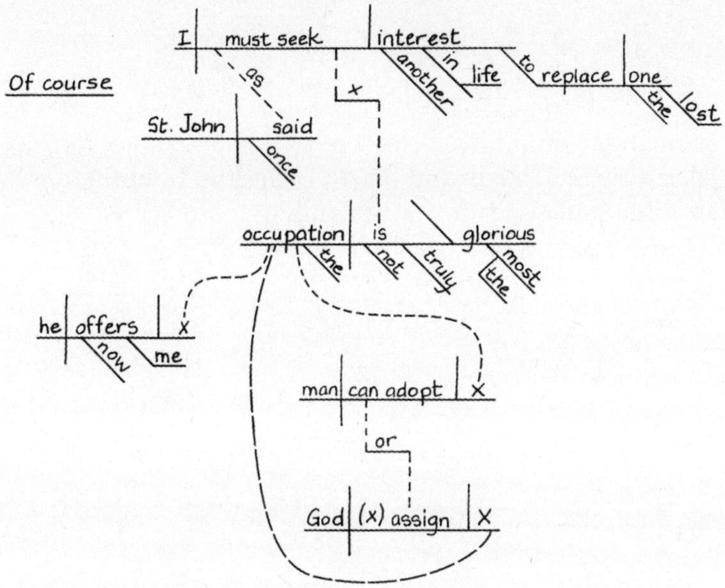

She had no great talents, no marked traits of character, no peculiar development of feeling or taste which raised her one inch above the ordinary level of childhood; but neither had she any deficiency or vice which sunk her below it.

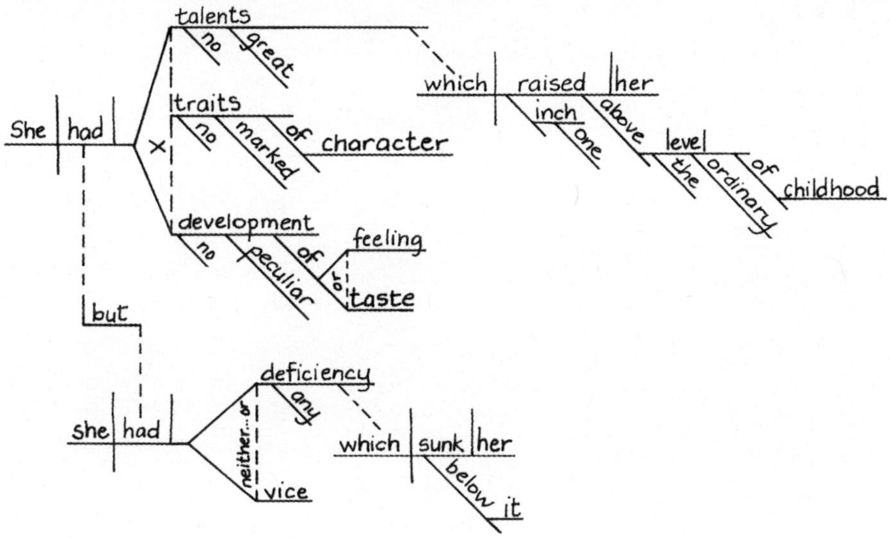

You are not to suppose, reader, that Adèle has all this time been sitting motionless on the stool at my feet.

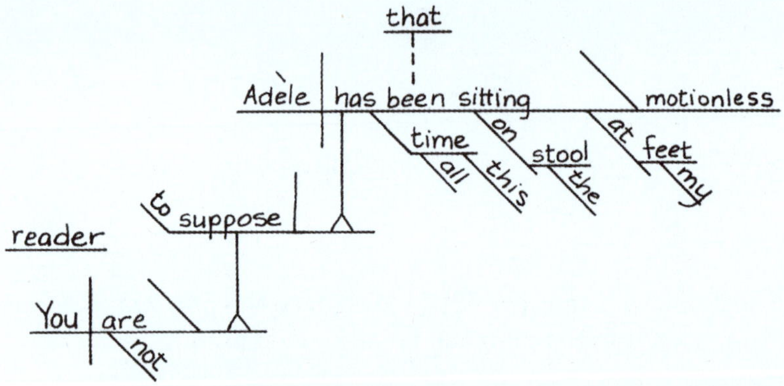

Note to Instructor: The modifier *motionless* could also be diagrammed as an adverb modifying *has been sitting*; Adèle is motionless, but so is her action of sitting.

A ridge of lighted heath, alive, glancing, devouring, would have been a meet emblem of my mind when I accused and menaced Mrs. Reed: the same ridge, black and blasted after the flames are dead, would have represented as neatly my subsequent condition, when half an hour's silence and reflection had shown me the madness of my conduct, and the dreariness of my hated and hating position.

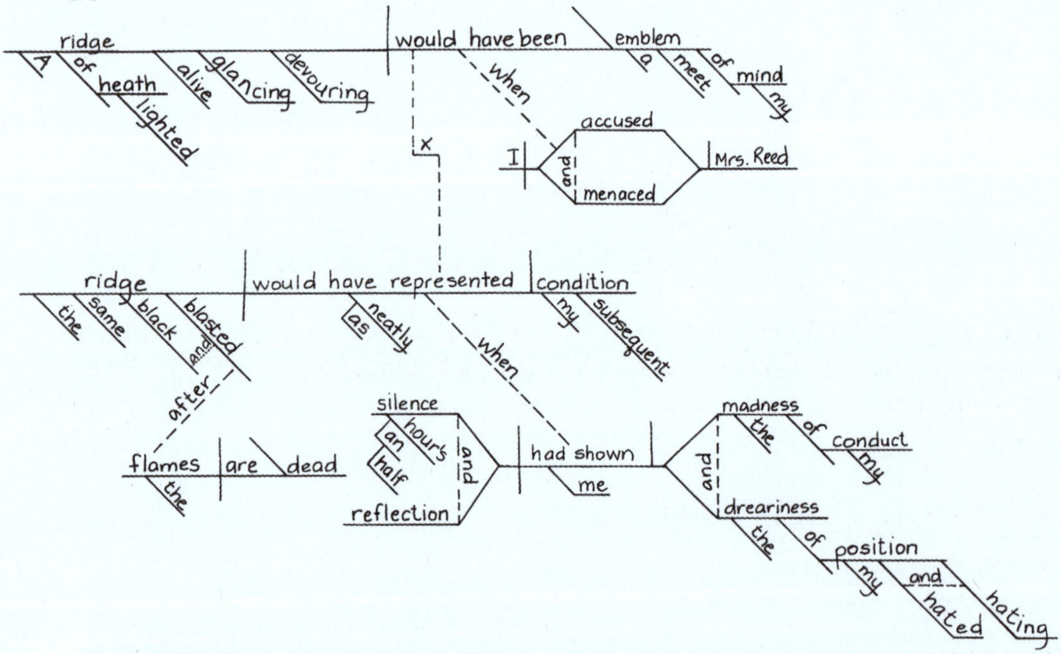

Note to Instructor: The phrase *half an hour's* could also be diagrammed with *half* and *an* both modifying *hour's*, or with *half an hour's* all on a single line as a compound adjective.

WEEK 29

Still More Verbs

— LESSON 109 —

Hortative Verbs

Subjunctive Verbs

Exercise 109A: Identifying Hortative Verbs

Sacred and religious texts are often exhorting their readers—so they tend to use many hortative verbs! In the following sentences, underline twice every element of each hortative verb (*let* or *may*, any other helping verbs, and the main verb). Above the verb, identify it as state-of-being, active, or passive. If the person or thing being exhorted is present in the sentence, circle the noun or pronoun that identifies him/her/it, and identify it as *S* for subject or *O* for object.

Be careful—some sentences may not include any hortative verbs!

The first is done for you.

passive
S
So may we be acquainted with thine innermost benevolence:
Neglect us not, come hitherward.
—Rig Veda

Though one may conquer a thousand times a thousand men in battle, yet he is indeed the noblest victor who conquers himself.
—The Dhammapada

active
O
Come, let me speak with you.
—The *Analects* of Confucius

active O ... active O
Let us arm ourselves with the armor of righteousness, and let us teach ourselves first to walk in the commandment of the Lord.
—Polycarp 4:1

active O ... active
So let them answer Me, and have faith in Me, that they may be rightly guided.
—Qur'an 186

Note to Instructor: In the sentence above, *let* is acting as a hortative verb for both action verbs (*answer* and *have*).

active O
Let not a mortal's evil will obstruct us.
—*Rig Veda*

Indeed, angry speech hurts, and retaliation may overtake you.
—The *Dhammapada*

And God said, Let there be lights in the firmament of the heaven to divide the day from the night; and let them be for signs, and for seasons, and for days, and years.
—Genesis 1:14 (King James Version)

May He grant unto you a lot and portion among His saints.
—Polycarp 12:2

The Guru has given me this one understanding: there is only the One, the Giver of all souls. May I never forget Him!
—Guru Granth Sahib

May the swift Wanderer, Lord of refreshments, listen to our songs, who speeds through cloudy heaven:
And may the Waters, bright like castles, hear us, as they flow onward from the cloven mountain.
—*Rig Veda*

The Master having visited Nan-tsze, Tsze-lu was displeased, on which the Master swore, saying, "Wherein I have done improperly, may Heaven reject me, may Heaven reject me!"
—The *Analects* of Confucius

But let all those that put their trust in thee rejoice: let them ever shout for joy, because thou defendest them: let them also that love thy name be joyful in thee.
—Psalm 5:11 (King James Version)

Only let thy heart be with God, and doubt not in thy mind about that which thou seest.
—*Shepherd of Hermas*

Abandoning the dark way, let the wise man cultivate the bright path. Having gone from home to homelessness, let him yearn for that delight in detachment, so difficult to enjoy.
—The *Dhammapada*

The Master said, "Let the will be set on the path of duty. Let every attainment in what is good be firmly grasped. Let perfect virtue be accorded with. Let relaxation and enjoyment be found in the polite arts."
—The *Analects* of Confucius

Let all the earth fear the Lord: let all the inhabitants of the world stand in awe of him.
—Psalm 33:8 (King James Version)

state-of-being O passive O

And let there be witnesses whenever you conclude a contract, and let no harm be done to either scribe or witness.

—Qur'an 282

Exercise 109B: Rewriting Indicative Verbs as Hortative Verbs

Hortative verbs are also common in speeches. In the excerpts from famous speeches below, the statements and commands in bold type originally contained hortative verbs. On your own paper, rewrite each bolded clause so that the main verbs are hortative. Then, compare your answers with the original.

If you need help, ask your instructor.

Note to Instructor: Each excerpt with bolded clauses is followed by the original, hortative version. Accept any reasonable answers, but ask the student to read both her rewritten sentences and the originals out loud, listening carefully to both.

If the student needs help, give her the first three or four words of the original sentence and ask her to continue rewriting from there.

But if anyone has a better proposal to make, **he should make it, and give us his advice.**

But if anyone has a better proposal to make, let him make it, and give us his advice.

—Demosthenes, "The Third Philippic" (341 BC)

Tyrants ought to fear; I have always so behaved myself that, under God, I have placed my chiefest strength and safeguard in the loyal hearts and good will of my subjects.

Let tyrants fear; I have always so behaved myself that, under God, I have placed my chiefest strength and safeguard in the loyal hearts and good will of my subjects.

—Queen Elizabeth I, "Against the Spanish Armada" (1588)

He should make up his mind to do his duty in politics without regard to holding office at all, and he should know that often the men in this country who have done the best work for our public life have not been the men in office.

Let him make up his mind to do his duty in politics without regard to holding office at all, and let him know that often the men in this country who have done the best work for our public life have not been the men in office.

—Theodore Roosevelt, "The Duties of American Citizenship" (1883)

I will hope this movement will spread throughout all branches of applied science and industry and that women may come to share with men the joy of doing.

May I hope this movement will spread throughout all branches of applied science and industry and that women may come to share with men the joy of doing.

—Amelia Earhart, "A Woman's Place in Science" (1935)

We will begin, then, with Grammar.

Let us begin, then, with Grammar.

—Dorothy Sayers, "The Lost Tools of Learning" (1947)

Exercise 109C: Diagramming

On your own paper, diagram every word of the following sentences.

The war is inevitable—and let it come!

—Patrick Henry, "Liberty or Death" (1775)

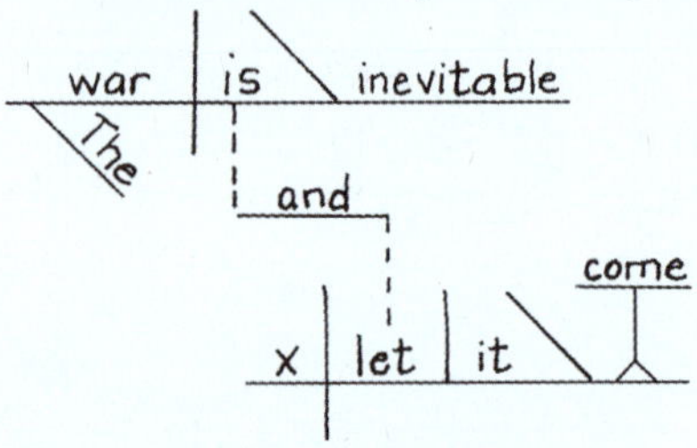

Sir, well may you start at the suggestion that such a series of wrongs, so clearly proved by various testimony, so openly confessed by the wrong-doers, and so widely recognized throughout the country, should find apologies.

—Charles Sumner, "The Crime Against Kansas" (1856)

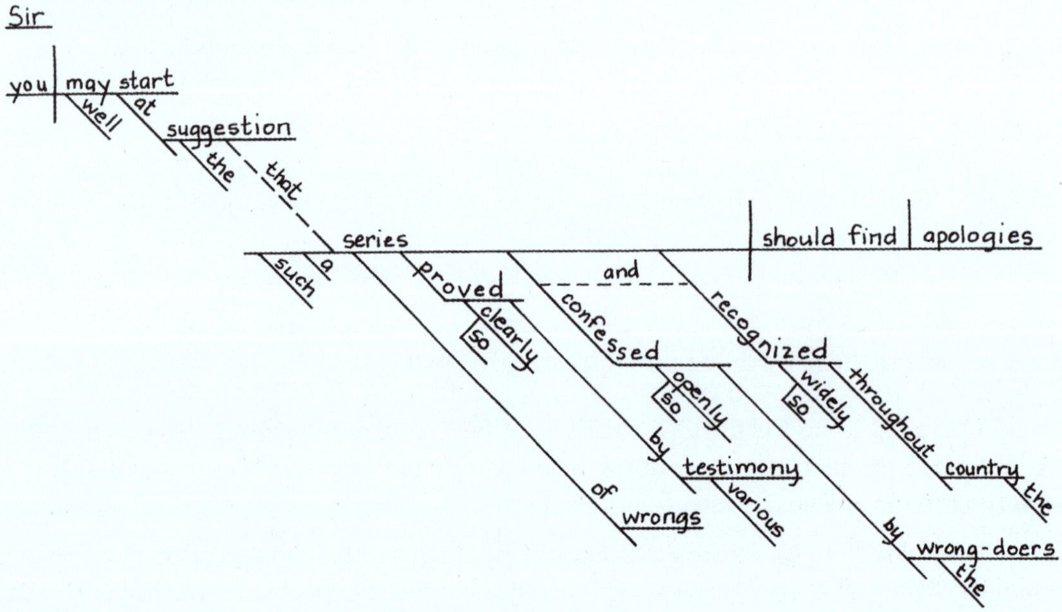

My fellow citizens: let no one doubt that this is a difficult and dangerous effort on which we have set out.

John F. Kennedy, "On the Cuban Missile Crisis" (1962)

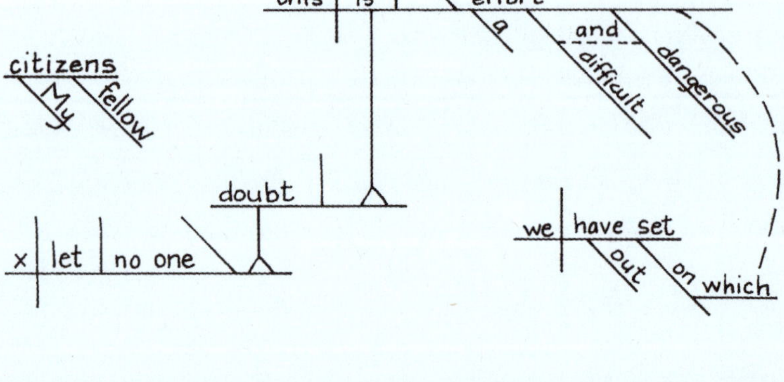

— LESSON 110 —

Transitive Verbs
Intransitive Verbs
Sit/Set, Lie/Lay, Rise/Raise
Ambitransitive Verbs

Exercise 110A: Ambitransitive Verbs

The sentences below have been adapted from traditional Peruvian folktales. For each sentence, carry out the following steps:

a) Underline the verbs that are acting as predicates (of both subordinate AND independent clauses), and label each one as *TR* for transitive or *INT* for intransitive.

b) Label each transitive verb as *A* for active or *P* for passive.

c) Circle the direct object of each active transitive verb and label it as *DO (TR)*. Circle the subject of each passive transitive verb and label it as *S (TR)*.

d) Choose two sentences with passive transitive verbs. On your own paper, rewrite them so that the verb becomes active. You may need to invent your own subject!

TR A DO (TR) TR A DO (TR)
Ayar Cachi, the strongest of all, threw rocks with his slingshot and knocked down mountains.

TR A DO (TR) TR A DO (TR)
I will throw out of this world anyone who throws me out of my house.

S (TR) TR P
The first pomegranate was grown in Lima.

INT INT
The skirmish grew in intensity, and the onlookers whispered worriedly.

TR A DO (TR) INT
Ahar Acu grew wings, and flew away to Pampa del Sol.

TR A DO (TR)
They whispered foul gossip through the streets.

INT INT TR A DO (TR)
The creature El Tunche whistles; if you listen, you will give away your place in the rainforest.

TR A DO (TR)
You there! Give these scoundrels a good beating!

TR A DO (TR)
You can only recognize El Tunche by looking at his goat-like hooves.

S (TR) TR P
Her authority was recognized by the royal tribunal.

TR A DO(TR) INT TR A DO (TR)
Sink this stick into the ground. Where it sinks, build your kingdom there.

INT INT
The flagship blazed up and then sank.

TR A DO (TR) TR A DO (TR) INT
They hid the letter, and then ate a second melon, that delicious fruit which acts gold in the morning, silver at noon, and death in the evening.

TR A INT TR A DO (TR)
They were eating in holy peace, when suddenly the dog growled, and the cat arched its back.

INT INT
A dry throat can neither growl nor sing.

INT TR A DO (TR)
The minions of the law fell upon him, and took him to jail.

S (TR) TR P TR A DO (TR)
They were felled by the sickness and growled their pain to the skies.

REWRITTEN SENTENCES

The people of Lima grew the first pomegranate. [As long as the verb is grew, the student may assign any reasonable subject.]

The royal tribunal recognized her authority.

The sickness felled them, and they growled their pain to the skies.

Exercise 110B: The Prefix *Ambi-*

Find two more words using the prefix *ambi-*, where the prefix carries the meaning of "both." On your own paper, write the words and their definitions, and then use each correctly in a sentence. If the word is too technical for you to write an original sentence, you may locate a sentence using an Internet search and write it down.

Note to Instructor: These are sample answers; the student's answers may vary. Make sure that the words the student chooses carry the meaning of *both* rather than *around*, another possible meaning of the prefix *ambi-* (so, *ambivalent*, but not *ambiance* or *ambition*).

The following answers from The Purple Workbook are still acceptable:

ambivalent: having mixed feelings or more than one feeling, having trouble choosing between two different options
The six-year-old felt ambivalent about the family's enormous new dog.

ambilateral: affecting both sides
The patient's muscle weakness was ambilateral.

ambipolar: having both positive and negative charge carriers
"Ambipolar diffusion is important in redistributing magnetic flux." *(From* Issues in Astronomy and Astrophysics*)*

ambisinister: equally clumsy with both hands
The ambisinister cook dropped the tureen of soup, cut both hands with his paring knife, and burned his left elbow while trying to turn on the burner with his right hand.

ambivert: someone who is both introverted and extroverted
Ambiverts make good salespeople because they enjoy talking to customers but don't overwhelm them with too much attention.

as well as these additional possible answers:

ambisyllabic: a word with a single sound that is shared by two different syllables
The word *apple* is ambisyllabic, because the "p" sound belongs to both the first and the last syllable.

ambitendency: contradictory behaviors rising out of conflicting thoughts or impulses
Her ambitendency appeared when she put out her hand for a handshake, drew it away, put it back out, and then withdrew it again.

Exercise 110C: Diagramming

On your own paper, diagram every word of the following quotations.

When you are finished, label each action verb occupying a predicate space with *T* for transitive or *INT* for intransitive.

When the sword is once drawn, the passions of men observe no bounds of moderation.
—Alexander Hamilton

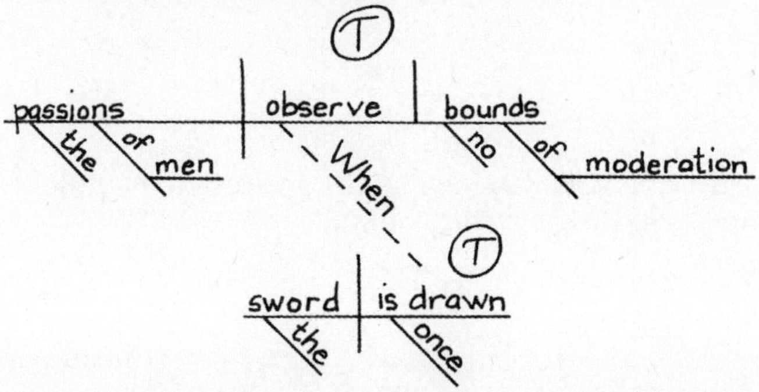

She who succeeds in gaining the mastery of the bicycle will gain the mastery of life.
—Susan B. Anthony

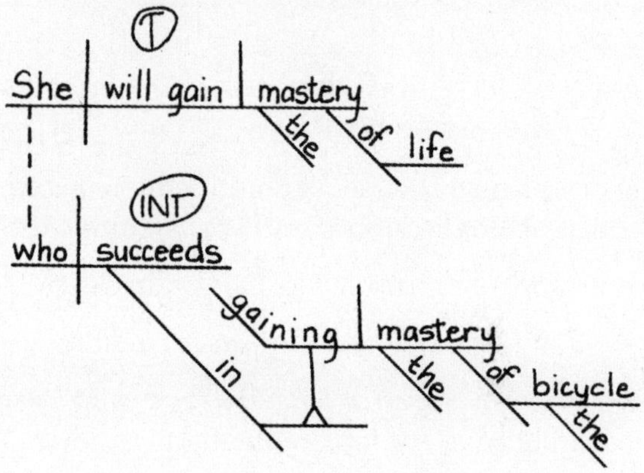

The freedom which we enjoy in our government extends also to our ordinary life.
—Pericles

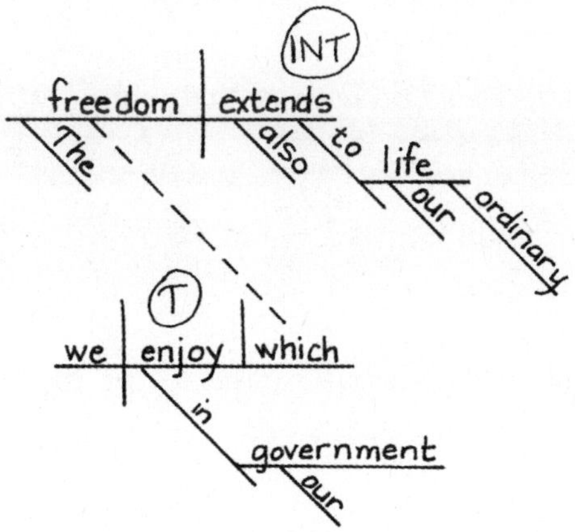

I agree to this Constitution with all its faults, if they are such; because I think a general Government necessary for us.
—Benjamin Franklin

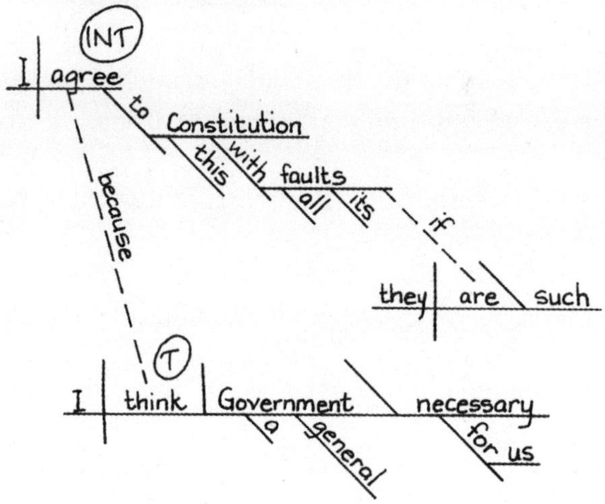

Without peace, all other dreams vanish and are reduced to ashes.
—Jawaharlal Nehru

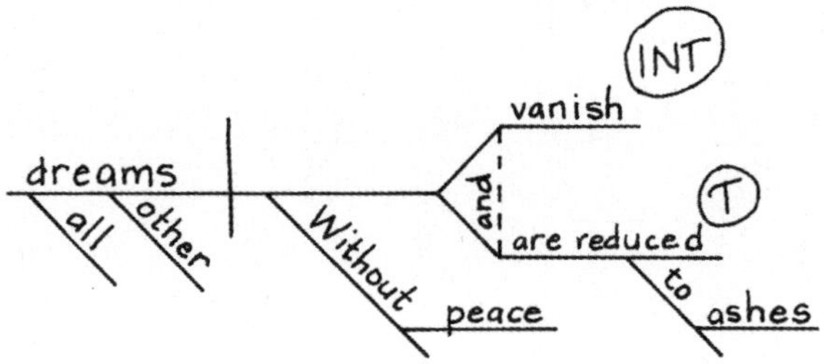

Note to Instructor: The prepositional phrase *Without peace* is an adverb that modifies both verbs, so is diagrammed after the subject/predicate division line but before the branching compound predicate lines.

— LESSON 111 —

Ambitransitive Verbs
Gerunds and Infinitives
Infinitive Phrases as Direct Objects
Infinitive Phrases With Understood *To*

Exercise 111A: Infinitives and Other Uses of "To"

In the following sentences from Johann David Wyss's *The Swiss Family Robinson*, underline every phrase that incorporates the word *to*. For infinitives, underline just the infinitive itself; for prepositional phrases and verbs, underline the entire phrase.

- Label each phrase as *INF* for infinitive, *PREP* for prepositional, or *V* for verb.
- For prepositional phrases, also label the object of the preposition as *OP*.
- Further identify each entire phrase as *S* for subject, *DO* for direct object, *PA* for predicate adjective, *PN* for predicate nominative, *ADJ* for adjective, or *ADV* for adverb.
- For adjective and adverb phrases, draw an arrow to the word modified.
- For verbs, parse the verb.

The first one is done for you.

Fritz completed a dish and some plates, to his great satisfaction [PREP ADV; OP: satisfaction; → completed], but we considered that, being so frail, we could not carry them with us.

We therefore filled them with sand, that the sun might not warp them, and left them to dry [INF ADV; → left], till we returned.

We began to consider [INF DO] how we should come at the contents of the hogshead without exposing the perishable matter to the heat [PREP ADV; OP: heat; → exposing] of the sun.

I then tied the flamingo to a stake [PREP ADV; OP: stake; → tied], near the river, by a cord long enough to allow [INF ADV; → long] him to fish [INF DO] at his pleasure, and in fact, in a few days, he learned to know [INF DO] us, and was quite domesticated.

> **Note to Instructor:** The infinitive *to fish* serves as the direct object of the infinitive *to allow*. The pronoun *him* is the indirect object of *to allow*.

This reconciled them a little to their lot [PREP ADV; OP: lot; → reconciled], and they left us.

I proceeded to suspend [INF ADV; → proceeded] this infernal machine against the side of the ship near our work.

> **Note to Instructor:** *Proceed* is intransitive, so *to suspend* is a modifier rather than a direct object.

INF ADV

It could not be worse than the buffalo they had assisted me to subdue.

> **Note to Instructor:** The pronoun *me* is the direct object of the verb *had assisted.*

V simple present, active, modal

Especially I warned them against the *manchineel*, which ought to grow in this part of the world.

INF ADV INF ADV PREP ADV OP INF ADJ

To accustom them to come to this shelter of themselves, we took care to fill their racks with the food they liked best, mingled with salt.

INF PN PREP ADJ OP

Our first care, when we stepped in safety on land, was to kneel down and thank God, to whom we

INF PN PREP ADV OP

owed our lives, and to resign ourselves wholly to his fatherly kindness.

Exercise 111B: Diagramming

On your own paper, diagram every word of the following sentences, adapted from *The Swiss Family Robinson.*

I had neglected to take my cloak and boots, and my dear little fellow had volunteered to bring them to Tent House.

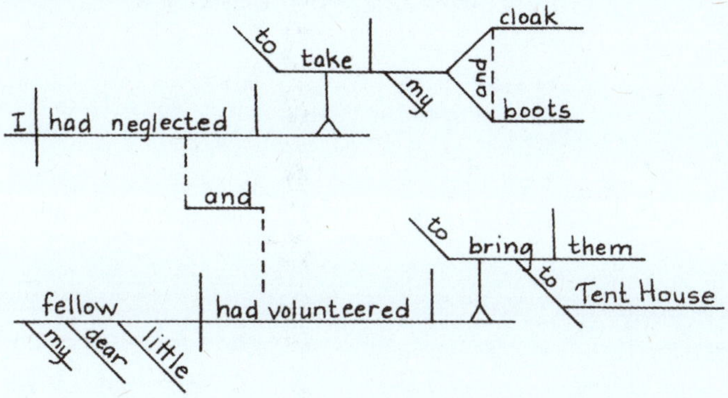

I am impatient to learn if Fritz has any tidings of Captain Johnson, for it was on the shore near Tent House that he and Jack passed the night.

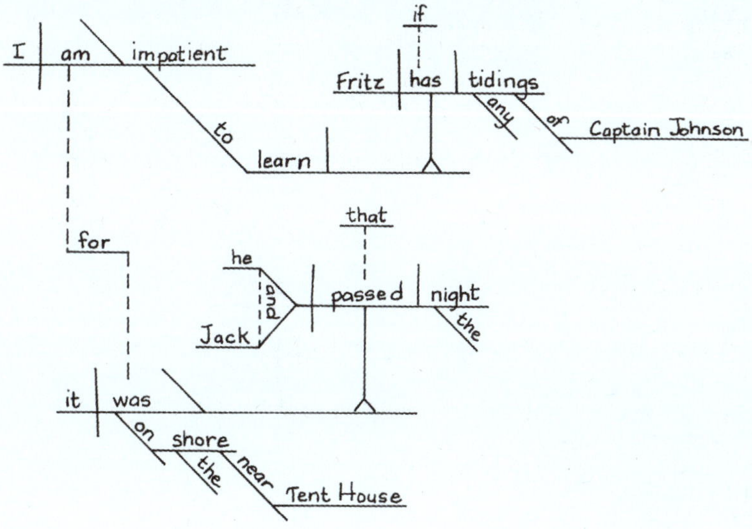

I agreed to this reasonable request, and only begged to know how they would procure water for their fountains.

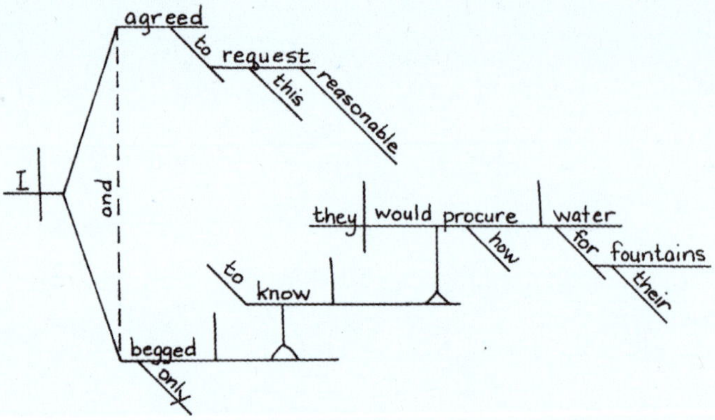

I saw that my presence was necessary to restrain and aid him; and I decided, with a heavy heart, to leave Ernest alone to protect the vessel.

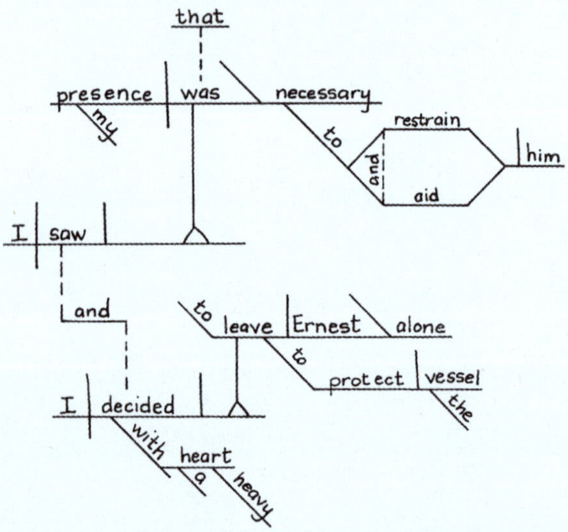

Note to Instructor: *Alone* is ambiguous and could also be diagrammed as an adverb beneath the infinitive *to leave.*

Exhausted by fatigue, we were glad to take a good night's rest in the captain's cabin, on an elastic mattress, of which our hammocks had made us forget the comfort.

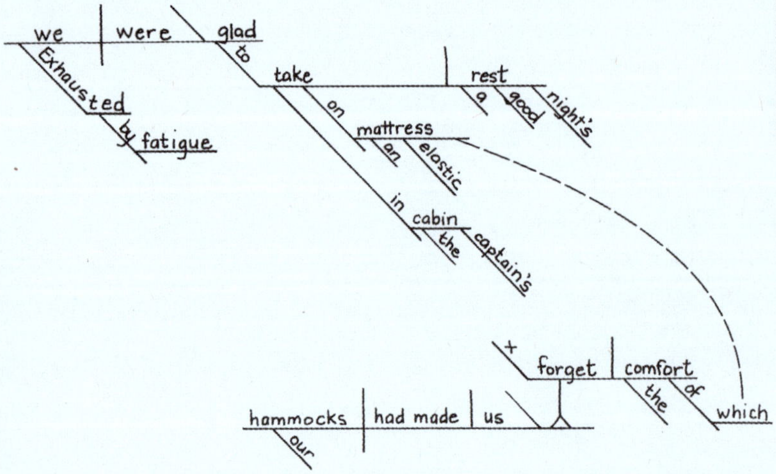

Note to Instructor: The infinitive phrase *forget the comfort* has an understood *to* and serves as an object complement. *Us* is the direct object of *had made,* since the *making* action most directly affects *us.*

— LESSON 112 —

Principal Parts

Yet More Troublesome Verbs

Exercise 112A: Verb Definitions

For each definition, choose the best term from the word bank. Write it into the blank next to the definition.

ambitransitive verb	first principal part	gerund
hortative	imperative	indicative
infinitive	intransitive verb	modal
perfect verb	present participle	progressive verb
second principal part	simple verb	subjunctive
third principal part	transitive verb	

Expresses action that is not received by any person or thing	intransitive verb
The simple past	second principal part
Describes an action which has been completed before	perfect verb
Expresses situations that are unreal, wished for, or uncertain	subjunctive
A verb form ending in -ing	present participle
Formed by combining *to* and the first-person singular present form of a verb	infinitive
Expresses action that is received by some person or thing	transitive verb
Can be either transitive or intransitive	ambitransitive verb
The perfect past, minus helping verbs	third principal part
Describes an ongoing or continuous action	progressive verb
Affirms or declares what actually is	indicative
Expresses possible actions	modal
The simple present (first-person singular)	first principal part
Expresses intended actions	imperative
Simply tells whether an action takes place in the past, present, or future	simple verb
Present participle acting as a noun	gerund
Encourages or recommends an action	hortative

Exercise 112B: Using Troublesome Verbs Correctly

In the following sentences from *Turkish Fairy Tales and Folk Tales* (collected by Dr. Ignácz Kúnos, translated by R. Nisbet Bain), fill in the blanks. The first blank (above the sentence) should be filled in with the first principal part of the correct verb: *lie* or *lay* in the first set of sentences, *sit* or *set* in the second set, and *rise* or *raise* in the third set. You will be able to tell from the context of the sentence whether you should use the transitive verbs *lay*, *set*, and *raise* (the verb is passive, or has a direct object) or the intransitive verbs *lie*, *sit*, and *rise* (the action of the verb is not passed on to any other word in the sentence).

The second blank in the sentence itself should be filled in with the correct form of that verb.

The first sentence in each section is done for you.

(simple past active indicative of lie)
There in the rippling water in front of the prince, like a dream-shape, lay a large garden.

(simple past active indicative of lie)
They lay down together, and together they rose up.

(perfect past active indicative of lay)
One day she put her ring upon her sewing-table, but scarcely had she laid it down when there came a little dove and took up the ring and flew away with it.

(perfect present active modal of lie)
Then, auguring some evil, he beat in the door, and lo! the place where the damsel should have lain was cold.

Note to Instructor: The original sentence uses *should*, but the student may make use of any of the modal helping verbs.

(infinitive of lie)
They were just going to lie down to sleep when all at once such a roaring, such a bellowing arose that the very mountains fell down from their places.

(simple present active imperative of lay)
Moisten these three wooden tablets with water, lay them on the face of the damsel, and I will come out of her, and a rich reward will be thine.

(simple present active hortative of lay)
"Come now!" said some of them, "let us steal a march upon Mehmed one day and lay hands upon his table, and then there will be an end to the fool's glory."

Note to Instructor: The hortative verb here must be *let*, not *may*, because the word *us* is an object pronoun. The hortative verb applies to both *steal* and *lay* in this sentence.

(simple past active indicative of lay)
Now his mother knew that thou wert my destined bride, so she laid the curse of her spells upon me.

(simple past active indicative of lie)
He sent to the cemetery, had the tomb opened, and there in her coffin lay the Rose-beauty of his dreams.

(simple present active indicative of __lie__)
The wise men and the leeches cannot help the damsel; the only medicine that can cure her __lies__ hidden elsewhere.

(simple past active indicative of __set__)
She put the room tidy, cooked the meal, __set__ everything in order, and then leaped back upon the rafter and became a feather again.

(simple past passive indicative of __set__)
Then rich meats on rare and precious dishes __were set__ before him, and then the dancers and the jugglers diverted him till the evening.

(progressive passive infinitive of __sit__)
His wife chanced just then __to be sitting__ at the window, and when she saw her husband she leaped clean out of the window to him.

(simple past active indicative of __set__)
The crow begged and prayed till at last he let her go free, and again he __set__ the
(simple past active indicative of __sit__)
snare in the tree and __sat__ down at the foot of it to wait.

(simple past active indicative of __sit__)
Here they __sat__ down to rest a while, and as they were looking about them to the right hand and to the left, the valley was suddenly shaken as if by an earthquake.

(perfect past active indicative of __sit__)
In the evening the lion came home sure enough, and when they __had sat__ down together and begun to talk, the girl asked him what he would do if any of her brothers should chance to come there.

(simple past active indicative of __set__)
But the young man brought out his table, __set__ it in the midst, and cried: "Little table, give me to eat!"

(simple past active indicative of __raise__)
When Aleodor heard these words, and how the ant called him by his name, he __raised__ his foot again and let the ant go where it would.

(simple past active indicative of __rise__)
On the morning of the reception of guests she __rose__ up early and commanded that on the
(simple present active modal of __rise__)
spot where the little hut stood a palace __should rise__, the like of which eye hath never seen nor ear heard.

> **Note to Instructor:** The original sentence uses *should*, but the student may make use of any of the modal helping verbs.

(simple past active indicative of __rise__)
She __rose__ from her bed and promised the youth a great treasure if he would bring her to that tower.

(simple active infinitive of __raise__)
His eyelids were so heavy that he had __to raise__ them on high with his hands.

(simple present active imperative of rise)
" Rise up, poor man, and fear not," said the ghost.

(simple past active indicative of rise)
But the good steed rose into the air like a dart, and Boy Beautiful shot an arrow which struck off one of the witch's three heads.

(simple past active indicative of rise)
They lay down together, and together they rose up.

Exercise 112C: More Irregular Principal Parts

Fill in the chart below with the missing principal parts of each verb. (You may use a dictionary if necessary.) Then, in the sentences below (from *The Wind in the Willows* by Kenneth Grahame), fill in the blanks with the correct verb, in the tense, mood, and voice indicated in brackets at the end of each sentence. Each verb is used one time.

	First Principal Part **Present**	Second Principal Part **Past**	Third Principal Part **Past Participle**
I	forbid	forbade	forbidden OR forbid
	burst	burst	burst
	shrink	shrank	shrunk
	bind	bound	bound
	overtake	overtook	overtaken
	beset	beset	beset
	cling	clung	clung
	ride	rode	ridden
	drive	drove	driven

The rapid nightfall of mid-December had quite beset the little village as they approached it on soft feet over a first thin fall of powdery snow. [perfect past active indicative]

"Seize him!" they cried, "seize the Toad, the wicked animal who stole our motor-car! Bind him, chain him, drag him to the nearest police-station!" [simple present active imperative]

Then out of the tunnel burst the pursuing engine, roaring and whistling, her motley crew waving their various weapons and shouting, "Stop! stop! stop!" [simple past active indicative]

Though it was past ten o'clock at night, the sky still clung to and retained some lingering skirts of light from the departed day. [simple past active indicative]

Who persuaded them into letting him see if he ____could drive____? [simple present active modal]

The Mole recollected that animal-etiquette ____forbade____ any sort of comment on the sudden disappearance of one's friends at any moment, for any reason or no reason whatever. [simple past active indicative]

You ____can____ easily ____overtake____ me on the road, for you are young. [simple present active modal]

As the sun rose royally behind us, we ____rode____ into Venice down a path of gold. [simple past active indicative]

But the constant chorus of the orchards and hedges ____had shrunk____ to a casual evensong from a few yet unwearied performers. [perfect past active indicative]

WEEK 30

Still More About Clauses

— LESSON 113 —

Clauses and Phrases

Exercise 113A: Phrases and Clauses

In the sentences below from Johnny Gruelle's *Raggedy Ann Stories*, identify each bolded set of words as *PH* for phrase or *CL* for clause.

- Then, identify the part of the sentence (*S, DO, IO, OP, PN, PA, ADV, ADJ*) that each set of words functions as.
- For adjective and adverb phrases and clauses, draw an arrow to the word modified.
- For phrases, further identify the phrase as *PREP, INF* (infinitive), *PRESP* (present participle) or *PASTP* (past participle).
- For clauses, underline the subject of the clause once and the predicate twice.

The first sentence is done for you. Notice that it contains two separate sets of bolded words—*to be nice children* is one set of words (a phrase), and *while she was away* is a second set of words (a clause). If a phrase contains a clause, mark both the phrase and the clause. If a clause or phrase contains additional phrases, there is no need to mark each phrase separately—just label the overall clause or phrase.

PH DO INF

Their little mistress had placed them all around the room and told them **to be nice children**

CL ADV

while she was away.

PH ADV PREP PH ADV PREP

They swarmed **upon the pantry shelves** and **in their eagerness** spilled a pitcher of cream **which**

CL ADJ

ran all over the French dolly's dress.

CL DO

Raggedy Ann knew just **how it all happened** and her remaining shoe-button eye twinkled.

CL ADV had been

When a tail had been fastened to the kite and a large ball of heavy twine tied to the front, one of

PH ADV PREP PH ADV PRESP

the boys held the kite up **in the air** and another boy walked off, **unwinding the ball of twine.**

Note to Instructor: The helping verbs *had been* are understood in the predicate of the subject *ball*. Prompt the student if she does not insert them. The adverbial prepositional phrase *in the air* could also be modifying the adverb *up*; the construction is ambiguous.

PH ADJ PREP CL DO

But I had no way **of telling your mistress where Fido was**, for she cannot understand dog language!

> **Note to Instructor:** The clause *where Fido was* is technically contained within the prepositional phrase, but should be marked as a clause. It serves as the direct object of the present participle *telling*, which itself serves as the object of the preposition *of*. The noun *mistress* is the indirect object of *telling*.

PH OP PRESP

The dolls lost no time in **scrambling into bed and pulling up the covers**, for they were very sleepy.

> **Note to Instructor:** Since *in* is not bolded, the focus is on the phrase formed by the present participles *scrambling* and *pulling*, which are gerunds (participles acting as nouns) serving as the compound objects of the preposition *in*.

CL ADJ / CL DO

Well, I know you will not tell anyone **who would not be glad to know about it**, so I will tell you the secret and **why I am wearing my smile a trifle broader**!

CL ADV

The puppy dog ran up to Raggedy Ann and twisted his head about **as he looked at her**.

CL DO

I did not notice **how pleasant her face looked** last night!

CL ADV / PH DO GER / PH ADV PREP

"Play something lively!" said the French doll, **as she giggled behind her hand**, so Uncle Clem began **hammering the eight keys** upon the piano **with all his might** until a noise was heard upon the stairs.

CL ADV / PH ADV PREP / PH ADJ PRESP

As Raggedy watched, her candy heart went pitty-pat **against her cotton stuffing**, for she saw a tiny pink foot **sticking out of the bundle of light**.

CL DO / CL DO

So we can hardly tell **when it is day** and **when it is night**.

PH ADV PREP / CL OP

I was so interested **in looking out of the window** I did not pay any attention to **what they said**, for we were on a train and the scenery was just flying by!

Exercise 113B: Diagramming

On your own paper, diagram every word of the following sentences, taken from *Raggedy Ann Stories* by Johnny Gruelle.

When Mistress had me out playing with me this morning, she carried me by a door near the back of the house and I smelled something which smelled as if it would taste delicious!

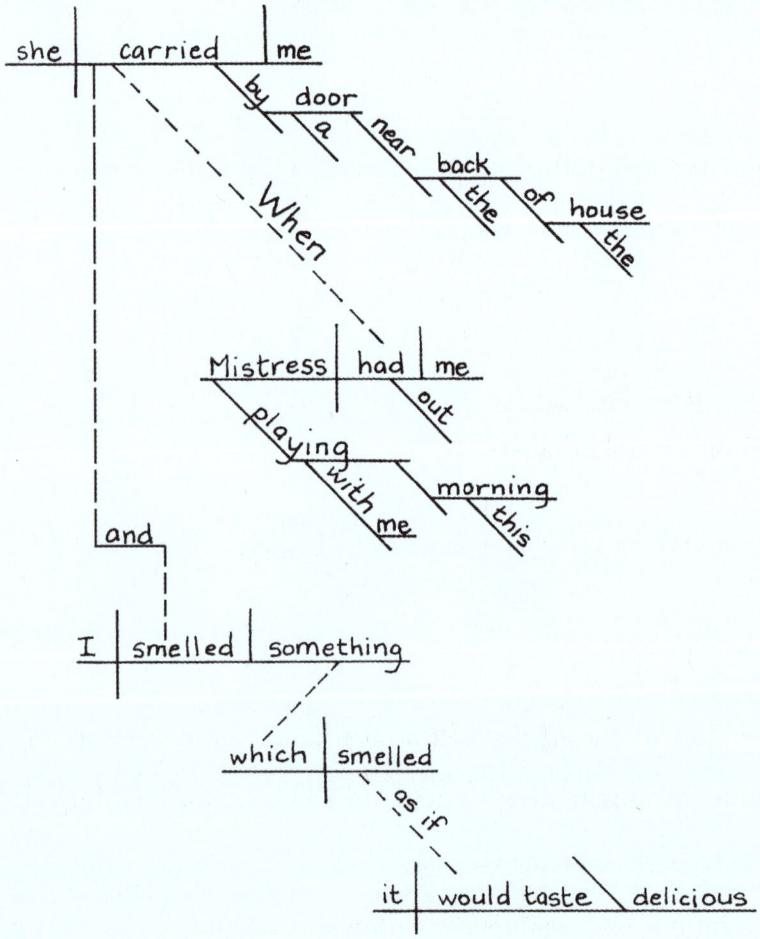

I think it would be a good plan to elect Raggedy Ann as our leader on this expedition!

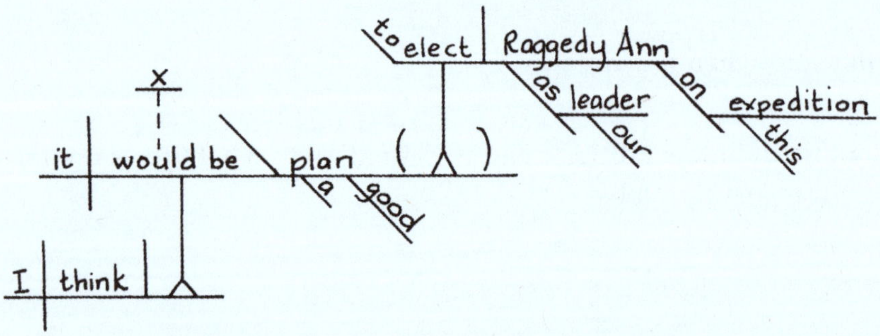

Note to Instructor: Since the plan is *to elect Raggedy Ann*, it is diagrammed as an appositive. There is an understood "that" introducing the clause *it would be a good plan...*

They swarmed upon the pantry shelves and in their eagerness spilled a pitcher of cream which ran all over the French dolly's dress.

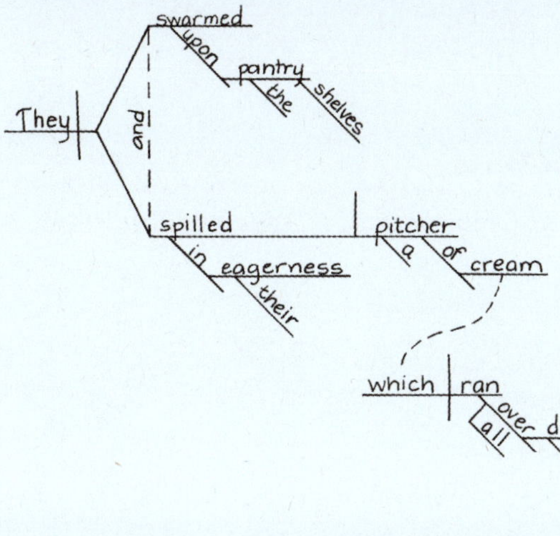

Once a strange dog ran out at them, but Peterkins told him to mind his own business and the strange dog returned to his own yard.

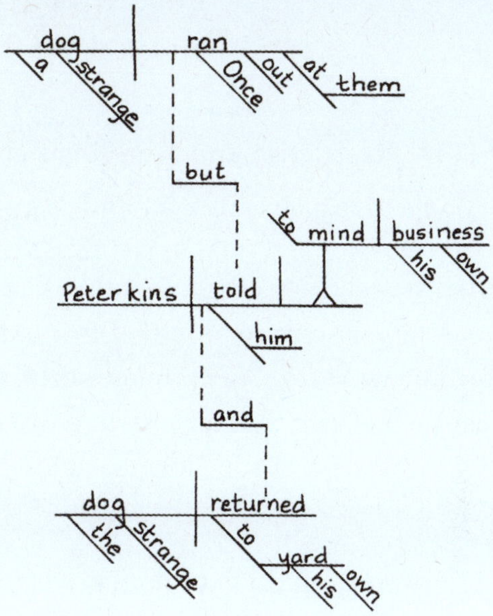

She kicked and twisted as much as she could, but the puppy dog thought Raggedy was playing.

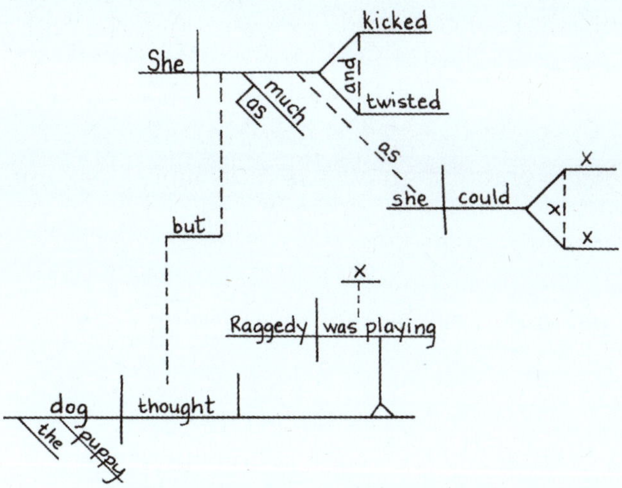

Note to Instructor: The understood completion of the comparison is "as much as she could kick and twist." Since *could* goes with both understood verbs, it is diagrammed after the predicate line but before the branch into the compound understood predicate. *That* is also understood in the final clause ("the puppy dog thought that Raggedy was playing").

Both new dolls were silent for a while, thinking deeply.

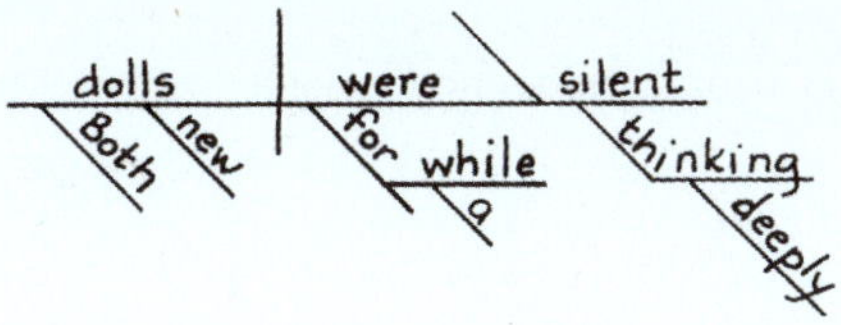

— LESSON 114 —

Restrictive and Non-Restrictive Modifying Clauses
Punctuating Modifying Clauses
Which and *That*

Exercise 114A: Restrictive and Non-Restrictive Adjective Clauses

Find every adjective clause in the following sentences, taken from *Symbolic Logic* by John Venn, and then follow these steps:

1) Underline each adjective clause.
2) Circle the relative pronoun that introduces each clause.
3) Draw an arrow from the pronoun back to the word modified.
4) Label each clause as *R* for restrictive or *NR* for non-restrictive.
5) Draw an asterisk or star next to each sentence that does *not* follow the *which/that* rule.

* What we here have to do is to conceive, and invent a notation for, all the possible combinations which any number of class terms can yield. (R)

* I may heap up one such term upon another, provided I put in some expression at the end which shall neutralize the surplus. (R)

When it is asked, What are the limits of not-x? the symbolic answer is invariably the same, "all that is excluded from x is taken up by not-x." (R)

* On this plan of notation *xy* stands for the compartment, or class, of things which are both *x* and *y*. (R)

To one point, which has already been noticed, attention must be very persistently directed, as any vagueness of apprehension here will be fatal to the proper understanding of symbolic reasoning. (NR)

The assertion that Dr. Boole's system is in any way founded on the doctrine of the Quantification of the Predicate—is, in fact, not directly hostile to that doctrine—is so astonishing that one is inclined to suspect some lurking confusion of meaning. (R)

Note to Instructor: The underlined clause above is treated as though the subject *system* takes the compound predicate *is founded* and *is*. The student may also choose to treat the phrase between the hyphens as a parenthetical expression, and only underline the clause *that Dr. Boole's...of the Predicate*.

The vanishing of every term is an indication that no information whatever is obtainable. R

The accurate language of symbols requires us to insert a final term which common language had rejected for the sake of brevity. NR

The disproval of this fact, which would be equivalent to showing that the subject had no existence, would at most show that I had been hasty. NR

The only complication that is thus produced is that the final elements or subdivisions of such an ill-expressed fractional form may possess other numerical factors, positive or negative, besides the true typical four. R

Exercise 114B: Dependent Clauses within Dependent Clauses

The following sentences, adapted from George Boole's *An Investigation of the Laws of Thought*, all contain dependent clauses that have other dependent clauses within them.

Underline the entire dependent clause, including additional dependent clauses that act as nouns or modifiers within it. Place a box around the subject of the main dependent clause and underline its predicate twice. In the right-hand margin, write the abbreviation for the part of the sentence that the main dependent clause is fulfilling: *N-SUB* for a noun clause acting as subject, *N-PN* for predicate nominative, *N-DO* for direct object, *N-OP* for object of the preposition, and then *ADJ* for adjective and *ADV* for adverb. For *ADJ* and *ADV* clauses, also write the word that the clause modifies.

Then, circle any additional clauses that fall within the main dependent clause. Label each clause, above the circle, as *N* for noun, *ADJ* for adjective, or *ADV* for adverb. Then, also label noun clauses as *S, PN, DO,* or *OP*. For these additional *ADJ* and *ADV* clauses, draw a line from the circle to the word in the main dependent clause modified.

The first sentence is done for you.

But if the general truths of Logic are of a nature that at once commands the mind's assent (ADJ) wherein consists the difficulty of constructing the Science of Logic? ADV consists

The reader may be curious to inquire what effect would be produced if we literally translated this expression. (ADV) N-DO

Note to Instructor: The clause serves as the direct object of the infinitive *to inquire*.

A little consideration will here show that the class represented by 1 must be "the Universe," since this is the only class in which are found *all* the individuals that exist in *any* class. (ADV; ADJ; ADJ) N-DO

Note to Instructor: The subject and predicates of the clauses contained within the main dependent clause are, respectively: *this is*; *individuals are found*; *that exist*.

Now the above system of processes would conduct us to no intelligible result, unless the final equations resulting therefrom were in a form which should render their interpretation, after we have restored to the symbols their logical significance, possible.

ADV
would conduct

> **Note to Instructor:** The entire underlined subordinate clause beginning with *unless* is adverbial and modifies the verb ***would conduct*** (it answers the question *How?*). This clause contains within itself the subordinate clause *which should render their interpretation possible.* That subordinate clause is divided by a third subordinate clause, *after we have restored to the symbols their logical significance.*

It is necessary that the reader should apprehend what are the specific ends of the investigation upon which we are entering, as well as the principles which are to guide us to the attainment of them.

ADV
necessary

> **Note to Instructor:** The compound direct objects of the verb *should apprehend* are the noun clause *what are the specific...we are entering* and the noun *principles.*

It now remains to show that those constituent parts of ordinary language which have not been considered in the previous sections of this chapter are either resolvable into the same elements as those which have been considered, or are subsidiary to those elements by contributing to their more precise definition.

N-DO

I apprehend therefore that the solution indicates, that when a particular condition has prevailed through the whole of our *recorded experience*, it assumes the above character with reference to the class of phaenomena over which that experience has extended.

N-DO

> **Note to Instructor:** The entire underlined subordinate clause acts as the direct object of the main predicate, *apprehend.* Within that subordinate clause, the clause *that when a particular...has extended* acts as the direct object of the predicate *indicates.*

Such knowledge is, indeed, unnecessary for the ends of science, which properly concerns itself with what is, and seeks not for grounds of preference or reasons of appointment.

ADJ
science

I do not here speak of that perfection only which consists in power, but of that also which is founded in the conception of what is fit and beautiful.

N-OP

ADJ perfection

ADJ that

Note to Instructor: The second *that* is here serving as a demonstrative pronoun that does *not* introduce a subordinate clause. The second relative pronoun *which* refers back to the demonstrative pronoun *that*—a rare case of a pronoun referring back to another pronoun.

Exercise 114C: Diagramming

On your own paper, diagram every word of the following sentences from Mary Everest Boole's *The Preparation of the Child for Science.* If you need help, ask your instructor.

Some readers may be tempted to think that in mathematics there are no tolerated and mutually corrective errors.

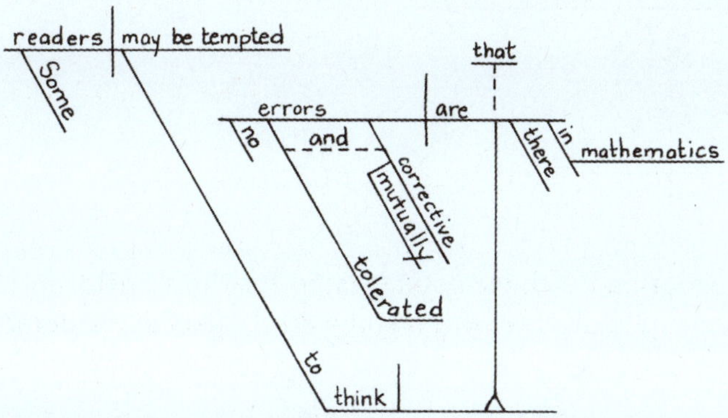

The efficient and intelligent teacher learns all he or she can of principles of psychology and general tendencies, and then carries them out by methods which, in detail, are his or her own.

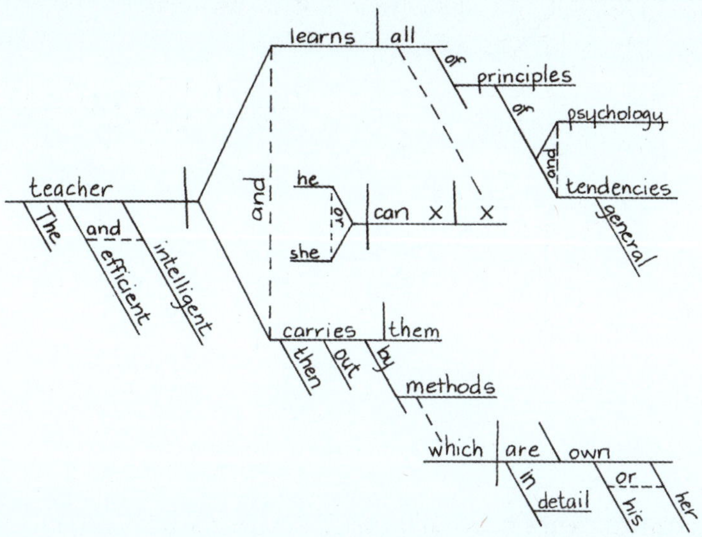

Note to Instructor: The subordinate clause *he or she can* contains two understood elements: *[that] he or she can [learn]*. The understood *that* has been diagramed as a pronoun referring back to *all*.

The first thing we must do is to resolve seriously that a good deal of time before the age of ten, and of the vacations afterwards, shall be resolutely dedicated to the training of the unconscious mind.

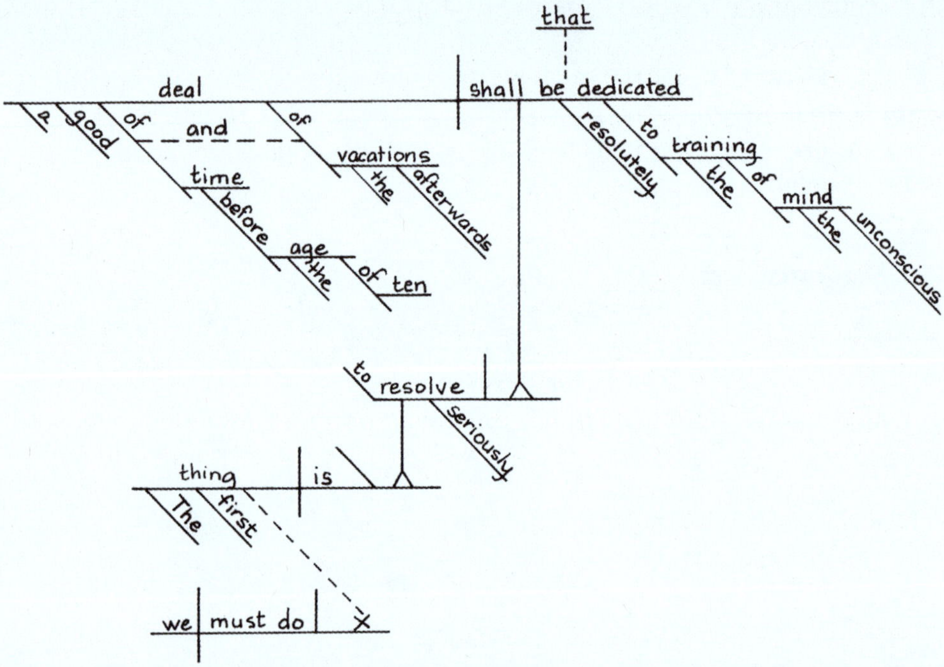

Many parents seem to think that all the time is wasted for their children which is not spent in taking in consciously some special idea which some adult already understands.

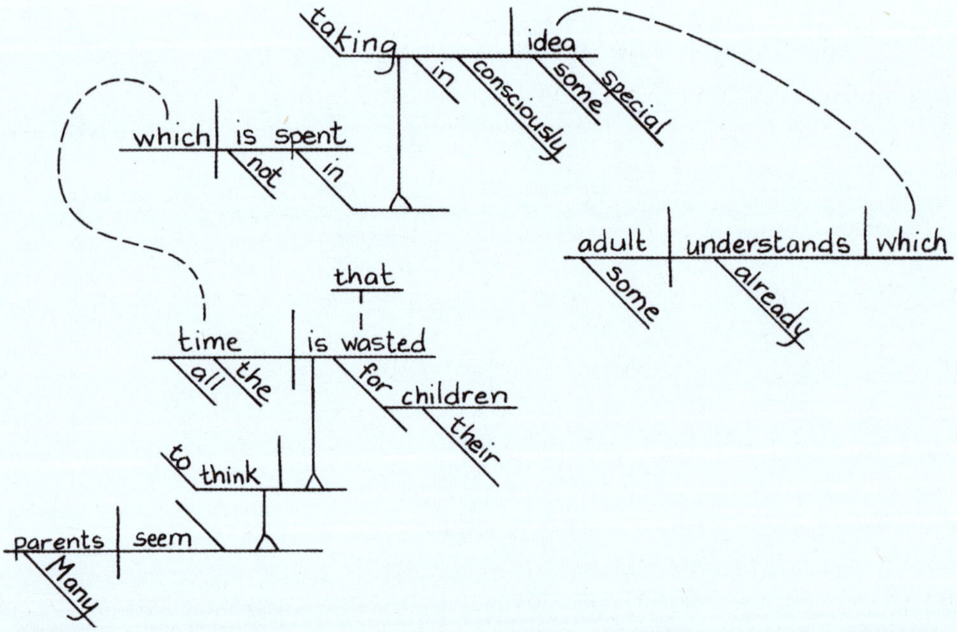

Note to Instructor: Since the infinitive *to think* describes the noun *parents*, it has been diagrammed here as a predicate adjective. An argument could be made for diagramming the infinitive underneath the predicate *seem*, as an adverb answering the question *how.*

There are some conceptions in physical science which present no difficulty to one who, years before he hears any discussion about matter and force, has made a long series of experiments with the same object rotating under varied conditions.

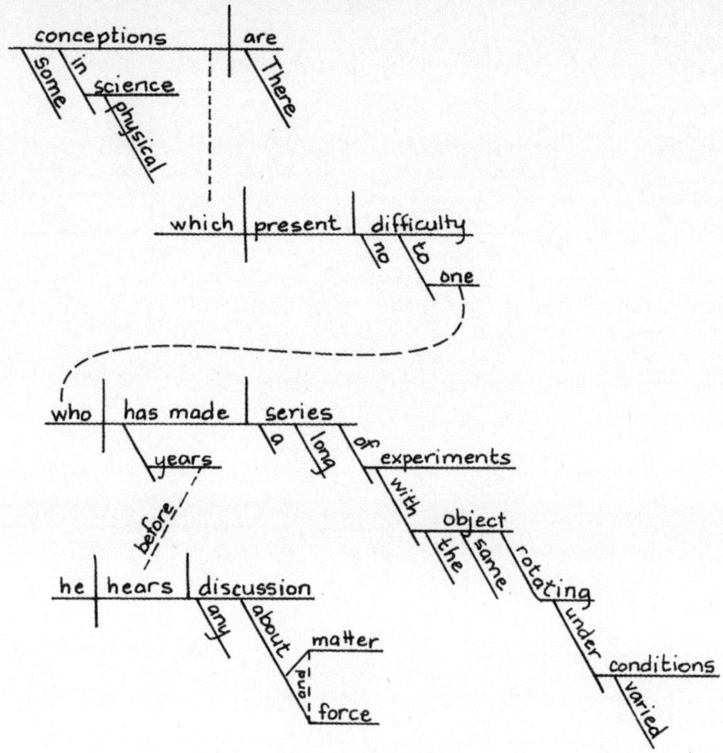

— LESSON 115 —

Conditional Sentences
Conditional Sentences as Dependent Clauses
Conditional Sentences with Missing Words
Formal *If* Clauses

Exercise 115A: Conditional Clauses

In the following sentences, from *World War Z: An Oral History of the Zombie War* by Max Brooks, circle every conditional sentence. This may mean circling the entire sentence, or circling simply the part of it that makes up the conditional-consequence clause set, or circling the conditional and consequence clauses separately if they are divided by other words.

After you have circled the conditional sentences, underline twice and then parse the predicate in each conditional and consequence clause.

Finally, write a *1, 2,* or *3* in the blank to indicate *First, Second,* or *Third Conditional.*

The first is done for you.

(simple past, active, subjunctive) (simple present, active, modal)
If you showed any signs of advanced infection, they wouldn't go near you. 2

simple present, active, indicative (emphatic) — simple present, state-of-being, subjunctive

Zombies don't really smell that bad, not individually and not if they're fresh. 1

simple past, active, subjunctive — simple past, active, subjunctive — simple present, state-of-being, modal

He thought that if we abandoned our tribal homeland and relocated to a city, there would be a brand-new house and high-paying jobs just sitting there waiting for us. 2

simple past, active, subjunctive (emphatic) — simple past, active, subjunctive (emphatic) — simple present, active, modal

If you didn't know the true story, if you didn't know it from my end, you'd think it was an efficient crackdown. 2

simple past, active, subjunctive — simple past, active, subjunctive — simple present, active, modal

If you had a loved one, a family member, a child, who was infected, and you thought there was a shred of hope in some other country, wouldn't you do everything in your power to get there? 2

perfect past, active, subjunctive — perfect present, active, modal

At least if we had gone north, we might have had a chance. 3

simple past, active subjunctive — progressive present, active, modal — progressive present, active, modal

If we blew it now, not only would we be sending dozens of people hurtling to their deaths, but we would be trapping thousands on the other side. 2

Note to Instructor: This is a conditional sentence with a compound sentence (two independent clauses connected by *not only . . . but*) acting as the consequence clause.

simple present, active, modal — simple present, state-of-being, modal

If we could provide them with the necessary equipment, they might be able to start raising enough food to stretch our existing provisions for years. 1

simple past, active, subjunctive — simple present, active, modal

I know that if we had the resources to clear them all we would. 2

Note to Instructor: The consequence clause, *we would*, has understood elements: *we would clear them*. Because the full verb is *would clear*, it is modal. (See the diagram of this sentence in 115B below.)

simple present, state-of-being, modal — progressive past, active, subjective

The only risk might be if Zack were clinging to you during the ascent. 2

Exercise 115B: Diagramming

On your own paper, diagram every word of the following sentences from Exercise 115A.

He thought that if we abandoned our tribal homeland and relocated to a city, there would be a brand-new house and high-paying jobs just sitting there waiting for us.

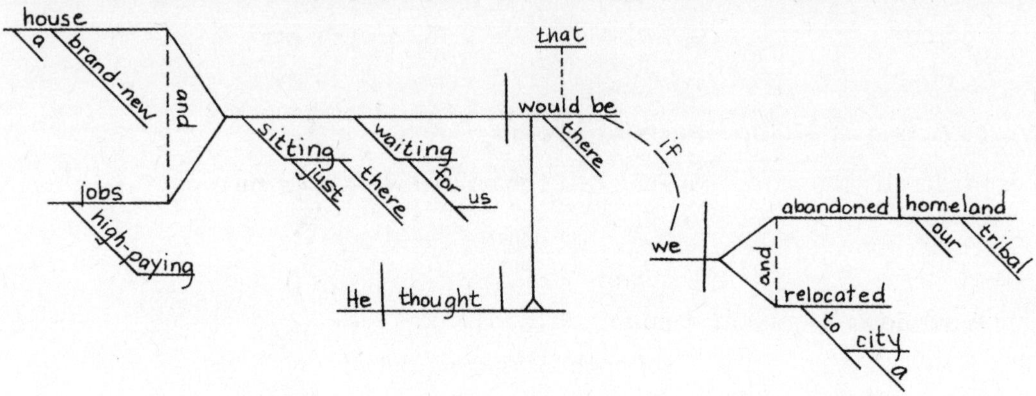

If you didn't know the true story, if you didn't know it from my end, you'd think it was an efficient crackdown.

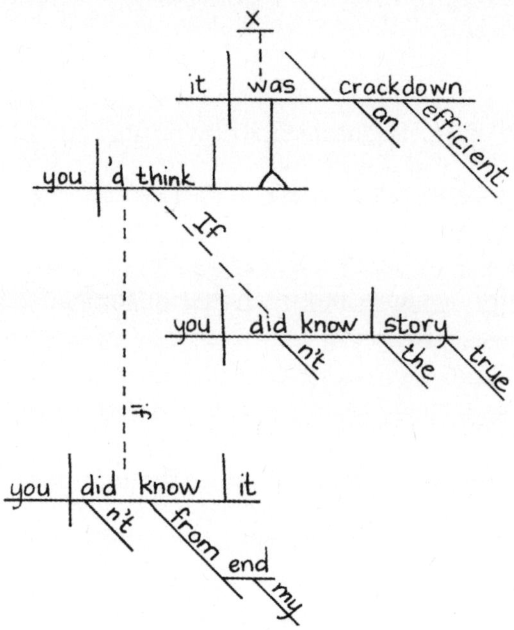

I know that if we had the resources to clear them all we would.

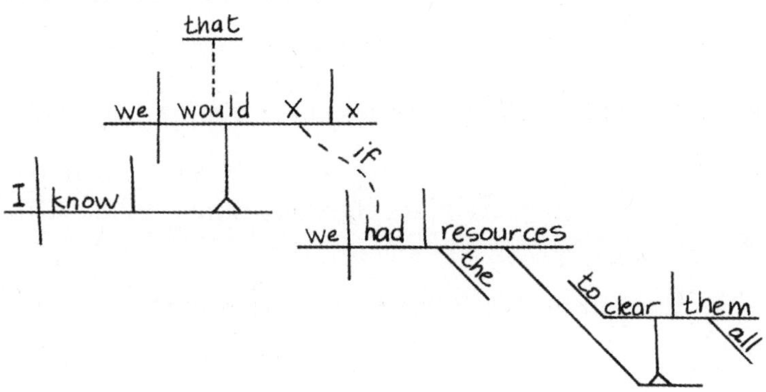

—LESSON 116—

Words That Can Be Multiple Parts of Speech
Interrogatives
Demonstratives
Relative Adverbs and Subordinating Conjunctions

Exercise 116A: Words Acting as Multiple Parts of Speech

Use these sentences to identify the parts of speech that the bolded words can serve as. Fill in the blanks with the correct labels from the following list:

adjective	adverb
coordinating conjunction	noun
preposition	subordinating conjunction

The following sentences are from *The Moffats* by Eleanor Estes.

Down preposition adverb

She looked up the street and down the street.

Here she refreshed herself with a deep drink from a sparkling spring and sank down into the moss to await the White Prince.

Until subordinating conjunction preposition

So we will just forget about that old sign until Dr. Witty actually does sell the house to someone.

Hurrah! School was all over until next September.

Before preposition adverb subordinating conjunction

But this little nod did not come naturally to Jane and required some practice before the mirror.

Rufus had never been in school before except for one day last year when Jane brought him to her class for Visiting Day.

He had seen now where the hatch was and he meant to escape before that ghost could catch up with him.

Still adverb adjective coordinating conjunction

However, she still walked on tiptoe when she passed his house, in order not to disturb him should he be napping.

And the red steed sent sparks from his nostrils that disappeared like shooting stars into the still night air.

Why, he knew nothing of that, of course, and although he was inclined to toss the matter lightly aside, still he blanched visibly when again from some mysterious dark recess of the house came the same wild howl.

About preposition adverb

Mama did not like this business about the yards.

Everybody on the street stopped to stare and wave their arms about in excitement.

The following sentences are from *Ginger Pye* by Eleanor Estes.

After subordinating conjunction preposition

"That is all book stuff," Jerry had reasoned ruefully after it was all over and Rachel had skipped off with Addie Egan.

After the singing there was quiet for a time, with only an occasional sharp command from the one in charge of all these goings-on.

Around adverb preposition

This time, however, there weren't any other people around and it was a splendid opportunity.

When Uncle Bennie got tired of the new game, Rachel and Jerry tied the dusters around their own waists and slid back and forth across the pews themselves.

Since preposition subordinating conjunction

After all she had been up since dawn with bee-bite.

Since they were already hungry they ate these.

Below adverb preposition

Of course he dropped Jerry's pencil but fortunately it dropped on the windowsill and not down below.

Early in the morning Rachel and Jerry set out to explore the great field below the railroad station for wild strawberries which usually grew there in abundance and which they were very fond of, crushed up with milk and sugar.

Past adverb noun preposition adjective

The trains went streaking past, running back and forth from Boston to New York, from New York to Boston.

Concealing his impatience, since the leash was still handy, Ginger looked up at Mrs. Pye with what, in the past, he had found to be a winning pose, head to side, tongue dangling out.

Now Ginger was going past the Carruthers' driveway.

When Rachel recovered from the surprise she said to herself, "That man is more interested in sudden perils than in past ones."

Exercise 116B: Words Introducing Clauses

In the following sentences, taken from *Around the World in Eighty Days* by Jules Verne, circle each subordinate clause. Then, carry out the following steps:

1) Underline the introductory word of the clause. (Note: When the introductory word is the object of a preposition, underline the word itself, not the preposition that precedes it. See the first sentence below.)
2) Label the entire clause as noun, *ADJ* (for adjective), or *ADV* (for adverb).
3) For noun clauses, further identify them as subject or object.
4) For adjective or adverb clauses, draw an arrow from the circle to the word modified.
5) Finally, label the introductory word as one of the following: *RP* for relative pronoun, *RAdj* for relative adjective (a relative pronoun functioning as an adjective and introducing an adjective clause), *RAdv* for relative adverb, *SC* for subordinating conjunction, or *A-SC* for adverb functioning as a subordinating conjunction.

Note to Instructor: Explanatory notes follow as needed. Use them to prompt the student if necessary.

He was pleased, on the day after leaving Suez, to find on deck the obliging person (ADJ) with whom (RP) he had walked and chatted on the quays.

Aouda seized a moment (ADV) when (RAdv) Mr. Fogg was asleep to tell Fix and Passepartout (noun object) whom (RP) she had seen.

Note to Instructor: Although the first descriptive clause describes a noun, it is an adverb clause, introduced by a relative adverb, because it modifies a place. The relative adverb *when* relates the clause back to *moment*. Show the student the diagram below:

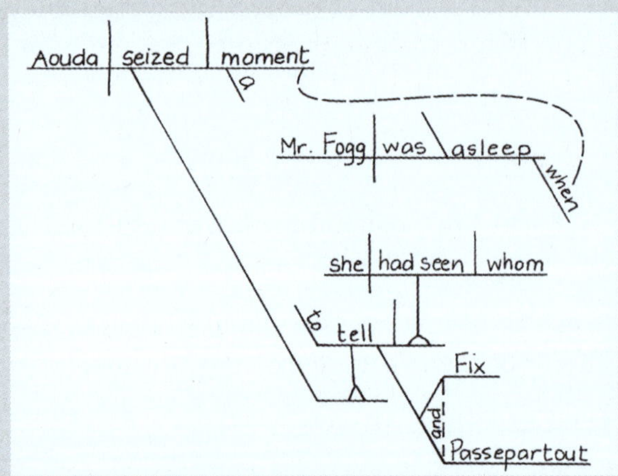

It was Phineas Fogg, (ADJ) whose (RAdj) head now emerged from behind his newspapers, (ADJ) who (RP) made this remark.

ADV
SC
But could he even wait till they reached Hong Kong?

ADJ
RP
This was Fix, one of the detectives who had been despatched from England in search of

ADJ
RP
the bank robber; it was his task to narrowly watch every passenger who arrived at Suez,

ADJ
RP
and to follow up all who seemed to be suspicious characters, or bore a resemblance to the

ADJ
RP
description of the criminal, which he had received two days before from the police head-
quarters at London.

Who dares to say the contrary?

> **Note to Instructor:** This is a trick sentence—"who" is the subject of the sentence and there are no independent clauses.

The other was a small, slight-built personage, with a nervous, intelligent face, and bright eyes

ADJ
RP
peering out from under eyebrows which he was incessantly twitching.

ADV
A-SC
A true Englishman doesn't joke when he is talking about so serious a thing as a wager.

> **Note to Instructor:** Because *when* does not refer back to a noun or pronoun in the main clause, it is an adverb acting as a subordinating conjunction, rather than a relative adverb. The verb in the main clause is *does joke*, so the clause modifying *joke* is an adverb. (You may need to remind the student that *joke* can serve as a verb as well as a noun.)

noun object
SC
But how could Passepartout have discovered that he was a detective?

ADJ
RAdj
Fix looked intently at his companion, whose countenance was as serene as possible, and laughed with him.

Half an hour later several members of the Reform came in and drew up to the fireplace,

ADV
RAdv
where a coal fire was steadily burning.

> **Note to Instructor:** The clause is adverbial because it modifies a place (fireplace).

He gazed with wonder upon the fortifications which make this place the Gibraltar of the Indian Ocean, and the vast cisterns where the English engineers were still at work, two thousand years after the engineers of Solomon.

Note to Instructor: The second clause is adverbial because it describes the place where this was happening (at the cisterns). If the modifying clause had been *that the English engineers were still working on*, it would describe the noun *cisterns* directly and would be adjectival.

You must know that I shall lose twenty thousand pounds, unless I arrive in London by a quarter before nine on the evening of the 21st of December.

They chatted about the journey, and Passepartout was especially merry at the idea that Fix was going to continue it with them.

Note to Instructor: The clause is in apposition to *idea*, which is the object of the preposition *at*, so the clause is also an object.

Mudge was not afraid of being stopped by the Platte River, because it was frozen.

Exercise 116C: Diagramming

On your own paper, diagram every word of the following sentences from Jules Verne's *The Clipper of the Clouds*.

Aeronef is an archaic word for airplane (derived from the French).

Here Frycollin gave vent to a long groan, which might have been taken for his last had he not followed it up with several more.

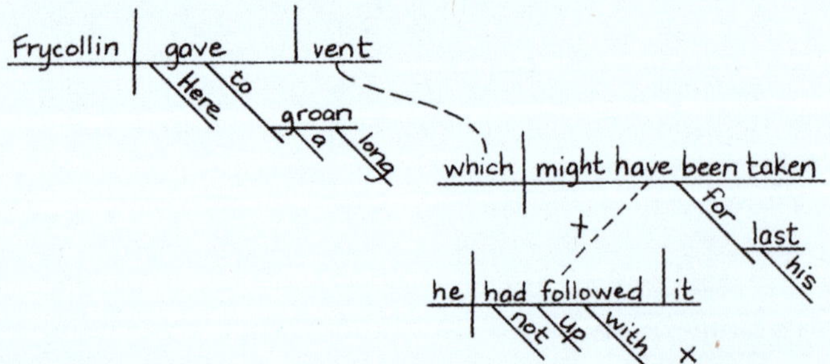

Who was this Robur, of whom up to the present we know nothing but the name?

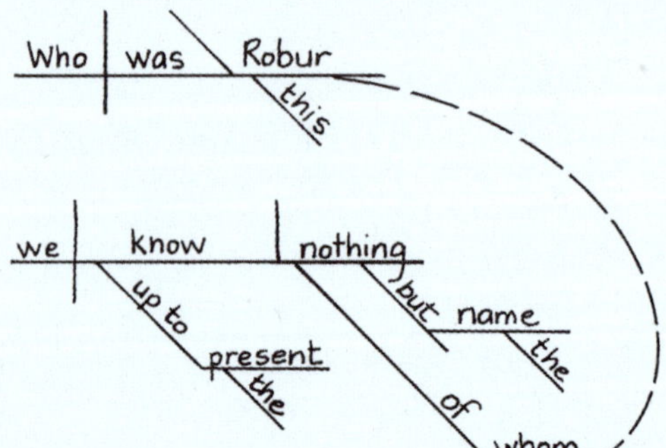

The prisoners, although they did not understand how the help had come to them, broke their bonds, while the soldiers were firing at the aeronef.

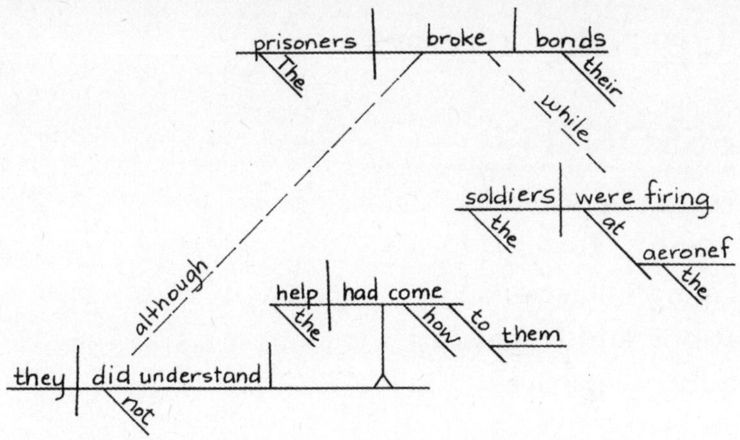

Rewards were offered to whoever would give news of the three absentees, and even to those who would find some clue to put the police on the track.

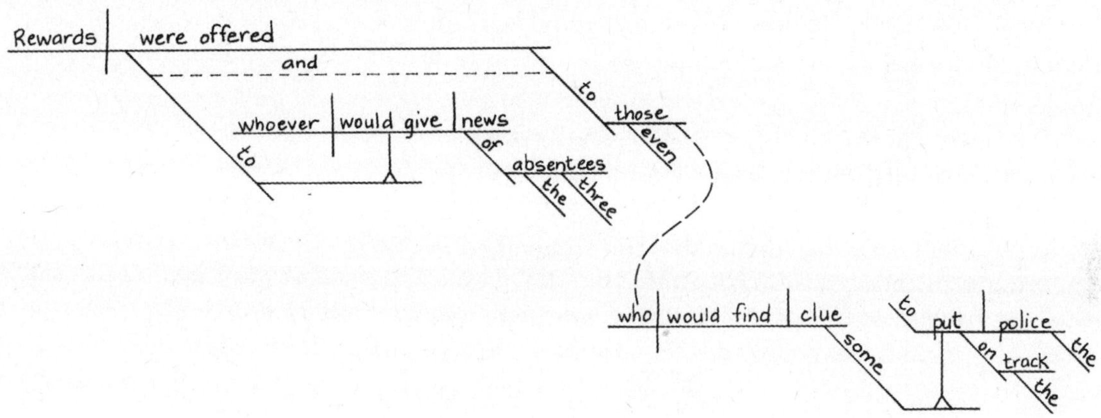

When she reached Port Famine the *Albatross* resumed her course to the south.

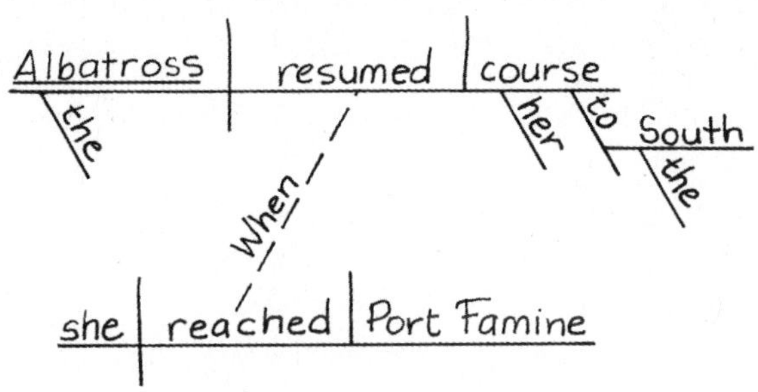

WEEK 31

Filling Up the Corners

— LESSON 117 —

Interrogative Adverbs
Noun Clauses
Forming Questions
Affirmations and Negations
Double Negatives

Exercise 117A: Identifying Adverbs, Interrogative and Demonstrative Pronouns and Adjectives, and Relatives

In the following sentences from Roald Dahl's *James and the Giant Peach*, follow these steps:

a) Label each bolded word as one of the following:

ADV for adverb.
Draw an arrow from the adverb to the word modified.
If the adverb also introduces a clause, underline the clause.

PRO for pronoun.
If the pronoun has an antecedent, label the antecedent as *ANT*.
If the pronoun introduces a clause, underline the clause.
Label each pronoun as *S* for subject, *PN* for predicate nominative, *DO* for direct object, *IO* for indirect object, or *OP* for object of the preposition.

ADJ for adjective.
Draw an arrow from the adjective to the word modified.
If the adjective introduces a clause, underline the clause.

N for noun.
Label the noun as *S*, *PN*, *DO*, *IO*, or *OP*.

b) Label each underlined clause as *ADV-C* for adverb clause, *ADJ-C* for adjective clause, or *N-C* for noun clause.

c) Draw an arrow from each *ADV-C* and *ADJ-C* clause to the word modified. Label each *N-C* noun clause as *S* for subject, *DO* for direct object, *IO* for indirect object, or *OP* for object of the preposition.

The first is done for you.

PRO S
But **who's** telling this story anyway?

PRO OP ADJ
And don't whisper a word of **this** to **those** two horrible aunts of yours!

ADV ADV ADV-C ANT PRO OP ADJ-C ADV

Then at last, **when** it had become nearly as tall as the tree **that** it was growing on, as tall and wide, in fact, as a small house, the bottom part of it gently touched the ground—and **there** it rested.

> **Note to Instructor:** *that it was growing* on is an adjective clause, modifying *tree,* within the longer adverbial clause *when it had become . . . small house,* modifying *touched.* The word *that* is a relative pronoun referring back to *tree*; it introduces the adjective clause, and within that clause, it serves as the object of the preposition *on.* (The prepositional phrase *on that* is adverbial and modifies the verb *growing* (it was growing where? *on that*).

N OP ADJ

And meanwhile I wish you'd come over **here** and give me a hand with **these** boots.

> **Note to Instructor:** The adverb *here* functions as a noun—the entire prepositional phrase *over* [preposition] *here* [object of the preposition] functions as an adverb and modifies *come.*

ADV N-C DO

He can't see **how** splendid I look.

PRO S ADV ANT PRO S ADJ-C N-C DO

That is **why** people **who** travel in airplanes never see anything.

> **Note to Instructor:** The entire noun clause *why people . . . see anything* functions as a predicate nominative renaming *That.* Within the noun clause, the adjective clause *who travel in airplanes* modifies *people.*

PRO S ADV N-C DO

"And **who** knows **where** it will end," muttered the Earthworm, "if *you* have anything to do with it."

ADV ADV-C ADV

He stopped **when** he was about three yards away, and he stood **there** leaning on his stick and staring hard at James.

ADV

Then **why** did we start sinking?

ADV

Where, for example, do you think that I keep my ears?

> **Note to Instructor:** This is a tricky sentence! The word *where* belongs to the subordinate clause *that I keep my ears,* but it is separated from it and does not actually introduce it. To see the structure of the sentence more clearly, it may be helpful to remove the absolute construction "for example" and reword the sentence as a statement instead of a question: "You do think that I keep my ears **where**." This makes it easier to see that *that I keep my ears where* is a noun clause serving as the direct object of the verb *think. That* is a subordinating conjunction introducing the clause, and *where* is an adverb modifying *keep.*

Exercise 117B: Forming Questions

On your own paper, rewrite the following statements as questions.

Use each of the three methods for forming questions (adding an interrogative pronoun, reversing the subject and helping verb, adding the helping verb *do*, *does*, or *did* in front of the subject and adjusting the tense of the main verb) at least once. You may change tenses, add or subtract words, or alter the statements in any other necessary ways, as long as the meaning remains the same.

These statements are all adapted from famous questions in books and movies. When you have transformed your statements into questions, compare them with the originals.

Note to Instructor: The student's questions do not need to be identical to the originals, but each question should be grammatically correct, and each method should be used at least once.

STATEMENT	QUESTION
You solve a problem like Maria in some way.	How do you solve a problem like Maria? *The Sound of Music*
It is secret. It is safe. [two questions]	Is it secret? Is it safe? *The Fellowship of the Ring*
She even has that lever.	Why does she even have that lever? *The Emperor's New Groove*
You are crying.	Are you crying? *A League of Their Own*
There is somebody else in this house.	Is there anybody else in this house? *Clue*
You have considered piracy.	Have you ever considered piracy? *The Princess Bride*
Your dog is wearing glasses.	Why is your dog wearing glasses? *Meet the Robinsons*
When you got a hundred voices singing, someone can hear a lousy whistle blow.	When you got a hundred voices singing, who can hear a lousy whistle blow? *Newsies*
You are telling me that you built a time machine out of a DeLorean.	Are you telling me that you built a time machine out of a DeLorean? *Back to the Future*
You would do something with a brain if you had one.	What would you do with a brain if you had one? *The Wizard of Oz*
The name of his other leg is something.	What's the name of his other leg? *Mary Poppins*

Exercise 117C: Affirmations and Negations

On your own paper, rewrite each of the following statements.

- Change affirmative statements into negations, using one adverb or adjective of negation. You may add or subtract words or change tenses as necessary.
- Change negative statements into affirmatives, using at least one adverb of affirmation.
- Change double negations into affirmatives, also using at least one adverb of affirmation.

When you are finished, compare your answers with the original sentences, adapted from *Beeton's Book of Poultry and Domestic Animals.*

Note to Instructor: The student's answers do not need to be identical to the original sentences, as long as the guidelines above are followed. Check to see that the student has included adverbs or adjectives of affirmation and negation in each sentence; these are bolded in the original sentences below.

ASSIGNED SENTENCES	ORIGINAL VERSIONS
Small stones or pebbles are not essential to the existence of fowls.	Small stones or pebbles are, of course, **absolutely** essential to the existence of fowls.
A person dared venture within the line of devastation.	**No** person dared venture within the line of devastation.
The turtle dove will not take advantage of the door of its cage or aviary being left open to escape.	The turtle dove will almost **certainly** take advantage of the door of its cage or aviary being left open to escape.
They're not quick in none of their movements.	They are **very** quick in their movements.
A well-behaved bird may tumble.	A well-behaved bird **never** tumbles.
Handle the pups during the first week more than is necessary.	Do**n't** handle the pups during the first week any more than is necessary.
The impatience which prompted the purchase will not manifest itself now that the longed-for treasure is obtained.	The impatience which prompted the purchase will **surely** manifest itself now that the longed-for treasure is obtained.
There seems to be something of use or value in these unusual characteristics.	There does **not** seem to be anything of use or value in these unusual characteristics.

— LESSON 118 —

Diagramming Affirmations and Negations
Yet More Words That Can Be Multiple Parts of Speech
Comparisons Using *Than*
Comparisons Using *As*

Exercise 118A: Identifying Parts of Speech

Label each of the bolded words in these sentences (from A. A. Milne's *The Red House Mystery*) with one of the following abbreviations.

ADJ: adjective	ADV: adverb
ADV-N: adverb of negation	ADV-A: adverb of affirmation
ADV-R: relative adverb	SC: subordinating conjunction
PREP: preposition	RP: relative pronoun
DP: demonstrative pronoun	P: plain ol' pronoun
N: noun	

Where a subordinating conjunction introduces a comparison clause with missing words, draw a caret and insert the missing words.

SC DP
But, as soon as Antony suggested trying the windows, Cayley saw **that that** was the obvious thing to do.

ADV SC
"Well," he said eagerly, **as** he sat **down** to the business of the meal, "what are we going to do this morning?"

ADV-N ADV ADV
If he **never** went into the office at all, then **where** is he **now**?

ADV RP ADV-N
Bill was silent, wondering **how** to put into words thoughts **which** had **never** formed themselves
ADV-A ADV-A
very definitely in his own mind.

P P
I was never the **one** to pretend to be **what** I wasn't.

ADV-A P
You asked me to be **quite** frank, you know, and tell you **what** I thought.

> **Note to Instructor:** The subordinate clause *what I thought* is the direct object of the verb *tell* (*you* is the indirect object). *What* is the direct object of *thought*. I have classified it simply as a pronoun, not a relative pronoun, because it doesn't refer back to a word in the main clause.

ADJ RP RP
He was supposed, by his patron and **any** others **who** inquired, to be "writing"; but **what** he wrote,
ADV-N
other than letters asking for more time to pay, has **never** been discovered.

ADV PREP
Audrey threaded a needle, held her hand **out** and looked **at** her nails critically for a moment, and
ADV
then began to sew.

ADV P SC
Why did Mark need to change from brown to blue, or **whatever** it was, **when** Cayley was the only
RP
person **who** saw him in brown?

> **Note to Instructor:** *When* is not acting as an adverb because it does not express the idea of *time*—instead, it expresses a condition. If the student is confused, ask him to substitute *if* for *when*, and point out that the sentence still makes sense.

SC ADV ADV
As he came **down** the drive and approached the old red-brick front of the house, **there** was a lazy murmur of bees in the flower-borders, a gentle cooing of pigeons in the tops of the elms, and from distant lawns the whir of a mowing-machine.

ADJ P
He had a sponge in **one** hand, a handkerchief in the **other**.

SC PREP
Miss Norris was hurried away **because** she knew **about** the secret passage.

ADV-A RP ADV ADV ADV-A
The window was open, and he felt **very** sorry for the owner of it all, **who** was **now** mixed **up** in **so** grim a business.

ADV SC are interesting ADV
Anyway, biographies are just **as** interesting **as** most novels^; so **why** linger?

Exercise 118B: Diagramming

On your own paper, diagram every word of the following sentences from A. A. Milne's *The Sunny Side.* Ask your instructor for help if you need it.

Yes, dear reader, you are right.

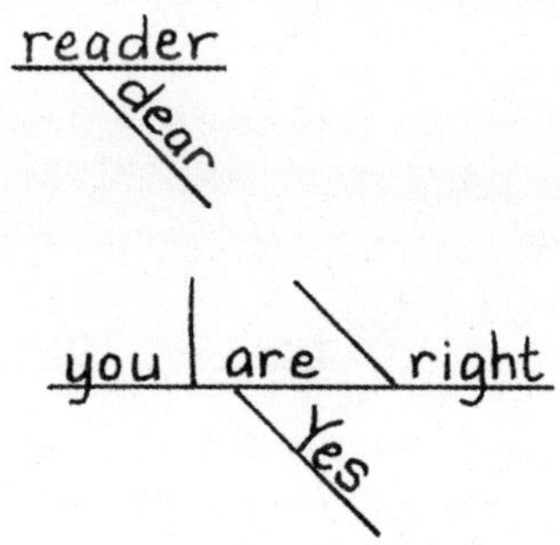

And if the young dramatist answers callously, "Yes," it simply shows that he has no feeling for the stage whatever.

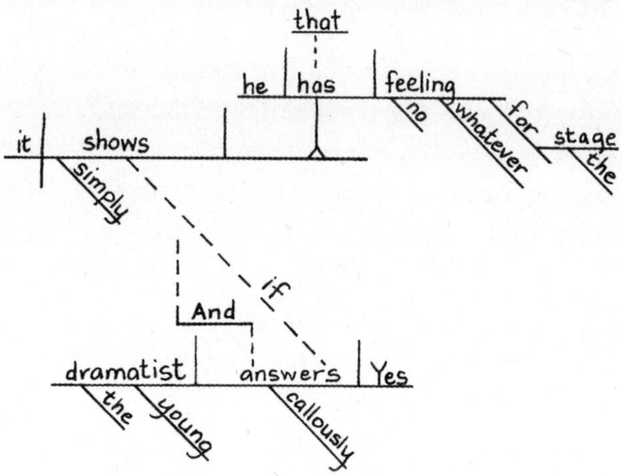

No, I have had enough of writing in the Army and I never want to sign my own name again.

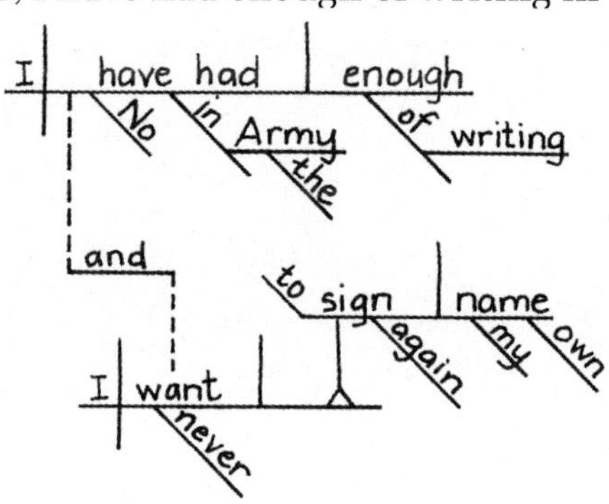

What you want to do is to write a really long letter to Mrs. Cardew, acquainting her with all the facts.

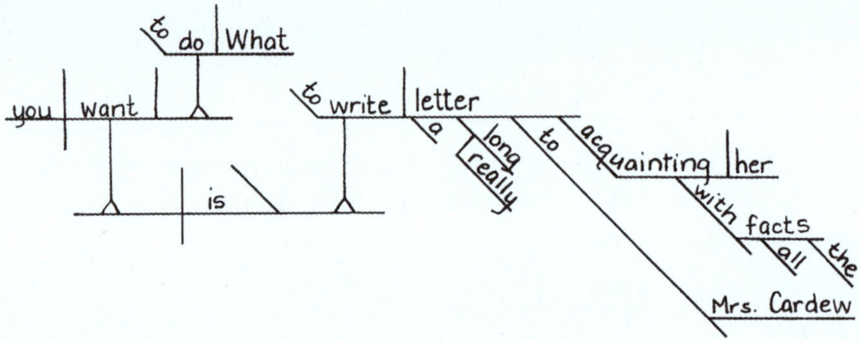

When we arrive you will introduce us as your friends, Mr. and Mrs. Mannering.

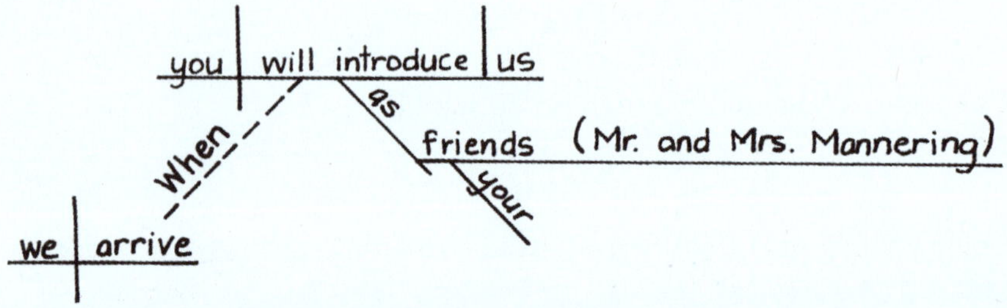

Note to Instructor: The phrase *as your friends* is adverbial (rather than modifying *friends*) because it answers the question *How?*.

For we cannot listen always for that FLOP, and hear it always; nothing in this world is as inevitable as that.

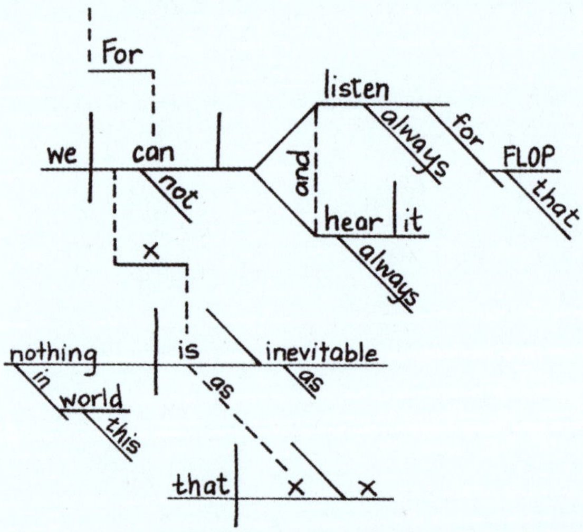

Note to Instructor: The understood clause is *that [is][inevitable]*.

Yes, he was to be a writer; there could be no doubt about that.

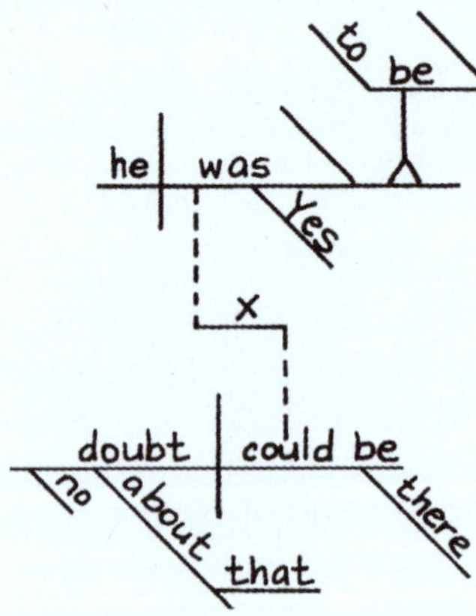

— LESSON 119 —

Idioms

> **Note to Instructor:** The dialogue from the Core Instructor Text is continued here, in the Answer Key, so that instructor and student can study different idioms each year.
>
> If the student is unfamiliar with any idiom covered, provide the meaning.

Instructor: We can divide idioms into two types. In the first type, all of the words in the idiom are serving a clear, familiar grammatical function—but the idiom itself means something completely different than its literal meaning. The next sentences in your workbook are this type of idiom. Read me the first sentence.

Student: *Kerensa found the dress quite ugly but decided to* ***hold her tongue****.*

Instructor: The verb *decide* can be transitive. If you say, for example, "I decided to eat my vegetables" the infinitive phrase *to eat my vegetables* is the direct object of the verb *decide*. It is the thing that you decided.

The infinitive phrase *to hold her tongue* is also the direct object of the verb *decide*. It is the thing Kerensa decided. But she probably wasn't grabbing her tongue and holding onto it. What does *hold your tongue mean*?

Student: *To stay quiet* OR *to not say anything.*

Instructor: Put your right index finger on the diagram of I *decided to eat my vegetables* and your left index finger on the diagram of *to hold her tongue*. Do they look the same?

Student: *Yes.*

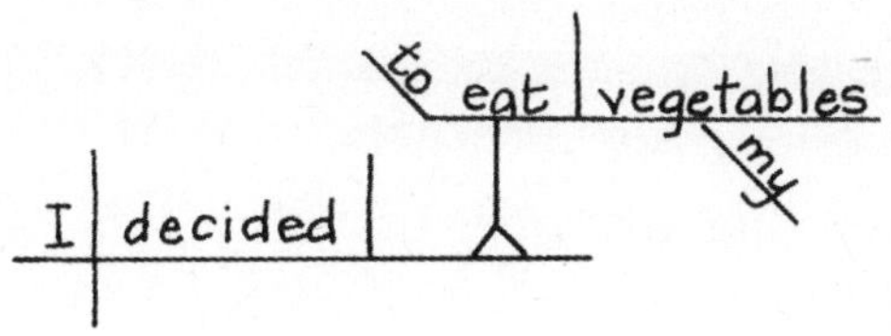

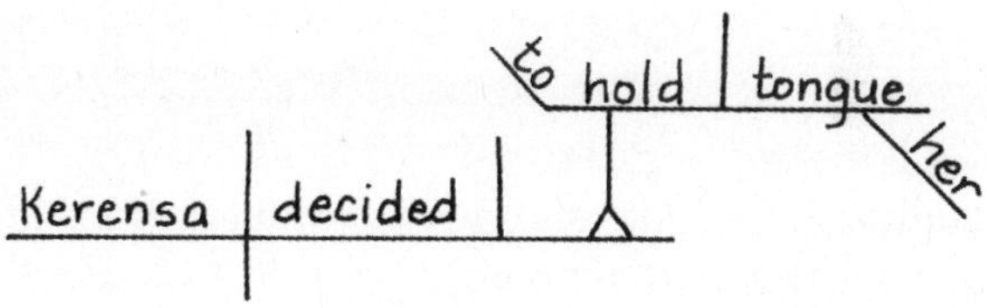

Instructor: Except for the fact that you wouldn't ever grab onto your tongue and hold it, the idiom works just like any other transitive verb with an infinitive phrase as the direct object. Read me the next sentence.

Student: *For Diana's surprise party, we'll have a big cake, party hats,* ***the whole nine yards****.*

Instructor: Diana is getting a literal cake and literal party hats for her surprise party. Is she also getting nine yards?

Student: *No.*

Instructor: What does *the whole nine yards* mean?

Student: *As much as possible* OR *the full extent of party supplies and activities* OR *[something similar].*

Instructor: Put the sentence on the frame in your workbook.

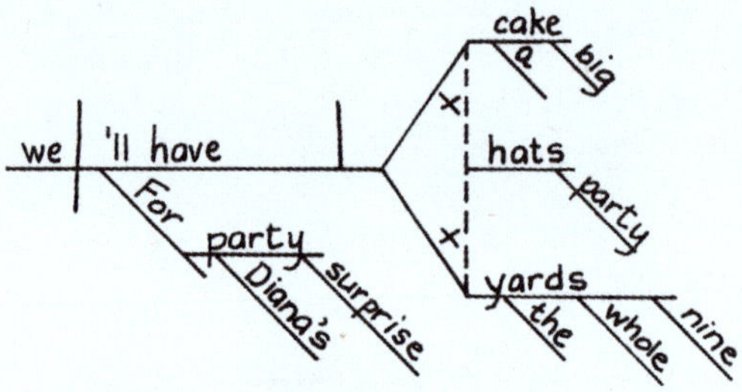

Instructor: If you can diagram an idiom without any trouble, you know that it has regular grammar—even if it has an unusual meaning.

The second type of idiom uses combinations of words that might not fit into the patterns you've already learned. Read me the next sentence.

Student: *Did I just say that **out loud**?*

Instructor: Underline the subject once and the predicate twice.

Did I just say that out loud?

Instructor: *Just* is an adverb modifying *did say*. But how about *loud*? It's an adjective, so it can't modify a verb. In this sentence, though, it is combined with *out* to form a single compound adverb describing *how* something was said: It was said so that everyone could hear. Usually, you wouldn't be able to diagram an adjective such as *loud* beneath the predicate—but when the two words *out* and *loud* are combined, they become an idiom that functions as an adverb. Diagram this sentence onto the frame in your workbook.

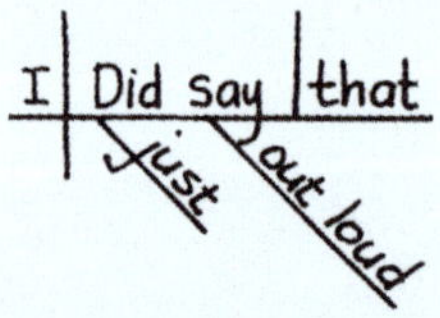

Instructor: Let's look at another example of an idiom working as a single part of speech. Read me the next sentence.

Student: *I would like to **make sure** we're **on the same page**.*

Instructor: Look at the partial diagram in your workbook.

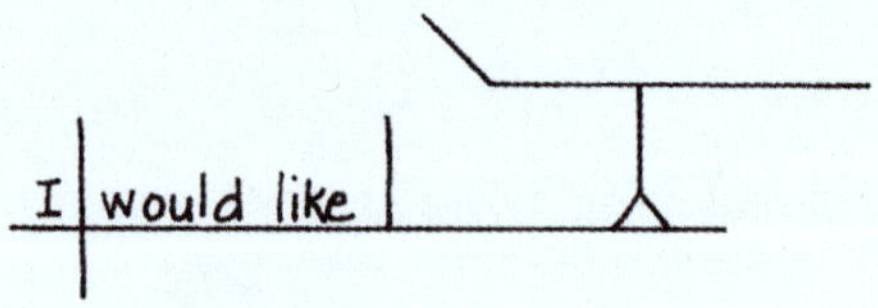

Instructor: What are the subject and predicate of the sentence?

Student: *I would like.*

Instructor: *To make sure* is the direct object of the verb *like*. But what is the actual infinitive?

> **Note to Instructor:** If the student responds, "To make," point out that *sure* then has to function as the object. Ask, "Why can't *sure* be an object?" The answer: *Sure* is an adjective. Offer the student the sentences *I am sure* and *It is a sure thing*, and ask, "What part of speech is *sure* in these sentences?" (predicate adjective in the first, attributive adjective in the second).
>
> *To sure* is nonsensical, but if the student suggests this, ask him to construct a sentence with *suring* as the predicate.

Instructor: *Make sure* is an idiom that serves as a single verb. You can't separate *make* and *sure*, because both words would change meaning.

What is the second idiom in the sentence?

Student: *On the same page.*

Instructor: What does it mean?

Student: *We agree with each other.*

Instructor: *On the same page* is a simple prepositional phrase—but with a difference. It follows a linking verb and describes the subject. That is the definition of what part of speech?

Student: *Predicate adjective.*

Instructor: There is no good way to diagram a prepositional phrase as a predicate adjective—because prepositional phrases that aren't idioms never act like predicate adjectives! Instead, you would diagram the phrase *on the same page* all on the same line, as a single predicate adjective.

Using the partial frame in your workbook, try to complete the diagram of the sentence now. Here's a hint: *To make sure* is an idiom serving as a *transitive* verb.

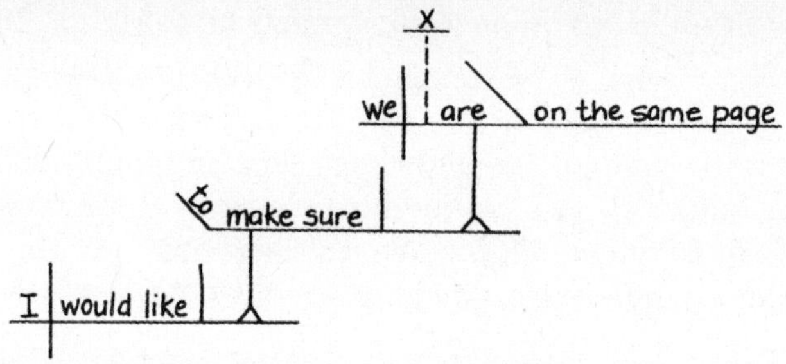

Note to Instructor: If the student becomes frustrated, show her the answer above.

Instructor: Instead of diagramming the next three sentences, we'll circle the idioms. See if you can find them yourself.

As a rule of thumb, the pH of an aquarium should be between 6.5 and 8 for fresh water.
—Terry Fairfield, *A Common Sense Guide to Fish*

Note to Instructor: It is acceptable for the student to circle the entire phrase *As a rule of thumb.*

I had an ugly dream, which I can't remember. I went to pieces. I don't know what came over me.

—J. R. R. Tolkien, *The Fellowship of the Ring*

We've got you dead to rights, so no monkey business.
—George Barr, *Anderson Crow, Detective*

Instructor: In the first sentence, *rule of thumb* means *a basic principle, a general guideline. Rule of thumb* has the sense of "something you do usually, but there might be exceptions." In the entire phrase *As a rule of thumb*, what part of speech is the word *as*?

Note to Instructor: If the student has trouble identifying *as*, give her the answer.

Student: Preposition.

Instructor: In this case, you could diagram the idiom like any other prepositional phrase. It modifies the verb *should be*, rule is the object of the preposition, and *of thumb* modifies *rule*.

In the second sentence, *went to pieces* functions as a single verb. What happens when you go to pieces?

Student: *You lose your self-control [cannot function normally, collapse, malfunction, become insane]*

> **Note to Instructor:** If the student answers with another idiom, such as *fall apart*, *come unglued*, *flip*, or *lose it*, point out that these too are idioms. Work with the student until she comes up with a more literal definition. This is a complex idiom because it describes a mental state. (*Freak out* is also an idiom.)

Instructor: The verb *went* and the prepositional phrase *to pieces* mean something completely different if you separate them, so *went to pieces* is an idiom acting like one verb meaning *collapse* or *malfunction*.

The final sentence has two idioms in it! The phrase *dead to rights* means *absolutely, without question*. It's almost always used with the verbs *get* or *have*. You get someone dead to rights, or you have someone dead to rights. Together with the verb, the idiom means that they are guilty of something, and there's no way they can argue innocence.

The phrase *so no monkey business* has two complications. First, *so* is actually a subordinating conjunction introducing a clause with understood elements. The missing words are *you must not try*. What's the problem with inserting those words? Try putting them in and see how it sounds.

you shouldn't try

We've got you dead to rights so ^ no monkey business

—George Barr, *Anderson Crow, Detective*

Student: *It's a double negative.*

Instructor: Second, what is *monkey business*?

Student: *Something illegal [something unusual, fighting back, resisting].*

Instructor: What kind of business?

Student: *Monkey.*

Instructor: What part of speech is *monkey*?

Student: *A noun.*

Instructor: *Monkey* modifies *business*, but it's a noun, not an adjective! A noun can't modify another noun. So you wouldn't try to separate these words—*monkey business* together functions as a single word.

You also probably wouldn't try to diagram that last sentence, because it's an example of what's called *colloquial speech*—a way people talk to each other that really doesn't follow grammatical rules. But the sentences in your exercises are grammatical, so finish them now.

Exercise 119A: Identifying Idioms

Circle each complete idiom in the following sets of sentences. (Sometimes, more than one sentence has been provided for context.) There is one obvious idiom in each set, but you may find others.

Write the meaning of each idiom above it in your own words. (You can use more than one word!) The first is done for you.

You will notice that the last set of sentences is from a play. Instead of having traditional dialogue tags such as "he said" or "she answered," the sentences are preceded by the name of the speaker in all capitals, followed by a period. Play dialogue can also be written so that the speaker's name is bolded or italicized and is followed by a colon, like this:

Note to Instructor: If the student cannot find at least one idiom in each set of sentences, point the idiom(s) out and ask the student to describe (or act out) its literal meaning. Encourage the student to include helping verbs when idioms contain a verb. If the student cannot explain the meaning of the idiom, allow her to look it up in a print or online reference tool; idioms are often listed in dictionaries under the first or primary word in the idiom.

The definitions below are suggestions; any explanation that carries a similar meaning is acceptable.

Remember that identifying idioms is not an exact science! Some of the idioms below are very close to the literal meanings of the words. As long as the student finds one idiom in each set of sentences, accept the answer but also point out the additional idiomatic expressions.

progress normally / a lot of turnips

If you plant a couple of turnips and let nature (take its course) you'll have turnips (all over the place)

this always happens

With good things (it were always thus)

a problem

There is always (a fly in the custard)

contrary to, notwithstanding, in opposition to / in the presence of, in defiance of

(In spite of) his sarcasm, and (in the face of) all criticism, I insist that I was beginning to learn.

—From *That House I Bought: A Little Leaf From Life*, by Henry Edward Warner

She was the youngest of the two daughters of a most affectionate, indulgent father; and had,

because of, as a result of

(in consequence of) her sister's marriage, been mistress of his house from a very early period.

had the desired effect, brought about the result / loves her

Her visit to Abbey-Mill, this summer, seems to have (done his business) He is desperately (in love) and means to marry her.

Note to Instructor: The phrase *in love* occurs twice in this exercise, both times as a prepositional phrase acting as a predicate adjective. It isn't exactly an idiom, since it describes a mental state (these phrases are always difficult to classify) and commonly expresses an emotion that can't be literally defined. However, it isn't incorrect for the student to identify it; just ask him to define *done his business* as well.

Ah! there I am—thinking of him directly. Always the first person to be thought of! How I

discover a truth about myself, realize something about myself

(catch myself out)!

it's almost here

The evening is closing in and grandmama will be looking for us.

in the right company,
given proper attention

Her character depends upon those she is with; but in good hands she will turn out a valuable woman.

agree to,
be willing to
help her,
let her lean on you

I am sure if Jane is tired, you will be so kind as to give her your arm.

> **Note to Instructor:** The phrase "so kind as to" is a common one. When diagrammed, *so kind as* should be diagrammed as a single predicate adjective, with the following infinitive (in this case, *to give*) diagrammed as an adverb modifying the predicate adjective.

loves someone
escape the worst consequences of

I shall do very well again after a little while—and then, it will be a good thing over; for they say everybody is in love once in their lives, and I shall have been let off easily.

> **Note to Instructor**: For *in love*, see previous page.

assigning little or no importance to something

It was adventuring too far, assuming too much, making light of what ought to be serious, a trick of what ought to be simple.

> **Note to Instructor:** *To make light* is an idiom because there is no actual reduction of weight involved, whereas *adventuring* and *assuming* here carry their literal meanings.

support, be on the same side as

No, indeed, I shall grant you nothing. I always take the part of my own sex.

—From *Emma*, by Jane Austen

So what? Why is this important?

THE MOTHER. Yes, and what of it? You are always asking all sorts of questions, and in that way you spoil the better part of your life—There is Lena, now.

This is difficult.

MASTER OF Q. Yes, it comes hard. But here every one must stop who hails from plague-stricken places.

now that I reconsider

THE OFFICER. But she will come—She will come! [*Walks up and down*] But come to think of it,

this is my final conclusion,
now that I've considered everything else

perhaps I had better call off the dinner after all—as it is late?

> **Note to Instructor:** *After all* is such a common idiom that it almost doesn't qualify for idiom status any more—but it doesn't mean *after everything else*, so it does carry a meaning that isn't exactly literal. It is bolded here in case the student identifies it; if she does, ask her to also find the second idiom in the speech.

enjoy, prefer

MASTER OF Q. I wish often that I could forget—especially myself. That is why I go in for masquerades and carnivals and amateur theatricals.

—From *The Dream Play*, by August Strindberg

Exercise 119B: Diagramming

On your own paper, diagram every word of the following sentences.

These sentences are taken from Marie Brennan's novel *A Natural History of Dragons: A Memoir by Lady Kent.*

dined at house
Whether he dined at our house, or we^at his^, we talked of little else, and the earl made good on his promise (or perhaps threat) to pick my brain about my readings.

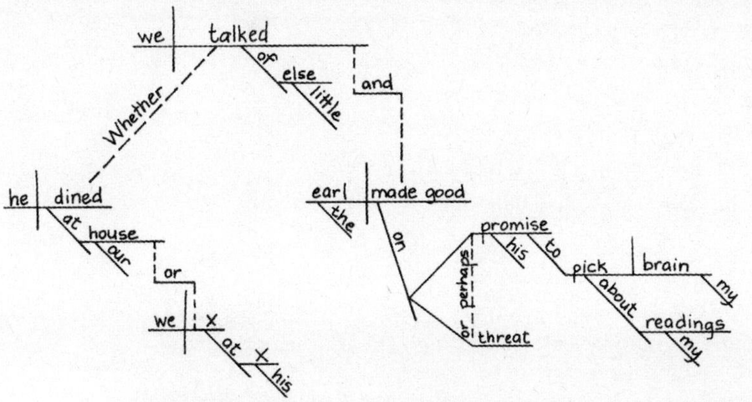

Note to Instructor: The second subordinate clause contains understood elements which are diagrammed as Xs, and which are inserted above for your reference. *Promise* and *threat* are diagrammed as double objects of the preposition *on*, linked by the semicoordinator *or perhaps*. It is also correct to diagram *or perhaps threat* as a parenthetical expression. In that case, *promise* becomes the single object of the preposition *on* (with *to pick my brain about my readings* diagrammed exactly as above), and the parenthetical expression could appear like this:

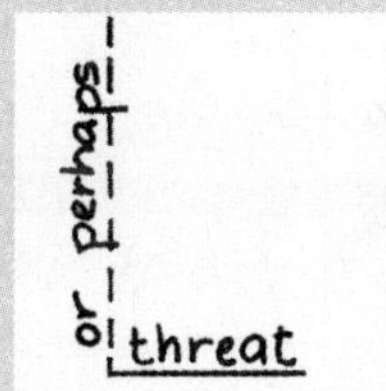

The phrase *made good* operates as a single verb. If the student diagrams *good* as the direct object of *made*, accept the answer but show him the diagram and point out that *make good* is an idiom serving as the single verb *fulfill* or *complete*.

The idiom *pick my brain* can be diagrammed grammatically.

The astute among you will have noticed that almost all of my expeditions have been to the warmer regions of the world: Akhia, the Broken Sea, and so forth.

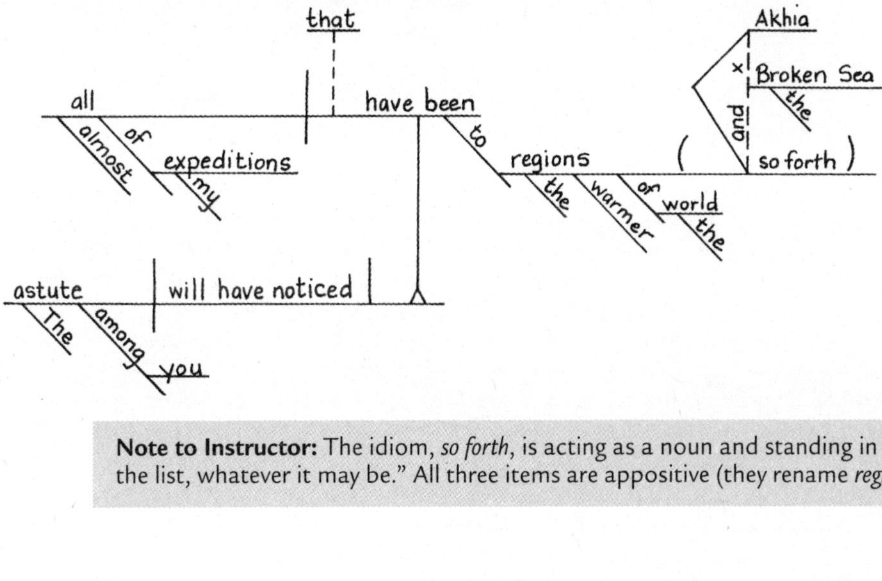

Note to Instructor: The idiom, *so forth*, is acting as a noun and standing in for "the next item in the list, whatever it may be." All three items are appositive (they rename *regions*).

Come to that, Astimir had "found" the first print, behind our house; he'd even been the one to cry out the monster's name, setting everyone's thoughts in the proper direction.

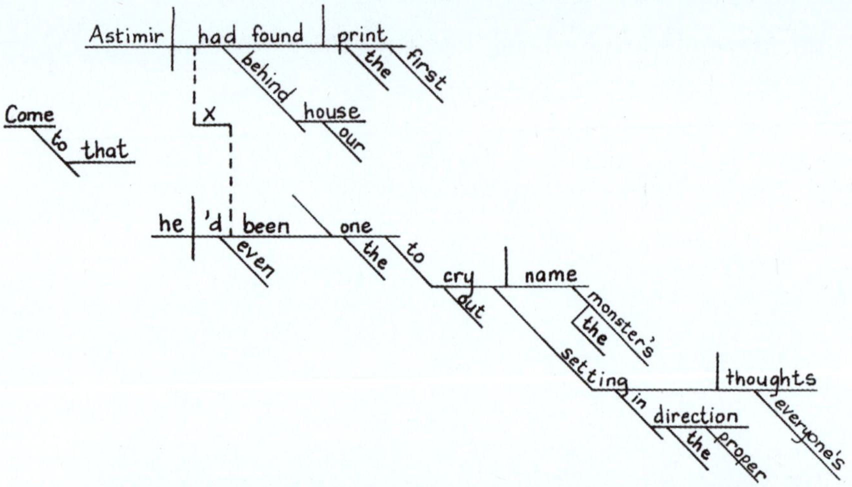

> **Note to Instructor:** *Come to that* is an idiomatic expression equivalent to *in fact*. In this sentence, it is parenthetical because it doesn't have a grammatical relationship with another part of the sentence.

Crawling in a dress, for those gentlemen who have never had occasion to try it, is an exercise in frustration, all but guaranteed to produce feelings of homicidal annoyance in the crawler.

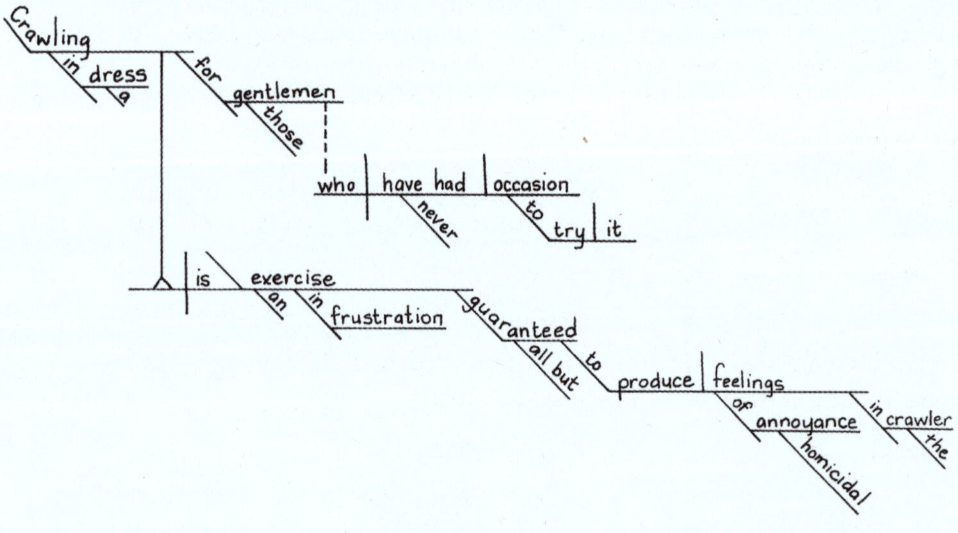

— LESSON 120 —

Troublesome Sentences

Exercise 120A: A Selection of Oddly Constructed Sentences

After your instructor discusses each sentence with you, diagram it on your own paper.

> **Note to Instructor:** For each sentence, go through the dialogue provided and then ask the student to diagram the sentence before moving on to the next. Prompt the student for answers as necessary.

Instructor: Let's start with a fairly simple sentence. The first sentence in your workbook comes from the memoir of Frederick Douglass. He was born as a slave in 1818 and escaped from slavery in 1838. Once he was free, he became a strong voice for abolition—outlawing slavery. Read the sentence out loud now.

Student: *Freedom now appeared, to disappear no more forever.*

Instructor: What are the subject and predicate of the main clause?

Student: *Freedom appeared.*

Instructor: *Now* is simply an adverb modifying *appeared.*

Let's look at the second part of the sentence: *to disappear no more forever.* It has two ambiguous parts! First, the infinitive *to disappear* could be describing freedom, but it is simpler to take it as an adverbial phrase describing *appeared.* How does freedom appear? *To disappear no more forever.* So although it would not be incorrect to diagram the phrase below *freedom,* we'll diagram it below *appeared.*

The three adverbs *no more forever* are also a little tricky. *No* clearly modifies *more.* What does *forever* modify?

Student: *To disappear.*

Instructor: How about *more*?

> **Note to Instructor:** It isn't clear whether *more* modifies *forever* or *to disappear.* Whichever answer the student gives, point out that *more* can also modify the other option.

Instructor: Together, the phrase *no more forever* makes perfect sense—it means that freedom will never disappear. But when you pull the three words apart, they become a little bit unclear! When you diagram this sentence, you can choose three different ways to place those three adverbs on the diagram. Diagram it now in the best way you can, and then I'll show you the other two options.

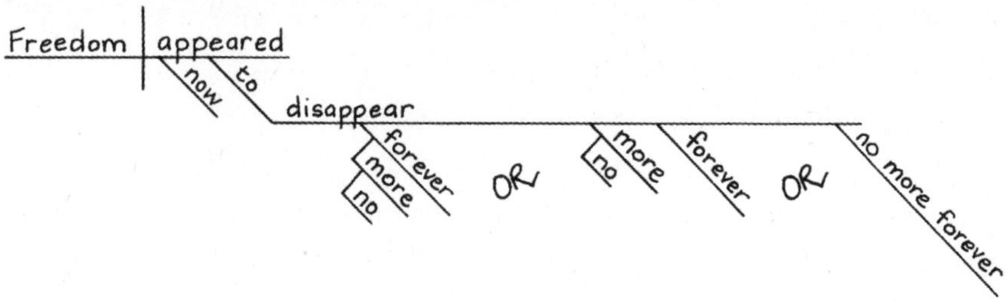

> **Note to Instructor:** When the student is finished, show her the diagram above and point out the three options for diagramming *no more forever.*

Instructor: Your second sentence is from a speech made in 1789 by the British politician William Wilberforce. He was arguing, in the British House of Commons, that slavery should be abolished in Britain. Read the sentence out loud.

Student: *Let this enlightened country take precedence in this noble cause, and we shall soon find that France is not backward to follow, nay, perhaps to accompany our steps.*

Instructor: What kind of sentence is *Let this enlightened country take precedence in this noble cause*? If you can't remember, look back at Lesson 109 in Week 29.

Student: *It is a hortative verb.*

Instructor: In Lesson 109, you learned that when you diagram a hortative sentence, you put an *x* in the subject space. Where does *let* go?

Student: *In the predicate space.*

Instructor: The main verb, *take*, goes up on a tree in the object complement space. What is the direct object of *take*?

Student: *Precedence.*

Instructor: What prepositional phrase modifies *precedence*?

Student: *In this noble cause.*

Instructor: What demonstrative adjective modifies *country*?

Student: *This.*

Instructor: What past participle modifies *country*?

Student: *Enlightened.*

Instructor: That's all fairly simple! Let's look at the second independent clause. It is linked to the first independent clause by the coordinating conjunction *and*. Read me the entire second independent clause.

Student: *We shall soon find that France is not backward to follow, nay, perhaps to accompany our steps.*

Instructor: That independent clause contains a subordinate clause. This entire sentence contains two independent clauses and a subordinate clause. What do we call this kind of sentence?

Student: *Compound complex.*

> **Note to Instructor:** If the student cannot remember, ask her to turn back to Lesson 80.

Instructor: The subordinate clause beginning *that France is not backward* is an object. What is it the object of?

Student: *The verb* shall find.

Instructor: The clause describes the thing being found, so it serves as a direct object. Within the clause what does *backward* describe?

Student: *France.*

Instructor: Usually, *backward* is an adverb, but in this sentence it serves as a predicate adjective. Two infinitive phrases describe *backward*. What are they?

Student: To follow *and* to accompany.

Instructor: *To follow* and *to accompany* what?

Student: *Steps.*

Instructor: *Steps* is actually the object of both infinitives. It is understood to follow both. So you would diagram it after one of the infinitives, and then place an *x* in the direct object space after the other infinitive to show that *steps* is understood to follow it as well.

Now let's look at *nay, perhaps*. *Perhaps* describes *one* of the infinitives. Which one?

Student: *To accompany.*

Instructor: France will definitely follow, but only *perhaps* accompany. So *perhaps* here acts as an adverb meaning *maybe* and modifying *to accompany.*

Nay is an old fashioned way to say *no*, so usually it acts as an adverb of negation. But in this sentence it's doing something odd. It connects the two infinitives together—so it is acting not like an adverb, but like a coordinating conjunction.

Do your best to diagram the sentence now, and then we'll compare it to the diagram I have here.

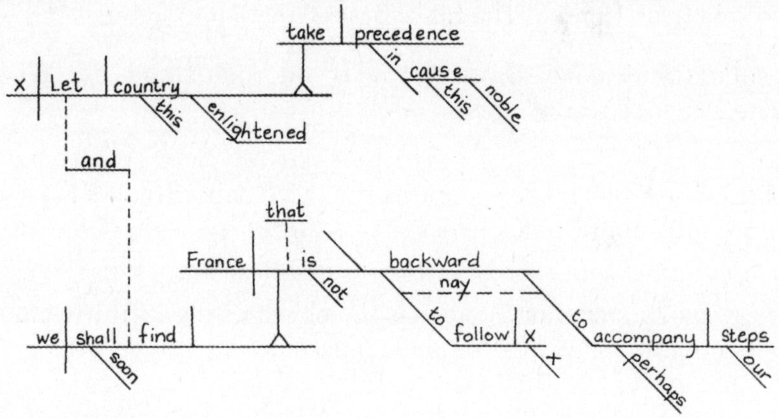

Instructor: Your next sentence isn't complicated—but it does have an unusual idiom in it. Read it out loud now.

Student: Hence he had made himself out of whole cloth a life full of complications and drama.

Instructor: *Out of whole cloth* is an expression that means "completely invented" or "made up with no basis in fact." In this sentence, it means that a man has created a lot of problems for himself that didn't really exist.

The expression comes from the days when cloth was very expensive. Tailors would often put a piece of clothing together from previously made items. But for more expensive clothes, they would get down a brand new bolt of cloth that had never been used before. That was called *whole cloth*. So *whole cloth* developed the meaning of something completely new, not based on something that existed before.

This idiom can *almost* be diagrammed grammatically. The adverb *out* and the preposition *of* are actually functioning as a single preposition. If you separate *out* from *of*, it changes meaning. So diagram them together on the preposition line.

Try diagramming the sentence now.

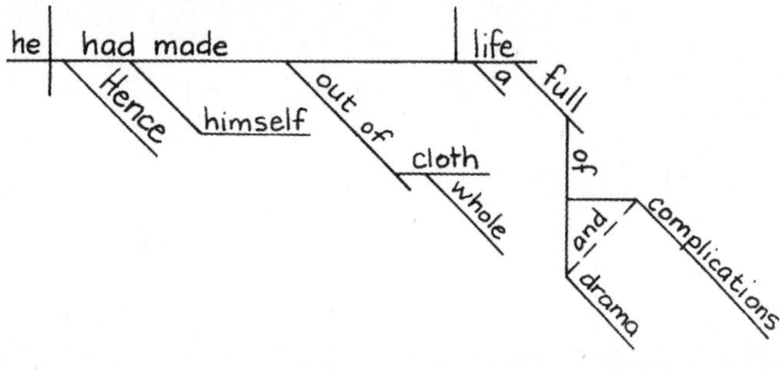

Note to Instructor: *Out of whole cloth* is adverbial because it describes the process of making, rather than the life itself. *Himself* functions as an indirect object. The prepositional phrase of *complications and drama* describes the adjective *full*.

Instructor: Your next sentence is short—but it has a lot of subordinate clauses in it, for a short sentence! How many can you find?

Note to Instructor: The three subordinate clauses are underlined below.

> It is a debt ^(that) we owe to the purity of our religion to show that it is at variance with that law which warrants slavery.
>
> —Patrick Henry, "The Slave Trade" (personal letter, 1773)

Instructor: The first subordinate clause is introduced by an understood *that*. What does the first subordinate clause describe?

Student: *Debt.*

Instructor: The second subordinate clause contains the third subordinate clause within it. What is the entire second subordinate clause?

Student: *That it is at variance with that law which warrants slavery.*

Instructor: The entire second subordinate clause is the object of the infinitive to *show*. What are the subject and predicate of the second clause?

Student: *It is.*

Instructor: The prepositional phrase *at variance* is acting as a predicate nominative, renaming *it*. There are two different uses of *that* within the clause. What is the first *that* functioning as?

Student: *A subordinating conjunction.*

Instructor: How about the second?

Student: *A demonstrative adjective.*

Instructor: What is the third subordinate clause?

Student: *Which warrants slavery.*

Instructor: What does it describe?

Student: *Law.*

Instructor: Diagram the sentence now.

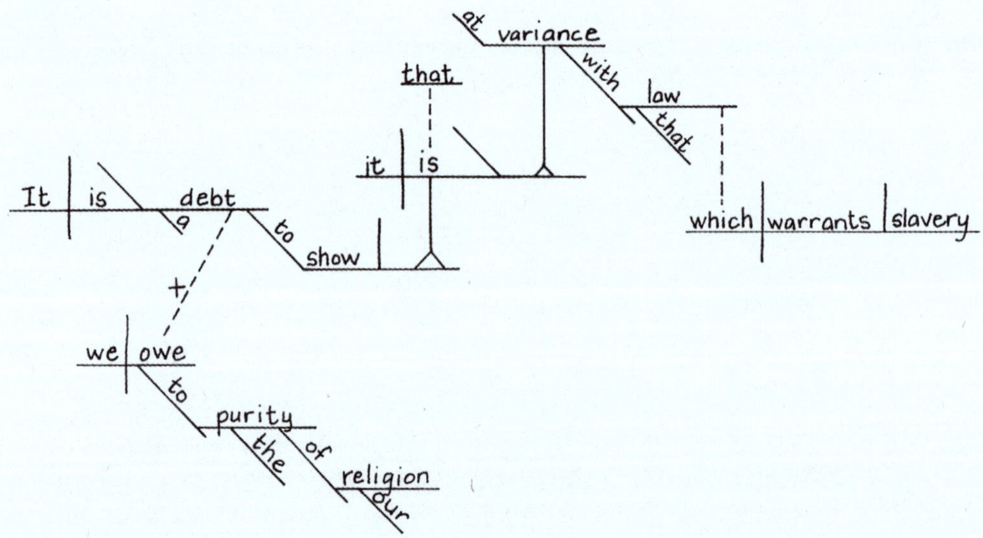

Instructor: Your last sentence is a long one—but it only has *one* subordinate clause in it! Read it out loud now.

Student: *In such a society, also, our private economies will depend less and less upon the private ownership of real, usable property, and more and more upon property that is institutional and abstract, beyond individual control, such as money, insurance policies, certificates of deposit, stocks, and shares.*

Instructor: What are the subject and predicate of the main clause?

Student: *Economies will depend.*

Instructor: This sentence has two different uses of the word *such*. In the introductory phrase, *In such a society*, *such* and *a* are both acting as adjectives. What word do they modify?

Student: *Society.*

Instructor: The entire prepositional phrase answers the question *where* and acts as an adverb, modifying the main predicate. *Also* is an adverb modifying the predicate as well. And the two prepositional phrases *upon the private ownership of real, usable property* and *upon property that is institutional and abstract* also are acting as adverbs and modifying *will depend*. The tricky words are *less and less* and *more and more*. For clarity, you're going to intentionally diagram them in the *wrong* place!

First of all, what parts of speech are *less* and *more*? If you're not sure, listen to these sentences: *I hurried less. I rested more.*

Student: *Adverbs.*

Instructor: *Less and less* and *more and more* are technically adverbs that modify *will depend*. But here's the problem—if you diagram them below *will depend*, they cancel each other out. You depend *less and less* AND *more and more*. Instead, diagram them *beneath* the two things that you are depending less and less on, and more and more on. In that way, the diagram will be a clearer explanation of the what the sentence really means.

Look at the partial diagram in your workbook. *Less and less* is already diagrammed beneath *ownership*. Add *more and more* beneath *property*.

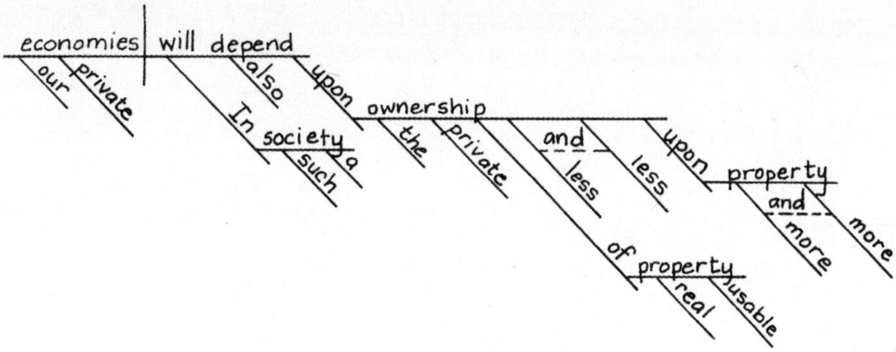

Instructor: The subordinate clause *that is institutional and abstract, beyond individual control, such as money, insurance policies, certificates of deposit, stocks and shares* modifies what noun?

Student: *Property.*

Instructor: This subordinate clause has two odd things in it. First, what *three* words or phrases follow the linking verb *is* and describe *that*?

Student: *Institutional, abstract, beyond individual control.*

Instructor: These three predicate adjectives are made up of two actual adjectives, and one prepositional phrase *acting* like an adjective! All three should be diagrammed on the right-hand side of a slanting predicate adjective line—but the prepositional phrase will need to go up on a little tree.

Second, what does *such as* mean? Can you substitute a single word for *such as*?

Note to Instructor: Prompt the student with the answer if necessary.

Student: *Like.*

Instructor: In this sentence, the expression *such as* works like a single preposition. You would diagram *such as* on one preposition line—with five different objects of the preposition! What are those five objects? (Just one word each.)

Student: *Money, policies, certificates, stocks, shares.*

Instructor. Complete the diagram of the sentence now.

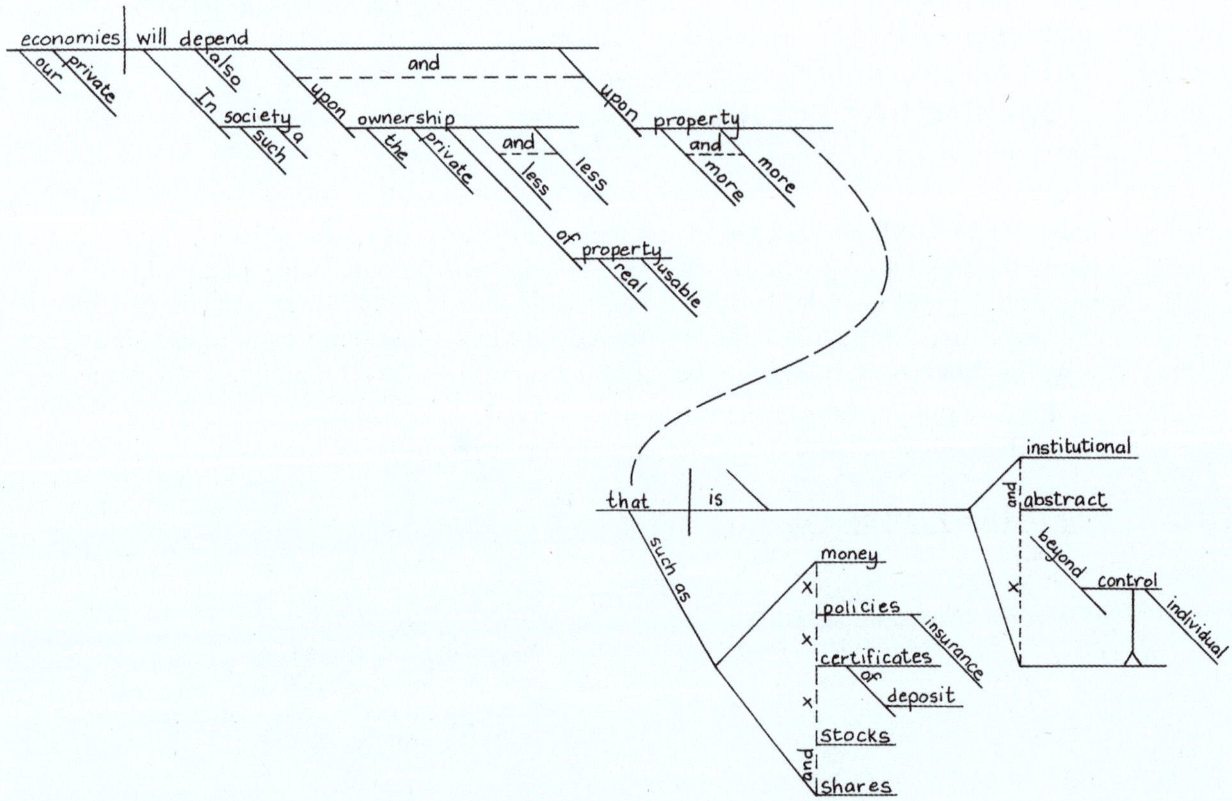

WEEK 32

—REVIEW 10—

Weeks 29-31

Topics
Hortative Verbs
Ambitransitive Verbs
Infinitive Phrases as Objects
Infinitive Phrases With Understood "To"
Principal Parts of Irregular Verbs
Noun Clauses as Appositives
Which/That in Restrictive and Non-Restrictive Clauses
Formal Conditionals
Words Acting as Multiple Parts of Speech
Affirmations and Negations
Idioms

All of the sentences in this exercise are taken from (or slightly adapted from) the 19th-century magazine called *Prairie Farmer: A Weekly Journal for the Farm, Orchard and Fireside*. It first appeared in 1841 and continued to be published from the city of Chicago for the next half-century.

Review 10A: The Missing Words Game

Fill in each blank below with the exact form described—but choose your own words!

Read each word to your instructor, who will insert them into the matching blanks in the short essay in the Key.

Your instructor will then show you the original essay—and your version.

(Verbs are indicative unless another mood is specified.)

Note to Instructor: Write the student's answers in the blanks below. The fill-in-the-blank version of the essay is followed by the original. You may decide which version to show the student first. Ask the student to read the explanatory notes that precede the original.

Bad ___________ (present active participle of transitive verb), which means under-cooking, over-cooking or flavorless cooking, renders food inedible, and ___________ (adjective) food contributes to world shortage.

Fats are wasted in cooking by ___________ (present passive participle) and by not being carefully utilized as dripping and shortening. The water in which salt meat, fresh meat, or poultry ___________ (present perfect passive verb, third-person singular) should be allowed ___________ (active infinitive of intransitive verb) and the fat removed before ___________ (singular concrete noun) is made of it. Such fat can be used, ___________ (ordinal number) of all, in cooking, and then any inedible portions can be used in soap ___________ (present active participle of transitive verb).

Tough _________ of meat not _________ enough to appear on the table are ________ wasted.
(idiom functioning as a noun and meaning "remnants") (adjective) (adverb)

They can be transformed by long cooking into savory _________, ragouts, _________ and hashes,
(plural concrete noun) (plural concrete noun)

whereas, if _________ and _________ cooked, they are _________ and indigestible. Scraps
(regular adverb) (regular adverb) (adjective formed with un-)

of left-over _________ meat should be ground in the food-chopper and made into appetizing,
(past participle of transitive verb)

_________hashes or sandwich paste. If you happen _________ a soft-cooked egg left over,
(compound plural concrete noun) (active infinitive of transitive verb)

_________it hard at once. It _________ for garnishes, _________, salads or sandwich paste.
(active imperative verb) (simple present passive modal verb, third-person singular) (plural concrete noun)

Use all bits of bread, that cannot be used as toast, in puddings, _________, scalloped dishes or
(plural concrete noun)

_________ soup.
(active infinitive of transitive verb)

_________ away cold muffins and _________ breads. Split and _________ them for next
(active imperative, negative form, of transitive verb) (adjective) (active imperative of transitive verb)

_________ breakfast.
(possessive noun acting as an adjective)

_________ the serving of food should be carefully planned so as to prevent waste, _________
(subordinating conjunction introducing an adverb clause) (singular abstract noun)

_________ that growing children have _________ food. It is a mistake to suppose that a _________
(simple present modal passive verb, third-person singular) (adjective) (present participle of intransitive verb)

child can be nourished on less than a _________ adult. A boy of _________ who wants to eat more
(adjective) (cardinal number)

than his _________ probably needs all that he asks for. We _________ on the children; but it will
(singular concrete noun) (simple present modal active verb, first person plural, negative form)

be well ________ them plain food for the most part, which will ______ tempt them to overeat, and
(active infinitive of transitive verb) (adverb of negation)

tactfully combat _________, overfastidious likes and dislikes.
(adjective)

The United States Food Administration _________ the gospel of the _________ plate, and
(progressive present, active, third-person singular of transitive verb) (adjective)

_________ can be accomplished by serving _________ portions, insisting that all food accepted
(singular demonstrative pronoun) (adjective in the comparative form)

_________; by keeping down _________ waste, cutting the _________ at the table a slice at a time
(past passive participle) (concrete noun acting as an adjective) (same concrete noun as in previous blank)

as needed; by _________ only sufficient to supply _________ the number _________, and no more.
(present active participle of transitive verb) (adverb) (passive infinitive)

It is a ________ idea of good providing that ________ must leave the table with a generous ________.
(adjective) (plural concrete noun) (singular concrete hyphenated compound noun)

Waste of cooked food is a serious item in _________ economy, and no matter _________ skillfully
(compound adjective) (adverb introducing a subordinate adverb clause)

_________ are utilized, it is always less _________ and more appetizing _________ fresh-cooked
(plural compound noun) (adjective) (active infinitive of transitive verb)

foods at _________ meal.
(singular indefinite adjective)

________ would think that with the various uses to which all kinds of ________ may be put
(singular indefinite pronoun) (plural compound concrete noun)
that there ________ little left for the ________ garbage pail. ________ the Secretary of the
(simple present modal state-of-being verb, third-person singular) (present participle of intransitive verb) (coordinating conjunction)
United States Department of Agriculture is ________ for the statement that $750,000,000 worth of
(adjective)
food ________ annually in the American kitchen. Undoubtedly a large part of ________ wastefulness
(present perfect passive verb, third-person singular) (singular demonstrative adjective)
was due to ________ on the part of the housewife, and the rest of it to the ________
(abstract singular noun) (abstract singular noun)
of co-operation on the part of the employees who ________ the food but not paid the ________.
(perfect present active indicative transitive verb, third-person plural) (plural concrete noun)

According to a ________ domestic scientist, the only things ________ should find their
(compound adjective) (relative pronoun)
way to the garbage pail are:

Egg shells—after being used ________ coffee.
(active infinitive of transitive verb)

________ skins—after having been cooked on the ________ .
(concrete noun that is acting as an adjective modifying another noun) (same concrete noun as in previous blank)

Banana skins—if there are no tan shoes ________ .
(passive infinitive)

Bones—after ________ in soup kettle.
(perfect present passive participle)

Coffee grounds—if there is ________ garden where ________ can be used for fertilizer, or
(adjective of negation) (plural subject pronoun)
if they are not desired as filling for ________ .
(concrete plural compound noun)

Tea leaves—after every tea-serving, if they are not needed for ________ carpets or rugs
(present active participle of transitive verb)
when swept.

Asparagus ends—after ________ and drained for soup.
(present passive participle)

Spinach, etc.— ________ leaves and dirty ends of roots.
(past participle acting as an adjective)

If more than ________ is now thrown away, you ________ the family income and not
(singular demonstrative pronoun) (present progressive of transitive verb, second-person singular)
fulfilling ________ part in the ________ world struggle. Your government says ________ it
(possessive personal pronoun) (adjective) (subordinating conjunction introducing a noun clause)
is your business to know what ________ your family needs to be efficient; that you ________
(singular concrete noun) (simple present modal verb, second-person singular)
how to make the ________ of the foods you buy; that it is your duty ________ the nature and
(indefinite pronoun that can be either singular or plural) (active infinitive of transitive verb)
uses of ________ foods and to get the ________ possible nourishment out of every pound of
(adjective) (adjective in the superlative form)
food that ________ to your home.
(simple present intransitive verb, third-person singular)

The art of utilizing left-overs is an important factor in this prevention of waste. The thrifty have always known it. The careless have always ignored it. But now as a measure of home
________ as well as a patriotic ________, the left-over must be handled ________.
(abstract singular noun) (abstract singular noun) (adverb)

The original excerpt is found below. This is taken from a cookbook, published in 1918, called *Foods That Will Win the War and How to Cook Them*. Right at the end of World War I (1914–1918), shortages of food were a major problem for the nations who were fighting the war, and cooks ("housewives," in 1918) were encouraged to waste as little as possible.

Bad ___cooking___ (present active participle of transitive verb), which means under-cooking, over-cooking or flavorless cooking, renders food inedible, and ___inedible___ (adjective) food contributes to world shortage.

Fats are wasted in cooking by ___being burned___ (present passive participle) and by not being carefully utilized as dripping and shortening. The water in which salt meat, fresh meat, or poultry ___has been boiled___ (present perfect passive verb, third-person singular) should be allowed ___to cool___ (active infinitive of intransitive verb) and the fat removed before ___soup___ (singular concrete noun) is made of it. Such fat can be used, ___first___ (ordinal number) of all, in cooking, and then any inedible portions can be used in soap ___making___ (present active participle of transitive verb).

Tough ___odds and ends___ (idiom functioning as a noun and meaning "remnants") of meat not ___sightly___ (adjective) enough to appear on the table are ___often___ (adverb) wasted. They can be transformed by long cooking into savory ___stews___ (plural concrete noun), ragouts, ___croquettes___ (plural concrete noun) and hashes, whereas, if ___carelessly___ (regular adverb) and ___insufficiently___ (regular adverb) cooked, they are ___unpalatable___ (adjective formed with un-) and indigestible. Scraps of left-over ___cooked___ (past participle of transitive verb) meat should be ground in the food-chopper and made into appetizing ___meatballs___ (compound plural concrete noun), hashes or sandwich paste. If you happen ___to have___ (active infinitive of transitive verb) a soft-cooked egg left over, ___boil___ (active imperative verb) it hard at once. It ___can be used___ (simple present passive modal verb, third-person singular) for garnishes, ___sauces___ (plural concrete noun), salads or sandwich paste.

Use all bits of bread, that cannot be used as toast, in puddings, ___croquettes___ (plural concrete noun), scalloped dishes or ___to thicken___ (active infinitive of transitive verb) soup.

___Don't throw___ (active imperative, negative form, of transitive verb) away cold muffins and ___fancy___ (adjective) breads. Split and ___toast___ (active imperative of transitive verb) them for next ___day's___ (possessive noun acting as an adjective) breakfast.

___Although___ (subordinating conjunction introducing an adverb clause) the serving of food should be carefully planned so as to prevent waste, ___care___ (singular abstract noun) ___should be taken___ (simple present modal passive verb, third-person singular) that growing children have ___ample___ (adjective) food. It is a mistake to suppose that a ___growing___ (present participle of intransitive verb) child can be nourished on less than a ___sedentary___ (adjective) adult. A boy of ___fourteen___ (cardinal number) who wants to eat more than his ___father___ (singular concrete noun) probably needs all that he asks for. We ___must not save___ (simple present modal active verb, first person plural, negative form) on the children; but it will be well ___to give___ (active infinitive of transitive verb) them plain food for the most part, which will ___not___ (adverb of negation) tempt them to overeat, and tactfully combat ___persnickety___ (adjective), overfastidious likes and dislikes.

The United States Food Administration is preaching the gospel of the clean plate, and
(progressive present, active, third-person singular of transitive verb) (adjective)
this can be accomplished by serving smaller portions, insisting that all food accepted be eaten;
(singular demonstrative pronoun) (adjective in the comparative form) (past passive participle)
by keeping down bread waste, cutting the bread at the table a slice at a time as needed;
(concrete noun acting as an adjective) (same concrete noun as in previous blank)
by cooking only sufficient to supply moderately the number to be fed, and no more.
(present active participle of transitive verb) (adverb) (passive infinitive)
It is a false idea of good providing that platters must leave the table with a generous left-over.
(adjective) (plural concrete noun) (singular concrete hyphenated compound noun)
Waste of cooked food is a serious item in household economy, and no matter how skillfully
(compound adjective) (adverb introducing a subordinate adverb clause)
left-overs are utilized, it is always less expensive and more appetizing to provide fresh-cooked
(plural compound noun) (adjective) (active infinitive of transitive verb)
foods at each meal.
(singular indefinite adjective)

One would think that with the various uses to which all kinds of foodstuffs may be put
(singular indefinite pronoun) (plural compound concrete noun)
that there would be little left for the yawning garbage pail. But the Secretary of the
(simple present modal state-of-being verb, third-person singular) (present participle of intransitive verb) (coordinating conjunction)
United States Department of Agriculture is responsible for the statement that $750,000,000 worth of
(adjective)
food has been wasted annually in the American kitchen. Undoubtedly a large part of this wastefulness
(present perfect passive verb, third-person singular) (singular demonstrative adjective)
was due to ignorance on the part of the housewife, and the rest of it to the lack
(abstract singular noun) (abstract singular noun)
of co-operation on the part of the employees who have handled the food but not paid the bills.
(perfect present active indicative transitive verb, third-person plural) (plural concrete noun)

According to a well-known domestic scientist, the only things which should find their
(compound adjective) (relative pronoun)
way to the garbage pail are:

Egg shells—after being used to clear coffee.
(active infinitive of transitive verb)

Potato skins—after having been cooked on the potato.
(concrete noun that is acting as an adjective modifying another noun) (same concrete noun as in previous blank)

Banana skins—if there are no tan shoes to be cleaned.
(passive infinitive)

Bones—after having been boiled in soup kettle.
(perfect present passive participle)

Coffee grounds—if there is no garden where they can be used for fertilizer, or
(adjective of negation) (plural subject pronoun)
if they are not desired as filling for pincushions.
(concrete plural compound noun)

Tea leaves—after every tea-serving, if they are not needed for brightening carpets or rugs when swept.
(present active participle of transitive verb)

Asparagus ends—after being cooked and drained for soup.
(present passive participle)

Spinach, etc.— decayed leaves and dirty ends of roots.
(past participle acting as an adjective)

If more than this is now thrown away, you are wasting the family income and not
(singular demonstrative pronoun) (present progressive of transitive verb, second-person singular)
fulfilling your part in the great world struggle. Your government says that it is your business
(possessive personal pronoun) (adjective) (subordinating conjunction introducing a noun clause)
to know what food your family needs to be efficient; that you must learn how to make the
(singular concrete noun) (simple present modal verb, second-person singular)
most of the foods you buy; that it is your duty to learn the nature and uses of various foods and
(indefinite pronoun that can be either singular or plural) (active infinitive of transitive verb) (adjective)
to get the greatest possible nourishment out of every pound of food that comes to your home.
(adjective in the superlative form) (simple present intransitive verb, third-person singular)

The art of utilizing left-overs is an important factor in this prevention of waste. The thrifty have always known it. The careless have always ignored it. But now as a measure of home economy as well as a patriotic service, the left-over must be handled intelligently.
(abstract singular noun) (abstract singular noun) (adverb)

Review 10B: Identifying Infinitive Phrases, Noun Clauses, and Modifying Clauses

In the following excerpt, follow these four steps:

a) Identify every set of underlined words as *INF* for infinitive phrase, *PREP* for prepositional phrase, or *CL* for clause.
b) Infinitive phrases, prepositional phrases, or clauses may occur within other phrases or clauses. If words are double-underlined (or even triple underlined!), identify them as a separate element within the single-underlined phrase or clause.
c) Label each phrase or clause as *ADV* for adverb, *ADJ* for adjective, or *N* for noun.
d) For adjective and adverb phrases and clauses, draw an arrow from the label to the word modified.
e) For noun phrases and clauses, add the appropriate part of the sentence label: *S* for subject, *DO* for direct object, *IO* for indirect object, *PN* for predicate nominative, *OP* for object of the preposition, *APP* for appositive.

The first is done for you.

This is taken from a book called *Thrilling Stories of the Great War: On Land and Sea, In the Air, Under the Water*, by Logan Marshall. It was written in 1915, during the second year of World War I. (World War I was known simply as the Great War until World War II.) Here, Mr. Marshall tells the story of the sinking of the RMS *Lusitania*, a British passenger ship that was torpedoed by a German submarine on May 7, 1915.

Because the *Lusitania* was a civilian ship, not a military vessel, the German attack was against internationally recognized rules of warfare. Over a thousand passengers died, and anger over the sinking was one of the factors that eventually led the United States to enter the war—although this did not happen for two more years.

CL ADV
One of the passengers, Dr. Daniel Moore, of Yankton, S. D., declared that before he
CL N DO
went downstairs to luncheon shortly after one o'clock he and others with him noticed
PREP ADV
through a pair of marine glasses, a curious object in the sea, possibly two miles or more away.
CL N DO PREP ADV
What it was he could not determine, but he jokingly referred to it later at luncheon as a submarine.

CL ADV
While the first cabin passengers were chatting over their coffee cups they felt the ship give a great leap forward. Full speed ahead had suddenly been signaled from the bridge . . .

The *Lusitania* began to swerve to starboard, heading for the submarine, but before she could really answer her helm a torpedo was flashing through the water toward her at express speed. Myers and his companions, like many others of the passengers, saw the white wake of the torpedo and its metal casing gleaming in the bright sunlight . . .

In far less time than it takes to tell, the torpedo had crashed into the *Lusitania's* starboard side, just abaft the first funnel, and exploded with a dull boom in the forward stoke-hole.

Captain Turner at once ordered the helm put over and the prow of the ship headed for land, in the hope that she might strike shallow water while still under way. The boats were ordered out, and the signals calling the boat crews to their stations were flashed everywhere through the vessel. . . .

Down in the dining saloon the passengers felt the ship reel from the shock of the explosion and many were hurled from their chairs. Before they could recover themselves, another explosion occurred. There is a difference of opinion as to the number of torpedoes fired. Some say there were two; others say only one torpedo struck the vessel, and that the second explosion was internal.

In any event, the passengers now realized their danger. The ship, torn almost apart, was filled with fumes and smoke, the decks were covered with débris that fell from the sky, and the great *Lusitania* began to list quickly to starboard. Before the passengers below decks could make their way above, the decks were beginning to slant ominously, and the air was filled with the cries of terrified men and women, some of them already injured by being hurled against the sides of the saloons. Many passengers were stricken unconscious by the smoke and fumes from the exploding torpedoes.

The stewards and stewardesses, recognizing the too evident signs of a sinking ship, rushed about urging and helping the passengers to put on life-belts, of which more than 3,000 were aboard. . . .

The first life-boat that struck the water capsized with some sixty women and children aboard her, and all of these must have been drowned almost instantly. Ten more boats were lowered, the desperate expedient of cutting away the ropes being resorted to to prevent them from being dragged along by the now halting steamer.

The great ship was sinking by the bow, foot by foot, and in ten minutes after the first explosion she was already preparing to founder. Her stern rose high in the air, so that those in the boats that got away could see the whirring propellers, and even the boat deck was awash.

Captain Turner urged the men to be calm, to take care of the women and children, and megaphoned the passengers to seize life-belts, chairs—anything they could lay hands on to save themselves from drowning. There was never any question in the captain's mind that the ship was about to sink, and if, as reported, some of the stewards ran about advising

the passengers not to take to the boats, that there was no danger of the vessel going down till
CL ADV
she reached shore, it was done without his orders. But many of the survivors have denied this,
CL N DO CL ADJ
and declared that all the crew, officers, stewards and sailors, even the stokers, who dashed up from their flaming quarters below, showed the utmost bravery and calmness in the face of the
INF N DO INF ADJ
disaster, and sought in every way to aid the panic-stricken passengers to get off the ship.

Review 10C: Parsing

Parse every bolded verb in the following.

This was written by the British politician David Lloyd George, who was prime minister during World War I. In this excerpt, Lloyd George, writing twenty years after the fact, reflects back on 1914, when Great Britain first joined the Allied fight against the Central Powers.

Provide the following information:

Person:	First, second, or third
Number:	Sing. or pl.
Tense:	Simple past, present, or future; perfect past, present, or future; progressive past, present, or future; or progressive perfect present
Voice:	Active, passive, or state-of-being
Mood:	Indicative, subjunctive, imperative, hortatory, or modal If the verb is also emphatic, add this label to the mood.

The first is done for you.

"Boom!"

third pl, simple past, active, indicative

The deep notes of Big Ben **rang** out into the night, the first strokes in Britain's most

third sing., simple past, active, indicative

fateful hour since she arose out of the deep. A shuddering silence **fell** upon the room. Every face

third sing., simple past, passive, indicative

was suddenly **contracted** in a painful intensity.

third sing., simple past, active, indicative

"Doom!" "Doom!" "Doom!" to the last stroke. The big clock **echoed** in our ears like the

third sing., simple present, active, modal — first pl., perfect past, active, indicative

hammer of destiny. What destiny? Who **could tell**? We **had challenged** the most powerful military

third sing., perfect present, active, indicative — third sing., simple past, state-of-being, indicative

empire the world **has** yet **brought** forth. France **was** too weak alone to challenge its might and

third sing., simple present, active, modal

Russia was ill-organised, ill-equipped, corrupt. We knew what brunt Britain **would have** to bear.

third sing., simple present, active, modal

Could she **stand** it? There was no doubt or hesitation in any breast.

third sing., simple present, passive, hortatory

But **let** it **be admitted** without shame that a thrill of horror quickened every pulse.

third sing., simple present, passive, modal — first pl., simple present, active, modal

Did we know that before peace **would be restored** to Europe we **should have** to wade through four years of the most concentrated slaughter, mutilation, suffering, devastation and savagery

third sing., perfect present, active, indicative

which mankind **has** ever **witnessed**?

third pl., simple present,
passive, modal

That 12 millions of the gallant youth of the nations **would be slain**, that another 20 mil-

third sing., simple present,
passive, modal

lions would be mutilated? That Europe **would be crushed** under the weight of a colossal war debt?

third pl., simple present,
active, modal

That only one empire **would stand** the shock? That the three other glittering empires of the world

third pl., perfect present,
passive, modal

would have been flung to the dust, and shattered beyond repair? That revolution, famine and anarchy would sweep over half of Europe, and that their menace would scorch the rest of this hapless continent?

third sing., perfect present,
passive, indicative
first pl., perfect past,
active, indicative

Has the full tale yet **been told**? Who can tell? But **had** we **foreseen** it all on the fourth of

first pl., perfect present,
passive, modal

August, we **could have done** no other.

Twenty minutes after the hour, Mr. Winston Churchill came in and informed us the wires

first sing., perfect present,
passive, indicative

had already **been sent** to the British ships of war in every sea, announcing that war had been declared and that they were to act accordingly. Soon afterward we dispersed. There was nothing

third sing., simple present,
active, modal

more to say that night. Tomorrow **would bring** us novel tasks and new bearings. As I left, I felt

third sing., perfect past,
passive, indicative

like a man standing on a planet that **had been** suddenly **wrenched** from its orbit by a demoniacal

third sing., progressive past,
active, indicative

hand, and that **was spinning** wildly into the unknown.

—From *The War Memoirs of David Lloyd George* (Nicholson & Watson, 1933–38)

Review 10D: Which and That Clauses

In the following sentences, taken from the 1919 book *History of the World War: An Authentic Narrative of the World's Greatest War* by Francis March and Richard Beamish, underline each clause introduced by *which* or *that.*

- If *that* is understood, underline the clause and use a caret to insert the missing *that.*
- If a *which* or *that* clause falls within another clause, underline the entire larger clause once, and the clause-within-a-clause a second time.
- Label each underlined clause as *ADJ* for adjective, *ADV* for adverb, or *N* for noun.
- For adjective and adverb clauses, draw an arrow back to the word modified.
- For noun clauses, label the part of the sentence that the clause fulfills (*S, PN, DO, IO, APP*).
- Finally, label each adjective clause as R for restrictive or NON-R for nonrestrictive.

The first clause is done for you.

ADJ R

Germany's military machine was ready. A gray-green uniform that at a distance would fade into misty obscurity had been devised after exhaustive experiments by optical, dye and cloth experts co-operating with the military high command . . . German soldiers had received instructions

ADJ R

which enabled each man at a signal to go to an appointed place where he found everything in readiness for his long forced marches into the territory of Germany's neighbors.

Messages which might help any of the belligerents in any way were barred.

German cruisers that had raided sea-going commerce were destroyed.

There had been no time to intrench the position properly, but the troops showed a magnificent front to the terrible fire which confronted them.

The Allies found they had a formidable army to aid them, and the enemy learned finally that he had one to reckon with.

An examination of exploded shells indicated that the new German gun was less than nine inches in caliber, and that the projectiles, which weighed about two hundred pounds, contained two charges, in two chambers connected by a fuse, which often exploded more than a minute apart.

The Air Service, the Tank Corps, the development of heavy mobile artillery, the proper organization of divisions, corps, and armies, all will be set forth in the scheme which will be submitted to you with the recommendation that it be transmitted for the consideration of Congress.

We made steady headway in the almost impenetrable and strongly held Argonne Forest, for, despite this reinforcement, it was our army that was doing the driving.

The role of the French army, which was operating to the right of the British army, was threefold. It had to support the British attacking on its left. It had on its right to support the center, which, from September 7th, had been subjected to a German attack of great violence. Finally, its mission was to throw back the three active army corps and the reserve corps which faced it.

To give this victory all its meaning it is necessary to add that it was gained by troops which for two weeks had been retreating, and which, when the order for the offensive was given, were found to be as ardent as on the first day. It has also to be said that these troops had to meet the whole German army.

> **Note to Instructor:** The entire clause *that it was gained . . . on the first day* is the object of the active infinitive *to add*. The entire clause *that these troops had to meet the whole German army* cannot be the direct object of *to be said* because this is a passive infinitive (serving as the direct object of the verb *has*).

Knowing that the war was over for other American soldiers, the morale of the troops declined throughout the winter.

Our Third Corps crossed the Meuse on the 5th and the other corps, in the full confidence that the day was theirs, eagerly cleared the way of machine guns as they swept northward. . . . The strategical goal which was our highest hope was gained.

Review 10E: Words Acting as Multiple Parts of Speech

In the sentences below, identify the part of speech of each underlined word. Label them as *N* for noun, *V* for verb, *PRO* for pronoun, *ADV* for adverb, *ADJ* for adjective, *PREP* for preposition, *CC* for coordinating conjunction, or *SC* for subordinating conjunction.

When you are finished, write each word (once) in the left-hand column. In the right-hand column, list the parts of speech that it fulfills.

The first is done for you.

These sentences are all taken from poems written by Wilfred Owen, an English poet who fought in World War I. Owen was killed in action in November 1918, just a week before the end of the war, at the age of 25.

And by [PREP] his smile, I knew that sullen hall;
With a thousand fears that vision's face was grained;
Yet [CC] no blood reached there from the upper ground,
And no [ADJ] guns thumped, or down [PREP] the flues made moan.

And He, picking a manner of worm, which half had hid
Its bruises in the earth, but crawled no [ADV] further,
Showed me its feet . . .

Rain, guttering down [ADV] in waterfalls of slime
Kept slush waist high, that rising hour by [CC] hour,
Choked up [ADV] the steps too thick with clay to climb.

A few [N], a few, too few for drums and yells,
May creep back, silent, to still [ADJ] village wells
Up [PREP] half-known roads.

But many there stood still [ADV]
To face the stark, blank sky beyond the ridge,
Knowing their feet had come to the end of the world.

Now, he will spend a few [ADJ] sick years in Institutes . . .

Also, they read of Cheap Homes, not yet [ADV] planned;
For [CC], said the paper, "When this war is done
The men's first instinct will be making homes."

And there's no light to see the voices by [ADV]—
No time to dream, and ask—he knows not what.

Let us lie [V] down [ADV] and dig ourselves in thought.

Smiling they wrote his lie [N]; aged nineteen years.

Courage leaked, as [PREP] sand
From the best [ADJ] sandbags after [PREP] years of rain.

PREP ADV
About this time Town used to swing so gay
When glow-lamps budded in the light-blue trees
SC
And girls glanced lovelier as the air grew dim,
SC ADV
—In the old times, before he threw away his knees.

ADV
Dullness best solves
N
The tease and doubt of shelling . . .

PREP
. . . Where once an hour a bullet missed its aim
V
And misses teased the hunger of his brain.

Move him into the sun—
ADV
Gently its touch awoke him once,
At home, whispering of fields unsown.

CC
Hour after hour they ponder the warm field—
ADJ ADV
And the far valley behind, where the buttercups
Had blessed with gold their slow boots coming up . . .

ADV
We two will stay behind and keep our troth.

I forgot him there
PREP
In posting next for duty, and sending a scout . . .
ADV
To beg a stretcher somewhere, and floundering about
PREP
To other posts under the shrieking air.

ADV
Why speak they not of comrades that went under?

PRO PREP
In all my dreams before my helpless sight
He plunges at me, guttering, choking, drowning.

Northward incessantly, the flickering gunnery rumbles,
ADV ADV
Far off, like a dull rumour of some other war.

ADV ADJ
Nurse looks so far away. And everywhere
PREP
Music and roses burnt through crimson slaughter.

CC
. . . shell on frantic shell
PREP ADV
Hammered on top, but never quite burst through.

> **Note to Instructor:** The compound subjects *shell* and *shell* are linked by *on*. It would not be incorrect to identify the phrase *on frantic shell* as a prepositional phrase modifying the first *shell*. However, the sense of the line is clearly that the shells were multiple (compound). If the student identifies *on* as a preposition, do not mark the answer as incorrect, but point out that *on* also functions as a connector between compound subjects.

ADV
I, too, have dropped off fear—
PREP
Behind the barrage . . .

ADJ ADJ
I'd ask no night off when the bustle's over . . .

CC
So, soon they topped the hill, and raced together
PREP
Over an open stretch of herb and heather
Exposed.

How cold steel is, and keen with hunger of blood;
ADJ
Blue with all malice, like a madman's flash . . .

by	preposition, coordinating conjunction, adverb	so	adverb, coordinating conjunction
yet	coordinating conjunction, adverb	before	subordinating conjunction, preposition
no	adjective, adverb	tease	noun, verb
down	preposition, adverb	once	preposition, adverb
up	adverb, preposition	behind	adverb, preposition
few	noun, adjective	under	preposition, adverb
still	adjective, adverb	all	pronoun, adjective
for	coordinating conjunction, preposition	far	adverb, adjective
lie	verb, noun	through	preposition, adverb
as	preposition, subordinating conjunction	on	coordinating conjunction, preposition
best	adjective, adverb	off	adverb, adjective
after	preposition, coordinating conjunction	over	adjective, preposition
about	preposition, adverb		

Review 10F: Idioms

Circle each idiom in the following sentences. Above each one, write its meaning within the sentence. These sentences are taken from *The Untold Story of the First World War*, by Anna Revell.

changed everything, made the situation different
World War I (turned the world on its head) and prepared the way for the coming of our own world.

These wars were generally viewed as proof that the Great Powers had the sense to compromise
in great danger
when they could see they were (on the edge of the precipice).

in chaos, ready for war, in a state of disturbance
In July 1914 Europe was (a powder keg waiting to go off).

so that he could do something else instead, to make a new priority of
Franz Ferdinand decided to change his plans for the rest of the day (in favour of) visiting the wounded in hospital.

everything except for
China was forced to concede (all but) the most savage of the demands.

everyone paid attention to
Now (all eyes looked) to Great Britain.

after the event

When the smoke had cleared the British had lost fourteen warships and almost seven thousand men, to the Germans' eleven ships and three thousand men.

ignored, decided not to notice

The Tsar and his wife seemed blind to these things.

keep on being king

He hoped that he might save his crown by personally leading the troops back from the front.

Review 10G: Transitive, Intransitive, and State-of-Being Verbs

The following poem, "In Flanders Fields," is probably the most famous piece of literature from World War I. It was written by the Canadian doctor John McCrae in 1915, right after McCrae conducted the funeral of his friend and fellow officer Alexis Helmer. Helmer was killed in battle on May 2, 1915.

Flanders Fields is the name for an area of World War I battlefields that now lie in Belgium and France.

Poppies grew on the battlefields because they flourish where the ground has been disturbed. Because of this poem, the red poppy became an international symbol for the memory of those who have died in battle.

Underline each predicate in the poem (in both independent and subordinate clauses).

- Mark each as *T* for transitive, *IT* for intransitive or *SB* for state-of-being.
- For transitive verbs, circle the word that receives the action of the verb and draw a line from the circled word to the appropriate transitive verb.

In Flanders fields the poppies blow (IT)
Between the crosses, row on row,
That mark (T) our place and in the sky
The larks, still bravely singing, fly (IT)
Scarce heard (T) amid the guns below.

Note to Instructor: The line above is tricky; *heard* is the passive form *are heard,* with the helping verb *are* understood; the poet has left it out to keep the meter of the poem even.

We are (SB) the Dead. Short days ago
We lived (IT), felt (T) dawn, saw (T) sunset glow,
Loved (IT) and were loved (T), and now we lie (IT)
In Flanders fields.

Take (T) up our quarrel with the foe:
To you from failing hands we throw (T)
The torch; be (SB) yours to hold it high.
If ye break (T) faith with us who die (IT)
We shall not sleep (IT), though poppies grow (IT)
In Flanders fields.

Review 10H: Hunt and Find

In the following excerpt, from the first chapter of the classic World War I adventure novel *The Thirty-Nine Steps* by John Buchan, find, underline, and label one example of each of the following:

Restrictive adjective clause
Nonrestrictive adjective clause
Infinitive phrase with an understood *to*
Ordinal number acting as a noun
Appositive
Present participle acting as direct object of verb
Past participle phrase acting as an adverb
Adverb clause
Third conditional sentence
Indirect object
Clause with an understood *that*
To as a preposition
Idiom (be ready to explain it)
Noun clause acting as a direct object
Compound Modifier
Infinitive phrase acting as a noun
Comparison
Superlative adjective
Adverbial noun
Present participle phrase acting as object of preposition
Predicate nominative
Clause introduced by a relative adverb
Infinitive phrase acting as an adjective
Infinitive phrase acting as an adverb
That acting as a demonstrative pronoun
Reflexive pronoun acting as direct object
Adjective clause modifying an idiom

Note to Instructor: Multiple possible answers are underlined below; the student needs to find only one example of each. If she identifies an idiom that is not underlined, accept the answer as long as she can explain the idiom's meaning.

CHAPTER ONE

The Man Who Died

past participle phrase, acting as an adverb

I returned from the City about three o'clock on that May afternoon pretty well disgusted with life.

adverbial noun — idiom meaning "finished" — indirect object — adverbial noun

I had been three months in the Old Country, and was fed up with it. If anyone had told me a year

Third conditional sentence — noun clause acting as a direct object — *that* acting as a demonstrative pronoun

ago that I would have been feeling like that I should have laughed at him; but there was the fact . . .

comparison

I couldn't get enough exercise, and the amusements of London seemed as flat as soda-water that has

reflexive pronoun acting as direct object — idiom meaning "in the wrong place" or "doing the wrong thing"

been standing in the sun. "Richard Hannay," I kept telling myself, "you have got into the wrong ditch, my friend, and you had better climb out."

idiom meaning "wealthy"

. . . I had got my pile—not one of the big ones, but good enough for me; and I had figured out all kinds of ways of enjoying myself. My father had brought me out from Scotland at the age of

predicate nominative — *to* as a preposition

six, and I had never been home since; so England was a sort of Arabian Nights to me, and I counted on stopping there for the rest of my days.

ordinal number acting as a noun
But from the first I was disappointed with it. In about a week I was tired of seeing sights, and in
compound modifier
less than a month I had had enough of restaurants and theatres and race-meetings. I had no real pal
infinitive phrase acting as an adjective — adverb clause — infinitive phrase acting as an adverb
to go about with, which probably explains things. Plenty of people invited me to their houses, but
indirect object
they didn't seem much interested in me. They would fling me a question or two about South Africa,
infinitive phrase acting as an adverb
and then get on their own affairs. A lot of Imperialist ladies asked me to tea to meet schoolmasters
infinitive phrase acting as an adverb — *that* acting as a demonstrative pronoun — superlative adjective — predicate nominative
from New Zealand and editors from Vancouver, and that was the dismalest business of all. Here was
infinitive phrase acting as an adjective
I, thirty-seven years old, sound in wind and limb, with enough money to have a good time, yawning
adverbial noun — infinitive phrase acting as a noun (DO) — infinitive phrase w/ understood *to*, acting as a noun (DO) — *to* as preposition
my head off all day. I had just about settled to clear out and get back to the veld, for I was the best
predicate nominative
bored man in the United Kingdom.

adverbial noun — infinitive phrase acting as an adverb
That afternoon I had been worrying my brokers about investments to give my mind something
infinitive phrase, acting as an adjective — appositive — nonrestrictive adjective clause
to work on, and on my way home I turned into my club—rather a pot-house, which took in Colonial
members. I had a long drink, and read the evening papers. They were full of the row in the Near
appositive
East, and there was an article about Karolides, the Greek Premier. I rather fancied the chap. From
idiom meaning "the most important man" — idiom meaning "he was honest"
all accounts he seemed the one big man in the show; and he played a straight game too, which was
adjective clause modifying an idiom/nonrestrictive adjective clause — compound modifier — noun clause acting as direct object
more than could be said for most of them. I gathered that they hated him pretty blackly in Berlin
noun clause acting as direct object — idiom meaning "support him"
and Vienna, but that we were going to stick by him, and one paper said that he was the only barrier
noun clause acting as direct object — present participle acting as direct object of verb
between Europe and Armageddon. I remember wondering if I could get a job in those parts. . .

About six o'clock I went home, dressed, dined at the Cafe Royal, and turned into a music-hall. It
predicate nominative — adverb clause
was a silly show . . . and I did not stay long. The night was fine and clear as I walked back to the flat
clause with an understand *that*/ restrictive adjective clause
I had hired near Portland Place. The crowd surged past me on the pavements, busy and chattering,
present participle phrase acting as object of preposition
and I envied the people for having something to do. These shop-girls and clerks and dandies and
restrictive adjective clause — *to* acting as a preposition
policemen had some interest in life that kept them going. I gave half-a-crown to a beggar because
adverb clause — predicate nominative
I saw him yawn; he was a fellow-sufferer. At Oxford Circus I looked up into the spring sky and I
made a vow. I would give the Old Country another day . . . if nothing happened, I would take the
next boat for the Cape.

predicate nominative
My flat was the first floor in a new block behind Langham Place...I was just fitting my key into the door when I noticed a man at my elbow. . . . He was a slim man, with a short brown beard and small, gimlety blue eyes. I recognized him as the occupant of a flat on the top floor, with whom I had passed the time of day on the stairs.
adverb clause; nonrestrictive adjective clause

to acting as a preposition
"Can I speak to you?" he said. "May I come in for a minute?" He was steadying his voice with an effort, and his hand was pawing my arm.

compound modifier; clause introduced by a relative adverb
I got my door open and motioned him in. No sooner was he over the threshold than he made a dash for my back room, where I used to smoke and write my letters. Then he bolted back.

"Is the door locked?" he asked feverishly, and he fastened the chain with his own hand.

predicate nominative; predicate nominative; restrictive adjective clause; adverb clause; idiom meaning "help me"
"I'm very sorry," he said humbly. "It's a mighty liberty, but you looked the kind of man who would understand. I've had you in my mind all this week when things got troublesome. Say, will you do me a good turn?"

to acting as a preposition; predicate nominative
"I'll listen to you," I said. "That's all I'll promise." I was getting worried by the antics of this nervous little chap.

nonrestrictive adjective clause; adverb clause
There was a tray of drinks on a table beside him, from which he filled himself a stiff whisky-and-soda. He drank it off in three gulps, and cracked the glass as he set it down.

idiom meaning "upset"; adverbial noun; infinitive acting as an adverb
"Pardon," he said, "I'm a bit rattled tonight. You see, I happen at this moment to be dead."

Note to Instructor: Since *happen* is an intransitive verb and is not a linking verb, *to be* cannot serve as either a predicate adjective or an object; therefore it must be adverbial.

Review 10I: Conditionals and Formal Conditionals

In each of the following conditional sentences, parse the underlined verbs, giving tense, voice (active, passive, or state-of-being), and mood. Then, classify the sentences as first, second, or third conditional by placing a *1*, *2*, or *3* in the blank at the end.

If the sentence is a formal conditional, write *FC* next to the blank.

The first is done for you.

These sentences are taken from *Tales of War*, a short story collection about World War I published in 1918. The author, Lord Dunsany (Edward Plunkett, the 18th Baron of Dunsany), was best known for his fantasy novels, such as *The King of Elfland's Daughter* and *The Book of Wonder*, but he also wrote plays, poems, poetry, and stories.

simple past, active, subjunctive (emphatic); simple present, active, modal
And even if it did end, that would not bring their four sons home now. 2

simple present, active, subjunctive — simple future, active, indicative

If we do not see in them the saga and epic, how shall we tell of them? 1

Note to Instructor: *do see* is not emphatic because the helping verb *do* is present in order to form the negative (as opposed to *did end*, which could have been phrased *ended* for a nonemphatic form)

perfect past, active, subjunctive — perfect present, active, modal

Had he not done it we might have had ruins and German orders everywhere. 3 FC

simple present, active, indicative — simple, present, active, subjunctive

It is curious, after such a colossal event as this explosion must be in the life of a bar of steel, that anything should remain at all of the old bell-like voice of the metal, but it appears to, if you listen attentively. 1

simple past, active, subjunctive — simple present, active, modal

If you went to them after great suffering they might speak to you; after nights and nights of shelling over in France, they might speak to you and you might hear them clearly. 2

perfect past, state-of-being, subjunctive — perfect present, active, modal

Had it not been for him the crafty Belgians would have attacked the Fatherland, but they were struck down before they could do it. 3 FC

simple past, active, subjunctive — simple present, active, modal

If they fought among themselves, which is quite unthinkable, the police would run them in. 2

perfect past, state-of-being, subjunctive — perfect present, active, modal

Probably had it not been for this the two men would have died among those desolate craters. 3 FC

progressive present, active, subjunctive — simple present, active, indicative

One's horse, if one is riding, does not very much like it. 1

perfect past, active, subjunctive — simple present, active, modal

If shells had come, or the Germans, or anything at all, you would know how to take it; but that quiet mist over huge valleys, and stillness! 3

simple past, state-of-being, subjunctive

If a part of the moon were to fall off in the sky and come tumbling to earth, the comment on the lips of the imperturbable British watchers that have seen

simple present, state-of-being, modal

so much would be, "Hullo, what is Jerry up to now?" 2

Review 10J: Affirmations and Negations

The following sentences, from the standard one-volume history *World War I* by S. L. A. Marshall, all contain adverbs of affirmation and negation. Circle each one, and label them as *AFF* or *NEG*.

Then, choose three sentences and rewrite them on your own paper, turning affirmatives into negatives and vice versa. Show your sentences to your instructor.

The first is done for you.

Note to Instructor: The rewritten sentences below are just examples; the student may choose to use other affirmative or negative adverbs.

From the first go, both sides remained (absolutely) [AFF] committed.

From the first go, both sides remained uncommitted. OR
From the first go, both sides were not committed.

Turning to Count Godard, Wilhelm said: "And now I must have a cup of good, hot, strong English tea, (yes) [AFF] make it English."

Turning to Count Godard, Wilhelm said: "And now I must have a cup of good, hot, strong English tea, no, don't make it English."

Wilhelm had reached the end of his emotional reserves, which were (never) [NEG] abundant.

Wilhelm had reached the end of his emotional reserves, which were extremely abundant.

A large, mysterious object shipped around the country under canvas would (surely) [AFF] whet public curiosity.

A large, mysterious object shipped around the country under canvas would not whet public curiosity.

So while trenches had been carried, the line, in effect, was (not) [NEG] broken.

So while trenches had been carried, the line, in effect, was absolutely broken.

No worthwhile subordinate could abide him for (very) [AFF] long.

Worthwhile subordinates could not abide him for long!

Note to Instructor: The first *No* is an adjective, not an adverb, so it is not circled. In order to reverse the sentence, the student must delete the initial *No* and then transform the affirmative adverb into an adverb of negation.

He had (never) [NEG] commanded in combat in his life.

He had certainly commanded in combat in his life.

Here is a general (definitely) [AFF] (not) [NEG] commanding.

Here is a general never absolutely commanding.
Here is a general absolutely commanding.

Note to Instructor: The combination of an affirmative and negative adverb side by side results in a strengthening of the negation. The first italicized sentence replaces the affirmative with a negative, and the negative with an affirmative—but the sense of the sentence remains the same. The second italicized sentence simply replaces both with a single affirmative—which flips the meaning. Either approach is acceptable.

Every word of it was (positively)[AFF] true—and (absolutely)[AFF] deceptive.

Every word of it was not true—and never deceptive.

Note to Instructor: You may want to point out to the student that since *true* is a positive adjective and *deceptive* is a negative one, replacing both affirmations with negations creates a meaningless sentence, since it creates a double negative in the second half of the sentence.

The German cruisers Goeben and Breslau were then steaming around in mid-Mediterranean, possibly in anticipation of this very contingency, and (certainly)[AFF] too far from home base to risk returning.

The German cruisers Goeben and Breslau were then steaming around in mid-Mediterranean, possibly in anticipation of this very contingency, and not too far from home base to risk returning.

Note to Instructor: In this sentence, *very* acts as an adjective and so can't be replaced by an adverb of affirmation.

Review 10K: Diagramming

On your own paper, diagram every word of the following sentences, taken from Lucy Maud Montgomery's *Rilla of Ingleside* (the final novel in the Anne of Green Gables series, set during the final years of World War I).

No, we have lost—let us face the fact as other peoples in the past have had to face it.

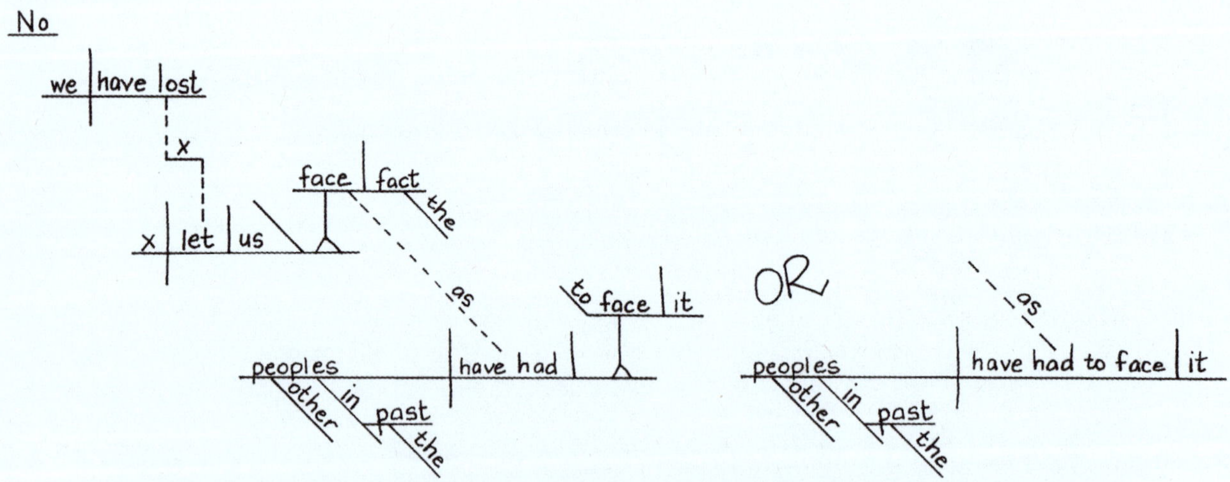

Note to Instructor: In this sentence, *No* is an interjection rather than an adverb of negation.

The verb phrase *have had to face it* can be diagrammed in two ways. *Have had* can be interpreted as a transitive verb with the infinitive *to face* as its direct object (the infinitive is the thing *had*). However, *have had to* can also be interpreted as an idiom which carries the single meaning *must*:

Other peoples must face it.

In that case, it could be diagrammed on a single line.

Both options are acceptable and both are seen on the diagram above.

It did not say where the wound was, which is unusual, and we all feel worried.

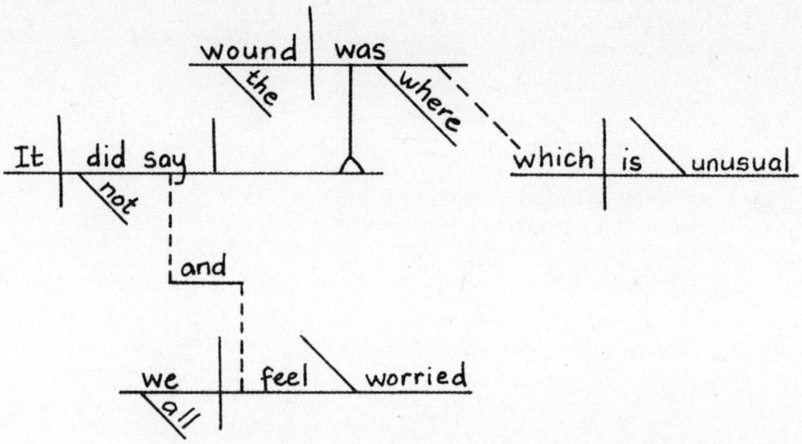

Note to Instructor: In this sentence, *not* is simply an adverb of negation.

However, the clauses *where the wound was, which is unusual* present a challenge. *Where the wound was* is the direct object of the verb *did say. Which is unusual* actually modifies the entire direct object clause. I have chosen to link the relative pronoun *which* (referring to the whole direct object clause) to the predicate of the direct object clause, in order to show the close connection. However, an argument could be made for linking *which* to *did say*.

Remember that diagramming is a tool, not an exact science, and accept any reasonable answers.

Lloyd George began to heckle the Allies regarding equipment and guns and Susan said you would hear more of Lloyd George yet.

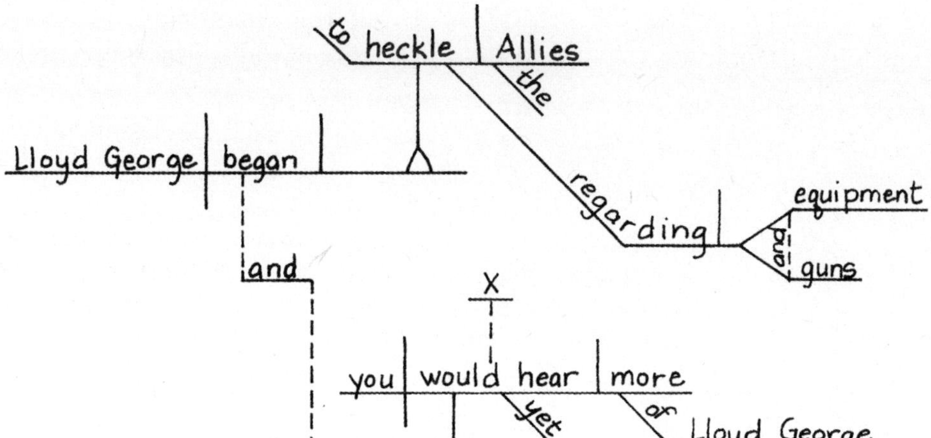

Note to Instructor: The noun clause *you would hear more of Lloyd George yet* serves as the direct object and is introduced by an understood *that*. The word *more* can be an adjective, but here functions as a noun—the direct object of *would hear*.

In the big living-room at Ingleside Susan Baker sat down with a certain grim satisfaction hovering about her like an aura; it was four o'clock and Susan, who had been working incessantly since six that morning, felt that she had fairly earned an hour of repose and gossip.

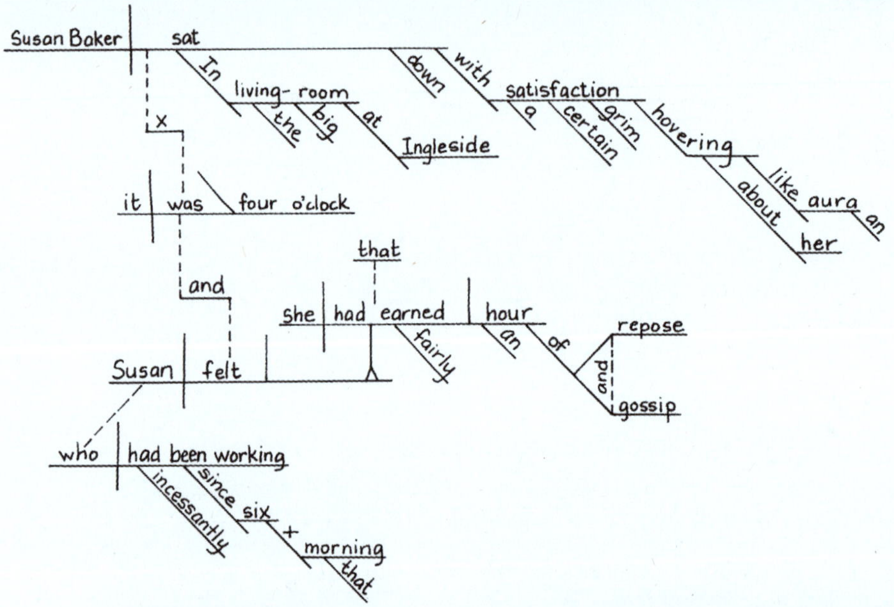

Note to Instructor: In this sentence, *four o'clock* functions as a single noun (predicate nominative renaming *it*). The noun clause *that she had fairly earned an hour of repose and gossip* is the direct object of *felt*, which is acting as a transitive verb (not linking verb) in this sentence. *Morning* is the direct object of the understood preposition *in/on*: "since six in/on that morning."

For the first time since the blow had fallen Rilla felt—a different thing from tremulous hope and faith—that Walter, of the glorious gift and the splendid ideals, still lived, with just the same gift and just the same ideals.

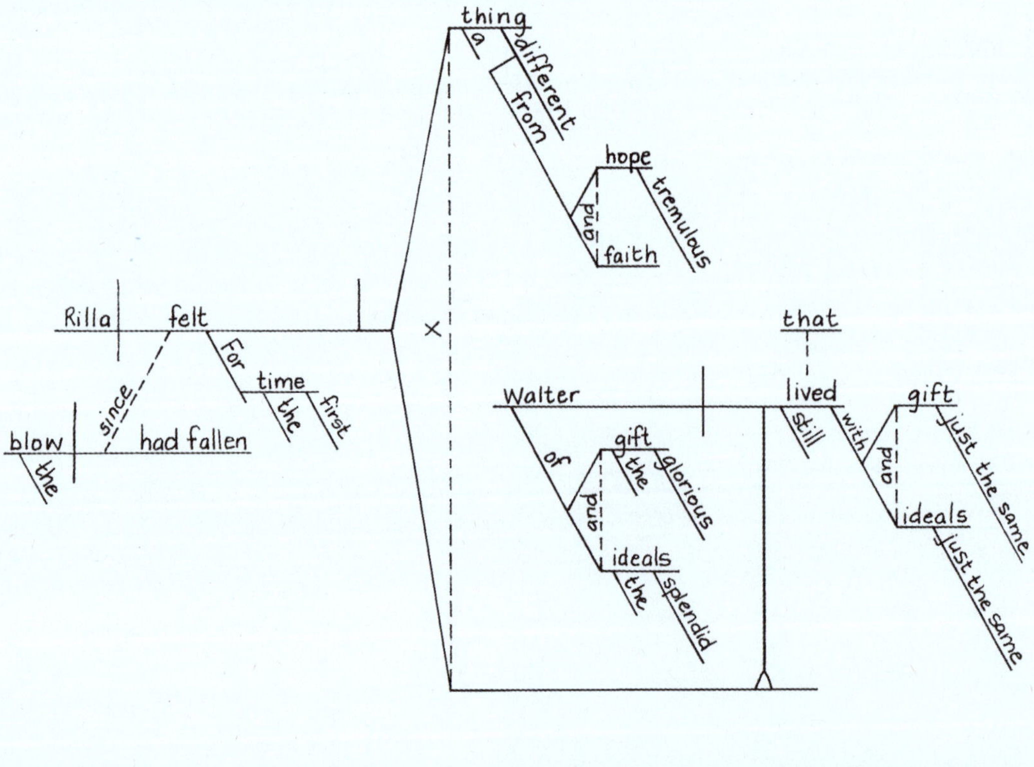

Note to Instructor: *For the first time* is a prepositional phrase acting as an adverb; *since the blow had fallen* is a clause acting as an adverb. Both are diagrammed modifying the verb *felt*. *For the first time* cannot modify *had fallen* (the blow didn't fall for the first time; Rilla *felt* for the first time) so it must modify the verb in the independent clause.

If the student diagrams the phrase *a different thing from tremulous hope and faith* as a parenthetical expression, accept the answer, but point out that grammatically Rilla feels two things: *a different thing* and *that Walter still lived* (a noun clause acting as a direct object).

In meaning, *a different thing* actually renames or describes *that Walter still lived*, but grammatically, *thing* and the noun clause serve as compound direct objects of the verb *felt*.

Just the same is an idiom: a phrase expressing a single meaning. If the student attempts to diagram *just*, *the*, and *same* beneath *gift* and *ideals*, ask whether it is a *just gift* or *just ideals*. (That doesn't make sense!) *Just the same* is an idiom meaning *identical*: "Walter still lived, with identical ideals."

Review 10L: Explaining Sentences

Tell your instructor every possible piece of grammatical information about the following sentences. Follow these steps:

a) Underline each clause. Describe the identity and function of each clause and give any other useful information (introductory word, relationship to the rest of the sentence, etc.)

b) Circle each phrase. Describe the identity and function of each phrase and give any other useful information.

c) Parse all verbs acting as predicates.

d) Describe the identity and function of each individual remaining word.

If you need help, ask your instructor.

Note to Instructor: Use the information in the Notes, below, to prompt the student as necessary. The purpose of this exercise is to build the student's confidence in defining and explaining sentences out loud. Give all necessary help and encourage the student to answer loudly and in complete sentences.

All was to stay well for a time at least, for the war suddenly moved away from us that spring.

—Michael Morpurgo, *War Horse*

a) All was to stay well for a time at least, for the war suddenly moved away from us that spring.

Note to Instructor: This compound sentence is made up of two independent clauses connected by a comma and the coordinating compound *for*.

b) All was (to stay well (for a time (at least))) for the war suddenly moved away (from us) (that spring).

Note to Instructor: The entire infinitive phrase *to stay well for a time at least* serves as a predicate nominative renaming *all*.

Within the infinitive phrase, the prepositional phrase *for a time at least* acts as an adverb modifying *stay*. Within the prepositional phrase, the secondary prepositional phrase *at least* acts as an adjective modifying the noun *time*.

The prepositional phrase *from us* acts as an adverb modifying *away* (it answers the question *away where?*). Finally, *that spring* is an adverbial noun phrase modifying *moved* and also answering the question *when? Spring* is the adverbial noun and *that* is a demonstrative adjective modifying *spring*.

c) The predicate *was* is simple past, state-of-being, indicative.

The predicate *moved* is simple past, active, indicative.

d) The indefinite pronoun *all* is the subject of the first clause and is singular.

The singular noun *war*, modified by the article *the*, is the subject of the second clause.

The adverbs *suddenly* and *away* both modify the predicate *moved*.

He told me how in the same action in which Captain Nicholls had been killed, his horse had been shot down from beneath him, and how only a few weeks before he had been an apprentice blacksmith with his father.

—Michael Morpurgo, *War Horse*

a) He told me how in the same action in which Captain Nicholls had been killed, his horse had been shot down from beneath him, and how only a few weeks before he had been an apprentice blacksmith with his father.

> **Note to Instructor:** This sentence is made up of one independent clause (*He told me . . . with his father*), with *He* as the subject and *told* as the predicate. The independent clause contains within it two subordinate clauses introduced by the subordinating adverb *how.*
>
> Both subordinate clauses (*how in the same action . . . from beneath him* and *how only a few weeks . . . with his father*) are acting as direct objects of the verb *told*.
>
> Within the first subordinate clause, the subordinate clause *in which Captain Nicholls had been killed* is an adjective clause modifying the noun *action*. It is introduced by the relative pronoun *which*, referring back to action, and within the clause which acts as the object of the preposition *in*.

b) He told me how (in the same action) (in which) Captain Nicholls had been killed, his horse had been shot down (from beneath him) and how only (a few weeks before) he had been an apprentice blacksmith (with his father)

> **Note to Instructor:** The prepositional phrase *in the same action* is an adverb phrase modifying the predicate of the first subordinate clause, *had been shot*. It answers the question *when?*
>
> The prepositional phrase *in which* acts, within the subordinate clause, as an adverb—it answers the question *where?* and modifies *had been killed*. The relative pronoun *which* refers back to *action*. (If you were to diagram the sentence, *in which* would be diagrammed beneath *had been killed* and a dotted line would connect *which* to *action*.)
>
> The prepositional phrase *from beneath him* is adverbial and modifies *had been shot*. This is a very tricky prepositional phrase! *From beneath* acts as a compound preposition—together, the two words represent a single *place*, with *him* as the object of the compound preposition. (If the student has trouble with this, ask him to think about how the phrase would be diagrammed if either *from him* or *beneath him* were a single prepositional phrase—in that case, there's nothing to do with the other preposition except make it modify the first preposition (and generally in English, prepositions don't get modifiers!).
>
> *Only a few weeks before* is an adverbial noun phrase. *Weeks* modifies *had been*. *Few* and *before* modify *weeks*. *Only* and *a* modify *few*. (It wasn't *only weeks*, it was *only a few*).
>
> The prepositional phrase *with his father* modifies the noun *blacksmith*. *Father* is the object of the preposition.

c) The predicate *told*, in the independent clause, is simple past, active, indicative.

The predicate *had been killed*, in the subordinate clause contained within the first object clause, is perfect past, passive, indicative.

The predicate *had been shot*, in the first object clause, is perfect past, passive, indicative.

The predicate *had been*, in the second object clause, is perfect past, state-of-being, indicative.

d) The pronoun *He* is the subject of the independent clause.

The pronoun *me* is the indirect object of the predicate *told*.

The adverb *how* introduces the first object clause and modifies *had been shot*.

The proper noun *Captain Nicholls* is the subject of the first object clause.

The noun *horse* is the subject of the subordinate clause within the first object clause. It is modified by the possessive pronoun *his*.

The adverb *down* modifies the verb *had been shot*.

The coordinating conjunction *and* connects the two object clauses.

The second adverb *how* introduces the second object clause and modifies *had been*.

The pronoun *he* is the subject of the second object clause.

The noun *blacksmith* is a predicate nominative renaming the subject *he*. It is modified by the article *an* and the adjective *apprentice*.

In March of the year of grace 1918 there was one week into which must have crowded more of searing human agony than any seven days had ever held before in the history of the world.

—L. M. Montgomery, *Rilla of Ingleside*

a) In March of the year of grace 1918 there was one week into which must have crowded more of searing human agony than any seven days had ever held before in the history of the world.

Note to Instructor: This sentence is made up of one independent clause (*there was one week . . . history of the world*). The subject of the independent clause is *week* and the predicate is *was*.

Within that independent clause, the subordinate clause *into which must have crowded . . . history of the world* modifies *week* and acts as an adjective. The subject of the subordinate clause is *more*, acting as a pronoun, and the predicate is *must have crowded*. The relative pronoun *which* introduces the clause and relates back to *week*.

Within that subordinate clause, the second subordinate clause *than any seven days . . . history of the world* acts as an adjective and modifies *more*. It is linked to *more* by the subordinating conjunction *than*. The subject of the clause is *days* and the verb is *had held*.

b) In March of the year of grace 1918 there was one week into which must have crowded more of searing human agony than any seven days had ever held before in the history of the world.

Note to Instructor: The prepositional phrase *In March of the year of grace 1918* is an adverbial phrase modifying the verb of the independent clause, *was*.

Within that prepositional phrase, *of the year of grace 1918* is a prepositional phrase acting as an adjective and modifying *March*. The prepositional phrase *of grace* is contained within the previous phrase, and acts as an adjective modifying *year*.

ADDITIONAL NOTE: The phrase year *of grace [date]* is rarely used in contemporary writing and can almost qualify as an idiom. In this phrase, the date (1918, in this case) acts as an appositive to the noun *year*: *The year 1918*. The prepositional phrase *of grace* comes between *year* and *1918* but does not affect their relationship.

As noted above, the prepositional phrase *into which* belongs to the first subordinate clause. Within the clause, it is adverbial and modifies *must have crowded* (answering the question *where?*). *Which* is the object of the preposition into and refers back to *week*.

Of searing human agony is an adjectival prepositional phrase modifying the pronoun *more*. *Agony* is the object of the preposition *of*; the present participle *searing* and the adjective *human* both modify *agony*.

The prepositional phrase *in the history of the world* is adverbial and modifies the verb *had held*. *History* is the object of *in*. Within that phrase, *of the world* is adjectival and modifies *history*; *world* is the object of *of*.

c) The predicate *was* is simple past, state-of-being, indicative.

The predicate *must have crowded* is perfect present, active, modal.

The predicate *had held* is perfect past, active, indicative.

d) In the main clause *there was one week*, *there* is an adverb modifying *was* and *one* is an adjective modifying the subject *week*.

Within the subordinate clause introduced by *than*, *any* and *seven* are both adjectives modifying the subject *days*.

The adverbs *ever* and *before* both modify the verb *had held*.

WEEK 33

Mechanics

— LESSON 121 —

Capitalization Review
Additional Capitalization Rules
Formal and Informal Letter Format
Ending Punctuation

Exercise 121A: Proofreading

Use proofreader's marks to insert the missing capital letters and punctuation marks into the following sentences.

capitalize letter: ≡ make letter lowercase: /

insert period: ⊙ insert exclamation point: ^!

insert comma: ^, insert question mark: ^?

insert apostrophe: ’ v

If a word or phrase should be italicized, indicate this by underlining.

Note to Instructor: The original sentences are below. Accept all reasonable corrections.

Bruce Fuoco drifted downward through the frigid water, suspended by a harness connected to a ship on the surface, and protected from the icy cold by a diving suit that looked as if it had been made for *Star Wars*.

The *Fitzgerald*, often called the *Titanic* of the Great Lakes, was not only the most famous freshwater shipwreck; it was also the biggest mystery in Great Lakes history.

That same year, Canadian folksinger Gordon Lightfoot recorded "The Wreck of the *Edmund Fitzgerald*," a ballad recalling the ship's last voyage and the perils of sailing on the Great Lakes in November.

A hotly disputed Coast Guard report, released after an extensive investigation into the accident, added to the *Fitzgerald's* growing legend.

Dr. Joseph MacInnis, an underwater explorer who had visited the wreckage of the *Titanic* in the North Atlantic in 1991, studied the *Fitzgerald* in 1994 as part of a government-sponsored project examining the Great Lakes and the St. Lawrence River.

Note to Instructor: You may need to point out to the student that the abbreviation St. stands for Saint. Dr. and St. both follow the same punctuation rule as Mr. and Mrs.

Both Shannon and the Shipwreck Society had substantial monetary investments in their respective projects, Shannon in paying for his dive to the wreck, the Shipwreck Society, along with the National Geographic Society and the Canadian navy, in assembling the recovery team.

> **Note to Instructor:** You may need to point out to the student that *Shipwreck Society* and *National Geographic Society* are proper names, while *Canadian* is a proper adjective modifying the common noun *navy*. If the student capitalizes *Navy*, point out that the actual proper name of Canada's navy is the *Royal Canadian Navy*. The phrase *Canadian navy* is not the same as the proper name. (But don't penalize the student, since this may not be clear, especially to non-Canadians.)

Down below, on the spar deck of the *Edmund Fitzgerald*, First Mate Jack McCarthy supervised the removal of the ship's hatch covers.

> **Note to Instructor:** The phrase *first mate* occurring alone would not be capitalized, but here it is used as a title, so it is treated like Captain, Mr., or Mrs. *McCarthy* and *Mccarthy* are both correct.

Fortunately, Dr. E. W. Davis of the University of Minnesota, working with other researchers and scientists, developed a way of separating the iron ore from taconite.

> **Note to Instructor:** The full proper name of the school is the University of Minnesota, so *University* must be capitalized.

On September 22, 1958, the *Edmund Fitzgerald*, skippered by Captain Bert Lambert, left Rouge River bound for Silver Bay, Minnesota, where it was scheduled to pick up a load of taconite pellets to be delivered to Toledo.

—Michael Schumacher, *Mighty Fitz: The Sinking of the Edmund Fitzgerald*

In 1914, Sir Ernest Shackleton set sail for Antarctica on the ship *Endurance*.

He planned to walk from the Weddell Sea on one side of Antarctica to the Ross Sea on the other.

Also on board *Endurance* were 69 sled dogs and Mrs. Chippy, the carpenter's cat.

Temperatures on the ice dipped to -30º Fahrenheit (-34º Celsius).

—Alfred Lansing, *Endurance: Shipwreck and Survival on a Sea of Ice*

Local knowledge of sandbanks, reefs, and rocks is simply negated at night; British lights in the Western Approaches, for example, were as important to British fishermen from the Isles of Scilly, bred in those waters, as they were to German U-boat captains from Wilhelmshaven who had never before ventured out of the North Sea.

> **Note to Instructor:** The student may not be aware that *U-boat* is capitalized. You may need to explain that this is a shortened, anglicized form of the German noun *Unterseeboot* ("undersea boat"). Since German nouns are capitalized, the *U* is capitalized in the shortened form as well.

Jack Binns, radio operator of the *Republic*, sent the first CQD message — the precursor of the SOS.

In August 1914 that war arrived, and not long after the declaration, the *Lusitania* was briefly commandeered by the Admiralty, but soon returned to the Cunard Line when it was discovered how much coal she used.

> **Note to Instructor:** Both *August 1914* and *August, 1914,* are correct. When a month and year are listed without a specific day, the commas are optional.
>
> You may need to explain to the student that *Admiralty* is the proper name of the government department that oversaw the British navy.

Although she was carefully searched by the special "neutrality squad" before she left New York, which certified that she carried no armament, her previous associations with the Admiralty had ensured that her silhouette—the means by which a ship was identified from the periscope of a U-boat—had appeared in *Jane's Fighting Ships* for 1914, and both the *Lusitania* and the *Mauretania* were categorized as "armed merchantmen" in the *British Naval Pocket Book* of the same year.

—Sam Willis, *Shipwreck: A History of Disasters at Sea*

Exercise 121B: Correct Letter Mechanics

The following text is a rejection letter sent to the comic book artist Jim Lee. Lee is now the copublisher at DC Comics and is the author of *X-Men #1*, which the *Guinness Book of World Records* lists as the best-selling comic book of all time. But at the beginning of his career, Lee's work was rejected repeatedly. This letter came from Marvel Comics.

On your own paper (or with your own word processor), rewrite or retype the text so that it is properly formatted, punctuated, and capitalized. You may choose either letter format from this lesson.

The text of the letter is a single paragraph. The closing is "Best," which is an acceptable way to end a letter. There is no date in the letter. The sender chose to spell out the states rather than abbreviating them, which is also acceptable. The salutation ("Dear Mr. Lee") is followed by a comma (a colon is more common in a business letter, but a comma is also correct).

When you are finished, compare your letter with the two versions in the Answer Key.

marvel comics group 135 west 50th street, 7th Floor new york new york 10020 jim lee 12848 topping meadows st louis missouri 63131 dear mr lee your work looks as if it were done by four different people. your best pencils are on page 7, panel with agents (lower left corner) and close up of face. the rest of the pencils are of much weaker quality. the same can be said for your inking. resubmit when your work is consistent and when you have learned to draw hands. best
eliot r brown Submissions Editor

Note to Instructor: Two correct versions of the letter are given below.

Marvel Comics Group
135 West 50th Street, 7th Floor
New York, New York 10020

Jim Lee
12848 Topping Meadows
St. Louis, Missouri 63131

Dear Mr. Lee,

Your work looks as if it were done by four different people. Your best pencils are on page 7, panel with agents (lower left corner) and close up of face. The rest of the pencils are of much weaker quality. The same can be said for your inking. Resubmit when your work is consistent and when you have learned to draw hands.

Best,

Eliot R. Brown
Submissions Editor

Marvel Comics Group
135 West 50th Street, 7th Floor
New York, New York 10020

Jim Lee
12848 Topping Meadows
St. Louis, Missouri 63131

Dear Mr. Lee,

Your work looks as if it were done by four different people. Your best pencils are on page 7, panel with agents (lower left corner) and close up of face. The rest of the pencils are of much weaker quality. The same can be said for your inking. Resubmit when your work is consistent and when you have learned to draw hands.

Best,

Eliot R. Brown
Submissions Editor

— LESSON 122 —

Commas
Semicolons
Additional Semicolon Rules
Colons
Additional Colon Rules

Exercise 122A: Comma Use

In the blank at the end of each sentence, write the number from the list above that describes the comma use. If more than one number seems to fit equally well, write all suitable numbers.

Note to Instructor: As long as the student writes at least one number, accept the answer. However, ask him if there is a second (or third) rule that could be applied. After the student answers, point out the additional numbers that could have been referenced.

"My dear friends," said Doctor Heidegger, motioning them to be seated, "I am desirous of your assistance in one of those little experiments with which I amuse myself here in my study." 5,16,17

They looked as if they had never known what youth or pleasure was, but had been the offspring of nature's dotage, and always the gray, decrepit, sapless, miserable creatures, who now sat stooping round the doctor's table, without life enough in their souls or bodies to be animated even by the prospect of growing young again. 2,6

Note to Instructor: The nonrestrictive adjective clause is *who now sat stooping round the doctor's table.*

There, in fact, stood the four glasses, brimful of this wonderful water, the delicate spray of which, as it effervesced from the surface, resembled the tremulous glitter of diamonds. 7,6

Note to Instructor: The parenthetical expression is *in fact*.
The nonrestrictive adjective phrase is *the delicate spray of which*.

The Widow Wycherley adjusted her cap, for she felt almost like a woman again. 1

"Dance with me, Clara!" cried Colonel Killigrew. 5

Had the changes of a lifetime been crowded into so brief a space, and were they now four aged people, sitting with their old friend, Doctor Heidegger? 1,8,19

Yes, they were old again! 10

With a shuddering impulse, that showed her a woman still, the widow clasped her skinny hands over her face, and wished that the coffin lid were over it, since it could be no longer beautiful. 6,11

Note to Instructor: The nonrestrictive adjective clause is *that showed her a woman still.*

—Nathaniel Hawthorne, "Dr. Heidegger's Experiment"

As a historical figure, Ponce de Leon left little evidence, and some basic facts, such as the exact year of his birth, remain uncertain. 1,6

Note to Instructor: The nonrestrictive adjective clause is *such as the exact year of his birth.*

By the 19th century, the story was a popular subject of painters, who often portrayed an aged Ponce de Leon in a long, flowing white beard. 3,6,11

Note to Instructor: The nonrestrictive adjective clause is *who often portrayed.*

Recent archaeological evidence combined with linguistic and DNA analysis suggests that the first migration to Australia and New Guinea was over a land bridge just before the last ice age, around 40,000 years ago, and a second migration occurred over water around 4,000 years ago. 1,15

Gilgamesh was told, however, that there was a fountain of healing waters on another island, and beside it grew a magical plant of immortality. 1

Note to Instructor: *However* is an adverb, not a parenthetical expression.

Over the course of two centuries, Robert de Boron's story was retold by a dozen other writers, and the story became deeply connected with the Fisher King, King Arthur, worthiness, and the right to rule over Britain. 1,2,4,11

Note to Instructor: Without the Oxford comma, the last phrase would read *Fisher King, King Arthur, worthiness and the right to rule over Britain.* Since these are not adjectives, the student may not recognize it—be sure to point it out.

Yet, the idea of a sacred, nonearthly object providing healing and rejuvenation for those very select few who could obtain it is constant. 3

Note to Instructor: *Yet* is a coordinating conjunction, not a parenthetical expression.

The oldest recorded human life span is a French woman, Jeanne Louise Calment, who smoked until she was 117 years old and ate a typical French diet that included heavy sauces, olive oil, red wine, and chocolate. 2, 4, 8

Note to Instructor: Without the Oxford comma, the last phrase would read *heavy sauces, olive oil, red wine and chocolate*. Since these are not adjectives, the student may not recognize it—be sure to point it out.

The clause beginning *who smoked . . .* is a restrictive adjective clause; the comma before it sets off the preceding appositive, not the clause itself.

Jeanne Calment was born in Arles, France, on February 21, 1875—the same year that Leo Tolstoy published *Anna Karenina* and a year before Alexander Graham Bell filed for a patent on his new telephone. 12, 13

Note to Instructor: Although this isn't an address, the principle that a city is separated from its state/larger geographical context still applies.

—Aharon W. Zorea, *Finding the Fountain of Youth: The Science and Controversy behind Extending Life and Cheating Death*

Exercise 122B: Capitalization and Punctuation

Insert all missing punctuation and correct all capitalization in the text that follows. Use these proofreader's marks:

capitalize letter: ≡	make letter lowercase: /
insert period: ⊙	insert exclamation point: ^!
insert comma: ^,	insert question mark: ^?
insert colon: ^:	insert semicolon: ^;
insert dash: (—)	insert quotation marks: ^"
insert hyphen: ^-v	

If a word or phrase should be italicized, indicate this by underlining.

Note to Instructor: The original sentences are found below. Where there is a legitimate judgement call over which punctuation mark to admit, a note has been inserted. Make sure that the student looks at the original sentences once the exercise is finished, so that she can be familiar with the different ways in which these punctuation marks may be used.

Be sure to check the student's proofing of the citations as well as the sentences themselves.

122B.1: Sentences

Millions of tons of ice pressed inexorably upon the little ship that had dared the challenge of the Antarctic. The *Endurance* was now leaking badly, and at 9 p.m. I gave the order to lower boats, gear, provisions, and sledges to the floe, and move them to the flat ice a little way from the ship.

Note to Instructor: The student should be able to deduce from context that *Endurance* is the name of a ship. Both *9 p.m.* and *9 PM* are correct.

Then came a fateful day—Wednesday, October 27.

Note to Instructor: The appositive *Wednesday, October 27* can be set off with a dash, colon, or comma.

We are now 346 miles from Paulet Island, the nearest point where there is any possibility of finding food and shelter.

It was a sickening sensation to feel the decks breaking up under one's feet, the great beams bending and then snapping with a noise like heavy gunfire.

Nothing more could be done at that moment, and the men turned in again; but there was little sleep.

> **Note to Instructor:** The semicolon before *but* could also be a comma. The comma before *and* could also be a semicolon. However, some punctuation mark should come before both of the conjunctions.

The cook got the blubber-stove going, and a little while later, when I was sitting round the corner of the stove, I heard one man say, "Cook, I like my tea strong."

> **Note to Instructor:** *Cook* should be capitalized and set off with commas because it is both a term of direct address and a title.

The ridges, or hedgerows, marking the pressure-lines that border the fast-diminishing pieces of smooth floe-ice, are enormous.

> **Note to Instructor:** The compound adjective *fast diminishing* is hyphenated because it precedes the noun. The commas around *or hedgerows* set off an appositive, but are optional because the appositive is brief. The remaining commas help to prevent misunderstanding. They are optional as well—but without any commas, the sentence would be grammatical but very hard to read!

The ice moves majestically, irresistibly.

> **Note to Instructor:** This comma stands in for a conjunction and is essential.

We are twenty-eight men with forty-nine dogs, including Sue's and Sallie's five grown-up pups.

I tore the fly-leaf out of the Bible that Queen Alexandra had given to the ship, with her own writing in it, and also the wonderful page of Job containing the verse:

Out of whose womb came the ice?
And the hoary frost of Heaven, who hath gendered it?
The waters are hid as with a stone,
And the face of the deep is frozen.

> **Note to Instructor:** A colon precedes the lines of poetry because they are a block quote. The question mark in the second line is demanded by context. In traditional poetry, each line begins with a capital letter.

We also possessed a few books on Antarctic exploration, a copy of Browning, and a copy of "The Ancient Mariner."

> **Note to Instructor:** The commas are necessary because *Antarctic exploration, a copy of Browning, and a copy of "The Ancient Mariner"* are three items in a row. The comma after *Browning* is an Oxford comma.

The ship left South Georgia just a year and a week ago, and reached this latitude four or five miles to the eastward of our present position on January 3, 1915, crossing the circle on New Year's Eve.

> **Note to Instructor:** You may need to explain that *South Georgia* is the name of an island in the southern reaches of the Atlantic Ocean. If it referred to the southern part of the American state of Georgia, it would be written as *south Georgia.*

—Ernest Shackleton, *The Heart of the Antarctic* and *South*

122B.2: Letter Format

The following letters are adapted from the book *Letters of Note,* compiled by Shaun Usher.

January 24, 1960

Buckingham Palace

Dear Mr. President,

Seeing a picture of you in today's newspaper, standing in front of a barbecue grilling quail, reminded me that I had never sent you the recipe of the drop scones which I promised you at Balmoral.

I now hasten to do so, and I do hope you will find them successful. Though the quantities are for 16 people, when there are fewer, I generally put in less flour and milk, but use the other ingredients as stated.

Yours sincerely,

Elizabeth R.

Note to Instructor: *President* is followed by a comma, not a colon, because the Queen was writing a friendly letter about scones rather than a business letter. However, if the student uses a colon, do not mark it as incorrect. The commas around *standing in front of . . . quail* are necessary to clarify that the newspaper is not standing in front of the grill.

10 Downing Street, Whitehall
June 27, 1940

My darling,

I hope you will forgive me if I tell you something that I feel you ought to know.

One of the men in your entourage (a devoted friend) has told me that there is a danger of your being generally disliked by your colleagues and subordinates because of your rough, sarcastic, and overbearing manner. My darling Winston, I must confess that I have noticed a deterioration in your manner, and you are not so kind as you used to be.

Your loving, devoted, and watchful
Clemmie

Note to Instructor: The appositive phrase *a devoted friend* could be set off with commas, hyphens, or parentheses. The commas after *sarcastic* and *devoted* are Oxford commas. There is no comma after *watchful* because it describes *Clemmie* and is not acting as a closing (as *sincerely* might do). The phrase *My darling Winston* is direct address and should be followed by a comma.

122B.3: Quotes

These excerpts are taken from the biography *Winston Churchill,* by John Keegan.

I felt my spine stiffen. Then the voice changed tempo, from rallentando to recitative:

> A tremendous battle is raging in France and Flanders. The Germans . . . by a remarkable combination of air bombing and heavily armoured tanks . . . have broken through the French defences north of the Maginot Line, and strong columns of their armoured vehicles are ravaging the open country, which for the first day or two was without defenders.

Churchill, however, rejected capitulation in absolute terms. "We shall not flag or fail," he insisted. "We shall go on to the end. . . . We shall fight on the beaches, we shall fight on the landing-grounds, we shall fight in the fields and in the streets, we shall fight in the hills. We shall never surrender." Those who heard those words, it is said, never forgot anything about them: the rhythm of his sentences, the timbre of his voice, above all the magnificently defiant "never" of "We shall never surrender."

> **Note to Instructor:** The parenthetical clause *it is said* must be set off with commas. A colon should precede the three items that explain *anything* because they must be separated by commas.

On May 9, 1945, the day five years later when victory was finally proclaimed in Europe, he spoke from a balcony in Whitehall to salute the crowds below: "God bless you all! This is *your* victory."

> **Note to Instructor:** The phrase/clause *the day . . . in Europe* should be surrounded by commas because it is an appositive renaming the date. The student may have difficulty figuring out that a colon should precede the quote. A comma cannot be used because the dialogue tag does not immediately precede the quote, and a period would isolate the quote from the rest of the sentence. Provide help as needed!

— LESSON 123 —

Colons
Dashes
Hyphens
Parentheses
Brackets

Exercise 123A: Hyphens

Some (but not all) of the following sentences contain words that should be hyphenated. Insert a hyphen into each word that needs one.

These sentences are adapted from *Of Six Medieval Women*, by Alice Kemp-Welch.

The abbess was generally a high–born and influential woman.

The legends are mainly based on well-known themes.

It has been maintained that the classic theatre decayed and disappeared as Christianity became all-powerful in Europe.

The first was taken from a Latin translation of a fourth-century Greek legend.

On went the easy-going company, singing by the way, and with horns blowing.

The fresh petals were sprinkled over the surface of the water in the bath, and were distilled to make the rose-water with which the knights and ladies washed their hands and faces when they left their much-curtained beds.

Note to Instructor: *rose water* is also correct.

Around Marie de France there must always remain an atmosphere of doubt and mystery, since she is only mentioned by an anonymous thirteenth-century poet, and by an Anglo-Saxon poet, Denys Pyramus.

Marie was born in Normandy, about the middle of the twelfth century.

These Courts of Love formed one of the semi-serious pastimes of the Middle Ages.

If I were to speak one little word of the choirs of heaven, it would be no more than the honey that a bee can carry away on its feet from a full-blown flower.

Odilio was Queen Adelheid's friend and one-time confessor.

This dialogue takes place between the sorrow-stricken nuns.

Serpents are often credited with a knowledge of life-giving plants.

French was established by then as the language of those who were high born.

Christine de Pisan was possessed of profound common sense, and of a generous-hearted nature.

She argued for the importance to France of a strong middle class.

She saw the thirst for knowledge as an ever-present want of the soul.

The king's infamous and all-powerful favorite was suddenly dismissed.

But the misery of France was ever increasing.

Exercise 123B: Parenthetical Elements

The following sentences are all from *A Journal of the Plague Year* by Daniel Defoe. Defoe liked to write very long sentences filled with parenthetical elements! Set off each bolded set of words with commas, dashes, or parentheses. Choose the punctuation marks that seem to fit best. Then, compare your answers with the original punctuation in the Answer Key.

NOTE: Depending on what punctuation marks you choose, you may have to add an additional comma, colon, or semicolon following some of the parenthetical elements. Be sure to look at the entire sentence to decide whether additional punctuation should be added. Keep in mind that, in contemporary English punctuation, a parenthesis can be followed by another punctuation mark, but a dash almost never is.

Note to Instructor: The original sentences are below, but unless otherwise noted, all three types of punctuation (commas, dashes, or parentheses) will work. If the student chooses different punctuation than Defoe, ask her to compare the two versions side by side and decide which one she prefers. This exercise is simply intended to demonstrate the many different correct ways in which sentences with parenthetical elements can be punctuated.

Another man—**I heard him**—adds to his words, "'Tis all wonderful; 'tis all a dream."

Note to Instructor: Because the parenthetical element is a complete sentence without a subordinating element, it can be set off by dashes or by parentheses, but not by commas (this would create a comma splice).

This was a very terrible and melancholy thing to see, and as it was a sight which I could not but look on from morning to night **(for indeed there was nothing else of moment to be seen)**, it filled me with very serious thoughts of the misery that was coming upon the city, and the unhappy condition of those that would be left in it.

Note to Instructor: The comma following *to be seen* separates the independent clause *it filled me with very serious thoughts . . .* from the adverbial clause and *it was a sight . . . morning to night*. It is technically optional, but it avoids confusion and ideally should be inserted.

Business led me out sometimes to the other end of the town, even when the sickness was chiefly there; and as the thing was new to me, **as well as to everybody else,** it was a most surprising thing to see those streets which were usually so thronged now grown desolate, and so few people to be seen in them, that if I had been a stranger and at a loss for my way, I might sometimes have gone the length of a whole street **(I mean of the by-streets)**, and seen nobody to direct me except watchmen set at the doors of such houses as were shut up, of which I shall speak presently.

Note to Instructor: The comma following *by-streets* separates the compound predicate phrases *have gone the length of a whole street* and *and seen nobody to direct me*. It is optional.

But I mention it here on this account, **namely,** that it was a rule with those who had thus two houses in their keeping or care, that if anybody was taken sick in a family, before the master of the family let the examiners or any other officer know of it, he immediately would send all the rest of his family, whether children or servants, **as it fell out to be,** to such other house which he had so in charge, and then giving notice of the sick person to the examiner, have a nurse or nurses appointed, and have another person to be shut up in the house with them **(which many for money would do)**, so to take charge of the house in case the person should die.

> **Note to Instructor:** Because *namely* is a short parenthetical expression, commas are more appropriate than dashes or parentheses. The comma following *do* separates the adverbial phrase *so to take charge* from the clause before, and is optional.

That abundance of them died is certain—**many of them came within the reach of my own knowledge**—but that all of them were swept off I much question.

> **Note to Instructor:** Because the parenthetical element is a complete sentence without a subordinating element, it can be set off by dashes or by parentheses, but not by commas (this would create a comma splice).

One thing, however, must be observed: that as to ships coming in from abroad **(as many, you may be sure, did)**, some who were out in all parts of the world a considerable while before, and some who when they went out knew nothing of an infection, or at least of one so terrible—these came up the river boldly, and delivered their cargoes as they were obliged to do, except just in the two months of August and September, when the weight of the infection lying, **as I may say,** all below Bridge, nobody durst appear in business for a while.

> Note to Instructor: The parenthetical phrase *as many did* contains the second parenthetical clause *you may be sure*. If the phrase is set off with parentheses, as above, the clause can be set off with commas or dashes (but not parentheses). If the phrase is set off with commas, the clause can be set off with any of the three punctuation marks. (This does not create a comma splice because the clause is within a phrase, not within another independent clause.) If the phrase is set off by dashes, the clause can be set off with commas or parentheses, but not with dashes.

But even those wholesome reflections—**which, rightly managed, would have most happily led the people to fall upon their knees, make confession of their sins, and look up to their merciful Saviour for pardon, imploring His compassion on them in such a time of their distress, by which we might have been as a second Nineveh**—had a quite contrary extreme in the common people, who, ignorant and stupid in their reflections as they were brutishly wicked and thoughtless before, were now led by their fright to extremes of folly; and**, as I have said before,** that they ran to conjurers and witches, and all sorts of deceivers, to know what should become of them **(who fed their fears, and kept them always alarmed and awake on purpose to delude them and pick their pockets)**, so they were as mad upon their running after quacks and mountebanks, and every practicing old woman, for medicines and remedies; storing themselves with such multitudes of pills, potions, and preservatives, **as they were called,** that they not only spent their money but even poisoned themselves beforehand for fear of the poison of the infection; and prepared their bodies for the plague, instead of preserving them against it.

> **Note to Instructor:** Because there are so many commas within the first parenthetical expression, it would be better set off with dashes or parentheses than with commas (to avoid confusion).
>
> The comma following *and pick their pockets* acts with the conjunction *so* to separate the clauses *they ran to conjurers and witches* . . . and *they were as mad upon their running* . . . and is necessary.

— LESSON 124 —

Italics
Quotation Marks
Ellipses
Single Quotation Marks
Apostrophes

Exercise 124A: Proofreading Practice

The sentences below have lost most punctuation and capitalization. Insert all missing punctuation marks, and correct all capitalization errors. When you are finished, compare your sentences with the originals.

Use these proofreader's marks:

capitalize letter: ≡	make letter lowercase: /
insert period: ⊙	insert exclamation point: ^!
insert comma: ^,	insert question mark: ^?
insert colon: ^:	insert semicolon: ^;
insert apostrophe: ’v	insert quotation marks: “v
insert dash: (—)	insert hyphen: ^=v

If a word or phrase should be italicized, indicate this by underlining.

Note to Instructor: The original sentences are below.

The following sentences are taken from the book *A History of the Vietnamese* by K. W. Taylor; it has thirteen chapters, including "The Ly Dynasty," "The French Conquest," and "Franco-Vietnamese Colonial Relations."

Note to Instructor: An optional comma can be placed after the book title. The semicolon could also be a period followed by a capitalized *it*. The comma after *chapters* is useful, but optional. The comma after *Conquest* is an Oxford comma.

The plain of the Red River, along with the smaller plains of the Ma and Ca Rivers immediately to the south, make up the scene in which Vietnamese history was lived until the fifteenth century.

Yue had been the name of a state on the south-central coast of China (the modern province of Zhejiang) during the sixth to fourth centuries BCE.

Note to Instructor: Although this text hyphenates *south-central* (making a compound adjective modifying *coast*), this could also be written as *south central* (meaning that *south* modifies *central*). The appositive *the modern province of Zhejiang* renames *state* and can also be surrounded by commas. BCE can also be written B.C.E.

Thereafter, King An Duong lost the magic crossbow and was defeated.

Note to Instructor: The comma after *Thereafter* is optional.

An imperial census was taken in the year 2 CE. It recorded 143,643 households and 981,755 people in the three prefectures of Giao Chi, Cuu Chan, and Nhat Nam.

> **Note to Instructor:** *CE* can also be written *C.E.* The period after *CE* could also be a semicolon, followed by a lowercase *it*. The comma after *Cuu Chan* is an Oxford comma. The student should be able to figure out from context that each prefecture has a two-word name, but provide help if needed.

Another month passed and, after the annual blood oath was administered, Le Quy Ly met with Tran Phu, who is reported to have said: "You and I are of the same family."

> **Note to Instructor:** Although the commas around *after the annual blood oath was administered* are technically optional, they prevent misunderstanding and should be inserted. The colon after *said* could also be a comma.

Trinh Tung then raised Le Duy Bang's fifth son, Le Duy Dam, to the throne.

> **Note to Instructor:** Although the appositive *Le Duy Dam* is technically one name, because it is more than one word, it is best set off with commas.

They laid the basis for what became, in the independent Vietnam of recent decades, the academic fields of anthropology, ethnology, archaeology, art, geography, history, linguistics, music, philology, religion, and sociology.

> **Note to Instructor:** The comma after *religion* is an Oxford comma.

At the same time, French security agents were busy with a clandestine struggle to thwart Japanese cultivation of anti-French Vietnamese nationalists.

> **Note to Instructor:** The comma after *time* is optional (but recommended).

Phan Khoi (1887-1959) had participated in the reformist movement led by Phan Chu Trinh in the 1900s.

> **Note to Instructor:** The student may not be familiar with the convention of placing birth and death dates in parentheses following a proper name. If he chooses commas instead, accept the answer but point out the original. Dashes should not be used due to confusion with the hyphen. No apostrophe should be placed in the word *1900s*! It is not a possessive.

In 1932 he published a poem entitled "Old Love" which criticized the practice of arranged marriage.

> **Note to Instructor:** An optional comma could be placed after *In 1932* and another could be placed after the title of the poem.

This man had chosen his revolutionary name to celebrate the Long March (*truong chinh* in Vietnamese) that had been a defining event in the history of the Chinese Communist Party during the 1930s.

> **Note to Instructor:** No apostrophe should be placed in the word *1900s!* It is not a possessive. The phrase *truong chinh* is italicized because it is a foreign phrase.

Exercise 124B: Foreign Phrases That Are Now English Words

The following phrases and words are now part of English and are usually not italicized. Using a dictionary, look up each one. In the blank, write the original language that the word belongs to, the meaning in English, and the meaning in the original language. The first is done for you.

cul-de-sac	French, a dead-end street, "bottom of the sack"
ad nauseam	Latin, something repeated until you're sick of it, "to sickness"
prima donna	Italian, someone who's temperamental and arrogant, "first lady" (the lead singer in an opera company)
faux pas	French, a socially embarrassing mistake, "false step"
mano a mano	Spanish, a direct confrontation or fight with another, "hand to hand"
per capita	Latin, for each person, "by the head"
double entendre	French, having more than one meaning or implication, "double understanding"
per se	Latin, as such, in itself, intrinsically, "by itself"
et al.	Latin, and others, and the rest, short for et alia, "and others"
hoi polloi	Greek, the common people, the masses, "the many"

WEEK 34

Advanced Quotations & Dialogue

LESSONS 125 and 126

No exercises in these lessons.

— LESSON 127 —

Practicing Direct Quotations and Correct Documentation

Note to Instructor: The student's instructions and the resources given are provided below for your reference. You will need to check the paper for each of the seven required elements and compare the student's formatting to the rules in the workbook.

A simple summary of each source, incorporating direct quotes as described in the student instructions, is all that's necessary. The essay may be any length, as long as it is over 250 words.

A sample essay is provided at the end of this lesson for your reference. If the student has trouble getting started, read her the first paragraph of the sample essay (don't let her look at it, since formatting the quotes properly is part of the challenge) and tell her she can use it as a model for the first paragraph of her own essay.

The student's Works Cited section should be identical to the Works Cited section of the sample essay.

The student may write an introduction and conclusion, but since the focus of this assignment is on documentation, four paragraphs that simply present information about the four animals described in the sources are perfectly acceptable.

After the assignment is completed, ask the student to read the sample essay and the explanatory notes.

Your assignment: Write a short essay called "Four Extraordinary Animals." It should be at least 250 words, although it will probably need to be longer.

You must quote directly from all four of the sources listed below, footnote each direct quote, and put all four on your Works Cited page.

Your essay must include the following:

a) A brief quote that comes before its attribution tag.
b) A brief quote that comes after its attribution tag.
c) A brief quote divided by its attribution tag.
d) A block quote.
e) A quote that is incorporated into a complete sentence and serves a grammatical function within that sentence.
f) A quote that has been altered with either brackets or ellipses.
g) A second quote from the same source.

One quote can fulfill more than one of these requirements.

If you need help, ask your instructor.

Author: C. William Beebe
Title of Book: The Pangolin or Scaly Anteater
City of Publication: New York
Publisher: New York Zoological Society
Date: 1914

Page 41

Hidden deep below the surface of the ground beneath the dry plains of central and southern Africa and the humid jungles of India, Burma and the great East Indian Islands, are thousands of great reptile-like creatures, some a full six feet in length, covered from nose to tail-tip with a complete armature of scales; lizards in appearance; mammals in truth; orphans in classification. The Malays call them Tanjiling, which English tongues have twisted to Pangolin.

Under his armor of scales, the Pangolin, or Scaly Anteater, conceals a bodily structure as confusing to the scientist as is his general appearance to the layman. In common with other toothless or nearly toothless devourers of ants, the Pangolin has usually been classed with armadillos and hairy anteaters. But his structure is so peculiarly Pangolin, his resemblances to other living creatures so slight, and the absence of fossil relatives so complete, that he has finally been assigned to an order of his own, Pholidota.

Throughout the days of violent sunshine or of tropical downpours, not one of the hosts of Pangolins ever shows himself; but in the dusk of evening the round, shingled ball stirs in its underground chamber, unrolls, stretches, and comes forth timidly, hesitating long at the entrance of the burrow before daring to shuffle forth on its quest for food.

In the embryo Pangolin, the scales are little more than a mass of felted hairs, which harden after birth. This armor is for defense alone, his muscles impel no offensive blows, his powerful claws are sheathed. With such perfect defense, flight is useless, so his fastest gait is a man's slow walk. And his normal position on the march is very unlike that conceived and executed by the average museum taxidermist. His tail drags, his head is held low and his back is steeply arched,

Page 42

reminding one of the old Stegosaurus of Jurassic days. Indeed flight is as impossible as it would be for an average man to attempt to run with armor of fifty pounds weight.

The Pangolin is made for ants, and ants alone: without them, he would starve at once. The mouth is tiny, as only ants pass in; the tongue is very long, serpent-like in its mobility and covered with glutinous saliva. Twenty very strong claws, backed by muscles of immense power, allow them to tear through the anthills, hard almost as concrete. I have counted five hundred fire ants in the gizzard of a Pangolin, their bites and stings powerless against the sticky, merciless tongue. Lacking teeth, the creature swallows tiny pebbles which, as in a chicken, aid in crushing the hard bodies of the ants.

Author: L. Hussakof
Title of Article: The Newly Discovered Goblin Shark of Japan
Magazine: Scientific American
Date: February 26, 1910
Volume and Issue Number: Vol. CII, No. 9
Page range of article: 186–187

Page 186

Japanese fishermen occasionally take on their lines a shark whose grotesqueness has won him among natives the name of "goblin shark." One of these "goblins" came into the hands of

President David Starr Jordan of Leland Stanford University a dozen years ago and was at once recognized as an interesting archaic type whose close relatives had long since become extinct. President Jordan described it under the name of *Mitsukurina owstoni*—the name being given to honor at the same time the late Prof. Kakichi Mitsukuri, who for a quarter of a century was the leading light of Japanese zoology, and Mr. Alan Owston, a natural history dealer of Yokohama, who was instrumental in securing the specimen.

This name, by the way, does not stand at the present day, but must be replaced by *Scapanorhynchus*—a name which had previously been applied to the teeth of the extinct species of this type of shark found in the rocks of the Chalk period, in different parts of the world. In accordance with scientific usage, therefore, the Japanese shark described by President Jordan must now be known as *Scapanorhynchus owstoni.*

It is now to be recorded that a second species of goblin shark has turned up in a most unexpected way. It happened thus: All of the sharks caught in Japan in the past years and sent to the various museums—about twenty in all—were looked upon as belonging to the same species, *S. owstoni.* No one had ever thought of comparing several specimens; in fact, these sharks are so rare in museums that comparison is generally quite out of the question. It was therefore a pleasure for the writer to have had the opportunity of comparing several specimens in the collections at Columbia University, and the American Museum of Natural History, and to find among them a new species of the goblin shark. This has recently been described in the Bulletin of the American Museum of Natural History as *Scapanorhynchus jordani*—the specific name being given in honor of President Jordan, our greatest authority on the fish of Japan.

Now to come to the fish himself: The new shark is certainly grotesque, well deserving his sobriquet "goblin." The largest specimen in this country is one in the National Museum at Washington, measuring over eleven feet; and the species probably attains a length of fifteen. Fortunately it is not given to frequenting the bathing beach, but keeps to deeper waters—usually about fifty fathoms. As is generally the case with fish from deeper water, this shark is soft and pliable. Even after hardening in a preservative for several months, it can be rolled into a ball. The most remarkable feature is the curiously elongated "nose." It is this, together with its protruding jaw and small beady eyes, that gives the shark that ugly appearance. The teeth are sharp and slender, each like the pointed end of an awl. They constitute a most effective weapon, which must be fingered with discretion even on the laboratory table.

Page 187

As to the differences between the new species and the one already known, the new form is distinguished by a much less protruding jaw, by a very much smaller spiracle (the minute accessory gill-pore seen at some distance back of the eye), and by the fact that the eye is situated opposite the middle of the jaw instead of back of it. These features are quite sufficient, in the opinion of experts, for separating our goblin as a distinct "kind."

Author/Editor/Sponsoring Organization: Green Global Travel
Name of Web Article: 60 Weird Animals around the World
URL: https://greenglobaltravel.com/weird-animals-around-the-world/#WEIRD%20MAMMALS
Date of Access: Use the date on which you are writing your essay

Chinese Water Deer: More similar to a Musk Deer than a true Deer, Water Deer are proficient swimmers who live along the rivers and islands of China and Korea. But the Chinese subspecies is particularly unusual, with no antlers and prominent tusks (which are actually elongated canine teeth) that led to its English nickname, the Vampire Deer. Able to swim for several miles, the Chinese Water Deer can also pull their canine tusks back by using their facial muscles.

Author: George Brown Goode
Title of Book: *The Fisheries and Fishery Industries of the United States*
City of Publication: Washington, D. C.
Publisher: Government Printing Office
Date: 1884

Page 19

The Narwhal, *Monodon monoceros Linn.*, whose long spiral tusk has always been an object of curiosity, and gave rise to the stories of the imaginary creature known as the unicorn, is now found in only one part of the United States—along the northern shores of Alaska. It is still abundant in the Arctic Ocean. It has long since ceased to appear on the coasts of Great Britain, the last having been seen off Lincolnshire in 1800. There is a record of one having been seen in the Elbe at Hamburg in 1736.

The Narwhal is ten to fourteen feet long, somewhat resembling the white whale in form, is black, and in old age mottled or nearly white. The tusk, a modified tooth, grows out of the left side of the upper jaw, to the length of eight or ten feet. All its teeth, except its tusks, are early lost, and it is said to feed on fish and soft sea-animals.

> **Note to Instructor:** The letters of the required elements are in marginal brackets below, followed by additional explanation where necessary at the end of the essay.

SAMPLE ESSAY

The Scaly Anteater, or Pangolin, belongs to its own order. It lives in southern Africa, in India, and in the East Indies. When asleep, the Pangolin looks like a "round, shingled ball."[1] [e] But as author C. William Beebe points out, when the Pangolin wakes up and stretches out, it looks like "one of the old Stegosaurus of Jurassic days" and can be "a full six feet in length."[2] The Pangolin lives on nothing but ants. It rips down hard anthills with its strong [b, e, g] claws and licks up the ants with its long, sticky tongue. Because it doesn't have teeth, Beebe writes, it "swallows tiny pebbles which . . . aid in crushing the hard bodies of the ants."[3] [b, f, g]

Goblin sharks are just as odd looking as Pangolin are. They are "soft and pliable," according to L. Hussakof's article "The Newly Discovered Goblin Shark of Japan," and can even be "rolled into a ball."[4] It has a long nose, prominent jaw, small beady eyes, and [a, c, e] sharp pointed teeth. There are two different species of goblin sharks. Hussakof writes that

> . . . the new form is distinguished by a much less protruding jaw, by a very much smaller spiracle (the minute accessory gill-pore seen at some distance back of the eye), and by the fact that the eye is situated opposite the middle of the jaw instead of back of it.[5] [d, f, g]

The Chinese Water Deer can swim long distances, and it can be found along rivers and on islands both in China and in Korea. Sometimes, the Chinese Water Deer is called a Vampire Deer because, as the article "60 Weird Animals around the World" points out, it has "prominent tusks . . . actually elongated canine teeth."[6] [b, f]

Finally, the Narwhal, which looks like a white whale (but is much smaller), has a "long spiral tusk" which once made fishermen think that they had seen a unicorn.[7] This tusk is the [e] only tooth that it has—it loses all the others very early.

---

[1] C. William Beebe, *The Pangolin or Scaly Anteater* (New York Zoological Society, 1914), p. 41.
[2] Beebe, pp. 41-42.

[3] Beebe, p. 42.

[4] L. Hussakof, "The Newly Discovered Goblin Shark of Japan." *Scientific American*, February 26, 1910, p. 186.

[5] Hussakof, p. 187.

[6] Green Global Travel, "60 Weird Animals around the World," https://greenglobaltravel.com/weird-animals-around-the-world/#WEIRD%20MAMMALS (accessed April 4, 2018).

[7] George Brown Goode, *The Fisheries and Fishery Industries of the United States* (Government Printing Office, 1884), p. 19.

WORKS CITED

Beebe, C. William. *The Pangolin or Scaly Anteater.* New York: New York Zoological Society, 1914.

Goode, George Brown. *The Fisheries and Fishery Industries of the United States.* Washington, D.C.: Government Printing Office, 1884.

Green Global Travel. "60 Weird Animals around the World." https://greenglobaltravel.com/weird-animals-around-the-world/#WEIRD%20MAMMALS (accessed April 4, 2018).

Hussakof, L. "The Newly Discovered Goblin Shark of Japan." *Scientific American* CII:9 (February 26, 1910), pp. 186–187.

Instructor Notes to Bracketed Letters

[e]	The direct quote "round, shingled ball" is the object of the preposition *like*.
[b, e, g]	Both quotes come after the attribution tag "as author C. William Beebe points out." The first quote is the object of the preposition *like* and the second is a predicate adjective. The second quote is from the same source as the first.
[b, f, g]	Both quotes come after the attribution tag "Beebe writes." The ellipses indicate words that have been cut. Technically, when a footnote cites the same information as the footnote immediately before it, you merely write Ibid. However, that's advanced documentation, and this assignment is intended to give the student a chance to practice the second quote format, so the student should use the second quote format even though the reference is identical.
[a, c, e]	The first part of the quote comes before the attribution tag "according to . . . ." The quote is also divided by the attribution tag. The quote "soft and pliable" is a predicate adjective, and "rolled into a ball" makes up the verb phrase along with the helping verbs *can* and *be*.
[d, f, g]	The block quote is introduced by ellipses that represent cut words. This is the second quote from Hussakof.
[b, f]	The quote follows the attribution tag. Words have been eliminated.
[e]	The quote acts as the direct object of the verb *has*.

WEEK 35

Introduction to Sentence Style

— LESSON 128 —

Sentence Style: Equal and Subordinating
Sentences with Equal Elements: Segregating, Freight-Train, and Balanced

Exercise 128A: Identifying Sentence Types

In the blank that follows each sentence or set of sentences, write *S* for segregating, *FT* for freight-train, or *B* for balanced.

There was no ship in sight, and the sea-gulls were motionless upon its even greyness. The sky was dark with lowering clouds, but there was no wind.
—W. Somerset Maugham, *The Explorer* ____B____

He must wish her good night; he was going; he should get home as fast as he could.
—Jane Austen, *Persuasion* ____FT____

To me, she was in the place of a parent. Do not mistake me, however. I am not saying that she did not err in her advice.
—Jane Austen, *Persuasion* ____S____

Is this a costume? Does this say anything? It barely covers one man's nakedness!
—Robert Bolt, *A Man for All Seasons* ____S____

Let him die without an heir and we'll have them back again.
—Robert Bolt, *A Man for All Seasons* ____B____

Let them all be gathered together, let them stand up; yet they shall fear, and they shall be ashamed together.
—Isaiah 44:11 (KJV) ____FT, B____

Note to Instructor: Although this is a freight-train sentence, the semicolon in the middle also creates a balance between the first two independent clauses and the last two, so either answer can be considered as correct. Point this out to the student.

It is cold, and we have no blankets; the little children are freezing to death.
—Chief Joseph, "Surrender Speech" ____FT____

I am tired of fighting. Our Chiefs are killed; Looking Glass is dead. Shute is dead. The old men are all dead.
—Chief Joseph, "Surrender Speech" ____S____

I know you're scared. That's okay. I think there may be things in there and we have to take a look. There's no place else to go. This is it. I want you to help me.
—Cormac McCarthy, *The Road* ____S, B____

Note to Instructor: These are definitely segregating sentences, but among them, *I think there may be things in there* and *we have to take a look* is, individually, a balanced sentence. *S* is the correct answer, but also point out the balanced sentence to the student.

To be given dominion over another is a hard thing; to wrest dominion over another is a wrong thing; to give dominion of yourself to another is a wicked thing.
—Toni Morrison, *A Mercy* FT

Agitation, in the interval, certainly had held me and driven me, for I must, in circling about the place, have walked three miles; but I was to be, later on, so much more overwhelmed that this mere dawn of alarm was a comparatively human chill.
—Henry James, *The Turn of the Screw* B

The bay-sheltered islands and the great sea beyond stretched away to the far horizon southward and eastward; the little procession in the foreground looked futile and helpless on the edge of the rocky shore.
—Sarah Orne Jewett, *The Country of the Pointed Firs* B

Time was growing short. His time was growing short. It had to be enough. He had to make it enough.
—Robert Jordan, *The Dragon Reborn* S

And if you continue to give orders, they will continue to obey, for you will be the one who saved them, and who better to lead?
—Robert Jordan, *The Dragon Reborn* FT

— LESSON 129 —

Subordinating Sentences: Loose, Periodic, Cumulative, Convoluted, and Centered

Exercise 129A: Identifying Subordinating Sentences

In each sentence, underline the subject(s) of the main clause once and the predicate twice.

Label each sentence in the blank that follows it as *L* for loose, *P* for periodic, *CUMUL* for cumulative, *CONV* for convoluted, or *CENT* for centered.

For the purposes of this exercise, any sentence with four or more phrases and dependent clauses before or after the main clause should be considered cumulative. If two or three phrases or dependent clauses come before or after the main clause, the sentence should be classified as loose or periodic.

A single modifying phrase before or after the main clause does not turn it into a periodic or loose sentence.

If phrases or clauses come before and after the main clause, the sentence is centered, no matter how many phrases or clauses there are.

If any phrases or clauses come between the subject, predicate, or any essential parts of the main clause (objects, predicate nominatives, or predicate adjectives), the sentence is convoluted.

A phrase serving as an object or predicate nominative should be considered a single part of speech, not a subordinate phrase.

In the documentary, a man afflicted with cerebral palsy, his movements jerky and his speech low and drawled, detailed his life and his tribulations. CONV

I still see the image of him clearly, sitting in a small courtyard with a knife in his hand, whittling ever so slowly, his forearms moving like two gears in mesh—a short burst of motion, then a pause, his eyes wide open behind wide-rimmed glasses, his mouth constantly open, not closing even as he tried to speak. CUMUL

—Henry Jay Przybylo, MD, *Counting Backwards: A Doctor's Notes on Anesthesia*

King tides are driven by a particular alignment of the sun and moon and Earth that maximizes the gravitational tug on the oceans, as well as changes in the Gulf Stream current and the way the heat of a long summer causes the ocean to expand. CUMUL

When the king tides arrived in 2014 it was clear that the mayor's political gamble had paid off. CENT

—Jeff Goodell, *The Water Will Come: Rising Seas, Sinking Cities, and the Remaking of the Civilized World*

While the advantages of going to an elite college aren't questioned as often as they should be, the disadvantages are even less frequently broached, perhaps because a great many people can't imagine that there'd be any. CENT

And he contended that the homogeneous group of overachievers who make it to Princeton or Yale have, to that point, known only one triumph after another, largely because they've been given extensive preparation to master precisely those tasks that the elite educational track values. CUMUL

—Frank Bruni, *Where You Go Is Not Who You'll Be: An Antidote to the College Admissions Mania*

And if I have the gift of prophecy, and know all mysteries and all knowledge; and if I have all faith, so as to remove mountains, but have not love, I am nothing. CUMUL

—1 Corinthians 13:2, NASB

The rest of us, bathed and changed into a required green velvet dress for evenings, sat in descending order of age and class until the youngest and most recently arrived sat at the distant foot of the table. CONV

Telling myself that I would get her through one set of changes at a time, I temporized about my departure. P

These I ate at favorite spots: in the middle of a deserted pear orchard alive with bees, or on the roadside at the brow of a hill where the patterns of agriculture—green, brown, gold, and red—could be looked at with half-closed eyes to produce an instant impressionist painting. CUMUL

—Jill Ker Conway, *The Road from Coorain*

But I must confess, we're drawn here by other things as well: by the feeling of history in this city, more than 500 years older than our own nation; by the beauty of the Grunewald and the Tiergarten; most of all, by your courage and determination. CUMUL

Standing before the Brandenburg Gate, every man is a German, separated from his fellow men. CENT

—Ronald Reagan, "Tear Down This Wall"

Out of the bosom of the Air,
Out of the cloud-folds of her garments shaken,
Over the woodlands brown and bare,
Over the harvest-fields forsaken,
Silent, and soft, and slow
Descends the snow. CUMUL

This is the secret of despair,
Long in its cloudy bosom hoarded,
Now whispered and revealed
To wood and field. L

—Henry Wadsworth Longfellow, "Snow-flakes"

Five or six wild duck flew overhead in a swiftly moving V, intent on some far-off destination. L

Note to Student: *duck* is an unusual, but acceptable, plural version of *duck*.

As a bull, with a slight but irresistible movement, tosses its head from the grasp of a man who is leaning over the stall and idly holding its horn, so the sun entered the world in smooth, gigantic power. P

Note to Instructor: I have classified this as periodic because two dependent clauses precede the main clause, but since those clauses contain multiple elements, it is acceptable for the student to categorize this as cumulative.

Fiver stayed with him, keeping the wounds clean and watching his recovery. L

If ever great danger arose, he would come back to fight for those who honored his name. CENT

—Richard Adams, *Watership Down*

The Good Friday Agreement, overwhelmingly endorsed by the people on both sides of the Border, holds out the prospect of a peaceful long-term future for Northern Ireland, and the whole island of Ireland. CONV

Those urges to belong, divergent as they are, can live together more easily if we, Britain and the Irish Republic, can live closer together too. CONV

—Tony Blair, "Address to the Irish Parliament"

Unprovided with original learning, unformed in the habits of thinking, unskilled in the arts of composition, I resolved to write a book. P

The various modes of worship, which prevailed in the Roman world, were all considered by the people as equally true, by the philosopher as equally false, and by the magistrate as equally useful. CONV

Note to Instructor: This sentence must be marked as convoluted, since the clause *which . . . world* comes between subject and predicate, but the three phrases at the end also give aspects of a loose sentence.

It has always been my practice to cast a long paragraph in a single mould, to try it by my ear, to deposit it in my memory, but to suspend the action of the pen till I had given the last polish to my work. L

—Edward Gibbon, *The History of the Decline and Fall of the Roman Empire*

She was listening to the third woman, a stout, pleasant-faced, elderly woman who was talking in a slow clear monotone which showed no signs of pausing for breath or coming to a stop. CUMUL

Gathering up her despised money, the American lady followed suit, followed by the lady like a sheep. CENT

This crime, we have reason to believe, took place at a quarter past one last night. CONV

—Agatha Christie, *Murder on the Orient Express*

And then there were apple pies, and peach pies, and pumpkin pies; besides slices of ham and smoked beef; and moreover delectable dishes of preserved plums, and peaches, and pears, and quinces; not to mention broiled shad and roasted chickens; together with bowls of milk and cream, all mingled higgledy-piggledy, pretty much as I have enumerated them, with the motherly teapot sending up its clouds of vapor from the midst—Heaven bless the mark! CUMUL

All the stories of ghosts and goblins that he had heard in the afternoon now came crowding upon his recollection. CONV

About two hundred yards from the tree, a small brook crossed the road, and ran into a marshy and thickly-wooded glen, known by the name of Wiley's Swamp. CENT

All these tales, told in that drowsy undertone with which men talk in the dark, the countenances of the listeners only now and then receiving a casual gleam from the glare of a pipe, sank deep in the mind of Ichabod. CONV

—Washington Irving, "The Legend of Sleepy Hollow"

Like the waters of the river, like the motorists on the highway, and like the yellow trains streaking down the Santa Fe tracks, drama, in the shape of exceptional happenings, had never stopped there. CONV, P

—Truman Capote, *In Cold Blood*

Note to Instructor: This sentence is convoluted, but the three deliberate phrases coming before the subject are clearly designed to produce a periodic feel.

Is it not astonishing that, while we are plowing, planting, and reaping, using all kinds of mechanical tools, erecting houses, constructing bridges, building ships, working in metals of brass, iron, copper, silver, and gold; that while we are reading, writing, and ciphering, acting as clerks, merchants, and secretaries, having among us lawyers, doctors, ministers, poets, authors, editors, orators, and teachers; that we are engaged in all the enterprises common to other men—digging gold in California, capturing the whale in the Pacific, feeding sheep and cattle on the hillside, living, moving, acting, thinking, planning, living in families as husbands, wives, and children, and above all, confessing and worshipping the Christian God, and looking hopefully for life and immortality beyond the grave—we are called upon to prove that we are men? CUMUL

—Frederick Douglass, "The Hypocrisy of American Slavery"

— LESSON 130 —

Practicing Sentence Style

Choose one of the following assignments:

Exercise 130A: Rewriting

The following list of events, from the traditional Japanese fable "The Sagacious Monkey and the Boar," needs to be rewritten as a story.

This story must have at least one of each of the following types of sentences:

Segregating (at least three sentences in a row)
Freight-Train
Balanced
Loose
Periodic
Cumulative (with four or more subordinate phrases/clauses; main clause can come either first or last)
Convoluted
Centered

You may add, change, and subtract, as long as the finished story is at least 400 words long and makes good sense.

a traveling monkey-man had a monkey
he took it around and showed off its tricks
he came home angry
he told his wife to send for the butcher
the monkey kept forgetting his tricks
the monkey-man wanted to sell the monkey for meat
the wife pleaded for the monkey
the man was determined to sell him to the butcher
the monkey heard the conversation
the monkey knew there was a wise boar in the forest

he went to see the boar
he told the boar his problem
the boar asked if the monkey-man and his wife had a baby
the monkey said yes
the boar said that he had seen the baby playing by the door in the mornings
the monkey agreed
the boar offered to grab the baby and run away
he told the monkey to follow him
the monkey would rescue the baby
then the man and his wife would keep the monkey
the monkey went home
he did not sleep much
the next morning the wife put the baby on the floor
she started to do her morning chores
the baby gave a cry
she saw the boar carrying off the baby
she woke her husband up
they saw the monkey
the monkey was running after the boar
the monkey brought the baby back
the wife praised the monkey
they sent the butcher away
the monkey was petted
the monkey lived out his days in peace

Note to Instructor: This sample composition shows one way in which the assignment could be completed. Each sentence fulfilling one of the required elements is underlined, with the label of the required element written in the margin next to the line where the sentence ends. The original fable, which does not meet the requirements for sentence styles, is also included. If the student has trouble rewriting, allow her to read the original tale.

The student does not necessarily need to use direct dialogue in the story, as I have done below.

SAMPLE COMPOSITION

Once upon a time, there was a traveling monkey man. He used to travel around Japan with his monkey, showing off its tricks. But one day, he came home horribly angry. He told his wife to send for the butcher. The monkey kept forgetting its tricks, falling asleep in the middle of shows, wandering off into the crowds, getting distracted by birds flying by overhead or children in the crowd, stopping for a snack when it was supposed to be working. **cumulative**

No matter what the man did, he could not get the monkey to perform. He decided that the only way to get money for the monkey was to sell it for meat.

His wife was horrified! She loved the monkey. She pleaded for the monkey. She begged for its life. **segregating**

But the man had no pity. He insisted on calling the butcher, and the butcher agreed to come first thing in the morning.

The monkey overheard, and he was terrified. He knew he had to do something to save himself. But what? He didn't know. **balanced**

But he had heard that a wise boar lived in the forest nearby, spending his days snoozing in the sun, dispensing advice to the forest creatures. So late that night, he slipped from the house and made his way to the boar's den. **loose**

"O wise boar," he said, humbly, "I have a problem. I am older than I used to be. I cannot always remember the tricks that my master teaches me. And he is so angry that he wants to sell me to the butcher for meat. What should I do?"

"Hmm," said the boar. "Let me think about it."

He thought for a long time, and then he said, "I believe that your master and his wife have a baby."

"Yes," the monkey said, "they do."

"I have seen the baby playing by the door, early in the mornings."

"Yes," the monkey agreed, "my mistress often puts her baby there to play."

"In the morning, I will grab the baby and run away with it," the boar said. "You run after me; run as fast as you can; leap onto my back; rescue the baby; and take it home. Your master and his wife will be so grateful that they will keep you forever." **freight train**

The monkey agreed to this plan, and went home. Filled with fear and uncertainty, tossing and turning, terrified of the morning, he did not sleep that night! But the next morning, it all unfolded as the boar had described. His mistress put the baby on the floor next to the door, where it could play in the morning sun, and began to fix breakfast and do her morning chores. **periodic**

Suddenly, the baby gave a cry. The mother looked up and saw the boar, carrying her baby away.

She ran to wake up her husband. They dashed out into the yard—and saw the monkey, running at top speed after the boar. A few moments later, the monkey returned, holding the baby. **centered**

"Oh, beautiful monkey!" the mother exclaimed. "How could we ever have thought of sending you to the butcher? I owe you my child's life!"

Just then, the butcher came in the front gate. But the monkey-man and his wife sent the butcher away. The monkey, patted and praised, given treats, tucked at night into a warm bed, now a treasured member of the family, lived in peace for the rest of its days. **convoluted**

THE SAGACIOUS MONKEY AND THE BOAR
(Original Japanese Fable)

Long, long ago, there lived in the province of Shinshin in Japan, a traveling monkey-man, who earned his living by taking round a monkey and showing off the animal's tricks.

One evening the man came home in a very bad temper and told his wife to send for the butcher the next morning.

The wife was very bewildered and asked her husband:

"Why do you wish me to send for the butcher?"

"It's no use taking that monkey round any longer, he's too old and forgets his tricks. I beat him with my stick all I know how, but he won't dance properly. I must now sell him to the butcher and make what money out of him I can. There is nothing else to be done."

The woman felt very sorry for the poor little animal, and pleaded for her husband to spare the monkey, but her pleading was all in vain; the man was determined to sell him to the butcher.

Now the monkey was in the next room and overheard every word of the conversation. He soon understood that he was to be killed, and he said to himself:

"Barbarous, indeed, is my master! Here I have served him faithfully for years, and instead of allowing me to end my days comfortably and in peace, he is going to let me be cut up by the butcher, and my poor body is to be roasted and stewed and eaten? Woe is me! What am I to do? Ah! a bright thought has struck me! There is, I know, a wild boar living in the forest nearby. I have often heard tell of his wisdom. Perhaps if I go to him and tell him the strait I am in he will give me his counsel. I will go and try."

There was no time to lose. The monkey slipped out of the house and ran as quickly as he could to the forest to find the boar. The boar was at home, and the monkey began his tale of woe at once.

"Good Mr. Boar, I have heard of your excellent wisdom. I am in great trouble, you alone can help me. I have grown old in the service of my master, and because I cannot dance properly now he intends to sell me to the butcher. What do you advise me to do? I know how clever you are!"

The boar was pleased at the flattery and determined to help the monkey. He thought for a little while and then said:

"Hasn't your master a baby?"

"Oh, yes," said the monkey, "he has one infant son."

"Doesn't it lie by the door in the morning when your mistress begins the work of the day? Well, I will come round early and when I see my opportunity I will seize the child and run off with it."

"What then?" said the monkey.

"Why, the mother will be in a tremendous scare, and before your master and mistress know what to do, you must run after me and rescue the child and take it home safely to its parents, and you will see that when the butcher comes they won't have the heart to sell you."

The monkey thanked the boar many times and then went home. He did not sleep much that night, as you may imagine, for thinking of the morrow. His life depended on whether the boar's plan succeeded or not. He was the first up, waiting anxiously for what was to happen. It seemed to him a very long time before his master's wife began to move about and open the shutters to let in the light of day. Then all happened as the boar had planned. The mother placed her child near the porch as usual while she tidied up the house and got her breakfast ready.

The child was crooning happily in the morning sunlight, dabbing on the mats at the play of light and shadow. Suddenly there was a noise in the porch and a loud cry from the child. The mother ran out from the kitchen to the spot, only just in time to see the boar disappearing through the gate with her child in its clutch. She flung out her hands with a loud cry of despair and rushed into the inner room where her husband was still sleeping soundly.

He sat up slowly and rubbed his eyes, and crossly demanded to know what his wife was making all that noise about. By the time that the man was alive to what had happened, and they both got outside the gate, the boar had got well away, but they saw the monkey running after the thief as hard as his legs would carry him.

Both the man and wife were moved to admiration at the plucky conduct of the sagacious monkey, and their gratitude knew no bounds when the faithful monkey brought the child safely back to their arms.

"There!" said the wife. "This is the animal you want to kill—if the monkey hadn't been here we should have lost our child forever."

"You are right, wife, for once," said the man as he carried the child into the house. "You may send the butcher back when he comes, and now give us all a good breakfast and the monkey too."

When the butcher arrived he was sent away, and the monkey was petted and lived the rest of his days in peace, nor did his master ever strike him again.

Exercise 130B: Original Composition

Write an original composition of at least 400 words, with at least one of each of the following types of sentences:

Segregating (at least three sentences in a row)
Freight-Train
Balanced
Loose
Periodic
Cumulative (with four or more subordinate phrases/clauses; main clause can come either first or last)
Convoluted
Centered

This composition may be one of the following:

a) A plot summary of one of your favorite books or movies.

b) A narrative of some event, happening, trip, or great memory from your past.

c) A scene from a story that you create yourself.

d) Any other topic you choose.

Note to Instructor: Answers will vary! If you have trouble checking for the required elements, consider posting your student's work on forums.welltrainedmind.com to get a "group sourced" check.

WEEK 36

— REVIEW 11 —

Final Review

Note to Instructor: This is not a "test"—it is a review and a challenge to the student to use the knowledge acquired. Give all necessary assistance.

Review 11A: Explaining Sentences

Tell your instructor every possible piece of grammatical information about the following sentences. Follow these steps (notice that these are slightly different than the instructions in your previous "explaining" exercise):

1) Identify the sentence type and write it in the left-hand margin.
2) Underline each subordinate clause. Describe the identity and function of each clause and give any other useful information (introductory word, relationship to the rest of the sentence, etc.)
3) Label each preposition as *P* and each object of the preposition as *OP*. Describe the identity and function of each prepositional phrase.
4) Parse, out loud, all verbs acting as predicates.
5) Describe the identity and function of each individual remaining word. Don't worry about the articles and coordinating conjunctions, though.
6) Provide any other useful information that you might be able to think of.

Note to Instructor: Use the information below to prompt the student as necessary. (Numbered information sections correspond to instruction steps above.) Give all necessary help. Encourage the student to answer loudly and in complete sentences.

Among the most common residents of Alaska's forests (and northern cousins of the gray squirrels that inhabit most of the United States), red squirrels remain active year-round.

I had simply assumed the birds to be either tree swallows or violet-green swallows, the kinds most commonly seen in and around Anchorage.

—Bill Sherwonit, *Animal Stories: Encounters with Alaska's Wildlife*

1) periodic **Among the most common residents of Alaska's forests (and northern cousins of the gray squirrels that inhabit most of the United States), red squirrels remain active year-round.**

2) **Among the most common residents of Alaska's forests (and northern cousins of the gray squirrels <u>that inhabit most of the United States</u>), red squirrels remain active year-round.**

Note to Instructor: The single subordinate clause, introduced by the relative pronoun *that*, acts as an adjective modifying *squirrels*.

3) P OP P OP
Among the most common residents of Alaska's forests (and northern
P OP P OP
cousins of the gray squirrels <u>that inhabit most of the United States</u>),
red squirrels remain active year-round.

Note to Instructor: All four prepositional phrases act as adjectives. The first modifies *red squirrels*, the second modifies *residents*, the third modifies *cousins*, and the fourth modifies *most*.

4) *Inhabits* is simple present, active, indicative. *Remain* is simple present, linking, indicative. The student may identify this as active, but notice that in this context *remain* connects *red squirrels* with the adjective describing them, so it cannot be an action verb.

5) *Common* is an adjective modifying residents; *most* is an adverb modifying *common.*

Alaska's is a proper adjective modifying *forests.*

Cousins is an appositive renaming *red squirrels.* It is unusual in that it comes before the noun it renames, rather than afterwards, which may confuse the student. *Northern* is an adjective modifying *cousins. Gray squirrels* is a single compound noun, not an adjective and a noun, since removing *gray* changes the meaning of the word. (See 6, below, for additional information.)

Within the subordinate clause, *that* is the relative pronoun whose antecedent is *gray squirrels. Most* is a noun serving as the direct object of *inhabit.* (Notice that *most* has two different functions in this sentence!)

Red squirrels is a compound noun acting as the subject of the independent clause (see *gray squirrels*, above). *Active* is a predicate adjective describing the subject and following the linking verb *remain. Year-round* is a compound adverb describing *remain* and answering the question *when.* (If the student says that it describes *active,* you may accept this—the phrase is ambiguous.)

6) The entire appositive renaming *red squirrels* is *and northern cousins of the gray squirrels that inhabit most of the United States.* It is unusual because the writer has chosen to turn it into a parenthetical element and place it before the noun renamed. This cannot be a second object of the preposition *among,* because red squirrels *are* northern cousins of gray squirrels—they are not *among* northern cousins of gray squirrels.

1) periodic **I had simply assumed the birds to be either tree swallows or violet-green swallows, the kinds most commonly seen in and around Anchorage.**

2) **I had simply assumed <u>the birds to be either tree swallows or violet-green swallows</u>, the kinds most commonly seen in and around Anchorage.**

Note to Instructor: This is an unusual subordinate clause that makes use of an idiom. In meaning, it is identical to *that the birds were either tree swallows or violet-green swallows*: a noun clause serving as the direct object of *had assumed.* However, in this form, *that* disappears, and the linking verb *were* is transformed into the infinitive form *to be.* This acts as a linking verb connecting *birds* to the predicate nominatives *tree swallows* and *violet-green swallows.*

3) **I had simply assumed the birds to be either tree swallows or violet-green swallows, the kinds most commonly seen in (P) and around (P) Anchorage (OP).**

> **Note to Instructor:** *Anchorage* is the object of both prepositions! Together, the two prepositions and the single object form a single prepositional phrase. It acts as an adverb modifying *seen* and answering the question *where.*

4) *Had assumed* is a perfect past, active, indicative verb.

As noted above, *to be* is an present active infinitive, but in the clause, it functions as a simple present state-of-being indicative verb.

Note that *seen* is not acting as a predicate—it is a past participle! (See below.)

5) *I* is a personal subject pronoun, serving as the subject of the main clause.

Simply is an adverb modifying *had assumed.*

Birds is the subject of the noun clause.

Tree swallows and *violet-green swallows* are compound nouns (removing *tree* and *violet-green* would change the meaning of the noun) serving as predicate nominatives and renaming *birds.*

Either . . . or are coordinating correlative conjunctions joining the predicate nominatives.

Kinds is an appositive that renames both predicate nominatives.

Seen is a past participle acting as an adjective and describing *kinds. Commonly* is an adverb describing *seen*, and *most* is an adverb describing *commonly.*

6) This sentence stands out not only for the idiom, but because in two places, a single noun is related to two words preceding—*kinds* renaming both *tree swallows* and *violet-green swallows*, and *Anchorage* serving as the object of both *in* and *around.*

There was just one very small improvement—after swearing that he wouldn't use her to send letters to any of his friends, Harry had been allowed to let his owl, Hedwig, out at night.

—J. K. Rowling, *Harry Potter and the Prisoner of Azkaban*

1) loose/ compound-complex **There was just one very small improvement—after swearing that he wouldn't use her to send letters to any of his friends, Harry had been allowed to let his owl, Hedwig, out at night.**

> **Note to Instructor:** In feel, this is a loose sentence, with the main independent clause *There was just one very small improvement* followed by a long prepositional phrase that includes a dependent clause.
>
> However, the second half of the sentence is *Harry had been allowed to let his owl, Hedwig, out at night*, which is an independent clause. If there were a semicolon between *improvement* and *after,* this would be a compound-complex sentence made up of one independent clause (sentence), and one periodic sentence (the independent clause *Harry had been . . .*) preceded by the long prepositional phrase.
>
> But because Rowling chose to use a dash rather than a semicolon, the weight of the sentence is on the first independent clause, with everything following the dash having the feel of falling away from the main thought of the sentence.
>
> Discuss this with the student, and point out that sometimes sentences do not fall easily into a single category!

2) **There was just one very small improvement—after swearing that he wouldn't use her to send letters to any of his friends, Harry had been allowed to let his owl, Hedwig, out at night.**

> **Note to Instructor:** The single subordinate clause is a noun clause, acting as the object of the present participle *swearing*. The introductory *that* is not a relative pronoun, just a subordinating word—in a diagram, it would be placed on a horizontal line above the diagram with a dotted line connecting it to the verb *would use*.

3) **There was just one very small improvement—after** (P) **swearing** (OP) **that he wouldn't use her to send letters to** (P) **any** (OP) **of** (P) **his friends** (OP), **Harry had been allowed to let his owl, Hedwig, out at** (P) **night** (OP).

> **Note to Instructor:** *After swearing that he wouldn't use her to send letters to any of his friends* is, all together, an adverbial prepositional phrase modifying *had been allowed* and answering the question *when*. (See further explanation in 6), below.) *To any* is an adverbial prepositional phrase modifying *send* (send where?). *Of his friends* is an adjectival prepositional phrase modifying the indefinite pronoun *any*. *At night* is an adverbial prepositional phrase modifying the infinitive *to let*.
>
> Notice that *to send* and *to let* are infinitives, while *to any* is a prepositional phrase.

4) *Was* is simple past, state-of-being, indicative.

Would use is simple present, active, modal.

Had been allowed is perfect past, passive, indicative.

5) *There* is an adverb modifying the state-of-being verb *was*.

Improvement is the subject of the first main clause. *Small* is an adjective modifying *improvement*. *Very* is an adverb modifying *small*. *One* is an adjective modifying *improvement*. *Just* is an adverb modifying *one*.

Swearing is a present participle acting as the object of the preposition *after*.

The personal pronoun *he* is the subject of the subordinate clause.

n't is the condensed form of the negative particle *not*.

The personal pronoun *her* is the object of the verb *would use*.

The infinitive *to send* modifies *would use* and answers the question *how*. *Letters* is the object of the infinitive.

His is a possessive adjective (pronoun) modifying *friends*.

Harry is the subject of the second independent clause.

To let is an infinitive acting as an adverb and modifying the verb *had been allowed*. (Notice that it cannot be the object of the verb because the verb is passive.)

Owl is the object of the infinitive *to let*. *His* is a possessive adjective (pronoun) modifying *owl*. *Hedwig* is an appositive renaming *owl*.

Out is an adverb modifying *to let*.

6) The entire phrase *after swearing that he wouldn't use her to send letters to any of his friends* is a prepositional phrase, with *swearing* as the object of the preposition *after*, and the subordinate noun clause as the object of *swearing*.

From a long habit of listening admiringly to everything that was said in her presence, and looking at the speakers as if she were mentally engaged in taking off impressions of their images upon her soul, never to part with the same but with life, her head had quite settled on one side.

—Charles Dickens, *Dombey and Son*

1) cumulative **From a long habit of listening admiringly to everything that was said in her presence, and looking at the speakers as if she were mentally engaged in taking off impressions of their images upon her soul, never to part with the same but with life, her head had quite settled on one side.**

Note to Instructor: Although technically everything from the initial *From* to *life* consists of one prepositional phrase, I have classified this as cumulative because of the length of the elements within that phrase and the inclusion of two subordinate clauses.

2) **From a long habit of listening admiringly to everything that was said in her presence, and looking at the speakers as if she were mentally engaged in taking off impressions of their images upon her soul, never to part with the same but with life, her head had quite settled on one side.**

Note to Instructor: The first subordinate clause is an adjectival clause modifying *everything*, introduced by the relative pronoun *that*, which also serves as the subject of the clause. The second subordinate clause is an adverbial clause modifying *looking* and introduced by the compound adverb *as if* (this functions in the same way as the single adverb *like*).

3) **From** (P) **a long habit** (OP) **of** (P) **listening** (OP) **admiringly to** (P) **everything** (OP) **that was said in** (P) **her presence** (OP)**, and looking** (OP) **at** (P) **the speakers** (OP) **as if she were mentally engaged in** (P) **taking** (OP) **off impressions of** (P) **their images** (OP) **upon** (P) **her soul** (OP)**, never to part with the same but with life, her head had quite settled on** (P) **one side** (OP)**.**

Note to Instructor: Technically, the entire section *From a long . . . but with life* is a single prepositional phrase, acting as an adverb and modifying the verb *had settled* in the independent clause. The object of the preposition *from* is the noun *habit*; everything else in the phrase modifies something within it (see 5 below).

Of listening acts as an adjective and modifies *habit*; *looking* is the second object of the same *of* (compound objects of the preposition).

To everything acts as an adverb and modifies the present participle *listening*; *in her presence* acts as an adverb and modifies *was said* (answering the question *where*); *at the speakers* acts as an adverb and modifies the present participle *looking*; *in taking* acts as an adverb and modifies *were engaged*; *of their images* acts as an adjective and modifies *impressions*; *upon her soul* also acts as an adjective and modifies *impressions* (NOT *images*; the *impressions* are upon her soul); *on one side* is adverbial and modifies *had settled*.

The student may be confused by the phrase *never to part with the same but with life*. The meaning is, "she will never part with the impressions of those images until she parts with life." *With* does not here serve as a preposition; rather, it is part of the verb. "To part with" is an idiomatic verb with the single meaning of "abandon" or "relinquish." The repetition of *with* before *life* is not the repetition of a pronoun or adverb, but rather a condensed form of the infinitive: the full use would be "never to part with the same but to part with life." You may show the student the partial diagram below in explanation.

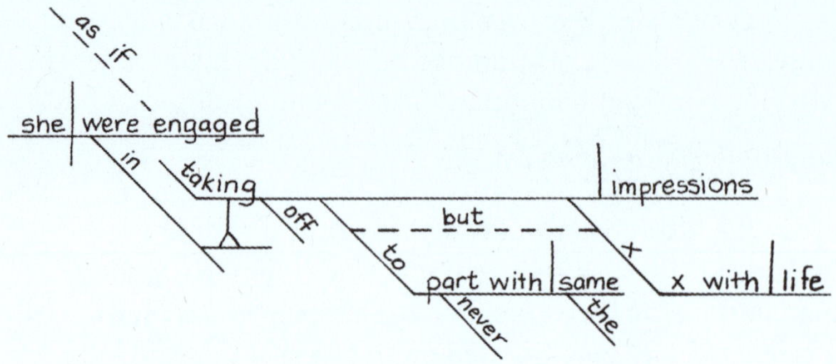

4) *Was said* is simple past, passive, indicative.
Were engaged is simple past, passive, subjunctive.
Had settled is perfect past, passive, indicative.

5) *Long* is an adjective modifying *habit.*
Admiringly is an adverb modifying the present participle *listening.*
The first *her* is a possessive adjective (pronoun) modifying *presence.*
Mentally is an adverb modifying *were engaged.*
Off is an adverb modifying the present participle *taking.*
Their is a possessive adjective (pronoun) modifying *images.*
The second *her* is a possessive adjective (pronoun) modifying *soul.*
Never is an adverb of negation, modifying the infinitive *to part with.*
As noted above, *to part with* is an idiomatic infinitive verb.
Same is a noun acting as the object of the infinitive *to part with.*
As noted above, *life* is the object of the partially elided infinitive *(to part) with.*
The third *her* is a possessive adjective (pronoun) modifying *head.*
Head is the subject of the independent clause.
Quite is an adverb modifying the verb *had settled.*
One is an adjective modifying the noun *side.*

6) As noted above, although this sentence is cumulative with the independent clause coming at the end, it is also made up of a single independent clause with all other elements contained within the single prepositional phrase preceding the independent clause.

Throughout his papacy, the whole family of Rodrigo Borgia, who ascended the papal throne as Alexander VI, was surrounded by a buzz of scandal.

But if the whole is unsatisfactory, the David, taken part by part, is a work of overwhelming power and magnificence, and it is Michelangelo's first great assertion of the quality that is so often in our minds when we think of him — the heroic.

—J. H. Plumb, *The Italian Renaissance*

1) convoluted **Throughout his papacy, the whole family of Rodrigo Borgia, who ascended the papal throne as Alexander VI, was surrounded by a buzz of scandal.**

> **Note to Instructor:** This convoluted sentence (the subject, *family,* is separated by the subordinate clause *who ascended the papal throne as Alexander VI* from the predicate, was *surrounded*) also has the rhythm of a centered sentence, since *Throughout his papacy* precedes the subject and *by a buzz of*

> *scandal* follows the predicate. You may wish to point this out to the student, as an example of how sentence rhythms can work on multiple levels.

2) **Throughout his papacy, the whole family of Rodrigo Borgia, who ascended the papal throne as Alexander VI, was surrounded by a buzz of scandal.**

> **Note to Instructor:** The single subordinate clause is adjectival and modifies *Rodrigo Borgia*. It is introduced by the relative pronoun *who*, which also serves as the subject of the clause.

P OP P OP

3) **Throughout his papacy, the whole family of Rodrigo Borgia, who ascended**

P OP P OP P OP

the papal throne as Alexander VI, was surrounded by a buzz of scandal.

> **Note to Instructor:** *Throughout his papacy* is adverbial and modifies *was surrounded*; *of Rodrigo Borgia* is adjectival and modifies *family*; *as Alexander VI* is adverbial and modifies *ascended* (it answers the question *how?*); *by a buzz* is adverbial and modifies *was surrounded*; *of scandal* is adjectival and modifies *buzz*.

4) *Ascended* is simple past, active, indicative.
Was surrounded is simple past, passive, indicative.

5) *His* is a possessive adjective (pronoun) modifying *papacy*.
Whole is an adjective modifying *family*; *family* is the subject of the main independent clause.
Throne is the object of the verb *ascended*; *papal* is an adjective modifying *throne*.

6) This is a relatively simple sentence, included to show how a sentence can have rhythms of more than one sentence type (see 1, above).

1) convoluted/ compound-complex/ loose

But if the whole is unsatisfactory, the *David*, taken part by part, is a work of overwhelming power and magnificence, and it is Michelangelo's first great assertion of the quality that is so often in our minds when we think of him—the heroic.

> **Note to Instructor:** This compound-complex sentence consists of two independent clauses joined by a comma and a coordinating conjunction. The first sentence is convoluted (the past participle phrase *taken part by part* divides the subject, *the David*, from the predicate, *is*. The second sentence is loose; the main clause *it is Michelangelo's first great assertion* is followed by a series of prepositional phrases and subordinate clauses.
>
> Do not expect the student to realize immediately that these are two sentences with two different sentence structures, but give all help necessary to reach this conclusion.

2) **But if the whole is unsatisfactory, the *David*, taken part by part, is a work of overwhelming power and magnificence, and it is Michelangelo's first great assertion of the quality that is so often in our minds when we think of him—the heroic.**

> **Note to Instructor:** The first subordinate clause is adverbial and modifies the first predicate *is*; it is introduced by the adverb *if*. The second subordinate clause is adjectival and modifies *quality*; it is introduced by the relative pronoun *that*, which also serves as the subject of the clause. The third subordinate clause is actually part of the second clause; it is adverbial and modifies the second predicate *is*. It is introduced by the adverb *when*.

3)

P OP

But if the whole is unsatisfactory, the *David*, taken part by part,

P OP OP

is a work of overwhelming power and magnificence, and it is

P OP

Michelangelo's first great assertion of the quality that is so often

P OP P OP

in our minds when we think of him—the heroic.

> **Note to Instructor:** *By part* is one element of the idiom *part by part*, which (all together) is an adverbial idiom modifying the past participle *taken* and has the meaning of "piecemeal" or "bit by bit."
>
> *Of overwhelming power and magnificence* is adjectival and modifies *work* (*power and magnificence* are the compound objects of the preposition *of*); *of the quality* is adjectival and modifies *assertion*.
>
> *In our minds* is actually a prepositional phrase acting as a predicate adjective; it follows the linking verb *is* and describes the subject. It could also be interpreted as an adverbial phrase modifying the state-of-being verb *is* and answering the question *where*. You may want to point out to the student that the phrase is ambiguous.
>
> *Of him* is adverbial and modifies *think*.

4) In the first subordinate clause, *is* is simple present, state-of-being, indicative. (Note that the *if* introducing the clause does not introduce a condition contrary to reality, so this cannot be subjunctive.)

In the first main clause, *is* is simple present, state-of-being, indicative.

In the second main clause, *is* is simple present, state-of-being, indicative.

In the second subordinate clause, *is* is simple present, state-of-being, indicative.

In the third subordinate clause, *think* is simple present, active, indicative.

5) *Whole* is a noun serving as the subject of the first dependent clause.

Unsatisfactory is a predicate adjective describing *whole*.

The David is a proper noun serving as the subject of the first main clause.

Taken is the past participle of *take* and describes *the David*.

Part by part is an idiom acting as an adverb and describing *taken* (it answers the question *how*).

Work is a predicate nominative renaming *the David*.

Overwhelming is a present participle acting as an adjective and describing both *power* and *magnificence*.

It is a third person singular pronoun serving as the subject of the second main clause.

Michelangelo's is a possessive adjective describing *assertion*. *First* and *great* are also adjectives describing assertion. *Assertion* is a predicate nominative renaming *it*.

Often is an adverb describing the predicate adjective phrase *in our minds*; *so* is an adverb describing *often*.

Our is a possessive adjective (pronoun) describing *minds*.

We is a personal pronoun serving as the subject of the third dependent clause.

Heroic is an appositive; it serves as a noun (*the heroic*) and it renames *quality*. In this sentence, it is a parenthetical element that serves a grammatical function within the sentence.

Review 11B: Correcting Errors

Rewrite the following sets of sentences on your own paper (or with a word-processing program), inserting all necessary punctuation and capitalization.

Include the citations in your corrections!

> **Note to Instructor:** The original sentences are listed below. In some cases, there are multiple correct options for punctuation. As many acceptable alternatives as possible are listed below, but if the student chooses an option not listed and it appears to follow the rules, you may choose to accept it.
>
> When the student is finished, show him the original sentences for comparison.

"I feel like a salt crystal," he often said, "in a mountain stream, being washed away. We don't belong here. We're Earth people. This is Mars. It was meant for Martians. For heaven's sake, Cora, let's buy tickets for home!"

> **Note to Instructor:** The dialogue tag must be punctuated exactly as above. The comma after *stream* could also be a dash, but there must be some punctuation there, since the stream is not being washed away—the salt crystal is. The periods between these sentences could be semicolons; grammatical variations on separating the complete sentences, such as a semicolon after *here* and dashes setting off *This is Mars*, are acceptable, but the sentences cannot be linked together merely by commas. *Earth* should be capitalized since it is a proper adjective. *Cora* is a term of direct address and must be surrounded by commas. The exclamation point after *home* could be a period. The quotation marks must be placed exactly as above.

But the American-built town of cottages, peach trees, and theatres was silent.

> **Note to Instructor:** *American-built* is a compound adjective in the attribute position and must be hyphenated. The commas should be placed exactly as above.

—Ray Bradbury, "Dark They Were, and Golden Eyed."

The account of Michelangelo's career begins with his auspicious birth and early training and it chronicles his early works, including the *Bacchus* (1496-7) and the St. Peter's *Pietà* (1497-9) in Rome, before coming to the colossal and extraordinary statue of the *David* (1501-4) in Florence and his unexecuted scheme for the enormous painting *Battle of Cascina* (1504-5).

> **Note to Instructor:** A comma could follow *training*. Another could follow *Florence*.

—Giorgio Vasari, *The Life of Michelangelo*

Michelangelo chafed at any restrictions placed on his freedom. "If Your Holiness wishes me to accomplish anything," he wrote to Pope Clement VIII, "I beg you not to have authorities set over me in my own trade, but to have faith in me and give me a free hand."

> **Note to Instructor:** A colon could follow *freedom*. The comma after *trade* is preferable but not necessary. *Your Holiness* is a formal title; both words should be capitalized.

In 1475, about 50,000 people lived within the Tuscan capital's high walls; at least an equal number lived in the contado, the surrounding countryside where for thousands of years a large number of peasants and a smaller number of gentleman farmers had cultivated wine, grain, and olives in the rocky hillsides.

> **Note to Instructor:** The semicolon after *walls* could be a period, with *At* capitalized.

Michelangelo will employ the same complex, twisting pose—suggestive of struggle and internal contradictions—in mature works like the famous *Night* from the Medici tombs.

> **Note to Instructor:** The comma between *complex* and *twisting* is necessary, since the two adjectives can be exchanged freely. The dashes could also be commas or parentheses.

Miles J. Unger, *Michelangelo: A Life in Six Masterpieces*

> **Note to Instructor:** The student may put a comma after *Michelangelo*; if so, do not mark this as wrong, but point out that a colon usually separates title from subtitle.

Worms can not only survive in faux-Martian soil—they can start a new generation. That's the conclusion from biologist Wieger Wamelink, who recently discovered two baby worms in his simulated Mars soil experiment.

> **Note to Instructor:** The dash after *soil* can also be a semicolon, but not a period (the "not only" in the first clause gives it too close a relationship to the second) or comma (that would be comma splice). The period after *generation* could also be a semicolon.

Since 2013, scientists from Wageningen University & Research have been growing crops in Mars and moon-soil simulants designed by NASA.

> **Note to Instructor:** The comma after *Since 2013* is preferable but not necessary,as the prepositional phrase is so short.

Lauren Sigfusson, "Good News! Worms Make Babies in 'Martian' Soil." In *Discover: Science for the Curious*, December 4, 2017.

> **Note to Instructor:** The quotes around *'Martian'* are there because the soil isn't really Martian, but since the student has not covered this rule, point out that quotes are sometimes used to set off something that isn't actually true. The exclamation point after *News* could also be a colon. The colon between *Discover* and *Science* is not necessary, as the title of the journal could easily be *Discover Science for the Curious*.

Review 11C: Fill in the Blank

Each of the following sentences is missing one of the elements listed. Provide the correct required form of a word that seems appropriate to you. When you are finished, compare your sentences with the originals.

In __contrast__ (singular abstract noun), the German infantry __involved__ (past participle) in the crossing __were__ absolutely __exhausted__ (simple past, passive, indicative action verb), having had __no__ (adjective of negation) sleep to speak of __since__ (preposition) 10 May and __having been involved__ (perfect present passive participle, action verb) in heavy fighting the __previous__ (adjective) day.

__Soon__ (adverb) after, he spoke to General Georges, who __seemed__ (linking verb, simple past) to have __partially__ (adverb) recovered from the previous __day's__ (possessive adjective) breakdown. Georges admitted __that__ (subordinating word) there had been a __serious__ (adjective) breach of more than ten miles, but assured Churchill __that it was now plugged__ (noun clause acting as object of *assured*). In this, __of course__ (short parenthetical expression),

Georges was ___hopelessly___ misinformed. ___In fact___, the French Ninth Army ___had crumpled___ apart at
adverb — short parenthetical expression — perfect past, active, indicative action verb

the seams and a gap of ___some___ fifty miles ___had been punched___ in the line up to sixty miles deep.
adverb — perfect past, passive, indicative action verb

—James Holland, *The Battle of Britain: Five Months That Changed History: May-October, 1940*

In the days ___when___ the Cheyennes ___numbered___ in the thousands, they had more ___horses___ than
relative adverb — past participle — plural concrete noun

any of the Plains tribes. They ___were called___ the Beautiful People, but fate ___had turned___ against
simple past, passive, indicative action verb — perfect past, active, indicative action verb

them both in the south and in the north. ___After___ twenty years of ___decimation___ they were
preposition — abstract noun

___closer___ to ___obliteration___ than the buffalo.
comparative adjective — abstract noun

The treaty commissioners ___promised___ Captain Jack and the ___other___ head men that if they
simple past, active, indicative action verb — adjective

___would move___ ___north___ to a reservation in Oregon ___every___ family ___would have___ ___its___ own
simple present, active, modal action verb — adverbial noun — adjective — simple present, active, modal action verb — possessive adjective (pronoun)

land, teams of horses, ___wagons___, ___farming___ implements, tools, clothing, and food—all ___provided___
plural concrete noun — present participle — past participle

___by___ the government.
preposition

—Dee Brown, *Bury My Heart at Wounded Knee: An Indian History of the American West*

Sometimes it is not ___easy___ for people ___to remember___ clearly what ___was read___. It is storytelling
predicate adjective — active infinitive — simple past, passive, indicative action verb

___that___ people tend ___to remember___ ___easily___.
relative pronoun — active infinitive — adverb

Fox ___had left___ his home village of Fenny Drayton in Leicestershire four ___years___ earlier and
perfect past, active, indicative action verb — adverbial noun, plural

___had been searching___ across England for ___someone___ who ___might help___ him with his religious
progressive perfect past, active, indicative action verb — indefinite pronoun — simple present, active, modal action verb

quest. He ___had spent___ a year with a ___Baptist___ uncle in London and ___had visited___ the army
perfect past, active, indicative action verb — proper adjective — perfect past, active, indicative action verb

camps of the English Civil War ___where___ the ___most___ ___radical___ religious ideas ___were circulating___.
relative adverb — adverb — adjective — progressive past, active, indicative action verb

—Stephen W. Angell and Ben Pink Dandelion, eds., *The Cambridge Companion to Quakerism*

Within four days of running out of food, he'll barely be able to stand up, let alone control
preposition — present participle — active infinitive — adverb

a rover. Plus, his mental faculties will rapidly decline. He'd have a hard time even
possessive pronoun — adjective — simple future, active, indicative action verb — simple present, active, modal action verb, condensed

staying awake.
present participle — adverb

It should have been my call from the beginning, but you two stepped in and overrode me.
perfect present, state-of-being, active, modal verb — abstract noun — simple past, active, indicative action verb — simple past, indicative action verb

Ignoring all that, we agreed we'd tell them when there was hope.
present participle — simple present, active, modal action verb, condensed — relative adverb — abstract noun

—Andy Weir, *The Martian*

They should have had an orientation program before they came to Mars to tell them
perfect past, active, modal action verb — preposition — infinitive

how to look and how to walk around and be good for a few days.
noun clause acting as the object of the infinitive

Its six legs fell upon the ancient highway with the sounds of a sparse rain which
possessive pronoun — adjective — plural concrete noun — adjective

dwindled away, and from the back of the machine a Martian with melted gold for eyes
simple past, active, indicative action verb — singular concrete noun — past participle

looked down at Tomás as if he were looking into a well.
simple past, active, indicative action verb — progressive past, active, subjunctive action verb — singular concrete noun

—Ray Bradbury, *The Martian Chronicles*

Review 11D: Diagramming

On your own paper, diagram every word of the following sentences.

According to more than one astronaut memoir, one of the most beautiful sights in space is that of a sun-illumined flurry of flash-frozen waste-water droplets.

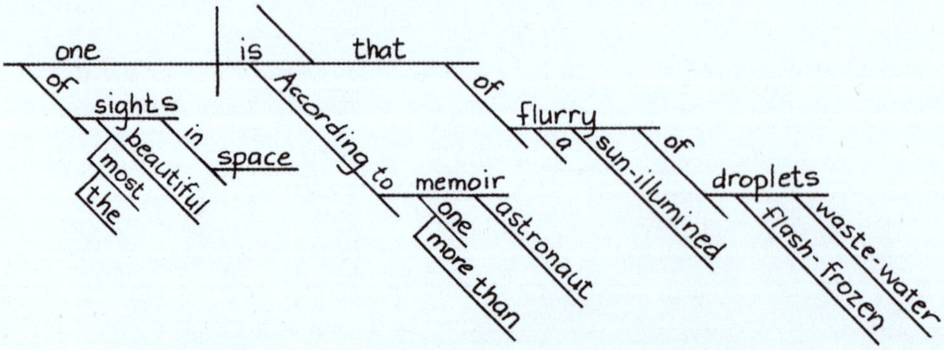

Note to Instructor: In the phrase *the most beautiful sights, the* functions as an adverb. Both *According to* and *more than* function as single words; *According to* is a preposition, while *more than* is an adverb.

The astronaut's job is stressful for all the same reasons yours or mine is—overwork, lack of sleep, anxiety, other people—but two things compound the usual stresses: the deprivations of the environment and one's inability to escape it.

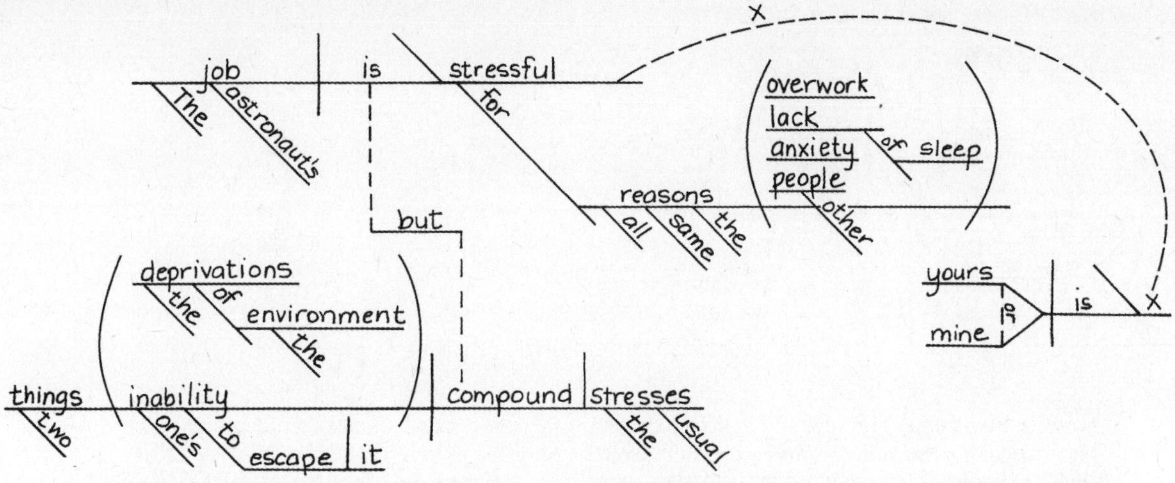

Note to Instructor: This sentence contains two sets of appositives that must be diagrammed in parentheses following the words they rename. The phrase *yours or mine is* is tricky to diagram. It is a condensation of *(that) yours or mine is (stressful)*, with the pronouns *yours* or *mine* standing in for *your job* and *my job*. I have chosen to connect the two occurrences of *stressful* with the understood *that*, since this is a type of comparison, but the student could also argue that the understood *(stressful)* should be connected to *reasons*, since the reasons are stressful.

—Mary Roach, *Packing for Mars: The Curious Science of Life in the Void*

Since Liddell first became public property—always walking in the arc light of fame—wherever he went and whatever he did or had once done was brightly illuminated.

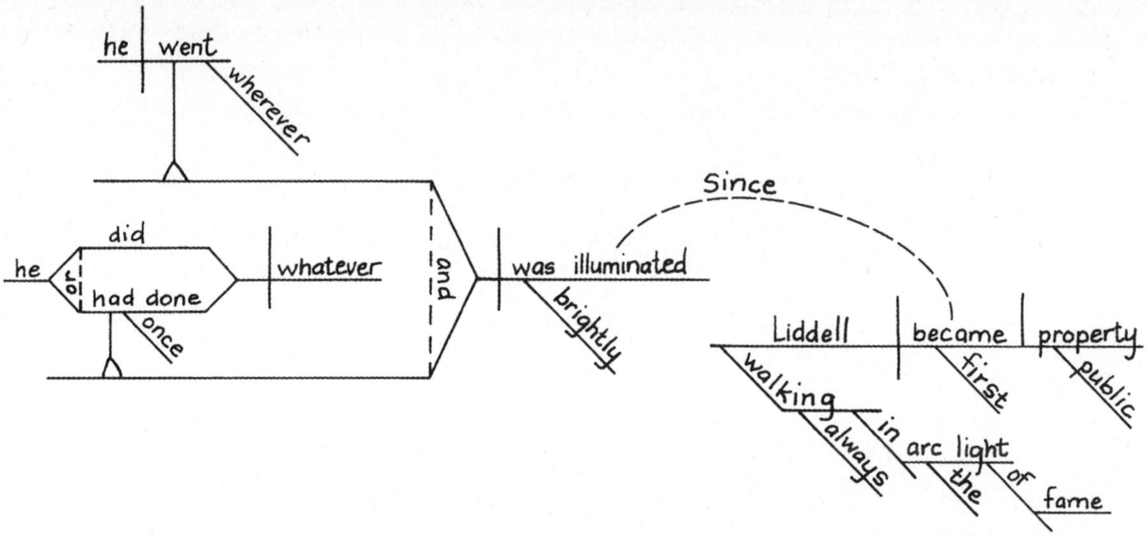

Note to Instructor: The two subordinate noun clauses *wherever he went* and *whatever he did* or *had once done* serve as the compound subject of the main clause. I have diagrammed the present participle phrase *always walking in the arc light of fame* as an adjective describing *Liddell*, but the student could argue that it is adverbial and modifies the verb *became*. However, despite the dashes, it is not an absolute construction.

The images, the music, the man, and what he achieved in the Olympics in 1924 are familiar to us because cinema made them so.

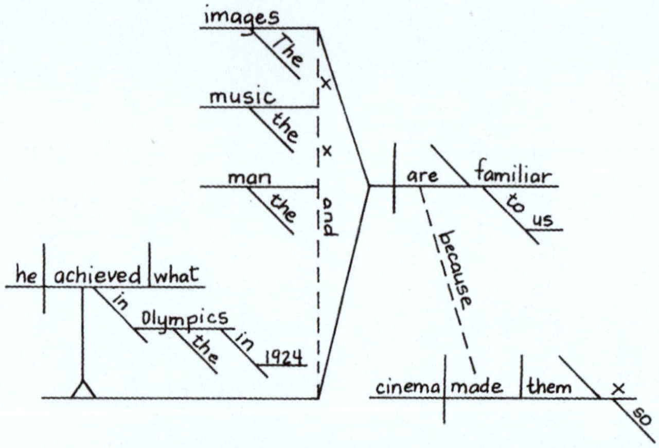

Note to Instructor: The subordinate clause contains an understood object complement: because *cinema made them so (familiar)*. You know that there is an understood *familiar* because *so* doesn't modify any other word in the clause.

—Duncan Hamilton, *For the Glory: The Untold and Inspiring Story of Eric Liddell, Hero of Chariots of Fire*

The master and thirty sailors escaped in the boat; but they were dragged in chains to the Porte: the chief was impaled; his companions were beheaded; and the historian Ducas beheld, at Demotica, their bodies exposed to the wild beasts.

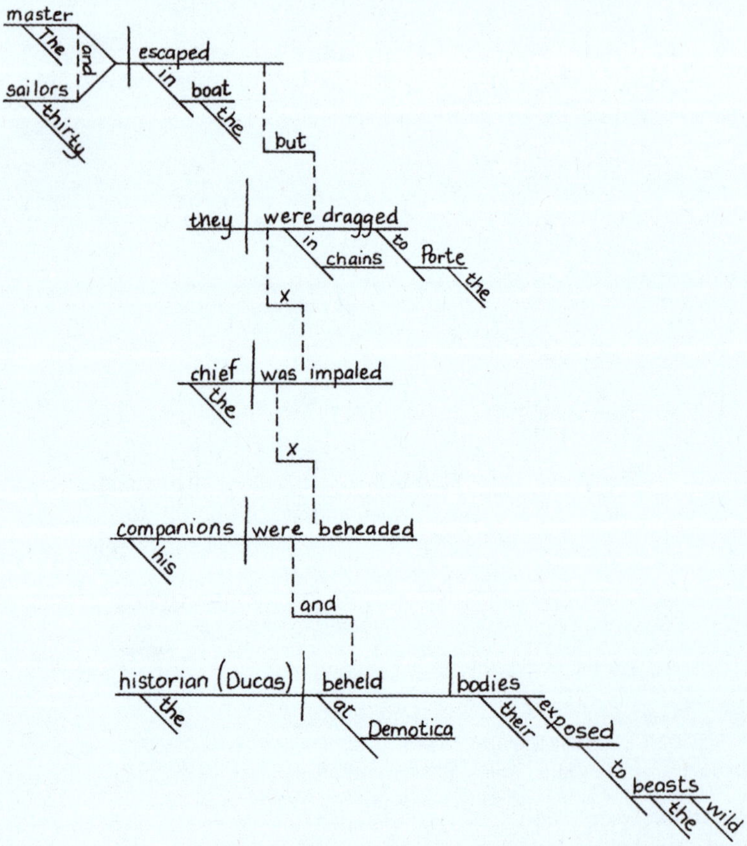

—Edward Gibbon, *History of the Decline and Fall of the Roman Empire*

There remained two growing girls; a shy midget of eight; John, tall, awkward, and eighteen; Jim, younger, quicker, and better looking; and two babies of indefinite age.

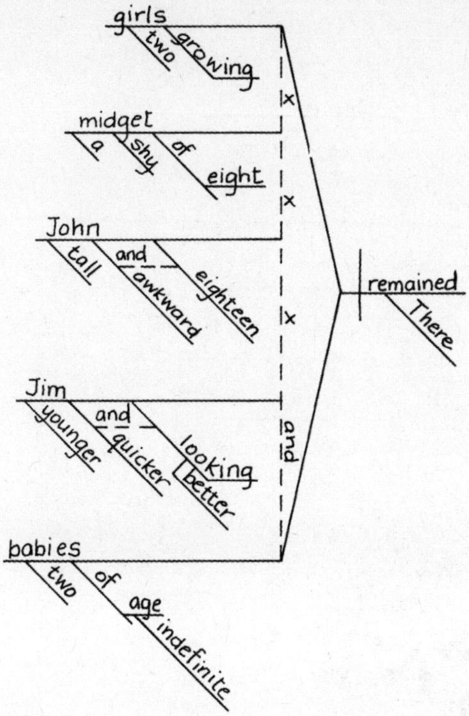

The function of the university is not simply to teach bread-winning, or to furnish teachers for the public schools or to be a center of polite society; it is, above all, to be the organ of that fine adjustment between real life and the growing knowledge of life, an adjustment which forms the secret of civilization.

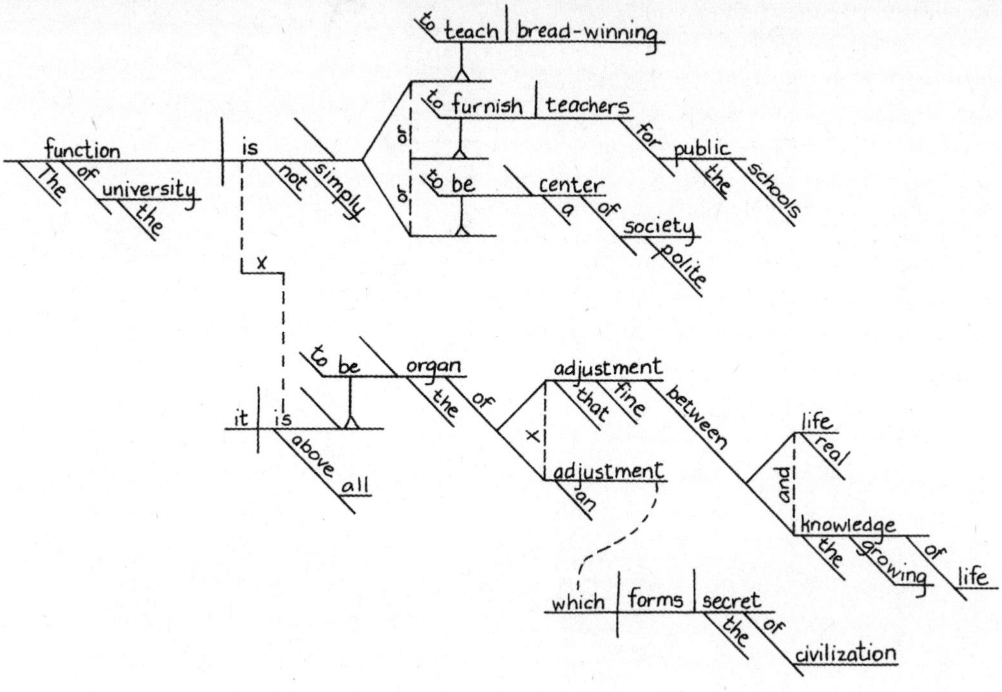

—W. E. B. Du Bois, *The Souls of Black Folk*

I thought of my dead godmother, of the night when I read to her, of her frowning so fixedly and sternly in her bed, of the strange place I was going to, of the people I should find there, and what they would be like, and what they would say to me, when a voice in the coach gave me a terrible start.

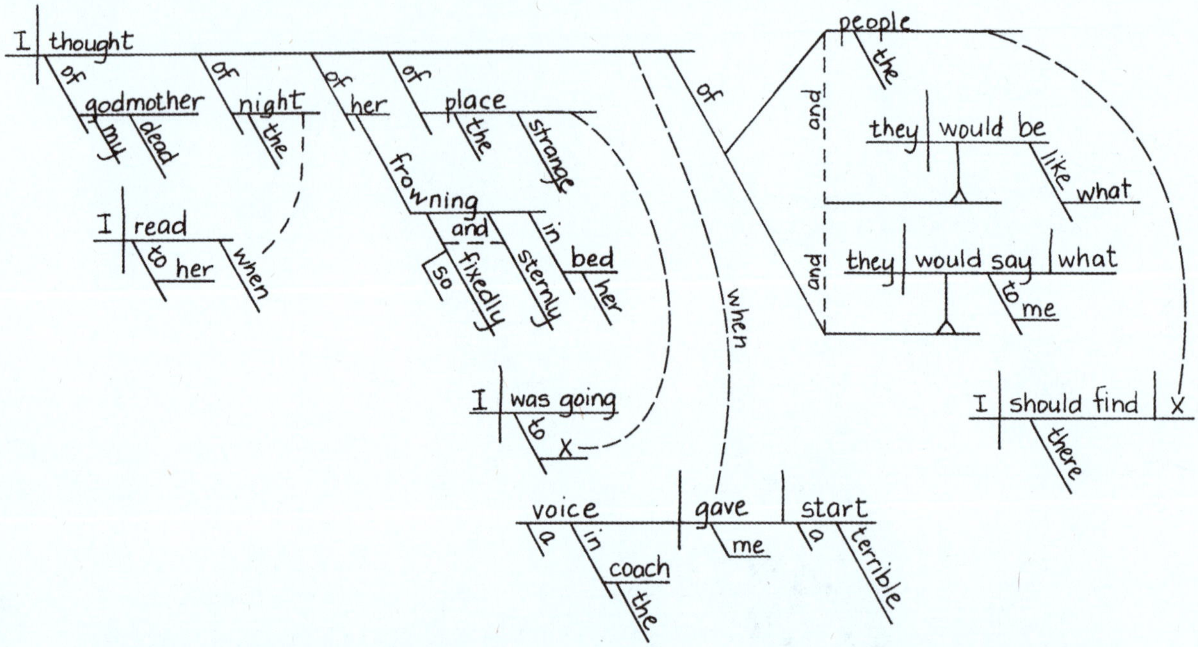

Note to Instructor: The two-word main clause contains multiple adverbial prepositional phrases. The last, *of the people I should find there, and what they would be like, and what they would say to me,* is a single prepositional phrase with three objects of the preposition *of.* The second and third objects are noun clauses acting as objects of the preposition.

The noun clause *of the people (that) I should find there* has an understood relative pronoun that refers back to *people* and serves as the direct object of *should find.*

The prepositional phrase *of the strange place (that) I was going to* has an understood relative pronoun that refers back to *place* and serves as the object of the preposition *to.*

Notice that *when* in *the night when I read to her* is a relative adverb referring back to *place,* while the *when* in *when a voice in the coach gave me a terrible start* is an adverb working as a subordinating conjunction.

—Charles Dickens, *Bleak House*